**10367 Reisterstown Road
Garrison Forest Plaza
Owings Mills, MD 21117 U.S.A.
Phone: 301-356-4567**
FAX: 301-356-4693

Established in 1973, Music Machine has built its reputation as one of the best sources for rock collectibles. We always stock a large selection of 7" and 12" singles, albums and compact discs from the U.S. and abroad. We regularly visit England and Europe to hand-pick the finest vinyl at collector's shops, conventions and from personal collections. We also feature a vast selection of promotional records, compact discs & oddities for the discriminating collector. You'll find it easy to shop with us in any of these ways:

 ☆ **MUSIC MACHINE MAIL ORDER**

Please check out our full page ad and 'Collector's Showcase' ads featured in every issue of "Goldmine". We feature the latest releases plus a selection of our collectibles in each ad. You can call and find out what we have by your favorite artist(s) or write for our latest catalogue. Your 'want lists' are welcome! We make it easy to shop with us. Just call and say, "Charge It!" Or send in a check or money order. FAX us your order if you like! We sincerely do our level best to get you your order as soon as possible, and in the best possible condition!

☆ **MUSIC MACHINE RETAIL STORE**

Hours: Monday, Thursday, Friday 10-9
Tuesday, Wednesday, Saturday 10-6
Sundays 12-6

When in The Baltimore/Washington DC area, please visit our store! 2,000 square feet jam-packed with records, tapes, t-shirts, posters and collectibles. Being vinyl junkies ourselves, we do our best to stock as much vinyl as possible! An extensive assortment of compact disc albums and singles is also featured. Please drop by and browse!

Take Baltimore Beltway (695) To Exit #19 (795) ... Get Off 795 At 1st Exit (Owing's Mill's Blvd) ... Bear To Right ... Go Thru 1 Light & 1 Stop Sign, Turn Up Right Into Our Large Parking Lot.

☆ **MUSIC MACHINE AT CONVENTIONS**

Come Visit Us When We Come To Your Town!

We do our best to regularly set up a large display of our best merchandise at many of the country's leading record conventions! It's always great to meet you face to face! We travel from Baltimore to Boston to Chicago to Texas to show off our goodies! We try to attend these conventions as much as possible: Montvale, NJ; Boston, MA; Cleveland, OH; Tysons Corner, VA; Silver Springs, MD; Chicago, IL; Long Island, NY; Cranford, NJ; Austin, TX; Akron, OH; Pittsburgh, PA; Albany, NY; Meadowlands, NY; Waterbury, CT & Detroit, MI. Please check "Goldmine's" convention listings and check with us to see where we'll be ... and when!

Hello & Thanks to all the great convention promoters we know: John Godlewski, Larry Garland, Burt at Randolph Music, Clete at Convergence, George & Sally Gelestino, Steve Petryszyn, Marvelous Marv, Richie Ranno, Mary & Leonard Laferriere, Pat McCardle, Arc, Judith Tukich, Doug Hanners, Jim Furlong and of course, Mark & Debbie Zakarin!

Music Machine ... Dealing In The Past, Present And Future Of Rock!

Goldmine's

Price Guide to Collectible Record Albums

by
Neal Umphred

Published by Krause Publications, Inc.
700 E. State St.
Iola, WI 54990
Phone: (715) 445-2214

Printed in the United States of America

This book is dedicated to the memories of
John L. O' Sullivan and Buddy Wall

"Who flies afar from the sphere of our sorrow
is here today and here tomorrow."

Acknowledgements
The following people contributed to making this book:

Steve Andrews
Bellevue, WA

Athanesas
Redmond, WA

Benjamin Blake
Alan Shaw
Kingston Korner
Naperville, IL

Frank Brockel
Jefferson City, MO

Ralph Bukofzer
Rockville Centre, NY

Joe Carter
Graceland Records

Christopher Chatman
Los Angeles, CA

John Christensen
Seattle, WA

John De Blaiso
Renton, WA

Paul Dowling
Brooklandville, MD

Ed Heath
Lexington, IN

Dwayne Heeter
Richmond, IN

Paul Hochsprung
Tucson, AZ

Claudius Hunerwadel
Sunset Records
Switzerland

Allan Johnson
Rockaway Records
Mesa, AZ

Gary Johnson
Wayne Johnson
Rockaway Records
Los Angeles, CA

Linda Jones
Austin, TX

Lars Keilhau
Oslo, Norway

Pete Kellner
Marquette, WI

Peter Kirchheimer
Pompton Lakes, NJ

Richard Kohler
Strabane, PA

L.P. Larry
Brooklyn, NY

Mad Louie
Buffalo, NY

David Michelak
Earwax
San Francisco, CA

Bill Paquin
Lambertville, NJ

Joe Pfeiffer
Chandler, AZ

Walter Piotrowski
Dearborn, MI

John Rogers
Rubato Records
Bellevue, WA

Bill Shonk
Jazz Grooveyard
Seattle, WA

Todd Van Sittert
Phoenix, AZ

Neal Skok
Redmond, WA

Vicky Sokoloff
Reading, PA

Betty Smith
Amber's Records
Spokane, WA

David Smith
New Carrolton, MD

Zari Smith
Record Vault
Pleasanton, CA

John Tefteller
Grant's Pass, OR

Jack & Barb Thuemmler
Saugus, CA

Tom Ventris, Jr.
Long Beach, CA

Barry Wickham
Terra Linda, CA

Thanks to the many readers who wrote concerning my work in *Goldmine* over the past two years.

For technical assistance;
Michael McIntyre, Pam Stanton-Wyman, Steve Smith and Tony Hoagland.

For advice, Don Woodside.

To Buddy Wall, for the photography.

Special thanks to Davie Allan and John Fred.

"Major Albums by Major Artists on Major Labels"

Introduction to Goldmine's Price Guide to Collectible Record Albums

Neal Umphred

As anyone who has been active in record collecting in the past few years will attest, there is a real need for a single book addressing the general state of the current market. That is, a book that covers a major portion of the field and provides reasonable discographical information with accurate values. *Goldmine's Price Guide to Collectible Record Albums* was created for that general market: included here is virtually every genre of collectible records with the exception of instrumentals (most pop and all jazz) and "classical music," each of which requires a book of its own.

First and foremost: this is a price *guide*. It is not intended to be "a bible" for the business. It is intended solely to assist the general collector and dealer in developing a reliable overview of the market and ascertain where his or her interests lie. The prices quoted are, without exception, *an average* that reflects the broad differences in markets from region to region, state to state and city to city. Attention was given to the foreign market (i.e., overseas collectors of American made records). Collectors from some countries are able to pay twice — or more — the going rate for a record and come out ahead, due to inflation and the weakness of the U.S. dollar. While this was, of necessity, taken into account, I did not allow it to excessively or unduly affect the pricing.

Any book of this nature must first define its own limitations, what will be included and what will be omitted. Many of these decisions were defined by the actual physical boundaries of the book, especially page size and page count. Regarding content, the rule of thumb I used is that of the title of this introduction: major albums by major artists on major labels. Due to the need to cover as much music and as many artists as possible, the listings were restricted to commercial pressings: records that were made available to the retail market, either those that you could purchase in the stores or through record clubs, and then only first pressings. With the exception of the *creme de la creme* (Elvis and the Beatles), this makes perfect sense, as second pressings of most records are of negligible value. Exceptions were made for albums originally issued as 10" discs and then reissued as 12" LPs; repackages of previous material with a new title; reissuing titles on a new label; mis-pressings or colored vinyl; and most importantly, for small label punk/psychedelic albums from the late '60s.

So, what's not here? Lots. There is no attempt at completeness; rather, the reader will find approximately 20,000 listings that cover, more or less: 1) the most collectible records in the business (excluding promotional records); 2) those records that exchange hands the most often; and 3) those records most in need of attention at this point in time. While the discographies of many artists are complete, for others they are obviously incomplete. Let's use the group Chicago as an example: their eponymous first album, issued in 1969 under their original name, *Chicago Transit Authority*, was pressed on Columbia's "360 Sound Stereo" label. The album was a huge hit, reaching the Top 20 and spending over three years on the charts!

During the course of this stay, Columbia switched from the "360 Sound" label to the one they have used since: a red label with gold "Columbias" circling the label perimeter. This was an album that was bought and played, not set on the shelf after a few spins. Consequently, the original "360 Sound" pressings are rather difficult to find in mint condition and fetch a reasonable price on the collector's market.

Shortening their name to Chicago, their second album, *Chicago II*, was also issued on the "360 Sound Stereo" label in the early part of 1970. This was another big seller and the first pressings are also sought after. With the release of *Chicago III*, all of their albums have appeared on the red and gold label and sold millions of copies. These are readily available and are a clear case where the supply vastly outweighs the demand. Consequently, all of the Chicago albums on the red and gold label, including second pressings of the first two albums, have negligible value on the collector's market. In many stores they are staples of the 99¢ bargain bin, regardless of the fact that many of them are nearly two decades old! For this reason *they are not listed* in this book.

Columbia was the one label who most actively pursued the quadraphonic potential in the early 1970s, issuing thousands of their catalog titles in new quad mixes. Few of these sold very well. *Chicago III* through *Chicago X* were all issued in quad (I have no information on the first two being issued in this format, although the possibility that they were does exist). These are highly sought after by Chicago collectors, with prices of $25-30 for certain titles in some markets not being out of line, At the same time, in other markets, where neither Chicago nor quads have any real followers, these will turn up for $3.99-5.99 *and sit*. The prices listed in this book, of course, represent a compromise between these two extremes. Finally, with the advent of the "audiophile" market, several Chicago albums were issued as half-speed masters; one on the Mobile Fidelity label and two others under Columbia's own imprint.

Thus for the highly popular and hugely successful Chicago, only the original pressings of their first two albums, the quadraphonic versions from 1974-75 and the more recent half-speeds are listed in this book, with the regular, common pressings ignored. This approach was used on many artists and *is not meant as an artistic judgement on my behalf but rather an economical one.*

Additions, corrections and suggestions are welcome, please address them to: Neal Umphred, Krause Publications, 700 East State Street, Iola, WI 54990.

Page Breakdown

The records are listed chronologically in the manner which *Goldmine* readers are accustomed. Broken down, the page set-up lists the label and catalogue number (first column), each record's sound (mono, stereo, etc.); year of release and values. Necessary notes are usually listed in italics in parenthesis below the appropriate section or selections. Once again using Chicago as our example:

CHICAGO(CHICAGO TRANSIT AUTHORITY)

Columbia GP-8	(S)	Chicago Transit Authority	1969	10.00	25.00
Columbia GP-24	(S)	Chicago II	1970	6.00	15.00

(Columbia albums above have "360 Sound" labels.)

The first column indicates the label (Columbia) and catalog number. The second column features a single capitol letter italicized in parenthesis. This is a notation for the record's sound. An "(M)" denotes a monaural recording, while an "(S)" means the entire record is in true stereo. An "(E)" indicates that the stereo effect of the album has been electronically created. A "(P)" indicates a partially true stereo record; i.e., while most of the tracks are true stereo, one or more are either mono or electronic stereo. Finally, "(Q)" indicates quadraphonic.

The record's title is the middle column followed by the year of release. Dating the records was the most problematic. The final two columns, the prices, are for two conditions, very-good-plus (VG+) and near-mint (NM) and are dealt with at length below.

The short parenthetical note listed below the second title tells the reader that all of the above titles (in this case only two) were originally issued on Columbia's "360 Sound" label and that the prices quoted are for those copies and those alone.

Regarding the artist listings: when a group's name is followed by another name in parenthesis, it means that the group has recorded under two names. If the two names are similar, the records are listed together under the first name. For instance, "CHICAGO (CHICAGO TRANSIT AUTHORITY)," tells the reader that albums listed under either of those two names can be found under that one listing.

If the names are very different, then there is another listing in the book that the group recorded under. For instance, Creedence Clearwater originally recorded as the Golliwogs. After their success, Fantasy gathered up the early singles as an album by the Golliwogs. When looking up Creedence the reader will find "CREEDENCE CLEARWATER REVIVAL (THE GOLLIWOGS)." Likewise, the reader will find "GOLLIWOGS, THE (CREEDENCE CLEAR-WATER REVIVAL)." In each case the parenthetical title tells the reader that there is another listing for that group in the book under the second name. Common sense should prevail.

For single artists, some of the parenthetical names are used similarly, indicating that the artists recorded under another name and that those records are included in this book. Other times the parenthetical name is the artists' real name, and that the popular name is a pseudonym.

For the sake of usefulness, certain artists who started out as members of a group and who then rose to dominate the group have all of the recordings listed under the individual artist's usually better known name. For instance, while the Midnighters originally recorded under just that name the Midnighters, the bulk of their material was recorded under the name Hank Ballard & The Midnighters, under which all of their recordings are grouped in this book. Similarly, the Crickets first album is listed under Buddy Holly; the Teenagers under Frankie Lymon; the Stone Poneys under Linda Ronstadt; etc.

References are kept to a bare minimum and refer the reader to another artist only when the artist or group in question is named in the title of an album or is inseparably linked with the recording. Listing references for artists who appeared on other artist's recording is a book in itself. Should the reader desire one, Terry Hounsome and Tim Chambre's "Rock Record" is highly recommended, with thousands upon thousands of listings of who played on what, when, and where!

Finally: All records are on black vinyl unless otherwise noted.

Still Sealed

Please note that the prices quoted are for opened copies in either VG+ or nearly mint condition. In many cases collectors are willing to pay a reasonable premium for still-sealed copies. Depending on the age and desirability of the record, the premium may be a modest 10% above the NM price to 50%. In the case of certain items, the increase would be dramatically greater. Sealed copies of Beatles mono albums on Capitol are worth three to four times the NM price listed in these pages. Certain Elvis Presley albums with a "bonus" sticker on the sealed shrinkwrap would be worth two or more times the NM price. As in all cases, common sense should be used.

One major point on purchasing still-sealed albums: generally, a dealer cannot be held responsible for what is inside a sealed jacket. For example, during Elvis' career RCA often printed far more covers than records and subsequently used the covers until they ran out. Thus it is rather common to find second and third pressing records in original first pressing covers. Consequently, Elvis collectors are not as obsessed with sealed copies and would rather see an opened mint copy than take a chance on a sealed one.

There is also the practice of re-sealing albums. This was done over the years by the record companies and by firms specializing in remainders (I don't remember anyone calling them cut-outs in the '60s). Prior to the sales boom of the mid 1970s the industry had a very loose policy regarding returns; many of us over "thirtysomething" grew up able to test a purchase out on the store's turntable before taking it home. We were often able to return records that we just plain didn't like! Of course, those were the days when most retail operations were independently owned and operated and the proprietor knew most of his customers and catered to their needs...

When purchasing a valuable sealed collectible at a shop or show, pay for the record *with the mutual understanding* that you will open it *immediately after purchase, in front of the dealer,* and if the record inside is not what it should be, *you may return it on the spot.* Do not purchase a sealed record, leave the store or dealer's table, and return a half-hour later claiming that you got the wrong record or a damaged copy. Naturally, very few dealers will offer a refund in such a case.

On a less savory note, there are more than a few dealers and shops that do their own shrink-wrapping.

The Market... Recently

The market is in its most volatile state in nearly a decade. The most visible example is the enormous rise in prices on '50s and early '60s records — along with virtually every other high-ticket item. As Gary Johnson pointed out in the preface, a still-sealed copy of a first-state, stereo "butcher cover" of the Beatles' *Yesterday And Today* recently sold for $10,000. While this might be the kind of eye-opener that the news media gloms onto, even more interesting to the market as a whole is the growing interest in late '60s/early '70s soul and progressive music and the continually accelerating demand for "alternate" rock from the last ten years.

While country and "pop" have slowly established themselves in the market, especially female vocals from the '40s and '50s and country music recorded prior to 1969, some music still lags behind. Popular instrumental music, whether it is the lushly arranged orchestral type of Mantovani or the piano stylings of Peter Nero and Ferrante & Teicher, generates little interest in most markets. Hence its unfortunate exclusion from this book. Likewise, the phenomenally popular disco music of the '70s has not really caught on with collectors, although interest in the original 12" singles intended for club spins is growing.

Several labels have reached a point where virtually everything on them is collectible: Sun and its subsidiary, Philips International; labels specializing in rhythm & blues, such as Aladdin and Score; King's rhythm & blues, rock & roll and country titles continue to escalate, as does the small Audio Lab label, which produced a slew of interesting country/western titles in the late '50s and early '60s. Original Atlantic albums are finally being recognized and virtually any stereo release on Atlantic or Atco prior to 1963 is in demand. Early Motown albums have come into their own as has anything related to Phil Spector's various entrepreneurial endeavors.

Mono, Stereo and the Audiophile

One interesting facet of record collecting eschews the emulation of individual artists or bands in favor of the collecting of the recording technique. As more and more listeners grow more and more disenchanted with the contemporary approach to recording (dubbed "wide channel mono" by one observer), the demand for earlier sounds has increased. Early stereo recordings from the late 1950s through the end of the '60s, known affectionately as wide-channel stereo due to the placement of the signals in the sound stage, made no attempt at reality but went for effect. The placement of individual instruments in the two separate channels made for a more involving listening experience, essentially inviting the brain to participate in completing the mixdown from the widely disparate signals emanating from the two speakers. Collectors of this type of technology pursue the best examples of it, not necessarily concentrating on the particular type of music involved.

Much of the best rock, r&b and country was done under less than state-of-the-art conditions and the technicians involved in making the master tapes were far more adept in mixing down to mono than creating a good stereo two-track. This takes its extreme with most of the pre-70s Motown albums, where legend has it that Berry Gordy assigned his best technicians to mix down the mono albums and left the stereo mixing to the fledglings. So, while the current market still seeks out the stereo versions, the demand for mono originals is growing.

In record collecting, the term "audiophile" is generally applied to those who specialize in high-quality recordings on high-quality vinyl. While every album could be an audiophile pressing, very few are, and the standard of quality, especially in the amount of pressings done from each stamper to the quality of the vinyl used, has dropped dramatically in the past fifteen years. Thus the door was open for several independent companies to enter the field and provide the market with better records. The most popular of these have been the half-speed masters made most successfully by Mobile Fidelity Sound Laboratories. Virtually the entire catalog of this small label is now collectible, although only those that concern popular music are listed in this book. The Nautilus label half-speeds were less successful on the market that MFSL and consequently their titles are a bit harder to find. Similarly, CBS did

pour out a large number of their Columbia and Epic catalog in this format, but these were done in relatively small printings, did not fare well on the retail racks and thus, the demand for certain titles is increasing.

This is similar to the situation of quadraphonic pressings from the first half of the 1970s, many of which are listed in this book. Quads are attractive for a variety of reasons, scarcity being the most obvious. But of far more interest is the fact that many quads have radically different, and sometimes superior, mixes to the original stereo.

Caveat Emptor: Second Pressings and Counterfeits

The Term "second pressing" has two contradictory meanings amongst record collectors. The first and legitimate use refers to any pressing of a record by the original record company that is noticeably different from the original pressing. And this is the term that will suffice for our purposes in this book.

(Lee Cotten and Howard DeWitt, in their book, "Jailhouse Rock: The Bootleg Records Of Elvis Presley," take the whole thing a step further and define a "second pressing" as a release by the original record company with identical covers but a different record inside; either the label or the color of the vinyl is changed. A "second edition" is a release by the original record company with an identical record but a different cover. Finally, a "second issue" is a release by the original record company with both the cover and the record are different in some manner. This is noted for the reader's edification and has no real bearing on the contents of this book.)

Now, for the confusing aspect: records that have gone out of print but are still sought after by a small audience are often "reissued" without the consent of the legitimate copyright holders. These pressings, far more common amongst singles, are also referred to as "second pressings." (In an equally confusing manner they are also referred to as bootlegs, although they have nothing in common with "bootlegs" as they have come to be known since the early 1970s.)

This then brings us to the subject of counterfeits. A counterfeit is an exact copy (or an attempt at an exact copy) of a legitimate record. These are far more common than one might expect. Counterfeits range from the not-so-professional to the perfect. Examples of the former include copies of all of the Epic Yardbirds albums, the Mothers Of Inventions on Verve, the Left Banke on Smash and Todd Rundgren's two *Runt* albums on Apex. Each of these is fairly obvious, as the covers are blurred photo-copies of the originals, the labels tend to be uneven and the sound quality is obviously "mastered" from another record. At the time of their "release" they were almost always sold on the collectors market as second pressings or bootlegs. Unfortunately, ten years after the fact, they are readily confused for the originals by novice collectors.

On the opposite end of the scale is the professional duplication. The most famous case may be the instance of a large retailer who was busted for possession of 500,000 copies of *Saturday Night Fever* in 1978. These copies, while farily obviously counterfeits to an eye looking for them or when held against an original, were good enough to fool countless customers. Similarly, some sources claim there are more bogus copies of the Beatles' *Let It Be* album on Apple than there are real ones! Cotten and DeWitt in "Jailhouse Rock" note that "in a recent RIAA report, it was brought out that Elvis'

records are among those which were among the most counterfeited." Since this was not common knowledge at the time, nor is it, for that matter, well known six years after the book's publication, I would infer that the counterfeits are damn near perfect.

The business of counterfeits is not confined to vinyl: there has been a proliferation of acetates on the market in recent years and, apparently, some of them are bogus. Thus the active buyer should always be alert for "original pressings" that just didn't look quite original enough, or, to borrow a time honored phrase, "Let the buyer beware."

The Psychedelic Sixties

Listed in these pages are several of the albums that fall under the punk/psychedelic umbrella. Briefly, this is the music that was recorded in miniscule studios around the country from approximately 1966-1972 and captures what happens when the garage meets the cosmos. Most of these records were pressed in minute quantities (500 or more being a normal run), of which only a handful exist. Their scarcity and the enthusiasm that the collectors of this type of music bring to their endeavors make many of these amongst the more valuable rock albums. But, the problem is that a lot of the records bear reputations for their rarity that the music in the grooves doesn't quite match, leaving many a purchaser hard pressed to justify his expensive purchase. The demand for these records ebbs and flows (often with the availability of cheap European repressings) and I have attempted to list reasonable, steady market values. Thus albums that have sold for as much as $750-800 (when they were hot) are listed here at a conservative but reliable $500.

Pricing the Records
Current Values Based on Recent Sales
or Purchases

This book is not the work of one man. It does not reflect my opinions of what *your records* are worth. Instead, I solicited the assistance of many collectors and dealers whom I had known for several years, both personally and professionally. Each dealer and collector was requested to provide *current values based on recent sales or purchases,* not transactions from years ago.

By dealing with people I knew personally, I was able to take into account each individual's personal bias when arriving at prices. While a collector or dealer who specializes in a certain field (such as '60s psych, popular vocals, "old fashioned" country, etc.) would be inclined to assign higher values than would the more general, centralized market, these collectors/dealers were also more awasre of which individual albums were difficult to find and what the current trens in their field were. All of this was taken into account.

Following the publication of O'Sullivan Woodside's 1985-1986 edition of their *Rock Record Album Price Guide,* for which I served as editor, I received an enormous amount of input from countless sources around the country. Much of it was conveyed aurally at record shows and stores in various states (New York, Pennsylvania, Texas, Tennessee, Arizona, California and my current home state, Washington). All of this information and a constant scrutiny of the set-sale and auctions placed in the pages of *Goldmine,* also played a part in the make-up of this book.

Several collectors stressed the need for a sense of

internal consistency with the pricing. That is, do not attach east coast prices to oldies, northwest prices to garage, midwest prices to Motown, L.A. prices to surf, etc., but rather seek a balance between them all so that the book as a whole works as a guideline for each region of the country to use as an outline for their own market. Thus every item in this book has been scrutinized by several individuals. The values that were decided upon represent a ballpark value that takes into account each of the prices submitted. In no instance was the highest price submitted the one that has been printed.

There is a tremendous variance in prices around the country; the point of this book is to provide realistic figures that will assist both buyers and sellers everywhere in their dealings. It should always be borne in mind that the geographic/economic area in which you live plays a great role in whether the price here seem a bit high or a bit low. That is, someone in a major seller's market (high density population areas such as New York or Los Angeles) should expect to see local prices somewhat higher than those listed. Conversely, a reader living in a buyer's market should expect to see many of these prices lower in their local market. Also, many geographic areas have particular interests that make certain artists or types of music more popular there than elsewhere; consequently, prices for these records would be higher, perhaps much higher.

There are some cases where realistic values for a record could not be assigned due to the record's rarity and subsequent lack of documented sales (several items are virtually unknown except for a handful of diligent collectors). Consequently there are no known sales upon which to base a value. In these few cases the record is listed with an "___," meaning it has an as yet undetermined value.

For those artists who achieved a long lasting popularity that saw their recordings repeatedly re-issued I have attempted to list brief notations concerning the label that applies to a particular record. As in the case of our Chicago example, which begins "Columbia albums above...," the note applies to all of the albums above it. For this work one book was invaluable: Joe Lindsay's "Record Label Guide For Domestic LPs." Published by BioDisc, this is an absolute must for serious album collectors.

There are two prices listed for each title with the first representing VG+ (usually the lowest condition a serious collector will accept into his or her collection; for records in less than VG condition refer to the section on grading records below). The second price represents a nearly perfect, or NM, copy. The prices are meant to convey some idea of the spread between a fairly common copy and the exceedingly scarce nearly mint ones.

The NM price reflects the consensus of opinions from which I had to choose while the VG+ reflects a percentage of the NM price. Briefly, the percentage of the NM price that most collectors are willing to pay for a lesser copy varies with the age and value of the record. For this reason I devised the following sliding scale:

Near Mint Value	VG+ Value (%)
Less than $50	40%
$60-200	50%
$250-500	60%
$600-1,800	66%
$2,000 and up	70%

The normal rule of thumb for pricing is that the cover makes up 40-50% of the value and the record 50-

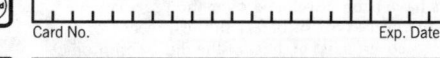

60%, although there are many, many exceptions to this rule. While some collectors are mainly concerned with the disc alone and are satisfied if the cover is whole, the purpose of this book is to take into consideration both and the pricing does just that. Please remember that the two prices listed here in the book stand for copies of albums that have either a VG+ record in a VG+ cover or a NM record in a NM cover.

So, what then, if the cover is merely VG but it holds a NM record? I will use our Chicago example once again, this time as a hypothetical copy with a VG cover and a NM record:

CHICAGO(CHICAGO TRANSIT AUTHORITY)

Columbia GP-8	(S)	Chicago Transit Authority	1969	10.00	25.00
Columbia GP-24	(S)	Chicago II	1970	6.00	15.00

Columbia albums above have "360 Sound" labels.)

In the case of the first Chicago album, I will say that a NM copy of the record is worth $13 and a NM copy of the cover $12. Since the hypothetical album has a NM record, then we have at least a $13 value. Using the percentage breakdown for pricing as a guide, a VG+ copy of the cover would be worth $6, and a VG cover $3. So the hypothetical album would be worth $16.

Always keep in mind that the accuracy of these prices are meaningless without a corresponding accuracy in the grading of records.

On Grading the Records

Even attempting to tackle this matter is troublesome; the reader should bare in mind that no matter how eloquent and descriptive my choice of words, they will not replace even the most modest hands-on experience. The best and quickest way to get a handle on grading is to become active with a variety of dealers and other collectors. Visit the used record stores in your area; attend swaps and collector shows; *make friends with other collectors,* especially the ones that collect music seemingly alien to you; subscribe to trade publications and try a few mail-order firms.

Records are graded by visual standards, not aural; the reason being that when purchasing a record at a show or through the mail the buyer does not get to listen to it. The biggest complaints against the visual method are 1) the subjectivity of the grader's eyes or viewpoint, and 2) the fact that records do not always play as good — or bad — as they look. Both of these are justifiable arguments and, of course, it is the first point that causes the need for discussions such as this: records always look better when selling than when buying. The arguments against play-grading are similar: the subjectivity of the listener is also a factor, a factor that is multiplied by the type of equipment the grader is playing the record on to form his or her judgement. So, for the sake of convenience *and* necessity, visual grading is the standard by which almost all dealers and collectors work.

When grading a disc, grade the overall wear of the vinyl. A record advertised as "NM" or "VG" should tell the prospective buyer the shape of the playable vinyl (although common sense should be used: perfectly unplayed records that are warped cannot be Mint.) Such defects as name stickers on the label, tape on the jacket, etc, should be addressed separately with abbreviated notations. A reliable set of these notations have been developed over the years covering virtually every type of defect that can occur to a record or its cover; a list of most of the more common abbreviations and their meanings follow the grading definitions below. When defining the grades, it is difficult to describe several without discussing certain defects and/or the way the disc plays; these are included to help define the grade, not to cause confusion. If a seller accurately describes the overall condition of the vinyl and lists each defect, the buyer should have no problem with the record when he or she receives it.

Visual grading is most important in mail-order transactions where a buyer doesn't see his purchase until his check has cleared the bank. Grading needs to be as strict, as accurate as possible. Put simply, the aim of grading is to make the buyer visualize the record he or she is purchasing through an advertisement and not be disappointed when that record arrives! A record that is accurately graded will play the same (or better) than the grading! In-person deals do not require a grade of any sort; if you are holding a record that has obviously been played a hundred times, you don't need a grade to determine whether or not you are going to purchase the disc.

Always grade records under a good, steady light. A 100 watt bulb in a common desk-lamp will do an adequate job; most major defects will jump out at you and allow you to make an accurate assessment of the vinyl. Grading a record using light from the ceiling or from deflected sunlight entering the window will often "hide" paper scuffs, discoloration, groove wear and even some fingerprints. Everyone makes mistakes in grading. This is a problem all dealers and collectors are prone to make and must be aware of. So don't condemn a dealer for one mistake; but, when the mistake is the norm, find someone else to buy your records from. Think of these definitons as guidelines around which your experience will build a better understanding of conditons.

Mint. A Mint ("M") record should appear to have just left the manufacturers without any handling; that is, it should appear perfect! No scuffs or scratches, blotches or stains, labels or writing, tears or splits; nothing. *Perfect.* And age has nothing to do with it; *the same standards for Mint apply to a 78 from 1949 as they do to an album for 1989!* There are no sliding values for Mint.

A Mint album cover should appear to have never have had a record in it; no ring-wear, dog-eared corners, writing, seam-splits, or even circular impressions, especially on single picture sleeves. Similarly, a Mint picture sleeve should essentially appear as though a record were never placed in it! No slight seam splits, no turned down tops or dog-eared corners, no prices or dates stamped or written anywhere, including inside the sleeve. And, most importantly, no ring-wear! Any of these all too common signs of age would reduce the sleeve to VG+!

I will define ring-wear as any imprint on the sleeve from the record that it formerly held. *Any* imprint. To many dealers and collectors the ink has to be worn off of the picture for them to recognize ring-wear and grade a sleeve down. I have been handed sleeves where each of the four corners were virtually bent

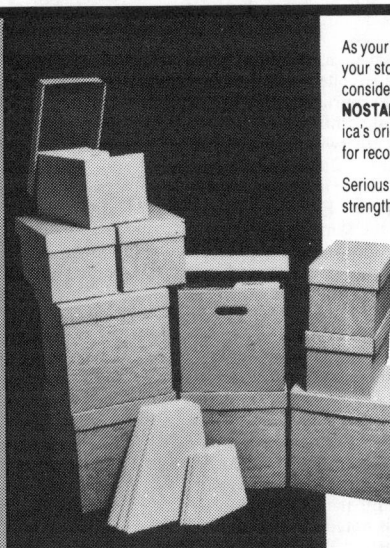

back from the pressure of the disc inside but there is no ink rubbed off so the dealer/collector claims the sleeve is Mint and asks an appropriately high price. Uh-uh. Mint means perfect and nothing else.

Near Mint. A record that is otherwise Mint but has one or two tiny, inconsequential flaws that do not affect the play is Near Mint ("NM") and should command 85-95% of the Mint price. For many, Near Mint and Mint-Minus mean the same thing; for the sake of this article, they are interchangeable. When dealing with a seller that discriminates between the two grades, inquire as to what the dealer means when he calls one record M- and another NM. Many dealers and collectors take the position that any used (opened) record cannot be verified as Mint so they use M- to describe what appears to be a perfect record that has been opened.

A sleeve for a single may have a slight impression from the record having been in it (no ring-wear; ring-wear should always be listed as a defect with the appropriate notation). An otherwise Mint sleeve or cover with a price stamped on it is acceptable to many collectors as long as it is noted in the ad; writing of any sort is not. Similarly, LP and EP covers should be close to perfect with minor signs of wear or age just becoming evident: slight ring-wear, minor denting to a corner, or writing on the cover should all be noted properly.

Very Good Plus. Sometimes referred to as "Excellent," a Very Good Plus ("VG+") record has been handled and played either infrequently or very carefully. That is, an item obviously not perfect, but not too far from it. On a disc, this could mean that there are light paper scuffs from sliding in and out of a dust jacket; the vinyl may have lost some — not all — of its original lustre. A slight scratch that did not affect the play in an otherwise nearly Mint disc would be acceptably VG+ for most collectors; a scratch of any sort that audibly clicked throughout at a level greater than or equal to the music would not be acceptable. Always list the flaws in a VG+ record or cover.

As a rule of thumb, a VG+ item is worth 50%, or one-half, of the Near Mint value, although this ratio varies with the rarity of the item. That is, a record that is fairly common in NM/M condition has little real value in VG+ to most collectors; consequently 25-35% may be more appropriate. On the other hand, truly rare records will fetch 75% in VG+. (By rare, I am referring to items in which the supply is merely a fraction of the demand and the record sells for hundreds of dollars...) On covers and sleeves, some wear from storage is acceptable, especially light wear that does not affect the beauty of the artwork. Again, listing the flaws when selling is safest.

Very Good. Very Good ("VG") records will display visible signs of handling and playing, such as loss of vinyl lustre, light surface scratches, groove wear, and spindle trails from countless spins on the turntables. A VG record looks like it will have some audible surface noise when it is played, although any such noise should not overwhelm the music or otherwise ruin the listening experience. VG record should appear to have been well-played although well-loved by a responsible owner. Gouges, rips in the label, cracks,

maple syrup in the grooves are all unacceptable.

As more and more collectors spend more and more money on their acquisitions, the lower limits of acceptability for an item to be admitted into their collection rises. That is, to many collectors, a record in VG condition is not acceptable unless the item is truly rare and virtually unavailable in any other condition! And then, only if the price is scaled appropriately to match the condition. Used but not abused might sum up this grade. A VG record should command approximately 20-30% of the Near Mint price.

This is a difficult grade when discussing paper goods. Like a disc, usually a cover is VG when a variety of problems are evident: ring wear, seam splits, bent corners, loss of gloss on the photo, stains, etc. An aggravated combination of two of these problems — *never all of them* — would likely cause a sleeve to be graded VG.

Good. Good ("G") in record collecting parlance all too often means a beat, trashed, take-it-to-the-flea-market frisbee. This should not be (obviously). Good should mean that the record is well-played with any number of defects that collectors normally shy away from, such as an almost complete loss of surface sheen, aggravating surface noise, etc. Still, the purchaser, knowing full well that he or she is buying a Good record, should be able to take it home, slap it onto the turntable and have a *good* time listening to it. Records that do not provide this most fundamental requirement *are just no good.* A Good record should command 10-15% of the Near Mint price.

A Good cover has seen considerable handling over a course of years and displays the obvious physical signs: ring-wear on the front and back; some seam-splitting, particularly along the bottom and/or the left side, which would receive the brunt of the record's sliding in and out; corners may be dog-eared to a light degree; an infatuated owner may have written his or her name somewhere; etc. If a record or cover is beneath your contempt, it is not in "G" condition; look below for the appropriate grade.

Poor. Any record or cover that does not qualify for the above "Good" grading. A "P" record should command 0-5% of the Mint price.

Finally, it should always be borne in mind that visual evidence can be deceiving: the quality of the vinyl and the plating make all the difference in the world. A record properly manufactured with a high quality plating may *look VG+* and *play* Near Mint; this is particularly true of older albums from the '50s through the mid-'60s, when print runs were dramatically smaller, vinyl was fresher and more care was paid to the entire procedure. Albums from this period are a better investment in VG+ condition than the more recent American product. In fact, many albums from the '50s can be purchased in VG condition at reasonable prices and will play far better than the price paid would indicate. A record manaufactured from recycled vinyl with poor plating (too many albums from the past 15 years or so) may look Mint and play VG. Still, most dealers do not have the time to listen to each item in their inventory, so visual standards remain.

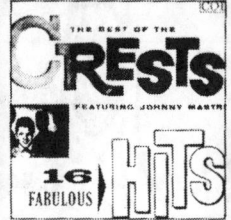

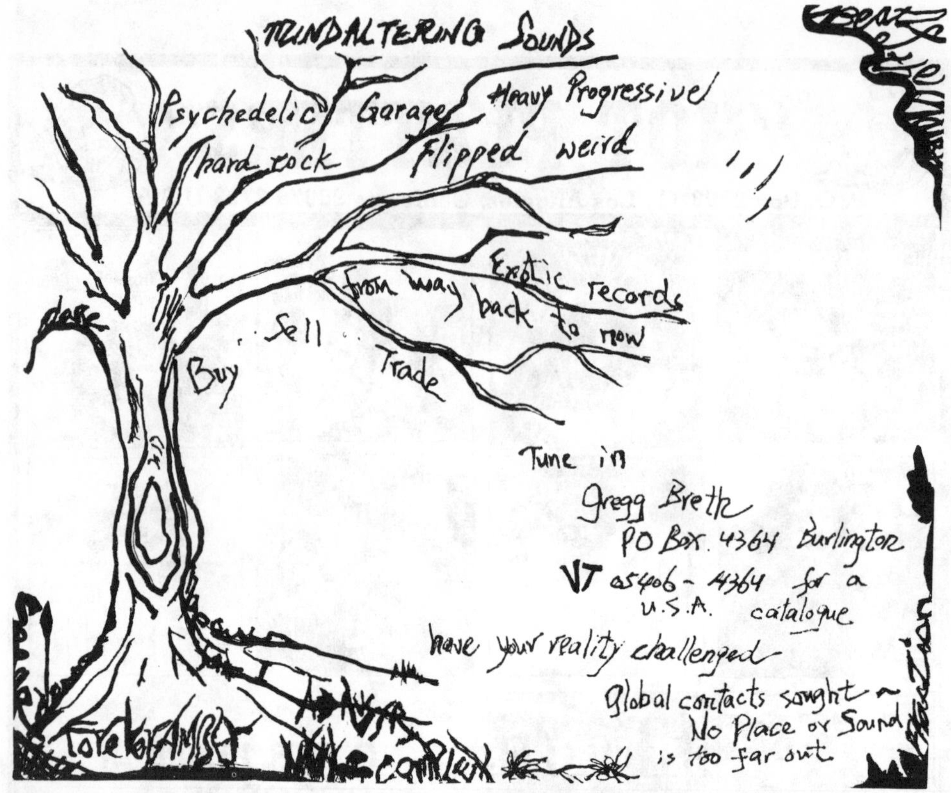

Gold and Platinum Record Award Collecting:

By Christopher Chatman

The purpose of this article is to give the reader a general acquaintance with the terms and descriptions commonly used in the field of gold and platinum record award collecting. This is being done in order to provide added information about an aspect of record collecting of which little is commonly known.

The easiest way to go about this is to take a listing of an item as an example, examine it section by section; define each term; and, by so doing, go through the basics of collecting these awards. In other words, for those of you with both the interest and the financial means of doing so, this is how you "go for the gold."

Example: 1) Aerosmith; 2) *Permanent Vacation;* 3) R.I.A.A.; 4) Double Platinum; 5) Hologram; 6) Awarded to Geffen Records; and 7) $750.00.

1) **Artist.** Obviously the artist whose records, cassettes or compact discs the award commemorates is of immense importance. An award for The Beatles or Bruce Springsteen is generally worth more than one for Aerosmith (though probably not to an Aerosmith fan, for whom a Double-Platinum Award for their *Permanent Vacation* album may be the ultimate collectible). But generally, the same rules of collecting that help determine the values of records and related memorabilia hold for collecting awards. Just remember that all generalizations stink (including the one I just made).

2) **Title.** It is my opinion that the title of the record impacts greatly on the desirability of a given award. This opinion is not held by every dealer or collector. I would rather have an award for Bob Dylan's *Bringing It All Back Home* than one for *Nashville Skyline,* all other factors being equal because to me, *Bringing It All Back Home* is more of a classic. Different people are going to have different opinions about what is classic or desirable. There are certain constants, such as an artist's first

gold or platinum award; most collectors would place a premium on that. Again, personal preference and the generalization rule referred to earlier also apply here.

3) **Organization Recognizing Sales Achievement.** *This section deserves special notation because so many record award collectors place high emphasis on this.* Most collectors in the United States prefer to have R.I.A.A. certified awards. R.I.A.A. stands for Record Industry Association of America, the official organization in the U.S. which certifies the number of records, tapes and compact discs sold. The R.I.A.A. has many other functions but the main one which concerns us here is that it acts as an unbiased accounting firm to verify the actual number of units sold. It is for this reason that most award collectors give R.I.A.A. certification so much importance. However, it is important to note that record awards that are certified by the record company itself (commonly referred to as "in-house awards") are also desirable. Besides the beauty of some in-house awards, even after 1958 (the year the R.I.A.A. was formed), many record companies did not become members (Motown comes instantly to mind).

Another thing to keep in mind is that Platinum status (described below), was recognized by individual record companies years before the R.I.A.A. did in 1976. So Platinum in-house award presented prior to 1976 can be just as valid as an R.I.A.A. gold award presented at the same time.

The official organization certifying sales achievement in the United Kingdom is the B.P.I., or British Phonographic Industry. Because of the blue, red and black cloth backgrounds of these awards, they can be especially nice to acquire.

4). **R.I.A.A. Award Designation** (Gold Platinum or Multi-Platinum). Qualification for R.I.A.A. awards have varied over the years as the following chart illustrates:

1958-1974:	45 Gold Award	1,000,000	units in sales.
	LP Gold Award	1,000,000	dollars in sales.
1975-1988	45 Gold Award	1,000,000	units in sales.
	LP Gold Award	500,000	units in sales.
1976	45 Platinum Award	2,000,000	units in sales.
	LP Platinum Award	1,000,000	units in sales.
1984	LP Multi-Platinum Awards		
	LP Double-Platinum Awards	2,000,000	units in sales.
	LP Triple-Platinum Awards	3,000,000	units in sales.
	Etc.		
1989	45 Gold Award*	500,000	units in sales.

Single and album requirements are now the same.

5) **R.I.A.A. Styles or Formats of Awards.**

A. White Matte (1958-1974): The plaque background is an off-white linen material in an unpainted wood frame.

B. Floater (1975-1981): The plaque background is dark (usually black). The record, mini-cover (in the case of albums) and award plate appear to be floating between the background and the Plexiglas in an unpainted wood frame.

C. Strip-Plate (1982-1984): The plaque background is dark. The engraving and R.I.A.A. logo (and mini-cover for album awards) are on the same strip of metal. These came with and without a cassette inside.

D. Hologram (1984-1989): Same as the strip-plate above except the R.I.A.A. logo is designated in a hologram, rainbow-fashion, to avoid copying. All come with the cassette inside.

Because of the increased popularity of collecting these puppies in the last few years, many recipients have taken to ordering extra R.I.A.A. awards to sell to the collector market. Therefore, when buying a hologram (or any other style of award for that matter), try to make sure the award is in the *original format.* Original format means that the style of the award coincides with the time period in which the album or single was originally certified by the R.I.A.A. The original format of

any award will be the most desirable (most of the time).

Another thing to remember is that sometimes record companies have been known to reframe awards in a style other than the standard frame of a given style. This was done to replace damaged frames or because someone in the record company didn't like the standard frame. This practice was not met with favor by the R.I.A.A, and has been discontinued for the most part.

6) **Recipient.** In my opinion, the best way to get an award "Presented to" is listed below in descending order.

    A. The artist.
    B. The record company.
    C. Someone closely connected with the production of the record. Example: anyone listed in the album credits.
    D. Production company.
    E. Radio station.
    F. A record company executive.

7) **Price.** Compare prices. Prices are going to vary, depending on how a dealer has invested in a given item and what the dealer thinks he can get out of that award. Consider all the preceding factors but be sure to consider a dealer's reputation. A good price is a *bad* price if you never receive the item or get a bogus one.

Gold and platinum awards are a great investment if you invest in an artist who will maintain collector interest over the years. As the interest in this field of collecting continues to grow, a wise purchase in the present has the potential to grow into a healthy investment for the future.

Revised from "Welcome To the Wonderful World Of Gold And Platinum Award Collecting; An Introduction," an advertisement in June 30, 1989, issue of Goldmine magazine. Christopher Chatman, owner of Beyond Records, is a collector/dealer who has specialized in rare records and memorabilia- including gold and platinum awards-for several years.

GOLDMINE publisher's foreward by John Koenig

For the eleven years of my professional involvement with GOLDMINE magazine, and my twenty years of 'collecting records,' just what an item is worth has always been a subject of discussion. Cold hard cash hasn't been the primary focus for all that time, but it's safe to say that these days it's one of the first topics to come up. As the field evolves and grows, valuations become more and more important. Hundreds, perhaps thousands, of people in this country are making their living selling used recordings.

Discographies and detailed listings of records have always been a mainstay of GOLDMINE magazine's editorial offerings. Collectors, dealers and casual readers alike find this reference information entertaining and useful. A few years ago we determined that adding pricing information would increase the value of our articles. Neal Umphred was the logical choice to assist us in this project. We knew him as an advertiser in our pages, and we were aware of his work in books as a price-guide editor for O'Sullivan Woodside Publishing in Arizona.

In recent years we've slowly increased the volume of pricing in the GOLDMINE discographies and articles. Our readership applauds these moves. They reflect changes in the record collecting marketplace. Records are worth more money today than ever before. The rare and desirable discs have been rapidly increasing in value. Collectors and dealers need current, accurate and realistic pricing information. We've been providing this in GOLDMINE magazine.

Over the years, Neal and I often talked about price guides and the current state of the record collecting hobby. Krause Publications is a longtime book publisher, and we agreed with Neil that a general price guide to record albums was a good idea. This book is the result.

One of the hardest tasks in putting together a project such as this is determining what should and should not be included. We wanted the book to be useful to the average album buyer, not just the specialist or hardcore collector. Neil's original manuscript was 600 pages; the resulting volume has had many records, and entire artists, deleted. There is no way to satisfy every need, and we haven't tried.

What we have produced is a realistic, current, interesting, and useful price guide to popular record albums from the late '40s to the early '80s. This book might be only the first of a series of books serving recorded music collectors of all types. Whatever your interests, I think you will find information of value to you in these pages. If you have ideas for future volumes, or changes, additions or corrections for this one, please let us know. This book is for everyone who loves popular music and the long-playing records it's recorded on.

"How Much Is It Worth?"

By Gary Johnson of Rockaway Records

In recent years, collectible records have seen a tremendous surge in value — so much so that some people will be amazed or even bewildered when they read the prices that this book indicates rare records are worth today. Although to some they may seem high, due to Neal Umphred's essentially conservative approach to pricing, many items might be undervalued.

Let's examine some of the factors that have caused rare records to escalate in value in the past few years:

1. **DEMAND:** The demand for rarities by major collectible artists (e.g. Beatles, Elvis Presley, Buddy Holly, etc.) is at an all-time high. In the case of Beatles rarities, the demand is growing all the time.

2. **SCARCITY:** This dates the book. As time goes on, the amount of older rarities available decreases. An original Gene Vincent LP is now over 30 years old! Although a certain record was seen for sale often in 1975, it may rarely, if ever, be offered for sale today. Original sources and quantities of many older items have now dried up.

3. **CONDITION:** I can't stress this factor enough. Many of today's collectors seem far more educated about condition than ever before. With 1950's Rock and Roll and Rhythm & Blues LP's and 1960's Beatles records, condition is probably the most important factor in determining a current market value.

   For example, original Beatles and Elvis Presley LP's are not very rare. Remember, they sold millions of copies. However, a mint copy (in the truest sense of the word) is a genuine rarity and will command a price many times greater than usual simply because of its immaculate condition.

   If you often see a particular record for sale at $100, then suddenly someone is asking $300 for the same record, it does not necessarily mean the $300 price is outrageous. Look at the disc. If the expensive copy is in beautiful condition, it's certainly worth three times the price of the average condition copy. The $300 price may even be conservative in this case due to it's extreme rarity in this exceptional condition.

4. **INFLATION:** As much of what we buy today increases in price, so do records. Many of the older rarities actually seem cheap compared to prices of newer collectibles. For example, a 1989 Madonna promotional gold compact disc is worth approximately the same price as a 1950's Elvis Presley 7 inch EP with picture cover!

Many dealers have $12-$15 minimum bids on LP's for auction today. In my opinion, this is fair since the price of a new CD is $15, and the item the collector is purchasing is most likely a 10-year-old out-of-print LP!

5. **COMPACT DISCS:** As fewer records become available, many collectors are buying rare records for fear of not finding them later. This fear may or may not reflect reality. It is true that trying to find new records in stores is very difficult today, but it is also true that, as more people convert to compact disc, many more used and out-of-print records are available for sale. Theoretically, the supply should outweigh the demand, and prices will come down.

Although this is somewhat true for common used LP's, it is certainly not true for collectible out-of-print items. My feeling is that common used records will continue to be worth less while out-of-print rarities will only continue to escalate in value. This will be due to a continuing decrease in the amount of quality items offered for sale and the increased demand by the specialty market (i.e. record collectors).

Everyone should applaud the bold accurate price info in this book. The prices in this book reflect the changing nature of records as a "legitimate" collectible such as comic books and baseball cards. Even at today's prices, most records are worth relatively little compared to other collectibles. As we enter the 1990's, I believe we will see many records approach the value of other established collectibles.

The trend has already begun in this respect in the case of extremely rare R&B 45's, Beatles, and Elvis records reaching unprecendented prices at auction. Also, recent sales of Rock and Roll memorabilia at prestigious auction houses such as Sotheby's and Christie's has assisted in making Rock and Roll collecting "legitimate."

In the past, these auction houses have shied away from selling rare records, but recent sales have shown that this is now changing. Many people are now discovering that rare records can be a great investment item. (It is also nostalgic and fun!) For example, a still-sealed stereo first-state Beatles "Butcher Cover" was worth $4,000, in 1985. In 1988 one was sold for $10,000, and this was no fluke. This is a more than 40% increase per year!

I believe the next five years will show that records as an investment-quality collectible will finally achieve the notoriety they deserve, and prices today of true rarities will seem like a steal compared to tomorrow's prices. Time will tell.

The 100 Most Valuable Albums 1948-1988
From Goldmine's Price Guide To Collectible Record Albums

The Beatles
Capitol ST-2553

Yesterday And Today — 1966 — $5,000.00
(Stereo. First state butcher cover. The original cover with the Fab Four in doctor's smocks covered with pieces of meat and baby doll parts!)

Bob Dylan
Columbia CL-1986

The Freewheelin' Bob Dylan — 1963 — 4,000.00
(Mono. Original pressing with "Talkin" John Birch Society Blues," "Let Me Die In My Footsteps," "Ramblin,' Gamblin,' Willie's Dead Man's Hand," and "Rocks And Gravel." Stereo copies are not known to exist.)

David Bowie
RCA APL1-0576

Diamond Dogs — 1974 — 3,000.00
(The cover painting features the Bowiedog with its genitals plainly visible.)

The Beatles/Frank Ifield
Vee Jay LP-1085

The Beatles And Frank Ifield On Stage — 1964 — 3,000.00
(Stereo. The cover has a painting of the Beatles on the front.)

The Beatles
Vee Jay LPS-1062

Introducing The Beatles — 1963 — 2,500.00
(Stereo. Black rainbow label with "Love Me Do." The back cover features ads for 25 other albums.)

Elvis Presley
RCA VPSX-6089

Aloha From Hawaii Via Satellite — 1973 — 2,000.00
(Commercial copy of the album with a sticker on the cover with the Chicken Of The Sea mermaid that reads "Sneak Preview. Chicken Of The Sea Sponsors Elvis Presley's Greatest TV Performance." Also included was an insert explaining Van Camp's involvement.)

Ike & Tina Turner
Philles PHLP-4011

River Deep-Mountain High — 1966 — 2,000.00
(A very small quantity of the album was pressed and most subsequently destroyed. There were no covers manufactured.)

The Beatles/The Four Seasons
Vee Jay DXS-30

The Beatles Vs. The Four Seasons — 1964 — 1,500.00
(Stereo. A repackage of "Introducing The Beatles" with "The Golden Hits Of The Four Seasons." The price may be affected by which version of "Introducing" is used. Issued with a large, full-color poster of the moptops, which is worth $150.)

The Beatles
Capitol T-2553

Yesterday And Today — 1966 — 1,500.00
(Mono, First state butcher cover.)

The Beatles
Vee Jay LP-1062

Introducing The Beatles — 1963 — 1,200.00
(Mono. Black rainbow label with "Love Me Do." The back cover features ads for 25 other albums.)

Billy Ward & The Dominoes
Federal 295-94 (10")

Billy Ward & His Dominoes — 1954 — 1,200.00

The Beatles
Vee Jay LPS-1062

Introducing The Beatles — 1963 — 1,000.00
(Stereo. Black rainbow label with "Love Me Do." The back cover is blank.)

The Beatles/Frank Ifield
Vee Jay LP-1085

The Beatles And Frank Ifield On Stage — 1964 — 1,000.00
(Mono. The cover has a painting of the Beatles on the front.)

The Beatles
Vee Jay LPS-1092

Songs, Pictures And Stories — 1964 — 1,000.00
(Stereo. The fold-open front cover is 8" across.)

The Beatles
Capitol ST-2553

Yesterday And Today — 1966 — 1,000.00
(Stereo. Second state butcher cover. The trunk cover is pasted over the original butcher cover with no attempts at removal.)

Ruth Brown
King 115 (10")

Ruth Brown — 1956 — 1,000.00

Boyd Bennett
King 594

Boyd Bennett — 1957 — 1,000.00

BRISK PRODUCTIONS
27 Old Gloucester Street, London, England WCIN 3XX

Yardbirds' Jim McCarty, The Downliners Sect & Chris Youlden have the following products available only by mail order (not in any stores) solely from Brisk Productions. Price includes airmail postage.

A. Yardbirds World-The Book. This superb privately printed paperback book, personally autographed by Jim McCarty, is a best of compilation of Richard MacKay's famous Yardbirds magazine. Jam packed with more never before published information on the Yardbirds and their off-shoot bands than you could ever imagine. Your wildest dreams come true. Featuring interviews with Jim McCarty and Jane Relf, Jeff Beck and Jimmy Page Studio Sessions, The 1983 Yardbirds Reunion Concerts, The Beck/ Page Yardbirds, unreleased recordings, radio/ TV sessions, Renaissance, Illusion, The Resurfacing Of Top Topham, Videographies, The Jim McCarty-Top Topham Band, rare 1980's photos and much more. $27.50

B. CD's and official cassettes - All are personally autographed by Jim McCarty:
   1. Illusion - "Enchanted Caress" - The Unreleased Third Album By Jane Relf, Jim Mc-Carty, John Hawken, Loui Cennamo and John Knightsbridge, including as a bonus Keith Relf's last unreleased recording "All The Fallen Angels" is now officially available on CD or cassette only from brisk productions by special arrangement with Jim McCarty. Illusion, The Original Renaissance, were the Beatles of progressive rock and this masterpiece is their Sergeant Pepper. These are the completed demos for their unreleased 3rd LP and they sound unbelievably beautiful. CD is $26.50. Cassette is 20.50
   2. Jim McCarty & Loui Cennammo's Stairway Moonstone CD or Cassette. Exceedingly hard to find fantastic recording featuring Jane Relf on vocals doing beautiful melodic originals in the Renaissance mode backed by Jim & Loui. Jim sings too. CD has over an hour of great music. Cassette has 45 minutes of music. CD is $35.00. Cassette is 22.50
   3. Jim McCarty & Loui Cennammo's Stairway Aquamarine Cassette. Exceedingly hard to find. Beautiful originals from the boys, mainly instrumentals, with Jane Relf singing The Incredible Aquamarine 22.50

C. Official authorized VHS Videos (available in both the American System NTSC format or the European Pal Format. U.S. orders automatically sent NTSC format). All personally autographed by Jim McCarty except #5&6:
   1. The Yardbird-Downliners Sect Summer Jam of 89. Incredible Ballsy Live R&B Jam between Yardbird Jim McCarty and The Downliners Sect. 60 minutes 42.00
   2. Jim McCarty and Loui Cennammo's Stairway Live In Concert Jim and Loui perform beautiful original songs in the Renaissance mode featuring Jim on lead vocals. Wonderful! 75 minutes 45.00
   3. Jim McCarty: The Yardbird Interview. Revealing interview in which Jim talks openly with Richard MacKay about the Yardbirds and his musical career & plays little Yardbirds snippets on drums. 75 minutes 45.00
   4. Intro to Rock Drumming The Yardbirds Style By Jim McCarty. This is a drum instruction video by Jim in which he demonstrates basic rock drumming by playing various Yardbirds numbers on drums. 60 minutes 41.00
   5. Chris Youlden: The Interview. Former Savoy Brown Singer Chris talks about his career before, during and after Savoy Brown. 60 minutes 41.00
   6. The Downliners Sect Story Vol. 1. The Downliners Sect perform great rockers and tell their story. 60 minutes 41.00

D. To Order: Send regular U.S. money order only (postal, bank, etc.) in U.S. dollars to: Brisk Productions, 27 Old Gloucester Street, London, England WCIN 3XX.

E. To Order From England, Europe, Japan, Australia, Etc.: Checks, Postal Orders, International Money Orders in pounds sterling drawn on a UK bank. Use a conversion rate of $1.50 to a pound. Send to address listed above.

Little Esther (Philips)
King 622 — Memory Lane/The Greatest Songs Little Esther Ever Recorded — 1,000.00

Johnny Burnette & The Rock 'N' Roll Trio
Coral CRL-57080 — Johnny Burnette & The Rock 'N' Roll Trio — 1956 — 1,000.00

Elvis Presley
RCA Victor LPM-1382 — Elvis — 1956 — 1,000.00
(Contains an alternate take of "Old Shep." Copies with the matrix number in the trail-off vinyl that end with either "17S" or "19S" may or may not have the rare track; listening is required. In the common version Elvis sings the lines in the first verse "we were both full of fun" without pause. In the rare version here Elvis sings "we were both...full of fun," pausing between "both" and "full.")

Elvis Presley
RCA Victor LPM-3989 — Speedway — 1968 — 1,000.00
(Issued with a bonus photo, which is worth $50.)

Frank Frost & The Nighthawks
Phillips International
1975 — Hey Boss Man! — 1961 — 750.00

The Beatles/The Four Seasons
Vee Jays DX-30 — The Beatles Vs. The Four Seasons — 1964 — 600.00
(Mono. The price may be affected by which version of "Introducing" is used. Issued with a poster, which is worth $150.)

Roy Brown, Wynonie Harris & Eddie Vinson
King 668 — Battle Of The Blues, Volume 4 — 1960 — 600.00

The Fendermen
Soma MG-1240 — Mule Skinner Blues — 1960 — 600.00

The Five Satins
Ember ELP-100 — The Five Satins Sing (Blue vinyl) — 1957 — 600.00
(The price is a very conservative estimate.)

Jim Reeves
Abbott LP-5001 — Jim Reeves Sings — 1956 — 600.00

Marty Robbins
Columbia CL-2544 (10") — Rock 'N' Roll 'N' Robbins — 1956 — 600.00

Hank Ballard & The Midnighters
Federal 295-90 (10") — The Midnighters — 1954 — 500.00

The Beatles
Vee Jay LP-1062 — Introducing The Beatles — 1963 — 500.00
(Mono. Black rainbow label with "Love Me Do." The back cover is blank.)

The Beatles
Vee Jay LPS-1062 — Introducing The Beatles — 1964 — 500.00
(Stereo. Black rainbow label with the "Vee Jay" logo on top. Includes "Please Please Me.")

The Chantels
End LP-301 — We're The Chantels — 1958 — 500.00
(The cover features a photo of the girls.)

Fats Domino
Reprise RS-6439 — Fats — 1971 — 500.00
(This album was pressed in miniscule quantities and appears on virtually every Fats Domino collectors want-list. The price is a conservative estimate.)

The Five Keys
Aladdin 806 — The Best Of The Five Keys (Blue label) — 1956 — 500.00

The Four Lovers
RCA Victor LPM-1317 — Joyride — 1956 — 500.00

The Four Tops
Workshop 217 — Jazz Impressions — 1962 — 500.00

Bill Haley & The Comets
Decca DL-5560 (10") — Shake, Rattle And Roll — 1954 — 500.00

Buddy Holly Decca DL-8707	That'll Be The Day (Black label.)	1958	**500.00**
Carl Mann Phillips International 1960	Like Mann	1960	**500.00**
Gatemouth Moore King 684	I'm A Fool To Care	1960	**500.00**
The Platters Federal 395-549	The Platters	1955	**500.00**
Elvis Presley RCA Victor LPM-3921	Elvis' Gold Records, Volume 4 *(Issued with a bonus photo, which is worth $100.)*	1968	**500.00**
The Teddy Bears Imperial LP-12067	The Teddy Bears Sings!	1959	**500.00**
Billy Ward & The Dominoes Federal 395-94	Billy Ward & His Dominoes	1956	**500.00**
Billy Ward & The Dominoes Federal 559	Clyde McPhatter With Billy Ward	1957	**500.00**
The C.A. Quintet Candy Floss 7764	A Trip Through Hell	1969	**500.00**
The Marble Phrogg Derrick 8868	The Marble Phrogg	1968	**500.00**
The New Tweedy Brothers Ridon 234	The New Tweedy Brothers		**500.00**
The Rising Storm Remnant 3571	A Calm Before The Rising Storm	1968	**500.00**
West Coast Pop Art Fifo M1001	The West Coast Pop Art Experimental Band *(The five albums listed above are pivotal pieces in the collecting of '60s garage/punk/pshychedelia. Each was limited to a pressing of several hundred copies and each has sold for considerably more than $500 each.)*	1956	**500.00**
Eddie Vinson & Jimmy Witherspoon King 634	Battle Of The Blues, Volume 3	1959	**450.00**
Frank Ballard Phillips International 1985	Rhythm-Blues Party	1962	**400.00**
Charlie Rich Phillips International 1970	Lonely Weekends	1960	**400.00**
The Beatles Capitol T-2553	Yesterday And Today *(Mono. Second state butcher cover.)*	1966	**400.00**
The Beatles/The George Martin Orchestra United Artists UAL-3366	A Hard Day's Night *(Mono. Black label record club release.)*	1964	**400.00**
Grandma's Rockers Fredlo 6727	Homemade Apple Pie	1967	**400.00**
The Iveys Apple SAPCOR-8S	Maybe Tomorrow *(This Italian version is included due to the fact that it has been heavily counterfeited and sold as legitimate. The real one has the common green Apple label while the bootleg has a black label.)*	1968	**400.00**
Kenny & The Kasuals Mark 5000	The Impact Sound Of Kenny & the Kasuals	1966	**400.00**

The Kinks
Warners/Reprise
PRO-328 — **The Kinks Box** — 1969 — **400.00**
(Alternately known as either the "God Save The Kinks" box or the "Then, Now And In Between" box. The contents include a Victorian postcard; a "God Save The Kinks" button; a bag of grass; a decal; a Union Jack lapel pin; a decal; a letter; a Kinks Konsumer Guide; and an album, "Then, Now And In Between.")

Carl Perkins
Sun 1225 — **The Dance Album Of Carl Perkins** — 1957 — **400.00**

Elvis Presley
RCA Victor LOC-1035 — **Elvis' Christmas Album** — 1957 — **400.00**
(Gatefold cover with ten pages of photos bound to the inner spine. Some copies came with a "gift certificate" sticker that read "To ___/ From ___/ Elvis Sings" with the contents of the album. Some stickers were adhered to the back cover while others were applied to a loose plastic bag. The sticker is worth $100.)

Elvis Presley
RCA Victor LSP-2999 — **Roustabout** — 1964 — **400.00**
(Black label with "Living Stereo" in silver on the bottom.)

Del Shannon
Big Top S12-3003 — **Runaway** — 1961 — **400.00**

Charles Brown
Aladdin 702 (10") — **Mood Music** (Red vinyl) — 1954 — **400.00**

Amos Milburn
Aladdin 704 (10") — **Rockin' The Boogie** (Red vinyl) — 1956 — **400.00**

The Five Royales
Apollo LP-488 — **The Rockin' Five Royales** — 1956 — **400.00**

The Five Keys
Score LP-4003 — **On The Town** — 1957 — **400.00**

Johnny Ace
Duke DLP-70 (10") — **Memorial Album For Johnny Ace** — 1955 — **350.00**

The Beatles
Vee Jay LPS-1062 — **Introducing The Beatles** — 1964 — **350.00**
(Stereo. Black rainbow label with the "VJ" logo on top. Includes "Please Please Me.")

Wynonie Harris, Amos Milburn & Crown Prince Waterford
Aladdin 703 (10") — **Party After Hours** (Red vinyl) — 1956 — **350.00**

Dale Hawkins
Chess 1429 — **Suzie-Q** — 1958 — **350.00**

John Lennon
Adam VIII LP-8018 — **The Great Rock & Roll Hits/Roots** — 1975 — **350.00**

Fapardokly
U.I.P. 250 — **Fapardokly** — 1966 — **350.00**

The Tempos
Justice 104 — **Speaking Of The Tempos** — 1966 — **350.00**

The Beatles
Vee Jay LPS-1062 — **Introducing The Beatles** — 1964 — **300.00**
(Stereo. Solid black label with the "Vee Jay" logo on top. Includes "Please Please Me.")

The Big Bopper (J.P. Richardson)
Mercury MG-20402 — **Chantilly Lace** (Black label) — 1959 — **300.00**

Roy Brown & Wynonie Harris
King 607 — **Battle Of The Blues, Volume 1** — 1958 — **300.00**

Roy Brown & Wynonie Harris
King 607 — **Battle Of The Blues, Volume 2** — 1959 — **300.00**

The Champs Challenge CHL-601	**Go Champs, Go** (Blue vinyl)	1958	**300.00**
The Clovers Atlantic 1248	**The Clovers** (Black label)	1956	**300.00**
Esquerita Capitol T-1186	**Esquerita**	1959	**300.00**
Screamin' Jay Hawkins Epic LN-3448	**At Home With Screamin' Jay Hawkins**	1956	**300.00**
Buddy Holly & The Crickets Brunswick BL-54038	**The "Chirping" Crickets**	1957	**300.00**
Amos Milburn Aladdin 704 (10")	**Rockin' The Boogie**	1956	**300.00**
Shirley & Lee Aladdin 807	**Let The Good Times Roll**	1956	**300.00**
The Platters King 549	**The Platters**	1956	**300.00**
Lulu Reed King 604	**Moody And Blue**	1959	**300.00**
Frankie Lymon & the Teenagers Gee GLP-701	**The Teenagers** (Red label)	1957	**300.00**
The Spaniels Vee Jay LP-1002	**Goodnite, It's Time To Go** (Maroon label)	1958	**300.00**
The Del Vikings Luniverse LP-1000	**Come Go With The Del Vikings**	1957	**300.00**
The Fugitives Hideout 1001	**The Fugitives At Dave's Hideout**	1968	**300.00**
Mickey Gilley Astro 101	**Lonely Wine**	1964	**300.00**
Paul Revere & The Raiders Sande 1001	**Paul Revere & The Raiders**	1962	**300.00**
Shep & The Limelites Hull 1001	**Our Anniversary**	1962	**300.00**
The Stowaways Justice	**The Stowaways**		**300.00**
The Teddy Bears Imperial LP-9067	**The Teddy Bears Sing!**	1959	**300.00**
Gene Vincent Capitol T-764	**Bluejean Bop!**	1957	**300.00**
Gene Vincent Capitol T-811	**Gene Vincent & The Blue Caps**	1957	**300.00**
Gene Vincent Capitol T-970	**Gene Vincent Rocks! And The Blue Caps Roll**	1958	**300.00**
Gene Vincent Capitol T-1059	**A Gene Vincent Record Date**	1958	**300.00**

Honorable Mention
Records That Would Make The Top 100 If I Could Determine A Value For Them!

Jan & Dean
Columbia CL-2661   **Save For A Rainy Day**   1967
Columbia CS-9461   **Save For A Rainy Day**   1967
                     (Long rumored to exist, there are no copies known. A
                     Conservative estimate would be $2,000.)

The Crests
Coed LPS-904   **The Best Of The Crests**   1961
                     (Long rumored to exist, a stereo cover has been found but a stereo copy
                     of the record has not. A conservative estimate would be $2,000.)

The Rolling Stones
London LL-3402   **12 X 5**   1964
                     (Blue vinyl. A conservative estimate would be $2,000.)

Record Collecting Abbreviations

Listed here are several common abbreviatons used when advertising to describe flaws and their locations on a record or cover. Different collectors/dealers have different ways of using these abbreviations; some capitalize them ("DJ"), some use periods after each letter ("n.a.p.") and some use a slash ("c/o"). Those defects marked with an asterisk (*) should *always be listed* when advertising an item for sale or auction.

alt	alternate (take)
cc	cut corner*
co	cut out*
coh	cut-out hole*
c-33	compact-33⅓ rpm single or EP
cvr	cover
dj	disc jockey, or promotional, copy
flexi	flexible plastic disc
imp	import
ips	inches per second
lbl	label
lp	12" 33⅓ rpm long playing album
mo	mono, or monaural
nap	(does) not affect play
ol	on label
org	original
pln cvr	plain paper jacket (no picture or titles)
promo	promotional copy
quad	quadraphonic
re	reissue

reel	reel to reel tape
repro	reproduction, or counterfeit
sdtk	soundtrack
se	stereo effect electronically produced
2nd pr	second pressing
slt wrp	slight warp*
sm	saw mark (a cut-out mark)*
sm splt	seam split*
sol	sticker on the label*
sr	slight ring-wear on the front cover*
ss	still sealed
st	stereo
stkr	sticker
10"	10" 33⅓ rpm album
t&ts	(disc jockey) title & timing strip
toc	tape on the cover*
tol	tape on the label*
ts	taped seams*
wlp	white label promo
wol	writing on the label*

Label		Title	Year	VG+	NM
A.F.O. EXECUTIVES, THE					
A.F.O. LP-0002	(M)	A Compendium		75.00	150.00
ABBA					
Nautilus 20	(S)	Arrival		8.00	20.00
ACE, JOHNNY					
Duke DLP-70 (10")	(M)	Memorial Album For Johnny Ace	1955	210.00	350.00
Duke DLP-71	(M)	Memorial Album For Johnny Ace	1956	75.00	150.00
		(Purple & yellow label.)			
ACUFF, ROY					
Columbia CL-9004 (10")	(M)	Songs Of The Smokey Mountains		16.00	40.00
Columbia CL-9010 (10")	(M)	Old Time Barn Music		16.00	40.00
Capitol T-617	(M)	Songs Of The Smokey Mountains	1955	10.00	25.00
MGM E-3707	(M)	Favorite Hymns	1958	10.00	25.00
MGM E-4044	(M)	Hymn Time	1962	5.00	12.00
MGM SE-4044	(S)	Hymn Time	1962	6.00	15.00
Capitol T-1870	(M)	Songs Of The Smokey Mountains	1963	6.00	15.00
Capitol T-2103	(M)	The Great Roy Acuff	1964	5.00	12.00
Capitol ST-2103	(S)	The Great Roy Acuff	1964	6.00	15.00
Capitol T-2276	(M)	The Voice Of Country Music	1965	5.00	12.00
Capitol ST-2276	(S)	The Voice Of Country Music	1965	6.00	15.00
ADAMS, EDIE					
MGM E-3751	(M)	Music To Listen To Records To		6.00	15.00
MGM SE-3751	(S)	Music To Listen To Records To		8.00	20.00
ADAMS, FAYE					
Warwick 2031	(M)	Shake A Hand	1961	40.00	80.00
ADAMS, MIKE, & THE RED JACKETS					
Crown CST-312	(S)	Surfer's Beat (Colored vinyl)	1963	16.00	40.00
ADRIAN & THE SUNSETS					
Sunset 63-601	(M)	Breakthrough	1963	30.00	60.00
Sunset 63-601	(M)	Breakthrough (Multi-colored vinyl)	1963	45.00	90.00
Sunset SE-63-601	(S)	Breakthrough	1963	35.00	70.00
Sunset SE-63-601	(S)	Breakthrough (Multi-colored vinyl)	1963	50.00	100.00
ADVENTURERS, THE					
Columbia CL-2147	(M)	Can't Stop Twistin'	1961	8.00	20.00
Columbia CS-8547	(S)	Can't Stop Twistin'	1961	10.00	25.00
AEROSMITH					
Columbia KCQ-32847	(Q)	Get Your Wings	1974	6.00	15.00
Columbia JCQ-33479	(Q)	Toys In The Attic	1975	6.00	15.00
Columbia PCQ-34165	(Q)	Rocks	1976	6.00	15.00
AESOPS FABLE					
Cadet Concept LPS-323	(S)	In Due Time	1969	8.00	20.00
AFFINITY					
Paramount PAS-5027	(S)	Affinity	1970	10.00	25.00
AFTERGLOW					
M.T.A. 5010	(M)	Afterglow	1967	8.00	20.00
AGGREGATION					
L.H.I. 12008	(S)	Mind Odyssey	1967	40.00	80.00

Label		Title	Year	VG+	NM
AIR SUPPLY					
Mobile Fidelity 1-113	(S)	The One That You Love		5.00	12.00
Nautilus 31	(S)	Lost In Love		8.00	20.00
AKENS, JEWEL					
End EL-110	(M)	The Birds And The Bees	1965	8.00	20.00
End ES-110	(S)	The Birds And The Bees	1965	10.00	25.00
ALAIMO, STEVE					
Checker LP-2981	(M)	Twist With Steve Alaimo	1961	14.00	35.00
Checker LP-2983	(M)	Mashed Potatoes	1962	14.00	35.00
Checker LP-2986	(M)	Every Day I Have To Cry	1963	14.00	35.00
ABC-Paramount 501	(M)	Starring Steve Alaimo	1965	8.00	20.00
ABC-Paramount S-501	(S)	Starring Steve Alaimo	1965	10.00	25.00
ABC-Paramount 531	(M)	Where The Action Is	1965	8.00	20.00
ABC-Paramount S-531	(S)	Where The Action Is	1965	10.00	25.00
ABC-Paramount 551	(M)	Steve Alaimo Sings And Swings	1966	8.00	20.00
ABC-Paramount S-551	(S)	Steve Alaimo Sings And Swings	1966	10.00	25.00
ALBERTS, AL					
Coral CRL-57259	(M)	Man Has Got To Sing	1959	10.00	25.00
Coral CRL7-57259	(S)	Man Has Got To Sing	1959	12.00	30.00
ALBRIGHT, LOLA					
Columbia CL-1327	(M)	Dreamsville	1959	6.00	15.00
Columbia CS-8133	(S)	Dreamsville	1959	8.00	20.00
ALEONG, ALI, & THE NOBLES					
Reprise R-6020	(M)	C'Mon Baby, Let's Dance	1962	6.00	15.00
Reprise R9-6020	(S)	C'Mon Baby, Let's Dance	1962	8.00	20.00
Reprise R-6011	(M)	Twistin' The Hits	1962	6.00	15.00
Reprise R9-6011	(S)	Twistin' The Hits	1962	8.00	20.00
Vee Jay LP-1060	(M)	Come Surf With Me	1963	8.00	20.00
Vee Jay SR-1060	(S)	Come Surf With Me	1963	10.00	25.00
ALEXANDER, ARTHUR					
Dot DLP-3434	(M)	You Better Move On	1962	16.00	40.00
Dot DLP-25434	(S)	You Better Move On	1962	30.00	60.00
Warners B-2592	(S)	Arthur Alexander	1972	6.00	15.00
ALEXANDER'S TIMELESS BLOOZBAND					
Smack 1001	(M)	Alexander's Timeless Bloozband	1967	65.00	130.00
ALL STARS, THE					
Gramophone 20192	(M)	Boogie Woogie		20.00	50.00
ALLAN, CHAD, & THE EXPRESSIONS					
Scepter SP-533	(M)	Chad Allan And The Expressions	1966	10.00	25.00
Scepter SPS-533	(E)	Chad Allan And The Expressions	1966	6.00	15.00
ALLAN, DAVIE (& THE ARROWS)					
Tower T-5002	(M)	Apache '65	1965	8.00	20.00
Tower DT-5002	(E)	Apache '65	1965	6.00	15.00
Tower T-5043	(M)	The Wild Angels (Sdtk)	1966	6.00	15.00
Tower DT-5043	(E)	The Wild Angels (Sdtk)	1966	5.00	12.00
Tower T-5053	(M)	Dr. Goldfoot And The Girl Bombs (Sdtk)	1967	5.00	12.00
Tower DT-5053	(E)	Dr. Goldfoot And The Girl Bombs (Sdtk)	1967	4.00	10.00
Tower T-5056	(M)	The Wild Angels, Volume 2 (Sdtk)	1967	8.00	20.00
Tower DT-5056	(E)	The Wild Angels, Volume 2 (Sdtk)	1967	6.00	15.00
Tower T-5065	(M)	Riot On Sunset Strip (Sdtk)	1967	14.00	35.00
Tower DT-5065	(E)	Riot On Sunset Strip (Sdtk)	1967	12.00	30.00
Tower T-5074	(M)	Devil's Angels (Sdtk)	1967	8.00	20.00
Tower DT-5074	(E)	Devil's Angels (Sdtk)	1967	6.00	15.00
Tower T-5078	(M)	Blues Theme	1967	10.00	25.00
Tower DT-5078	(E)	Blues Theme	1967	8.00	20.00
Sidewalk T-5902	(M)	Thunder Alley (Sdtk)	1967	6.00	15.00
Sidewalk ST-5902	(S)	Thunder Alley (Sdtk)	1967	8.00	20.00
Sidewalk T-5903	(M)	Teenage Rebellion (Sdtk)	1967	10.00	25.00
Sidewalk DT-5903	(E)	Teenage Rebellion (Sdtk)	1967	8.00	20.00
Sidewalk T-5907	(M)	Albert Peckingpaw's Revenge (Sdtk)	1967	5.00	12.00
Sidewalk ST-5907	(S)	Albert Peckingpaw's Revenge (Sdtk)	1967	6.00	15.00

Label		Title	Year	VG+	NM
Sidewalk T-5910	(M)	Glory Stompers (Sdtk)	1968	8.00	20.00
Sidewalk DT-5910	(E)	Glory Stompers (Sdtk)	1968	6.00	15.00
Sidewalk T-5911	(M)	Mary Jane (Sdtk)	1968	10.00	25.00
Sidewalk DT-5911	(E)	Mary Jane (Sdtk)	1968	8.00	20.00
Sidewalk T-5914	(M)	Wild Racers (Sdtk)	1968	6.00	15.00
Sidewalk ST-5914	(S)	Wild Racers (Sdtk)	1968	8.00	20.00
Tower DT-5083	(E)	Mondo Hollywood (Sdtk)	1968	10.00	25.00
Tower DT-5094	(E)	Cycledelic Sounds	1968	10.00	25.00
Tower DT-5099	(S)	Wild In The Streets (Sdtk)	1968	8.00	20.00
Tower DT-5124	(E)	Hellcats (Sdtk)	1968	8.00	20.00
Tower DT-5141	(S)	Killers Three (Sdtk)	1968	8.00	20.00

ALLEN, DAVE

Label		Title	Year	VG+	NM
International Arts. 11	(S)	Color Blind	1969	20.00	50.00

ALLEN, LEE

Label		Title	Year	VG+	NM
Ember ELP-200	(M)	Walkin' With Mr. Lee (Red label)	1958	75.00	150.00

ALLEN, REX

Label		Title	Year	VG+	NM
Decca DL-8402	(M)	Under Western Skies	1956	10.00	25.00
Decca DL-8776	(M)	Mister Cowboy	1959	8.00	20.00
Decca DL7-8776	(S)	Mister Cowboy	1959	10.00	25.00
Buena Vista BV-3307	(M)	Rex Allen Sings 16 Favorites	1961	10.00	25.00
Mercury MG-20752	(M)	Rex Allen Sings And Tells Tales	1962	6.00	15.00
Mercury SR-60752	(S)	Rex Allen Sings And Tells Tales	1962	8.00	20.00

ALLEN, RAY, & THE UPBEATS

Label		Title	Year	VG+	NM
Blast BLP-6804	(M)	A Tribute To Six		20.00	50.00

ALLEN, RITCHIE

Label		Title	Year	VG+	NM
Imperial LP-9212	(M)	Stranger From Durango	1963	12.00	30.00
Imperial LP-12212	(S)	Stranger From Durango	1963	16.00	40.00
Imperial LP-9229	(M)	The Rising Surf	1963	12.00	30.00
Imperial LP-12229	(S)	The Rising Surf	1963	16.00	40.00
Imperial LP-9243	(M)	Surfer's Slide	1963	12.00	30.00
Imperial LP-12243	(S)	Surfer's Slide	1963	16.00	40.00

ALLEN, TONY, & THE NIGHT OWLS

Label		Title	Year	VG+	NM
Crown CLP-5231	(M)	Rock And Roll With Tony Allen	1960	16.00	40.00

ALLEN, WOODY

Label		Title	Year	VG+	NM
Colpix CP-488	(M)	Woody Allen	1964	6.00	15.00
Colpix SCP-488	(S)	Woody Allen	1964	8.00	20.00
Colpix CP-518	(M)	Woody Allen 2	1965	6.00	15.00
Colpix SCP-518	(S)	Woody Allen 2	1965	8.00	20.00
Capitol T-2986	(M)	The Third Woody Allen Album	1968	6.00	15.00
Bell 6008	(S)	Wonderful Wacky World Of Woody Allen	1968	5.00	12.00

ALLISON, GENE

Label		Title	Year	VG+	NM
Vee Jay LP-1009	(M)	Gene Allison (Maroon label)	1959	30.00	60.00

ALLISON, KEITH

Label		Title	Year	VG+	NM
Columbia CL-2641	(M)	Keith Allison In Action	1967	6.00	15.00
Columbia CS-9441	(S)	Keith Allison In Action	1967	8.00	20.00

ALLMAN, DUANE & GREGG

Label		Title	Year	VG+	NM
Bold 33-301	(S)	Duane And Gregg Allman	1972	8.00	20.00

ALLMAN, SHELDON

Label		Title	Year	VG+	NM
Hi Fi R-415	(M)	Folk Songs For The 21st Century	1960	8.00	20.00
Del Fi 1213	(M)	Sing Along With Drac	1961	8.00	20.00
Del Fi ST-1213	(S)	Sing Along With Drac	1961	10.00	25.00

ALLMAN BROTHERS BAND, THE

Label		Title	Year	VG+	NM
Atco SD-33-308	(S)	The Allman Brothers Band	1969	5.00	12.00
Atco SD-33-342	(S)	Idlewild South	1970	5.00	12.00
Atco SD-33-805	(S)	Beginnings	1973	6.00	15.00
Capricorn CP4-0102	(Q)	Eat A Peach	1972	10.00	25.00
Mobile Fidelity 2-157	(S)	Eat A Peach		10.00	25.00

Label		Title	Year	VG+	NM
ALLSUP, TOMMY					
Reprise R-6182	(M)	The Buddy Holly Songbook	1965	20.00	50.00
Reprise RS-6182	(S)	The Buddy Holly Songbook	1965	30.00	60.00
ALPERT, HERB (& THE TIJUANA BRASS)					
A&M LP-101	(M)	The Lonely Bull (Cream label)	1962	5.00	12.00
A&M SP-101	(S)	The Lonely Bull (Cream label)	1962	6.00	15.00
Colgems COL-5005	(M)	Casino Royale (Sdtk)	1967	12.00	30.00
Colgems COS-5005	(S)	Casino Royale (Sdtk)	1967	45.00	90.00
A&M QU-54110	(Q)	Whipped Cream And Other Delights	1974	5.00	12.00
A&M QU-54245	(Q)	Herb Alpert's Greatest Hits	1974	5.00	12.00
Mobile Fidelity 1-053	(S)	Rise		8.00	20.00
AMBOY DUKES, THE					
Mainstream 56104	(M)	The Amboy Dukes	1968	12.00	30.00
Mainstream 6104	(S)	The Amboy Dukes	1968	10.00	25.00
Mainstream 6112	(S)	Journey To The Center Of The Mind	1968	10.00	25.00
Mainstream 6118	(S)	Migration	1968	8.00	20.00
Mainstream 6125	(S)	The Best Of The Original Amboy Dukes	1969	6.00	15.00
Mainstream 421	(S)	Ted Nugent & The Amboy Dukes		6.00	15.00
Polydor 24-4012	(S)	Marriage On The Rocks	1970	8.00	20.00
Polydor 24-4035	(S)	Survival Of The Fittest	1970	6.00	15.00
DiscReet 2181	(S)	Call Of The Wild	1974	5.00	12.00
DiscReet 2203	(S)	Tooth, Fang And Claw	1974	5.00	12.00
AMBROSE SLADE (SLADE)					
Fontana SRF-67598	(S)	Ballzy	1969	20.00	50.00
AMERICAN BLUES, THE					
Karma KLP-1001	(M)	The American Blues Is Here	1967	75.00	150.00
Uni 73044	(S)	The American Blues Do Their Thing	1969	10.00	25.00
AMERICAN BREED, THE					
Atca 8003	(M)	The American Breed	1967	6.00	15.00
Atca 38003	(S)	The American Breed	1967	8.00	20.00
Atca 38003	(S)	Bend Me, Shape Me	1968	8.00	20.00
AMERICAN DREAM, THE					
Ampex 10101	(S)	The American Dream	1970	16.00	40.00
AMERICAN EAGLE					
Decca DL7-5258	(S)	American Eagle	1971	8.00	20.00
AMON DUUL					
Prophesy PRS-1003	(S)	Amon Duul	1970	10.00	25.00
ANCIENT GREASE					
Mercury SR-61305	(S)	Women And Children First	1970	8.00	20.00
ANDERSON, CASEY					
Elektra EKL-192	(M)	Goin' Places	1960	6.00	15.00
Elektra EKS7-192	(S)	Goin' Places	1960	8.00	20.00
Atco 33-149	(M)	The Bag I'm In	1962	6.00	15.00
Atco SD-33-149	(S)	The Bag I'm In	1962	8.00	20.00
Atco 33-166	(M)	More Pretty Girls Than One	1964	6.00	15.00
Atco SD-33-166	(S)	More Pretty Girls Than One	1964	8.00	20.00
Atco 33-172	(M)	Live At The Ice House	1965	6.00	15.00
Atco SD-33-172	(S)	Live At The Ice House	1965	8.00	20.00
Atco 33-176	(M)	Blues Is A Woman Gone	1965	6.00	15.00
Atco SD-33-176	(S)	Blues Is A Woman Gone	1965	8.00	20.00
ANDERSON, ERNESTINE					
Mercury MG-20354	(M)	Hot Cargo	1958	10.00	25.00
Mercury MG-20400	(M)	Ernestine Anderson	1959	8.00	20.00
Mercury SR-60074	(S)	Ernestine Anderson	1959	10.00	25.00
Mercury MG-20492	(M)	Fascinating Ernestine	1959	8.00	20.00
Mercury SR-60171	(S)	Fascinating Ernestine	1959	10.00	25.00
Mercury MG-20496	(M)	My Kinda Swing	1959	8.00	20.00
Mercury SR-60175	(S)	My Kinda Swing	1959	10.00	25.00
Mercury MG-20582	(M)	Moanin,' Moanin,' Moanin'	1959	8.00	20.00
Mercury SR-60242	(S)	Moanin,' Moanin,' Moanin'	1959	10.00	25.00

Casino Royale. This soundtrack is collected mainly for its sparkling stereo sound. From conception through recording and mastering to the final pressing and plating, this is one of the best sounding stereo albums of popular music ever made. Features Herb Alpert performing the title track and Dusty Springfield's definitive performance of "The Look Of Love."

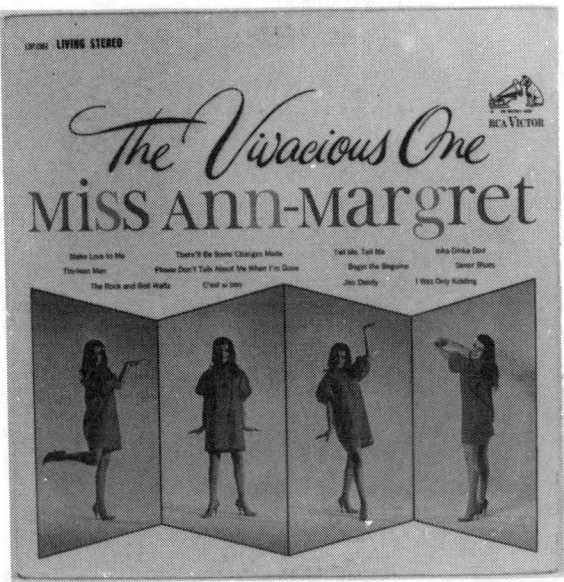

Ann-Margret, *The Vivacious One.* For all of her many successes, Ann-Margret has never had one of her solo albums make the charts! This, her third RCA effort, sports a cover worth framing. Collectors are still waiting for RCA to release a *Viva Las Vegas* soundtrack, which pairs her with Elvis Presley.

Label		Title	Year	VG+	NM
Mercury MG-12281	(M)	Ernestine Anderson	1964	6.00	15.00
Mercury SR-16281	(S)	Ernestine Anderson	1964	8.00	20.00

ANDERSON, PINK

Bluesville BV-1038	(M)	Carolina Blues Man	1961	8.00	20.00
Bluesville BV-1051	(M)	Medicine Show Man	1962	8.00	20.00
Bluesville BV-1071	(M)	Ballad And Folksinger	1963	8.00	20.00

ANDREWS SISTERS, THE
Also refer to Bing Crosby.

Decca DL-5019 (10")	(M)	Merry Christmas	1950	10.00	25.00
Decca DL-5020 (10")	(M)	Christmas Greetings	1950	10.00	25.00
Decca DL-5065 (10")	(M)	Tropical Songs	1951	10.00	25.00
Decca DL-5120 (10")	(M)	The Andrews Sisters	1951	10.00	25.00
Decca DL-5155 (10")	(M)	Club 15	1951	10.00	25.00
Decca DL-5264 (10")	(M)	Berlin Songs	1951	10.00	25.00
Decca DL-5282 (10")	(M)	Christmas Cheer	1951	10.00	25.00
Decca DL-5284 (10")	(M)	Mr. Music (Sdtk)	1951	14.00	35.00
Decca DL-5306 (10")	(M)	I Love To Tell The Story	1952	10.00	25.00
Decca DL-5331 (10")	(M)	Country Style	1952	10.00	25.00
Decca DL-5423 (10")	(M)	My Isle Of Golden Dreams	1952	10.00	25.00
Decca DL-5438 (10")	(M)	Sing, Sing, Sing	1952	10.00	25.00
Decca DL-7019	(M)	Curtain Call	1956	8.00	20.00
Decca DL-8354	(M)	Jingle Bells	1956	8.00	20.00
Decca DL-8360	(M)	By Popular Demand	1957	8.00	20.00
Capitol T-790	(M)	The Andrews Sisters In Hi-Fi	1957	8.00	20.00
Capitol T-860	(M)	Fresh And Fancy Free	1957	8.00	20.00
Capitol T-973	(M)	Dancing Twenties	1958	8.00	20.00
Dot DLP-3406	(M)	The Andrews Sisters' Greatest Hits	1961	5.00	12.00
Dot DLP-25406	(S)	The Andrews Sisters' Greatest Hits	1961	6.00	15.00
Dot DLP-3452	(M)	Great Golden Hits	1962	5.00	12.00
Dot DLP-25452	(S)	Great Golden Hits	1962	6.00	15.00
Dot DLP-3529	(M)	The Andrews Sisters Present	1963	5.00	12.00
Dot DLP-25529	(S)	The Andrews Sisters Present	1963	6.00	15.00
Dot DLP-3543	(M)	The Andrews Sisters' Greatest Hits	1963	5.00	12.00
Dot DLP-25543	(S)	The Andrews Sisters' Greatest Hits	1963	6.00	15.00
Capitol T-1924	(M)	The Hits Of The Andrews Sisters	1964	5.00	12.00
Capitol ST-1924	(S)	The Hits Of The Andrews Sisters	1964	6.00	15.00
Dot DLP-3567	(M)	Great Country Hits	1964	5.00	12.00
Dot DLP-25567	(S)	Great Country Hits	1964	6.00	15.00
Dot DLP-3632	(M)	The Andrews Sisters Go Hawaiian	1965	5.00	12.00
Dot DLP-25632	(S)	The Andrews Sisters Go Hawaiian	1965	6.00	15.00

ANGELS, THE

Caprice LP-1001	(M)	And The Angels Sing	1962	16.00	40.00
Caprice SLP-1001	(P)	And The Angels Sing	1962	20.00	50.00
Smash MGS-27039	(M)	My Boyfriend's Back	1963	14.00	35.00
Smash SRS-67039	(S)	My Boyfriend's Back	1963	16.00	40.00
Smash MGS-27048	(M)	A Halo To You	1964	10.00	25.00
Smash SRS-67048	(S)	A Halo To You	1964	12.00	30.00
Ascot AM-13009	(M)	Twelve Of Their Greatest Hits	1964	8.00	20.00
Ascot ALS-6009	(P)	Twelve Of Their Greatest Hits	1964	10.00	25.00

ANIMALS, THE (ERIC BURDON & THE ANIMALS)

MGM E-4264	(M)	The Animals	1964	8.00	20.00
MGM SE-4264	(E)	The Animals	1964	6.00	15.00
MGM E-4273	(M)	Get Yourself A College Girl (Sdtk)	1964	6.00	15.00
MGM SE-4273	(S)	Get Yourself A College Girl (Sdtk)	1964	8.00	20.00
MGM E-4281	(M)	The Animals On Tour	1965	8.00	20.00
MGM SE-4281	(E)	The Animals On Tour	1965	6.00	15.00
MGM E-4305	(M)	Animal Tracks	1965	10.00	25.00
MGM SE-4305	(E)	Animal Tracks	1965	8.00	20.00
ABC-Paramount 536	(M)	The Dangerous Christmas Of Red Riding Hood (Sdtk)	1965	10.00	25.00
ABC-Paramount S-536	(S)	The Dangerous Christmas Of Red Riding Hood (Sdtk)	1965	12.00	30.00
MGM E-4324	(M)	The Best Of The Animals	1966	6.00	15.00
MGM SE-4324	(P)	The Best Of The Animals	1966	6.00	15.00
MGM E-4384	(M)	Animalization	1966	8.00	20.00
MGM SE-4384	(P)	Animalization	1966	6.00	15.00

Label		Title	Year	VG+	NM
MGM E-4414	(M)	Animalism	1966	8.00	20.00
MGM SE-4414	(E)	Animalism	1966	6.00	15.00
MGM E-4433	(M)	Eric Is Here	1967	3.50	8.00
MGM SE-4433	(S)	Eric Is Here	1967	4.00	10.00
MGM E-4446	(M)	The Biggest Bundle Of Them All (Sdtk)	1967	5.00	12.00
MGM SE-4446	(S)	The Biggest Bundle Of Them All (Sdtk)	1967	6.00	15.00
MGM E-4454	(M)	The Best Of The Animals, Volume 2	1967	5.00	12.00
MGM SE-4454	(P)	The Best Of The Animals, Volume 2	1967	6.00	15.00
MGM E-4484	(M)	Winds Of Change	1967	5.00	12.00
MGM SE-4484	(S)	Winds Of Change	1967	6.00	15.00
MGM E-4537	(M)	The Twain Shall Meet	1968	6.00	15.00
MGM SE-4537	(S)	The Twain Shall Meet	1968	6.00	15.00
MGM E-4553	(M)	Every One Of Us	1968	5.00	12.00
MGM SE-4553	(S)	Every One Of Us	1968	5.00	12.00
MGM SE-4591	(S)	Love Is	1969	10.00	25.00

ANIMATED EGG

Label		Title	Year	VG+	NM
Alshire SF-5104	(S)	Animated Egg		8.00	20.00

ANKA, PAUL

Label		Title	Year	VG+	NM
ABC-Paramount 240	(M)	Paul Anka	1958	16.00	40.00
ABC-Paramount S-240	(S)	Paul Anka	1958	20.00	50.00
ABC-Paramount 296	(M)	My Heart Sings	1959	12.00	30.00
ABC-Paramount S-296	(S)	My Heart Sings	1959	16.00	40.00
ABC-Paramount 323	(M)	Paul Anka Sings His Big 15	1960	10.00	25.00
ABC-Paramount S-323	(S)	Paul Anka Sings His Big 15	1960	12.00	30.00
ABC-Paramount 347	(M)	Paul Anka Swings For Young Lovers	1960	8.00	20.00
ABC-Paramount S-347	(S)	Paul Anka Swings For Young Lovers	1960	10.00	25.00
ABC-Paramount 353	(M)	Anka At The Copa	1960	8.00	20.00
ABC-Paramount S-353	(S)	Anka At The Copa	1960	10.00	25.00
ABC-Paramount 360	(M)	It's Christmas Everywhere	1960	10.00	25.00
ABC-Paramount S-360	(S)	It's Christmas Everywhere	1960	12.00	30.00
ABC-Paramount 371	(M)	Strictly Instrumental	1961	10.00	25.00
ABC-Paramount S-371	(S)	Strictly Instrumental	1961	12.00	30.00
ABC-Paramount 390	(M)	Paul Anka Sings His Big 15, Volume 2	1961	8.00	20.00
ABC-Paramount S-390	(S)	Paul Anka Sings His Big 15, Volume 2	1961	10.00	25.00
ABC-Paramount 409	(M)	Paul Anka Sings His Big 15, Volume 3	1962	8.00	20.00
ABC-Paramount S-409	(S)	Paul Anka Sings His Big 15, Volume 3	1962	10.00	25.00
ABC-Paramount 420	(M)	Diana	1962	8.00	20.00
ABC-Paramount S-420	(S)	Diana	1962	10.00	25.00
RCA LPM-2502	(M)	Young, Alive And In Love!	1962	6.00	15.00
RCA LSP-2502	(S)	Young, Alive And In Love!	1962	8.00	20.00
RCA LPM-2575	(M)	Let's Sit This One Out!	1962	6.00	15.00
RCA LSP-2575	(S)	Let's Sit This One Out!	1962	8.00	20.00
RCA LPM-2614	(M)	Our Man Around The World	1963	6.00	15.00
RCA LSP-2614	(S)	Our Man Around The World	1963	8.00	20.00
RCA LPM-2691	(M)	Paul Anka's 21 Golden Hits	1963	6.00	15.00
RCA LSP-2691	(S)	Paul Anka's 21 Golden Hits	1963	8.00	20.00
		(Mono RCA albums above have "Long Play"			
		on the bottom of the label. Stereo albums			
		have "Living Stereo" on the bottom.)			
RCA LPM-2744	(M)	Songs I Wish I'd Written	1963	5.00	12.00
RCA LSP-2744	(S)	Songs I Wish I'd Written	1963	6.00	15.00
RCA LPM-2996	(M)	Excitement On Park Avenue	1964	5.00	12.00
RCA LSP-2996	(S)	Excitement On Park Avenue	1964	6.00	15.00
RCA LPM-3580	(M)	Strictly Nashville	1966	5.00	12.00
RCA LSP-3580	(S)	Strictly Nashville	1966	6.00	15.00
RCA LPM-3875	(M)	Paul Anka Alive	1967	5.00	12.00
RCA LSP-3875	(S)	Paul Anka Alive	1967	6.00	15.00
		(Stereo RCA albums above have black labels.)			

ANN-MARGRET

Label		Title	Year	VG+	NM
RCA LPM-2399	(M)	And Here She Is	1961	6.00	15.00
RCA LSP-2399	(S)	And Here She Is	1961	8.00	20.00
RCA LPM-2453	(M)	On The Way Up	1961	6.00	15.00
RCA LSP-2453	(S)	On The Way Up	1961	8.00	20.00
Dot DLP-9011	(M)	State Fair (Sdtk)	1962	6.00	15.00
Dot DLP-25011	(S)	State Fair (Sdtk)	1962	8.00	20.00
RCA LPM-2551	(M)	The Vivacious One	1962	6.00	15.00
RCA LSP-2551	(S)	The Vivacious One	1962	8.00	20.00

Label		Title	Year	VG+	NM
RCA LPM-2659	(M)	Bachelor's Paradise	1963	6.00	15.00
RCA LSP-2659	(S)	Bachelor's Paradise	1963	8.00	20.00
RCA LPM-2690	(M)	Beauty And The Beard (With Al Hirt)	1963	5.00	12.00
RCA LSP-2690	(S)	Beauty And The Beard (With Al Hirt)	1963	6.00	15.00
		(Mono RCA albums above have "Long Play" on the bottom of the label. Stereo albums have "Living Stereo" on the bottom.)			
RCA LOC-1081	(M)	Bye Bye Birdie (Sdtk)	1963	6.00	15.00
RCA LSO-1081	(S)	Bye Bye Birdie (Sdtk)	1963	8.00	20.00
		(Ann-Margret is not on the cover.)			
RCA LPM-2947	(M)	Hits From Broadway Shows	1964	4.00	10.00
RCA LSP-2947	(S)	Hits From Broadway Shows	1964	5.00	12.00
RCA LOC-1101	(M)	The Pleasure Seekers (Sdtk)	1965	14.00	35.00
RCA LSO-1101	(S)	The Pleasure Seekers (Sdtk)	1965	16.00	40.00
RCA LPM-3710	(M)	The Swinger (Sdtk)	1966	8.00	20.00
RCA LSP-3710	(S)	The Swinger (Sdtk)	1966	10.00	25.00
		(Stereo RCA albums above have black labels.)			

ANNETTE (ANNETTE FUNICELLO)

Label		Title	Year	VG+	NM
Mickey Mouse MM-24	(M)	Songs From Annette		30.00	60.00
Buena Vista BV-3301	(M)	Annette	1959	30.00	60.00
Buena Vista BV-3302	(M)	Annette Sings Anka	1960	20.00	50.00
Buena Vista BV-3303	(M)	Hawaiiannette	1960	20.00	50.00
Buena Vista BV-3304	(M)	Italianette	1960	20.00	50.00
Buena Vista BV-3305	(M)	Dance Annette	1961	20.00	50.00
Buena Vista BV-3309	(M)	The Parent Trap (Sdtk)	1961	10.00	25.00
Buena Vista BVS-3309	(S)	The Parent Trap (Sdtk)	1961	16.00	40.00
Buena Vista BV-4022	(M)	Babes In Toyland (Sdtk)	1961	10.00	25.00
Buena Vista BVS-4022	(S)	Babes In Toyland (Sdtk)	1961	16.00	40.00
Buena Vista BV-4037	(M)	Annette Funicello	1962	20.00	50.00
Buena Vista BV-3312	(M)	The Story Of My Teens	1962	30.00	60.00
Buena Vista BV-3313	(M)	Teen Street	1962	20.00	50.00
Buena Vista BV-3314	(M)	Muscle Beach Party (Sdtk)	1963	14.00	35.00
Buena Vista STER-3314	(S)	Muscle Beach Party (Sdtk)	1963	20.00	50.00
Buena Vista BV-3316	(M)	Annette's Beach Party (Sdtk)	1963	16.00	40.00
Buena Vista STER-3316	(S)	Annette's Beach Party (Sdtk)	1963	30.00	60.00
Buena Vista BV-3320	(M)	Annette On Campus	1964	16.00	40.00
Buena Vista STER-3320	(S)	Annette On Campus	1964	30.00	60.00
Buena Vista BV-3324	(M)	Annette At Bikini Beach	1964	16.00	40.00
Buena Vista STER-3324	(S)	Annette At Bikini Beach	1964	30.00	60.00
Buena Vista BV-3325	(M)	Annette's Pajama Party	1964	16.00	40.00
Buena Vista STER-3325	(S)	Annette's Pajama Party	1964	30.00	60.00
Buena Vista BV-3327	(M)	Annette Sings Golden Surfin' Hits	1964	16.00	40.00
Buena Vista STER-3327	(S)	Annette Sings Golden Surfin' Hits	1964	30.00	60.00
Buena Vista BV-3328	(M)	Something Borrowed, Something Blue	1964	16.00	40.00
Buena Vista BV-3508	(M)	Annette And Hayley Mills		50.00	100.00
Wand 671	(M)	How To Stuff A Wild Bikini (Sdtk)	1965	6.00	15.00
Wand S-671	(S)	How To Stuff A Wild Bikini (Sdtk)	1965	8.00	20.00
Disneyland DQ-1245	(M)	Walt Disney's Wonderful World Of Color	1964	10.00	25.00
Disneyland DQS-1245	(S)	Walt Disney's Wonderful World Of Color	1964	16.00	40.00
Disneyland DQ-1267	(M)	The Best Of Broadway	1965	12.00	30.00
Disneyland DQ-1287	(M)	Tubby The Tuba	1966	10.00	25.00
Disneyland DQS-1287	(S)	Tubby The Tuba	1966	16.00	40.00
Disneyland DQ-1293	(M)	State And College Songs	1967	10.00	25.00
Disneyland DQS-1293	(S)	State And College Songs	1967	16.00	40.00
Sidewalk T-5902	(M)	Thunder Alley (Sdtk)	1967	6.00	15.00
Sidewalk ST-5902	(S)	Thunder Alley (Sdtk)	1967	8.00	20.00

ANT TRIP CEREMONY

Label		Title	Year	VG+	NM
C.R.C. 2129	(M)	Twenty-Four Hours	1967	100.00	200.00

AORTA

Label		Title	Year	VG+	NM
Columbia CS-9785	(S)	Aorta	1968	8.00	20.00
Happy Tiger HT-1010	(S)	Aorta 2	1970	12.00	30.00

APHRODITE'S CHILD

Label		Title	Year	VG+	NM
Vertigo 2500	(S)	666		8.00	20.00

APPEL, DAVE

Label		Title	Year	VG+	NM
Cameo C-1004	(M)	Alone Together	1959	12.00	30.00

Label		Title	Year	VG+	NM
APPLETREE THEATRE					
Forecast FTS-302	(S)	Playback	1968	6.00	15.00
APOSTLES, THE					
Sound Recording 1245	(M)	An Hour Of Prayer		75.00	150.00
AQUATONES, THE					
Fargo 3001	(M)	The Aquatones Sing	1964	100.00	200.00
ARCHIES, THE					
Calendar KES-101	(S)	The Archies	1968	6.00	15.00
Calendar KES-103	(S)	Everything's Archie	1969	4.00	10.00
Calendar KES-105	(S)	Jingle Jangle	1969	4.00	10.00
Kirshner KES-107	(S)	Sugar Sugar	1969	5.00	12.00
Kirshner KES-109	(S)	The Archies' Greatest Hits	1970	4.00	10.00
Kirshner KES-110	(S)	This Is Love	1971	6.00	15.00
ARDEN, TONI					
Decca DL-8651	(M)	Miss Toni Arden	1957	10.00	25.00
Decca DL-8875	(M)	Besame	1959	6.00	15.00
Decca DL7-8875	(S)	Besame	1959	8.00	20.00
ARISTOCATS, THE					
High Fidelity R-610	(M)	Boogie And Blues	1959	12.00	30.00
High Fidelity SR-610	(S)	Boogie And Blues	1959	16.00	40.00
ARK 2					
Uni 73075	(S)	Flaming Youth	1969	16.00	40.00
ARMAGEDDON					
Amos 73075	(S)	Armageddon	1969	8.00	20.00
ARNOLD, EDDY					
RCA LPM-3027 (10")	(M)	Anytime	1952	16.00	40.00
RCA LPM-3031 (10")	(M)	All-Time Hits From The Hills	1952	16.00	40.00
RCA LPM-3117 (10")	(M)	All-Time Favorites	1953	16.00	40.00
RCA LPM-3219 (10")	(M)	The Chapel On The Hill	1954	16.00	40.00
RCA LPM-3230 (10")	(M)	An American Institution	1954	16.00	40.00
RCA LPM-1111	(M)	Wanderin'	1955	12.00	30.00
RCA LPM-1223	(M)	All-Time Favorites	1955	12.00	30.00
RCA LPM-1224	(M)	Anytime	1955	12.00	30.00
RCA LPM-1225	(M)	The Chapel On The Hill	1955	12.00	30.00
RCA LPM-1293	(M)	A Dozen Hits	1956	12.00	30.00
RCA LPM-1377	(M)	A Little On The Lonely Side	1956	12.00	30.00
RCA LPM-1484	(M)	When They Were Young	1957	12.00	30.00
RCA LPM-1575	(M)	My Darling, My Darling	1957	12.00	30.00
RCA LPM-1733	(M)	Praise Him, Praise Him	1958	10.00	25.00
RCA LPM-1928	(M)	Have Guitar, Will Travel	1959	8.00	20.00
RCA LSP-1928	(S)	Have Guitar, Will Travel	1959	10.00	25.00
RCA LPM-2036	(M)	Thereby Hangs A Tale	1959	6.00	15.00
RCA LSP-2036	(S)	Thereby Hangs A Tale	1959	8.00	20.00
RCA LPM-2185	(M)	Eddy Arnold Sings Them Again	1960	6.00	15.00
RCA LSP-2185	(S)	Eddy Arnold Sings Them Again	1960	8.00	20.00
RCA LPM-2268	(M)	You Gotta Have Love	1960	5.00	12.00
RCA LSP-2268	(S)	You Gotta Have Love	1960	6.00	15.00
RCA LPM-2337	(M)	Let's Make Memories Tonight	1961	5.00	12.00
RCA LSP-2337	(S)	Let's Make Memories Tonight	1961	6.00	15.00
RCA LPM-2471	(M)	One More Time	1961	5.00	12.00
RCA LSP-2471	(S)	One More Time	1961	6.00	15.00
RCA LPM-2554	(M)	Christmas With Eddy Arnold	1961	5.00	12.00
RCA LSP-2554	(S)	Christmas With Eddy Arnold	1961	6.00	15.00
RCA LPM-2578	(M)	Cattle Call	1962	5.00	12.00
RCA LSP-2578	(S)	Cattle Call	1962	6.00	15.00
RCA LPM-2596	(M)	Our Man Down South	1962	5.00	12.00
RCA LSP-2596	(S)	Our Man Down South	1962	6.00	15.00
RCA LPM-2629	(M)	Faithfully Yours	1963	5.00	12.00
RCA LSP-2629	(S)	Faithfully Yours	1963	6.00	15.00

(Mono RCA albums above have "Long Play"
on the bottom of the label. Stereo albums
have "Living Stereo" on the bottom.)

The Archies, *This Is Love.* This one is so scarce many of the band's fans are not even aware of its existence! Their 1971 swan song, this failed to even dent the charts and regularly sells for surprising amounts of money to hardcore Archies collectors.

Chet Atkins' Workshop. The king of country guitar; a mainstay in Nashville's finest studios; mandatory listening for every aspiring country guitarist; producer of some of the finest records in the past thirty years. And he makes good records, too.

Label		Title	Year	VG+	NM
ARNOLD, P.P.					
Immediate Z1252016	(S)	Kafunta		8.00	20.00
ARZACHEL					
Roulette SR-42036	(S)	Arzachel	1969	20.00	50.00
ASHER, JANE					
London OSA-1206	(M)	Alice In Wonderland	1965	14.00	35.00
ASHES					
Vault 125	(S)	Ashes	1968	10.00	25.00
ASHKAN					
Sire SES-97017	(S)	In From The Cold	1970	8.00	20.00
ASTAIRE, FRED					
Verve V-2010	(M)	Mr. Top Hat		10.00	25.00
Verve V-2114	(M)	Easy To Dance With		10.00	25.00
Epic LN-3137	(M)	The Best Of Fred Astaire		10.00	25.00
Epic LN-13103	(M)	Nothing Thrilled Us Half As Much		10.00	25.00
Kapp KL-1165	(M)	Now		10.00	25.00
ASTRONAUTS, THE					
RCA LPM-2760	(M)	Surfin' With The Astronauts	1963	10.00	25.00
RCA LSP-2760	(S)	Surfin' With The Astronauts	1963	12.00	30.00
RCA LPM-2782	(M)	Everything Is A-OK	1964	8.00	20.00
RCA LSP-2782	(S)	Everything Is A-OK	1964	10.00	25.00
RCA LPM-2858	(M)	Competition Coupe	1964	8.00	20.00
RCA LSP-2858	(S)	Competition Coupe	1964	10.00	25.00
RCA LPM-2903	(M)	The Astronauts Orbit Campus	1964	8.00	20.00
RCA LSP-2903	(S)	The Astronauts Orbit Campus	1964	10.00	25.00
RCA PRM-183	(M)	Rockin' With The Astronauts	1964	10.00	25.00
20th Century TFM-3131	(M)	Surf Party (Sdtk)	1964	8.00	20.00
20th Century TFS-4131	(S)	Surf Party (Sdtk)	1964	10.00	25.00
RCA LPM-3441	(M)	Wild On The Beach (Sdtk)	1965	6.00	15.00
RCA LSP-3441	(S)	Wild On The Beach (Sdtk)	1965	8.00	20.00
RCA LPM-3307	(M)	The Astronauts Go Go Go	1965	8.00	20.00
RCA LSP-3307	(S)	The Astronauts Go Go Go	1965	10.00	25.00
RCA LPM-3359	(M)	Favorites For You, Our Fans, From Us	1965	8.00	20.00
RCA LSP-3359	(S)	Favorites For You, Our Fans, From Us	1965	10.00	25.00
RCA LPM-3454	(M)	Down The Line	1965	8.00	20.00
RCA LSP-3454	(S)	Down The Line	1965	10.00	25.00
Decca DL-4699	(M)	Wild, Wild Winter (Sdtk)	1966	6.00	15.00
Decca DL7-4699	(S)	Wild, Wild Winter (Sdtk)	1966	8.00	20.00
Decca DL-4751	(M)	Out Of Sight (Sdtk)	1966	6.00	15.00
Decca DL7-4751	(S)	Out Of Sight (Sdtk)	1966	8.00	20.00
RCA LPM-3733	(M)	Travelin' Men	1967	6.00	15.00
RCA LSP-3733	(S)	Travelin' Men	1967	8.00	20.00
ATCHER, BOBBY, & THE COUNTRYMEN					
Columbia HL-9006 (10")	(M)	Early American Folk Songs		10.00	25.00
Columbia HL-9013 (10")	(M)	Songs Of The Saddle		10.00	25.00
ATKINS, CHET					
RCA LPM-3079 (10")	(M)	Chet Atkins' Gallopin' Guitar	1952	30.00	60.00
RCA LPM-3169 (10")	(M)	Stringin' Along With Chet Atkins	1953	20.00	50.00
RCA LPM-3167 (10")	(M)	String Dustin'	1953	20.00	50.00
RCA LPM-1090	(M)	A Session With Chet Atkins	1955	14.00	35.00
RCA LPM-1197	(M)	Chet Atkins In Three Dimensions	1956	14.00	35.00
RCA LPM-1236	(M)	Stringin' Along With Chet Atkins	1956	14.00	35.00
RCA LPM-1383	(M)	Finger Style Guitar	1956	14.00	35.00
RCA LPM-1544	(M)	Chet Atkins At Home	1957	12.00	30.00
RCA LPM-1577	(M)	Hi Fi In Focus	1957	12.00	30.00
RCA LPM-1993	(M)	Chet Atkins In Hollywood	1959	5.00	12.00
RCA LSP-1993	(S)	Chet Atkins In Hollywood	1959	8.00	20.00
RCA LPM-2025	(M)	Hum And Strung Along (With booklet)	1959	6.00	15.00
RCA LSP-2025	(S)	Hum And Strung Along (With booklet)	1959	10.00	25.00
RCA LPM-2103	(M)	Mister Guitar	1959	4.00	10.00
RCA LSP-2103	(S)	Mister Guitar	1959	6.00	15.00
RCA LPM-2161	(M)	Teensville	1960	4.00	10.00
RCA LSP-2161	(S)	Teensville	1960	6.00	15.00

Label		Title	Year	VG+	NM
RCA LPM-2175	(M)	The Other Chet Atkins	1960	4.00	10.00
RCA LSP-2175	(S)	The Other Chet Atkins	1960	5.00	12.00
RCA LPM-2232	(M)	Chet Atkins' Workshop	1961	4.00	10.00
RCA LSP-2232	(S)	Chet Atkins' Workshop	1961	5.00	12.00
RCA LPM-2346	(M)	The Most Popular Guitar	1961	4.00	10.00
RCA LSP-2346	(S)	The Most Popular Guitar	1961	5.00	12.00
RCA LPM-2424	(M)	Christmas With Chet Atkins	1961	4.00	10.00
RCA LSP-2424	(S)	Christmas With Chet Atkins	1961	5.00	12.00
RCA LPM-2450	(M)	Down Home	1962	4.00	10.00
RCA LSP-2450	(S)	Down Home	1962	5.00	12.00
RCA LPM-2549	(M)	Caribbean Guitar	1962	4.00	10.00
RCA LSP-2549	(S)	Caribbean Guitar	1962	5.00	12.00
RCA LPM-2601	(M)	Back Home Hymns	1962	4.00	10.00
RCA LSP-2601	(S)	Back Home Hymns	1962	5.00	12.00
RCA LPM-2616	(M)	Our Man In Nashville	1963	4.00	10.00
RCA LSP-2616	(S)	Our Man In Nashville	1963	5.00	12.00
RCA LPM-2678	(M)	Travelin'	1963	4.00	10.00
RCA LSP-2678	(S)	Travelin'	1963	5.00	12.00
RCA LPM-2719	(M)	Teen Scene	1963	4.00	10.00
RCA LSP-2719	(S)	Teen Scene	1963	5.00	12.00

*(Mono RCA albums above have "Long Play"
on the bottom of the label. Stereo albums
have "Living Stereo" on the bottom.)*

ATLANTA RHYTHM SECTION, THE

Mobile Fidelity 1-038	(S)	Champagne Jam		6.00	15.00

ATTILA

Epic E-30030	(S)	Attila	1970	12.00	30.00

AU-GO-GO SINGERS, THE

Roulette R-25280	(M)	They Call Us The Au Go-Go Singers	1964	16.00	40.00
Roulette SR-25280	(S)	They Call Us The Au Go-Go Singers	1964	20.00	50.00

AUTOSALVAGE

RCA LSP-3940	(S)	Autosalvage	1968	8.00	20.00

AUTRY, GENE

Columbia JL-8001 (10")	(M)	Gene Autry At The Rodeo	1949	20.00	50.00
Columbia JL-8009 (10")	(M)	Stampede		20.00	50.00
Columbia HL-9001 (10")	(M)	Western Classic, Volume 1		20.00	50.00
Columbia HL-9002 (10")	(M)	Western Classic, Volume 2		20.00	50.00
Columbia MJV-82 (10")	(M)	The Story Of The Nativity		20.00	50.00
Columbia MJV-83 (10")	(M)	Little Johnny Pilgrim		20.00	50.00
Columbia MJV-94 (10")	(M)	Rusty, The Rocking Horse		20.00	50.00
Columbia CL-2547 (10")	(M)	Merry Christmas	1955	20.00	50.00
Columbia CL-2568 (10")	(M)	Gene Autry Sings Peter Cottontail	1955	20.00	50.00
Columbia CL-677	(M)	Champion Western Adventures	1955	14.00	35.00
Challenge CHL-600	(M)	Christmas With Gene Autry	1958	14.00	35.00
Columbia CL-1575	(M)	Gene Autry's Greatest Hits	1961	14.00	35.00
RCA LPM-2623	(M)	Gene Autry's Golden Hits	1962	10.00	25.00
RCA LSP-2623	(S)	Gene Autry's Golden Hits	1962	10.00	25.00

AVALON, FRANKIE

Chancellor CHL-5001	(M)	Frankie Avalon	1958	20.00	50.00
Chancellor CHL-5002	(M)	The Young Frankie Avalon	1959	16.00	40.00
Chancellor CHLX-5004	(M)	Swingin' On A Rainbow	1959	16.00	40.00
Chancellor CHL-5009	(M)	Fabian And Avalon: The Hit Makers	1960	20.00	50.00
Chancellor CHL-69801	(M)	Young And In Love	1960	20.00	50.00

(Boxed set with photos and a 3-D portrait.)

Chancellor CHL-5011	(M)	Summer Scene	1960	12.00	30.00
Chancellor CHLS-5011	(S)	Summer Scene	1960	14.00	35.00
Chancellor CHL-5018	(M)	A Whole Lot Of Frankie	1961	12.00	30.00
Chancellor CHL-5022	(M)	And Now About Mr. Avalon	1961	8.00	20.00
Chancellor CHLS-5022	(S)	And Now About Mr. Avalon	1961	10.00	25.00
Chancellor CHL-5025	(M)	Italiano	1962	8.00	20.00
Chancellor CHLS-5025	(S)	Italiano	1962	10.00	25.00
Chancellor CHL-5027	(M)	You Are Mine	1962	8.00	20.00
Chancellor CHLS-5027	(S)	You Are Mine	1962	10.00	25.00

Label		Title	Year	VG+	NM
Chancellor CHL-5031	(M)	Frankie Avalon's Christmas Album	1962	10.00	25.00
Chancellor CHLS-5031	(S)	Frankie Avalon's Christmas Album	1962	12.00	30.00
Chancellor CHL-5032	(M)	Cleopatra Plus 13 Other Great Hits	1963	10.00	25.00
Chancellor CHLS-5032	(S)	Cleopatra Plus 13 Other Great Hits	1963	12.00	30.00
Buena Vista BV-3314	(M)	Muscle Beach Party (Sdtk)	1964	14.00	35.00
Buena Vista STER-3314	(S)	Muscle Beach Party (Sdtk)	1964	20.00	50.00
United Arts. UAL-3371	(M)	Songs From Muscle Beach Party	1964	8.00	20.00
United Arts. UAS-6371	(S)	Songs From Muscle Beach Party	1964	10.00	25.00
United Arts. UAL-3382	(M)	Frankie Avalon's 15 Greatest Hits	1964	8.00	20.00
United Arts. UAS-6382	(P)	Frankie Avalon's 15 Greatest Hits	1964	8.00	20.00
United Arts. UAL-4121	(M)	I'll Take Sweden (Sdtk)	1965	6.00	15.00
United Arts. UAS-5121	(S)	I'll Take Sweden (Sdtk)	1965	8.00	20.00
Metromedia 1034	(S)	I Want You Near Me	1970	6.00	15.00

AVENGERS VI, THE

Mark 56 Records	(M)	Real Cool Hits	1965	60.00	120.00

AVONS, THE

Hull HLP-1000	(M)	The Avons	1960	150.00	250.00

AZTECS, THE

World Artists WAM-2001	(M)	Live At The AD-Lib Club Of London	1964	50.00	100.00

BABY

Lone Starr 9782	(S)	Baby	1974	8.00	20.00

BABY HUEY

Curtom CRS-8007	(S)	The Living Legend	1970	16.00	40.00

BADFINGER (THE IVEYS)

Commonwealth Un. 6004	(S)	The Magic Christian (Sdtk)	1970	8.00	20.00
Apple ST-3364	(S)	Magic Christian Music	1970	10.00	25.00
Apple SKAO-3367	(S)	No Dice	1970	12.00	30.00
Apple SW-3387	(S)	Straight Up	1971	40.00	80.00
Apple SW-3411	(S)	Ass	1973	8.00	20.00
Warners BS-2762	(S)	Badfinger	1974	6.00	15.00
Warners BS-2827	(S)	Wish You Were Here	1974	8.00	20.00
Elektra 6E-175	(S)	Airwaves	1979	4.00	10.00

BAEZ, JOAN

Vanguard VRS-2077	(M)	Joan Baez	1960	10.00	25.00
Vanguard VRS-2097	(M)	Joan Baez, Volume 2	1961	8.00	20.00
Vanguard VRS-2122	(M)	Joan Baez In Concert, Volume 1	1962	8.00	20.00
Vanguard VRS-2123	(M)	Joan Baez In Concert, Volume 2	1963	8.00	20.00
Vanguard VRS-9160	(M)	Joan Baez/5	1964	8.00	20.00

BAGDASARIAN, ROSS (DAVID SEVILLE)

Bagdasarian as David Seville was the mastermind behind the Chipmunks.

Liberty LRP-3451	(M)	The Crazy, Mixed-Up World	1966	8.00	20.00
Liberty LST-7451	(S)	The Crazy, Mixed-Up World	1966	10.00	25.00

BAIN, BOB

Capitol T-965	(M)	Rockin,' Rollin'	1958	20.00	50.00

BAKER, LAVERN

Atlantic 8002	(M)	LaVern	1956	50.00	100.00
Atlantic 8007	(M)	LaVern Baker	1957	30.00	60.00

Badfinger, *Straight Up.* Their most successful album both commercially (#31 in early 1972 and 32 weeks on the chart) and artistically, this was a cut-out bin staple within a year of release. *Straight UP* has become a highly collectible example of early "power pop," a short-lived phenomenon of the late '70s, most fully realized by Eric Carmen's Raspberries.

The Beach Boys, *Surfer Girl.* The Beach Boys third album and the first to show their real abilities as record makers was, not coincidentally, the first produced entirely by Brian Wilson, who also wrote or arranged all twelve of the songs. While Brian mixed the mono version, the stereo was mixed by engineer Chuck Britz and is currently available in all its wide channel wonder from Mobile Fidelity's Original Master Recording series.

Label		Title	Year	VG+	NM
Atlantic 1281	(M)	LaVern Baker Sings Bessie Smith	1958	20.00	50.00
Atlantic 8030	(M)	Blues Ballads	1959	20.00	50.00
Atlantic 8036	(M)	Precious Memories	1959	20.00	50.00
		(Atlantic albums above have black labels.)			
Atlantic 8050	(M)	Saved	1961	16.00	40.00
Atlantic SD-8050	(S)	Saved	1961	30.00	60.00
Atlantic 8071	(M)	See See Rider	1963	16.00	40.00
Atlantic SD-8071	(S)	See See Rider	1963	30.00	60.00
Atlantic 8078	(M)	The Best Of LaVern Baker	1963	10.00	25.00
Atlantic SD-8078	(S)	The Best Of LaVern Baker	1963	20.00	50.00

BAKER, MICKEY
Formerly one half of Mickey & Sylvia. Also refer to Brother John Sellers.

Atlantic 8035	(M)	Wildest Guitar	1959	50.00	100.00
Atlantic SD-8035	(S)	Wildest Guitar	1959	75.00	150.00
King K-839	(M)	But Wild	1963	20.00	50.00
King KS-839	(S)	But Wild	1963	35.00	70.00
Sire 97010	(S)	In Heavy Blues (With Jack Dupree)	1969	6.00	15.00

BALLADEERS, THE

Del-Fi DF-1204	(M)	Alive-O	1959	16.00	40.00

BALLARD, FRANK

Phillips International 1985	(M)	Rhythm-Blues Party	1962	240.00	400.00

BALLARD, HANK (& THE MIDNIGHTERS)

Federal 295-90 (10")	(M)	The Midnighters	1954	300.00	500.00
Federal 395-541	(M)	The Midnighters	1956	150.00	250.00
Federal 395-581	(M)	The Midnighters, Volume 2	1957	100.00	200.00
King 395-541	(M)	The Midnighters	1958	50.00	100.00
King 395-581	(M)	The Midnighters, Volume 2	1958	50.00	100.00
King 618	(M)	Singin And Swingin'	1959	20.00	50.00
King 674	(M)	The One And Only Hank Ballard	1960	20.00	50.00
King 700	(M)	Mr. Rhythm And Blues	1960	20.00	50.00
King 740	(M)	Spotlight On Hank Ballard	1961	20.00	50.00
King KS-740	(S)	Spotlight On Hank Ballard	1961	50.00	100.00
King 748	(M)	Let's Go Again	1961	20.00	50.00
King 759	(M)	Sing Along	1961	20.00	50.00
King 781	(M)	The Twistin' Fools	1962	20.00	50.00
King 793	(M)	Jumpin' Hank Ballard	1962	20.00	50.00
King 815	(M)	The 1963 Sound Of Hank Ballard	1963	20.00	50.00
King 867	(M)	Biggest Hits	1963	20.00	50.00
King 896	(M)	A Star In Your Eyes	1964	20.00	50.00
		(King albums above have crownless black labels.)			
King 913	(M)	Those Lazy, Lazy Days	1965	14.00	35.00
King 927	(M)	Glad Songs, Sad Songs	1966	10.00	25.00
King 950	(M)	24 Hit Tunes	1966	10.00	25.00
King 981	(M)	24 Great Songs	1968	8.00	20.00
King KSD-1052	(S)	You Keep A Good Man Down	1969	8.00	20.00

BAND, THE

Capitol SKAO-2955	(S)	Music From Big Pink (Black label)	1968	6.00	15.00
Capitol ST-132	(S)	The Band (Green label)	1969	5.00	12.00
Mobile Fidelity 1-039	(S)	Music From Big Pink		8.00	20.00

BANTAMS, THE

Warners W-1625	(M)	Beware The Bantams	1966	8.00	20.00
Warners WS-1625	(S)	Beware The Bantams	1966	10.00	25.00

BARBARIANS, THE

Laurie LLP-2033	(M)	Are You A Boy Or Are You A Girl?	1966	16.00	40.00
Laurie SLP-2033	(S)	Are You A Boy Or Are You A Girl?	1966	30.00	60.00

BARDOT, BRIGITTE

Poplar 33-1002	(M)	The Girl In The Bikini (Sdtk)	1952	100.00	200.00
Decca DL-8685	(M)	And God Created Woman (Sdtk)	1957	30.00	60.00
Warners W-1371	(M)	Behind Brigitte Bardot	1960	8.00	20.00
Warners WS-1371	(S)	Behind Brigitte Bardot	1960	10.00	25.00
Philips PC-204	(M)	Brigitte Bardot Sings	1963	8.00	20.00
Philips PCC-604	(S)	Brigitte Bardot Sings	1963	10.00	25.00

Label		Title	Year	VG+	NM
BARE, BOBBY					
RCA LPM-2835	(M)	500 Miles Away From Home	1963	8.00	20.00
RCA LSP-2835	(S)	500 Miles Away From Home	1963	10.00	25.00
BARGE, GENE					
Checker 2994	(M)	Dance With Daddy G	1965	12.00	30.00
BARNES, MAE					
Atlantic ALS-404 (10")	(M)	Songs By Mae Barnes		75.00	150.00
BAROQUES, THE					
Chess 1516	(M)	The Baroques	1967	10.00	25.00
Chess S-1516	(S)	The Baroques	1967	12.00	30.00
BARRACUDAS, THE					
Justice 143	(M)	A Plane View	1968	75.00	150.00
BARRY & THE TAMERLANES					
A&M W-406	(M)	I Wonder What She's Doing Tonight	1963	40.00	80.00
BARRY, GENE					
RCA LPM-2975	(M)	The Star Of Burke's Law Sings	1964	5.00	12.00
RCA LSP-2975	(S)	The Star Of Burke's Law Sings	1964	6.00	15.00
BARRY, LEN					
Decca DL-4720	(M)	1-2-3	1965	8.00	20.00
Decca DL7-4720	(P)	1-2-3	1965	10.00	25.00
RCA LPM-3823	(M)	My Kind Of Soul	1967	5.00	12.00
RCA LSP-3823	(S)	My Kind Of Soul	1967	6.00	15.00
BARTHOLOMEW, DAVE					
Imperial LP-9162	(M)	Fats Domino Presents David Bartholomew	1961	16.00	40.00
Imperial LP-12076	(S)	Fats Domino Presents David Bartholomew	1961	20.00	50.00
Imperial LP-9217	(M)	New Orleans House Party	1963	16.00	40.00
Imperial LP-12217	(S)	New Orleans House Party	1963	20.00	50.00
BATTERED ORNAMENTS					
Harvest SKAO-422	(S)	Mantle-Piece	1970	8.00	20.00
BAYSIDERS, THE					
Everest LPBR-5124	(M)	Over The Rainbow	1961	20.00	50.00
Everest BRST-5124	(S)	Over The Rainbow	1961	30.00	60.00
BEACH BOYS, THE					
Also refer to Jan & Dean and Spring.					
Capitol T-1808	(M)	Surfin' Safari	1962	14.00	35.00
Capitol DT-1808	(E)	Surfin' Safari	1962	12.00	30.00
Capitol T-1890	(M)	Surfin' U.S.A.	1963	12.00	30.00
Capitol ST-1890	(S)	Surfin' U.S.A.	1963	12.00	30.00
Capitol T-1981	(M)	Surfer Girl	1963	12.00	30.00
Capitol ST-1981	(S)	Surfer Girl	1963	12.00	30.00
Capitol T-1998	(M)	Little Deuce Coupe	1963	12.00	30.00
Capitol ST-1998	(P)	Little Deuce Coupe	1963	12.00	30.00
Capitol T-2027	(M)	Shut Down, Volume 2	1964	12.00	30.00
Capitol ST-2027	(P)	Shut Down, Volume 2	1964	12.00	30.00
Capitol T-2110	(M)	All Summer Long	1964	16.00	40.00
Capitol ST-2110	(P)	All Summer Long	1964	16.00	40.00
		(Cover lists "Don't Break Down.")			
Capitol T-2110	(M)	All Summer Long	1964	12.00	30.00
Capitol ST-2110	(P)	All Summer Long	1964	12.00	30.00
		(Cover lists "Don't Back Down.")			
Capitol T-2164	(M)	The Beach Boys' Christmas Album	1964	10.00	25.00
Capitol ST-2164	(S)	The Beach Boys' Christmas Album	1964	12.00	30.00
Capitol TAO-2198	(M)	Beach Boys Concert	1964	10.00	25.00
Capitol STAO-2198	(S)	Beach Boys Concert	1964	12.00	30.00
Capitol T-2269	(M)	The Beach Boys Today!	1965	12.00	30.00
Capitol DT-2269	(E)	The Beach Boys Today!	1965	10.00	25.00
Capitol T-2354	(M)	Summer Days And Summer Nights!	1965	12.00	30.00
Capitol DT-2354	(E)	Summer Days And Summer Nights!	1965	10.00	25.00
		(The front cover reads "Duophonic Stereo.")			

Label		Title	Year	VG+	NM
Capitol DT-2354	(E)	Summer Days And Summer Nights!	1965	12.00	30.00
		(The front cover reads "New Improved			
		Full Dimensional Stereo.")			
Capitol MAS-2398	(M)	The Beach Boys Party (With bonus cards)	1965	14.00	35.00
Capitol DMAS-2398	(E)	The Beach Boys Party (With bonus cards)	1965	12.00	30.00
Capitol T-2458	(M)	Pet Sounds	1966	8.00	20.00
Capitol DT-2458	(E)	Pet Sounds	1966	6.00	15.00
Capitol T-2545	(M)	Best Of The Beach Boys	1966	6.00	15.00
Capitol DT-2545	(P)	Best Of The Beach Boys	1966	6.00	15.00
Capitol T-2706	(M)	Best Of The Beach Boys, Volume 2	1967	6.00	15.00
Capitol DT-2706	(P)	Best Of The Beach Boys, Volume 2	1967	6.00	15.00
Brother T-9001	(M)	Smiley Smile	1967	8.00	20.00
Brother ST-9001	(E)	Smiley Smile	1967	6.00	15.00
		(Back cover does not mention Barry Turnbull.)			
Capitol TCL-2813	(M)	The Beach Boys Deluxe Set (3 LPs)	1967	60.00	120.00
Capitol DTCL-2813	(E)	The Beach Boys Deluxe Set (3 LPs)	1967	35.00	70.00
Capitol T-2859	(M)	Wild Honey	1967	8.00	20.00
Capitol ST-2859	(E)	Wild Honey	1967	6.00	15.00
Capitol ST8-2891	(E)	Smiley Smile (Record Club)	1968	75.00	150.00
Capitol DKAO-2893	(E)	Stack-O-Tracks (With booklet)	1968	50.00	100.00
Capitol ST-2895	(S)	Friends	1968	6.00	15.00
Capitol DKAO-2945	(P)	The Best Of The Beach Boys, Volume 3	1969	6.00	15.00
Capitol SKAO-133	(P)	20/20	1969	6.00	15.00
Capitol SKAO-8-0133	(P)	20/20 (Record Club)	1969	8.00	20.00
Capitol SWBB-253	(E)	Close-Up	1969	6.00	15.00
		(Capitol albums above have black labels.)			
Sears SPS-609	(E)	Summertime Blues	1970	50.00	100.00
Capitol ST-442	(P)	Good Vibrations	1970	8.00	20.00
Capitol SKAO-93352	(S)	Sunflower (Record Club)	1970	20.00	50.00
Reprise RS-6382	(S)	Sunflower (Orange label)	1970	8.00	20.00
Reprise RS-6453	(S)	Surf's Up (With lyric sheet)	1971	5.00	12.00
Reprise R-113793	(S)	Surf's Up (Record Club)	1971	8.00	20.00
Asylum R-113793	(S)	Surf's Up (Record Club)	1971	50.00	100.00
		(A printing mishap with two labels caused			
		"Surf's Up" to appear on Asylum while a			
		Jackson Browne album appears on Reprise.)			
Reprise 2MS-2083	(S)	Carl And The Passion/Pet Sounds	1972	6.00	15.00
Reprise MS-2118	(S)	Holland (With "Mt.Vernon & Fairway" EP)	1973	6.00	15.00
Mobile Fidelity 1-116	(S)	Surfer Girl		5.00	12.00

BEACON STREET UNION

Label		Title	Year	VG+	NM
MGM SE-4517	(S)	The Eyes Of The Beacon Street Union	1968	6.00	15.00
MGM SE-4568	(S)	The Clown Died In Marvin Gardens	1968	5.00	12.00

BEARCATS, THE

Label		Title	Year	VG+	NM
Somerset P-20800	(M)	Beatlemania	1964	12.00	30.00

BEASLEY, JIMMY

Label		Title	Year	VG+	NM
Modern LMP-1214	(M)	The Fabulous Jimmy Beasley	1956	50.00	100.00
Crown CLP-5014	(M)	The Fabulous Jimmy Beasley	1957	20.00	50.00

BEATLE BUDDIES, THE

Label		Title	Year	VG+	NM
Diplomat 2313	(M)	The Beatle Buddies	1964	10.00	25.00

BEATLES, THE
Also refer to Pete Best and George Martin.

Label		Title	Year	VG+	NM
Vee Jay LP-1062	(M)	Introducing The Beatles	1963	800.00	1,200.00
Vee Jay LPS-1062	(P)	Introducing The Beatles	1963	1,750.00	2,500.00
		(Black label with a rainbow border includes			
		"Love Me Do" and "P.S. I Love You." The back			
		cover features ads for 25 other albums.)			
Vee Jay LP-1062	(M)	Introducing The Beatles	1963	300.00	500.00
Vee Jay LPS-1062	(P)	Introducing The Beatles	1963	660.00	1,000.00
		(Black label with a rainbow border includes			
		"Love Me Do" and "P.S. I Love You." The back			
		cover is glossy white and completely blank.)			
Vee Jay LP-1062	(M)	Introducing The Beatles	1963	100.00	200.00
		(Black label with a rainbow border includes			
		"Love Me Do" and "P.S. I Love You." The back			
		cover lists the song titles in two columns.			
		Stereo copies are not known to exist.)			

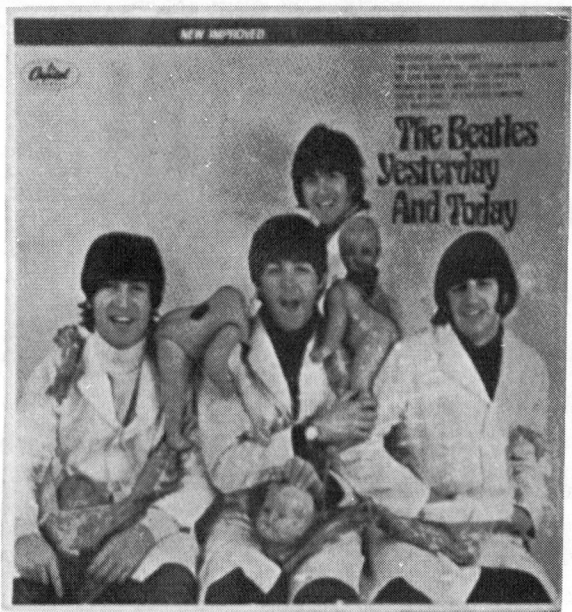

The Beatles, *Yesterday And Today*. The most collectible album of all, though far from the rarest, this is affectionately referred to as the "butcher cover," due to the cover graphics, which was a Beatles' design and a rather obvious comment on Capitol's, their American label, butchering of their albums. A normal Beatles album in Europe was 14 new songs; in the U.S. it was eleven, often containing hit singles still available or re-packaged, older material. The stereo version is far, far rarer than the mono, with an original, still-sealed stereo copy selling for $10,000 in 1988.

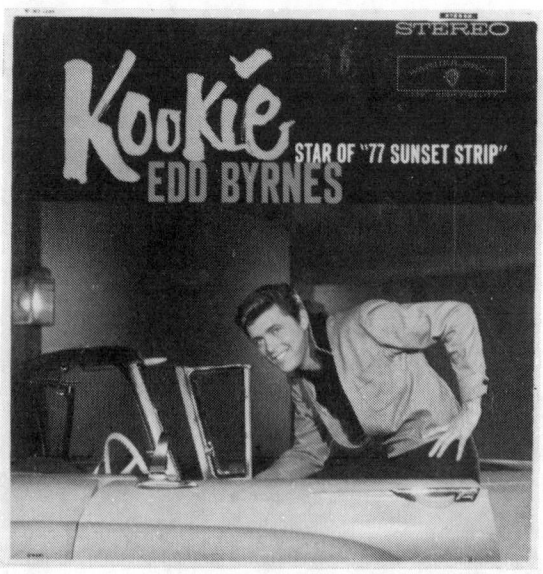

Edd Byrnes, *Kookie*. A manufactured teen heart-throb, Eddie Byrnes was bestown as the character "Kookie," in television's "77 Sunset Strip" (he parked cars). This album presents an amiable young actor pretending to be an amiable young singer.

Label		Title	Year	VG+	NM
Vee Jay LP-1062	(M)	Introducing The Beatles	1964	75.00	150.00
Vee Jay LPS-1062	(P)	Introducing The Beatles	1964	300.00	500.00
		(Black label with a rainbow border and the "Vee Jay" oval logo. Includes "Please Please Me" and "Ask Me Why.")			
Vee Jay LP-1062	(M)	Introducing The Beatles	1964	60.00	120.00
Vee Jay LPS-1062	(P)	Introducing The Beatles	1964	300.00	500.00
		(Black label with a rainbow border and the "VJ" logo. Includes "Please Please Me" and "Ask Me Why.")			
Vee Jay LP-1062	(M)	Introducing The Beatles	1964	50.00	100.00
Vee Jay LPS-1062	(P)	Introducing The Beatles	1964	300.00	500.00
		(Solid black label with the "Vee Jay" oval logo. Includes "Please Please Me" and "Ask Me Why.")			
Vee Jay LP-1062	(M)	Introducing The Beatles	1964	50.00	100.00
		(Solid black label with the "VJ" in brackets. Includes "Please Please Me" and "Ask Me Why." Stereo copies are not known to exist.)			
Vee Jay LP-1062	(M)	Introducing The Beatles	1964	50.00	100.00
		(Solid black label with a plain "VJ" logo. Includes "Please Please Me" and "Ask Me Why." Stereo copies are not known to exist.)			
Vee Jay LP-1085	(M)	The Beatles And Frank Ifield On Stage	1964	50.00	100.00
Vee Jay LP-1085	(P)	The Beatles And Frank Ifield On Stage	1964	150.00	250.00
		(The purple cover has a drawing of an old man with a Beatles haircut.)			
Vee Jay LP-1085	(M)	The Beatles And Frank Ifield On Stage	1964	1,065.00	1,600.00
Vee Jay LP-1085	(P)	The Beatles And Frank Ifield On Stage	1964	2,500.00	3,500.00
		(The cover has a painting of the Beatles with printing along the spine.)			
Vee Jay DX-30	(M)	The Beatles Vs. The Four Seasons	1964	400.00	600.00
Vee Jay DXS-30	(P)	The Beatles Vs. The Four Seasons	1964	1,000.00	1,500.00
		(Double album couples "Introducing The Beatles" with "The Golden Hits Of The Four Seasons." Issued with a poster, priced separately below.)			
		The Beatles Vs. The Four Seasons Poster	1964	75.00	150.00
		(12" x 23" full-color poster of the Fab Four.)			
Vee Jay LP-1092	(M)	Songs, Pictures And Stories	1964	75.00	150.00
Vee Jay LPS-1092	(P)	Songs, Pictures And Stories	1964	660.00	1,000.00
		(The fold-open front cover is 8" across.)			
Capitol T-2047	(M)	Meet The Beatles	1964	20.00	50.00
Capitol ST-2047	(P)	Meet The Beatles	1964	16.00	40.00
		(The title on the cover is brown.)			
Capitol T-2047	(M)	Meet The Beatles	1964	16.00	40.00
Capitol ST-2047	(P)	Meet The Beatles	1964	12.00	30.00
		(The title on the cover is green.)			
Capitol ST-82047	(P)	Meet The Beatles	1964	50.00	100.00
		(Record Club issue on the black label.)			
MGM E-4215	(M)	The Beatles With Tony Sheridan	1964	40.00	80.00
MGM SE-4215	(P)	The Beatles With Tony Sheridan	1964	90.00	180.00
Capitol T-2080	(M)	The Beatles Second Album	1964	16.00	40.00
Capitol ST-2080	(P)	The Beatles Second Album	1964	12.00	30.00
Capitol ST-82080	(P)	The Beatles Second Album	1964	50.00	100.00
		(Record Club issue on the black label.)			
United Arts. UAL-3366	(M)	A Hard Day's Night (Black label)	1964	20.00	50.00
United Arts. UAS-6366	(P)	A Hard Day's Night (Black label)	1964	16.00	40.00
United Arts. UAL-3366	(M)	A Hard Day's Night	1964	240.00	400.00
United Arts. UAS-6366	(P)	A Hard Day's Night	1964	100.00	200.00
		(Record Club issue on the black label.)			
Capitol T-2108	(M)	Something New	1964	16.00	40.00
Capitol ST-2108	(S)	Something New	1964	12.00	30.00
Capitol ST-82108	(S)	Something New	1964	50.00	100.00
		(Record Club issue on the black label.)			
Atco 33-169	(M)	Ain't She Sweet	1964	60.00	120.00
Atco SD-33-169	(P)	Ain't She Sweet	1964	75.00	150.00
Capitol TBO-2222	(M)	The Beatles' Story	1964	20.00	50.00
Capitol STBO-2222	(P)	The Beatles' Story	1964	16.00	40.00
Capitol T-2228	(M)	Beatles '65	1964	16.00	40.00
Capitol ST-2228	(P)	Beatles '65	1964	12.00	30.00
Capitol T-2309	(M)	The Early Beatles	1965	16.00	40.00
Capitol ST-2309	(P)	The Early Beatles	1965	12.00	30.00

Label		Title	Year	VG+	NM
Capitol T-2358	(M)	Beatles VI	1965	16.00	40.00
Capitol ST-2358	(P)	Beatles VI	1965	12.00	30.00
		(The back cover of first pressings read "See label for correct playing order.")			
Capitol ST-82358	(P)	Beatles VI	1965	50.00	100.00
		(Record Club issue on the black label.)			
Capitol MAS-2386	(M)	Help!	1965	16.00	40.00
Capitol SMAS-2386	(P)	Help!	1965	12.00	30.00
Capitol SMAS-82386	(P)	Help!	1965	50.00	100.00
		(Record Club issue on the black label.)			
Capitol T-2442	(M)	Rubber Soul	1965	16.00	40.00
Capitol ST-2442	(S)	Rubber Soul	1965	12.00	30.00
Capitol ST-82442	(S)	Rubber Soul	1965	50.00	100.00
		(Record Club issue on the black label.)			
Capitol T-2553	(M)	Yesterday And Today	1966	1,000.00	1,500.00
Capitol ST-2553	(P)	Yesterday And Today	1966	3,500.00	5,000.00
		(First state butcher cover. The original cover with the Fab Four in doctor's smocks covered with pieces of meat and baby doll parts!)			
Capitol T-2553	(M)	Yesterday And Today	1966	240.00	400.00
Capitol ST-2553	(P)	Yesterday And Today	1966	660.00	1,000.00
		(Second state butcher cover. The trunk cover is pasted over the original butcher cover with no attempts at removal.)			
Capitol T-2553	(M)	Yesterday And Today	1966	16.00	40.00
Capitol ST-2553	(S)	Yesterday And Today	1966	12.00	30.00
		(The trunk cover.)			
Capitol ST-82553	(S)	Yesterday And Today	1966	50.00	100.00
		(Record Club issue on the black label.)			
Capitol T-2576	(M)	Revolver	1966	16.00	40.00
Capitol ST-2576	(S)	Revolver	1966	12.00	30.00
Capitol ST-82576	(S)	Revolver	1966	50.00	100.00
		(Record Club issue on the black label.)			
Clarion 601	(M)	The Amazing Beatles	1966	35.00	70.00
Clarion SD-601	(P)	The Amazing Beatles	1966	50.00	100.00
		(The back cover lists the song titles.)			
Clarion 601	(M)	The Amazing Beatles	1966	50.00	100.00
Clarion SD-601	(P)	The Amazing Beatles	1966	75.00	150.00
		(The back cover does not list the song titles.)			
Capitol MAS-2653	(M)	Sgt. Pepper's Lonely Heart's Club Band	1967	30.00	60.00
Capitol SMAS-2653	(S)	Sgt. Pepper's Lonely Heart's Club Band	1967	10.00	25.00
		(With insert and psychedelic inner sleeve.)			
Capitol MAL-2835	(M)	Magical Mystery Tour	1967	50.00	100.00
Capitol SMAL-2835	(P)	Magical Mystery Tour	1967	10.00	25.00
		(Capitol albums above have black labels.)			
Apple SWBO-101	(S)	The Beatles	1968	20.00	50.00
		(The cover has "The Beatles" in raised white letters with a number stamped in black. The price includes a poster and four glossy, color portraits of John, Paul, George and Ringo.)			
Apple SW-153	(S)	Yellow Submarine (Sdtk)	1968	8.00	20.00
Apple SO-383	(S)	Abbey Road	1969	8.00	20.00
Polydor 24-4504	(P)	In The Beginning (Red label)	1970	10.00	25.00
Apple SO-385	(S)	Hey Jude/The Beatles Again	1970	10.00	25.00
Apple SW-385	(S)	Hey Jude/The Beatles Again	1970	8.00	20.00
		(Original pressings of the record were titled "The Beatles Again" with either the "SO" or "SW" prefix. The cover reads "Hey Jude.")			
Apple SBC-100	(P)	The Beatles Christmas Album	1970	75.00	150.00
		(Issued to fan club members only.)			
Apple SW-385	(S)	Hey Jude	1970	8.00	20.00
Apple AR-34001	(S)	Let It Be	1970	8.00	20.00
Apple ST-2047	(P)	Meet The Beatles	1970	8.00	20.00
Apple ST-2080	(P)	The Beatles Second Album	1970	8.00	20.00
Apple ST-2108	(S)	Something New	1970	8.00	20.00
Apple ST-2222	(P)	The Beatles' Story	1970	8.00	20.00
Apple ST-2228	(P)	Beatles '65	1970	8.00	20.00
Apple ST-2309	(P)	The Early Beatles	1970	8.00	20.00
Apple ST-2358	(P)	Beatles VI	1970	8.00	20.00
Apple ST-2386	(P)	Help!	1970	8.00	20.00
Apple ST-2442	(S)	Rubber Soul	1970	8.00	20.00

Label		Title	Year	VG+	NM
Apple ST-2553	(S)	Yesterday And Today	1970	8.00	20.00
Apple ST-2576	(S)	Revolver	1970	8.00	20.00
Apple SMAS-2653	(S)	Sgt. Pepper's Lonely Heart's Club Band	1970	8.00	20.00
Apple SMAL-2835	(P)	Magical Mystery Tour	1970	8.00	20.00
		(Apple albums above have "A Subsidiary of			
		Capitol" on the bottom of the label.)			
Apple ST-2047	(P)	Meet The Beatles	1970	6.00	15.00
Apple ST-2080	(P)	The Beatles Second Album	1970	6.00	15.00
Apple ST-2108	(S)	Something New	1970	6.00	15.00
Apple ST-2222	(P)	The Beatles' Story	1970	6.00	15.00
Apple ST-2228	(P)	Beatles '65	1970	6.00	15.00
Apple ST-2309	(P)	The Early Beatles	1970	6.00	15.00
Apple ST-2358	(P)	Beatles VI	1970	6.00	15.00
Apple ST-2386	(P)	Help!	1970	6.00	15.00
Apple ST-2442	(S)	Rubber Soul	1970	6.00	15.00
Apple ST-2553	(S)	Yesterday And Today	1970	6.00	15.00
Apple ST-2576	(S)	Revolver	1970	6.00	15.00
Apple SMAS-2653	(S)	Sgt. Pepper's Lonely Heart's Club Band	1970	6.00	15.00
Apple SMAL-2835	(P)	Magical Mystery Tour	1970	6.00	15.00
Apple SW-385	(S)	Hey Jude	1970	6.00	15.00
		(Apple albums above have "Mfd. by Apple			
		Records" on the bottom of the label.)			
Apple SKBO-3403	(P)	The Beatles 1962-1966	1973	8.00	20.00
Apple SKBO-3404	(P)	The Beatles 1967-1970	1973	8.00	20.00
Capitol SKBO-11537	(P)	Rock 'N' Roll Music	1977	8.00	20.00
Capitol SMAS-11638	(S)	The Beatles At The Hollywood Bowl	1977	6.00	15.00
		(The title and graphics on the cover are raised.)			
Lingasong LS-2-7001	(M)	The Beatles Live At The Star Club	1977	6.00	15.00
Capitol SKBL-11711	(S)	Love Songs (Embossed cover)	1977	10.00	25.00
		(Picture disc.)			
Capitol SEAX-11840	(S)	Sgt. Pepper's Lonely Heart's Club Band	1978	12.00	30.00
Capitol SEBX-11841	(S)	The Beatles (White vinyl)	1978	12.00	30.00
Capitol SEBX-11842	(S)	The Beatles 1962-1966 (Red vinyl)	1978	12.00	30.00
Capitol SEBX-11843	(S)	The Beatles 1967-1970 (Blue vinyl)	1978	12.00	30.00
Capitol SEAX-11900	(S)	Abbey Road (Picture disc)	1978	12.00	30.00
Capitol SN-12009	(P)	The Beatles Rarities (Green label)	1978	35.00	70.00
Capitol BC-13	(P)	The Beatles Collection (14 LPs)	1978	210.00	350.00
Mobile Fidelity 1-023	(S)	Abbey Road	1979	14.00	35.00
Capitol SHAL-12060	(P)	Rarities (Black label)	1980	4.00	10.00
Mobile Fidelity 1-047	(P)	Magical Mystery Tour	1981	16.00	40.00
Capitol SV-12199	(S)	Reel Music (Gold vinyl)	1982	20.00	50.00
		(The back cover has a "limited edition" number			
		in the upper right corner.)			
Capitol SV-12199	(S)	Reel Music (Gold vinyl)	1982	10.00	25.00
		(The back cover does not have a "limited edition"			
		number in the upper right corner.)			
Mobile Fidelity	(P)	The Beatles Collection (14 LPs)	1982	210.00	350.00
Mobile Fidelity 1-072	(S)	The Beatles	1982	10.00	25.00
Mobile Fidelity 1-100	(S)	Sgt. Pepper's Lonely Heart's Club Band	1982	5.00	12.00
Mobile Fidelity 1-100	(S)	Sgt. Pepper's Lonely Heart's Club Band		75.00	150.00
		(U.H.Q.R. boxed set.)			
Mobile Fidelity 1-101	(S)	Please Please Me	1984	5.00	12.00
Mobile Fidelity 1-102	(S)	With The Beatles	1984	20.00	50.00
		(Due to a manufacturing mishap, production			
		was halted after a brief press run.)			
Mobile Fidelity 1-103	(S)	A Hard Day's Night	1984	5.00	12.00
Mobile Fidelity 1-104	(S)	Beatles For Sale	1984	5.00	12.00
Mobile Fidelity 1-105	(S)	Help	1984	5.00	12.00
Mobile Fidelity 1-106	(S)	Rubber Soul	1984	5.00	12.00
Mobile Fidelity 1-107	(S)	Revolver	1984	5.00	12.00
Mobile Fidelity 1-108	(P)	Yellow Submarine (Sdtk)	1984	5.00	12.00
Mobile Fidelity 1-109	(S)	Let It Be	1984	5.00	12.00

BEATS, THE (THE LIVERPOOL BEATS)

Rondo 2026	(M)	The New Merseyside Sound	1964	12.00	30.00

BEAU BRUMMELS, THE

Autumn LP-103	(M)	Introducing The Beau Brummels	1965	10.00	25.00
Autumn SLP-103	(S)	Introducing The Beau Brummels	1965	14.00	35.00
Autumn LP-104	(M)	The Beau Brummels, Volume 2	1965	10.00	25.00
Autumn SLP-104	(S)	The Beau Brummels, Volume 2	1965	12.00	30.00

Label		Title	Year	VG+	NM
Decca DL-4699	(M)	Wild, Wild Winter (Sdtk)	1966	6.00	15.00
Decca DL7-4699	(S)	Wild, Wild Winter (Sdtk)	1966	8.00	20.00
Warners WS-1644	(M)	Beau Brummels '66	1966	6.00	15.00
Warners WS-1644	(S)	Beau Brummels '66	1966	8.00	20.00
Warners W-1692	(M)	Triangle	1967	6.00	15.00
Warners WS-1692	(S)	Triangle	1967	8.00	20.00
Warners WS-1760	(S)	Bradley's Barn	1968	8.00	20.00

BEAUREGARDE

F-Empire	(S)	Beauregarde		40.00	80.00

BEAVER, PAUL

Rapture 11111	(S)	Perchance To Dream		12.00	30.00

BEAVER & KRAUSE (PAUL BEAVER & BERNIE KRAUSE)

Limelight 86069	(S)	Ragnarok	1969	10.00	25.00

BECK (GROUP), JEFF

Epic BN-26413	(S)	Truth (Yellow label)	1968	6.00	15.00
Epic BN-26478	(S)	Beck-Ola (Yellow label)	1969	5.00	12.00
Epic EQ-30973	(Q)	Rough And Ready	1972	6.00	15.00
Epic EQ-31331	(Q)	The Jeff Beck Group	1972	6.00	15.00
Epic PEQ-33409	(Q)	Blow By Blow	1975	6.00	15.00
Epic PEQ-33849	(Q)	Wired	1976	6.00	15.00
Epic PEQ-34433	(Q)	Live	1977	6.00	15.00

BEDIENT, JACK, & THE CHESSMEN

Trophy 101	(M)	Two Sides Of Jack Bedient	1964	16.00	40.00
Fantasy 3365	(M)	Live At Harvey's	1965	14.00	35.00
Executive Productions	(M)	Jack Bedient		16.00	40.00
Satori LP-1001	(M)	Where Did She Go?	1966	14.00	35.00

BEE GEES, THE (BARRY, MAURICE & ROBIN GIBB)

Atco 33-223	(M)	The Bee Gees First	1967	6.00	15.00
Atco SD-33-223	(S)	The Bee Gees First (Purple & white label)	1967	6.00	15.00
Atco 33-233	(M)	Horizontal	1968	6.00	15.00
Atco SD-33-233	(S)	Horizontal (Purple & white label)	1968	6.00	15.00
Atco SD-33-253	(S)	Idea	1968	5.00	12.00
Atco SD-33-264	(E)	Rare, Precious And Beautiful	1968	5.00	12.00
Atco SD-33-292	(S)	The Best Of The Bee Gees	1969	5.00	12.00
Atco SD-2-702	(S)	Odessa (Red felt cover)	1969	6.00	15.00
Atco SD-2-702	(S)	Odessa (Plain red cover)	1969	12.00	30.00
Atco SD-33-321	(E)	Rare, Precious And Beautiful, Volume 2	1970	4.00	10.00
Atco SD-33-327	(S)	Cucumber Castle	1970	5.00	12.00
Atco SD-33-353	(S)	Two Years On	1971	5.00	12.00
Atco SD-33-363	(S)	Melody (Sdtk)	1971	6.00	15.00
		(Atco albums above have yellow labels with "1841 Broadway" on the bottom.)			
Nautilus 17	(S)	Spirits Having Flown		6.00	15.00

BEEFHEART, CAPTAIN (& THE MAGIC BAND)
Also refer to Fran Zappa.

Buddah BDM-1001	(M)	Safe As Milk	1967	14.00	35.00
Buddah BDS-5001	(E)	Safe As Milk (Red label)	1967	12.00	30.00
		(With custom inner sleeve & bumper sticker.)			
Blue Thumb BTS-1	(S)	Strictly Personal	1968	8.00	20.00
Straight STS-1053	(S)	Trout Mask Replica	1969	12.00	30.00
Reprise RS-6420	(S)	Lick My Decals Off, Baby	1970	12.00	30.00
		(Orange label with a lyric sheet)			
Buddah BDS-5077	(S)	Mirror Man (Fold open, die-cut cover)	1971	8.00	20.00
Reprise MS-2050	(S)	Spotlight Kid (Orange label)	1972	8.00	20.00
Reprise MS-2115	(S)	Clear Spot (Clear jacket)	1972	10.00	25.00
Mercury SRM-1-1018	(S)	Bluejeans And Moonbeams	1974	6.00	15.00

BEETHOVEN SOUL

Dot DLP-3821	(M)	The Beethoven Soul	1967	6.00	15.00
Dot DLP-25821	(S)	The Beethoven Soul	1967	8.00	20.00

BELAFONTE, HARRY

RCA LPM-1022	(M)	Mark Twain And Other Folk Favorites	1955	8.00	20.00
RCA LPM-1150	(M)	Three For Tonight (Sdtk)	1955	8.00	20.00

Label		Title	Year	VG+	NM
RCA LPM-1150	(M)	Belafonte	1956	8.00	20.00
RCA LPM-1248	(M)	Calypso	1956	8.00	20.00
RCA LPM-1402	(M)	An Evening With Belafonte	1957	8.00	20.00
RCA LPM-1505	(M)	Belafonte Sings Of The Caribbean	1957	8.00	20.00
RCA LOP-1006	(M)	Belafonte Sings The Blues	1958	8.00	20.00
RCA LPM-1887	(M)	To Wish You A Merry Christmas	1958	8.00	20.00
RCA LPM-1927	(M)	Love Is A Gentle Thing	1959	5.00	12.00
RCA LSP-1927	(S)	Love Is A Gentle Thing	1959	6.00	15.00
RCA LOC-1507	(M)	Porgy And Bess	1959	5.00	12.00
RCA LSO-1507	(S)	Porgy And Bess	1959	6.00	15.00
RCA LOC-6006	(M)	Belafonte At Carnegie Hall	1959	5.00	12.00
RCA LSO-6006	(S)	Belafonte At Carnegie Hall	1959	6.00	15.00
RCA LPM-2022	(M)	My Lord What A Mornin'	1960	4.00	10.00
RCA LSP-2022	(S)	My Lord What A Mornin'	1960	5.00	12.00
RCA LOC-6007	(M)	Belafonte Returns To Carnegie Hall	1960	4.00	10.00
RCA LSO-6007	(S)	Belafonte Returns To Carnegie Hall	1960	5.00	12.00
RCA LPM-2194	(M)	Swing Dat Hammer	1960	4.00	10.00
RCA LSP-2194	(S)	Swing Dat Hammer	1960	5.00	12.00
RCA LPM-2388	(M)	Jump Up Calypso	1961	4.00	10.00
RCA LSP-2388	(S)	Jump Up Calypso	1961	5.00	12.00
RCA LPM-2499	(M)	The Midnight Special	1962	6.00	15.00
RCA LSP-2499	(S)	The Midnight Special	1962	8.00	20.00
RCA LPM-2574	(M)	The Many Moods Of Belafonte	1962	4.00	10.00
RCA LSP-2574	(S)	The Many Moods Of Belafonte	1962	5.00	12.00
RCA LPM-2626	(M)	To Wish You A Merry Christmas	1962	4.00	10.00
RCA LSP-2626	(S)	To Wish You A Merry Christmas	1962	5.00	12.00
RCA LPM-2695	(M)	Streets I Have Walked	1963	4.00	10.00
RCA LSP-2695	(S)	Streets I Have Walked	1963	5.00	12.00

*(Mono RCA albums above have "Long Play"
on the bottom of the label. Stereo albums
have "Living Stereo" on the bottom.)*

BELL, ARCHIE, & THE DRELLS

Atlantic SD-8181	(S)	Tighten Up	1968	10.00	25.00
Atlantic SD-8204	(S)	I Can't Stop Dancing	1968	8.00	20.00
Atlantic SD-8226	(S)	There's Gonna Be A Showdown	1969	6.00	15.00

BELL, FREDDIE, & THE BELL BOYS

Mercury MG-20289	(M)	Rock And Roll—All Flavors	1958	50.00	100.00
20th Century 4146	(M)	Bells Are Swinging	1964	8.00	20.00
20th Century S-4146	(S)	Bells Are Swinging	1964	10.00	25.00
MGM E-4273	(M)	Get Yourself A College Girl (Sdtk)	1964	6.00	15.00
MGM SE-4273	(S)	Get Yourself A College Girl (Sdtk)	1964	8.00	20.00

BELLINE, DENNY, & THE RICH KIDS

RCA LPM-3655	(M)	Denny Belline And The Rich Kids	1966	6.00	15.00
RCA LSP-3655	(S)	Denny Belline And The Rich Kids	1966	8.00	20.00

BELLUS, TONY

N.R.C. LPA-8	(M)	Robbin' The Cradle	1960	50.00	100.00

BELMONTS, THE
Also refer to Dion & The Belmonts.

Sabina SALP-5001	(M)	The Belmonts' Carnival Of Hits	1962	75.00	150.00
Dot DLP-25949	(S)	Summer Love	1969	10.00	25.00
Buddah BDS-5123	(S)	Cigars, Acappella, Candy	1972	10.00	25.00
Strawberry 6001	(S)	Cheek To Cheek	1978	6.00	15.00

BELVIN, JESSE

RCA LPM-2089	(M)	Just Jesse Belvin	1959	12.00	30.00
RCA LSP-2089	(S)	Just Jesse Belvin	1959	16.00	40.00
RCA LPM-2105	(M)	Mr. Easy	1960	12.00	30.00
RCA LSP-2105	(S)	Mr. Easy	1960	16.00	40.00

BENETAR, PAT

Mobile Fidelity 1-057	(S)	In The Heat Of The Night		6.00	15.00

BENNETT, BOYD

King 594	(M)	Boyd Bennett	1957	660.00	1,000.00

Label		Title	Year	VG+	NM
BENNETT, TONY					
Columbia CL-613	(M)	Treasure Chest Of Song Hits	1955	10.00	25.00
Columbia CL-621	(M)	Cloud Seven	1955	10.00	25.00
Columbia CL-938	(M)	Tony	1957	10.00	25.00
Columbia CL-1079	(M)	The Best Of My Heart	1957	8.00	20.00
Columbia CL-1186	(M)	Long Ago And Far Away	1958	8.00	20.00
Columbia CL-1229	(M)	Tony's Greatest Hits	1958	8.00	20.00
Columbia CL-1292	(M)	Blue Velvet	1959	8.00	20.00
Columbia CL-2343	(M)	If I Ruled The World	1959	8.00	20.00
Columbia CL-2507	(M)	Alone At Last With Tony Bennett	1959	8.00	20.00
Columbia CL-2550	(M)	Because Of You	1959	8.00	20.00
Columbia CL-1294	(M)	Tony Bennett In Person	1959	5.00	12.00
Columbia CS-8104	(S)	Tony Bennett In Person	1959	6.00	15.00
Columbia CL-1301	(M)	Hometown, My Hometown	1959	5.00	12.00
Columbia CS-8107	(S)	Hometown, My Hometown	1959	6.00	15.00
Columbia CL-1429	(M)	To My Wonderful One	1960	5.00	12.00
Columbia CS-8226	(S)	To My Wonderful One	1960	6.00	15.00
Columbia CL-1446	(M)	Tony Sings For Two	1960	5.00	12.00
Columbia CS-8242	(S)	Tony Sings For Two	1960	6.00	15.00
Columbia CL-1471	(M)	Alone Together	1960	5.00	12.00
Columbia CS-8262	(S)	Alone Together	1960	6.00	15.00
Columbia CL-1535	(M)	More Tony's Greatest Hits	1960	5.00	12.00
Columbia CS-8335	(S)	More Tony's Greatest Hits	1960	6.00	15.00
Columbia CS-1559	(M)	A String Of Harold Arlen	1960	5.00	12.00
Columbia CS-8359	(S)	A String Of Harold Arlen	1960	6.00	15.00
Columbia CL-1658	(M)	My Heart Sings	1961	5.00	12.00
Columbia CS-8458	(S)	My Heart Sings	1961	6.00	15.00
Columbia CL-1763	(M)	Mr. Broadway	1962	5.00	12.00
Columbia CS-8563	(S)	Mr. Broadway	1962	6.00	15.00
		(Columbia albums above have six black & white "eye" logos on each label.)			
Roulette R-25072	(M)	Count Basie Swings/Tony Sings	1961	6.00	15.00
Roulette SR-25072	(S)	Count Basie Swings/Tony Sings	1961	8.00	20.00
Roulette R-25231	(M)	Bennett And Basie Strike Up The Band	1961	6.00	15.00
Roulette SR-25231	(S)	Bennett And Basie Strike Up The Band	1961	8.00	20.00
Columbia CL-1852	(M)	Tony's Greatest Hits	1962	6.00	15.00
Columbia CS-8652	(E)	Tony's Greatest Hits	1962	4.00	10.00
Columbia CL-1869	(M)	I Left My Heart In San Francisco	1962	5.00	12.00
Columbia CS-8669	(S)	I Left My Heart In San Francisco	1962	6.00	15.00
Columbia C2L-23	(M)	Tony Bennett At Carnegie Hall	1962	5.00	12.00
Columbia C2S-23	(S)	Tony Bennett At Carnegie Hall	1962	6.00	15.00
		(Columbia albums above have "360 Sound" labels.)			
Mobile Fidelity 1-117	(S)	The Bennett/Evans Albums		6.00	15.00
BENSON, GEORGE					
Mobile Fidelity 1-011	(S)	Breezin'	1979	8.00	20.00
BENTON, BARBI					
Playboy 404	(S)	Barbi Doll (With poster)	1974	6.00	15.00
Playboy 406	(S)	Barbi Benton	1975	4.00	10.00
Playboy 411	(S)	Something New	1976	4.00	10.00
BENTON, BROOK					
Epic LN-3573	(M)	Brook Benton At His Best		6.00	15.00
Mercury MG-20421	(M)	It's Just A Matter Of Time	1959	8.00	20.00
Mercury MG-20464	(M)	Brook Benton	1959	6.00	15.00
Mercury SR-60146	(S)	Brook Benton	1959	8.00	20.00
Mercury MG-20565	(M)	So Many Ways I Love You	1959	6.00	15.00
Mercury SR-60217	(S)	So Many Ways I Love You	1959	8.00	20.00
Mercury MG-20588	(M)	The Two Of Us (With Dinah Washington)	1960	5.00	12.00
Mercury SR-60244	(S)	The Two Of Us (With Dinah Washington)	1960	6.00	15.00
Mercury MG-20602	(M)	Songs I Love To Sing	1960	5.00	12.00
Mercury SR-60602	(S)	Songs I Love To Sing	1960	6.00	15.00
Mercury MG-20607	(M)	Brook Benton's Golden Hits	1961	5.00	12.00
Mercury SR-60607	(S)	Brook Benton's Golden Hits	1961	6.00	15.00
Mercury MG-20619	(M)	If You Believe	1961	5.00	12.00
Mercury SR-60619	(S)	If You Believe	1961	6.00	15.00
Mercury MG-20641	(M)	The Boll Weevil Song	1961	5.00	12.00
Mercury SR-60641	(S)	The Boll Weevil Song	1961	6.00	15.00
Mercury MG-20673	(M)	There Goes That Song Again	1962	5.00	12.00
Mercury SR-60673	(S)	There Goes That Song Again	1962	6.00	15.00

Label		Title	Year	VG+	NM
Mercury MG-20740	(M)	Singing The Blues	1962	5.00	12.00
Mercury SR-60740	(S)	Singing The Blues	1962	6.00	15.00
Mercury MG-20774	(M)	Brook Benton's Golden Hits, Volume 2	1963	5.00	12.00
Mercury SR-60774	(S)	Brook Benton's Golden Hits, Volume 2	1963	6.00	15.00
Mercury SR-60830	(M)	Best Ballads Of Broadway	1963	5.00	12.00
Mercury SR-60830	(S)	Best Ballads Of Broadway	1963	6.00	15.00
Mercury MG-20886	(M)	Born To Sing The Blues	1964	5.00	12.00
Mercury SR-60886	(S)	Born To Sing The Blues	1964	6.00	15.00
Mercury MG-20918	(M)	On The Country Side	1964	4.00	10.00
Mercury SR-60918	(S)	On The Country Side	1964	5.00	12.00
Mercury MG-20934	(M)	This Bitter Earth	1964	4.00	10.00
Mercury SR-60934	(S)	This Bitter Earth	1964	5.00	12.00
RCA LPM-3514	(M)	That Old Feeling	1966	4.00	10.00
RCA LSP-3514	(S)	That Old Feeling	1966	5.00	12.00
RCA LPM-3526	(M)	Mother Nature, Father Time	1966	4.00	10.00
RCA LSP-3526	(S)	Mother Nature, Father Time	1966	5.00	12.00
RCA LPM-3590	(M)	My Country	1966	4.00	10.00
RCA LSP-3590	(S)	My Country	1966	5.00	12.00
Reprise R-6268	(M)	Laura, What's He Got That I Ain't Got?	1967	4.00	10.00
Reprise RS-6268	(S)	Laura, What's He Got That I Ain't Got?	1967	5.00	12.00

BERGEN, POLLY

Label		Title	Year	VG+	NM
Columbia CL-994	(M)	Bergen Sings Morgan	1957	12.00	30.00
Columbia CL-1031	(M)	The Party's Over	1957	12.00	30.00
Columbia CL-1138	(M)	Polly And Her Pop	1958	10.00	25.00
Columbia OL-2014	(M)	First Impressions	1959	10.00	25.00
Columbia CL-1218	(M)	My Heart Sings	1959	8.00	20.00
Columbia CS-8018	(S)	My Heart Sings	1959	10.00	25.00
Columbia CL-1300	(M)	All Alone By The Telephone	1959	8.00	20.00
Columbia CS-8100	(S)	All Alone By The Telephone	1959	10.00	25.00
Columbia CL-1481	(M)	Four Seasons Of Love	1960	6.00	15.00
Columbia CS-8246	(S)	Four Seasons Of Love	1960	8.00	20.00
Columbia CL-1632	(M)	"Do Re Mi" And "Annie Get Your Gun"	1961	6.00	15.00
Columbia CS-8432	(S)	"Do Re Mi" And "Annie Get Your Gun"	1961	8.00	20.00
		(Columbia albums above have six black "eye" logos on each label.)			

BERNARD, ROD

Label		Title	Year	VG+	NM
Jin LP-4007	(M)	Rod Bernard		20.00	50.00

BERRY, CHUCK

Label		Title	Year	VG+	NM
Chess LP-1425	(M)	Rock, Rock, Rock (Sdtk)	1957	50.00	100.00
Chess LP-1426	(M)	After School Session	1958	40.00	80.00
Chess LP-1432	(M)	One Dozen Berrys	1958	40.00	80.00
Chess LP-1435	(M)	Berry Is On Top	1959	35.00	70.00
Chess LP-1448	(M)	Rockin' At The Hops	1960	35.00	70.00
Chess LP-1456	(M)	New Juke Box Hits	1961	20.00	50.00
Chess LP-1465	(M)	Chuck Berry Twist	1962	30.00	60.00
Chess LP-1465	(M)	More Chuck Berry	1963	20.00	50.00
Chess LP-1480	(M)	Chuck Berry On Stage	1963	20.00	50.00
Chess LP-1485	(M)	Chuck Berry's Greatest Hits	1964	16.00	40.00
Chess LP-1488	(M)	St. Louis To Liverpool	1964	20.00	50.00
Chess LPS-1488	(P)	St. Louis To Liverpool	1964	30.00	60.00
		(Chess albums above have black & silver labels.)			
Checker LP-2991	(M)	Two Great Guitars (With Bo Didley)	1964	10.00	25.00
Checker LPS-2991	(S)	Two Great Guitars (With Bo Didley)	1964	12.00	30.00
Chess LP-1495	(M)	Chuck Berry In London	1965	14.00	35.00
Chess LPS-1495	(S)	Chuck Berry In London	1965	16.00	40.00
Chess LP-1498	(M)	Fresh Berrys	1965	14.00	35.00
Chess LPS-1498	(S)	Fresh Berrys	1965	16.00	40.00
Chess LP-1514	(M)	Chuck Berry's Golden Decade	1967	10.00	25.00
Chess LPS-1514	(E)	Chuck Berry's Golden Decade	1967	6.00	15.00
Mercury MG-21103	(M)	Chuck Berry's Golden Hits	1967	6.00	15.00
Mercury SR-61103	(S)	Chuck Berry's Golden Hits	1967	6.00	15.00
Mercury MG-21123	(M)	Chuck Berry In Memphis	1967	8.00	20.00
Mercury SR-61123	(S)	Chuck Berry In Memphis	1967	10.00	25.00
Mercury MG-21138	(M)	Live At The Fillmore Auditorium	1967	8.00	20.00
Mercury SR-61138	(S)	Live At The Fillmore Auditorium	1967	10.00	25.00
		(Features the Steve Miller Blues Band.)			
Mercury SR-61176	(S)	From St. Louis To Frisco	1968	8.00	20.00
Mercury SR-61223	(S)	Concerto In B. Goode	1969	8.00	20.00

Label		Title	Year	VG+	NM
Chess LPS-1550	(S)	Back Home	1970	8.00	20.00
Chess CH-50008	(S)	San Francisco Dues	1971	8.00	20.00
Chess CH-60020	(P)	The London Sessions (Fold-open jacket.)	1972	6.00	15.00
		(Chess albums above have blue & white labels.)			

BERRY, RICHARD (& THE SOUL SEARCHERS)

Crown CLP-5371	(M)	Richard Berry And The Dreamers	1963	10.00	25.00
Pam 1001	(M)	Live At The Century Club		20.00	50.00
Pam 1002	(M)	Wild Berry		20.00	50.00

BEST, PETE
Best was a member of the Beatles before they recorded for EMI/Parlophone.

Savage BM-71	(M)	Best Of The Beatles	1965	75.00	150.00

BIG BEATS, THE

Liberty LRP-3407	(M)	The Big Beats Live	1965	8.00	20.00
Liberty LST-7407	(S)	The Big Beats Live	1965	10.00	25.00

BIG BOPPER (J.P. "JAPE" RICHARDSON)

Mercury MG-20402	(M)	Chantilly Lace (Black label)	1959	180.00	300.00

BIG BROTHER

All American 5770	(M)	Confusion	1970	50.00	100.00

BIG BROTHER & THE HOLDING COMPANY

Mainstream 56099	(M)	Big Brother & The Holding Company	1967	6.00	15.00
Mainstream S-6099	(S)	Big Brother & The Holding Company	1967	6.00	15.00
Columbia KCS-9700	(S)	Cheap Thrills ("360 Sound" label)	1968	5.00	12.00
Columbia C-30222	(S)	Be A Brother	1970	6.00	15.00
Columbia C-30738	(S)	How Hard It Is	1971	6.00	15.00

BIG DADDY

Gee G-704	(M)	Big Daddy's Blues	1960	12.00	30.00
Gee SG-704	(S)	Big Daddy's Blues	1960	16.00	40.00
Regent 6106	(M)	Twist Party	1962	10.00	25.00

BIG FOOT

Winro 1004	(S)	Big Foot	1968	8.00	20.00

BIG MAYBELLE

Savoy MG-14005	(M)	Big Maybelle Sings	1958	20.00	50.00
Savoy MG-14011	(M)	Blues, Candy And Big Maybelle	1958	20.00	50.00
Brunswick BL-54107	(M)	What More Can A Woman Do	1962	10.00	25.00
Brunswick BL7-54107	(S)	What More Can A Woman Do	1962	12.00	30.00
Scepter S-522	(M)	The Soul Of Big Maybelle	1964	5.00	12.00
Scepter SS-522	(S)	The Soul Of Big Maybelle	1964	6.00	15.00
Rajac S-522	(M)	Got A Brand New Bag	1967	5.00	12.00
Rajac SS-522	(S)	Got A Brand New Bag	1967	6.00	15.00
Brunswick BL-754142	(S)	Gospel Soul Of Big Maybelle	1968	5.00	12.00

BIG STAR

Ardent ADS-2803	(S)	#1 Record	1972	10.00	25.00
Ardent ADS-1501	(S)	Radio City	1974	10.00	25.00

BIG THREE, THE (CASS ELLIOTT, JIM HENDRICKS & TIM ROSE)

FM 307	(M)	The Big Three	1963	8.00	20.00
FM FS-307	(S)	The Big Three	1963	10.00	25.00
FM 311	(M)	Live At The Recording Studio	1964	8.00	20.00
FM FS-311	(S)	Live At The Recording Studio	1964	10.00	25.00
Roulette R-42000	(M)	The Big Three Featuring Cass Elliott	1967	5.00	12.00
Roulette SR-42000	(S)	The Big Three Featuring Cass Elliott	1967	6.00	15.00

BLACK, CILLA

Capitol T-2308	(M)	Is It Love?	1965	5.00	12.00
Capitol ST-2308	(S)	Is It Love?	1965	6.00	15.00

BLACK PEARL

Atlantic SD-8220	(S)	Black Pearl	1969	6.00	15.00
Prophesy PRS-1001	(S)	Black Pearl Live	1970	8.00	20.00

Label		Title	Year	VG+	NM
BLACKFOOT, J. D.					
Mercury SRM-1-61288	(S)	The Ultimate Prophecy	1970	14.00	35.00
BLACKWELL, OTIS					
Davis 109	(M)	Singin' The Blues	1956	65.00	130.00
BLANC, MEL					
Capitol H-436 (10")	(M)	Party Panic		16.00	40.00
Capitol JAO-3251	(M)	Woody Woodpecker And His Talent Show	1961	10.00	25.00
Capitol J-3257	(M)	Bugs Bunny And His Friends	1961	10.00	25.00
Capitol J-3261	(M)	Tweety Pie And Other Favorites	1962	10.00	25.00
Capitol J-3263	(M)	Woody Woodpecker's Picnic	1962	10.00	25.00
Capitol J-3266	(M)	Bugs Bunny In Storyland	1963	10.00	25.00
Colpix CP-472	(M)	Hey There, It's Yogi Bear (Sdtk)	1964	10.00	25.00
Colpix SCP-472	(S)	Hey There, It's Yogi Bear (Sdtk)	1964	14.00	35.00
Hanna-Barbera 2055	(M)	A Man Called Flintstone (Sdtk)	1967	10.00	25.00
BLAND, BOBBY "BLUE"					
Duke DLP-74	(M)	Two Steps From The Blues	1961	10.00	25.00
Duke DLP-75	(M)	Here's The Man	1962	10.00	25.00
Duke DLP-77	(M)	Call On Me	1963	10.00	25.00
Duke DLP-78	(M)	Ain't Nothing You Can Do	1964	10.00	25.00
Duke DLP-79	(M)	The Soul Of The Man	1966	6.00	15.00
Duke DLPS-79	(S)	The Soul Of The Man	1966	8.00	20.00
Duke DLP-84	(M)	The Best Of Bobby Bland	1967	5.00	12.00
Duke DLPS-84	(S)	The Best Of Bobby Bland	1967	6.00	15.00
Duke DLP-88	(M)	Touch Of The Blues	1967	5.00	12.00
Duke DLPS-88	(S)	Touch Of The Blues	1967	6.00	15.00
Duke DLP-86	(M)	The Best Of Bobby Bland, Volume 2	1968	5.00	12.00
Duke DLPS-86	(S)	The Best Of Bobby Bland, Volume 2	1968	6.00	15.00
Duke DLPS-89	(S)	Spotlighting The Man	1969	6.00	15.00
Duke X-90	(S)	If Loving You Is Wrong	1970	5.00	12.00
BLASTERS, THE					
Rollin' Rock 021	(S)	American Music	1980	20.00	50.00
BLIND FAITH					
Atco SD-33-304A	(S)	Blind Faith (Naked girl on cover)	1969	8.00	20.00
BLOCKER, DAN					
RCA LPM-2896	(M)	Our Land, Our Heritage	1964	5.00	12.00
RCA LSP-2896	(S)	Our Land, Our Heritage	1964	6.00	15.00
BLODWYN PIG					
A&M SP-4210	(S)	Ahead Rings Out	1969	6.00	15.00
A&M SP-4243	(S)	Getting To This	1970	6.00	15.00
BLOND					
Fontana SRF-67607	(S)	Blond	1969	8.00	20.00
BLONDIE					
Private Stock PS-2035	(S)	Blondie	1975	8.00	20.00
Chrysalis CHP-5001	(S)	Parallel Lines (Picture disc)	1978	8.00	20.00
Mobile Fidelity 1-050	(S)	Parallel Lines	1981	6.00	15.00
BLOOD, SWEAT & TEARS					
Columbia CS-9616	(S)	Child Is Father To The Man	1968	5.00	12.00
Columbia CS-9720	(S)	Blood, Sweat And Tears	1969	4.00	10.00
		(Columbia albums above have "360 Sound" labels.)			
Columbia CQ-30994	(Q)	Blood, Sweat And Tears	1973	8.00	20.00
Columbia CQ-31170	(Q)	Blood, Sweat And Tears' Greatest Hits	1973	6.00	15.00
Columbia PCQ-32929	(Q)	Mirror Image	1974	6.00	15.00
Columbia HC-49619	(S)	Child Is Father To The Man (1/2 speed)	1981	6.00	15.00
BLOOMFIELD, MICHAEL, AL KOOPER & STEPHEN STILLS					
Columbia CS-9701	(S)	Super Session ("360 Sound" label)	1968	6.00	15.00
Mobile Fidelity 1-178	(S)	Super Session		5.00	12.00
BLUE BARONS, THE					
Phillips PHM-200017	(M)	Twist To The Great Blues Hits	1962	8.00	20.00
Phillips PHS-600017	(S)	Twist To The Great Blues Hits	1962	10.00	25.00

Label		Title	Year	VG+	NM
BLUE BEATS, THE					
A.A. 133	(M)	The Beatle Beat	1964	20.00	50.00
BLUE CHEER					
Philips PHM-200264	(M)	Vincebus Eruptum	1968	8.00	20.00
Philips PHS-600264	(S)	Vincebus Eruptum	1968	6.00	15.00
Philips PHS-600278	(S)	Outsideinside	1968	6.00	15.00
Philips PHS-600305	(S)	New! Improved! Blue Cheer	1969	6.00	15.00
Philips PHS-600333	(S)	Blue Cheer	1970	6.00	15.00
Philips PHS-600347	(S)	The Original Human Being	1970	6.00	15.00
Philips PHS-600350	(S)	Oh! Pleasant Hope	1971	6.00	15.00
BLUE DIAMONDS, THE					
London LL-3235	(M)	Ramona	1963	10.00	25.00
BLUE EMOTIONS, THE					
Ambient Sound 38346	(S)	Doo-Wop Doo-Wop	1982	4.00	10.00
BLUE JAYS, THE					
Milestone 1001	(M)	The Blue Jays Meet Little Caesar		20.00	50.00
BLUE MOUNTAIN EAGLE					
Atco SD-33-324	(S)	Blue Mountain Eagle	1970	8.00	20.00
BLUE OYSTER CULT, THE					
Columbia PCQ-32017	(Q)	Tyranny And Mutation	1973	6.00	15.00
Columbia PCQ-32858	(Q)	Secret Treaties	1974	6.00	15.00
BLUE RIDGE RANGERS (JOHN FOGERTY)					
Fantasy F-9415	(S)	The Blue Ridge Rangers	1973	5.00	12.00
BLUE THINGS, THE					
RCA LPM-3603	(M)	The Blue Things	1966	16.00	40.00
RCA LSP-3603	(S)	The Blue Things	1966	20.00	50.00
BLUES CLIMAX					
Horne JC-333	(S)	Blues Climax		20.00	50.00
BLUES MAGOOS, THE					
Mercury MG-21096	(M)	Psychedelic Lollipop	1966	8.00	20.00
Mercury SR-61096	(S)	Psychedelic Lollipop	1966	10.00	25.00
Mercury MG-21104	(M)	Electric Comic Book (With comic book)	1967	10.00	25.00
Mercury SR-61104	(S)	Electric Comic Book (With comic book)	1967	12.00	30.00
Mercury SR-61167	(M)	Basic Blues Magoos	1968	8.00	20.00
Mercury SR-61167	(S)	Basic Blues Magoos	1968	10.00	25.00
		(Mercury albums above have red labels.)			
ABC S-697	(S)	Never Goin' Back To Georgia	1969	6.00	15.00
ABC S-710	(S)	Gulf Coast Bound	1970	6.00	15.00
BLUES PROJECT, THE					
Folkways FV-9025	(M)	Live At The Cafe Au-Go-Go	1966	6.00	15.00
Folkways FVS-9025	(S)	Live At The Cafe Au-Go-Go	1966	8.00	20.00
Folkways FT-3008	(M)	Projections	1966	6.00	15.00
Folkways FTS-3008	(S)	Projections	1966	8.00	20.00
Forecast FT-3025	(M)	Live At Town Hall	1967	6.00	15.00
Forecast FTS-3025	(S)	Live At Town Hall	1967	8.00	20.00
Forecast FTS-3046	(S)	Planned Obsolescence	1968	5.00	12.00
Forecast FTS-3069	(S)	Flanders/Kalb/Katz, Etc.	1969	5.00	12.00
BOB & EARL (BOB GARRETT & EARL COSBY)					
Tip TLP-1011	(M)	Harlem Shuffle	1964	8.00	20.00
Tip TLS-9011	(S)	Harlem Shuffle	1964	10.00	25.00
BOB & RAY					
RCA LPM-2131	(M)	On A Platter	1960	5.00	12.00
RCA LSP-2131	(S)	On A Platter (Black label)	1960	8.00	20.00
BOBB B. SOXX & THE BLUE JEANS					
Philles PHLP-4002	(M)	Zip-A-Dee-Doo-Dah	1963	80.00	160.00

Label		Title	Year	VG+	NM
BOHEMIAN VENDETTA					
Mainstream 56106	(M)	Bohemian Vendetta	1968	14.00	35.00
Mainstream 6106	(S)	Bohemian Vendetta	1968	14.00	35.00
BOMBERS, THE					
West End 104	(S)	The Bombers	1979	5.00	12.00
West End 106	(S)	The Bombers 2	1979	5.00	12.00
BOND, EDDIE					
Philips International 1980	(M)	The Greatest Country Gospel Hits	1961	50.00	100.00
BONDS, GARY "U.S."					
Legrand LLP-3001	(M)	Dance 'Til Quarter To Three	1961	50.00	100.00
Legrand LLP-3002	(M)	Twist Up Calypso	1962	40.00	80.00
Legrand LLP-3003	(M)	Greatest Hits Of Gary U.S. Bonds	1962	40.00	80.00
BONNEVILLES, THE					
Drum Boy DLM-1001	(M)	Meet The Bonnevilles	1963	14.00	35.00
Drum Boy LS-1001	(S)	Meet The Bonnevilles	1963	18.00	45.00
BONNIE LOU					
King 595	(M)	Bonnie Lou Sings	1958	20.00	50.00
BONNIWELL, T.S.					
Capitol ST-277	(S)	Close	1969	8.00	20.00
BONNIWELL'S MUSIC MACHINE (THE MUSIC MACHINE)					
Warners W-1732	(M)	Bonniwell's Music Machine	1967	8.00	20.00
Warners WS-1732	(S)	Bonniwell's Music Machine	1967	10.00	25.00
BONZO DOG (DOO DAH) BAND, THE					
Imperial LP-12370	(S)	Gorilla	1968	8.00	20.00
Imperial LP-12432	(S)	Urban Spaceman	1969	8.00	20.00
Imperial LP-12445	(S)	Tadpoles	1969	8.00	20.00
Imperial LP-12457	(S)	Keynsham	1970	8.00	20.00
United Arts. UAS-5584	(S)	Let's Make Up And Be Friendly	1972	6.00	15.00
		(With postcard still attached to the cover.)			
BOOGIE KINGS, THE					
Montel-Michelle 104	(M)	The Boogie Kings	1966	8.00	20.00
Montel-Michelle 109	(M)	Blue Eyed Soul	1967	8.00	20.00
BOOKER T. & THE M.G.'S					
Stax 701	(M)	Green Onions	1962	8.00	20.00
Stax 705	(M)	Soul Dressing	1965	5.00	12.00
Stax STS-705	(S)	Soul Dressing	1965	6.00	15.00
Stax 711	(M)	And Now	1966	5.00	12.00
Stax STS-711	(S)	And Now	1966	6.00	15.00
Stax 713	(M)	In The Christmas Spirit	1966	5.00	12.00
Stax STS-713	(S)	In The Christmas Spirit	1966	6.00	15.00
Stax 717	(M)	Hip Hug-Her	1967	5.00	12.00
Stax STS-717	(S)	Hip Hug-Her	1967	6.00	15.00
Stax 720	(S)	Back To Back (With the Mar-Keys)	1967	5.00	12.00
Stax STS-720	(S)	Back To Back (With the Mar-Keys)	1967	6.00	15.00
Stax 724	(M)	Doin' Our Thing	1968	5.00	12.00
Stax STS-724	(S)	Doin' Our Thing	1968	6.00	15.00
Stax STS-2001	(S)	Soul Limbo	1968	5.00	12.00
Atlantic 8202	(S)	The Best Of Booker T. And The MG's	1968	6.00	15.00
BOOMTOWN RATS					
Mercury SRM-1-1188	(S)	The Boomtown Rats	1977	4.00	10.00
BOONE, PAT					
Dot DLP-3012	(M)	Pat Boone	1956	8.00	20.00
Dot DLP-3030	(M)	Howdy	1956	8.00	20.00
Dot DLP-3050	(M)	Pat	1957	8.00	20.00
Dot DLP-3068	(M)	Hymns We Love	1957	8.00	20.00
Dot DLP-3071	(M)	Pat's Great Hits	1957	8.00	20.00
Dot DLP-9000	(M)	April Love (Sdtk)	1957	8.00	20.00
Dot DLP-3077	(M)	Pat Boone Sings Irving Berlin	1958	6.00	15.00
Dot DLP-3077	(S)	Pat Boone Sings Irving Berlin	1958	8.00	20.00

Label		Title	Year	VG+	NM
Dot DLP-3118	(M)	Star Dust	1958	6.00	15.00
Dot DLP-25118	(S)	Star Dust	1958	8.00	20.00
Dot DLP-3121	(M)	Yes Indeed	1958	6.00	15.00
Dot DLP-3158	(M)	Pat Boone Sings	1958	6.00	15.00
Dot DLP-25158	(S)	Pat Boone Sings	1958	8.00	20.00
Dot DLP-3180	(M)	Tenderly	1959	6.00	15.00
Dot DLP-25180	(S)	Tenderly	1959	8.00	20.00
Dot DLP-3181	(M)	Great Millions	1959	6.00	15.00
Dot DLP-25181	(S)	Great Millions	1959	8.00	20.00
Dot DLP-3199	(M)	Side By Side	1959	6.00	15.00
Dot DLP-25199	(S)	Side By Side	1959	8.00	20.00
Dot DLP-3222	(M)	White Christmas	1959	6.00	15.00
Dot DLP-25222	(S)	White Christmas	1959	8.00	20.00
Dot DLP-3234	(M)	He Leadeth Me	1960	5.00	12.00
Dot DLP-25234	(S)	He Leadeth Me	1960	6.00	15.00
Dot DLP-3261	(M)	Pat's Greatest Hits, Volume 2	1960	5.00	12.00
Dot DLP-25261	(S)	Pat's Greatest Hits, Volume 2	1960	6.00	15.00
Dot DLP-3270	(M)	Moonglow	1960	5.00	12.00
Dot DLP-25270	(S)	Moonglow	1960	6.00	15.00
Dot DLP-25270	(S)	Moonglow (Blue vinyl)	1960	16.00	40.00
Dot DLP-3285	(M)	This And That	1960	5.00	12.00
Dot DLP-25285	(S)	This And That	1960	6.00	15.00
Dot DLP-3346	(M)	Great, Great, Great	1961	5.00	12.00
Dot DLP-25346	(S)	Great, Great, Great	1961	6.00	15.00
Dot DLP-3384	(M)	Moody River	1961	5.00	12.00
Dot DLP-25384	(S)	Moody River	1961	6.00	15.00
Dot DLP-3386	(M)	My God And I	1961	4.00	10.00
Dot DLP-25386	(S)	My God And I	1961	5.00	12.00
Dot DLP-3399	(M)	I'll See You In My Dreams	1962	4.00	10.00
Dot DLP-25399	(S)	I'll See You In My Dreams	1962	5.00	12.00
Dot DLP-3402	(M)	Pat Boone Reads From The Holy Bible	1962	5.00	12.00
Dot DLP-3455	(M)	Pat Boone's Golden Hits	1962	4.00	10.00
Dot DLP-25455	(S)	Pat Boone's Golden Hits	1962	5.00	12.00
Dot DLP-9011	(M)	State Fair (Sdtk)	1962	8.00	20.00
Dot DLP-25011	(S)	State Fair (Sdtk)	1962	10.00	25.00
Dot DLP-3475	(M)	I Love You Truly	1962	4.00	10.00
Dot DLP-25475	(S)	I Love You Truly	1962	5.00	12.00
Dot DLP-3501	(M)	Pat Boone Sings Guss Who?	1963	12.00	30.00
Dot DLP-25501	(S)	Pat Boone Sings Guss Who?	1963	16.00	40.00

BOOT

Agape 2601	(S)	Boot		10.00	25.00
Guinness 36002	(S)	Turn The Other Cheek		6.00	15.00

BORDERSONG

Real Good 1001	(S)	Morning	1975	16.00	40.00

BOSTON

Epic E99-44188	(S)	Boston (Picture disc)	1978	6.00	15.00
Epic HE-44188	(S)	Boston (1/2 speed)	1980	8.00	20.00
Epic HE-45050	(S)	Don't Look Back (1/2 speed)	1981	8.00	20.00

BOSTON TEA PARTY, THE

Flick Disc 45000	(S)	The Boston Tea Party	1968	8.00	20.00

BOSWELL, CONNIE

Decca DL-5390 (10")	(M)	Bing And Connee (With Bing Crosby)	1951	10.00	25.00
RCA LPM-1426	(M)	Connie Boswell & The Original Memphis 5	1957	10.00	25.00
Decca DL-8356	(M)	Connie		10.00	25.00

BOW STREET RUNNERS, THE

B.T. Puppy BTPS-1026	(S)	The Bow Street Runners	1969	85.00	170.00

BOWEN, JIMMY

Roulette R-25004	(M)	Jimmy Bowen	1957	50.00	100.00
Roulette R-25048	(M)	Buddy Knox And Jimmy Bowen	1957	75.00	150.00
Reprise R-6210	(M)	Sunday Morning With The Comics	1966	10.00	25.00
Reprise RS-6210	(S)	Sunday Morning With The Comics	1966	12.00	30.00

Label		Title	Year	VG+	NM
BOWIE, DAVID					
Deram DE-16003	(M)	David Bowie	1967	50.00	100.00
Deram DES-18003	(S)	David Bowie	1967	75.00	150.00
Mercury SR-61246	(S)	Man Of Words, Man Of Music	1969	60.00	120.00
Mercury 61325	(S)	The Man Who Sold The World	1971	20.00	50.00
		(Original copies have the matrix number			
		stamped in the trail-off vinyl.)			
London 50007	(S)	Starting Point		8.00	20.00
London 61829	(P)	Images 1966-1967	1973	12.00	30.00
RCA LSP-4623	(S)	Hunky Dory	1972	6.00	15.00
RCA LSP-4702	(S)	The Rise And Fall Of Ziggy Stardust	1972	6.00	15.00
RCA LSP-4813	(S)	Space Oddity (With poster)	1972	10.00	25.00
RCA LSP-4816	(S)	The Man Who Sold The World (With poster)	1972	10.00	25.00
RCA LSP-4852	(S)	Aladdin Sane	1973	6.00	15.00
RCA APL1-291	(S)	Pin Ups	1974	6.00	15.00
RCA APL1-0576	(S)	Diamond Dogs	1974	2,100.00	3,000.00
		(The Bowiedog's genitals on the cover are visible;			
		all other copies have them airbrushed out.)			
RCA APL1-0576	(S)	Diamond Dogs	1974	6.00	15.00
RCA CPL2-0771	(S)	David Live	1974	6.00	15.00
RCA APL1-0998	(S)	Young Americans	1975	6.00	15.00
		(RCA albums above have orange labels.)			
Mobile Fidelity 1-064	(S)	The Rise And Fall Of Ziggy Stardust		10.00	25.00
Mobile Fidelity 1-083	(S)	Let's Dance		8.00	20.00
RCA CPL2-4862	(S)	Ziggy Stardust (Clear vinyl)	1983	50.00	100.00
BOX TOPS, THE					
Bell 6011	(M)	The Letter/Neon Rainbow	1967	6.00	15.00
Bell S-6011	(S)	The Letter/Neon Rainbow	1967	8.00	20.00
Bell S-6017	(S)	Cry Like A Baby	1968	8.00	20.00
Bell S-6023	(S)	Non-Stop	1968	6.00	15.00
Bell S-6032	(S)	Dimensions	1969	6.00	15.00
Cotillon SD-057	(S)	A Lifetime Believing	1971	5.00	12.00
BOYCE, TOMMY					
Camden CAL-2202	(M)	A Twofold Talent	1967	6.00	15.00
Camden CAS-2202	(S)	A Twofold Talent	1967	8.00	20.00
BOYCE, TOMMY, & BOBBY HART					
A&M SP-4126	(S)	Test Patterns	1967	6.00	15.00
A&M SP-4143	(S)	I Wonder What She's Doing Tonight	1968	6.00	15.00
A&M SP-4162	(S)	It's All Happening On The Inside	1968	6.00	15.00
BOYD, BILLY					
Crown CST-196	(S)	Twangy Guitars (Red vinyl)		10.00	25.00
BOYD, EDDIE					
Epic BN-26409	(S)	7936 South Rhodes	1968	10.00	25.00
London PS-554	(S)	I'll Dust My Broom	1969	10.00	25.00
BRADBURY, RAY					
Tower ST-5172	(S)	Dark Carnival		10.00	25.00
BRADLEY, WILL					
Columbia C-123	(M)	Will Bradley And Ray McKinley		16.00	40.00
Epic LN-1127	(M)	Will Bradley		16.00	40.00
Epic LN-3115	(M)	Boogie Woogie		16.00	40.00
Epic LN-3119	(M)	The House Of Bradley		16.00	40.00
BRADSHAW, TINY					
King 295-74 (10")	(M)	Off And On		100.00	200.00
King 395-501	(M)	Selections		40.00	80.00
King 653	(M)	Great Composer		20.00	50.00
King 953	(M)	24 Great Songs		10.00	25.00
BRAUTIGAN, RICHARD					
Harvest ST-424	(S)	Listening To Richard Brautigan	1969	6.00	15.00
BRENDA & THE TABULATIONS					
Dionn LPM-2000	(M)	Dry Your Eyes	1967	10.00	25.00
Dionn LPS-2000	(P)	Dry Your Eyes	1967	12.00	30.00

Label		Title	Year	VG+	NM
BRETT, PAUL					
ABC 672	(S)	Very Strange Brew	1969	8.00	20.00
Janus 3026	(S)	Paul Brett Sage	1971	6.00	15.00
BREWER, TERESA					
London AB-1006	(M)	Teresa Brewer		8.00	20.00
Coral CRL-56072	(M)	A Bouquet Of Hits	1954	12.00	30.00
Coral CRL-56093	(M)	Till I Waltz Again With You	1954	12.00	30.00
Coral CRL-57027	(M)	Music, Music, Music	1958	10.00	25.00
Coral CRL-57053	(M)	Teresa	1958	10.00	25.00
Coral CRL-57135	(M)	For Teenagers In Love	1958	10.00	25.00
Coral CRL-57144	(M)	Teresa Brewer At Christmas Time	1958	10.00	25.00
Coral CRL-57179	(M)	Miss Music	1958	10.00	25.00
Coral CRL-57232	(M)	Time For Teresa	1958	10.00	25.00
Coral CRL-57245	(M)	Teresa Brewer And The Dixieland Band	1959	8.00	20.00
Coral CRL7-57245	(S)	Teresa Brewer And The Dixieland Band	1959	10.00	25.00
Coral CRL-57257	(M)	When Your Love Has Gone	1959	8.00	20.00
Coral CRL7-57257	(S)	When Your Love Has Gone	1959	10.00	25.00
Coral CRL-57297	(M)	Heavenly Lover	1959	8.00	20.00
Coral CRL7-57297	(S)	Heavenly Lover	1959	10.00	25.00
Coral CRL-57315	(M)	Ridin' High	1960	6.00	15.00
Coral CRL7-57315	(S)	Ridin' High	1960	8.00	20.00
Coral CRL-57329	(M)	Naughty, Naughty, Naughty	1960	6.00	15.00
Coral CRL7-57329	(S)	Naughty, Naughty, Naughty	1960	8.00	20.00
Coral CRL-57351	(M)	My Golden Favorites	1960	6.00	15.00
Coral CRL7-57351	(S)	My Golden Favorites	1960	8.00	20.00
Coral CRL-57361	(M)	Songs Everybody Knows	1961	6.00	15.00
Coral CRL7-57361	(S)	Songs Everybody Knows	1961	8.00	20.00
Coral CRL-57374	(M)	Aloha From Teresa	1961	6.00	15.00
Coral CRL7-57374	(S)	Aloha From Teresa	1961	8.00	20.00
Coral CRL-57414	(M)	Don't Mess With Tess	1962	6.00	15.00
Coral CRL7-57414	(S)	Don't Mess With Tess	1962	8.00	20.00
Coral CXB-7	(M)	The Best Of Teresa Brewer	1965	6.00	12.00
Coral CXBS7-7	(S)	The Best Of Teresa Brewer	1965	6.00	15.00
Philips 200062	(M)	Teresa Brewer's Greatest Hits	1962	6.00	15.00
Philips 600062	(S)	Teresa Brewer's Greatest Hits	1962	8.00	20.00
Philips 200099	(M)	Terrific Teresa	1963	5.00	12.00
Philips 600099	(S)	Terrific Teresa	1963	6.00	15.00
Philips 200119	(M)	Moments To Remember	1964	5.00	12.00
Philips 600119	(S)	Moments To Remember	1964	6.00	15.00
Philips 200147	(M)	Golden Hits Of 1964	1964	5.00	12.00
Philips 600147	(S)	Golden Hits Of 1964	1964	6.00	15.00
Philips 200163	(M)	Goldfinger/Other Great Movie Songs	1965	5.00	12.00
Philips 600163	(S)	Goldfinger/Other Great Movie Songs	1965	6.00	15.00
Philips 200200	(M)	Songs For Our Fighting Men	1966	5.00	12.00
Philips 600200	(S)	Songs For Our Fighting Men	1966	6.00	15.00
Philips 200216	(M)	Gold Country	1966	5.00	12.00
Philips 600216	(S)	Gold Country	1966	6.00	15.00
Philips 200230	(M)	Texas Leather And Mexican Lace	1967	5.00	12.00
Philips 600230	(S)	Texas Leather And Mexican Lace	1967	6.00	15.00
BRILL, MARTY					
Mercury MG-20178	(M)	A Roving Balladeer	1956	10.00	25.00
BRILLIANT, ASHLEIGH					
Dorash 1001	(M)	In The Haight-Ashbury	1967	30.00	60.00
BRINSLEY SCHWARZ					
Capitol ST-589	(S)	Brinsley Schwarz	1970	6.00	15.00
Capitol ST-744	(S)	Despite It All	1971	6.00	15.00
United Arts. UAS-5566	(S)	Silver Pistol	1972	6.00	15.00
United Arts. UAS-5647	(S)	Nervous On The Road	1972	6.00	15.00
BRITT, ELTON					
RCA LPM-3222 (10")	(M)	Yodel Songs	1954	20.00	50.00
RCA LPM-1288	(M)	Yodel Songs	1956	14.00	35.00
ABC-Paramount 293	(M)	The Wandering Cowboy	1959	8.00	20.00
ABC-Paramount S-293	(S)	The Wandering Cowboy	1959	10.00	25.00
ABC-Paramount 322	(M)	Beyond The Sunset	1960	6.00	15.00
ABC-Paramount S-322	(S)	Beyond The Sunset	1960	8.00	20.00

Label		Title	Year	VG+	NM
ABC-Paramount 331	(M)	I Heard A Forest Praying	1960	6.00	15.00
ABC-Paramount S-331	(S)	I Heard A Forest Praying	1960	8.00	20.00
ABC-Paramount 521	(M)	The Singing Hills	1965	5.00	12.00
ABC-Paramount S-521	(S)	The Singing Hills	1965	6.00	15.00
ABC-Paramount 566	(M)	Somethin' For Everybody	1966	5.00	12.00
ABC-Paramount S-566	(S)	Somethin' For Everybody	1966	6.00	15.00

BROOKS, DONNIE

Era EL-105	(M)	The Happiest	1961	20.00	50.00
HBR HLP-8500	(M)	A Swingin' Summer (Sdtk)	1966	10.00	25.00
HBR HST-8500	(S)	A Swingin' Summer (Sdtk)	1966	12.00	30.00

BROOKS, HADDA

Modern LMP-1210	(M)	Femme Fatale	1956	50.00	100.00

BROONZY, BIG BILL

Period 1114 (10")	(M)	Big Bill Broonzy Sings		16.00	40.00
Vogue LO-60530	(M)	In Paris	1956	14.00	35.00
EmArcy MG-26034	(M)	Folk Blues	1957	14.00	35.00
EmArcy MG-26137	(M)	Blues By Broonzy	1957	14.00	35.00
Columbia WL-111	(M)	Big Bill's Blues	1958	16.00	40.00
Verve V-3001	(M)	Last Session, Part 1	1959	6.00	15.00
Verve V-3002	(M)	Last Session, Part 2	1959	6.00	15.00
Verve V-3003	(M)	Last Session, Part 3	1959	6.00	15.00
Folkways FA-2326	(M)	Country Blues		8.00	20.00
Folkways FA-3586	(M)	His Songs And Story		8.00	20.00
Folkways FA-3817	(M)	Big Bill Broonzy, Sonny Terry And Brownie Mc Ghee	1959	10.00	25.00
Chess LP-1468	(M)	Big Bill Broonzy And Washboard Sam	1962	16.00	40.00
Mercury MG-20822	(M)	Memorial	1963	6.00	15.00
Mercury SR-60822	(S)	Memorial	1963	8.00	20.00
Mercury MG-20905	(M)	Remembering Big Bill Broonzy	1964	6.00	15.00
Mercury SR-60905	(S)	Remembering Big Bill Broonzy	1964	8.00	20.00
Folkways FVS-9008	(S)	Big Bill Broonzy And Pete Seeger	1965	6.00	15.00
Period 1209	(M)	Josh White And Big Bill Broonzy		6.00	15.00
Epic EE-22017	(M)	Big Bill's Blues	1969	6.00	15.00

BROTHER FOX & TAR BABY

Capitol ST-544	(S)	Brother Fox And The Tar Baby	1969	12.00	30.00

BROTHERHOOD (FRIENDSOUND)

RCA LSP-4092	(S)	Brotherhood	1968	6.00	15.00
RCA LSP-4228	(S)	Brotherhood, Brotherhood	1969	6.00	15.00

BROWN, AL, & HIS TUNE TOPPERS

Amy A-1	(M)	The Madison Dance Party	1960	14.00	35.00
Amy AS-1	(P)	The Madison Dance Party	1960	16.00	40.00

BROWN, ARTHUR

Atlantic SD-8198	(S)	The Crazy World Of Arthur Brown	1968	8.00	20.00

BROWN, BOBBY

Destiny 4001	(S)	Bobby Brown Live	1972	6.00	15.00
Destiny 4002	(S)	The Enlightening Beam Of Axonda	1972	10.00	25.00

BROWN, BOOTS

RCA LG-1000	(M)	Rock That Beat	1958	20.00	50.00

BROWN, BUSTER

Fire FLP-102	(M)	The New King Of The Blues	1960	75.00	150.00

BROWN, CHARLES

Aladdin 702 (10")	(M)	Mood Music (Red vinyl)	1954	300.00	500.00
Aladdin 702 (10")	(M)	Mood Music	1954	150.00	250.00
Aladdin 809	(M)	Mood Music	1956	100.00	200.00
Score SLP-4011	(M)	Driftin' Blues	1957	50.00	100.00
Imperial A-9178	(M)	Million Sellers	1961	35.00	70.00
King 775	(M)	Sings Christmas Songs	1961	30.00	60.00
King 878	(M)	Great Charles Brown	1963	20.00	50.00
Mainstream 6035	(M)	Ballads My Way	1965	6.00	15.00
Mainstream 6035	(S)	Ballads My Way	1965	8.00	20.00

Label		Title	Year	VG+	NM
BROWN, HYLO					
Capitol T-1168	(M)	Hylo Brown	1959	12.00	30.00
BROWN, JAMES (& HIS FAMOUS FLAMES)					
King 395-610	(M)	Please Please Please	1959	50.00	100.00
King 395-635	(M)	Try Me	1959	50.00	100.00
King LP-683	(M)	Think	1960	35.00	70.00
King LP-743	(M)	The Always Amazing James Brown	1961	16.00	40.00
King LP-771	(M)	Jump Around	1962	16.00	40.00
King KS-771	(S)	Jump Around	1962	20.00	50.00
King LP-780	(M)	The Exciting James Brown	1962	16.00	40.00
King LP-826	(M)	James Brown Live At The Apollo!	1963	16.00	40.00
King KS-826	(S)	James Brown Live At The Apollo!	1963	20.00	50.00
King LP-851	(M)	Prisoner Of Love	1963	16.00	40.00
King KS-851	(S)	Prisoner Of Love	1963	20.00	50.00
King LP-883	(M)	Pure Dynamite! Live At The Royal	1964	16.00	40.00
Smash MGS-27054	(M)	Showtime	1964	5.00	12.00
Smash SRS-67054	(S)	Showtime	1964	6.00	15.00
King KS-909	(E)	Please Please Please	1964	16.00	40.00
King LP-919	(M)	The Unbeatable 16 Hits	1964	16.00	40.00
Smash MGS-27057	(M)	Grits And Soul	1965	5.00	12.00
Smash SRS-67057	(S)	Grits And Soul	1965	6.00	15.00
King LP-938	(M)	Papa's Got A Brand New Bag	1965	16.00	40.00
King KSD-938	(E)	Papa's Got A Brand New Bag	1965	12.00	30.00
Smash MGS-27072	(M)	Today And Yesterday	1965	5.00	12.00
Smash SRS-67072	(S)	Today And Yesterday	1965	6.00	15.00
King LP-946	(M)	I Got You, I Feel Good	1966	14.00	35.00
King KSD-946	(S)	I Got You, I Feel Good	1966	16.00	40.00
Smash MGS-27080	(M)	James Brown Plays New Breed	1966	5.00	12.00
Smash SRS-67080	(S)	James Brown Plays New Breed	1966	6.00	15.00
King LP-961	(M)	Mighty Instrumentals	1966	16.00	40.00
King LP-985	(M)	It's A Man's Man's Man's World	1966	14.00	35.00
King KS-985	(S)	It's A Man's Man's Man's World	1966	16.00	40.00
Smash MGS-27084	(M)	Handful Of Soul	1966	5.00	12.00
Smash SRS-67084	(S)	Handful Of Soul	1966	6.00	15.00
King LP-1010	(M)	Christmas Songs	1966	16.00	40.00
		(King albums above have crownless black labels.)			
King LP-1016	(M)	Raw Soul	1967	8.00	20.00
King KS-1016	(E)	Raw Soul	1967	10.00	25.00
King LP-1018	(M)	Live At The Garden	1967	8.00	20.00
King KS-1018	(S)	Live At The Garden	1967	10.00	25.00
Smash MGS-27093	(M)	James Brown Plays The Real Thing	1967	5.00	12.00
Smash SRS-67093	(S)	James Brown Plays The Real Thing	1967	6.00	15.00
Smash SRS-67109	(S)	James Brown Sings Out Of Sight	1968	6.00	15.00
King K-1020	(M)	Cold Sweat	1967	8.00	20.00
King KS-1020	(M)	Cold Sweat	1967	10.00	25.00
King KS-1022	(S)	Live At The Apollo, Volume 2	1968	8.00	20.00
King KS-1024	(S)	His Show Of Tomorrow	1968	6.00	15.00
King KS-1030	(S)	I Can't Stand Myself When You Touch Me	1968	6.00	15.00
King KS-1031	(S)	I Got The Feelin'	1968	6.00	15.00
King KS-1038	(S)	Thinking About Little Willie John	1968	16.00	40.00
King KS-1040	(S)	A Soulful Christmas	1968	6.00	15.00
King KS-1047	(S)	Say It Loud—I'm Black And I'm Proud	1969	6.00	15.00
King KS-1051	(S)	Gettin' Down To It	1969	6.00	15.00
King KS-1054	(S)	Nothing But Soul	1968	6.00	15.00
King KSO-1055	(S)	The Popcorn	1969	6.00	15.00
King KS-1063	(S)	It's A Mother	1969	6.00	15.00
King KSD-1092	(S)	Ain't It Funky	1970	6.00	15.00
King KS-1095	(S)	It's A New Day So Let A Man Come In	1970	6.00	15.00
King KS-1100	(S)	Soul On Top	1970	6.00	15.00
King KSD-1110	(S)	Sho Is Funky Down Here	1971	6.00	15.00
King KSD-1115	(S)	Sex Machine	1970	6.00	15.00
King KSD-1124	(S)	Hey America!	1970	6.00	15.00
King KS-1127	(S)	Super Bad	1971	6.00	15.00
BROWN, MAXINE					
Also refer to Chuck Jackson.					
Wand WD-656	(M)	The Fabulous Sound Of Maxine Brown	1963	8.00	20.00
Wand WD-663	(M)	Spotlight On Maxine Brown	1965	5.00	12.00
Wand WDS-663	(S)	Spotlight On Maxine Brown	1965	6.00	15.00

Label		Title	Year	VG+	NM
Wand WD-669	(M)	Saying Something	1965	6.00	15.00
Wand WDS-669	(S)	Saying Something	1965	8.00	20.00
Wand WD-678	(M)	Hold On, We're Coming	1966	6.00	15.00
Wand WDS-678	(S)	Hold On, We're Coming	1966	8.00	20.00
		(Wand 669 and 678 are with Chuck Jackson)			
Wand WD-684	(M)	Maxine Brown's Greatest Hits	1967	6.00	15.00
Wand WDS-684	(P)	Maxine Brown's Greatest Hits	1967	6.00	15.00

BROWN, NAPPY
Savoy MG-14002	(M)	Nappy Brown Sings	1958	40.00	80.00
Savoy MG-14025	(M)	The Right Time	1960	35.00	70.00

BROWN, ROY
King 607	(M)	Battle Of The Blues, Volume 1	1958	180.00	300.00
King 627	(M)	Battle Of The Blues, Volume 2	1959	180.00	300.00
		(King 607 and 627 feature Wynonie Harris.)			
King 668	(M)	Battle Of The Blues, Volume 4	1960	400.00	600.00
		(Features Wynonie Harris and Eddie Vinson.)			
King 956	(M)	Roy Brown Sings 24 Hits	1966	16.00	40.00
King KS-956	(S)	Roy Brown Sings 24 Hits	1966	20.00	50.00

BROWN, RUTH
Atlantic 115 (10")	(M)	Ruth Brown Sings	1956	660.00	1,000.00
Atlantic 8004	(M)	Ruth Brown (Black label)	1957	40.00	80.00
Atlantic 1308	(M)	Late Date With Ruth Brown (Black label)	1959	35.00	70.00
Atlantic SD-1308	(S)	Late Date With Ruth Brown (Green label)	1959	50.00	100.00
Atlantic 8026	(M)	Miss Rhythm (Black label)	1959	35.00	70.00
Atlantic 8026	(M)	Miss Rhythm (White label)	1959	35.00	70.00
Atlantic 8080	(M)	The Best Of Ruth Brown	1963	14.00	35.00
Atlantic SD-8080	(S)	The Best Of Ruth Brown	1963	20.00	50.00
Phillips PHM-200-028	(M)	Along Comes Ruth	1962	6.00	15.00
Phillips PHS-600-028	(S)	Along Comes Ruth	1962	8.00	20.00
Phillips PH-200-055	(M)	Gospel Time	1962	6.00	15.00
Phillips PHS-600-055	(S)	Gospel Time	1962	8.00	20.00
Mainstream 16044	(S)	Ruth Brown '65	1965	6.00	15.00
Mainstream S-6044	(S)	Ruth Brown '65	1965	8.00	20.00

BROWNE, JACKSON
Asylum SD-5051	(S)	Jackson Browne (With burlap cover)	1972	12.00	30.00
Reprise	(S)	Late For The Sky (Record Club)		12.00	30.00
		(A printing mishap with the labels caused "Late For The Sky" to appear on Reprise while a Beach Boys album appears on Asylum.)			
Mobile Fidelity 1-55	(S)	The Pretender		8.00	20.00

BROWNS, THE
RCA LPM-2144	(M)	Sweet Sounds By The Browns	1959	8.00	20.00
RCA LSP-2144	(S)	Sweet Sounds By The Browns	1959	10.00	25.00
RCA LPM-2174	(M)	Town And Country	1960	5.00	12.00
RCA LSP-2174	(S)	Town And Country	1960	8.00	20.00
RCA LPM-2260	(M)	The Browns Sing Their Hits	1960	5.00	12.00
RCA LSP-2260	(S)	The Browns Sing Their Hits	1960	8.00	20.00
RCA LPM-2333	(M)	Our Favorite Folk Songs	1961	5.00	12.00
RCA LSP-2333	(S)	Our Favorite Folk Songs	1961	8.00	20.00
RCA LPM-2345	(M)	The Little Brown Church Hymnal	1961	5.00	12.00
RCA LSP-2345	(S)	The Little Brown Church Hymnal	1961	8.00	20.00
		(Mono RCA albums above have "Long Play" on the bottom of the label. Stereo albums have "Living Stereo" on the bottom.)			

BROWNSVILLE STATION (BROWNSVILLE)
Palladium P-1004	(S)	Brownsville Station	1970	12.00	30.00
Warners WS-1888	(S)	No B.S.	1970	6.00	15.00

BRUCE, LENNY
Also refer to Lawrence Schiller.
Fantasy 7001	(M)	Interviews Of Our Times (Red vinyl)	1959	10.00	25.00
Fantasy 7001	(M)	Interviews Of Our Times	1959	8.00	20.00
Fantasy 7003	(M)	Sick Humor Of Lenny Bruce (Red vinyl)	1959	10.00	25.00
Fantasy 7003	(M)	Sick Humor Of Lenny Bruce	1959	8.00	20.00

Label		Title	Year	VG+	NM
Fantasy 7007	(M)	I Am Not A Nut, Elect Me (Red vinyl)	1960	10.00	25.00
Fantasy 7007	(M)	I Am Not A Nut, Elect Me	1960	8.00	20.00
Fantasy 7011	(M)	Lenny Bruce, American (Red vinyl)	1962	10.00	25.00
Fantasy 7011	(M)	Lenny Bruce, American	1962	8.00	20.00
Fantasy 7012	(M)	The Best Of Lenny Bruce	1962	8.00	20.00
Philles PHLP-4010	(M)	Lenny Bruce Is Out Again	1966	10.00	25.00
United Arts. UAL-3580	(M)	Lenny Bruce	1967	6.00	15.00
Douglas SD-788	(M)	The Essential Lenny Bruce	1968	6.00	15.00
Bizarre 6329	(M)	The Berkeley Concert	1969	10.00	25.00
Fantasy 7017	(M)	Thank You, Masked Man	1972	6.00	15.00
Fantasy 34201	(M)	Live At The Curran Theater	1972	6.00	15.00
United Arts. UAS-6794	(M)	The Midnight Concert		6.00	15.00

BRYANT, BOUDLEAUX

Label		Title	Year	VG+	NM
Monument MLP-8007	(M)	Boudleaux's Best Sellers	1963	5.00	12.00
Monument SLP-18007	(S)	Boudleaux's Best Sellers	1963	8.00	20.00

BRYANT (COMBO), RAY

Label		Title	Year	VG+	NM
Sue 1016	(M)	Groove House		10.00	25.00
Columbia CL-1449	(M)	Little Susie	1960	5.00	12.00
Columbia CS-8244	(S)	Little Susie	1960	6.00	15.00
Columbia CL-1467	(M)	Madison Time	1960	5.00	12.00
Columbia CS-8267	(S)	Madison Time	1960	6.00	15.00
Columbia CL-1746	(M)	Dancing The Big Twist	1962	5.00	12.00
Columbia CS-8546	(S)	Dancing The Big Twist	1962	6.00	15.00

BUBBLE GUM MACHINE, THE

Label		Title	Year	VG+	NM
Senate 21002	(M)	The Bubble Gum Machine	1967	5.00	12.00
Senate 21002	(S)	The Bubble Gum Machine	1967	6.00	15.00

BUBBLE PUPPY (DEMIAN)

Label		Title	Year	VG+	NM
International Arts. 10	(S)	A Gathering Of Promises	1969	16.00	40.00

BUCHANAN BROTHERS, THE

Label		Title	Year	VG+	NM
Event 101	(S)	Medicine Man	1969	10.00	25.00

BUCKINGHAM/NICKS (LINDSAY BUCKINGHAM & STEVIE NICKS)

Label		Title	Year	VG+	NM
Polydor PD-5058	(S)	Buckingham/Nicks (Fold-open cover)	1973	6.00	15.00

BUCKINGHAMS, THE

Label		Title	Year	VG+	NM
USA 107	(M)	Kind Of A Drag (With "I'm A Man")	1967	16.00	40.00
USA 107	(M)	Kind Of A Drag	1967	6.00	15.00
USA 107	(S)	Kind Of A Drag	1967	8.00	20.00
Columbia CL-2669	(M)	Time And Charges	1967	5.00	12.00
Columbia CS-9469	(S)	Time And Charges	1967	6.00	15.00
Columbia CL-2798	(M)	Portraits	1968	5.00	12.00
Columbia CS-9598	(S)	Portraits	1968	6.00	15.00
Columbia CS-9703	(S)	In One Ear And Gone Tomorrow	1968	5.00	12.00
		(Columbia albums above have "360 Sound" labels.)			

BUCKLEY, LORD

Label		Title	Year	VG+	NM
RCA LPM-3246 (10")	(M)	Hipsters, Flipsters And Finger Poppin' Daddies, Knock Me Your Lobes		50.00	100.00
World Pacific WP-1279	(M)	The Way Out Humor Of Lord Buckley	1959	20.00	50.00
Crestview CRV-801	(M)	The Best Of Lord Buckley	1963	14.00	35.00
Crestview CRV7-801	(S)	The Best Of Lord Buckley	1963	14.00	35.00
World Pacific WP-1815	(M)	Lord Buckley In Concert	1964	14.00	35.00
World Pacific WP-1849	(M)	Blowing His Mind And Your's, Too	1966	14.00	35.00
World Pacific WPS-21879	(S)	Buckley's Best	1968	14.00	35.00
World Pacific WPS-21889	(S)	Bad Rapping The Marquis De Sade	1969	14.00	35.00
Elektra EKS7-4047	(S)	The Best Of Lord Buckley	1969	8.00	20.00
Straight STS-1054	(S)	A Most Immaculately Hip Autocrat	1970	10.00	25.00
Bizarre RS-6389	(S)	Lord Buckley	1970	10.00	25.00

BUCKLEY, TIM

Label		Title	Year	VG+	NM
Elektra EKL	(M)	Tim Buckley	1966	6.00	15.00
Elektra EKS7	(S)	Tim Buckley	1966	8.00	20.00
Elektra EKL-318	(M)	Goodbye And Hello	1967	5.00	12.00
Elektra EKS7-318	(S)	Goodbye And Hello	1967	6.00	15.00
Elektra EKS7-4045	(S)	Happy Sad	1969	5.00	12.00
Elektra EKS7-4074	(S)	Lorca	1970	5.00	12.00

Label		Title	Year	VG+	NM
Straight STS-1060	(S)	Blue Afternoon	*1969*	**8.00**	**20.00**
Warners WS-1842	(S)	Blue Afternoon	*1970*	**5.00**	**12.00**
Warners WS-1881	(S)	Starsailor	*1970*	**5.00**	**12.00**
Warners B-2631	(S)	Greetings From L.A.	*1972*	**8.00**	**20.00**
		(Fold-open cover with postcard.)			
DiscReet 2157	(S)	Sefronia	*1973*	**5.00**	**12.00**
DiscReet 2201	(S)	Look At The Fool	*1974*	**5.00**	**12.00**

BUD & TRAVIS (BUD DASHIELL & TRAVIS EDMONSON)

Label		Title	Year	VG+	NM
Liberty LRP-3125	(M)	Bud And Travis	*1959*	**6.00**	**15.00**
Liberty LST-7125	(S)	Bud And Travis	*1959*	**8.00**	**20.00**
Liberty LDR-8001	(M)	Bud And Travis In Concert	*1960*	**6.00**	**15.00**
Liberty LDS-12001	(S)	Bud And Travis In Concert	*1960*	**8.00**	**20.00**
Liberty LRP-3138	(M)	Spotlight On Bud And Travis	*1961*	**4.00**	**12.00**
Liberty LST-7138	(S)	Spotlight On Bud And Travis	*1961*	**5.00**	**15.00**
Liberty LRP-3222	(M)	In Concert, Volume 2	*1962*	**4.00**	**12.00**
Liberty LST-7222	(S)	In Concert, Volume 2	*1962*	**5.00**	**15.00**
Liberty LRP-3295	(M)	Naturally	*1963*	**4.00**	**12.00**
Liberty LST-7295	(S)	Naturally	*1963*	**5.00**	**15.00**
Liberty LRP-3341	(M)	Perspective On Bud And Travis	*1964*	**4.00**	**12.00**
Liberty LST-7341	(S)	Perspective On Bud And Travis	*1964*	**5.00**	**15.00**
Liberty LRP-3386	(M)	Bud And Travis In Person	*1964*	**4.00**	**12.00**
Liberty LST-7386	(S)	Bud And Travis In Person	*1964*	**5.00**	**15.00**
Liberty LRP-3398	(M)	Bud And Travis' Latin Album	*1965*	**4.00**	**12.00**
Liberty LST-7398	(S)	Bud And Travis' Latin Album	*1965*	**5.00**	**15.00**

BUDDIES, THE

Label		Title	Year	VG+	NM
Wing MGW-12293	(M)	The Buddies And The Compacts	*1965*	**12.00**	**30.00**
Wing SRW-16293	(S)	The Buddies And The Compacts	*1965*	**16.00**	**40.00**
Wing MGW-12306	(M)	Go Go With The Buddies	*1965*	**8.00**	**20.00**
Wing SRW-16306	(S)	Go Go With The Buddies	*1965*	**10.00**	**25.00**

BUDGIE

Label		Title	Year	VG+	NM
Kapp KS-3656	(S)	Budgie	*1971*	**8.00**	**20.00**
Kapp KS-3669	(S)	Squawk	*1972*	**8.00**	**20.00**

BUFFALO NICKEL JUGBAND, THE

Label		Title	Year	VG+	NM
Happy Tiger 1018	(S)	The Buffalo Nickel Jugband	*1971*	**10.00**	**25.00**

BUFFALO SPRINGFIELD, THE

Label		Title	Year	VG+	NM
Atco 33-200	(M)	Buffalo Springfield	*1966*	**30.00**	**60.00**
Atco SD-33-200	(S)	Buffalo Springfield	*1966*	**20.00**	**50.00**
		(Originally issued with "Baby Don't Scold Me.")			
Atco 33-200-A	(M)	Buffalo Springfield	*1967*	**10.00**	**25.00**
Atco SD-33-200-A	(S)	Buffalo Springfield	*1967*	**6.00**	**15.00**
		(With "For What It's Worth.")			
Atco 33-226	(M)	Buffalo Springfield Again	*1967*	**8.00**	**20.00**
Atco SD-33-226	(S)	Buffalo Springfield Again	*1967*	**6.00**	**15.00**
		(Stereo albums above have purple & brown labels.)			
Atco SD-33-256	(S)	Last Time Around	*1968*	**5.00**	**12.00**
Cotillion SD-9037	(S)	Homer (Sdtk)	*1970*	**6.00**	**15.00**

BUGGS, THE

Label		Title	Year	VG+	NM
Coronet 212	(M)	The Beetle Beat	*1964*	**12.00**	**30.00**

BURKE, SOLOMON

Label		Title	Year	VG+	NM
Apollo ALP-498	(M)	Solomon Burke	*1962*	**35.00**	**70.00**
Atlantic 8067	(M)	Solomon Burke's Greatest Hits	*1962*	**12.00**	**30.00**
Atlantic SD-8067	(S)	Solomon Burke's Greatest Hits	*1962*	**20.00**	**50.00**
Atlantic 8085	(M)	If You Need Me	*1963*	**12.00**	**30.00**
Atlantic SD-8085	(S)	If You Need Me	*1963*	**20.00**	**50.00**
Atlantic 8096	(M)	Rock 'N' Roll Soul	*1964*	**12.00**	**30.00**
Atlantic SD-8096	(S)	Rock 'N' Roll Soul	*1964*	**20.00**	**50.00**
Atlantic 8109	(M)	The Best Of Solomon Burke	*1965*	**8.00**	**20.00**
Atlantic SD-8109	(S)	The Best Of Solomon Burke	*1965*	**10.00**	**25.00**
Atlantic SD-8185	(S)	I Wish I Knew	*1968*	**8.00**	**20.00**
Atlantic SD-8158	(S)	King Solomon	*1968*	**8.00**	**20.00**

BURNETTE, DORSEY

Label		Title	Year	VG+	NM
Era EL-102	(M)	Tall Oak Tree	*1960*	**75.00**	**150.00**
Era ELS-102	(S)	Tall Oak Tree	*1960*	**150.00**	**250.00**

Label		Title	Year	VG+	NM
Dot DLP-3456	(M)	Dorsey Burnette Sings	1963	16.00	40.00
Dot DLP-25456	(S)	Dorsey Burnette Sings	1963	20.00	50.00
Era ES-800	(S)	Dorsey Burnette's Greatest Hits	1969	10.00	25.00
Capitol ST-111094	(S)	Here And Now	1972	6.00	15.00
Capitol ST-11219	(S)	Dorsey Burnette	1973	6.00	15.00

BURNETTE, JOHNNY

Label		Title	Year	VG+	NM
Liberty LRP-3179	(M)	Dreamin'	1960	16.00	40.00
Liberty LST-7179	(S)	Dreamin'	1960	20.00	50.00
Liberty LRP-3183	(M)	Johnny Burnette	1961	16.00	40.00
Liberty LST-7183	(S)	Johnny Burnette	1961	20.00	50.00
Liberty LRP-3190	(M)	Johnny Burnette Sings	1961	16.00	40.00
Liberty LST-7190	(S)	Johnny Burnette Sings	1961	20.00	50.00
Liberty LRP-3206	(M)	Hits And Other Favorites	1962	16.00	40.00
Liberty LST-7206	(S)	Hits And Other Favorites	1962	20.00	50.00
Liberty LRP-3255	(M)	Roses Are Red	1962	16.00	40.00
Liberty LST-7255	(S)	Roses Are Red	1962	20.00	50.00
Liberty LRP-3389	(M)	The Johnny Burnette Story	1964	16.00	40.00
Liberty LST-7389	(S)	The Johnny Burnette Story	1964	20.00	50.00

BURNETTE, JOHNNY, & THE ROCK 'N' ROLL TRIO

Label		Title	Year	VG+	NM
Coral CRL-57080	(M)	Johnny Burnette & The Rock 'N' Roll Trio	1956	660.00	1,000.00

BURNT SUITE

Label		Title	Year	VG+	NM
B.J.W. 9	(M)	Burnt Suite	1967	35.00	70.00

BURROUGHS, WILLIAM

Label		Title	Year	VG+	NM
ESP 1050	(M)	Call Me Burroughs		20.00	50.00

BURTON, JAMES

Label		Title	Year	VG+	NM
Capitol ST-2822	(S)	Corn Pickin' And Slick Slidin'	1968	12.00	30.00
A&M SP-4293	(S)	James Burton	1971	6.00	15.00

BUTLER, BILLY

Label		Title	Year	VG+	NM
OKeh OKM-12115	(M)	Right Track	1966	6.00	15.00

BUTLER, JERRY

Label		Title	Year	VG+	NM
Abner R-2001	(M)	Jerry Butler Esquire	1959	75.00	150.00
Vee Jay LP-1027	(M)	Jerry Butler Esquire	1961	20.00	50.00
Vee Jay LP-1029	(M)	He Will Break Your Heart	1960	20.00	50.00
Vee Jay LP-1034	(M)	Love Me	1961	14.00	35.00
Vee Jay LP-1038	(M)	Aware Of Love	1961	10.00	25.00
Vee Jay SR-1038	(S)	Aware Of Love	1961	12.00	30.00
Vee Jay LP-1046	(M)	Moon River	1962	10.00	25.00
Vee Jay SR-1046	(S)	Moon River	1962	12.00	30.00
Vee Jay LP-1048	(M)	The Best Of Jerry Butler	1962	8.00	20.00
Vee Jay SR-1048	(P)	The Best Of Jerry Butler	1962	10.00	25.00
Vee Jay LP-1057	(M)	Folk Songs	1963	8.00	20.00
Vee Jay SR-1057	(S)	Folk Songs	1963	10.00	25.00
Vee Jay LP-1075	(M)	For Your Precious Love	1963	8.00	20.00
Vee Jay VJS-1075	(S)	For Your Precious Love	1963	10.00	25.00
Vee Jay LP-1076	(M)	Giving Up On Love/Need To Belong	1963	8.00	20.00
Vee Jay VJS-1076	(S)	Giving Up On Love/Need To Belong	1963	10.00	25.00
Vee Jay LP-1099	(M)	Delicious Together (With Betty Everett)	1964	6.00	15.00
Vee Jay VJS-1099	(S)	Delicious Together (With Betty Everett)	1964	8.00	20.00
Vee Jay 1119	(M)	More Of The Best Of Jerry Butler	1965	5.00	12.00
Vee Jay VJS-1119	(S)	More Of The Best Of Jerry Butler	1965	6.00	15.00

BUTTERFIELD, PAUL (THE BUTTERFIELD BLUES BAND)

Label		Title	Year	VG+	NM
Elektra EKL-7294	(M)	Paul Butterfield Blues Band	1965	6.00	15.00
Elektra EKS-7294	(S)	Paul Butterfield Blues Band	1965	8.00	20.00
Elektra EKL-7315	(M)	East-West	1966	6.00	15.00
Elektra EKS-7315	(S)	East-West	1966	8.00	20.00
Elektra EKL-4015	(M)	Resurrection Of Pigboy Crabshaw	1967	6.00	15.00
Elektra EKS-74015	(S)	Resurrection Of Pigboy Crabshaw	1967	8.00	20.00
Elektra EKS-74025	(S)	In My Own Dream	1968	6.00	15.00
Columbia OS-3240	(S)	You Are What You Eat (Sdtk)	1968	6.00	15.00
Cotillion CT3-500	(S)	Woodstock (Sdtk)	1970	8.00	20.00
Cotillion CT2-400	(S)	Woodstock Two	1970	6.00	15.00
Elektra EKS-75031	(S)	Sometimes I Just Feel Like Smilin'	1971	5.00	12.00
Elektra 7E-2001	(S)	Live	1971	6.00	15.00

Label		Title	Year	VG+	NM
BYRD, BOBBY (BOBBY DAY)					
King KS-1118	(S)	I Need Help	1970	6.00	15.00
BYRDS, THE					
Columbia CL-2372	(M)	Mr. Tambourine Man	1965	10.00	25.00
		(Label reads "Guaranteed High Fidelity.")			
Columbia CL-2372	(M)	Mr. Tambourine Man	1965	6.00	15.00
Columbia CS-9172	(P)	Mr. Tambourine Man	1965	6.00	15.00
Columbia CL-2454	(M)	Turn, Turn, Turn	1965	6.00	15.00
Columbia CS-9254	(P)	Turn, Turn, Turn	1965	5.00	12.00
Columbia CL-2549	(M)	Fifth Dimension	1966	6.00	15.00
Columbia CS-9349	(S)	Fifth Dimension	1966	5.00	12.00
Columbia CL-2642	(M)	Younger Than Yesterday	1967	6.00	15.00
Columbia CS-9442	(S)	Younger Than Yesterday	1967	5.00	12.00
MGM E-4484	(M)	Don't Make Waves (Sdtk)	1967	5.00	12.00
MGM SE-4484	(S)	Don't Make Waves (Sdtk)	1967	6.00	15.00
Columbia CL-2716	(M)	The Byrds' Greatest Hits	1967	6.00	15.00
Columbia CS-9516	(P)	The Byrds' Greatest Hits	1967	5.00	12.00
Columbia CL-2775	(M)	The Notorious Byrd Brothers	1968	8.00	20.00
Columbia CL-S-9575	(S)	The Notorious Byrd Brothers	1968	5.00	12.00
Columbia CS-9670	(S)	Sweetheart Of The Rodeo	1968	5.00	12.00
ABC OC-9	(S)	Candy (Sdtk)	1968	5.00	12.00
Columbia 9755	(S)	Dr. Byrds And Mr. Hyde	1968	5.00	12.00
Columbia CS-9942	(S)	The Ballad Of Easy Rider	1969	5.00	12.00
		(Columbia albums above have "360 Sound" labels.)			
Together ST-1001	(S)	Preflyte	1969	6.00	15.00
Dunhill DSX-50063	(S)	Easy Rider (Sdtk)	1970	8.00	20.00
Cotillion SD-9037	(S)	Homer (Sdtk)	1970	6.00	15.00
BYRNES, ED "KOOKIE"					
Warners W-1309	(M)	Kookie	1959	10.00	25.00
Warners WS-1309	(S)	Kookie	1959	12.00	30.00

Label		Title	Year	VG+	NM
C.A. QUINTET, THE					
Candy Floss 7764	(M)	A Trip Through Hell	1969	300.00	500.00
C.C.S.					
Rak KZ-30559	(S)	Whole Lotta Love	1971	8.00	20.00
Rak KZ-31569	(S)	C.C.S.	1972	8.00	20.00
CADETS, THE (THE JACKS)					
Crown CLP-5015	(M)	Rockin' 'N' Reelin	1957	50.00	100.00
Crown CLP-5370	(M)	The Cadets	1963	16.00	40.00
Crown CST-370	(E)	The Cadets	1963	10.00	25.00
CADILLACS, THE					
Jubilee JGM-1045	(M)	The Fabulous Cadillacs (Blue label)	1957	100.00	200.00
Jubilee JGM-1089	(M)	The Crazy Cadillacs (Flat black label)	1959	75.00	150.00
Jubilee JGM-1117	(M)	The Cadillacs Meet The Orioles	1961	50.00	100.00
Jubilee JGM-5009	(M)	Twisting With The Cadillacs	1962	50.00	100.00
CALIFORNIA POPPY PICKERS, THE					
Alshire 5152	(S)	Sounds Of '69	1969	6.00	15.00
Alshire 5153	(S)	Hair/Aquarius/Let The Sunshine In	1969	6.00	15.00
Alshire 5163	(S)	Today's Chart Busters	1969	6.00	15.00
Alshire	(S)	Honkey Tonk Women	1969	10.00	25.00

The Genius Of Ray Charles. The title of this album could aptly be applied to the bulk of Charles' recordings over the past three decades. This was his first album to be issued in stereo and, like all early Atlantic stereo releases, is highly sought after by Atlantic label collectors.

Pet Clark. After years as a successful entertainer in Europe, this album was issued by Imperial in 1959.
Ms. Clark had to wait another six years before her run of fifteen Top Forty hits made her one of the
most successful vocalist of the late '60s.

Label		Title	Year	VG+	NM
CALLIOPE					
Buddah BDS-5023	(S)	Steamed	1968	8.00	20.00
CAMPBELL, CHOKER					
Motown 620	(S)	Hits Of The Sixties	1965	8.00	20.00
CAMPBELL, DICK					
Mercury MG-21060	(M)	Dick Campbell Sings Where It's At	1966	6.00	15.00
Mercury SR-61060	(S)	Dick Campbell Sings Where It's At	1966	8.00	20.00
CAMPBELL, GLEN					
Also refer to the Green River Boys.					
Capitol T-1881	(M)	Too Late To Worry, Too Blue To Cry	1963	6.00	15.00
Capitol ST-1881	(S)	Too Late To Worry, Too Blue To Cry	1963	8.00	20.00
Capitol T-2023	(M)	The Astounding 12-String Guitar	1964	5.00	12.00
Capitol ST-2023	(S)	The Astounding 12-String Guitar	1964	6.00	15.00
Capitol T-2392	(M)	The Big Bad Rock Guitar Of Glen Campbell	1965	5.00	12.00
Capitol ST-2392	(S)	The Big Bad Rock Guitar Of Glen Campbell	1965	6.00	15.00
CAMPBELL, JO ANN					
End LP-306	(M)	I'm Nobody's Baby	1959	20.00	50.00
ABC-Paramount 393	(M)	Twistin' And Listenin'	1962	12.00	30.00
ABC-Paramount S-393	(S)	Twistin' And Listenin'	1962	16.00	40.00
Coronet CX-199	(M)	Starring Jo Ann Campbell		8.00	20.00
Coronet CXS-199	(S)	Starring Jo Ann Campbell		10.00	25.00
Cameo C-1026	(M)	All The Hits Of Jo Ann Campbell	1962	8.00	20.00
Cameo SC-1026	(S)	All The Hits Of Jo Ann Campbell	1962	12.00	30.00
Roulette R-25168	(M)	Hey, Let's Twist (Sdtk)	1962	8.00	20.00
Roulette SR-25168	(M)	Hey, Let's Twist (Sdtk)	1962	10.00	25.00
CAMPUS SINGERS, THE					
Argo 4023	(M)	The Campus Singers At The Fickle Pickle	1963	10.00	25.00
CANARIES, THE					
B.T. Puppy S-1007	(S)	Flying High With The Canaries	1970	12.00	30.00
CANDY STORE, THE					
Decca DL7-5147	(S)	Turned On Christmas	1969	10.00	25.00
CANNED HEAT					
Liberty LRP-3526	(M)	Canned Heat	1967	5.00	12.00
Liberty LST-7526	(S)	Canned Heat	1967	6.00	15.00
Liberty LST-7541	(S)	Boogie With Canned Heat	1968	6.00	15.00
Liberty LST-7618	(S)	Hallelujah	1969	5.00	12.00
Liberty LST-11000	(S)	Cookbook	1969	4.00	10.00
Liberty LST-11002	(P)	Future Blues	1970	4.00	10.00
Wand WDS-693	(S)	Live At Topanga Canyon	1970	8.00	20.00
Cotillion CT3-500	(S)	Woodstock (Sdtk)	1970	8.00	20.00
Cotillion CT2-400	(S)	Woodstock Two	1971	6.00	15.00
Liberty LST-35002	(S)	Hooker 'N' Heat	1971	6.00	15.00
United Arts. UAS-9955	(S)	Living The Blues	1971	6.00	15.00
United Arts. UAS-5509	(S)	Live In Europe	1971	4.00	10.00
United Arts. UAS-5557	(S)	Historical Figures And Ancient Heads	1972	4.00	10.00
		(With Little Richard, includes a comic book)			
CANNIBAL & THE HEADHUNTERS					
Rampart RM-3302	(M)	Land Of 1,000 Dances	1966	10.00	25.00
Rampart RS-3302	(S)	Land Of 1,000 Dances	1966	12.00	30.00
Date TEM-3001	(M)	Land Of 1,000 Dances	1966	8.00	20.00
Date TES-3001	(S)	Land Of 1,000 Dances	1966	10.00	25.00
CANNON, FREDDY					
Swan LP-502	(M)	The Explosive! Freddy Cannon	1960	40.00	80.00
Swan LPS-502	(P)	The Explosive! Freddy Cannon	1960	50.00	100.00
Swan LP-504	(M)	Happy Shades Of Blue	1960	40.00	80.00
Swan LP-505	(M)	Solid Gold Hits	1961	40.00	80.00
Swan LP-507	(M)	Freddy Cannon At Palisades Park	1962	40.00	80.00
Swan LP-511	(M)	Freddy Cannon Steps Out	1963	40.00	80.00
Warners W-1544	(M)	Freddy Cannon	1964	6.00	15.00
Warners WS-1544	(S)	Freddy Cannon	1964	8.00	20.00

Label		Title	Year	VG+	NM
Warners W-1612	(M)	Action!	1965	6.00	15.00
Warners WS-1612	(S)	Action!	1965	8.00	20.00
Warners W-1628	(M)	Freddy Cannon's Greatest Hits	1966	5.00	12.00
Warners WS-1628	(S)	Freddy Cannon's Greatest Hits	1966	6.00	15.00
CANNON, GUS					
Stax 702	(M)	Walk Right In	1962	16.00	40.00
CANTELON, WILLARD					
Supreme M-113	(M)	L.S.D. Battle For The Mind	1966	6.00	15.00
Supreme S-113	(S)	L.S.D. Battle For The Mind	1966	8.00	20.00
CAPES & MASKS, THE					
Mainstream 16069	(M)	Comic Book Heroes	1966	5.00	12.00
Mainstream 6069	(S)	Comic Book Heroes	1966	6.00	15.00
CAPITAL CITY ROCKETS, THE					
Elektra EKS-75059	(S)	Capital City Rockets	1973	6.00	15.00
CAPITOLS, THE					
Atco 190	(M)	Dance The Cool Jerk	1966	8.00	20.00
Atco SD-33-190	(S)	Dance The Cool Jerk	1966	10.00	25.00
Atco 201	(M)	We Got A Thing That's In The Groove	1966	5.00	12.00
Atco SD-33-201	(S)	We Got A Thing That's In The Groove	1966	6.00	15.00
CAPOTE, TRUMAN					
United Arts. UAS-6621	(S)	Christmas Memory	1968	6.00	15.00
United Arts. UAS-6682	(S)	Thanksgiving Visitor	1968	6.00	15.00
CAPRIS, THE					
Ambient Sound 37714	(S)	There's A Moon Out Tonight	1982	4.00	10.00
CAPTAIN BEYOND					
Capricorn CP-0105	(S)	Captain Beyond (3-D cover)	1972	8.00	20.00
CARAVAN, JIMMY					
Tower ST-5103	(S)	Look Into the Flower	1968	8.00	20.00
Vault 9007	(S)	Hey Jude	1969	6.00	15.00
CARAVELLES, THE					
Smash MGS-27044	(M)	You Don't Have To Be A Baby To Cry	1963	12.00	30.00
Smash SRS-67044	(E)	You Don't Have To Be A Baby To Cry	1963	10.00	25.00
CAREFREES, THE					
London LL-3379	(M)	We Love You All	1964	10.00	25.00
London PS-379	(S)	We Love You All	1964	12.00	30.00
CARLISLE BROTHERS, THE					
Mercury MG-20359	(M)	On Stage With The Carlisles	1958	16.00	40.00
King 643	(M)	Fresh From The Country	1959	16.00	40.00
CARNES, KIM					
Mobile Fidelity 1-073	(S)	Mistaken Identity	1982	6.00	15.00
CAROLINA SLIM					
Sharp 2002	(M)	Blues From The Cotton Fields		100.00	200.00
CARPENTER, IKE					
Aladdin LP-811	(M)	Lights Out	1956	75.00	150.00
Score SLP-4010	(M)	Lights Out	1957	40.00	80.00
CARPENTERS, THE (KAREN & RICHARD CARPENTER)					
A&M SP-4205	(S)	Offering	1969	16.00	40.00
A&M SP-4205	(S)	Ticket To Ride	1971	6.00	15.00
A&M QU-54271	(Q)	Close To You	1970	6.00	15.00
A&M QU-53502	(Q)	Carpenters	1971	6.00	15.00
A&M QU-53511	(Q)	A Song For You	1972	6.00	15.00
A&M QU-53519	(Q)	Now And Then	1973	6.00	15.00
A&M QU-53601	(Q)	The Singles 1969-1973	1973	6.00	15.00
A&M QU-54530	(Q)	Horizon	1975	6.00	15.00

Label		Title	Year	VG+	NM
CARR, CATHY					
Fraternity 1005	(M)	Ivory Tower		20.00	50.00
Dot DLP-3674	(M)	Ivory Tower		6.00	15.00
Dot DLP-25674	(S)	Ivory Tower		8.00	20.00
CARR, GEORGIA					
Tops 1617	(M)	Songs By A Moody Miss	1958	10.00	25.00
Vee Jay LP-1105	(M)	Rocks In My Bed	1964	6.00	15.00
Vee Jay VJS-1105	(S)	Rocks In My Bed	1964	8.00	20.00
Roulette R-25077	(M)	Shy		6.00	15.00
Roulette SR-25077	(S)	Shy		8.00	20.00
CARR, LEROY					
Columbia CL-1911	(M)	Blues Before Sunrise	1962	8.00	20.00
Columbia CS-8511	(S)	Blues Before Sunrise	1962	12.00	30.00
CARROLL, DIAHANN					
RCA LPM-1467	(M)	Diahann Carroll Sings Harold Arlen	1956	14.00	35.00
United Arts. UAL-4021	(M)	Porgy And Bess	1960	5.00	12.00
United Arts. UAS-5021	(S)	Porgy And Bess	1960	6.00	15.00
United Arts. UAL-3069	(M)	Diahann Carroll And Andre Previn	1960	5.00	12.00
United Arts. UAS-6069	(S)	Diahann Carroll And Andre Previn	1960	6.00	15.00
United Arts. UAL-3080	(M)	Diahann Carroll At The Persian Room	1960	5.00	12.00
United Arts. UAS-6080	(S)	Diahann Carroll At The Persian Room	1960	6.00	15.00
Atlantic 8048	(M)	Fun Life	1961	6.00	15.00
Atlantic SD-8048	(S)	Fun Life	1961	10.00	25.00
United Arts. UAL-4091	(M)	Goodbye Again (Sdtk)	1961	8.00	20.00
United Arts. UAS-5091	(S)	Goodbye Again (Sdtk)	1961	10.00	25.00
United Arts. UAL-3229	(M)	The Fabulous Diahann Carroll	1962	5.00	12.00
United Arts. UAS-6229	(S)	The Fabulous Diahann Carroll	1962	6.00	15.00
Columbia CL-2571	(M)	Nobody Sees Me Cry	1967	4.00	10.00
Columbia CS-9371	(S)	Nobody Sees Me Cry	1967	5.00	12.00
CARROLL BROTHERS					
Cameo C-1015	(M)	College Twist Party	1962	6.00	15.00
Cameo CS-1015	(S)	College Twist Party	1962	8.00	20.00
CARSON, MARTHA (LOU)					
RCA LPM-1145	(M)	Journey To The Sky	1955	12.00	30.00
RCA LPM-1490	(M)	Rock-A My Soul	1957	12.00	30.00
Sims LP-100	(M)	Martha Carson		6.00	15.00
Sims LP-109	(M)	Martha Carson		6.00	15.00
Capitol T-1507	(M)	Satisfied	1960	6.00	15.00
Capitol T-1607	(M)	A Talk With The Lord	1962	5.00	12.00
Capitol ST-1607	(S)	A Talk With The Lord	1962	6.00	15.00
CARTER, BETTY					
Epic LN-3202	(M)	Meet Betty Carter	1956	12.00	30.00
ABC-Paramount 363	(M)	The Modern Sound Of Betty Carter	1960	8.00	20.00
ABC-Paramount S-363	(S)	The Modern Sound Of Betty Carter	1960	10.00	25.00
ABC-Paramount 385	(M)	Ray Charles And Betty Carter	1961	16.00	40.00
ABC-Paramount S-385	(S)	Ray Charles And Betty Carter	1961	20.00	50.00
Atco 33-152	(M)	'Round Midnight	1963	6.00	15.00
Atco SD-33-152	(S)	'Round Midnight	1963	8.00	20.00
United Arts. UAL-3379	(M)	Inside Betty Carter	1963	8.00	20.00
United Arts. UAS-6379	(S)	Inside Betty Carter	1963	10.00	25.00
CARTER, CALVIN					
Vee Jay LP-1041	(M)	Twist Along With Calvin Carter	1962	8.00	20.00
Vee Jay SR-1041	(S)	Twist Along With Calvin Carter	1962	12.00	30.00
CARTER, CLARENCE					
Atlantic SD-8192	(S)	This Clarence Carter	1968	10.00	25.00
Atlantic SD-8199	(S)	The Dynamic Clarence Carter	1969	6.00	15.00
Atlantic SD-8238	(S)	Testifyin'	1969	6.00	15.00
Atlantic SD-8267	(S)	Patches	1970	6.00	15.00
Atlantic SD-8282	(S)	The Best Of Clarence Carter	1971	6.00	15.00
CARTER, LYNDA					
Epic JE-35309	(S)	Portrait (Picture disc)	1978	12.00	30.00

Label		Title	Year	VG+	NM
CARTER, MEL					
Derby LPM-702	(M)	When A Boy Falls In Love	1963	50.00	100.00
CASCADES					
Valiant W-405	(M)	Rhythm Of The Rain	1963	16.00	40.00
Valiant WS-405	(P)	Rhythm Of The Rain	1963	20.00	50.00
Cascade 681001	(S)	What Goes On	1968	20.00	50.00
Uni 73069	(S)	Maybe The Rain Will Fall	1969	8.00	20.00
CASEY, AL					
Prestige W-2007	(M)	Buck Jumpin'	1960	20.00	50.00
Prestige MV-12	(M)	The Al Casey Quartet	1961	16.00	40.00
Stacy STM-100	(M)	Surfin' Hootenanny	1963	20.00	50.00
Stacy STMS-100	(S)	Surfin' Hootenanny	1963	30.00	60.00
Stacy STMS-100	(S)	Surfin' Hootenanny (Blue vinyl)	1963	40.00	80.00
CASH, JOHNNY					
Sun 1220	(M)	Johnny Cash With His Hot & Blue Guitar	1956	20.00	50.00
Sun 1235	(M)	The Songs That Made Him Famous	1958	16.00	40.00
Sun 1240	(M)	Johnny Cash's Greatest!	1959	16.00	40.00
Sun 1245	(M)	Johnny Cash Sings Hank Williams	1960	16.00	40.00
Sun 1255	(M)	Now Here's Johnny Cash	1961	12.00	30.00
Sun 1270	(M)	All Aboard The Blue Train	1963	10.00	25.00
Sun 1275	(M)	The Original Sun Sound Of Johnny Cash	1965	10.00	25.00
Columbia CL-1253	(M)	The Fabulous Johnny Cash	1958	10.00	25.00
Columbia CS-8122	(S)	The Fabulous Johnny Cash	1958	12.00	30.00
Columbia CL-1284	(M)	Hymns By Johnny Cash	1959	8.00	20.00
Columbia CS-8125	(S)	Hymns By Johnny Cash	1959	10.00	25.00
Columbia CL-1339	(M)	Songs Of Our Soil	1959	8.00	20.00
Columbia CS-8148	(S)	Songs Of Our Soil	1959	10.00	25.00
Columbia CL-1463	(M)	Now, There Was A Song!	1960	8.00	20.00
Columbia CS-8254	(S)	Now, There Was A Song!	1960	10.00	25.00
Columbia CL-1464	(M)	Ride This Train	1960	6.00	15.00
Columbia CS-8255	(S)	Ride This Train	1960	8.00	20.00
Columbia CL-1622	(M)	The Lure Of The Grand Canyon	1961	8.00	20.00
Columbia CS-8422	(S)	The Lure Of The Grand Canyon	1961	10.00	25.00
Columbia CL-1722	(M)	Hymns From The Heart	1962	6.00	15.00
Columbia CS-8522	(S)	Hymns From The Heart	1962	8.00	20.00
Columbia CL-1802	(M)	The Sound Of Johnny Cash	1962	6.00	15.00
Columbia CS-8602	(S)	The Sound Of Johnny Cash	1962	8.00	20.00
		(Columbia albums above have six black & white "eye" logos on each label.)			
Columbia CL-1930	(M)	Blood, Sweat And Tears	1963	5.00	12.00
Columbia CS-8730	(S)	Blood, Sweat And Tears	1963	6.00	15.00
Columbia CL-2053	(M)	Ring Of Fire/The Best Of Johnny Cash	1963	5.00	12.00
Columbia CS-8853	(S)	Ring Of Fire/The Best Of Johnny Cash	1963	6.00	15.00
Columbia CL-2117	(M)	Christmas Spirit	1963	5.00	12.00
Columbia CS-8917	(S)	Christmas Spirit	1963	6.00	15.00
Columbia CL-2190	(M)	I Walk The Line	1964	5.00	12.00
Columbia CS-8990	(S)	I Walk The Line	1964	6.00	15.00
Columbia CL-2248	(M)	Bitter Tears	1964	6.00	15.00
Columbia CS-9048	(S)	Bitter Tears	1964	8.00	20.00
Columbia CL-2309	(M)	Orange Blossom Special	1965	5.00	12.00
Columbia CS-9109	(S)	Orange Blossom Special	1965	6.00	15.00
Columbia CL-2446	(M)	Mean As Hell	1965	5.00	12.00
Columbia CS-9246	(S)	Mean As Hell	1965	6.00	15.00
Columbia OL-6420	(M)	The Sons Of Katie Elder (Sdtk)	1965	14.00	35.00
Columbia OS-2820	(S)	The Sons Of Katie Elder (Sdtk)	1965	16.00	40.00
Columbia C2L-838	(M)	Ballads Of The True West	1965	6.00	15.00
Columbia C2S-838	(S)	Ballads Of The True West	1965	8.00	20.00
Columbia CL-2492	(M)	Everybody Loves A Nut	1966	5.00	12.00
Columbia CS-9292	(S)	Everybody Loves A Nut	1966	6.00	15.00
Columbia CL-2537	(M)	Happiness Is You	1966	5.00	12.00
Columbia CS-9337	(S)	Happiness Is You	1966	6.00	15.00
Columbia CL-2537	(M)	That's What You Get For Loving Me	1966	5.00	12.00
Columbia CS-9337	(S)	That's What You Get For Loving Me	1966	6.00	15.00
Columbia CL-2647	(M)	From Sea To Shining Sea	1967	5.00	12.00
Columbia CS-9447	(S)	From Sea To Shining Sea	1967	6.00	15.00
Columbia CL-2678	(M)	Johnny Cash's Greatest Hits, Volume 1	1967	5.00	12.00
Columbia CS-9478	(S)	Johnny Cash's Greatest Hits, Volume 1	1967	6.00	15.00

Label		Title	Year	VG+	NM
Columbia CL-2728	(M)	Carryin' On	1967	5.00	12.00
Columbia CS-9528	(S)	Carryin' On	1967	6.00	15.00
Columbia CS-9639	(S)	Johnny Cash At Folsom Prison	1968	5.00	12.00
Columbia CS-9726	(S)	The Holy Land (3D cover)	1969	8.00	20.00
Columbia CS-9726	(S)	The Holy Land	1969	5.00	12.00
Columbia CS-9827	(S)	Johnny Cash At San Quentin	1969	5.00	12.00
Columbia CS-9943	(S)	Hello, I'm Johnny Cash	1970	5.00	12.00
		(Columbia albums above have "360 Sound" labels.)			

CASINOS, THE

Fraternity 1019	(M)	Then You Can Tell Me Goodbye	1967	10.00	25.00
Fraternity LPS-1019	(S)	Then You Can Tell Me Goodbye	1967	12.00	30.00

CASTELLS, THE

Era EL-109	(M)	So This Is Love	1962	35.00	70.00
Era ES-109	(S)	So This Is Love	1962	50.00	100.00

CASTOR BUNCH, JIMMY

Smash MGS-27091	(M)	Hey Leroy!	1967	6.00	15.00
Smash SRW-67091	(S)	Hey Leroy!	1967	8.00	20.00

CATALINAS, THE

Ric M-1006	(M)	Fun, Fun, Fun	1964	14.00	35.00
Ric S-1006	(S)	Fun, Fun, Fun	1964	18.00	45.00

CATHY JEAN & THE ROOMATES

Valmor 789	(M)	At The Hop!	1961	75.00	150.00

CENTURIANS, THE (THE BRUCE JOHNSTON SURFING BAND)

Del-Fi DFLP-1228	(M)	Surfer's Pajama Party	1963	20.00	50.00
Del-Fi DFST-1228	(S)	Surfer's Pajama Party	1963	30.00	60.00

CESANA

Modern M-100	(M)	Tender Emotions	1964	8.00	20.00

CHAD & JEREMY (CHAD STUART & JEREMY CLYDE)

World Artists WAM-2002	(M)	Yesterday's Gone	1964	3.50	8.00
World Artists WAS-3002	(P)	Yesterday's Gone	1964	4.00	10.00
World Artists WAM-2005	(M)	Chad And Jeremy Sing For You	1965	3.50	8.00
World Artists WAS-3005	(P)	Chad And Jeremy Sing For You	1965	4.00	10.00
Columbia CL-2374	(M)	Before And After	1965	4.00	10.00
Columbia CS-9174	(S)	Before And After	1965	6.00	15.00
Columbia CL-2398	(M)	I Don't Want To Lose You Baby	1965	4.00	10.00
Columbia CS-9198	(S)	I Don't Want To Lose You Baby	1965	6.00	15.00
Capitol T-2470	(M)	The Best Of Chad And Jeremy	1966	3.50	8.00
Capitol ST-2470	(P)	The Best Of Chad And Jeremy	1966	4.00	10.00
Capitol TT-2546	(M)	More Chad And Jeremy	1966	3.50	8.00
Capitol ST-2546	(P)	More Chad And Jeremy	1966	4.00	10.00
Columbia CL-2564	(M)	Distant Shores	1966	4.00	10.00
Columbia CS-9364	(P)	Distant Shores	1966	6.00	15.00
Columbia CL-2657	(M)	Of Cabbages And Kings	1967	5.00	12.00
Columbia CS-9457	(S)	Of Cabbages And Kings	1967	6.00	15.00
Columbia CS-9699	(S)	The Ark	1968	6.00	15.00
Sidewalk ST-5918	(S)	Three In The Attic (Sdtk)	1969	8.00	20.00

CHALLENGERS, THE

Vault LP-100	(M)	Surfbeat	1963	16.00	40.00
Vault VS-100	(S)	Surfbeat	1963	20.00	50.00
Vault VS-100	(S)	Surfbeat (Orange vinyl)	1963	35.00	70.00
Vault VS-100	(S)	Surfbeat (Red vinyl)	1963	35.00	70.00
Vault VS-100	(S)	Surfbeat (Yellow vinyl)	1963	35.00	70.00
Vault LP-101	(M)	Surfing	1963	12.00	30.00
Vault VS-101	(S)	Surfing	1963	16.00	40.00
Vault VS-101	(S)	Surfing (Orange vinyl)	1963	30.00	60.00
Vault VS-101	(S)	Surfing (Red vinyl)	1963	30.00	60.00
Vault VS-101	(S)	Surfing (Yellow vinyl)	1963	30.00	60.00
		(The cover of Vault 101 notes it as part of the "Lloyd Thaxton Presents" series.)			
Vault VS-101	(S)	Surfing (Blue vinyl)	1963	35.00	70.00
		(Makes no mention of Lloyd Thaxton.)			

Label		Title	Year	VG+	NM
Vault LP-102	(M)	The Challengers On The Move	1963	12.00	30.00
Vault VS-102	(S)	The Challengers On The Move	1963	14.00	35.00
Vault LP-107	(M)	K-39	1964	20.00	50.00
Vault LP-109	(M)	The Surf's Up	1965	12.00	30.00
Vault VS-109	(S)	The Surf's Up	1965	14.00	35.00
Vault LP-110	(M)	The Challengers Au Go Go	1966	12.00	30.00
Vault VS-110	(S)	The Challengers Au Go Go	1966	14.00	35.00
Vault LP-111	(M)	The Challengers' Greatest Hits	1967	10.00	25.00
Vault VS-111	(S)	The Challengers' Greatest Hits	1967	8.00	20.00
Triumph 100	(M)	Sidewalk Surfing	1965	8.00	20.00
Triumph TR-100	(S)	Sidewalk Surfing	1965	10.00	25.00
GNP/Crescendo 2010	(M)	The Challengers At The Teenage Fair	1965	6.00	15.00
GNP/Crescendo S-2010	(S)	The Challengers At The Teenage Fair	1965	5.00	12.00
GNP/Crescendo 2018	(M)	The Man From U.N.C.L.E.	1965	6.00	15.00
GNP/Crescendo S-2018	(M)	The Man From U.N.C.L.E.	1965	5.00	12.00
GNP/Crescendo 2025	(M)	California Kicks	1966	6.00	15.00
GNP/Crescendo S-2025	(S)	California Kicks	1966	5.00	12.00
GNP/Crescendo 2030	(M)	Billy Strange And The Challengers	1967	6.00	15.00
GNP/Crescendo S-2030	(S)	Billy Strange And The Challengers	1967	5.00	12.00
GNP/Crescendo 2031	(M)	Wipe Out	1966	6.00	15.00
GNP/Crescendo S-2031	(S)	Wipe Out	1966	5.00	12.00
GNP/Crescendo 609	(M)	25 Great Instrumental Hits	1967	6.00	15.00
GNP/Crescendo S-609	(S)	25 Great Instrumental Hits	1967	5.00	12.00
GNP/Crescendo S-2045	(S)	Light My Fire With Classical Gas	1968	4.00	10.00
GNP/Crescendo S-2056	(S)	Vanilla Funk	1970	4.00	10.00
		(GNP albums above have red labels.)			

CHAMBERS BROTHERS, THE

Label		Title	Year	VG+	NM
Vault 9003	(M)	People Get Ready	1966	4.00	10.00
Vault 9003	(S)	People Get Ready	1966	5.00	12.00
Vault 115	(M)	The Chambers Brothers Now	1967	4.00	10.00
Vault 115	(S)	The Chambers Brothers Now	1967	5.00	12.00
Columbia CL-2722	(M)	The Time Has Come	1967	6.00	15.00
Columbia CS-9522	(S)	The Time Has Come	1967	6.00	15.00
Columbia CS-9671	(S)	A New Time/A New Day	1968	5.00	12.00
Vault 120	(S)	The Chambers Brothers Shout	1968	5.00	12.00
Vault 128	(S)	Feelin' The Blues	1969	5.00	12.00
Columbia KGP-20	(S)	Live At The Fillmore East	1969	6.00	15.00
		(Columbia albums above have "360 Sound" labels.)			
Vault 135	(S)	Chambers Brothers' Greatest Hits	1970	6.00	15.00
Columbia KC-31158	(S)	Oh, My God!	1972	10.00	25.00

CHAMPS, THE

Label		Title	Year	VG+	NM
Challenge CHL-601	(M)	Go Champs Go	1958	50.00	100.00
Challenge CHL-601	(M)	Go Champs Go (Blue vinyl)	1958	240.00	400.00
Challenge CHL-605	(M)	Everybody's Rockin' With The Champs	1959	40.00	80.00
Challenge CHS-605	(S)	Everybody's Rockin' With The Champs	1959	50.00	100.00
Challenge CHL-613	(M)	Great Dance Hits	1962	20.00	50.00
Challenge CHS-613	(S)	Great Dance Hits	1962	30.00	60.00
Challenge CHL-614	(M)	All American Music From The Champs	1962	20.00	50.00
Challenge CHS-614	(S)	All American Music From The Champs	1962	30.00	60.00

CHANDLER, GENE

Label		Title	Year	VG+	NM
Vee Jay MR-1040	(M)	The Duke Of Earl	1962	20.00	50.00
Vee Jay SR-1040	(S)	The Duke Of Earl	1962	40.00	80.00
Constellation LP-1421	(M)	Greatest Hits By Gene Chandler	1964	10.00	25.00
Constellation LP-1423	(M)	Just Be True	1964	10.00	25.00
Constellation LP-1425	(M)	Gene Chandler/Live On Stage In '65	1965	10.00	25.00
Checker LP-3003	(M)	The Duke Of Soul	1967	6.00	15.00
Checker LPS-3003	(E)	The Duke Of Soul	1967	5.00	12.00

CHANNEL, BRUCE

Label		Title	Year	VG+	NM
Smash MGS-27008	(M)	Hey! Baby	1962	30.00	60.00
Smash SRS-67008	(E)	Hey! Baby	1962	20.00	50.00

CHANTAYS, THE

Label		Title	Year	VG+	NM
Downey DLP-1002	(M)	Pipeline	1963	75.00	150.00
Dot DLP-3516	(M)	Pipeline	1963	10.00	25.00
Dot DLP-25516	(S)	Pipeline	1963	12.00	30.00
Dot DLP-3771	(M)	Two Sides Of The Chantays	1966	10.00	25.00
Dot DLP-25771	(S)	Two Sides Of The Chantays	1966	12.00	30.00

Label		Title	Year	VG+	NM
CHANTELS, THE					
End LP-301	(M)	We're The Chantels (Group photo cover)	1958	300.00	500.00
End LP-301	(M)	We're The Chantels (Jukebox cover)	1959	100.00	200.00
Carlton LP-144	(M)	The Chantels On Tour	1961	50.00	100.00
Carlton STLP-144	(P)	The Chantels On Tour	1961	100.00	200.00
End LP-312	(M)	There's Our Song Again	1962	20.00	50.00
CHARITY					
Uni 73061	(S)	Charity Now	1969	8.00	20.00
CHARLATANS, THE					
Phillips PHS-600-309	(S)	The Charlatans	1969	16.00	40.00
CHARLES, RAY					
Atlantic 8006	(M)	Ray Charles/Rock And Roll	1957	20.00	50.00
Atlantic 1259	(M)	The Great Ray Charles	1957	20.00	50.00
Atlantic 1279	(M)	Soul Brothers	1958	20.00	50.00
Atlantic 1289	(M)	Ray Charles At Newport	1958	20.00	50.00
Atlantic 8025	(M)	Yes, Indeed!	1959	12.00	30.00
Atlantic 8029	(M)	What'd I Say	1959	12.00	30.00
Atlantic 8039	(M)	Ray Charles In Person	1960	12.00	30.00
		(Atlantic albums above have black labels.)			
Atlantic 1312	(M)	The Genius Of Ray Charles	1960	12.00	30.00
Atlantic SD-1312	(S)	The Genius Of Ray Charles	1960	20.00	50.00
Atlantic 8052	(M)	The Genius Sings The Blues	1961	8.00	20.00
Atlantic SD-8052	(S)	The Genius Sings The Blues	1961	14.00	35.00
Atlantic 8054	(M)	Do The Twist With Ray Charles!	1961	10.00	25.00
Atlantic 1360	(M)	Soul Meeting	1961	8.00	20.00
Atlantic SD-1360	(S)	Soul Meeting	1961	14.00	35.00
Atlantic 1259	(M)	The Great Ray Charles	1961	8.00	20.00
Atlantic SD-1259	(S)	The Great Ray Charles	1961	14.00	35.00
Atlantic 1279	(M)	Soul Brothers	1961	8.00	20.00
Atlantic 1289	(M)	Ray Charles At Newport	1961	8.00	20.00
		(Mono Atlantic albums above have orange and purple labels with a white fan. Stereo albums have green and blue labels with a white fan.)			
Atlantic 1369	(M)	The Genius After Hours	1961	12.00	30.00
Atlantic SD-1369	(S)	The Genius After Hours	1961	16.00	40.00
Atlantic 8063	(M)	The Ray Charles Story, Volume 1	1962	8.00	20.00
Atlantic SD-8063	(P)	The Ray Charles Story, Volume 1	1962	8.00	20.00
Atlantic 8064	(M)	The Ray Charles Story, Volume 2	1962	8.00	20.00
Atlantic SD-8064	(P)	The Ray Charles Story, Volume 2	1962	8.00	20.00
Atlantic 8083	(M)	The Ray Charles Story, Volume 3	1963	8.00	20.00
Atlantic SD-8083	(P)	The Ray Charles Story, Volume 3	1963	8.00	20.00
Atlantic 8094	(M)	The Ray Charles Story, Volume 4	1964	8.00	20.00
Atlantic SD-8094	(P)	The Ray Charles Story, Volume 4	1964	8.00	20.00
Atlantic SD-7101	(S)	Great Hits Recorded On 8-Track Stereo	1964	8.00	20.00
ABC-Paramount 335	(M)	The Genius Hits The Road	1960	6.00	15.00
ABC-Paramount S-335	(S)	The Genius Hits The Road	1960	8.00	20.00
ABC-Paramount 355	(M)	Dedicated To You	1961	6.00	15.00
ABC-Paramount S-355	(S)	Dedicated To You	1961	8.00	20.00
ABC-Paramount 385	(M)	Ray Charles And Betty Carter	1961	16.00	40.00
ABC-Paramount S-385	(S)	Ray Charles And Betty Carter	1961	20.00	50.00
		(ABC albums above have black labels with "ABC-PARAMOUNT" on the top and "Am-Par Record Corp." on the bottom.)			
ABC-Paramount 410	(M)	Modern Sounds In Country And Western	1962	6.00	15.00
ABC-Paramount S-410	(S)	Modern Sounds In Country And Western	1962	8.00	20.00
		(Cover does not have the RIAA Gold Record logo.)			
ABC-Paramount 415	(M)	Ray Charles' Greatest Hits	1962	5.00	12.00
ABC-Paramount S-415	(S)	Ray Charles' Greatest Hits	1962	6.00	15.00
ABC-Paramount 435	(M)	Modern Sounds In Country And Western, Volume 2	1962	5.00	12.00
ABC-Paramount S-435	(S)	Modern Sounds In Country And Western, Volume 2	1962	6.00	15.00
ABC-Paramount 465	(M)	Ingredients In A Recipe For Soul	1963	4.00	10.00
ABC-Paramount S-465	(S)	Ingredients In A Recipe For Soul	1963	5.00	12.00
ABC-Paramount 480	(M)	Sweet And Sour Tears	1964	6.00	15.00
ABC-Paramount S-480	(S)	Sweet And Sour Tears	1964	8.00	20.00
ABC-Paramount 495	(M)	Have A Smile With Me	1964	5.00	12.00
ABC-Paramount S-495	(S)	Have A Smile With Me	1964	6.00	15.00

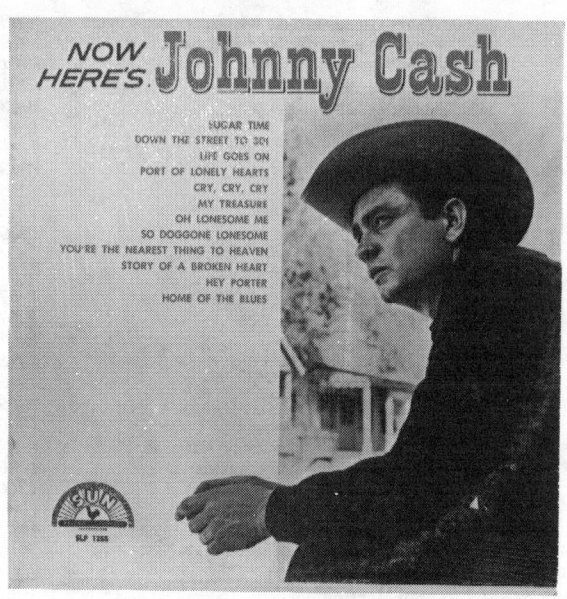

Now Here's Johnny Cash. While Cash was a mainstay with the Sun label for several years, he did not become a really big star until moving on to Columbia in 1958. Like many records from the pre-Beatles era, his Sun albums are drying up on the collector's market.

The Dave Clark Five. This two album set essentially reprises their two best of collections from the '60s., with one BIG exception, several of the hits are in true stereo for the first time. One of the most collectible albums of the early '70s.

Label		Title	Year	VG+	NM
MGM E-4313	(M)	The Cincinnati Kid (Sdtk)	1965	5.00	12.00
MGM SE-4313	(S)	The Cincinnati Kid (Sdtk)	1965	6.00	15.00
ABC-Paramount 500	(M)	Live In Concert	1965	4.00	10.00
ABC-Paramount S-500	(S)	Live In Concert	1965	5.00	12.00
ABC-Paramount 520	(M)	Country & Western Meets Rhythm & Blues	1965	6.00	15.00
ABC-Paramount S-520	(S)	Country & Western Meets Rhythm & Blues	1965	8.00	20.00
ABC-Paramount 520	(M)	Together Again	1966	5.00	12.00
ABC-Paramount S-520	(S)	Together Again	1966	6.00	15.00
ABC-Paramount 544	(M)	Crying Time	1966	5.00	12.00
ABC-Paramount S-544	(S)	Crying Time	1966	6.00	15.00
		(ABC albums above have black labels with "ABC-PARAMOUNT" on top.)			

CHASE, LINCOLN
Label		Title	Year	VG+	NM
Liberty LRP-3076	(M)	The Explosive Lincoln Chase	1958	12.00	30.00

CHECKER, CHUBBY (ERNEST EVANS)
Label		Title	Year	VG+	NM
Parkway 5001	(M)	Chubby Checker	1960	20.00	50.00
Parkway P-7001	(M)	Twist With Chubby Checker	1960	12.00	30.00
Parkway P-7002	(M)	For Twisters Only	1960	12.00	30.00
Parkway P-7003	(M)	It's Pony Time	1961	12.00	30.00
Parkway P-7004	(M)	Let's Twist Again	1961	12.00	30.00
Parkway P-7007	(M)	Your Twist Party	1961	12.00	30.00
Cameo C-1013	(M)	Bobby Rydell/Chubby Checker	1961	12.00	30.00
Parkway P-7008	(M)	Twistin' Round The World	1962	12.00	30.00
Parkway P-7009	(M)	For Teen Twisters Only	1962	12.00	30.00
Parkway P-7011	(M)	Don't Knock The Twist (Sdtk)	1962	12.00	30.00
Parkway P-7014	(M)	All The Hits For Your Dancin' Party	1962	12.00	30.00
Cameo C-1029	(M)	Down To Earth (With Dee Dee Sharp)	1962	8.00	20.00
Cameo SC-1029	(S)	Down To Earth (With Dee Dee Sharp)	1962	12.00	30.00
Parkway P-7020	(M)	Limbo Party	1962	8.00	20.00
Parkway SP-7020	(S)	Limbo Party	1962	12.00	30.00
Parkway P-7022	(M)	Chubby Checker's Biggest Hits	1962	10.00	25.00
Parkway SP-7022	(E)	Chubby Checker's Biggest Hits	1962	8.00	20.00
Parkway P-7026	(M)	Chubby Checker In Person	1963	8.00	20.00
Parkway SP-7026	(S)	Chubby Checker In Person	1963	12.00	30.00
Parkway P-7027	(M)	Let's Limbo Some More	1963	8.00	20.00
Parkway SP-7027	(S)	Let's Limbo Some More	1963	12.00	30.00
Parkway P-7030	(M)	Beach Party	1963	8.00	20.00
Parkway SP-7030	(S)	Beach Party	1963	12.00	30.00
Cameo C-1063	(M)	Chubby Checker And Bobby Rydell	1963	10.00	25.00
Parkway P-7040	(M)	Folk Album	1963	8.00	20.00
Parkway SP-7040	(S)	Folk Album	1963	12.00	30.00
Parkway P-7045	(M)	Discotheque	1965	8.00	20.00
Parkway SP-7045	(S)	Discotheque	1965	12.00	30.00
Parkway P-7048	(M)	Eighteen Golden Hits	1966	10.00	25.00
Parkway SP-7048	(P)	Eighteen Golden Hits	1966	10.00	25.00

CHER (CHER BONO ALLMAN)
Label		Title	Year	VG+	NM
Imperial LP-9292	(M)	All I Really Want To Do	1965	6.00	15.00
Imperial LP-12292	(S)	All I Really Want To Do	1965	8.00	20.00
Imperial LP-9301	(M)	The Sonny Side Of Cher	1966	5.00	12.00
Imperial LP-12301	(S)	The Sonny Side Of Cher	1966	6.00	15.00
Imperial 9320	(M)	Cher	1966	5.00	12.00
Imperial LP-12320	(S)	Cher	1966	6.00	15.00
Imperial LP-9358	(M)	With Love	1967	5.00	12.00
Imperial LP-12358	(S)	With Love	1967	6.00	15.00
Imperial LP-12373	(S)	Backstage	1968	5.00	12.00
Imperial LP-12406	(S)	Cher's Golden Greats	1968	5.00	12.00

CHESTER, GARY
Label		Title	Year	VG+	NM
DCP D-6803	(M)	Yeah, Yeah, Yeah	1964	6.00	15.00
DCP DS-6803	(S)	Yeah, Yeah, Yeah	1964	8.00	20.00

CHEVRONS, THE
Label		Title	Year	VG+	NM
Time T-10008	(M)	Sing A Long Rock And Roll	1961	20.00	50.00

CHICAGO (CHICAGO TRANSIT AUTHORITY)
Label		Title	Year	VG+	NM
Columbia GP-8	(S)	Chicago Transit Authority	1969	10.00	25.00
Columbia GP-24	(S)	Chicago II	1970	6.00	15.00
		(Columbia albums above have "360 Sound" labels.)			

Label		Title	Year	VG+	NM
Columbia C2Q-30110	(Q)	Chicago III	1974	8.00	20.00
Columbia CQ-30865	(Q)	Chicago At Carnegie Hall	1974	12.00	30.00
Columbia CQ-31102	(Q)	Chicago V	1974	6.00	15.00
Columbia CQ-32400	(Q)	Chicago VI	1974	6.00	15.00
Columbia C2Q-32810	(Q)	Chicago VII	1974	8.00	20.00
Columbia PCQ-33100	(Q)	Chicago VIII	1975	6.00	15.00
Columbia PCQ-33255	(Q)	Chicago Transit Authority	1975	8.00	20.00
Columbia GQ-33258	(Q)	Chicago II	1975	8.00	20.00
Columbia PCQ-33900	(Q)	Chicago IX/Greatest Hits	1975	6.00	15.00
Columbia PCQ-34200	(Q)	Chicago X	1976	6.00	15.00
Columbia HC-43900	(S)	Chicago IX/Greatest Hits (1/2 speed)	1981	6.00	15.00
Columbia HC-44200	(S)	Chicago X (1/2 speed)	1981	6.00	15.00
Mobile Fidelity 2-218	(S)	Chicago Transit Authority	1983	8.00	20.00

CHIFFONS, THE

Laurie LLP-2018	(M)	He's So Fine	1963	20.00	50.00
Laurie LLP-2020	(M)	One Fine Day	1963	20.00	50.00
Laurie LLP-2036	(M)	Sweet Talkin' Guy	1966	16.00	40.00
Laurie SLP-2036	(S)	Sweet Talkin' Guy	1966	20.00	50.00
B.T. Puppy S-1011	(S)	My Secret Love	1970	16.00	40.00

CHILDREN, THE

Cinema CLP-1	(S)	Rebirth	1967	12.00	30.00
Atco SD-33-271	(S)	Rebirth	1968	6.00	15.00

CHIPMUNKS, THE
The Chipmunks are the creation of Ross Bagdasarian, aka David Seville.

Liberty LRP-3132	(M)	Sing With The Chipmunks (Red vinyl)	1959	16.00	40.00
Liberty LST-7132	(S)	Sing With The Chipmunks (Red vinyl)	1959	20.00	50.00
Liberty LRP-3132	(M)	Sing With The Chipmunks	1959	8.00	20.00
Liberty LST-7132	(S)	Sing With The Chipmunks	1959	12.00	30.00
Liberty LRP-3159	(M)	Sing Again With The Chipmunks	1960	8.00	20.00
Liberty LST-7159	(S)	Sing Again With The Chipmunks	1960	12.00	30.00
Liberty LRP-3170	(M)	Around The World With The Chipmunks	1960	8.00	20.00
Liberty LST-7170	(S)	Around The World With The Chipmunks	1960	12.00	30.00
		(On the albums above the drawings of the Chipmunks on the cover are "realistic.")			
Liberty LRP-3209	(M)	The Alvin Show	1961	8.00	20.00
Liberty LST-7209	(S)	The Alvin Show	1961	10.00	25.00
Liberty LRP-3229	(M)	The Chipmunks Songbook	1962	8.00	20.00
Liberty LST-7229	(S)	The Chipmunks Songbook	1962	10.00	25.00
Liberty LRP-3256	(M)	Christmas With The Chipmunks	1962	8.00	20.00
Liberty LST-7256	(S)	Christmas With The Chipmunks	1962	10.00	25.00
Liberty LRP-3334	(M)	Christmas With The Chipmunks, Volume 2	1963	8.00	20.00
Liberty LST-7334	(S)	Christmas With The Chipmunks, Volume 2	1963	10.00	25.00
Liberty LRP-3388	(M)	The Chipmunks Sing The Beatles Hits	1964	10.00	25.00
Liberty LST-7388	(S)	The Chipmunks Sing The Beatles Hits	1964	12.00	30.00
Liberty LRP-3424	(M)	The Chipmunks A Go-Go	1965	6.00	15.00
Liberty LST-7424	(S)	The Chipmunks A Go-Go	1965	8.00	20.00
Liberty LRP-3405	(M)	The Chipmunks Sing With Children	1965	6.00	15.00
Liberty LST-7405	(S)	The Chipmunks Sing With Children	1965	8.00	20.00

CHOCOLATE WATCH BAND, THE

Tower T-5065	(M)	Riot On Sunset Strip (Sdtk)	1967	14.00	35.00
Tower DT-5065	(E)	Riot On Sunset Strip (Sdtk)	1967	12.00	30.00
Tower T-5096	(M)	No Way Out	1967	60.00	120.00
Tower ST-5096	(S)	No Way Out	1967	50.00	100.00
Tower ST-5016	(S)	The Inner Mystique	1968	60.00	120.00
Tower ST-5153	(S)	One Step Beyond	1969	40.00	80.00

CHORDETTES, THE

Columbia CL-6111 (10")	(M)	Harmony Time	1950	14.00	35.00
Columbia CL-6170 (10")	(M)	Harmony Time, Volume 2	1951	14.00	35.00
Columbia CL-6218 (10")	(M)	Harmony Encores	1953	14.00	35.00
Columbia CL-6285 (10")	(M)	Your Requests	1953	14.00	35.00
Columbia CL-956	(M)	Listen	1954	12.00	30.00
Columbia CL-2519	(M)	The Chordettes	1955	12.00	30.00
Cadence LP-3001	(M)	The Chordettes	1957	12.00	30.00
Cadence CLP-3002	(M)	Close Harmony	1957	12.00	30.00
Cadence CLP-3062	(M)	Never On Sunday	1962	8.00	20.00
Cadence CLP-25062	(S)	Never On Sunday	1962	12.00	30.00

Label		Title	Year	VG+	NM
CHOSEN FEW, THE					
RCA LSP-4242	(S)	The Chosen Few	1969	8.00	20.00
CHRISTIE, LOU (LUGEE GENO SACCO)					
Roulette R-25208	(M)	Lou Christie	1963	10.00	25.00
Roulette SR-25208	(P)	Lou Christie	1963	12.00	30.00
MGM E-4360	(M)	Lightnin' Strikes	1966	5.00	12.00
MGM SE-4360	(S)	Lightnin' Strikes	1966	6.00	15.00
Co&Ce LP-1231	(M)	Lou Christie Strikes Back	1966	16.00	40.00
Colpix CP-4001	(M)	Lou Christie Strikes Again	1966	8.00	20.00
Colpix SCP-4001	(S)	Lou Christie Strikes Again	1966	12.00	30.00
Roulette R-25332	(P)	Lou Christie Strikes Again	1966	6.00	15.00
Roulette SR-25332	(P)	Lou Christie Strikes Again	1966	8.00	20.00
MGM E-4394	(M)	Painter Of Hits	1966	5.00	12.00
MGM SE-4394	(P)	Painter Of Hits	1966	6.00	15.00
CHRISTY, JUNE					
Capitol H-516 (10")	(M)	Something Cool	1954	16.00	40.00
Capitol T-516	(M)	Something Cool	1955	12.00	30.00
Capitol T-656	(M)	Duet	1955	12.00	30.00
Capitol T-725	(M)	The Misty Miss Christy	1955	12.00	30.00
Capitol T-833	(M)	June Fair And Warmer	1957	12.00	30.00
Capitol T-902	(M)	Gone For The Day	1957	12.00	30.00
		(Capitol albums above have turquoise labels.)			
Capitol T-1076	(M)	June's Got Rhythm	1958	10.00	25.00
Capitol T-1114	(M)	The Song Is June!	1959	10.00	25.00
Capitol T-1202	(M)	June Christy Recalls Those Kenton Days	1959	10.00	25.00
Capitol T-1308	(M)	Ballads For Night People	1959	10.00	25.00
Capitol T-1398	(M)	The Cool School	1960	10.00	25.00
Capitol T-1498	(M)	Off Beat	1961	10.00	25.00
Capitol T-1586	(M)	Do Re Mi (Sdtk)	1961	6.00	15.00
Capitol ST-1586	(S)	Do Re Mi (Sdtk)	1961	8.00	20.00
Capitol T-1605	(M)	That Time Of Year	1961	6.00	15.00
Capitol ST-1605	(S)	That Time Of Year	1961	8.00	20.00
		(Capitol albums above have black labels with the Capitol logo on the left side.)			
Capitol T-1693	(M)	The Best Of June Christy	1962	6.00	15.00
Capitol ST-1693	(S)	The Best Of June Christy	1962	8.00	20.00
Capitol T-1845	(M)	Big Band Specials	1962	6.00	15.00
Capitol ST-1845	(S)	Big Band Specials	1962	8.00	20.00
Capitol T-1953	(M)	The Intimate June Christy	1962	6.00	15.00
Capitol ST-1953	(S)	The Intimate June Christy	1962	8.00	20.00
Capitol T-2410	(M)	Something Broadway, Something Latin	1965	5.00	12.00
Capitol ST-2410	(S)	Something Broadway, Something Latin	1965	6.00	15.00
		(Capitol albums above have black labels with the Capitol logo on the top.)			
CIRCUS					
Metromedia LPS-7401	(S)	Circus		10.00	25.00
CITY					
Ode Z-1244012	(S)	Now That Everythings Been Said	1969	20.00	50.00
		(The cover is in full color.)			
CLANTON, JIMMY					
Ace 1001	(M)	Just A Dream	1959	20.00	50.00
Ace 1007	(M)	Jimmy's Happy	1960	16.00	40.00
Ace 1007	(M)	Jimmy's Happy (Red vinyl)	1960	35.00	70.00
Ace 1008	(M)	Jimmy's Blue	1960	16.00	40.00
Ace 1008	(M)	Jimmy's Blue (Blue vinyl)	1960	35.00	70.00
Ace DLP-100	(M)	Jimmy's Happy/Jimmy's Blue	1960	30.00	60.00
Ace DLP-100	(M)	Jimmy's Happy/Jimmy's Blue	1960	70.00	140.00
		(The records for "Jimmy's Happy" and "Jimmy's Blue" have both the single album (1007 and 1008) and the double album (100) catalog numbers, making them interchangeable.)			
Ace 1011	(M)	My Best To You	1961	30.00	60.00
Ace 1014	(M)	Teenage Millionaire	1961	30.00	60.00
Ace 1026	(M)	Venus In Bluejeans	1962	35.00	70.00

Label		Title	Year	VG+	NM
Phillips PHM-200154	(M)	The Best Of Jimmy Clanton	1964	8.00	20.00
Phillips PHS-600154	(S)	The Best Of Jimmy Clanton	1964	10.00	25.00

CLAP

Nova Sol 1001	(S)	Have You Reached Yet?		100.00	200.00

CLAPTON, ERIC
Also refer to John Mayall.

RSO QD-4801	(Q)	461 Ocean Boulevard	1974	10.00	25.00
RSO QD-4806	(Q)	There's One In Every Crowd	1975	8.00	20.00
Mobile Fidelity 1-030	(S)	Slowhand	1980	10.00	25.00

CLARK, CHRIS

Motown 664	(M)	Soul Sounds	1967	5.00	12.00
Motown 664	(S)	Soul Sounds	1967	6.00	15.00

CLARK, CLAUDINE

Chancellor CHL-5029	(M)	Party Lights	1962	30.00	60.00

CLARK, DEE

Abner LP-2000	(M)	Dee Clark	1959	16.00	40.00
Abner SR-2000	(S)	Dee Clark	1959	30.000	60.00
Abner LP-2002	(M)	How About That	1960	16.00	40.00
Abner SR-2002	(S)	How About That	1960	30.00	60.00
Vee Jay LP-1019	(M)	You're Looking Good	1960	12.00	30.00
Vee Jay LP-1028	(M)	Dee Clark	1961	12.00	30.00
Vee Jay LP-1037	(M)	Hold On, It's Dee Clark	1961	10.00	25.00
Vee Jay SR-1037	(S)	Hold On, It's Dee Clark	1961	16.00	40.00
Vee Jay LP-1047	(M)	The Best Of Dee Clark	1964	8.00	20.00
Vee Jay SR-1047	(P)	The Best Of Dee Clark	1964	10.00	25.00

CLARK, GENE
Also refer to Dillard & Clark.

Columbia CL-2618	(M)	Gene Clark With The Gosdin Brothers	1967	10.00	25.00
Columbia CS-9418	(S)	Gene Clark With The Gosdin Brothers	1967	16.00	40.00

CLARK, PETULA

Imperial LP-9079	(M)	Pet Clark	1959	8.00	20.00
Imperial LP-12027	(S)	Pet Clark	1959	12.00	30.00
Warners W-1590	(M)	Downtown	1964	5.00	12.00
Warners WS-1590	(S)	Downtown	1964	6.00	15.00
Warners W-1598	(M)	I Know A Place	1965	5.00	12.00
Warners WS-1598	(S)	I Know A Place	1965	6.00	15.00
Warners W-1608	(M)	The World's Greatest International Hits	1965	5.00	12.00
Warners WS-1608	(S)	The World's Greatest International Hits	1965.	6.00	15.00
		(Warner albums above have grey labels.)			
Imperial LP-9281	(M)	Uptown With Petula Clark	1965	5.00	12.00
Imperial LP-12281	(S)	Uptown With Petula Clark	1965	6.00	15.00
Laurie LLP-2032	(M)	In Love	1965	5.00	12.00
Laurie LLPS-2032	(S)	In Love	1965	6.00	15.00
Laurie LLP-2043	(M)	Petula Clark Sings For Everybody	1966	5.00	12.00
Laurie LLPS-2043	(S)	Petula Clark Sings For Everybody	1966	6.00	15.00

CLARK SISTERS, THE

Coral CRL-57290	(M)	Beauty Shop Beat	1960	8.00	20.00
Coral CRL7-57290	(S)	Beauty Shop Beat	1960	10.00	25.00

CLARK FIVE, DAVE

Crown CLP-400	(M)	The Dave Clark Five With The Playbacks	1964	6.00	15.00
Crown CST-400	(S)	The Dave Clark Five With The Playbacks	1964	6.00	15.00
Crown CLP-473	(M)	Chaquita In Your Heart	1964	6.00	15.00
Crown CST-473	(E)	Chaquita In Your Heart	1964	6.00	15.00
Cortleight 1073	(M)	The Dave Clark Five With Ricky Astor	1964	8.00	20.00
Epic LN-24093	(M)	Glad All Over	1964	12.00	30.00
Epic BN-26093	(E)	Glad All Over	1964	10.00	25.00
		(The band has no instruments on the cover.)			
Epic LN-24093	(M)	Glad All Over	1964	10.00	25.00
Epic BN-26093	(E)	Glad All Over	1964	8.00	20.00
		(The band has their instruments on the cover.)			
Epic LN-24104	(M)	The Dave Clark Five Return	1964	10.00	25.00
Epic BN-26104	(E)	The Dave Clark Five Return	1964	8.00	20.00

Label		Title	Year	VG+	NM
Epic LN-24117	(M)	American Tour, Volume 1	1964	10.00	25.00
Epic BN-26117	(E)	American Tour, Volume 1	1964	8.00	20.00
Epic LN-24128	(M)	Coast To Coast	1965	10.00	25.00
Epic BN-26128	(E)	Coast To Coast	1965	8.00	20.00
Epic LN-24139	(M)	Weekend In London	1965	10.00	25.00
Epic BN-26139	(E)	Weekend In London	1965	8.00	20.00
Epic LN-24162	(M)	Having A Wild Weekend (Sdtk)	1965	10.00	25.00
Epic BN-26162	(E)	Having A Wild Weekend (Sdtk)	1965	8.00	20.00
Epic LN-24178	(M)	I Like It Like That	1965	10.00	25.00
Epic BN-26178	(E)	I Like It Like That	1965	8.00	20.00
Epic LN-24185	(M)	Dave Clark Five's Greatest Hits	1966	8.00	20.00
Epic BN-26185	(E)	Dave Clark Five's Greatest Hits	1966	6.00	15.00
Epic LN-24198	(M)	Try Too Hard	1966	8.00	20.00
Epic BN-26198	(E)	Try Too Hard	1966	6.00	15.00
Epic LN-24212	(M)	Satisfied With You	1966	8.00	20.00
Epic BN-26212	(E)	Satisfied With You	1966	6.00	15.00
Epic LN-24221	(M)	More Greatest Hits	1966	8.00	20.00
Epic BN-26221	(E)	More Greatest Hits	1966	6.00	15.00
Epic LN-24236	(M)	Five By Five	1967	6.00	15.00
Epic BN-26236	(S)	Five By Five	1967	10.00	25.00
Epic LN-24312	(M)	You Got What It Takes	1967	6.00	15.00
Epic BN-26312	(S)	You Got What It Takes	1967	10.00	25.00
Epic LN-24354	(M)	Everybody Knows	1968	8.00	20.00
Epic BN-26354	(S)	Everybody Knows	1968	10.00	25.00
Epic EG-30434	(P)	The Dave Clark Five	1971	30.00	60.00
Epic KEG-33459	(M)	Glad All Over Again	1975	10.00	25.00

CLASH, THE

Epic JE-35543	(S)	Give 'Em Enough Rope (Orange label)	1979	4.00	10.00
Epic 4E-36846 (10")	(S)	Black Market Clash	1980	4.00	10.00

CLAY, CASSIUS (MUHAMMAD ALI)

Columbia CL-2093	(M)	I Am The Greatest!	1963	14.00	35.00
Columbia CS-8893	(S)	I Am The Greatest!	1963	16.00	40.00

CLAY, JUDY, & BILLY VERA

Atlantic 8174	(M)	Storybook Children	1967	6.00	15.00
Atlantic 8174	(S)	Storybook Children	1967	8.00	20.00

CLAYTON, PAUL

Monument MLP-8017	(M)	Folk Singer	1965	5.00	12.00
Monument SLP-18017	(S)	Folk Singer	1965	6.00	15.00

CLEAR LIGHT

Elektra EKL-4011	(M)	Clear Light (With custom inner sleeve)	1967	6.00	15.00
Elektra EKS7-4011	(S)	Clear Light (With custom inner sleeve)	1967	8.00	20.00

CLEAVER, ELDRIDGE

More 4000	(S)	Soul On Wax	1968	6.00	15.00

CLEFTONES, THE

Gee GLP-705	(M)	Heart And Soul	1961	65.00	130.00
Gee SGLP-705	(S)	Heart And Soul	1961	100.00	200.00
Gee GLP-707	(M)	For Sentimental Reasons	1962	65.00	130.00
Gee SGLP-707	(S)	For Sentimental Reasons	1962	100.00	200.00

CLIFFORD, BUZZ

Columbia CL-1616	(M)	Baby Sittin' With Buzz	1961	12.00	30.00
Columbia CS-8416	(S)	Baby Sittin' With Buzz	1961	18.00	45.00

CLIFFORD, MIKE

United Arts. UAL-6409	(M)	For The Love Of Mike	1965	8.00	20.00
United Arts. UAS-6409	(P)	For The Love Of Mike	1965	10.00	25.00

CLINE, PATSY

Decca DL-8611	(M)	Patsy Cline	1957	20.00	50.00
		(Black & silver label.)			
Decca DL-4202	(M)	Patsy Cline Showcase	1960	10.00	25.00
Decca DL7-4202	(S)	Patsy Cline Showcase	1960	14.00	35.00
Decca DL-4282	(M)	Sentimentally Yours	1962	10.00	25.00
Decca DL7-4282	(S)	Sentimentally Yours	1962	14.00	35.00

Label		Title	Year	VG+	NM
Decca DXB-176	(M)	The Patsy Cline Story (With booklet)	1963	12.00	30.00
Decca DSXB7-176	(S)	The Patsy Cline Story (With booklet)	1963	16.00	40.00
Decca DL-4508	(M)	A Portrait Of Patsy Cline	1964	10.00	25.00
Decca DL7-4508	(S)	A Portrait Of Patsy Cline	1964	12.00	30.00
Decca DL-4586	(M)	That's How A Heartache Begins	1964	10.00	25.00
Decca DL7-4586	(S)	That's How A Heartache Begins	1964	12.00	30.00
		(Decca albums above have black labels with			
		"Mfrd. by Decca" beneath the rainbow.)			
Starday SLP-346	(M)	Gone, But Not Forgotten	1965	6.00	15.00
Decca DL-4854	(M)	Patsy Cline's Greatest Hits	1967	8.00	20.00
Decca DL7-4854	(S)	Patsy Cline's Greatest Hits	1967	10.00	25.00
Everest D-1200	(M)	Patsy Cline's Golden Hits	1962	6.00	15.00
Everest SD-1200	(S)	Patsy Cline's Golden Hits	1962	8.00	20.00
Everest D-1204	(M)	Encores	1963	6.00	15.00
Everest SD-1204	(S)	Encores	1963	8.00	20.00
Everest D-1217	(M)	In Memoriam	1963	6.00	15.00
Everest SD-1217	(S)	In Memoriam	1963	8.00	20.00
Everest D-1223	(M)	Patsy Cline-A Legend	1963	6.00	15.00
Everest SD-1223	(S)	Patsy Cline-A Legend	1963	8.00	20.00
Everest D-1229	(M)	Reflections	1964	6.00	15.00
Everest SD-1229	(S)	Reflections	1964	8.00	20.00

CLOONEY, ROSEMARY

Label		Title	Year	VG+	NM
Columbia CL-6338 (10")	(M)	White Christmas (Sdtk)	1954	16.00	40.00
Columbia CL-6282 (10")	(M)	Red Garters (Sdtk)	1954	16.00	40.00
Columbia CL-2525 (10")	(M)	Tenderly		16.00	40.00
Columbia CL-2567 (10")	(M)	Guys And Dolls (Studio Cast)		16.00	40.00
Columbia CL-2572 (10")	(M)	A Date With The King		16.00	40.00
MGM E-3153	(M)	Deep In My Heart (Sdtk; boxed set)	1954	20.00	50.00
MGM E-3153	(M)	Deep In My Heart (Sdtk)	1955	12.00	30.00
Columbia CL-585	(M)	Hollywood's Best	1955	8.00	20.00
Columbia CL-872	(M)	Blue Rose	1956	8.00	20.00
Columbia CL-969	(M)	Clooney Times	1957	8.00	20.00
Columbia CL-1006	(M)	Ring Around Rosie (With the Hi Lo's)	1957	8.00	20.00
Columbia CL-1230	(M)	Rosie's Greatest Hits	1958	8.00	20.00
Coral CRL-57266	(M)	Swing Around Rosie	1958	6.00	15.00
Coral CRL7-57266	(S)	Swing Around Rosie	1958	8.00	20.00
RCA LPM-1854	(M)	Fancy Meeting You Here	1958	6.00	15.00
RCA LSP-1854	(S)	Fancy Meeting You Here	1958	10.00	25.00
MGM E-3709	(M)	The Ferrers At Home		8.00	20.00
MGM E-3782	(M)	Hymns From The Heart	1959	6.00	15.00
MGM SE-3782	(S)	Hymns From The Heart	1959	8.00	20.00
MGM E-3834	(M)	Rosemary Clooney Swings Softly	1960	6.00	15.00
MGM SE-3834	(S)	Rosemary Clooney Swings Softly	1960	8.00	20.00
RCA LPM-2133	(M)	A Touch Of Tobasco	1960	6.00	15.00
RCA LSP-2133	(S)	A Touch Of Tobasco	1960	8.00	20.00
RCA LPM-2212	(M)	Clap Hands, Here Comes Rosie	1960	6.00	15.00
RCA LSP-2212	(S)	Clap Hands, Here Comes Rosie	1960	8.00	20.00
RCA LPM-2265	(M)	Rosie Solves The Swingin' Riddle	1961	6.00	15.00
RCA LSP-2265	(S)	Rosie Solves The Swingin' Riddle	1961	8.00	20.00
RCA LPM-2565	(M)	Country Hits From The Past	1963	5.00	12.00
RCA LSP-2565	(S)	Country Hits From The Past	1963	6.00	15.00
Reprise R-6088	(M)	Love	1963	5.00	12.00
Reprise R9-6088	(S)	Love	1963	6.00	15.00
Reprise R-6108	(M)	Thanks For Nothing	1964	5.00	12.00
Reprise R9-6108	(S)	Thanks For Nothing	1964	6.00	15.00
Capitol T-2300	(M)	That Travelin' Two Beat (With Bing Crosby)	1965	5.00	12.00
Capitol ST-2300	(S)	That Travelin' Two Beat (With Bing Crosby)	1965	6.00	15.00

CLOONEY SISTERS, THE (WITH ROSEMARY CLOONEY)

Label		Title	Year	VG+	NM
Epic LN-3160	(M)	The Clooney Sisters With Tony Pastor		12.00	30.00

CLOVERS, THE

Label		Title	Year	VG+	NM
Atlantic LP-1248	(M)	The Clovers	1956	180.00	300.00
Atlantic LP-8009	(M)	The Clovers (Black label)	1957	100.00	200.00
Poplar 1001	(M)	In Clover	1958	50.00	100.00
Atlantic LP-8034	(M)	Dance Party	1959	50.00	100.00
United Arts. UAL-3033	(M)	In Clover	1959	50.00	100.00
United Arts. UAS-6033	(E)	In Clover	1959	50.00	100.00
United Arts. UAL-3099	(M)	Love Potion Number Nine	1960	50.00	100.00
United Arts. UAS-6099	(S)	Love Potion Number Nine	1960	75.00	150.00

Patsy Cline, *Showcase*. Recorded with the Jordanaires, this was Ms Cline's first stereo recording and produced the cross-over hit, "Crazy." A great stylist, her untimely death in 1963 elevated her to mythic proportions in country circles. Widely regarded as the best female country vocalist of the post-war years, her influence is still strong.

The Cowsills, *On My Side*. Their first album for London, this was also their last gasp as a group. Spending one week at #200 in 1971, this is the rarest Cowsills album and, arguably, their shining moment as a pop group.

Label		Title	Year	VG+	NM
COASTERS, THE					
Atco 33-101	(M)	The Coasters (Yellow harp label)	1958	100.00	200.00
Atco 33-111	(M)	The Coasters' Greatest Hits	1959	50.00	100.00
Atco 33-123	(M)	One By One	1960	20.00	50.00
Atco SD-33-123	(S)	One By One	1960	35.00	70.00
Atco 33-135	(M)	Coast Along With The Coasters	1962	16.00	40.00
Atco SD-33-135	(P)	Coast Along With The Coasters	1962	30.00	60.00
COCHRAN, EDDIE					
Liberty LRP-3061	(M)	Singin' To My Baby (Green label)	1958	100.00	200.00
Liberty LRP-3172	(M)	Eddie Cochran/Memorial Album	1960	40.00	80.00
Liberty LRP-3220	(M)	Never To Be Forgotten	1962	30.00	60.00
Sunset SUM-1123	(M)	Summertime Blues	1966	10.00	25.00
United Arts. UAS-9959	(M)	Legendary Masters	1971	8.00	20.00
COCHRAN, WAYNE (& THE C.C. RIDERS)					
Chess LP-1519	(M)	Wayne Cochran	1967	6.00	15.00
Chess LPS-1519	(S)	Wayne Cochran	1967	8.00	20.00
King KS-1116	(S)	Livin' In A Bitch Of A World	1970	6.00	15.00
Bethlehem 10002	(S)	High And Ridin'	1970	6.00	15.00
Epic KE-30989	(S)	Cochran	1972	5.00	12.00
COHEN, SIDNEY					
Capitol TAO-2574	(M)	L.S.D.	1966	5.00	12.00
Capitol STAO-2574	(S)	L.S.D.	1966	6.00	15.00
COLDER, BEN (SHEB WOOLEY)					
MGM E-4117	(M)	Spoofing The Big Ones	1961	6.00	15.00
MGM SE-4117	(S)	Spoofing The Big Ones	1961	8.00	20.00
MGM E-4173	(M)	Ben Colder	1963	6.00	15.00
MGM SE-4173	(S)	Ben Colder	1963	8.00	20.00
MGM E-4421	(M)	Big Ben Strikes Again	1966	5.00	12.00
MGM SE-4421	(S)	Big Ben Strikes Again	1966	6.00	15.00
MGM E-4482	(M)	Wine, Women And Song	1967	5.00	12.00
MGM SE-4482	(S)	Wine, Women And Song	1967	6.00	15.00
COLE, JERRY					
Capitol T-2044	(M)	Outer Limits	1963	8.00	20.00
Capitol ST-2044	(S)	Outer Limits	1963	10.00	25.00
Capitol T-2061	(M)	Hot Rod Dance Party	1964	8.00	20.00
Capitol ST-2601	(S)	Hot Rod Dance Party	1964	10.00	25.00
Capitol T-2112	(M)	Surf Age	1964	14.00	35.00
Capitol ST-2112	(S)	Surf Age	1964	16.00	40.00
		(With bonus single "Thunder Wave" by Dick Dale.)			
COLE, NAT KING (KING COLE TRIO)					
Score SLP-4019	(M)	The King Cole Trio	1950	50.00	100.00
Capitol H-8 (10")	(M)	The King Cole Trio		14.00	35.00
Capitol H-29 (10")	(M)	The King Cole Trio, Volume 2	1950	14.00	35.00
Capitol H-59 (10")	(M)	The King Cole Trio, Volume 3	1950	14.00	35.00
Capitol H-139 (10")	(M)	The King Cole Trio, Volume 4	1951	14.00	35.00
Capitol H-156 (10")	(M)	Nat King Cole At The Piano	1952	14.00	35.00
Capitol H-177 (10")	(M)	The Nat King Cole Trio	1952	14.00	35.00
Capitol H-220 (10")	(M)	The Nat King Cole Trio	1952	14.00	35.00
Capitol H-332 (10")	(M)	Penthouse Serenade	1953	14.00	35.00
Capitol H-357 (10")	(M)	Unforgettable	1953	14.00	35.00
Capitol T-332	(M)	Penthouse Serenade	1955	8.00	20.00
Capitol T-357	(M)	Unforgettable	1953	8.00	20.00
Capitol T-420	(M)	Nat King Cole Sings For Two In Love	1954	8.00	20.00
Capitol W-514	(M)	Tenth Anniversary Album	1954	8.00	20.00
Capitol T-591	(M)	Vocal Classics	1955	8.00	20.00
Capitol T-592	(M)	Instrumental Classics	1955	8.00	20.00
Capitol T-680	(M)	Ballads Of The Day	1956	8.00	20.00
Capitol W-689	(M)	The Piano Style Of Nat King Cole	1956	8.00	20.00
Capitol W-782	(M)	After Midnight	1958	8.00	20.00
Capitol W-824	(M)	Love Is The Thing	1957	8.00	20.00
Capitol T-870	(M)	This Is Nat King Cole	1957	8.00	20.00
Capitol W-903	(M)	Just One Of Those Things	1957	8.00	20.00
Capitol W-993	(M)	Saint Louis Blues (Sdtk)	1958	12.00	30.00
		(Capitol albums above have turquoise labels.)			
Capitol W-1031	(M)	Cole Espanol	1958	5.00	12.00

Label		Title	Year	VG+	NM
Capitol W-1084	(M)	The Very Thought Of You	1958	5.00	12.00
Capitol SW-1084	(S)	The Very Thought Of You	1958	6.00	15.00
Capitol W-1120	(M)	Welcome To The Club	1959	5.00	12.00
Capitol SW-1120	(S)	Welcome To The Club	1959	6.00	15.00
Capitol W-1190	(M)	To Whom It May Concern	1959	5.00	12.00
Capitol SW-1190	(S)	To Whom It May Concern	1959	6.00	15.00
Capitol W-1220	(M)	A Mis Amigos	1959	5.00	12.00
Capitol SW-1220	(S)	A Mis Amigos	1959	6.00	15.00
Capitol T-1249	(M)	Every Time I Feel The Spirit	1960	5.00	12.00
Capitol ST-1249	(S)	Every Time I Feel The Spirit	1960	6.00	15.00
Capitol W-1331	(M)	Tell Me All About Yourself	1960	5.00	12.00
Capitol SW-1331	(S)	Tell Me All About Yourself	1960	6.00	15.00
Capitol WAK-1392	(M)	Wild Is Love	1960	5.00	12.00
Capitol SWAK-1392	(S)	Wild Is Love	1960	6.00	15.00
Capitol W-1444	(M)	The Magic Of Christmas	1960	5.00	12.00
Capitol SW-1444	(S)	The Magic Of Christmas	1960	6.00	15.00
Capitol W-1574	(M)	The Touch Of Your Lips	1961	5.00	12.00
Capitol ST-1574	(S)	The Touch Of Your Lips	1961	6.00	15.00
Capitol WCL-1613	(M)	The Nat King Cole Story (3 LPs)	1961	10.00	25.00
Capitol SWCL-1613	(P)	The Nat King Cole Story (3 LPs)	1961	10.00	25.00
		(Capitol albums above have black labels			
		with the Capitol logo on the left side.)			
Capitol W-1675	(M)	Nat King Cole Sings/George Shearing Plays	1962	5.00	12.00
Capitol ST-1675	(S)	Nat King Cole Sings/George Shearing Plays	1962	6.00	15.00
		(Includes the bonus album, PRO-2003.)			

COLE, NATALIE

Mobile Fidelity 1-032	(S)	Thankful		6.00	15.00
Mobile Fidelity 1-081	(S)	Natalie Cole Sings/George Shearing Plays		5.00	12.00

COLEMAN, EARL

Prestige 7045	(M)	Earl Coleman Returns	1956	16.00	40.00

COLLEGIANS, THE

Winley LP-6004	(M)	Sing Along With The Collegians		75.00	150.00

COLLINS, ALBERT

TCF Hall 8002	(M)	The Cool Sound Of Albert Collins	1965	12.00	30.00

COLLINS, TOMMY

Capitol T-776	(M)	Words And Music Country Style	1957	30.00	60.00
Capitol T-1125	(M)	Light Of The Lord	1959	20.00	50.00
Capitol T-1196	(M)	This Is Tommy Collins	1959	20.00	50.00
Capitol T-1436	(M)	Songs I Love To Sing	1961	16.00	40.00
Capitol ST-1436	(S)	Songs I Love To Sing	1961	20.00	50.00
Tower T-5021	(M)	Let's Live A Little	1966	8.00	20.00
Tower DT-5021	(E)	Let's Live A Little	1966	6.00	15.00
Tower T-5107	(M)	Shindig	1968	8.00	20.00
Tower DT-5107	(E)	Shindig	1968	6.00	15.00
Columbia CL-2510	(M)	The Dynamic Tommy Collins	1966	14.00	35.00
Columbia CS-9310	(S)	The Dynamic Tommy Collins	1966	20.00	50.00
Columbia CL-2778	(M)	On Tour	1968	14.00	35.00
Columbia CS-9578	(S)	On Tour	1968	20.00	50.00

COLWELL-WINFIELD BLUES BAND, THE

Forecast FVS-3056	(S)	Cold Wind Blues	1968	6.00	15.00
ZaZoo 1	(S)	Live Bust	1971	12.00	30.00

COMMON PEOPLE, THE

Capitol ST-266	(S)	Of The People, By The People	1969	20.00	50.00

COMO, PERRY

RCA LPC-109 (10")	(M)	Till The End Of Time	1948	16.00	40.00
RCA LPC-160 (10")	(M)	Perry Como	1948	16.00	40.00
RCA LPC-187 (10")	(M)	A Sentimental Date With Perry Como	1948	16.00	40.00
RCA LPM-1016	(M)	I Believe	1954	10.00	25.00
RCA LPM-1085	(M)	So Smooth	1955	10.00	25.00
RCA LPM-1137	(M)	I Believe	1955	10.00	25.00
RCA LPM-1176	(M)	Relaxing With Perry Como	1955	10.00	25.00
RCA LPC-1177	(M)	A Sentimental Date With Perry Como	1955	10.00	25.00
RCA LPM-1191	(M)	Hits From Broadway Shows	1956	10.00	25.00

Label		Title	Year	VG+	NM
RCA LPM-1463	(M)	We Get Letters	1957	10.00	25.00
RCA LPM-1243	(M)	Merry Christmas Music	1957	10.00	25.00
RCA LOP-1004	(M)	Saturday Night With Mr. C	1958	10.00	25.00
RCA LOP-1007	(M)	Como's Golden Records	1958	10.00	25.00
RCA LPM-1885	(M)	When You Come To The End Of The Day	1959	6.00	15.00
RCA LPM-2010	(M)	Como Swings	1959	6.00	15.00
RCA LSP-2010	(S)	Como Swings	1959	8.00	20.00
RCA LPM-2066	(M)	Season's Greetings	1959	6.00	15.00
RCA LSP-2066	(S)	Season's Greetings	1959	8.00	20.00
RCA LPM-2343	(M)	For The Young At Heart	1961	5.00	12.00
RCA LSP-2343	(S)	For The Young At Heart	1961	6.00	15.00
RCA LPM-2390	(M)	Sing To Me, Mr. C	1961	5.00	12.00
RCA LSP-2390	(S)	Sing To Me, Mr. C	1961	6.00	15.00
RCA LPM-2567	(M)	By Request	1962	5.00	12.00
RCA LSP-2567	(S)	By Request	1962	6.00	15.00
RCA LPM-2630	(M)	Irving Berlin's Songs For "Mr. President"	1962	5.00	12.00
RCA LSP-2630	(S)	Irving Berlin's Songs For "Mr. President"	1962	6.00	15.00
Columbia KOL-5870	(M)	Mr. President (Sdtk; fold-open jacket)	1962	8.00	20.00
Columbia KOS-2270	(S)	Mr. President (Sdtk; fold-open jacket)	1962	10.00	25.00
		(Mono RCA albums above have "Long Play" on the bottom of the label; stereo albums have "Living Stereo" on the bottom.)			

COMPETITORS, THE

Label		Title	Year	VG+	NM
Dot DLP-3542	(M)	Hits Of The Street And Strip	1963	16.00	40.00
Dot DLP-25542	(S)	Hits Of The Street And Strip	1963	20.00	50.00

COMSTOCK, BOBBY, & THE COUNTS

Label		Title	Year	VG+	NM
Ascot ALM-13026	(M)	Out Of Sight	1966	8.00	20.00
Ascot ALS-16026	(S)	Out Of Sight	1966	10.00	25.00

CONDELLO (MICHAEL CONDELLO)

Label		Title	Year	VG+	NM
Scepter SP-542	(M)	Phase 1	1968	8.00	20.00
Scepter SPS-542	(S)	Phase 1	1968	10.00	25.00

CONLEY, ARTHUR

Label		Title	Year	VG+	NM
Atco 33-215	(M)	Sweet Soul Music	1967	10.00	25.00
Atco SD-33-215	(S)	Sweet Soul Music	1967	12.00	30.00
Atco 33-220	(M)	Shake, Rattle And Roll	1967	8.00	20.00
Atco SD-33-220	(S)	Shake, Rattle And Roll	1967	10.00	25.00
Atco SD-33-243	(S)	Soul Directions	1968	8.00	20.00
Atco SD-33-276	(S)	More Sweet Soul	1969	8.00	20.00

CONNOR, CHRIS

Label		Title	Year	VG+	NM
Bethlehem 1001 (10")	(M)	Lullabys Of Birdland	1954	16.00	40.00
Bethlehem 1002 (10")	(M)	Lullabys For Lovers	1954	16.00	40.00
Bethlehem BCP-20	(M)	This Is Chris	1955	12.00	30.00
Bethlehem BCP-56	(M)	Chris	1956	12.00	30.00
Bethlehem BCP-6004	(M)	Lullabys Of Birdland	1954	12.00	30.00
Bethlehem BCP-6005	(M)	Lullabys For Lovers	1954	12.00	30.00
Bethlehem BCP-6006	(M)	Bethlehem Girls	1956	12.00	30.00
		(Bethlehem albums above have maroon labels.)			
Atlantic 8014	(M)	I Miss You So	1956	12.00	30.00
Atlantic 1240	(M)	He Loves Me, He Loves Me Not	1957	12.00	30.00
Atlantic 1228	(M)	Chris Connor	1957	12.00	30.00
Atlantic 1286	(M)	A Jazz Date With Chris Connor	1957	12.00	30.00
Atlantic 2-601	(M)	The George Gershwin Almanac Of Songs	1957	16.00	40.00
Atlantic 1290	(M)	Chris Craft	1958	12.00	30.00
		(Atlantic albums above have black labels.)			
Atlantic 1307	(M)	Ballads Of The Sad Cafe	1959	10.00	25.00
Atlantic SD-1307	(S)	Ballads Of The Sad Cafe	1959	16.00	40.00
Atlantic 8032	(M)	Witchcraft	1959	10.00	25.00
Atlantic SD-8032	(S)	Witchcraft	1959	16.00	40.00
Atlantic 8040	(M)	Chris In Person	1959	10.00	25.00
Atlantic SD-8040	(S)	Chris In Person	1959	16.00	40.00
Roulette R-52068	(M)	Two's Company	1960	10.00	25.00
Roulette SR-52068	(S)	Two's Company	1960	16.00	40.00
Atlantic 8046	(M)	A Portrait Of Chris	1960	10.00	25.00
Atlantic SD-8046	(S)	A Portrait Of Chris	1960	14.00	35.00
Atlantic 8049	(M)	Double Exposure	1961	10.00	25.00
Atlantic SD-8049	(S)	Double Exposure	1961	14.00	35.00

Label		Title	Year	VG+	NM
Atlantic 8061	(M)	Free Spirits	1962	8.00	20.00
Atlantic SD-8061	(S)	Free Spirits	1962	12.00	30.00
		(Mono Atlantic albums above have orange and			
		puple labels; stereo albums have green and blue			
		labels. Both mono and stereo have white fans.)			
FM 300	(M)	Chris Connor At The Village Gate	1963	6.00	15.00
FM S-300	(S)	Chris Connor At The Village Gate	1963	8.00	20.00
FM 312	(M)	A Weekend In Paris	1964	6.00	15.00
FM S-312	(S)	A Weekend In Paris	1964	8.00	20.00
ABC-Paramount 529	(M)	Gentle Bossa Nova	1965	6.00	15.00
ABC-Paramount S-529	(S)	Gentle Bossa Nova	1965	8.00	20.00
ABC-Paramount 585	(M)	Now	1966	6.00	15.00
ABC-Paramount S-585	(S)	Now	1966	8.00	20.00

CONRIED, HANS

Label		Title	Year	VG+	NM
RCA LPM-1923	(M)	Monster Rally	1959	6.00	15.00
RCA LSP-1923	(S)	Monster Rally	1959	8.00	20.00

CONTOURS, THE

Label		Title	Year	VG+	NM
Gordy 901	(M)	Do You Love Me	1962	40.00	80.00

COODER, RY

Label		Title	Year	VG+	NM
Reprise RS-6402	(S)	Ry Cooder	1970	6.00	15.00
Reprise MS-2117	(S)	Boomer's Story	1972	5.00	12.00
Reprise MS-2052	(S)	Into The Purple Valley	1972	5.00	12.00
Mobile Fidelity 1-085	(S)	Jazz		8.00	20.00

COOKE, SAM

Label		Title	Year	VG+	NM
Keen A-2001	(M)	Sam Cooke	1958	20.00	50.00
Keen 2003	(M)	Encore	1958	16.00	40.00
Keen 2004	(M)	Tribute To The Lady— Billie Holiday	1959	16.00	40.00
Keen 86101	(M)	Hit Kit	1959	16.00	40.00
Keen 86103	(M)	I Thank God	1960	14.00	35.00
Keen 86106	(M)	The Wonderful World Of Sam Cooke	1960	14.00	35.00
RCA LPM-2221	(M)	Cooke's Tour	1960	12.00	30.00
RCA LSP-2221	(S)	Cooke's Tour	1960	14.00	35.00
RCA LPM-2236	(M)	Hits Of The 50's	1960	12.00	30.00
RCA LSP-2236	(S)	Hits Of The 50's	1960	14.00	35.00
RCA LPM-2293	(M)	Swing Low	1960	12.00	30.00
RCA LSP-2293	(S)	Swing Low	1960	14.00	35.00
RCA LPM-2392	(M)	My Kind Of Blues	1961	10.00	25.00
RCA LSP-2392	(S)	My Kind Of Blues	1961	12.00	30.00
RCA LPM-2555	(M)	Twistin' The Night Away	1962	12.00	30.00
RCA LSP-2555	(S)	Twistin' The Night Away	1962	14.00	35.00
RCA LPM-2625	(M)	The Best Of Sam Cooke	1962	8.00	20.00
RCA LSP-2625	(E)	The Best Of Sam Cooke	1962	8.00	20.00
RCA LPM-2673	(M)	Mr. Soul	1963	8.00	20.00
RCA LSP-2673	(S)	Mr. Soul	1963	10.00	25.00
RCA LPM-2709	(M)	Night Beat	1963	8.00	20.00
RCA LSP-2709	(S)	Night Beat	1963	10.00	25.00
		(Mono RCA albums above have "Long Play"			
		on the bottom of the label; stereo albums			
		have "Living Stereo" on the bottom.)			
RCA LPM-2899	(M)	Ain't That Good News	1964	6.00	15.00
RCA LSP-2899	(S)	Ain't That Good News	1964	8.00	20.00
RCA LPM-2970	(M)	Sam Cooke At The Copa	1964	6.00	15.00
RCA LSP-2970	(S)	Sam Cooke At The Copa	1964	8.00	20.00
RCA LPM-3367	(M)	Shake	1965	6.00	15.00
RCA LSP-3367	(S)	Shake	1965	8.00	20.00
RCA LPM-3373	(M)	The Best Of Sam Cooke, Volume 2	1965	6.00	15.00
RCA LSP-3373	(P)	The Best Of Sam Cooke, Volume 2	1965	8.00	20.00
RCA LPM-3435	(M)	Try A Little Love	1965	6.00	15.00
RCA LSP-3435	(S)	Try A Little Love	1965	8.00	20.00
RCA LPM-3517	(M)	The Unforgettable Sam Cooke	1966	6.00	15.00
RCA LSP-3517	(S)	The Unforgettable Sam Cooke	1966	8.00	20.00
RCA LSP-3991	(S)	The Man Who Invented Soul	1968	6.00	15.00
		(RCA albums above have black labels.)			

COOL, CALVIN, & THE SURF KNOBS

Label		Title	Year	VG+	NM
Charter CLP-103	(M)	The Surfer's Beat	1963	10.00	25.00
Charter CLS-103	(S)	The Surfer's Beat	1963	12.00	30.00

Label		Title	Year	VG+	NM
COOLEY, SPADE					
RCA LPM-3041 (10")	(M)	Roy Rogers Souvenir Album	1952	20.00	50.00
Columbia HL-9007 (10")	(M)	Sagebrush Swing		35.00	70.00
Decca DL-5563 (10")	(M)	Dance-O-Rama	1955	35.00	70.00
Roulette R-25145	(M)	Fidoolin'	1961	8.00	20.00
Roulette SR-25145	(M)	Fidoolin'	1961	10.00	25.00
COOLIDGE, RITA					
Nautilus 16	(S)	Anytime, Anywhere		6.00	15.00
COOPER, ALICE					
Straight STS-1051	(S)	Pretties For You	1969	10.00	25.00
Straight WS-1845	(S)	Easy Action	1970	8.00	20.00
		("Alice Cooper" is in black letters on the cover)			
Warners WS-1883	(S)	Love It to Death	1971	10.00	25.00
		(Cooper's right thumb is visible on the cover.)			
Warners BS-2567	(S)	Killer (With calendar and poster)	1971	8.00	20.00
Warners BS-2623	(S)	School's Out (With panties)	1972	8.00	20.00
Warners BS4-2685	(Q)	Billion Dollar Babies	1974	8.00	20.00
Warners BS4-2748	(Q)	Muscle Of Love	1973	8.00	20.00
Mobile Fidelity 1-063	(S)	Welcome To My Nightmare	1980	8.00	20.00
COOPER, LES, & THE SOUL ROCKERS					
Everlast ELP-202	(M)	Wiggle Wobble	1963	16.00	40.00
CORBIN, HAROLD					
Roulette R-52079	(M)	Soul Brother	1961	8.00	20.00
Roulette SR-52079	(S)	Soul Brother	1961	10.00	25.00
CORNELLS, THE					
Garex 100	(M)	Beach Bound	1963	40.00	80.00
CORPORATION, THE					
Age of Aquarius 4150	(S)	Get On Our Swing	1969	10.00	25.00
Age of Aquarius 4250	(S)	Hassels In My Mind	1969	10.00	25.00
CORPORATION, THE					
Capitol ST-175	(S)	The Corporation	1969	8.00	20.00
CORTEZ, DAVE "BABY"					
RCA LPM-2099	(M)	Dave "Baby" Cortez And His Happy Organ	1959	10.00	25.00
RCA LSP-2099	(S)	Dave "Baby" Cortez And His Happy Organ	1959	14.00	35.00
Clock C-331	(M)	Dave "Baby" Cortez	1960	12.00	30.00
Chess LP-1473	(M)	Rinky Dink	1962	10.00	25.00
Roulette R-25298	(M)	Organ Shindig	1965	5.00	12.00
Roulette SR-25298	(S)	Organ Shindig	1965	6.00	15.00
Roulette R-25315	(M)	Tweety Pie	1966	5.00	12.00
Roulette SR-25315	(S)	Tweety Pie	1966	6.00	15.00
Roulette R-25328	(M)	In Orbit With Dave "Baby" Cortez	1966	5.00	12.00
Roulette SR-25328	(S)	In Orbit With Dave "Baby" Cortez	1966	6.00	15.00
COSTELLO, ELVIS (& THE ATTRACTIONS)					
Columbia JC-35037	(S)	My Aim Is True (Yellow back cover)	1977	5.00	12.00
Columbia JC-35331	(S)	This Year's Model ("Costello" label)	1978	6.00	15.00
Columbia JC-35709	(S)	Armed Forces	1979	6.00	15.00
		(Issued with a "Live At Hollywood High" EP.)			
Columbia HC-48157	(S)	Imperial Bedroom (1/2 speed)	1982	16.00	40.00
COTTON BLUES BAND, JAMES					
Folkways FT-3023	(M)	The James Cotton Blues Band	1967	5.00	12.00
Folkways FTS-3023	(S)	The James Cotton Blues Band	1967	6.00	15.00
Vanguard VSD-79283	(S)	Cut You Loose	1968	6.00	15.00
Folkways FTS-3038	(S)	Pure Cotton	1968	6.00	15.00
Forecast FTS-3060	(S)	Cotton In Your Ears	1969	6.00	15.00
COUNT FIVE, THE					
Double Shot DSM-1001	(M)	Psychotic Reaction	1966	10.00	25.00
Double Shot DSS-5001	(P)	Psychotic Reaction	1966	10.00	25.00
		(Yellow & black label.)			

Label		Title	Year	VG+	NM
COUNTRY JOE & THE FISH					
Vanguard VRS-9244	(M)	Electric Music For The Mind And Body	1967	6.00	15.00
Vanguard VSD-79244	(S)	Electric Music For The Mind And Body	1967	6.00	15.00
Vanguard VRS-9266	(M)	I-Feel-Like-I'm-Fixin'-To-Die	1967	6.00	15.00
Vanguard VSD-79266	(S)	I-Feel-Like-I'm-Fixin'-To-Die	1967	6.00	15.00
		(Issued with a poster, priced separately below.)			
		I-Feel-Like-I'm-Fixin'-To-Die Poster		4.00	10.00
		(Giant fold-open "Fish Game" poster.)			
Vanguard VSD-79277	(S)	Together	1968	5.00	12.00
Vanguard VSD-6545	(S)	Country Joe And The Fish's Greatest Hits	1969	4.00	10.00
Vanguard VSD-79299	(S)	Here We Are Again	1969	5.00	12.00
Vanguard VSD-6555	(S)	C.J. Fish	1970	4.00	10.00
ABC S-OC-13	(S)	Zachariah (Sdtk)	1970	5.00	12.00
Cotillion CT3-500	(S)	Woodstock (Sdtk; 3 LPs)	1970	8.00	20.00
COUSINS, THE					
Parkway P-7005	(M)	Music Of The Strip	1961	6.00	15.00
Parkway SP-7005	(S)	Music Of The Strip	1961	8.00	20.00
COVAY, DON					
Atlantic 8104	(M)	Mercy	1965	8.00	20.00
Atlantic SD-8104	(S)	Mercy	1965	10.00	25.00
Atlantic 8120	(M)	See Saw	1966	8.00	20.00
Atlantic SD-8120	(S)	See Saw	1966	10.00	25.00
Atlantic SD-8237	(S)	The House Of Blue Lights	1969	6.00	15.00
COWSILLS, THE					
MGM E-4498	(M)	The Cowsills	1967	4.00	10.00
MGM SE-4498	(S)	The Cowsills	1967	5.00	12.00
MGM SE-4534	(S)	We Can Fly	1968	4.00	10.00
MGM SE-4554	(S)	Captain Sad And His Ship Of Fools	1968	4.00	10.00
Wing SRW-16354	(S)	The Cowsills Plus The Lincoln Park Zoo	1968	4.00	10.00
MGM SE-4619	(S)	The Cowsills In Concert	1969	4.00	10.00
MGM SE-4639	(S)	II By II	1970	5.00	12.00
London 587	(S)	On My Side	1971	6.00	15.00
CRADDOCK, BILLY CRASH					
King 912	(M)	I'm Tore Up	1964	20.00	50.00
CRAIN, JIMMY					
Ray-O LP-2005	(M)	Miles To Go		50.00	100.00
CRANE, BOB					
Epic LN-246224	(M)	The Funny Side Of TV	1967	5.00	12.00
Epic BN-26224	(S)	The Funny Side Of TV	1967	6.00	15.00
CRAWFORD, JOHNNY					
Del-Fi LP-1220	(M)	The Captivating Johnny Crawford	1962	12.00	30.00
Del-Fi LP-1223	(M)	A Young Man's Fancy	1963	6.00	15.00
Del-Fi ST-1223	(S)	A Young Man's Fancy	1963	8.00	20.00
Del-Fi LP-1224	(M)	Rumors	1963	6.00	15.00
Del-Fi ST-1224	(S)	Rumors	1963	8.00	20.00
Del-Fi LP-1229	(M)	His Greatest Hits	1963	6.00	15.00
Del-Fi ST-1229	(S)	His Greatest Hits	1963	8.00	20.00
Del-Fi LP-1248	(M)	Greatest Hits, Volume 2	1964	6.00	15.00
Del-Fi ST-1248	(S)	Greatest Hits, Volume 2	1964	8.00	20.00
CRAYTON, PEE WEE					
Crown CLP-5175	(M)	Pee Wee Crayton	1959	20.00	50.00
CRAZY ELEPHANT					
Bell 6034	(S)	Crazy Elephant	1969	6.00	15.00
CREAM					
Atco 33-206	(M)	Fresh Cream	1967	12.00	30.00
Atco SD-33-206	(S)	Fresh Cream	1967	12.00	30.00
		(Originally released with "I Feel Free.")			
Atco 33-206	(M)	Fresh Cream	1967	6.00	15.00
Atco SD-33-206	(S)	Fresh Cream	1967	8.00	20.00
Atco 33-232	(M)	Disraeli Gears	1967	8.00	20.00
Atco SD-33-232	(S)	Disraeli Gears	1967	6.00	15.00

Label		Title	Year	VG+	NM
Atco SD-33-245	(S)	The Savage Seven (Sdtk)	1968	6.00	15.00
Atco SD-2-700	(S)	Wheels Of Fire	1968	8.00	20.00
Atco SD-7001	(S)	Goodbye	1969	6.00	15.00
		(Mono Atco albums above have gold & grey labels;			
		stereo albums have purple & brown labels.)			
Mobile Fidelity 2-066	(S)	Wheels Of Fire		8.00	20.00

CREATION OF SUNLIGHT
Windi 1001	(S)	Creation Of Sunlight		60.00	120.00

CREATURES, THE
RCA LPM-1923	(M)	Monster Rally	1959	12.00	30.00
RCA LSP-1923	(S)	Monster Rally	1959	16.00	40.00

CREEDENCE CLEARWATER REVIVAL (THE GOLLIWOGS)
Fantasy F-8382	(S)	Creedence Clearwater Revival	1968	6.00	15.00
		(Without the blurb for "Suzie Q" on the cover.)			
Fantasy F-8387	(P)	Bayou Country	1969	5.00	12.00
Fantasy F-8393	(S)	Green River	1969	5.00	12.00
Fantasy F-8397	(S)	Willy And The Poor Boys	1969	5.00	12.00
Fantasy F-8402	(S)	Cosmo's Factory	1970	5.00	12.00
Fantasy F-8410	(S)	Pendulum	1970	5.00	12.00
Fantasy F-9404	(S)	Mardi Gras	1972	5.00	12.00
		(Fantasy albums above have blue labels.)			
Liberty	(S)	Creedence Clearwater Revival		12.00	30.00
Liberty	(P)	Bayou Country		12.00	30.00
Liberty	(S)	Green River		12.00	30.00
Liberty	(S)	Willy And The Poor Boys		12.00	30.00
Liberty	(S)	Cosmo's Factory		12.00	30.00
Liberty	(S)	Pendulum		12.00	30.00
Liberty	(S)	Mardi Gras		12.00	30.00
		(CCR albums on Liberty are record club issues.)			
Mobile Fidelity 1-037	(S)	Cosmo's Factory	1979	10.00	25.00

CREME SODA
Trinity CST-11	(S)	Tricky Zingers (Group photo cover)		35.00	70.00

CRESCENDOS, THE
Guest Star G-1453	(M)	Oh Julie		12.00	30.00

CRESTS, THE
Coed LPC-901	(M)	The Crests Sing All The Biggies	1960	100.00	200.00
Coed LPC-904	(M)	The Best Of The Crests	1961	80.00	160.00
Coed LPS-904	(S)	The Best Of The Crests	1961	—	—
		(A stereo cover has been found,			
		although no stereo record.)			

CREW CUTS, THE
Mercury MG-20067	(M)	The Crew Cuts Go Longhair	1954	16.00	40.00
Mercury MG-20140	(M)	The Crew Cuts On The Campus	1954	16.00	40.00
Mercury MG-20143	(M)	Crew Cut Capers	1954	16.00	40.00
Mercury MG-20199	(M)	Music Ala Carte	1955	16.00	40.00
Mercury MG-21044	(M)	Rock And Roll Bash	1955	20.00	50.00
Wing MGW-12177	(M)	The Crew Cuts		8.00	20.00
Wing MGW-12180	(M)	High School Favorites		8.00	20.00
RCA LPM-1933	(M)	Surprise Package	1958	8.00	20.00
RCA LSP-1933	(S)	Surprise Package	1958	10.00	25.00
RCA LPM-2037	(M)	The Crew Cuts Sing	1959	8.00	20.00
RCA LSP-2037	(S)	The Crew Cuts Sing	1959	10.00	25.00
RCA LPM-2067	(M)	You Must Have Been A Beautiful Baby	1960	8.00	20.00
RCA LSP-2067	(S)	You Must Have Been A Beautiful Baby	1960	10.00	25.00
Camay CA-1002	(M)	The Crew Cuts Sing Folk		8.00	20.00
Camay CA-3002	(S)	The Crew Cuts Sing Folk		10.00	25.00

CRICKETS, THE
Liberty LRP-3272	(M)	Something Old, Something New	1962	20.00	50.00
Liberty LST-7272	(S)	Something Old, Something New	1962	30.00	60.00
Liberty LRP-7351	(M)	California Sun	1964	16.00	40.00
Liberty LST-7351	(S)	California Sun	1964	20.00	50.00
Barnaby Z-30268	(S)	Rockin' 50's Rock 'N' Roll	1970	8.00	20.00
Vertigo VEL-1020	(S)	Remnants	1973	8.00	20.00

Label		Title	Year	VG+	NM
CRISS, PETER					
Casablanca NBLP-7122	(S)	Peter Criss (With poster)	1978	6.00	15.00
Casablanca NBPIX-7122	(S)	Peter Criss (Picture disc)	1979	10.00	25.00
Casablanca NBPIX-7240	(S)	Out Of Control	1980	8.00	20.00
CRITTERS, THE					
Kapp KL-1485	(M)	Younger Girl	1966	6.00	15.00
Kapp KS-3485	(S)	Younger Girl	1966	8.00	20.00
CROCE, JIM					
Capitol ST-315	(S)	Croce	1969	6.00	15.00
Command QD-40006	(Q)	You Don't Mess Around With Jim	1974	6.00	15.00
Command QD-40007	(Q)	Life And Times	1974	6.00	15.00
Command QD-40008	(Q)	I Got A Name	1974	6.00	15.00
Command QD-40020	(Q)	Photographs And Memories	1974	6.00	15.00
Mobile Fidelity 1-079	(S)	You Don't Mess Around With Jim	1980	6.00	15.00
CROME CYRCUS, THE					
Command 925	(S)	Love Cycle	1968	8.00	20.00
CROSBY, BING					
Columbia CL-6027 (10")	(M)	Crosby Classics, Volume 1	1949	10.00	25.00
Columbia CL-6105 (10")	(M)	Crosby Classics, Volume 2	1950	10.00	25.00
Columbia CL-2502 (10")	(M)	Der Bingle		10.00	25.00
"X" 4250 (10")	(M)	Young Bing Crosby		10.00	25.00
Vik 1000	(M)	Young Bing Crosby		8.00	20.00
Decca DL-5001 (10")	(M)	Jerry Kern Songs	1949	10.00	25.00
Decca DL-5010 (10")	(M)	Foster	1950	10.00	25.00
Decca DL-5011 (10")	(M)	El Bingo	1950	10.00	25.00
Decca DL-5020 (10")	(M)	Christmas Greetings	1950	10.00	25.00
Decca DL-5037 (10")	(M)	St. Patrick's Day	1950	10.00	25.00
Decca DL-5039 (10")	(M)	St. Valentine's Day	1950	10.00	25.00
Decca DL-5042 (10")	(M)	Blue Skies	1950	10.00	25.00
Decca DL-5052 (10")	(M)	The Bells Of St. Mary's (Sdtk)	1950	10.00	25.00
Decca DL-5063 (10")	(M)	Don't Fence Me In	1950	10.00	25.00
Decca DL-5064 (10")	(M)	Bing Sings Cole Porter	1950	10.00	25.00
Decca DL-5081 (10")	(M)	Bing Sings George Gershwin	1950	10.00	25.00
Decca DL-5092 (10")	(M)	Holiday Inn (Sdtk)	1950	10.00	25.00
Decca DL-5105 (10")	(M)	Blue Of The Night	1950	10.00	25.00
Decca DL-5107 (10")	(M)	Cowboy Songs	1950	10.00	25.00
Decca DL-5119 (10")	(M)	Drifting And Dreaming	1950	10.00	25.00
Decca DL-5126 (10")	(M)	Stardust	1950	10.00	25.00
Decca DL-5129 (10")	(M)	Cowboy Songs, Volume 2	1950	10.00	25.00
Decca DL-5220 (10")	(M)	Bing Sings Hits	1950	10.00	25.00
Decca DL-5272 (10")	(M)	Top O' The Morning (Sdtk)	1950	10.00	25.00
Decca DL-5284 (10")	(M)	Mr. Music (Sdtk)	1950	20.00	50.00
Decca DL-5298 (10")	(M)	Hits From Broadway Shows	1951	10.00	25.00
Decca DL-5299 (10")	(M)	Favorite Hawaiian Songs	1951	10.00	25.00
Decca DL-5302 (10")	(M)	Go West, Young Man	1951	10.00	25.00
Decca DL-5310 (10")	(M)	Way Back Home	1951	10.00	25.00
Decca DL-5323 (10")	(M)	Bing And The Dixieland Bands	1951	10.00	25.00
Decca DL-5326 (10")	(M)	Yours Is My Heart Alone	1951	10.00	25.00
Decca DL-5331 (10")	(M)	Country Style	1951	10.00	25.00
Decca DL-5340 (10")	(M)	Down Memory Lane	1951	10.00	25.00
Decca DL-5343 (10")	(M)	Down Memory Lane, Volume 2	1951	10.00	25.00
Decca DL-5390 (10")	(M)	Bing And Connee Boswell	1951	10.00	25.00
Decca DL-5403 (10")	(M)	When Irish Eyes Are Smiling	1952	10.00	25.00
Decca DL-5444 (10")	(M)	The Road To Bali (Sdtk)	1952	10.00	25.00
Decca DL-5499 (10")	(M)	Song Hits Of Paris	1954	10.00	25.00
Decca DL-5556 (10")	(M)	Country Girl	1953	10.00	25.00
Decca DL-6000 (10")	(M)	The Small One	1955	10.00	25.00
Decca DL-6001 (10")	(M)	Ichabod Crane	1955	10.00	25.00
Decca DL-6009 (10")	(M)	Two For Tonight (Sdtk)	1956	10.00	25.00
Decca DL-6010 (10")	(M)	Rhythm On The Range (Sdtk)	1956	10.00	25.00
Decca DL-6011 (10")	(M)	Waikiki Wedding (Sdtk)	1956	10.00	25.00
Decca DL-6015 (10")	(M)	The Road To Singapore	1956	10.00	25.00
Decca DL-6013 (10")	(M)	The Star Maker (Sdtk)	1956	10.00	25.00
Decca DL-8020	(M)	A Man Without A Country	1956	6.00	15.00
Decca DL-8083	(M)	White Christmas (Sdtk)	1956	6.00	15.00
Decca DL-8110	(M)	Lullabye Time	1956	6.00	15.00
Decca DL-8128	(M)	Merry Christmas	1956	6.00	15.00

Label		Title	Year	VG+	NM
Decca DL-8207	(M)	Shillelaghs And Shamrocks	1956	6.00	15.00
Decca DL-8210	(M)	Home On The Range	1956	6.00	15.00
Decca DL-8262	(M)	When Irish Eyes Are Smiling	1956	6.00	15.00
Decca DL-8268	(M)	Drifting And Dreaming	1956	6.00	15.00
Decca DL-8269	(M)	Blue Hawaii	1956	6.00	15.00
Decca DL-8272	(M)	High Tor (Sdtk)	1956	50.00	100.00
Capitol W-750	(M)	High Society (Sdtk)	1956	10.00	25.00
RCA LPM-1473	(M)	Bing With A Beat	1957	6.00	15.00
Decca DL-8352	(M)	Songs I Wish I Had Sung	1958	6.00	15.00
Decca DL-8365	(M)	Twilight On The Trail	1958	6.00	15.00
Decca DL-8374	(M)	Some Fine Old Chestnuts	1958	6.00	15.00
Decca DL-8419	(M)	A Christmas Sing Around The World	1958	6.00	15.00
Decca DL-8493	(M)	Bing And The Dixieland Bands	1958	6.00	15.00
Decca DL-8575	(M)	New Tricks	1958	6.00	15.00
Decca DL-8687	(M)	Around The World	1958	6.00	15.00
Decca DL-8780	(M)	Bing In Paris	1958	6.00	15.00
Decca DL-8781	(M)	That Christmas Feeling	1958	6.00	15.00
		(Decca albums above have black & silver labels.)			
United Arts. UAL-4001	(M)	Paris Holiday (Sdtk)	1958	12.00	30.00
RCA LPM-2071	(M)	Young Bing Crosby	1959	6.00	15.00
Brunswick BL-54005	(M)	The Voice Of Bing In The 30s	1959	6.00	15.00
Decca DL-8846	(M)	In A Little Spanish Town	1959	6.00	15.00
Decca DL-9054	(M)	A Musical Autobiography 1927-1934	1959	8.00	20.00
Decca DL-9064	(M)	A Musical Autobiography 1934-1941	1959	8.00	20.00
Decca DL-9067	(M)	A Musical Autobiography 1941-1944	1959	8.00	20.00
Decca DL-9077	(M)	A Musical Autobiography 1944-1947	1959	8.00	20.00
Decca DL-9078	(M)	A Musical Autobiography 1947-1953	1959	8.00	20.00
Decca DL-9106	(M)	Ichabod	1959	6.00	15.00
RCA LPM-2314	(M)	High Time (Sdtk)	1960	8.00	20.00
RCA LSP-2314	(S)	High Time (Sdtk)	1960	12.00	30.00
Decca DL-4086	(M)	My Golden Favorites	1961	6.00	15.00
Decca DL-4250	(M)	Easy To Remember	1962	6.00	15.00
Decca DL-4251	(M)	Pennies From Heaven	1962	6.00	15.00
Decca DL-4252	(M)	Pocketful Of Dreams	1962	6.00	15.00
Decca DL-4253	(M)	East Side Of Heaven	1962	6.00	15.00
Decca DL-4254	(M)	The Road Begins	1962	6.00	15.00
Decca DL-4255	(M)	Only Forever	1962	6.00	15.00
Decca DL-4256	(M)	Holiday Inn	1962	6.00	15.00
Decca DL-4257	(M)	Swinging On A Star	1962	6.00	15.00
Decca DL-4258	(M)	Accentuate The Positive	1962	6.00	15.00
Decca DL-4259	(M)	Blue Skies	1962	6.00	15.00
Decca DL-4260	(M)	But Beautiful	1962	6.00	15.00
Decca DL-4261	(M)	Sunshine Cake	1962	6.00	15.00
Decca DL-4262	(M)	Cool Of The Evening	1962	6.00	15.00
Decca DL-4263	(M)	Zing A Little Zong	1962	6.00	15.00
Decca DL-4264	(M)	Anything Goes	1962	6.00	15.00
Decca DL-4281	(M)	Holiday In Europe	1962	5.00	12.00
Decca DL7-4281	(S)	Holiday In Europe	1962	6.00	15.00
Decca DL-4283	(M)	The Small One	1962	5.00	12.00
Decca DL7-4283	(S)	The Small One	1962	6.00	15.00
Decca DL-4415	(M)	Songs Everybody Knows	1964	5.00	12.00
Decca DL7-4415	(S)	Songs Everybody Knows	1964	6.00	15.00
Decca DX-184	(M)	The Best Of Bing Crosby	1965	6.00	15.00
Decca DXS7-184	(S)	The Best Of Bing Crosby	1965	6.00	15.00
		(Decca albums above have black labels with			
		"Mfrd By Decca" beneath the rainbow.)			
Verve V-2020	(M)	Bing Sings Whilst Bergman Swings		6.00	15.00
Warners W-1363	(M)	Join With Bing And Sing Along	1960	5.00	12.00
Warners WS-1363	(S)	Join With Bing And Sing Along	1960	6.00	15.00
Warners 2W-1401	(M)	101 Gang Songs	1961	8.00	20.00
Warners 2WS-1401	(S)	101 Gang Songs	1961	8.00	20.00
Warners W-1422	(M)	Join Bing In A Gang Sing Along	1961	5.00	12.00
Warners WS-1422	(S)	Join Bing In A Gang Sing Along	1961	6.00	15.00
Warners W-1435	(M)	Join Bing And Sing Along	1962	5.00	12.00
Warners WS-1435	(S)	Join Bing And Sing Along	1962	6.00	15.00
Warners W-1482	(M)	On The Happy Side	1962	5.00	12.00
Warners WS-1482	(S)	On The Happy Side	1962	6.00	15.00
Warners W-1484	(M)	I Wish You A Merry Christmas	1962	5.00	12.00
Warners WS-1484	(S)	I Wish You A Merry Christmas	1962	6.00	15.00
		(Warner albums above have grey labels.)			

Label		Title	Year	VG+	NM
Liberty LOM-16002	(M)	The Road To Hong Kong (Sdtk)	1962	8.00	20.00
Liberty LOS-17002	(S)	The Road To Hong Kong (Sdtk)	1962	12.00	30.00
Reprise R-6106	(M)	Return To Paradise Islands	1964	5.00	12.00
Reprise R9-6106	(S)	Return To Paradise Islands	1964	6.00	15.00
MGM E-3882	(M)	Bing And Satchmo	1960	6.00	15.00
MGM SE-3882	(S)	Bing And Satchmo	1960	8.00	20.00
MGM E-3890	(M)	Senor Bing	1961	5.00	12.00
MGM SE-3890	(S)	Senor Bing	1961	6.00	15.00
MGM E-4129	(M)	The Great Standards	1963	5.00	12.00
MGM SE-4129	(S)	The Great Standards	1963	6.00	15.00
MGM E-4203	(M)	The Very Best Of Bing Crosby	1964	5.00	12.00
MGM SE-4203	(S)	The Very Best Of Bing Crosby	1964	6.00	15.00
Metro M-523	(M)	Bing Crosby	1965	4.00	10.00
Metro MS-523	(S)	Bing Crosby	1965	5.00	12.00
Capitol T-2346	(M)	Great Country Hits	1965	4.00	10.00
Capitol ST-2346	(S)	Great Country Hits	1965	5.00	12.00
Columbia C2L-43	(M)	Bing In Hollywood	1967	6.00	15.00

CROSBY, STILLS, NASH & YOUNG

Mobile Fidelity 1-088	(S)	Deja Vu		8.00	20.00

CROTHERS, SCATMAN

Tops 1511	(M)	Rock 'N Roll With Scatman	1956	12.00	30.00
Craftsman 8036	(M)	Gone With Scatman	1960	10.00	25.00

CRUDUP, ARTHUR "BIG BOY"

Fire 103	(M)	Mean Ol' Frisco	1960	75.00	150.00
Delmark DS-614	(S)	Look On Yonders Wall	1969	10.00	25.00
Delmark DS-621	(S)	Crudup's Mood	1969	10.00	25.00
RCA LVP-573	(M)	Father Of Rock And Roll	1971	8.00	20.00

CRYAN' SHAMES, THE

Columbia CL-2589	(M)	Sugar And Spice	1966	6.00	15.00
Columbia CS-9389	(P)	Sugar And Spice ("360 Sound" label)	1966	8.00	20.00
Columbia CL-9586	(M)	A Scratch In The Sky	1967	5.00	12.00
Columbia CS-9586	(S)	A Scratch In The Sky ("360 Sound" label)	1967	6.00	15.00
Columbia CS-9719	(S)	Synthesis	1969	4.00	10.00

CRYSTALS, THE

Philles PHLP-4000	(M)	Twist Uptown	1962	90.00	180.00
Philles PHLP-4001	(M)	He's A Rebel	1963	80.00	160.00
Philles PHLP-4003	(M)	The Crystals Sing The Greatest Hits	1963	80.00	160.00

CUMBERLAND THREE, THE

Roulette R-25121	(M)	Folk Scene, U.S.A.	1960	6.00	15.00
Roulette SR-25121	(S)	Folk Scene, U.S.A.	1960	8.00	20.00
Roulette R-25132	(M)	Civil War Almanac/The Yankees	1960	5.00	12.00
Roulette SR-25132	(S)	Civil War Almanac/The Yankees	1960	6.00	15.00
Roulette R-25133	(M)	Civil War Almanac/The Rebels	1960	5.00	12.00
Roulette SR-25133	(S)	Civil War Almanac/The Rebels	1960	6.00	15.00

CURTIS, KEN

Capitol T-2418	(M)	Gunsmoke's Festus	1965	5.00	12.00
Capitol ST-2418	(S)	Gunsmoke's Festus	1965	6.00	15.00

CURTIS, SONNY

Imperial LP-9276	(M)	Beatle Hits Flamenco Guitar Style	1964	10.00	25.00
Imperial LP-12276	(S)	Beatle Hits Flamenco Guitar Style	1964	12.00	30.00

CYKLE, THE

Label 9-261	(S)	The Cykle	1969	180.00	300.00

CYMBAL, JOHNNY

Kapp KL-1324	(M)	Mr. Bass Man	1963	10.00	25.00
Kapp KS-3324	(S)	Mr. Bass Man	1963	14.00	35.00

CYRKLE, THE

Columbia CL-2544	(M)	Red Rubber Ball	1966	8.00	20.00
Columbia CS-9344	(S)	Red Rubber Ball	1966	10.00	25.00

Label		Title	Year	VG+	NM
DALE & GRACE					
Montel/Michelle LP-100	(M)	I'm Leaving It Up To You	1964	35.00	70.00
DALE, DICK (& HIS DEL-TONES)					
Also refer to Jerry Cole.					
Deltone LPM-1001	(M)	Surfer's Choice	1962	16.00	40.00
Deltone T-1886	(M)	Surfer's Choice	1962	10.00	25.00
Deltone DT-1886	(E)	Surfer's Choice	1962	8.00	20.00
Capitol T-1930	(M)	King Of The Surf Guitar	1963	16.00	40.00
Capitol ST-1930	(S)	King Of The Surf Guitar	1963	20.00	50.00
Capitol T-2002	(M)	Checkered Flag	1963	14.00	35.00
Capitol ST-2002	(S)	Checkered Flag	1963	16.00	40.00
Capitol T-2053	(M)	Mr. Eliminator	1964	14.00	35.00
Capitol ST-2053	(S)	Mr. Eliminator	1964	16.00	40.00
Capitol T-2111	(M)	Summer Surf	1964	20.00	50.00
Capitol ST-2111	(S)	Summer Surf	1964	30.00	60.00
		(With bonus single "Racing Waves" by Jerry Cole.)			
Capitol T-2293	(M)	Rock Out/Live At Ciro's	1965	14.00	35.00
Capitol ST-2293	(S)	Rock Out/Live At Ciro's	1965	16.00	40.00
DALE, JIMMY					
Decca DL-8429	(M)	Rock Pretty Baby		14.00	35.00
DAMITA JO					
ABC 378	(M)	The Big Fifteen	1961	10.00	25.00
Mercury MGC-201	(M)	Damita Jo	1961	8.00	20.00
Mercury MG-20642	(M)	I'll Save The Last Dance For You	1961	6.00	15.00
Mercury SR-60642	(S)	I'll Save The Last Dance For You	1961	8.00	20.00
Mercury MG-20734	(M)	Sing A Country Song	1962	6.00	15.00
Mercury SR-60734	(S)	Sing A Country Song	1962	8.00	20.00
Mercury MG-20703	(M)	Damita Jo At The Diplomat	1962	6.00	15.00
Mercury SR-60703	(S)	Damita Jo At The Diplomat	1962	8.00	20.00
Vee Jay LP-1137	(M)	Damita Jo Sings	1965	5.00	12.00
Vee Jay SR-1137	(S)	Damita Jo Sings	1965	6.00	15.00
Epic LN-24131	(M)	If You Go Away	1965	4.00	10.00
Epic BN-26131	(S)	If You Go Away	1965	5.00	12.00
Epic LN-24244	(M)	This Is Damita Jo	1967	4.00	10.00
Epic BN-26244	(S)	This Is Damita Jo	1967	5.00	12.00
Ranwood 8037	(S)	Miss Damita Jo	1968	5.00	12.00
DAMONE, VIC					
MGM E-86 (10")	(M)	Rich, Young And Pretty (Sdtk)	1951	20.00	50.00
Mercury MG-25202	(M)	Athena (Sdtk)	1954	50.00	100.00
MGM E-3153	(M)	Deep In My Heart (Sdtk; boxed set)	1954	20.00	50.00
MGM E-3153	(M)	Deep In My Heart (Sdtk)	1955	12.00	30.00
MGM E-3236	(M)	Rich, Young And Pretty (Sdtk)	1955	12.00	30.00
Mercury MG-20193	(M)	The Voice Of Vic Damone	1956	8.00	20.00
Columbia CL-900	(M)	That Towering Feeling!	1956	8.00	20.00
Columbia CL-950	(M)	The Stingiest Man In Town (Sdtk)	1956	16.00	40.00
Columbia CL-1113	(M)	The Gift Of Love (Sdtk)	1958	30.00	60.00
Columbia CL-1219	(M)	Closer Than A Kiss	1959	5.00	12.00
Columbia CS-8019	(S)	Closer Than A Kiss	1959	6.00	15.00
Columbia CL-1246	(M)	Angela Mia	1959	5.00	12.00
Columbia CS-8046	(S)	Angela Mia	1959	6.00	15.00
Columbia CL-1369	(M)	This Game Of Love	1959	5.00	12.00
Columbia CS-8169	(S)	This Game Of Love	1959	6.00	15.00
Columbia CL-1573	(M)	On The Swingin' Side	1961	5.00	12.00
Columbia CS-8373	(S)	On The Swingin' Side	1961	6.00	15.00
		(Columbia albums above have six black and white "eye" logos on each label.)			
Capitol T-1646	(M)	Linger Awhile With Vic Damone	1962	4.00	10.00
Capitol ST-1646	(S)	Linger Awhile With Vic Damone	1962	5.00	12.00

Label		Title	Year	VG+	NM
Capitol T-1691	(M)	Strange Enchantment	1962	4.00	10.00
Capitol ST-1691	(S)	Strange Enchantment	1962	5.00	12.00
Capitol T-1748	(M)	The Lively Ones	1962	4.00	10.00
Capitol ST-1748	(S)	The Lively Ones	1962	5.00	12.00
Capitol T-1811	(M)	My Baby Loves To Swing	1963	4.00	10.00
Capitol ST-1811	(S)	My Baby Loves To Swing	1963	5.00	12.00
Capitol T-1944	(M)	The Liveliest	1963	4.00	10.00
Capitol ST-1944	(S)	The Liveliest	1963	5.00	12.00
Capitol T-2123	(M)	On The Street Where You Live	1964	4.00	10.00
Capitol ST-2123	(S)	On The Street Where You Live	1964	5.00	12.00

DANTE & THE EVERGREENS

Label		Title	Year	VG+	NM
Madison MA-1002	(M)	Dante & The Evergreens	1961	150.00	250.00

DARIN, BOBBY

Label		Title	Year	VG+	NM
Atco 22-102	(M)	Bobby Darin	1958	30.00	60.00
Atco 33-104	(M)	That's All	1959	12.00	30.00
Atco SD-33-104	(S)	That's All	1959	16.00	40.00
Atco 33-115	(M)	This Is Darin	1960	12.00	30.00
Atco SD-33-115	(S)	This Is Darin	1960	16.00	40.00
Atco 33-122	(M)	Darin At The Copa	1960	10.00	25.00
Atco 33-122	(S)	Darin At The Copa	1960	14.00	35.00
Atco SP-1001	(M)	For Teenagers Only	1960	20.00	50.00
Atco 33-125	(M)	The 25th Of December	1960	8.00	20.00
Atco SD-33-125	(S)	The 25th Of December	1960	12.00	30.00
Colpix CP-507	(M)	Pepe (Sdtk)	1960	8.00	20.00
Colpix SCP-507	(S)	Pepe (Sdtk)	1960	12.00	30.00
Atco 33-126	(M)	Two Of A Kind	1961	8.00	20.00
Atco SD-33-126	(S)	Two Of A Kind	1961	10.00	25.00
Atco 33-131	(M)	The Bobby Darin Story	1961	10.00	25.00
Atco SD-33-131	(S)	The Bobby Darin Story (White cover)	1961	12.00	30.00
Atco 33-134	(M)	Love Swings	1961	8.00	20.00
Atco SD-33-134	(S)	Love Swings	1961	10.00	25.00
		(Atco albums above have yellow harp labels.)			
Atco 33-138	(M)	Twist With Bobby Darin	1961	8.00	20.00
Atco SD-33-138	(S)	Twist With Bobby Darin	1961	10.00	25.00
Atco 33-140	(M)	Bobby Darin Sings Ray Charles	1962	8.00	20.00
Atco SD-33-140	(S)	Bobby Darin Sings Ray Charles	1962	10.00	25.00
Atco 33-146	(M)	Things And Other Things	1962	8.00	20.00
Atco SD-33-146	(S)	Things And Other Things	1962	10.00	25.00
Atco 33-124	(M)	It's You Or No One	1963	8.00	20.00
Atco SD-33-124	(S)	It's You Or No One	1963	10.00	25.00
Atco 33-167	(M)	Winners	1964	6.00	15.00
Atco SD-33-167	(S)	Winners	1964	8.00	20.00
Dot DLP-9011	(M)	State Fair (Sdtk)	1962	8.00	20.00
Dot DLP-25011	(S)	State Fair (Sdtk)	1962	10.00	25.00
Capitol T-1791	(M)	Oh! Look At Me Now	1962	6.00	15.00
Capitol ST-1791	(S)	Oh! Look At Me Now	1962	8.00	20.00
Capitol T-1826	(M)	Earthy	1963	6.00	15.00
Capitol ST-1826	(S)	Earthy	1963	8.00	20.00
Capitol T-1866	(M)	You're The Reason I'm Living	1963	6.00	15.00
Capitol ST-1866	(S)	You're The Reason I'm Living	1963	8.00	20.00
Capitol T-1942	(M)	18 Yellow Roses	1963	6.00	15.00
Capitol ST-1942	(S)	18 Yellow Roses	1963	8.00	20.00
Capitol T-2007	(M)	Golden Folk Hits	1963	6.00	15.00
Capitol ST-2007	(S)	Golden Folk Hits	1963	8.00	20.00
Capitol T-2194	(M)	From "Hello Dolly" To "Goodbye Charlie"	1964	6.00	15.00
Capitol ST-2194	(S)	From "Hello Dolly" To "Goodbye Charlie"	1964	8.00	20.00
Decca DL-9119	(M)	The Lively Set (Sdtk)	1964	8.00	20.00
Decca DL7-9119	(S)	The Lively Set (Sdtk)	1964	10.00	25.00
Capitol T-2322	(M)	Venice Blue	1965	6.00	15.00
Capitol ST-2322	(S)	Venice Blue	1965	8.00	20.00
Capitol T-2571	(M)	The Best Of Bobby Darin	1966	6.00	15.00
Capitol ST-2571	(S)	The Best Of Bobby Darin	1966	8.00	20.00
Clarion 603	(M)	Clementine	1964	6.00	15.00
Clarion 603	(S)	Clementine	1964	8.00	20.00
Atlantic 8121	(M)	The Shadow Of Your Smile	1966	6.00	15.00
Atlantic SD-8121	(S)	The Shadow Of Your Smile	1966	8.00	20.00
Atlantic 8126	(M)	In A Broadway Bag	1966	6.00	15.00
Atlantic SD-8126	(S)	In A Broadway Bag	1966	8.00	20.00

Label		Title	Year	VG+	NM
Atlantic 8135	(M)	If I Were A Carpenter	1966	6.00	15.00
Atlantic SD-8135	(S)	If I Were A Carpenter	1966	10.00	25.00
Atlantic 8142	(M)	Inside Out	1967	6.00	15.00
Atlantic SD-8142	(S)	Inside Out	1967	8.00	20.00
Atlantic 8154	(M)	Bobby Darin Sings Doctor Doolittle	1967	6.00	15.00
Atlantic SD-8154	(S)	Bobby Darin Sings Doctor Doolittle	1967	8.00	20.00
Direction 1936	(S)	Born Walden Robert Cassotto	1968	8.00	20.00
Direction 1937	(S)	Commitment	1969	8.00	20.00
Motown M-753L	(S)	Bobby Darin	1972	5.00	12.00

DARLING, DENVER

Audio Lab 107	(M)	Denver Darling		20.00	50.00

DARLING, ERIC

Vanguard VRS-9099	(M)	True Religion	1961	6.00	15.00
Vanguard VRS-9131	(M)	Train Time	1962	6.00	15.00

DARTELLS, THE

Dot DLP-3522	(M)	Hot Pastrami	1963	8.00	20.00
Dot DLP-25522	(S)	Hot Pastrami	1963	10.00	25.00

DARTS, THE

Del-Fi DF-1244	(M)	Hollywood Drag	1963	8.00	20.00
Del-Fi DFST-1244	(S)	Hollywood Drag	1963	10.00	25.00

DASHIEL, BUD (& THE KINSMEN)
Also refer to Bud & Travis.

Warners W-1429	(M)	Bud Dashiell With The Kinsmen	1961	5.00	12.00
Warners WS-1429	(S)	Bud Dashiell With The Kinsmen	1961	6.00	15.00
Warners W-1432	(M)	Live Concert Extraordinaire	1962	5.00	12.00
Warners WS-1432	(S)	Live Concert Extraordinaire	1962	6.00	15.00
Warners WS-1731	(S)	I Think It's Gonna Rain Today	1968	4.00	10.00

DAVEY & THE BADMEN

K.R.W. WA-63054	(M)	Wanted		35.00	70.00

DAVID

U.M.C. 124	(S)	Another Day, Another Lifetime	1968	12.00	30.00

DAVIS, JIMMIE

Decca DL-5500 (10")	(M)	Jimmie Davis		20.00	50.00
Decca DL-8896	(M)	You Are My Sunshine		12.00	30.00

DAVIS, JOHNNY

King 626	(M)	Johnny "Scat" Davis	1959	12.00	30.00

DAVIS, JR., SAMMY

Decca DL-8118	(M)	Starring Sammy Davis, Jr.	1955	6.00	15.00
Decca DL-8170	(M)	Just For Lovers	1955	6.00	15.00
Decca DL-9032	(M)	Mr. Wonderful (Sdtk)	1956	16.00	40.00
Decca DL-8351	(M)	Here's Looking At You		8.00	20.00
Decca DL-8490	(M)	Boy Meets Girl (With Carmen McRae)		8.00	20.00
Decca DL-8641	(M)	It's All Over But The Swingin'		6.00	15.00
Decca DL-8676	(M)	Mood To Be Wooed		6.00	15.00
Decca DL-8779	(M)	All The Way And Then Some		6.00	15.00
Decca DL7-8779	(M)	All The Way And Then Some		6.00	15.00
Decca DL-8841	(M)	Sammy Davis, Jr. At Town Hall	1959	5.00	12.00
Decca DL7-8841	(S)	Sammy Davis, Jr. At Town Hall	1959	6.00	15.00
Decca DL-8854	(M)	Porgy And Bess	1959	5.00	12.00
Decca DL7-8854	(S)	Porgy And Bess	1959	6.00	15.00
Decca DL-8921	(M)	Sammy Awards	1960	5.00	12.00
Decca DL7-8921	(S)	Sammy Awards	1960	6.00	15.00
Decca DL-8981	(M)	I Got A Right To Swing	1960	5.00	12.00
Decca DL7-8981	(S)	I Got A Right To Swing	1960	6.00	15.00
		(Decca albums above have black & silver labels.)			

DAVIS, SKEETER

RCA LPM-2197	(M)	I'll Sing You A Song And Harmonize, Too	1960	10.00	25.00
RCA LPM-2327	(M)	Here's The Answer	1961	10.00	25.00
RCA LPM-2529	(M)	Duets (With Porter Wagoner)	1962	8.00	20.00
RCA LSP-2529	(S)	Duets (With Porter Wagoner)	1962	10.00	25.00

Label		Title	Year	VG+	NM
RCA LPM-2699	(M)	The End Of The World	1962	8.00	20.00
RCA LSP-2699	(S)	The End Of The World	1962	10.00	25.00
		(Mono RCA albums above have "Long Play"			
		on the bottom of the label. Stereo albums			
		have "Living Stereo" on the bottom.)			
RCA LPM-2736	(M)	Cloudy, With Occasional Tears	1963	6.00	15.00
RCA LPM-2736	(S)	Cloudy, With Occasional Tears	1963	8.00	20.00
RCA LPM-2980	(M)	Let Me Get Close To You	1964	6.00	15.00
RCA LSP-2980	(S)	Let Me Get Close To You	1964	8.00	20.00
RCA LPM-3374	(M)	The Best Of Skeeter Davis	1965	5.00	12.00
RCA LSP-3374	(P)	The Best Of Skeeter Davis	1965	6.00	15.00
RCA LPM-3382	(M)	Written By The Stars	1965	6.00	15.00
RCA LSP-3382	(S)	Written By The Stars	1965	8.00	20.00
RCA LPM-3463	(M)	Skeeter Sings Standards	1965	6.00	15.00
RCA LSP-3463	(S)	Skeeter Sings Standards	1965	8.00	20.00
RCA LPM-3567	(M)	Singin' In The Summer Sun	1966	6.00	15.00
RCA LSP-3567	(S)	Singin' In The Summer Sun	1966	8.00	20.00
RCA LPM-3667	(M)	My Heart's In The Country	1966	6.00	15.00
RCA LSP-3667	(S)	My Heart's In The Country	1966	8.00	20.00
RCA LPM-3763	(M)	Hand In Hand With Jesus	1967	6.00	15.00
RCA LSP-3763	(S)	Hand In Hand With Jesus	1967	8.00	20.00
RCA LPM-3790	(M)	Skeeter Davis Sings Buddy Holly	1967	10.00	25.00
RCA LSP-3790	(S)	Skeeter Davis Sings Buddy Holly	1967	12.00	30.00
RCA LPM-3876	(M)	What Does It Take	1967	6.00	15.00
RCA LSP-3876	(S)	What Does It Take	1967	8.00	20.00
RCA LSP-3960	(S)	Why So Lonely	1968	6.00	15.00
		(RCA albums above have black labels.)			

DAVIS GROUP, SPENCER

Label		Title	Year	VG+	NM
United Arts. UAL-3578	(M)	Gimme Some Lovin'	1967	12.00	30.00
United Arts. UAS-6578	(E)	Gimme Some Lovin'	1967	10.00	25.00
United Arts. UAL-3589	(M)	I'm A Man	1967	12.00	30.00
United Arts. UAS-6589	(P)	I'm A Man	1967	12.00	30.00
United Arts. UAL-3641	(M)	Spencer Davis' Greatest Hits	1968	8.00	20.00
United Arts. UAS-6641	(P)	Spencer Davis' Greatest Hits	1968	8.00	20.00
United Arts. UAS-6652	(S)	With Their New Face On	1968	5.00	12.00
United Arts. UAS-6691	(S)	Heavies	1969	5.00	12.00

DAWE, TIM

Label		Title	Year	VG+	NM
Straight STS-1058	(S)	Penrod	1969	10.00	25.00
Warners WS-1841	(S)	Penrod	1970	5.00	12.00

DAY, BOBBY

Label		Title	Year	VG+	NM
Class LP-5002	(M)	Rockin' With Robin	1959	75.00	150.00

DAY, CORA LEE

Label		Title	Year	VG+	NM
Roulette R-52048	(M)	My Crying Hour	1960	5.00	12.00
Roulette SR-52048	(S)	My Crying Hour	1960	6.00	15.00

DAY, DORIS

Label		Title	Year	VG+	NM
Columbia CL-6071 (10")	(M)	You're My Thrill	1949	14.00	35.00
Columbia CL-6106 (10")	(M)	Young Man With A Horn (Sdtk)	1950	16.00	40.00
Columbia CL-6149 (10")	(M)	Tea For Two (Sdtk)	1950	16.00	40.00
Columbia CL-6168 (10")	(M)	Lullaby Of Broadway (Sdtk)	1951	16.00	40.00
Columbia CL-6186 (10")	(M)	On Moonlight Bay (Sdtk)	1951	16.00	40.00
Columbia CL-6198 (10")	(M)	I'll See You In My Dreams (Sdtk)	1951	16.00	40.00
Columbia CL-6248 (10")	(M)	By The Light Of The Silvery Moon (Sdtk)	1953	16.00	40.00
Columbia CL-6273 (10")	(M)	Calamity Jane (Sdtk)	1953	16.00	40.00
Columbia CL-6339 (10")	(M)	Young At Heart (With Frank Sinatra)	1955	8.00	20.00
Columbia CL-2518 (10")	(M)	Lights, Cameras, Action		10.00	25.00
Columbia CL-2530 (10")	(M)	Boys And Girls Together		10.00	25.00
Columbia CL-2534 (10")	(M)	Hot Canaries (With Peggy Lee)		12.00	30.00
Columbia CL-582	(M)	Young Man With A Horn	1954	10.00	25.00
Columbia CL-624	(M)	Day Dreams	1955	10.00	25.00
Columbia CL-710	(M)	Love Me Or Leave Me (Sdtk)	1955	16.00	40.00
Columbia CL-749	(M)	Day In Hollywood	1955	10.00	25.00
Columbia CL-942	(M)	Day By Day	1957	10.00	25.00
Columbia OL-5210	(M)	The Pajama Game (Sdtk)	1957	10.00	25.00
Columbia CL-1210	(M)	Doris Day's Greatest Hits	1958	10.00	25.00
Columbia C2L-5	(M)	Hooray For Hollywood	1959	10.00	25.00
Columbia C2S-5	(S)	Hooray For Hollywood	1959	12.00	30.00

Label		Title	Year	VG+	NM
Columbia CL-1266	(M)	Hooray For Hollywood, Volume 1	1959	5.00	12.00
Columbia CS-8066	(S)	Hooray For Hollywood, Volume 1	1959	6.00	15.00
Columbia CL-1267	(M)	Hooray For Hollywood, Volume 2	1959	5.00	12.00
Columbia CS-8067	(S)	Hooray For Hollywood, Volume 2	1959	6.00	15.00
Columbia CL-1278	(M)	Cuttin' Capers	1959	6.00	15.00
Columbia CS-8078	(S)	Cuttin' Capers	1959	8.00	20.00
Columbia CL-1289	(M)	Day By Night	1959	6.00	15.00
Columbia CS-8089	(S)	Day By Night	1959	8.00	20.00
Columbia DD-1	(M)	Listen To Day	1960	6.00	15.00
Columbia DDS-1	(S)	Listen To Day	1960	8.00	20.00
Columbia CL-1434	(M)	What Every Girl Should Know	1960	6.00	15.00
Columbia CS-8234	(S)	What Every Girl Should Know	1960	8.00	20.00
Columbia CL-1461	(M)	Show Time	1960	6.00	15.00
Columbia CS-8261	(S)	Show Time	1960	8.00	20.00
Columbia CL-1660	(M)	I Have Dreamed	1961	6.00	15.00
Columbia CS-8460	(S)	I Have Dreamed	1961	8.00	20.00
Columbia OL-5860	(M)	Jumbo (Sdtk)	1962	6.00	15.00
Columbia OS-2260	(S)	Jumbo (Sdtk)	1962	8.00	20.00
Columbia CL-1752	(M)	Duet	1962	6.00	15.00
Columbia CS-8552	(S)	Duet	1962	8.00	20.00

(Columbia albums above have six black "eye" logos on each label.)

DAY BLINDNESS

Label		Title	Year	VG+	NM
Studio 10 DBX-101	(S)	Day Blindness	1969	12.00	30.00

DE-FENDERS, THE

Label		Title	Year	VG+	NM
World Pacific WP-1810	(M)	The Big Ones	1963	10.00	25.00
World Pacific WPS-1810	(S)	The Big Ones	1963	12.00	30.00
World Pacific WPS-1810	(S)	The Big Ones (Green vinyl)	1963	35.00	70.00
World Pacific WPS-1810	(S)	The Big Ones (Red vinyl)	1963	35.00	70.00
Del-Fi DFLP-1242	(M)	Drag Beat	1963	6.00	15.00
Del-Fi DFS-1242	(S)	Drag Beat	1963	8.00	20.00

DEAD BOYS, THE

Label		Title	Year	VG+	NM
Sire SR-6038	(S)	Young, Loud And Snotty	1977	10.00	25.00
Sire SRK-6054	(S)	We Have Come For Your Children	1978	10.00	25.00

DEAD KENNEDYS, THE

Label		Title	Year	VG+	NM
Alt. Tentacles	(S)	Fresh Fruit For Rotting Vegetables	1981	6.00	15.00

(Orange cover with a photo of an old band.)

DEADLY ONES, THE

Label		Title	Year	VG+	NM
Vee Jay LP-1090	(M)	It's Monster Surfing Time	1964	10.00	25.00
Vee Jay VS-1090	(S)	It's Monster Surfing Time	1964	12.00	30.00

DEAL, BILL, & THE RHONDELS

Label		Title	Year	VG+	NM
Heritage HTS-35006	(P)	The Best Of Bill Deal & The Rhondels	1969	5.00	12.00
Heritage HTS-35003	(P)	Vintage Rock	1969	5.00	12.00

DEBRIS

Label		Title	Year	VG+	NM
Static Disposal	(S)	Debris		14.00	35.00

DeCARLO, YVONNE

Label		Title	Year	VG+	NM
Masterseal	(M)	Yvonne DeCarlo Sings		12.00	30.00

DeCASTRO SISTERS, THE

Label		Title	Year	VG+	NM
Abbott 5002	(M)	The DeCastro Sisters		20.00	50.00
Capitol T-1402	(M)	The DeCastros Sing	1960	8.00	20.00
Capitol ST-1402	(S)	The DeCastros Sing	1960	10.00	25.00
Capitol T-1501	(M)	The Rockin' Beat	1961	8.00	20.00
Capitol ST-1501	(S)	The Rockin' Beat	1961	10.00	25.00

DEE, DAVE; DOZY, BEAKY, MICK & TICH

Label		Title	Year	VG+	NM
Fontana MGF-27567	(M)	Greatest Hits	1967	10.00	25.00
Fontana SRF-67567	(P)	Greatest Hits	1967	12.00	30.00
Imperial LP-12402	(P)	Time To Take Off	1968	10.00	25.00

DEE, JOEY (& THE STARLIGHTERS)

Label		Title	Year	VG+	NM
Roulette R-25166	(M)	Doin' The Twist	1961	10.00	25.00
Roulette SR-25166	(S)	Doin' The Twist	1961	12.00	30.00

Label		Title	Year	VG+	NM
Roulette R-25168	(M)	Hey, Let's Twist (Sdtk)	1962	8.00	20.00
Roulette SR-25168	(S)	Hey' Let's Twist (Sdtk)	1962	10.00	25.00
Roulette R-25171	(M)	All The World Is Twistin'	1962	8.00	20.00
Roulette SR-25171	(S)	All The World Is Twistin'	1962	10.00	25.00
Roulette R-25173	(M)	Back To The Peppermint Lounge Twistin'	1962	8.00	20.00
Roulette SR-25173	(S)	Back To The Peppermint Lounge Twistin'	1962	10.00	25.00
Roulette R-25182	(M)	Two Tickets To Paris (Sdtk)	1962	6.00	15.00
Roulette SR-25182	(S)	Two Tickets To Paris (Sdtk)	1962	8.00	20.00
Roulette R-25197	(M)	Joey Dee	1963	6.00	15.00
Roulette SR-25197	(S)	Joey Dee	1963	8.00	20.00
Roulette R-25221	(M)	Dance, Dance, Dance	1963	6.00	15.00
Roulette SR-25221	(S)	Dance, Dance, Dance	1963	8.00	20.00

DEEP, THE

Label		Title	Year	VG+	NM
Parkway 7051	(M)	Psychedelic Moods	1966	20.00	50.00
Parkway 7051	(S)	Psychedelic Moods	1966	35.00	70.00

DEEP PURPLE

Label		Title	Year	VG+	NM
Tetragrammaton 102	(S)	Shades Of Deep Purple	1968	6.00	15.00
Tetragrammaton 107	(S)	Book Of Taliesyn	1969	6.00	15.00
Tetragrammaton 119	(S)	Deep Purple	1969	6.00	15.00
Tetragrammaton	(S)	Concerto For Group And Orchestra	1969	50.00	100.00
Warners BS4-2607	(Q)	Machine Head	1974	8.00	20.00
Warners PR4-2832	(Q)	Stormbringer	1978	8.00	20.00

DEEP RIVER BOYS, THE

Label		Title	Year	VG+	NM
Waldorf 108 (10")	(M)	Spirituals And Jubilees	1956	50.00	100.00
Waldorf 120 (10")	(M)	Spirituals	1956	50.00	100.00
Vik LXA-1019	(M)	The Deep River Boys	1956	50.00	100.00
Camden CAL-303	(M)	Presenting The Deep River Boys	1956	35.00	70.00
Que FLS-104	(M)	Midnight Magic	1957	35.00	70.00
Capitol T-6050	(M)	Presenting The Deep River Boys		20.00	50.00

DEEP SIX, THE

Label		Title	Year	VG+	NM
Liberty LRP-3475	(M)	The Deep Six	1966	5.00	12.00
Liberty LST-7475	(S)	The Deep Six	1966	6.00	15.00

DEKKER, DESMOND (& THE ACES)

Label		Title	Year	VG+	NM
Uni 73059	(P)	Israelites	1969	10.00	25.00

DEL SATINS, THE

Label		Title	Year	VG+	NM
B.T. Puppy 1019	(S)	Out To Lunch	1972	20.00	50.00

DEL VIKINGS, THE (THE DELL VIKINGS)

Label		Title	Year	VG+	NM
Luniverse LP-1000	(M)	Come Go With The Del Vikings	1957	180.00	300.00
Mercury MG-20314	(M)	They Sing-They Swing	1957	100.00	200.00
Mercury MG-20353	(M)	A Swinging, Singing Record Session	1958	100.00	200.00
Crown CLP-5368	(M)	The Del Vikings & The Sonnets	1963	16.00	40.00
Dot DLP-3695	(M)	Come Go With Me	1966	75.00	150.00

DELFONICS, THE

Label		Title	Year	VG+	NM
Philly Groove 1150	(S)	La La Means I Love You	1968	8.00	20.00
Philly Groove 1151	(S)	The Sexy Sound Of Soul	1969	6.00	15.00
Philly Groove 1152	(S)	The Super Hits	1969	6.00	15.00
Philly Groove 1153	(S)	The Delfonics	1970	5.00	12.00

DELLS, THE

Label		Title	Year	VG+	NM
Vee Jay VJLP-1010	(M)	Oh What A Nite (Maroon labe!)	1959	100.00	200.00
Vee Jay LP-1141	(M)	It's Not Unusual	1965	10.00	25.00
Vee Jay LPS-1141	(S)	It's Not Unusual	1965	12.00	30.00

DELLWOODS, THE

Label		Title	Year	VG+	NM
Big Top 1306	(M)	Fink Along With Mad	1963	14.00	35.00

DELMORE BROTHERS, THE

Label		Title	Year	VG+	NM
King 589	(M)	Songs By The Delmore Brothers	1958	30.00	60.00
King 785	(M)	30th Anniversary Album	1962	20.00	50.00
King 910	(M)	In Memory	1964	14.00	35.00
King 920	(M)	In Memory, Volume 2	1964	14.00	35.00
King 983	(M)	24 Great Country Songs	1966	12.00	30.00
King S-983	(S)	24 Great Country Songs	1966	14.00	35.00

Jackie DeShannon. *Breakin' It Up On The Beatles Tour.* One of the neglected female talents in the past twenty years, Jackie's first two albums on Liberty are very hard to find. This, her second, is also sought after as a Beatles-related collectible. The title refers to her tour with the Fab Four, not to the material within.

Dolenz, Jones, Boyce & Hart. Essentially the Monkees Revisited, this featured two members of the original group teaming up with the multi-talented Tommy Boyce and Bobby Hart, song writers extraordinaire and recording artists on their own.

Label		Title	Year	VG+	NM
DELTA RHYTHM BOYS, THE					
RCA LPM-3085 (10")	(M)	Dry Bones	1950	50.00	100.00
Mercury MG-25153 (10")	(M)	The Delta Rhythm Boys	1953	75.00	150.00
Camden CAL-313	(M)	The Delta Rhythm Boys	1956	20.00	50.00
Elektra EKL-138	(M)	The Delta Rhythm Boys	1957	35.00	70.00
Jubilee LP-1022	(M)	In Sweden	1957	16.00	40.00
Jubilee LP-1022	(M)	In Sweden (Red vinyl)	1957	40.00	80.00
Coral CRL-57358	(M)	Swingin' Spirituals	1961	20.00	50.00
DEMIAN (BUBBLE PUPPY)					
ABC S-718	(S)	Demian	1970	12.00	30.00
DEREK & THE DOMINOS					
Atco SD-2-704	(S)	Layla	1970	10.00	25.00
DESANTO, SUGAR PIE					
Checker LP-2979	(M)	Sugar Pie	1961	20.00	50.00
DeSHANNON, JACKIE					
Liberty LRP-3320	(M)	Jackie DeShannon	1963	10.00	25.00
Liberty LST-7320	(S)	Jackie DeShannon	1963	12.00	30.00
Liberty LRP-3390	(M)	Breakin' It Up On The Beatles' Tour	1964	16.00	40.00
Liberty LST-7390	(S)	Breakin' It Up On The Beatles' Tour	1964	20.00	50.00
20th Century TFM-3131	(M)	Surf Party (Sdtk)	1964	8.00	20.00
20th Century TFS-3131	(S)	Surf Party (Sdtk)	1964	10.00	25.00
Imperial LP-9286	(M)	This Is Jackie DeShannon	1965	5.00	12.00
Imperial LP-12286	(S)	This Is Jackie DeShannon	1965	6.00	15.00
Imperial LP-9294	(M)	You Won't Forget Me	1965	5.00	12.00
Imperial LP-12294	(S)	You Won't Forget Me	1965	6.00	15.00
Imperial LP-9296	(M)	In The Wind	1965	5.00	12.00
Imperial LP-12296	(S)	In The Wind	1965	6.00	15.00
		(Imperial albums above have black & pink labels.)			
Liberty LRP-3430	(M)	C'Mon Let's Live A Little (Sdtk)	1966	6.00	15.00
Liberty LST-7430	(S)	C'Mon Let's Live A Little (Sdtk)	1966	8.00	20.00
DETERGENTS, THE					
Roulette R-25308	(M)	The Many Faces Of The Detergents	1965	16.00	40.00
Roulette SR-25308	(E)	The Many Faces Of The Detergents	1965	12.00	30.00
DEUCE COUPES, THE					
Del-Fi DFLP-1243	(M)	Hotrodders' Choice	1963	8.00	20.00
Del-Fi DFS-1243	(S)	Hotrodders' Choice	1963	10.00	25.00
DEVIANTS, THE					
Sire SES-97001	(S)	Poof	1969	16.00	40.00
Sire SES-97005	(S)	Disposable	1969	16.00	40.00
Sire SES-97016	(S)	The Deviants, No. 3	1969	16.00	40.00
DEVILED HAM					
Super K SKS-6003	(S)	I Had Too Much To Dream Last Night	1968	8.00	20.00
DEVIL'S ANVIL					
Columbia CL-2664	(M)	Hard Rock From The Middle East	1967	6.00	15.00
Columbia CS-9464	(S)	Hard Rock From The Middle East	1967	8.00	20.00
DEVROE, BILLY, &THE DEVILAIRES					
Tampa 31	(M)	Billy Devroe & The Devilaires, Volume 1		10.00	25.00
Tampa 39	(M)	Billy Devroe & The Devilaires, Volume 2		10.00	25.00
DIAMOND, NEIL					
Bang BLP-214	(M)	The Feel Of Neil Diamond	1966	14.00	35.00
Bang BLPS-214	(S)	The Feel Of Neil Diamond	1966	20.00	50.00
Bang BLP-217	(M)	Just For You	1967	8.00	20.00
Bang BLPS-217	(S)	Just For You	1967	10.00	25.00
Bang BLPS-219	(S)	Neil Diamond's Greatest Hits	1968	8.00	20.00
Bang BLPS-221	(S)	Shilo	1970	12.00	30.00
Bang BLPS-224	(S)	Do It!	1970	8.00	20.00
Bang BLPS-227	(P)	Double Gold	1970	6.00	15.00
		(Bang albums above have red & white labels.)			
Uni ST-73030	(S)	Velvet Gloves And Spit (Without "Shilo")	1968	10.00	25.00
Uni ST-73030	(S)	Velvet Gloves And Spit (With "Shilo")	1969	5.00	12.00

Label		Title	Year	VG+	NM
Uni ST-73047	(S)	Brother Love's Traveling Salvation Show *(Without "Sweet Caroline.")*	1969	10.00	25.00
Uni ST-73047	(S)	Brother Love's Traveling Salvation Show *(With "Sweet Caroline")*	1969	5.00	12.00
Uni ST-73071	(S)	Touching You Touching Me	1969	5.00	12.00
Uni ST-73084	(S)	Neil Diamond Gold	1970	5.00	12.00
Uni ST-73092	(S)	Tap Root Manuscript	1970	5.00	12.00
Uni ST-93106	(S)	Stones	1971	5.00	12.00
Uni ST-93136	(S)	Moods	1972	5.00	12.00
Frog King AAR-1	(S)	Early Classics	1972	12.00	30.00
MCA SM-734727	(S)	It's Happening! Diana Ross/Neil Diamond		12.00	30.00
Mobile Fidelity 2-024	(S)	Hot August Night		16.00	40.00
Mobile Fidelity 2-071	(S)	Jazz Singer		8.00	20.00
Columbia PCQ-32919	(Q)	Serenade	1974	10.00	25.00
Columbia HC-45625	(S)	You Don't Bring Me Flowers (1/2 speed)	1980	10.00	25.00

DIAMONDS, THE

Label		Title	Year	VG+	NM
Mercury MG-20213	(M)	Collection Of Golden Hits	1956	20.00	50.00
Mercury MG-20309	(M)	The Diamonds	1958	16.00	40.00
Mercury MG-20368	(M)	The Diamonds Meet Pete Rugolo	1958	14.00	35.00
Mercury SR-60076	(S)	The Diamonds Meet Pete Rugolo	1958	18.00	45.00
Wing MGW-12114	(M)	The Diamonds	1958	12.00	30.00
Wing MGW-12178	(M)	Pop Hits By The Diamonds	1959	12.00	30.00

DICK & DEE DEE

Label		Title	Year	VG+	NM
Liberty LRP-3236	(M)	Tell Me/The Mountain's High	1962	14.00	35.00
Liberty LST-7236	(E)	Tell Me/The Mountain's High	1962	12.00	30.00
Warners W-1500	(M)	Young & In Love	1963	6.00	15.00
Warners WS-1500	(S)	Young & In Love	1963	8.00	20.00
Warners W-1538	(M)	Turn Around	1964	6.00	15.00
Warners WS-1538	(S)	Turn Around	1964	8.00	20.00
Warners W-1586	(M)	Thou Shalt Not Steal	1965	6.00	15.00
Warners WS-1586	(S)	Thou Shalt Not Steal	1965	8.00	20.00
Warners W-1623	(M)	Songs We've Sung On Shindig	1965	6.00	15.00
Warners WS-1623	(S)	Songs We've Sung On Shindig	1965	8.00	20.00
Decca DL-4699	(M)	Wild, Wild Winter (Sdtk)	1966	6.00	15.00
Decca DL7-4699	(S)	Wild, Wild Winter (Sdtk)	1966	8.00	20.00

DICKEY DOO & THE DONT'S

Label		Title	Year	VG+	NM
United Arts. UAL-3094	(M)	Madison	1960	8.00	20.00
United Arts. UAS-6094	(S)	Madison	1960	10.00	25.00
United Arts. UAL-3097	(M)	Teen Scene	1960	8.00	20.00
United Arts. UAS-6097	(S)	Teen Scene	1960	10.00	25.00

DICTATORS, THE

Label		Title	Year	VG+	NM
Epic KE-33348	(S)	The Dictators Go Girl Crazy	1975	5.00	12.00
Asylum 7E-1109	(S)	Manifest Destiny	1977	4.00	10.00
Asylum 6E-147	(S)	Bloodbrothers	1978	4.00	10.00

DIDDLEY, BO (ELLAS McDANIEL)

Label		Title	Year	VG+	NM
Chess LP-1431	(M)	Bo Diddley	1957	35.00	70.00
Chess LP-1436	(M)	Go Bo Diddley	1958	20.00	50.00
Checker LP-2974	(M)	Have Guitar, Will Travel	1959	20.00	50.00
Checker LP-2976	(M)	Bo Diddley In The Spotlight	1960	16.00	40.00
Checker LP-2977	(M)	Bo Diddley Is A Gunslinger	1961	40.00	80.00
Checker LP-2980	(M)	Bo Diddley Is A Lover	1961	30.00	60.00
Checker LP-2982	(M)	Bo Diddley Is A Twister	1962	16.00	40.00
Checker LP-2982	(E)	Road Runner	1962	30.00	60.00
Checker LP-2984	(M)	Bo Diddley	1962	16.00	40.00
Checker LP-2985	(M)	Bo Diddley And Company	1963	35.00	70.00
Checker LP-2987	(M)	Surfin' With Bo Diddley	1963	16.00	40.00
Checker LPS-2987	(E)	Surfin' With Bo Diddley	1963	12.00	30.00
Checker LP-2988	(M)	Bo Diddley's Beach Party	1963	30.00	60.00
Checker LPS-2988	(E)	Bo Diddley's Beach Party	1963	20.00	50.00
Checker LP-2989	(M)	16 All Time Greatest Hits	1963	12.00	30.00
Checker LPS-2989	(E)	16 All Time Greatest Hits	1963	10.00	25.00
Checker LP-2991	(M)	Two Great Guitars (With Chuck Berry)	1964	10.00	25.00
Checker LPS-2991	(S)	Two Great Guitars (With Chuck Berry)	1964	12.00	30.00
Checker LP-2992	(M)	Hey! Good Lookin'	1964	12.00	30.00
Checker LPS-2992	(E)	Hey! Good Lookin'	1964	10.00	25.00

Label		Title	Year	VG+	NM
Checker LP-2996	(M)	500% More Man	1964	14.00	35.00
Checker LPS-2996	(S)	500% More Man	1964	12.00	30.00
		(Checker albums above have black & silver labels.)			
Checker LP-3001	(M)	The Originator	1966	10.00	25.00
Checker LPS-3001	(S)	The Originator	1966	12.00	30.00
		(Blue label with red & black checkers on top.)			
Checker LP-3006	(M)	Go Bo Diddley	1967	16.00	40.00
Checker LPS-3006	(E)	Go Bo Diddley	1967	14.00	35.00
Checker LP-3007	(M)	Boss Man	1967	35.00	70.00
Checker LPS-3007	(E)	Boss Man	1967	30.00	60.00
Checker LP-3008	(M)	Super Blues	1968	16.00	40.00
Checker LPS-3008	(S)	Super Blues	1968	20.00	50.00
		(Features Muddy Waters and Little Walter.)			
Checker LP-3010	(M)	Super, Super Blues Band	1968	16.00	40.00
Checker LPS-3010	(S)	Super, Super Blues Band	1968	20.00	50.00
		(Features Muddy Waters and Howlin' Wolf.)			
Checker LP-3013	(M)	The Black Gladiator	1969	12.00	30.00
Checker LPS-3013	(S)	The Black Gladiator	1969	14.00	35.00
Chess CH-50001	(S)	Another Dimension	1971	16.00	40.00
Chess CH-50016	(S)	Where It All Began	1972	16.00	40.00
Chess CH-50029	(S)	The London Sessions	1973	10.00	25.00
		(Checker and Chess albums above have blue & white labels.)			
Chess CH-50047	(S)	Big Bad Bo	1974	10.00	25.00
Chess 2CH-60005	(E)	Got My Own Bag Of Tricks	1974	10.00	25.00
RCA APL1-1229	(S)	The 20th Anniversary Of Rock N' Roll	1976	8.00	20.00
MF 2002	(S)	I'm A Man	1977	50.00	100.00
DIETRICH, MARLENE					
Columbia CL-105 (10")	(M)	American Songs In German For The OSS		16.00	40.00
Columbia CL-164 (10")	(M)	Marlene Dietrich In Rio		16.00	40.00
Decca DL-5100 (10")	(M)	Souvenir Album		16.00	40.00
Decca DL-8465	(M)	Marlene Dietrich		10.00	25.00
Columbia CL-1275	(M)	Lile Marlene		12.00	30.00
Capitol OTCR-300	(M)	The Magic Of Marlene	1969	10.00	25.00
Capitol T-10397	(M)	Marlene	1965	8.00	20.00
Capitol ST-10397	(S)	Marlene	1965	10.00	25.00
DIGA RHYTHM BAND, THE					
Round RX-110	(S)	The Diga Rhythm Band	1976	6.00	15.00
DILLARD, DOUG					
Together STT-1003	(S)	Banjo Album	1970	12.00	30.00
DILLARD & CLARK (DOUG DILLARD & GENE CLARK)					
A&M SD-4158	(S)	The Fantastic Expedition (Brown label)	1969	6.00	15.00
A&M SD-4203	(S)	Through The Morning, Through The Night	1970	5.00	12.00
DILLARDS					
Features Doug Dillard.					
Elektra EKL-232	(M)	Back Porch Bluegrass	1963	6.00	15.00
Elektra EKS-7232	(S)	Back Porch Bluegrass	1963	8.00	20.00
Elektra EKL-265	(M)	The Dillards Live! Almost!	1964	6.00	15.00
Elektra EKS-7265	(S)	The Dillards Live! Almost!	1964	8.00	20.00
Elektra EKL-285	(M)	Pickin' And Fiddlin' With Byron Berline	1965	6.00	15.00
Elektra EKS-7285	(S)	Pickin' And Fiddlin' With Byron Berline	1965	8.00	20.00
Elektra EKS-74035	(S)	Wheatstraw Suite	1969	6.00	15.00
Elektra EKS-74054	(S)	The Dillards-Copperfields	1969	6.00	15.00
DING DONGS, THE					
Motown 716	(S)	Gimme Dat Ding	1970	6.00	15.00
DINNING, MARK					
MGM E-3828	(M)	Teen Angel	1960	30.00	60.00
MGM SE-3828	(S)	Teen Angel	1960	35.00	70.00
MGM E-3855	(M)	Wanderin'	1960	16.00	40.00
MGM SE-3855	(S)	Wanderin'	1960	20.00	50.00
DION (& THE BELMONTS)					
Laurie LLP-2002	(M)	Presenting Dion & The Belmonts	1959	35.00	70.00
Laurie LLP-2004	(M)	Alone With Dion	1961	14.00	35.00

Label		Title	Year	VG+	NM
Laurie LLP-2006	(M)	Wish Upon A Star (With the Belmonts)	1960	16.00	40.00
Laurie LLP-2009	(M)	Runaround Sue	1961	14.00	35.00
Laurie LLP-2009	(M)	Runaround Sue (Blue vinyl)	1961	50.00	100.00
Laurie LLP-2012	(M)	Lovers Who Wander	1962	14.00	35.00
Laurie LLP-2013	(M)	Dion Sings His Greatest Hits	1962	14.00	35.00
Laurie LLP-2015	(M)	Love Came To Me	1963	14.00	35.00
Laurie LLP-2016	(M)	By Special Request (With the Belmonts)	1963	20.00	50.00
Laurie LLP-2017	(M)	Dion Sings To Sandy & All Other Girls	1963	14.00	35.00
Laurie LLP-2019	(M)	Dion Sings The 15 Million Sellers	1963	14.00	35.00
Laurie LLP-2022	(M)	More Of Dion's Greatest Hits	1963	10.00	25.00
Laurie SLP-2047	(S)	Dion	1968	8.00	20.00
Columbia CL-2010	(M)	Ruby Baby	1963	8.00	20.00
Columbia CS-8810	(S)	Ruby Baby	1963	10.00	25.00
Columbia CL-2107	(M)	Donna The Prima Donna	1963	8.00	20.00
Columbia CS-8907	(S)	Donna The Prima Donna	1963	10.00	25.00
ABC 599	(M)	Together Again (With the Belmonts)	1967	10.00	25.00
ABC S-599	(S)	Together Again (With the Belmonts)	1967	12.00	30.00
Columbia CS-9773	(S)	Wonder Where I'm Bound	1969	6.00	15.00
Warners BS-2664	(S)	Dion & The Belmonts Live 1972	1973	8.00	20.00

DIXIE CUPS, THE

Label		Title	Year	VG+	NM
Red Bird RB-20-100	(M)	Chapel Of Love	1964	14.00	35.00
Red Bird RBS-20-100	(S)	Chapel Of Love	1964	20.00	50.00
Red Bird RB-20-103	(M)	Iko Iko	1965	14.00	35.00
Red Bird RBS-20-103	(S)	Iko Iko	1965	20.00	50.00
ABC-Paramount 525	(M)	Riding High	1965	10.00	25.00
ABC-Paramount S-525	(S)	Riding High	1965	14.00	35.00

DIXIEBELLES, THE

Label		Title	Year	VG+	NM
Sound Stage 7 SSM-5000	(M)	Down At Poppa Joe's	1963	12.00	30.00
Sound Stage 7 SM-1500	(E)	Down At Poppa Joe's	1963	10.00	25.00

DIXON, WILLIE

Label		Title	Year	VG+	NM
Columbia CS-9987	(S)	I Am The Blues ("360 Sound" label)	1970	6.00	15.00

DIXON, WILLIE, & MEMPHIS SLIM

Label		Title	Year	VG+	NM
Bluesville BV-1003	(M)	Willie's Blues	1960	12.00	30.00
Verve V-3007	(M)	Blues Every Which Way	1961	8.00	20.00
Verve V6-3007	(S)	Blues Every Which Way	1961	10.00	25.00
Battle BV-6122	(M)	In Paris	1963	8.00	20.00
Battle BVS-6122	(S)	In Paris	1963	10.00	25.00

DOBKINS, JR., CARL

Label		Title	Year	VG+	NM
Decca DL-8938	(M)	Carl Dobkins, Jr.	1959	20.00	50.00
Decca DL7-8938	(S)	Carl Dobkins, Jr.	1959	35.00	70.00

DR. FEELGOOD & THE INTERNS

Label		Title	Year	VG+	NM
OKeh M-12101	(M)	Doctor Feelgood	1962	14.00	35.00
OKeh S-14101	(S)	Doctor Feelgood	1962	20.00	50.00

DR. JOHN, THE NIGHT TRIPPER (MAC REBENNACK)

Label		Title	Year	VG+	NM
Atco SD-33-234	(S)	Gris-Gris	1968	6.00	15.00
Atco SD-33-270	(S)	Babylon	1969	6.00	15.00
Atco SD-33-316	(S)	Remedies	1970	5.00	12.00
Atco SD-33-362	(S)	The Sun, Moon And Herbs	1971	5.00	12.00
Atco SD-36-7006	(S)	Gumbo	1972	5.00	12.00
Atco SD-7018	(S)	In The Right Place	1973	5.00	12.00

DODD, DICK

Label		Title	Year	VG+	NM
Tower ST-5142	(S)	First Evolution Of Dick Dodd	1968	16.00	40.00

DOLENZ, JONES, BOYCE & HART

Label		Title	Year	VG+	NM
Capitol ST-11513	(S)	Dolenz, Jones, Boyce And Hart	1976	10.00	25.00

DOMINO, FATS

Label		Title	Year	VG+	NM
Imperial LP-9004	(M)	Rock And Rollin'	1956	50.00	100.00
Imperial LP-9009	(M)	Fats Domino	1956	50.00	100.00
Imperial LP-9028	(M)	This Is Fats Domino!	1957	50.00	100.00
Imperial LP-9038	(M)	Here Stands Fats Domino	1957	50.00	100.00
Imperial LP-9040	(M)	This Is Fats	1957	50.00	100.00

(Imperial albums above have maroon labels.)

Label		Title	Year	VG+	NM
Imperial LP-9055	(M)	The Fabulous Mr. D	1958	20.00	50.00
Imperial LP-9062	(M)	Fats Domino Swings	1959	20.00	50.00
Imperial LP-9065	(M)	Let's Play Fats Domino	1959	20.00	50.00
Imperial LP-9103	(M)	Million Record Hits	1960	20.00	50.00
Imperial LP-12103	(E)	Million Record Hits	1960	16.00	40.00
Imperial LP-9138	(M)	A Lot Of Dominos	1961	16.00	40.00
Imperial LP-12138	(S)	A Lot Of Dominos	1961	30.00	60.00
Imperial LP-9153	(M)	Let The Four Winds Blow	1961	16.00	40.00
Imperial LP-12153	(S)	Let The Four Winds Blow	1961	30.00	60.00
Imperial LP-9164	(M)	What A Party	1962	16.00	40.00
Imperial LP-9170	(M)	Twistin' The Stomp	1962	12.00	30.00
Imperial LP-9195	(M)	Million Sellers	1962	12.00	30.00
Imperial LP-9208	(M)	Just Domino	1963	12.00	30.00
Imperial LP-9227	(M)	Walkin' To New Orleans	1963	12.00	30.00
Imperial LP-9239	(M)	Let's Dance With Domino	1963	12.00	30.00
Imperial LP-9248	(M)	Here He Comes Again	1963	12.00	30.00

(Mono Imperial albums above have black labels with multi-color rays on top. Stereo albums have black & silver labels.)

ABC-Paramount 455	(M)	Here Comes Fats Domino	1963	6.00	15.00
ABC-Paramount S-455	(S)	Here Comes Fats Domino	1963	8.00	20.00
ABC-Paramount 479	(M)	Fats On Fire		6.00	15.00
ABC-Paramount S-479	(S)	Fats On Fire		8.00	20.00
ABC-Paramount 510	(M)	Getaway With Fats Domino	1965	6.00	15.00
ABC-Paramount S-510	(S)	Getaway With Fats Domino	1965	8.00	20.00
Mercury MG-21029	(M)	Fats Domino '65	1965	5.00	12.00
Mercury SR-61029	(S)	Fats Domino '65	1965	6.00	15.00
Mercury MG-21065	(M)	Southland U.S.A.	1966	5.00	12.00
Mercury MG-21065	(S)	Southland U.S.A.	1966	6.00	15.00
Reprise RS-6304	(S)	Fats Is Back	1968	6.00	15.00
Reprise RS-6439	(S)	Fats	1971	300.00	500.00

(Very few copies known to exist.)

United Arts. UAS-9958	(M)	Legendary Masters	1971	6.00	15.00
United Arts. LA122	(M)	Cookin' With Fats	1976	6.00	15.00

DON & THE GOOD TIMES
Also refer to Jim Valley.

Burdette 300	(M)	Don & The Goodtimes' Greatest Hits	1966	20.00	50.00
Epic LN-24311	(M)	So Good	1967	4.00	10.00
Epic BN-26311	(S)	So Good	1967	5.00	12.00
Wand WDS-679	(S)	Where The Action Is	1969	12.00	30.00

DON, DICK & JIMMY

Modern LMP-1205	(M)	Spring Fever		16.00	40.00

DONNER, RAL

Gone LP-5012	(M)	Takin' Care Of Business	1961	75.00	150.00

DONOVAN (DONOVAN LEITCH)

Hickory LPM-123	(M)	Catch The Wind	1965	6.00	15.00
Hickory LPS-123	(E)	Catch The Wind	1965	5.00	12.00
Hickory LPM-127	(M)	Fairy Tale	1965	6.00	15.00
Hickory LPS-127	(E)	Fairy Tale	1965	5.00	12.00
Hickory LPM-135	(M)	The Real Donovan	1966	6.00	15.00
Hickory LPS-135	(E)	The Real Donovan	1966	5.00	12.00
Hickory LPS-143	(E)	Like It Is, Was And Evermore Shall Be	1968	6.00	15.00
Hickory LPS-149	(E)	The Best Of Donovan	1969	5.00	12.00
Epic LN-24217	(M)	Sunshine Superman	1966	6.00	15.00
Epic BN-26217	(E)	Sunshine Superman	1966	4.00	10.00
Epic LN-24239	(M)	Mellow Yellow	1967	6.00	15.00
Epic BN-26239	(E)	Mellow Yellow	1967	4.00	10.00
Epic LN-24349	(M)	Wear Your Love Like Heaven	1967	4.00	10.00
Epic BN-26349	(S)	Wear Your Love Like Heaven	1967	4.00	10.00
Epic LN-24350	(M)	For Little Ones	1967	4.00	10.00
Epic BN-26350	(S)	For Little Ones	1967	4.00	10.00
Epic L2N-6071	(M)	A Gift From A Flower To A Garden	1968	8.00	20.00
Epic B2N-6071	(S)	A Gift From A Flower To A Garden	1968	8.00	20.00

(With a portfolio of drawings, lyrics and poetry.)

DOOBIE BROTHERS, THE

Warners BS4-2634	(Q)	Toulouse Street	1974	6.00	15.00

Label		Title	Year	VG+	NM
Warners BS4-2694	(Q)	The Captain And Me	1974	6.00	15.00
Warners WS4-2750	(Q)	What Were Once Vices Are Now Habits	1974	6.00	15.00
Warners BS4-2835	(Q)	Stampede	1975	6.00	15.00
Nautilus 5	(S)	The Captain And Me (1/2 speed)	1980	10.00	25.00
Mobile Fidelity 1-122	(S)	Takin' It To The Streets		5.00	12.00

DOORS, THE

Label		Title	Year	VG+	NM
Elektra EKL-4007	(M)	The Doors	1967	16.00	40.00
Elektra EKS-74007	(S)	The Doors	1967	10.00	25.00
Elektra EKL-4014	(M)	Strange Days	1967	12.00	30.00
Elektra EKS-74014	(S)	Strange Days	1967	8.00	20.00
Elektra EKS-74024	(S)	Waiting For The Sun	1968	6.00	15.00
		(Elektra albums above have brown labels.)			
Elektra EKS-75005	(S)	The Soft Parade	1969	5.00	12.00
Elektra EKS-75007	(S)	Morrison Hotel/Hard Rock Cafe	1970	5.00	12.00
		(Elektra albums above have red labels.)			
Elektra EKS-2-9002	(S)	Absolutely Live	1970	8.00	20.00
Elektra EKS-74079	(S)	The Doors 13	1970	5.00	12.00
Elektra EKS-75011	(S)	L.A. Woman (Window cover)	1971	8.00	20.00
Elektra EQ-5035	(Q)	The Best Of The Doors	1973	6.00	15.00
		(Elektra albums above have "butterfly" labels.)			
Mobile Fidelity 1-051	(S)	The Doors	1980	14.00	35.00

DORS, DIANA

Label		Title	Year	VG+	NM
Columbia CL-1436	(M)	Swinging Dors	1960	10.00	25.00
Columbia CS-8236	(M)	Swinging Dors	1960	14.00	35.00

DORSEY, LEE

Label		Title	Year	VG+	NM
Fury 1002	(M)	Ya Ya	1962	20.00	50.00
Sphere Sound SR-7003	(M)	Ya Ya		12.00	30.00
Sphere Sound SSR-7003	(E)	Ya Ya		8.00	20.00
Amy 8010	(M)	Ride Your Pony	1966	8.00	20.00
Amy S-8010	(S)	Ride your Pony	1966	10.00	25.00
Amy 8011	(M)	The New Lee Dorsey	1966	8.00	20.00
Amy 8011	(S)	The New Lee Dorsey	1966	10.00	25.00

DOUGLAS, K.C.

Label		Title	Year	VG+	NM
Cook LP-5002	(M)	A Dead-Beat Guitar And The Mississippi	1956	50.00	100.00

DOVELLS, THE

Label		Title	Year	VG+	NM
Parkway P-7006	(M)	The Bristol Stomp	1961	20.00	50.00
Parkway P-7010	(M)	All The Hits Of The Teen Groups	1962	14.00	35.00
Parkway P-7011	(M)	Don't Knock The Twist (Sdtk)	1962	14.00	35.00
Parkway P-7021	(M)	For Your Hully Gully Party	1963	14.00	35.00
Parkway P-7025	(M)	You Can't Sit Down	1963	14.00	35.00
Cameo C-1067	(M)	Golden Hits Of The Orlons & The Dovells	1963	14.00	35.00
Wyncote W-9052	(M)	Discotheque	1965	6.00	15.00
Wyncote SW-9052	(S)	Discotheque	1965	8.00	20.00
Wyncote 9114	(M)	The Dovells' Biggest Hits	1965	6.00	15.00
Wyncote SW-9114	(P)	The Dovells' Biggest Hits	1965	8.00	20.00

DOWELL, JOE

Label		Title	Year	VG+	NM
Smash MGS-27000	(M)	Wooden Heart	1961	8.00	20.00
Smash SRS-67000	(S)	Wooden Heart	1961	10.00	25.00

DRAGONFLY (THE LEGENDS)

Label		Title	Year	VG+	NM
Megaphone MS-1202	(S)	Dragonfly	1968	16.00	40.00

DREAMLOVERS, THE

Label		Title	Year	VG+	NM
Columbia CL-2020	(M)	The Bird/Other Golden Dancing Grooves	1963	8.00	20.00
Columbia CS-8820	(S)	The Bird/Other Golden Dancing Grooves	1963	10.00	25.00

DREW, PATTI

Label		Title	Year	VG+	NM
Capitol T-2804	(M)	Tell Him	1967	6.00	15.00
Capitol ST-2804	(S)	Tell Him	1967	8.00	20.00

DRIFTERS, THE

Label		Title	Year	VG+	NM
Atlantic 8003	(M)	Clyde McPhatter & The Drifters	1956	100.00	200.00
Atlantic 8022	(M)	Rockin' And Driftin'	1958	100.00	200.00
		(Atlantic albums above have black labels.)			
Atlantic 8041	(M)	The Drifters' Greatest Hits	1960	30.00	60.00

Diana Dors, *Swinging Dors.* Another must for female vocal collectors with another wowee cover!

Bob Dylan. The miniscule first pressing of this album was on Columbia's older "eyes" logo label. Dylan's most over-looked early album, this is a tour de force for the young singer, who mixes blues, folk and a little cheeky humor like a master. Had Dylan made a career of recording albums like this, his most over-looked, he would still have been an artist to be reckoned with.

Label		Title	Year	VG+	NM
Atlantic 8059	(M)	Save The Last Dance For Me	1962	30.00	60.00
Atlantic SD-8059	(S)	Save The Last Dance For Me	1962	50.00	100.00
Atlantic 8073	(M)	Up On The Roof	1963	20.00	50.00
Atlantic SD-8073	(S)	Up On The Roof	1963	35.00	70.00
Atlantic 8093	(M)	Our Biggest Hits	1964	16.00	40.00
Atlantic SD-8093	(S)	Our Biggest Hits	1964	30.00	60.00
Atlantic 8099	(M)	Under The Boardwalk	1964	20.00	50.00
Atlantic SD-8099	(S)	Under The Boardwalk	1964	35.00	70.00
Clarion 608	(M)	The Drifters	1964	8.00	20.00
Clarion SD-608	(P)	The Drifters	1964	12.00	30.00
Atlantic 8102	(M)	The Good Life With The Drifters	1965	12.00	30.00
Atlantic SD-8102	(S)	The Good Life With The Drifters	1965	20.00	50.00
Atlantic 8113	(M)	I'll Take You Where The Music's Playing	1965	12.00	30.00
Atlantic SD-8113	(S)	I'll Take You Where The Music's Playing	1965	20.00	50.00
Atlantic 8153	(M)	The Drifters' Golden Hits	1968	8.00	20.00
Atlantic SD-8153	(P)	The Drifters' Golden Hits	1968	8.00	20.00

(Mono Atlantic albums above have orange & purple labels. Stereo albums have green & blue labels. Both have a black fan.)

DRIFTIN' SLIM (ELMON MIVKLE)

Label		Title	Year	VG+	NM
Milestone 93004	(M)	Driftin' Slim And His Blues Band	1968	8.00	20.00

DRUIDS OF STONEHENGE, THE

Label		Title	Year	VG+	NM
Uni 3004	(M)	Creation	1967	8.00	20.00
Uni 73004	(S)	Creation	1967	10.00	25.00

DUALS, THE

Label		Title	Year	VG+	NM
Sue LP-2002	(M)	Stick Shift	1961	50.00	100.00

DUBS, THE

Label		Title	Year	VG+	NM
Josie JM-4001	(M)	The Dubs Meet The Shells		30.00	60.00
Josie JSS-4001	(P)	The Dubs Meet The Shells		40.00	80.00

DUPREE, "CHAMPION" JACK

Label		Title	Year	VG+	NM
Atlantic 8019	(M)	Blues From The Gutter (Black label)	1959	30.00	60.00
Atlantic SD-8019	(S)	Blues From The Gutter (Green label)	1959	50.00	100.00
King LP-735	(M)	Sings The Blues	1961	20.00	50.00
Atlantic 8045	(S)	Natural And Soulful Blues	1961	14.00	35.00
Atlantic SD-8045	(S)	Natural And Soulful Blues	1961	20.00	50.00
Atlantic 8056	(M)	Champion Of The Blues	1961	14.00	35.00
Atlantic SD-8056	(S)	Champion Of The Blues	1961	20.00	50.00
Folkways FS-3825	(M)	Women Blues Of Champion Jack Dupree	1961	10.00	25.00
OKeh OKM-12103	(M)	Cabbage Greens	1963	10.00	25.00
London PS-553	(S)	From New Orleans To Chicago	1969	6.00	15.00
Sire 97010	(S)	In Heavy Blues (With Mickey Baker)	1969	6.00	15.00
Blue Horizon 7702	(S)	When You Feel The Feeling	1969	5.00	12.00
King KS-1084	(S)	Walking The Blues	1970	5.00	12.00

DUPREE, SIMON, & THE BIG SOUND

Label		Title	Year	VG+	NM
Tower ST-5097	(S)	Without Reservations	1968	12.00	30.00

DUPREES, THE

Label		Title	Year	VG+	NM
Coed LPC-905	(M)	You Belong To Me	1962	30.00	60.00
Coed LPC-906	(M)	Have You Heard	1963	30.00	60.00

DUROCS, THE

Label		Title	Year	VG+	NM
Capitol ST-11981	(S)	The Durocs	1979	6.00	15.00

DYKE & THE BLAZERS

Label		Title	Year	VG+	NM
Original Sound LP-8876	(M)	The Funky Broadway	1967	12.00	30.00
Original Sound LPS-8876	(S)	The Funky Broadway	1967	12.00	30.00
Original Sound LPS-8877	(S)	Dyke's Greatest Hits	1969	10.00	25.00

DYLAN, BOB

Label		Title	Year	VG+	NM
Columbia CL-1779	(M)	Bob Dylan	1962	75.00	150.00
Columbia CS-8579	(S)	Bob Dylan	1962	100.00	200.00

(Six black "eye" logos on each label.)

Label		Title	Year	VG+	NM
Columbia CL-1779	(M)	Bob Dylan	1963	8.00	20.00
Columbia CS-8579	(S)	Bob Dylan	1963	8.00	20.00

(Label reads "Guaranteed High Fidelity.")

Label		Title	Year	VG+	NM
Columbia CL-1986	(M)	The Freewheelin' Bob Dylan	1963	2,800.00	4,000.00
		(Initial pressings contain "Rocks And Gravel,"			
		"Let Me Die In My Footsteps," "John Birch			
		Society Blues" and "Ramblin' Gamblin' Willie."			
		These four tracks were replaced on subsequent			
		pressings. On the few copies found, neither the			
		cover nor the label listed these four tracks, so			
		listening is advised. Stereo copies are not			
		known to exist; should one be found, it could			
		easily double the mono value listed above..)			
Columbia CL-1986	(M)	The Freewheelin' Bob Dylan	1963	8.00	20.00
Columbia CS-8786	(S)	The Freewheelin' Bob Dylan	1963	8.00	20.00
		(Label reads "360 Sound Stereo" in black			
		without on either side arrows.)			
Columbia CL-2105	(M)	The Times They Are A-Changin'	1964	8.00	20.00
Columbia CS-8905	(S)	The Times They Are A-Changin'	1964	8.00	20.00
		(With a sheet of poetry.)			
Columbia CL-2193	(M)	Another Side Of Bob Dylan	1964	8.00	20.00
Columbia CS-8993	(S)	Another Side Of Bob Dylan	1964	8.00	20.00
Columbia CL-2328	(M)	Bringing It All Back Home	1965	8.00	20.00
Columbia CS-9128	(S)	Bringing It All Back Home	1965	8.00	20.00
		(Mono Columbia labels above have "Guaranteed			
		High Fidelity" on the bottom of the label. Stereo			
		albums have "360 Sound Stereo" in black with			
		arrows on both sides.)			
Columbia CL-2389	(M)	Highway 61 Revisited	1965	12.00	30.00
Columbia CS-9189	(S)	Highway 61 Revisited	1965	8.00	20.00
Columbia CS-9189	(S)	Highway 61 Revisited	1965	75.00	150.00
		(Contains an alternate take of "From A Buick 6."			
		The matrix number in the trail-off vinyl ends			
		with a dash and the number "1.")			
Columbia C2L-41	(M)	Blonde On Blonde	1966	20.00	50.00
Columbia C2S-41	(S)	Blonde On Blonde	1966	14.00	35.00
		(The inside cover has nine photos,			
		including one of Claudia Cardinale.)			
Columbia C2S-41	(S)	Blonde On Blonde	1966	10.00	25.00
		(The inside cover has seven photos,			
		omitting Claudia Cardinale.)			
Columbia KCL-2663	(M)	Bob Dylan's Greatest Hits (With poster)	1967	10.00	25.00
Columbia KCS-9463	(S)	Bob Dylan's Greatest Hits (With poster)	1967	8.00	20.00
Columbia CL-2804	(M)	John Wesley Harding	1968	20.00	50.00
Columbia CS-9604	(S)	John Wesley Harding	1968	6.00	15.00
Columbia KCS-9825	(S)	Nashville Skyline	1969	6.00	15.00
Columbia C2X-30050	(S)	Self Portrait	1970	16.00	40.00
		(Columbia albums above have "360 Sound" labels.)			
Columbia KC-30290	(S)	New Morning	1970	3.50	8.00
Columbia KG-31120	(S)	Bob Dylan's Greatest Hits, Volume 2	1971	3.50	8.00
Columbia KC-32460	(S)	Pat Garrett And Billy The Kid (Sdtk)	1973	3.50	8.00
Columbia KC-32747	(S)	Dylan	1973	3.50	8.00
Columbia CQ-32875	(Q)	Nashville Skyline	1973	16.00	40.00
Asylum 7E-1003	(S)	Planet Waves (With wrap-around)	1974	4.00	10.00
Asylum EQ-1003	(Q)	Planet Waves	1974	16.00	40.00
Island AB-201	(S)	Before The Flood	1975	12.00	30.00
Asylum AB-201	(S)	Before The Flood	1975	3.50	8.00
Columbia PC-33235	(S)	Blood On The Tracks	1975	2.50	6.00
		(The liner notes on the back are in black print.)			
Columbia PC-33235	(S)	Blood On The Tracks	1975	8.00	20.00
		(Back cover features a full-cover drawing.)			
Columbia PS2-33682	(S)	The Basement Tapes	1975	3.50	8.00
Columbia PCQ-33893	(Q)	Desire	1976	12.00	30.00
Columbia PC-33893	(S)	Desire	1976	2.50	6.00
Columbia PC-34349	(S)	Hard Rain	1976	2.50	6.00
Columbia JC-35453	(S)	Street Legal	1978	2.50	6.00
Columbia PC2-36067	(S)	Bob Dylan At Budokan	1979	3.50	8.00
Columbia FC-36120	(S)	Slow Train Coming	1979	2.00	5.00
Columbia FC-36553	(S)	Saved	1980	2.00	5.00
Columbia HC-49825	(S)	Nashville Skyline (1/2 speed)	1981	12.00	30.00
Mobile Fidelity 1-114	(S)	The Times They Are A-Changin'		5.00	12.00

DYNAMICS

Label		Title	Year	VG+	NM
Bolo BLP-8001	(M)	The Dynamics With Jimmy Hanna	1962	20.00	50.00

Label		Title	Year	VG+	NM
EAGLE					
Janus JLS-3011	(S)	Come Under Nancy's Tent	1970	6.00	15.00
EAGLES, THE					
Mobile Fidelity 1-126	(S)	Hotel California	1981	8.00	20.00
EAGLIN, "BLIND" SNOOKS					
Folkways FA-2476	(M)	New Orleans Street Singer	1959	8.00	20.00
Bluesville BV-1046	(M)	That's All Right	1962	8.00	20.00
EARLS, THE					
Old Town LP-104	(M)	Remember Me Baby	1963	50.00	100.00
EARTH, WIND & FIRE					
Columbia CQ-32194	(Q)	Head To The Sky	1974	6.00	15.00
Columbia CQ-32712	(Q)	Open Our Eyes	1974	6.00	15.00
Columbia HC-45647	(S)	Best Of Earth, Wind & Fire (1/2 speed)	1981	8.00	20.00
Columbia HC-47548	(S)	Raise (1/2 speed)	1982	8.00	20.00
Mobile Fidelity 1-159	(S)	That's The Way Of The World		5.00	12.00
EAST SIDE KIDS, THE					
Uni 73032	(S)	Tiger And The Lamb	1968	8.00	20.00
EASTWOOD, CLINT					
Cameo C-1056	(M)	Cowboy Favorites	1963	10.00	25.00
Cameo CS-1056	(S)	Cowboy Favorites	1963	12.00	30.00
EASY RIDERS, THE					
Columbia CL-990	(M)	Marianne And Other Songs	1957	10.00	25.00
Columbia CL-1302	(M)	Wanderin' Folk Songs	1959	8.00	20.00
Epic LN-24033	(M)	Easy Riders	1963	5.00	12.00
Epic BN-26033	(S)	Easy Riders	1963	6.00	15.00
EASYBEATS, THE					
United Arts. UAL-3588	(M)	Friday On My Mind	1967	14.00	35.00
United Arts. UAS-6588	(P)	Friday On My Mind	1967	16.00	40.00
United Arts. UAS-6667	(S)	Falling Off The Edge Of The World	1968	12.00	30.00
EBSEN, BUDDY					
Reprise R-6174	(M)	Buddy Ebsen Says Howdy	1965	5.00	12.00
Reprise R9-6174	(S)	Buddy Ebsen Says Howdy	1965	6.00	15.00
ECKSTINE, BILLY					
National 2001 (10")	(M)	Billy Eckstine Sings	1950	20.00	50.00
MGM E-219 (10")	(M)	Tenderly	1953	16.00	40.00
MGM E-257 (10")	(M)	I Let A Song Go Out Of My Heart	1954	16.00	40.00
MGM E-523	(M)	Songs By Billy Eckstine	1954	14.00	35.00
MGM E-548	(M)	Favorites	1954	14.00	35.00
MGM E-3176	(M)	Mister B With A Beat	1955	12.00	30.00
MGM E-3209	(M)	Rendezvous	1955	12.00	30.00
MGM E-3275	(M)	That Old Feeling	1955	12.00	30.00
King 265-12 (10")	(M)	The Great Mr. B	1954	20.00	50.00
EmArcy 26025 (10")	(M)	Blues For Sale	1954	16.00	40.00
EmArcy 26027 (10")	(M)	Love Songs Of Mr. B	1954	16.00	40.00
EmArcy MG-36010	(M)	I Surrender, Dear	1955	14.00	35.00
EmArcy MG-36029	(M)	Blues For Sale	1955	14.00	35.00
EmArcy MG-36030	(M)	Love Songs Of Mr. B	1955	14.00	35.00
EmArcy MG-36129	(M)	Imagination	1956	14.00	35.00
Regent 6052	(M)	Prisoner Of Love	1957	12.00	30.00
Regent 6053	(M)	The Duke, The Blues And Me	1957	12.00	30.00
Regent 6054	(M)	My Deep Blue Dream	1957	12.00	30.00
Regent 6058	(M)	You Call It Madness	1957	12.00	30.00

Label		Title	Year	VG+	NM
Mercury MG-20316	(M)	Sarah Vaughan And Billy Eckstine Sing			
		The Best Of Irving Berlin	1957	8.00	20.00
Lion L-70088	(M)	Billy And Sarah (With Sarah Vaughan)	1959	12.00	30.00
Audio Lab AL-1549	(M)	Mr. B	1960	20.00	50.00
Roulette R-25052	(M)	No Cover, No Minimum	1960	6.00	15.00
Roulette SR-25052	(S)	No Cover, No Minimum	1960	8.00	20.00
Roulette R-25104	(M)	Once More With Feeling	1960	6.00	15.00
Roulette SR-25104	(S)	Once More With Feeling	1960	8.00	20.00
Mercury MG-20333	(M)	Billy's Best	1960	8.00	20.00
Mercury MG-20637	(M)	Broadway, Bongos And Mr. B	1961	6.00	15.00
Mercury SR-60637	(S)	Broadway, Bongos And Mr. B	1961	8.00	20.00
Mercury MG-20674	(M)	Basin St. East	1962	6.00	15.00
Mercury SR-60674	(S)	Basin St. East	1962	8.00	20.00
Mercury MG-20736	(M)	Don't Worry 'Bout Me	1962	6.00	15.00
Mercury SR-60736	(S)	Don't Worry 'Bout Me	1962	8.00	20.00
Mercury MG-20796	(M)	The Golden Hits Of Billy Eckstine	1963	6.00	15.00
Mercury SR-60796	(S)	The Golden Hits Of Billy Eckstine	1963	8.00	20.00
Motown 632	(M)	Prime Of My Life	1965	6.00	15.00
Motown S-632	(S)	Prime Of My Life	1965	8.00	20.00
Motown 646	(M)	My Way	1966	6.00	15.00
Motown S-646	(S)	My Way	1966	8.00	20.00
Motown 677	(S)	For Love Of Ivy	1969	8.00	20.00
EDDY, DUANE					
Jamie JLP-3000	(M)	Have Twangy Guitar Will Travel	1958	14.00	35.00
		(Yellow label; title in white on cover)			
Jamie JLP-3006	(M)	Especially For You	1959	12.00	30.00
Jamie JLP-3009	(M)	The Twangs The Thang	1959	12.00	30.00
Jamie JLP-3011	(M)	Songs Of Our Heritage (Fold open cover)	1960	12.00	30.00
Jamie JLP-70-3011	(S)	Songs Of Our Heritage (Fold open cover)	1960	16.00	40.00
Jamie JLP-70-3011	(S)	Songs Of Our Heritage (Blue vinyl)	1960	40.00	80.00
Jamie JLP-70-3011	(S)	Songs Of Our Heritage (Red vinyl)	1960	40.00	80.00
Jamie JLP-3014	(M)	$1,000,000 Worth Of Twang	1960	8.00	20.00
Jamie JLP-70-3014	(E)	$1,000,000 Worth Of Twang	1960	12.00	30.00
Jamie JLP-3019	(M)	Girls! Girls! Girls!	1961	8.00	20.00
Jamie JLP-70-3019	(S)	Girls! Girls! Girls!	1961	12.00	30.00
Jamie JLP-3021	(M)	$1,000,000 Worth Of Twang, Volume 2	1962	8.00	20.00
Jamie JLP-70-3021	(P)	$1,000,000 Worth Of Twang, Volume 2	1962	12.00	30.00
Jamie JLP-3022	(M)	Twisting With Duane Eddy	1962	8.00	20.00
Jamie JLP-70-3022	(S)	Twisting With Duane Eddy	1962	12.00	30.00
RCA LPM-2525	(M)	Twistin' And Twangin'	1962	8.00	20.00
RCA LSP-2525	(S)	Twistin' And Twangin'	1962	10.00	25.00
RCA LPM-2576	(M)	Twangy Guitar, Silky Strings	1962	8.00	20.00
RCA LSP-2576	(S)	Twangy Guitar, Silky Strings	1962	10.00	25.00
RCA LPM-2648	(M)	Dance With The Guitar Man	1962	8.00	20.00
RCA LSP-2648	(S)	Dance With The Guitar Man	1962	10.00	25.00
RCA LPM-2681	(M)	Twang A Country Song	1963	8.00	20.00
RCA LSP-2681	(S)	Twang A Country Song	1963	10.00	25.00
RCA LPM-2700	(M)	Twangin' Up A Storm	1963	8.00	20.00
RCA LSP-2700	(S)	Twangin' Up A Storm	1963	10.00	25.00
		(Mono RCA albums above have "Long Play"			
		on the bottom of the label. Stereo albums			
		have "Living Stereo" on the bottom.)			
Jamie JLP-3024	(M)	Surfin' With Duane Eddy	1963	8.00	20.00
Jamie JLP-70-3024	(S)	Surfin' With Duane Eddy	1963	12.00	30.00
Jamie JLP-3025	(M)	Duane Eddy In Person	1963	8.00	20.00
Jamie JLP-70-3025	(S)	Duane Eddy In Person	1963	12.00	30.00
Jamie JLP-3026	(M)	16 Greatest Hits	1964	10.00	25.00
Jamie JLP-70-3026	(E)	16 Greatest Hits	1964	8.00	20.00
RCA LPM-2798	(M)	Lonely Guitar	1964	6.00	15.00
RCA LSP-2798	(S)	Lonely Guitar	1964	8.00	20.00
RCA LPM-2918	(M)	Water Skiing	1964	6.00	15.00
RCA LSP-2918	(S)	Water Skiing	1964	8.00	20.00
RCA LPM-2993	(M)	Twangin' The Golden Hits	1965	6.00	15.00
RCA LSP-2993	(S)	Twangin' The Golden Hits	1965	8.00	20.00
RCA LPM-3432	(M)	Twangsville	1965	6.00	15.00
RCA LSP-3432	(S)	Twangsville	1965	8.00	20.00
RCA LPM-3477	(M)	The Best Of Duane Eddy	1966	6.00	15.00
RCA LSP-3477	(P)	The Best Of Daune Eddy	1966	8.00	20.00
		(RCA albums above have black labels.)			

Label		Title	Year	VG+	NM
Colpix CP-490	(M)	Duane A-Go-Go	1965	8.00	20.00
Colpix CPS-490	(S)	Duane A-Go-Go	1965	10.00	25.00
Colpix CP-494	(M)	Duane Eddy Does Bob Dylan	1965	10.00	25.00
Colpix CPS-494	(S)	Duane Eddy Does Bob Dylan	1965	12.00	30.00
Reprise R-6218	(M)	The Biggest Twang Of Them All	1966	6.00	15.00
Reprise RS-6218	(S)	The Biggest Twang Of Them All	1966	8.00	20.00
Reprise R-6240	(M)	The Roaring Twangies	1967	6.00	15.00
Reprise RS-6240	(S)	The Roaring Twangies	1967	8.00	20.00
Sire SASH-3707	(P)	Vintage Years	1975	6.00	15.00

EDEN, BARBARA

Label		Title	Year	VG+	NM
Dot DLP-3795	(M)	Miss Barbara Eden	1967	10.00	25.00
Dot DLP-25795	(S)	Miss Barbara Eden	1967	12.00	30.00

EDMONSON, TRAVIS
Also refer to Bud And Travis.

Label		Title	Year	VG+	NM
Reprise R-6035	(M)	Travis On His Own	1962	5.00	12.00
Reprise R9-6035	(S)	Travis On His Own	1962	6.00	15.00
Horizon T-1606	(M)	Travis On Cue	1962	5.00	12.00
Horizon ST-1606	(S)	Travis On Cue	1962	6.00	15.00

EDWARDS, TOMMY

Label		Title	Year	VG+	NM
Regent MG-6096	(M)	Tommy Edwards Sings		12.00	30.00
Lion 70120	(M)	Tommy Edwards		12.00	30.00
MGM E-3732	(M)	It's All In The Game	1959	8.00	20.00
MGM SE-3732	(S)	It's All In The Game	1959	10.00	25.00
MGM E-3760	(M)	For Young Lovers	1959	6.00	15.00
MGM SE-3760	(S)	For Young Lovers	1959	8.00	20.00
		(MGM albums above have yellow labels.)			
MGM E-3805	(M)	You Started Me Dreaming	1960	5.00	12.00
MGM SE-3805	(S)	You Started Me Dreaming	1960	6.00	15.00
MGM E-3822	(M)	Step Out Singing	1960	5.00	12.00
MGM SE-3822	(S)	Step Out Singing	1960	6.00	15.00
MGM E-3838	(M)	Tommy Edwards In Hawaii	1960	5.00	12.00
MGM SE-3838	(S)	Tommy Edwards In Hawaii	1960	6.00	15.00
MGM E-3884	(M)	Tommy Edwards' Greatest Hits	1961	5.00	12.00
MGM SE-3884	(S)	Tommy Edwards' Greatest Hits	1961	6.00	15.00
MGM E-3959	(M)	Golden Country Hits	1961	5.00	12.00
MGM SE-3959	(S)	Golden Country Hits	1961	6.00	15.00
MGM E-4020	(M)	Stardust	1962	5.00	12.00
MGM SE-4020	(S)	Stardust	1962	6.00	15.00
MGM E-4060	(M)	Soft Strings And Two Guitars	1962	5.00	12.00
MGM SE-4060	(S)	Soft Strings And Two Guitars	1962	6.00	15.00
MGM E-4141	(M)	The Very Best Of Tommy Edwards	1963	5.00	12.00
MGM SE-4141	(S)	The Very Best Of Tommy Edwards	1963	6.00	15.00
		(MGM albums above have black labels.)			

EIRE APPARENT

Label		Title	Year	VG+	NM
Buddah BDS-5031	(S)	Sunrise	1969	8.00	20.00

ELBERT, DONNIE

Label		Title	Year	VG+	NM
King 629	(M)	The Sensational Donnie Elbert Sings	1959	60.00	120.00

EL DORADOS, THE

Label		Title	Year	VG+	NM
Vee Jay VJLP-1001	(M)	Crazy Little Mama (Maroon label)	1959	150.00	250.00

ELECTRIC FLAG, THE

Label		Title	Year	VG+	NM
Sidewalk T-5908	(M)	The Trip (Sdtk)	1967	8.00	20.00
Sidewalk ST-5908	(S)	The Trip (Sdtk)	1967	10.00	25.00
Columbia CS-9597	(S)	A Long Time Comin'	1968	5.00	12.00
Columbia CS-9714	(S)	An American Music Band	1968	5.00	12.00
Columbia OS-3240	(S)	You Are What You Eat (Sdtk)	1968	5.00	12.00
		(Columbia albums above have "360 Sound" labels.)			

ELECTRIC LIGHT ORCHESTRA, THE (E.L.O.)

Label		Title	Year	VG+	NM
United Arts. LA823	(S)	Out Of The Blue (Blue vinyl)	1977	10.00	25.00
Jet HZ-45769	(S)	Discovery (1/2 speed)	1979	10.00	25.00
Jet HZ-46310	(S)	ELO's Greatest Hits (1/2 speed)	1979	10.00	25.00
Jet HZ-47371	(S)	Time (1/2 speed)	1981	10.00	25.00
Jet HZ-48490	(S)	Secret Messages (1/2 speed)	1983	10.00	25.00

Label		Title	Year	VG+	NM
ELECTRIC PRUNES, THE					
Reprise R-6248	(M)	I Had Too Much To Dream	1967	8.00	20.00
Reprise RS-6248	(S)	I Had Too Much To Dream	1967	10.00	25.00
Reprise R-6262	(M)	Underground	1967	8.00	20.00
Reprise RS-6262	(S)	Underground	1967	10.00	25.00
Reprise R-6275	(M)	Mass In F Minor	1967	6.00	15.00
Reprise RS-6275	(S)	Mass In F Minor	1967	6.00	15.00
Reprise RS-6316	(S)	Release Of An Oath	1968	6.00	15.00
Reprise RS-6342	(S)	Just Good Rock N' Roll	1969	6.00	15.00
ELEPHANT CANDY					
Uni 73042	(S)	The Fun And Games	1969	6.00	15.00
ELEPHANT'S MEMORY					
Apple SMAS-3389	(S)	Elephants Memory	1972	6.00	15.00
ELECTRIC TOILET					
Nasco 9004	(S)	In The Hands Of Karma	1970	35.00	70.00
ELF					
Epic KE-31789	(S)	Elf	1972	6.00	15.00
MGM M3G-4974	(S)	L.A. 59	1974	4.00	10.00
MGM M3G-4994	(S)	Trying To Burn The Sun	1975	4.00	10.00
ELGINS, THE					
VIP 400	(M)	Darling Baby	1966	12.00	30.00
VIP 400	(S)	Darling Baby	1966	16.00	40.00
ELIMINATORS, THE					
Liberty LRP-3365	(M)	Liverpool, Dragsters, Cycles & Surfing	1964	10.00	25.00
Liberty LST-7365	(S)	Liverpool, Dragsters, Cycles & Surfing	1964	12.00	30.00
ELLINGTON, HARVEY					
Stepheny MF-4010	(M)	I Can't Hide The Blues	1959	12.00	30.00
ELLIOT, RON					
Warners WS-1833	(S)	Candlestickmaker (With booklet)	1969	6.00	15.00
ELLIS, ANITA					
Epic LN-3280	(M)	I Wonder What Became Of Me	1956	16.00	40.00
Epic LN-3419	(M)	Him	1958	16.00	40.00
Elektra EKL-179	(M)	The World In My Arms	1960	12.00	30.00
Elektra EKS7-179	(S)	The World In My Arms	1960	16.00	40.00
ELLIS, JIMMY (ORION)					
Boblo 78-829	(S)	Ellis Sings Elvis By Request		20.00	50.00
ELLIS, SHIRLEY					
Congress CGL-3002	(M)	Shirley Ellis In Action	1964	5.00	12.00
Congress CGS-3002	(S)	Shirley Ellis In Action	1964	6.00	15.00
Congress CGL-3003	(M)	The Name Game	1965	5.00	12.00
Congress CGS-3003	(S)	The Name Game	1965	6.00	15.00
Columbia CL-2679	(M)	Sugar, Let's Shing A Ling	1967	5.00	12.00
Columbia CS-9479	(S)	Sugar, Let's Shing A Ling	1967	6.00	15.00
ELMER GANTRY'S VELVET OPERA					
Epic BN-26415	(S)	Elmer Gantry's Velvet Opera	1968	14.00	35.00
EMBERS, THE					
J.C.P. Recording 2006	(M)	Rock And Roll Eleven		75.00	150.00
EMERALD CHOIR, THE					
Boat 1017	(S)	Timber Timbre Burn		4.00	10.00
EMERSON, LAKE & PALMER					
Mobile Fidelity 1-031	(S)	Pictures At An Exhibition	1980	10.00	25.00
END, THE					
London PS-560	(S)	Introspection	1969	10.00	25.00

Label		Title	Year	VG+	NM
ENDLE ST. CLOUD					
International Arts. 12	(S)	Thank You All Very Much	1968	10.00	25.00
ENNIS, ETHEL					
Jubilee 1021	(M)	Lullabies For Losers	1956	12.00	30.00
Capitol T-941	(M)	Changes Of Scenery		5.00	12.00
Capitol T-1078	(M)	Have You Forgotten?		5.00	12.00
Jubilee 5024	(M)	Ethel Ennis Sings	1963	8.00	20.00
RCA LPM-2984	(M)	Eyes For You	1964	6.00	15.00
RCA LSP-2984	(S)	Eyes For You	1964	8.00	20.00
ENTWHISTLE, JOHN					
Decca DL-79183	(S)	Smash Your Head Against The Wall	1971	6.00	15.00
Decca DL-79190	(S)	Whistle Rhymes	1972	6.00	15.00
EPPS, PRESTON					
Original Sound 8851	(M)	Bongo, Bongo, Bongo	1960	8.00	20.00
Original Sound S-8851	(S)	Bongo, Bongo, Bongo	1960	10.00	25.00
Original Sound 8872	(M)	Surfin' Bongos	1963	8.00	20.00
Original Sound S-8872	(S)	Surfin' Bongos	1963	10.00	25.00
EQUALS, THE					
Laurie LP-2045	(M)	Unequalled	1967	8.00	20.00
Laurie SLP-2045	(S)	Unequalled	1967	10.00	25.00
RCA LSP-4078	(S)	Baby Come Back	1968	8.00	20.00
President PTL-1015	(S)	Equal Sensation	1968	6.00	15.00
President PTL-1020	(S)	The Sensational Equals	1968	6.00	15.00
President PTL-1025	(S)	Equal Sensation	1968	6.00	15.00
President PTL-1030	(S)	Strikeback	1969	6.00	15.00
ESQUERITA					
Capitol T-1186	(M)	Esquerita	1959	180.00	300.00
ESQUIRES, THE					
Bunky 300	(S)	Get On Up And Get Away	1968	10.00	25.00
ESSEX, THE					
Roulette R-25234	(M)	Easier Said Than Done	1963	14.00	35.00
Roulette SR-25234	(S)	Easier Said Than Done	1963	16.00	40.00
Roulette R-25235	(M)	A Walkin' Miracle	1963	8.00	20.00
Roulette SR-25235	(S)	A Walkin' Miracle	1963	10.00	25.00
Roulette R-25246	(M)	Young And Lively	1964	8.00	20.00
Roulette SR-25246	(S)	Young And Lively	1964	10.00	25.00
ETERNITY'S CHILDREN					
Tower ST-5123	(S)	Eternity's Children	1968	10.00	25.00
Tower ST-5144	(S)	Timeless	1968	10.00	25.00
EUPHORIA					
Heritage HTS-35,005	(S)	Euphoria	1969	20.00	50.00
EUPHORIA					
Capitol SKAO-363	(S)	A Gift From Euphoria	1969	40.00	80.00
EVANS, PAUL					
Guaranteed GUL-1000	(M)	Fabulous Teens	1960	16.00	40.00
Guaranteed GUS-1000	(S)	Fabulous Teens	1960	20.00	50.00
Carlton 129	(M)	Hear Paul Evans In Your Home Tonight	1961	10.00	25.00
Carlton STLP-129	(P)	Hear Paul Evans In Your Home Tonight	1961	12.00	30.00
Carlton 130	(M)	Folk Songs Of Many Lands	1961	10.00	25.00
Carlton STLP-130	(S)	Folk Songs Of Many Lands	1961	12.00	30.00
Kapp KL-1346	(M)	21 Years In A Tennessee Jail	1964	8.00	20.00
Kapp KS-3346	(S)	21 Years In A Tennessee Jail	1964	10.00	25.00
Kapp KL-1475	(M)	Another Town, Another Jail	1966	8.00	20.00
Kapp KS-3475	(S)	Another Town, Another Jail	1966	10.00	25.00
EVERETT, BETTY					
Vee Jay VJ-1077	(M)	It's In His Kiss		12.00	30.00
Vee Jay VJS-1077	(S)	It's In His Kiss		16.00	40.00
Vee Jay VJ-1099	(M)	Delicious Together (With Jerry Butler)	1964	6.00	15.00
Vee Jay VJS-1099	(S)	Delicious Together (With Jerry Butler)	1964	8.00	20.00

Label		Title	Year	VG+	NM
Vee Jay VJLP-1122	(M)	The Very Best Of Betty Everett	1965	6.00	15.00
Vee Jay VJS-1122	(S)	The Very Best Of Betty Everett	1965	8.00	20.00

EVERLY BROTHERS, THE (DON & PHIL EVERLY)

Label		Title	Year	VG+	NM
Cadence CLP-3003	(M)	The Everly Brothers	1958	20.00	50.00
Cadence CLP-3106	(M)	Songs Our Daddy Taught Us	1958	20.00	50.00
Cadence CLP-3025	(M)	The Everly Brothers' Best	1959	20.00	50.00
Cadence CLP-3040	(M)	The Fabulous Style Of The Everly Brothers	1960	20.00	50.00
Cadence CLP-25040	(P)	The Fabulous Style Of The Everly Brothers	1960	20.00	50.00
Cadence CLP-3059	(M)	Folk Songs Of The Everly Brothers	1962	20.00	50.00
Cadence CLP-25059	(E)	Folk Songs Of The Everly Brothers	1962	16.00	40.00
Cadence CLP-3062	(M)	15 Everly Hits 15	1963	20.00	50.00
Cadence CLP-25062	(P)	15 Everly Hits 15	1963	20.00	50.00
Warners W-1381	(M)	It's Everly Time	1960	8.00	20.00
Warners WS-1381	(S)	It's Everly Time	1960	10.00	25.00
Warners W-1395	(M)	A Date With The Everly Brothers	1960	14.00	35.00
Warners WS-1395	(S)	A Date With The Everly Brothers	1960	16.00	40.00
		(Fold-open cover with a sheet of photos.)			
Warners W-1418	(M)	Both Sides Of An Evening	1961	10.00	25.00
Warners WS-1418	(S)	Both Sides Of An Evening	1961	12.00	30.00
Warners W-1430	(M)	Instant Party	1962	12.00	30.00
Warners WS-1430	(S)	Instant Party	1962	16.00	40.00
Warners W-1471	(M)	The Everly Brothers' Golden Hits	1962	8.00	20.00
Warners WS-1471	(S)	The Everly Brothers' Golden Hits	1962	10.00	25.00
Warners W-1483	(M)	Christmas With The Everly Brothers	1962	8.00	20.00
Warners WS-1483	(S)	Christmas With The Everly Brothers	1962	10.00	25.00
Warners W-1512	(M)	Great Country Hits	1963	8.00	20.00
Warners WS-1512	(S)	Great Country Hits	1963	10.00	25.00
Warners W-1554	(M)	The Very Best Of The Everly Brothers	1964	6.00	15.00
Warners WS-1554	(S)	The Very Best Of The Everly Brothers	1964	8.00	20.00
		(The cover is yellow.)			
Warners W-1578	(M)	Rock N' Soul	1965	10.00	25.00
Warners WS-1578	(S)	Rock N' Soul	1965	12.00	30.00
Warners W-1585	(M)	Gone, Gone, Gone	1965	10.00	25.00
Warners WS-1585	(S)	Gone, Gone, Gone	1965	12.00	30.00
Warners W-1605	(M)	Beat N' Soul	1965	10.00	25.00
Warners WS-1605	(S)	Beat N' Soul	1965	12.00	30.00
Warners W-1620	(M)	In Our Image	1966	10.00	25.00
Warners WS-1620	(S)	In Our Image	1966	12.00	30.00
Warners W-1646	(M)	Two Yanks In London	1966	16.00	40.00
Warners WS-1646	(S)	Two Yanks In London	1966	20.00	50.00
		(Although uncredited, the Hollies back up the Everly's throughout this album.)			
Warners W-1676	(M)	The Hit Sound Of The Everly Brothers	1967	12.00	30.00
Warners WS-1676	(S)	The Hit Sound Of The Everly Brothers	1967	16.00	40.00
Warners W-1708	(M)	The Everly Brothers Sing	1967	12.00	30.00
Warners WS-1708	(S)	The Everly Brothers Sing	1967	16.00	40.00
Warners WS-1752	(S)	Roots	1968	12.00	30.00
Harmony HS-11304	(S)	The Everly Brothers	1968	6.00	15.00
Harmony HS-11350	(S)	Christmas With The Everly Brothers	1969	6.00	15.00
Harmony HS-11388	(S)	Chained To A Memory	1970	4.00	10.00
Warners WS-1858	(S)	The Everly Brothers' Show	1970	8.00	20.00
RCA LSP-4781	(S)	Pass The Chicken And Listen	1972	6.00	15.00
RCA LSP-4620	(S)	Stories We Could Tell	1972	6.00	15.00

EVERLY, DON

Label		Title	Year	VG+	NM
Ode 77005	(S)	Don Everly	1970	6.00	15.00
Ode 77023	(S)	Sunset Towers	1974	5.00	12.00
Hickory AH-44003	(S)	Brother Jukebox	1976	4.00	10.00

EVERLY, PHIL

Label		Title	Year	VG+	NM
RCA APL1-0092	(S)	Star Spangled Banner	1973	6.00	15.00
Pye 12104	(S)	Phil's Diner	1975	6.00	15.00
Pye 12121	(S)	Mystic Line	1976	5.00	12.00

EVERPRESENT FULLNESS

Label		Title	Year	VG+	NM
White Whale 7132	(S)	Everpresent Fullness	1970	12.00	30.00

EVERYTHING IS EVERYTHING

Label		Title	Year	VG+	NM
Vanguard VSD-6512	(S)	Everything Is Everything	1969	10.00	25.00

Label		Title	Year	VG+	NM
EXCITERS, THE					
United Arts. UAL-3264	(M)	Tell Him	1963	14.00	35.00
United Arts. UAS-6264	(S)	Tell Him	1963	16.00	40.00
Roulette R-25326	(M)	The Exciters	1966	6.00	15.00
Roulette SR-25326	(S)	The Exciters	1966	8.00	20.00

Label		Title	Year	VG+	NM
FABARES, SHELLY					
Colpix CLP-426	(M)	Shelly	1962	16.00	40.00
Colpix CST-426	(S)	Shelly	1962	30.00	60.00
Colpix CLP-431	(M)	The Things We Did Last Summer	1962	16.00	40.00
Colpix CST-431	(S)	The Things We Did Last Summer	1962	30.00	60.00
MGM SE-4540	(S)	A Time To Sing (Sdtk)	1968	5.00	12.00
FABIAN (FABIAN FORTE)					
Chancellor CHL-5003	(M)	Hold That Tiger	1959	16.00	40.00
Chancellor CHLS-5003	(S)	Hold That Tiger	1959	20.00	50.00
Chancellor CHL-5005	(M)	The Fabulous Fabian	1959	16.00	40.00
Chancellor CHLX-5005	(S)	The Fabulous Fabian	1959	20.00	50.00
Chancellor CHL-5009	(M)	Fabian And Avalon-The Hit Makers	1960	20.00	50.00
Chancellor CHL-5012	(M)	The Good Old Summertime	1960	12.00	30.00
Chancellor CHLS-5012	(S)	The Good Old Summertime	1960	16.00	40.00
RCA LPM-2314	(M)	High Time (Sdtk)	1960	8.00	20.00
RCA LSP-2314	(S)	High Time (Sdtk)	1960	10.00	25.00
Chancellor CHL-5019	(M)	Rockin' Hot	1961	20.00	50.00
Chancellor CHL-5024	(M)	Fabian's 16 Fabulous Hits	1962	16.00	40.00
FAGEN, DONALD					
Mobile Fidelity 1-120	(S)	Nightfly		5.00	12.00
FAINE JADE					
R.S.V.P. 8002	(S)	Introspection: A Faine Jade Recital	1968	60.00	120.00
FAITH (LIMOUSINE)					
Brown Bag LA085	(S)	Faith	1973	6.00	15.00
FAITH, ADAM					
MGM E-3591	(M)	England's Top Singer	1961	10.00	25.00
MGM SE-3591	(S)	England's Top Singer	1961	12.00	30.00
Amy 8005	(M)	Adam Faith	1965	6.00	15.00
Amy 8005	(S)	Adam Faith	1965	8.00	20.00
FAITHFULL, MARIANNE					
London LL-3423	(M)	Marianne Faithful	1965	6.00	15.00
London PS-423	(E)	Marianne Faithful	1965	4.00	10.00
London LL-3452	(M)	Go Away From My World	1965	5.00	12.00
London PS-452	(P)	Go Away From My World	1965	6.00	15.00
London LL-3482	(M)	Faithful Forever	1966	5.00	12.00
London PS-482	(S)	Faithful Forever	1966	6.00	15.00
London PS-547	(P)	Marianne Faithful's Greatest Hits	1969	5.00	12.00
FALLEN ANGELS, THE					
Roulette SR-25358	(S)	The Fallen Angels	1968	8.00	20.00
Roulette SR-42011	(S)	It's A Long Way Down	1968	16.00	40.00
FAME, GEORGIE					
Imperial 9282	(M)	Yeh, Yeh	1965	6.00	15.00
Imperial LP-12282	(E)	Yeh, Yeh	1965	5.00	12.00

Label		Title	Year	VG+	NM
Imperial 9331	(M)	Get Away	*1966*	6.00	15.00
Imperial 12331	(E)	Get Away	*1966*	5.00	12.00
Epic BN-26368	(S)	The Ballad Of Bonnie And Clyde	*1968*	8.00	20.00

FANKHAUSER, MERRELL

| Shamley SS-701 | (S) | Merrell Fankhauser & His HMS Bounty | | 8.00 | 20.00 |
| Maui 101 | (S) | Merrell Fankhauser | *1976* | 12.00 | 30.00 |

FANTASTIC BAGGYS, THE (PHIL SLOAN & STEVE BARRI)

Imperial LP-9270	(M)	Tell 'Em I'm Surfin'	*1964*	40.00	80.00
Imperial LP-12270	(S)	Tell 'Em I'm Surfin'	*1964*	50.00	100.00
Liberty LPR-3368	(M)	Ride The Wild Surf (Sdtk)	*1964*	10.00	25.00
Liberty LST-7368	(S)	Ride The Wild Surf (Sdtk)	*1964*	12.00	30.00

FANTASTIC DJ'S, THE

| Stone | (S) | The Fantastic DJ's | | 12.00 | 30.00 |

FANTASTIC JOHNNY C, THE (JOHNNY CORLEY)

| Phil-L.A. 4000 | (S) | Boogaloo Down Broadway | *1968* | 16.00 | 40.00 |

FAPARDOKLY

| U.I.P. 250 | (S) | Faperdokly | *1966* | 210.00 | 350.00 |

FARLOWE, CHRIS (& THE THUNDERBIRDS)

Columbia CL-2593	(M)	The Fabulous Chris Farlowe	*1967*	6.00	15.00
Columbia CS-9393	(S)	The Fabulous Chris Farlowe	*1967*	8.00	20.00
Immediate Z12-52010	(S)	Paint It Farlowe	*1968*	6.00	15.00

FARM BAND, THE

| Mantra 777 | (S) | The Farm Band (With poster) | | 14.00 | 35.00 |

FATHER YOD

| Higher Key 3301 | (S) | Kohoutek | *1973* | 50.00 | 100.00 |
| Higher Key 3304 | (S) | All Or Nothing At All | *1974* | 50.00 | 100.00 |

FAUN

| Gregar 7000 | (S) | Faun | *1969* | 12.00 | 30.00 |

FAYE, FRANCES

Capitol H-512 (10")	(M)	No Reservations	*1954*	16.00	40.00
Capitol T-512	(M)	No Reservations	*1955*	12.00	30.00
Bethlehem 23	(M)	I Am Wild Again	*1955*	10.00	25.00
Bethlehem 62	(M)	Relaxin' With Frances Faye	*1956*	10.00	25.00
Bethlehem 6017	(M)	Frances Faye Sings Folk Songs	*1957*	10.00	25.00
Gene Norman 41	(M)	Caught In The Act	*1958*	10.00	25.00
Imperial LP-9059	(M)	Frances Faye Swings Fats Domino	*1959*	8.00	20.00
Imperial LP-12059	(S)	Frances Faye Swings Fats Domino	*1959*	12.00	30.00
Imperial LP-9158	(M)	Frances Faye Sings The Blues	*1961*	6.00	15.00
Imperial LP-12158	(S)	Frances Faye Sings The Blues	*1961*	8.00	20.00
Verve V-2147	(M)	In Frenzy	*1961*	6.00	15.00
Verve V6-2147	(S)	In Frenzy	*1961*	8.00	20.00
Verve V-8434	(M)	Swinging All The Way	*1962*	6.00	15.00
Verve V6-8434	(S)	Swinging All The Way	*1962*	8.00	20.00
Crescendo 92	(M)	Caught In The Act	*1963*	5.00	12.00
Crescendo 92	(S)	Caught In The Act	*1963*	6.00	15.00
Regina 315	(M)	You Gotta Go! Go! Go!	*1964*	6.00	15.00

FEAR ITSELF

| Dot DLP-25942 | (S) | Fear Itself | *1969* | 8.00 | 20.00 |

FENDERMEN, THE

| Soma MG-1240 | (M) | Mule Skinner Blues | *1960* | 400.00 | 600.00 |

FERLINGHETTI, LAWRENCE

Fantasy 7002	(M)	Poetry Readings In The Cellar	*1957*	20.00	50.00
Fantasy 7004	(M)	Impeachment Of President Eisenhower	*1958*	20.00	50.00
		(Fantasy 7002 and 7004 are on red vinyl)			

FIELD, SALLY

| Colgems CO-106 | (M) | Star Of "The Flying Nun" | *1967* | 5.00 | 12.00 |
| Colgems COS-106 | (S) | Star Of "The Flying Nun" | *1967* | 6.00 | 15.00 |

Label		Title	Year	VG+	NM
FIFTY FOOT HOSE					
Limelight 86062	(S)	Cauldron	1969	16.00	40.00
FINCHLEY BOYS, THE					
Golden Throat 200-19	(S)	Everlasting Tribute	1968	60.00	120.00
FIFTH ESTATE, THE					
Jubilee JGM-8005	(M)	Ding Dong The Witch Is Dead	1967	6.00	15.00
Jubilee JGS-8005	(S)	Ding Dong The Witch Is Dead	1967	8.00	20.00
FIRE TOWN					
Boat 1013	(S)	In The Heart Of The Heart Country	1987	4.00	10.00
FIREBALLS, THE					
Also refer to Jimmy Gilmer & The Fireballs.					
Top Rank RM-324	(M)	The Fireballs	1960	30.00	60.00
Top Rank RM-343	(M)	Vaquero	1960	20.00	50.00
Top Rank RS-643	(S)	Vaquero	1960	35.00	70.00
Warwick W-2042	(M)	Here Are The Fireballs	1961	20.00	50.00
Atco SD-33-239	(S)	Bottle Of Wine	1968	6.00	15.00
Atco SD-33-275	(S)	Come On, React!	1969	6.00	15.00
FIREFLIES, THE					
Taurus 1002	(M)	You Were Mine	1961	50.00	100.00
Taurus S-1002	(S)	You Were Mine	1961	75.00	150.00
FIRESIGN THEATRE					
Also refer to Phil Proctor & Dave Bergman.					
Columbia CL-2719	(M)	Waiting For The Electrician	1968	6.00	15.00
Columbia CS-9519	(S)	Waiting For The Electrician	1968	4.00	10.00
Columbia CS-9884	(S)	How Can You Be In Two Places At Once	1969	4.00	10.00
		(Columbia albums above have "360 Sound" labels.)			
Columbia C-30102	(S)	Don't Crush That Dwarf	1970	5.00	12.00
		(Issued with a 22"x33" color poster.)			
Columbia CQ-30737	(Q)	I Think We're All Bozos On This Bus	1971	6.00	15.00
Columbia CQ-33141	(Q)	Everything You Know Is Wrong	1974	6.00	15.00
FISCHER & EPSTEIN					
Swan 514	(M)	It's A Beatle (Coo Coo) World	1964	10.00	25.00
FISCHER, WILDMAN					
Bizarre 2XS-6332	(S)	An Evening With Wildman Fischer	1969	12.00	30.00
FISHER, EDDIE					
RCA LPM-3025 (10")	(M)	Fisher Sings	1952	10.00	25.00
RCA LPM-3058 (10")	(M)	I'm In The Mood For Love	1952	10.00	25.00
RCA LPM-3065 (10")	(M)	Christmas With Fisher	1952	10.00	25.00
RCA LPM-3185 (10")	(M)	May I Sing To You?	1954	10.00	25.00
RCA LPM-3375 (10")	(M)	The Best Of Eddie Fisher	1954	10.00	25.00
RCA LPM-1097	(M)	I Love You	1955	8.00	20.00
RCA LPM-1180	(M)	I'm In The Mood For Love	1955	8.00	20.00
RCA LPM-1181	(M)	May I Sing To You?	1955	8.00	20.00
RCA LPM-1399	(M)	Bundle Of Joy (Sdtk)	1956	20.00	50.00
RCA LPM-1548	(M)	Thinking Of You	1957	8.00	20.00
RCA LPM-1647	(M)	As Long As There's Music	1958	8.00	20.00
RCA LSP-1647	(M)	As Long As There's Music	1958	10.00	25.00
Ramrod T-6001	(M)	Scent Of Mystery (Sdtk)	1960	16.00	40.00
Ramrod ST-6001	(S)	Scent Of Mystery (Sdtk)	1960	20.00	50.00
RCA LPM-2504	(M)	Eddie Fisher's Greatest Hits	1962	5.00	12.00
RCA LSP-2504	(S)	Eddie Fisher's Greatest Hits	1962	6.00	15.00
		(Mono RCA albums above have "Long Play"			
		on the bottom of the label. Stereo albums			
		have "Living Stereo" on the bottom.)			
Ramrod RR-1	(M)	Eddie Fisher At The Winter Garden	1963	6.00	15.00
Ramrod RRS-1	(S)	Eddie Fisher At The Winter Garden	1963	8.00	20.00
Dot DLP-3631	(M)	Eddie Fisher Today!	1965	4.00	10.00
Dot DLP-25631	(S)	Eddie Fisher Today!	1965	5.00	12.00
Dot DLP-3648	(M)	When I Was Young	1965	4.00	10.00
Dot DLP-25648	(S)	When I Was Young	1965	5.00	12.00
Dot DLP-3785	(M)	His Greatest Hits	1966	4.00	10.00
Dot DLP-25785	(S)	His Greatest Hits	1966	5.00	12.00

Miss Toni Fisher, *The Big Hurt*. A big hit, "The Big Hurt" owes more to the excesses of broadway than the excesses of pop or rock. In a gimmicky move, Signet issued this album in "stereomonic" sound only, meaning the hit single was in mono while the rest of the album was in stereo.

Rhonda Fleming, *Rhonda*. Highly collectible amongst fans of popular female vocals, this, like many albums in that genre, sports a captivatingly lovely cover.

Label		Title	Year	VG+	NM
RCA LPM-3726	(M)	Games That Lovers Play	1966	4.00	10.00
RCA LSP-3726	(S)	Games That Lovers Play	1966	5.00	12.00
RCA LPM-3820	(M)	People Like You	1967	4.00	10.00
RCA LSP-3820	(S)	People Like You	1967	5.00	12.00
		(RCA albums above have black labels.)			

FISHER, CHIP

Label		Title	Year	VG+	NM
RCA LPM-1797	(M)	Chipper At The Suger Bowl	1958	10.00	25.00
RCA LSP-1797	(S)	Chipper At The Suger Bowl	1958	12.00	30.00

FISHER, MISS TONI

Label		Title	Year	VG+	NM
Signet WP-509	(P)	The Big Hurt	1960	16.00	40.00

FITZGERALD, ELLA

Label		Title	Year	VG+	NM
Columbia CL-2531 (10")	(M)	Ella, Lena And Billie	1950	50.00	100.00
Decca DL-5084 (10")	(M)	Souvenir Album	1950	16.00	40.00
Decca DL-5300 (10")	(M)	Gershwin Songs	1951	16.00	40.00
Decca DL-8068	(M)	Songs In A Mellow Mood	1955	10.00	25.00
Decca DL-8155	(M)	Sweet And Hot	1955	10.00	25.00
Decca DL-8149	(M)	Lullabies Of Birdland	1955	10.00	25.00
Decca DL-8166	(M)	Pete Kelly's Blues (Sdtk)	1955	14.00	35.00
Decca DL-8378	(M)	Ella Fitzgerald Sings Gershwin Songs	1957	10.00	25.00
Decca DL-8477	(M)	Ella And Her Fellas	1957	10.00	25.00
Decca DL-8695	(M)	First Lady Of Song	1958	10.00	25.00
Decca DL-8696	(M)	Listen And Relax	1958	10.00	25.00
Decca DL-8832	(M)	For Sentimental Reasons	1958	10.00	25.00
Decca DX-156	(M)	The Best Of Ella	1958	12.00	30.00
		(Decca albums above have black & silver labels.)			
Decca DL-4129	(M)	Golden Favorites	1961	8.00	20.00
Decca DL-4447	(M)	Early Ella	1964	8.00	20.00
Decca DL7-4447	(E)	Early Ella	1964	6.00	15.00
Decca DL-4446	(M)	Stairway To The Stars	1964	8.00	20.00
Decca DL7-4446	(E)	Stairway To The Stars	1964	6.00	15.00
Decca DL-4451	(M)	Ella Fitzgerald Sings Gershwin Songs	1964	6.00	15.00
Decca DL7-4451	(E)	Ella Fitzgerald Sings Gershwin Songs	1964	5.00	12.00
Verve V-4001	(M)	The Cole Porter Songbook	1956	16.00	40.00
Verve V-4002	(M)	The Rodgers And Hart Songbook	1956	16.00	40.00
Verve V-4003	(M)	Ella And Louis	1956	16.00	40.00
Verve V-4004	(M)	Like Someone In Love	1957	12.00	30.00
Verve V-4006	(M)	Ella And Louis Again	1956	16.00	40.00
Verve V-4008	(M)	Duke Ellington Songbook, Volume 1	1957	16.00	40.00
Verve V-4009	(M)	Duke Ellington Songbook, Volume 2	1957	16.00	40.00
Verve V-4010	(M)	Duke Ellington Songbook	1957	35.00	70.00
Verve V-4011	(M)	Porgy And Bess	1957	16.00	40.00
Verve V-8234	(M)	Ella And Billie At Newport	1958	12.00	30.00
Verve V-8264	(M)	Ella Fitzgerald At The Opera House	1958	12.00	30.00
Verve V-4017	(M)	Ella And Louis Again, Volume 1	1958	8.00	20.00
Verve V-4018	(M)	Ella And Louis Again, Volume 2	1958	8.00	20.00
Verve V-4019	(M)	The Irving Berlin Songbook	1958	12.00	30.00
Verve V-8288	(M)	One O' Clock Jump	1959	10.00	25.00
Verve V-4021	(M)	Ella Swings Lightly	1959	10.00	25.00
Verve V-4029	(M)	George And Ira Gershwin Songbook	1959	50.00	100.00
Verve V-4032	(M)	Sweet Songs For Swingers	1959	10.00	25.00
Verve V-4034	(M)	Hello, Love	1959	10.00	25.00
Verve V-4036	(M)	Get Happy	1959	10.00	25.00
Verve V6-4036	(S)	Get Happy	1959	10.00	25.00
Verve V-4041	(M)	Mack The Knife/Ella In Berlin	1960	10.00	25.00
Verve V-4042	(M)	Wishes You A Merry Christmas	1960	10.00	25.00
Verve V6-4042	(S)	Wishes You A Merry Christmas	1960	10.00	25.00
Verve V-4043	(M)	Let No Man Write My Epitaph (Sdtk)	1960	10.00	25.00
Verve V6-4043	(S)	Let No Man Write My Epitaph (Sdtk)	1960	12.00	30.00
Verve V-4046	(M)	The Harold Glen Songbook	1961	10.00	25.00
Verve V6-4046	(S)	The Harold Glen Songbook	1961	10.00	25.00
Verve V-4049	(M)	Ella Fitzgerald Sings Cole Porter	1961	8.00	20.00
Verve V-4050	(M)	Ella Fitzgerald Sings More Cole Porter	1961	8.00	20.00
Verve V-4052	(M)	Ella Fitzgerald In Hollywood	1961	8.00	20.00
Verve V6-4052	(S)	Ella Fitzgerald In Hollywood	1961	8.00	20.00
Verve V-4053	(M)	Clap Hands, Here Comes Charlie	1962	8.00	20.00
Verve V-4053	(M)	Clap Hands, Here Comes Charlie	1962	8.00	20.00
Verve V6-4053	(S)	Clap Hands, Here Comes Charlie	1962	8.00	20.00

Label		Title	Year	VG+	NM
Verve V-4054	(M)	Ella Fitzgerald Swings Brightly	1962	8.00	20.00
Verve V6-4054	(S)	Ella Fitzgerald Swings Brightly	1962	8.00	20.00
Verve V-4055	(M)	Ella Fitzgerald Swings Gently	1962	8.00	20.00
Verve V6-4055	(S)	Ella Fitzgerald Swings Gently	1962	8.00	20.00
Verve V-4056	(M)	Rhythm Is My Business	1962	8.00	20.00
Verve V6-4056	(S)	Rhythm Is My Business	1962	8.00	20.00
Verve V-4057	(M)	The Harold Arlen Songbook	1962	10.00	25.00
Verve V6-4057	(S)	The Harold Arlen Songbook	1962	10.00	25.00
		(Verve albums above have black & silver labels with "Verve Records Inc" on the bottom.)			
Verve V-4059	(M)	Ella Sings Broadway	1963	8.00	20.00
Verve V6-4059	(S)	Ella Sings Broadway	1963	8.00	20.00
Verve V-4060	(M)	The Jerome Kern Songbook	1965	8.00	20.00
Verve V6-4060	(S)	The Jerome Kern Songbook	1965	8.00	20.00
Verve V-4061	(M)	Ella And Basie	1963	8.00	20.00
Verve V6-4061	(S)	Ella And Basie	1963	8.00	20.00
Verve V-4062	(M)	These Are The Blues	1963	8.00	20.00
Verve V6-4062	(S)	These Are The Blues	1963	8.00	20.00
Verve V-4063	(M)	The Best Of Ella Fitzgerald	1964	8.00	20.00
Verve V6-4063	(S)	The Best Of Ella Fitzgerald	1964	8.00	20.00
Verve V-4064	(M)	Hello Dolly	1964	8.00	20.00
Verve V6-4064	(S)	Hello Dolly	1964	8.00	20.00
Verve V-4066	(M)	A Tribute To Cole Porter	1964	8.00	20.00
Verve V-4067	(M)	The Johnny Mercer Songbook	1965	8.00	20.00
Verve V6-4067	(S)	The Johnny Mercer Songbook	1965	8.00	20.00
Verve V-8720	(M)	The Best Of Ella Fitzgerald	1967	6.00	15.00
Verve V6-8720	(S)	The Best Of Ella Fitzgerald	1967	6.00	15.00
		(Verve albums above have black & silver labels with "Metro Goldwyn Mayer" on the bottom.)			
Capitol T-2685	(M)	Brighten The Corner	1967	4.00	10.00
Capitol ST-2685	(S)	Brighten The Corner	1967	5.00	12.00
Capitol ST-2888	(S)	Misty Blue	1968	5.00	12.00
Reprise RS-6354	(S)	Ella	1969	5.00	12.00

FIVE AMERICANS, THE

Label		Title	Year	VG+	NM
Hanna Barbera LP-8503	(M)	I See The Light	1966	5.00	12.00
Hanna Barbera ST-9503	(S)	I See The Light	1966	6.00	15.00
Abnak AB-2067	(M)	Western Union/Sound Of Love	1967	5.00	12.00
Abnak ABST-2067	(S)	Western Union/Sound Of Love	1967	6.00	15.00
Abnak AB-2069	(M)	Progressions	1967	5.00	12.00
Abnak ABST-2069	(P)	Progressions	1967	6.00	15.00
Abnak ABST-2071	(P)	Now And Then	1968	6.00	15.00

FIVE EMPREES, THE

Label		Title	Year	VG+	NM
Freeport FR-3001	(M)	The Five Emprees	1965	30.00	60.00
Freeport FRS-4001	(S)	The Five Emprees	1965	40.00	80.00
Freeport FR-3001	(M)	Little Miss Sad	1966	12.00	30.00
Freepot FRS-4001	(S)	Little Miss Sad	1966	16.00	40.00

FIVE KEYS, THE

Label		Title	Year	VG+	NM
Aladdin 806	(M)	The Best Of The Five Keys (Blue label)	1956	300.00	500.00
Score LP-4003	(M)	The Five Keys On The Town	1957	240.00	400.00
Capitol T-828	(M)	The Five Keys On Stage	1957	60.00	120.00
		(The photo on the cover has the first member's hand against his body so that his thumb has a phallic appearance.)			
Capitol T-828	(M)	The Five Keys On Stage	1957	90.00	180.00
		(The cover has the thumb airbrushed out.)			
King 688	(M)	The Five Keys	1960	150.00	250.00
King 692	(M)	Rhythm And Blues Hits Past And Presant	1960	150.00	250.00
Capitol T-1769	(M)	The Fantastic Five Keys	1962	90.00	180.00

FIVE MAN ELECTRICAL BAND, THE

Label		Title	Year	VG+	NM
Capitol ST-165	(S)	The Five Man Electrical Band	1969	8.00	20.00

FIVE ROYALES, THE

Label		Title	Year	VG+	NM
Apollo LP-488	(M)	The Rockin 5 Royales	1956	240.00	400.00
King 580	(M)	Dedicated To You	1957	100.00	200.00
King 616	(M)	The 5 Royales Sing For You	1959	75.00	150.00
King 678	(M)	The Five Royales	1960	75.00	150.00
King 955	(M)	24 All Time Hits	1966	20.00	50.00

Label		Title	Year	VG+	NM
FIVE SATINS, THE					
Ember ELP-100	(M)	The Five Satins Sing (Red label)	1957	75.00	150.00
Ember ELP-100	(M)	The Five Satins Sing (Blue vinyl)	1957	400.00	600.00
		(The price listed is a conservative estimate.)			
Ember ELP-401	(M)	Encore, Volume 2 (Logs label)	1960	20.00	50.00
Mt. Vernon 108	(M)	The Five Satins Sing		12.00	30.00
FIVE STAIRSTEPS (& CUBIE), THE					
Windy C 6000	(M)	The Five Stairsteps	1967	5.00	12.00
Windy C S-6000	(S)	The Five Stairsteps	1967	6.00	15.00
FLAIRS, THE					
Crown CLP-5356	(M)	The Flairs		20.00	50.00
FLAME, THE					
Brother BR-2500	(Q)	Flame (With poster)	1970	10.00	25.00
FLAMIN' GROOVIES, THE					
Snazz (10")	(S)	Sneakers	1969	20.00	50.00
Epic BN-26487	(S)	Supersnazz	1969	12.00	30.00
Kama Sutra KSBS-2021	(S)	Flamingo (Pink label)	1970	6.00	15.00
Kama Sutra KSBS-2031	(S)	Teenage Head (Pink label)	1971	6.00	15.00
Sire D-7521	(S)	Shake Some Action	1976	5.00	12.00
Buddah BDS-5683	(S)	Still Shakin'	1977	5.00	12.00
Sire SRK-6059	(S)	The Flamin' Groovies (12 tracks)	1978	5.00	12.00
FLAMING YOUTH					
Uni 73075	(S)	Ark 2	1969	10.00	25.00
FLAMINGOS, THE					
Chess LP-1425	(M)	Rock, Rock, Rock (Sdtk)	1958	50.00	100.00
Checker LP-1433	(M)	The Flamingos (Blue label)	1959	75.00	150.00
Checker LPS-3005	(E)	The Flamingos (Blue label)	1959	60.00	120.00
End LP-304	(M)	Serenade	1959	20.00	50.00
End LPS-304	(E)	Serenade (Stereo cover)	1959	30.00	60.00
End LPS-304	(E)	Serenade (Rechanneled stereo cover)	1959	20.00	50.00
End LP-307	(M)	Favorites	1960	12.00	30.00
End LPS-307	(E)	Favorites	1960	16.00	40.00
End LP-308	(M)	Requestfully Yours	1960	12.00	30.00
End LPS-308	(E)	Requestfully Yours	1960	16.00	40.00
End LP-316	(M)	The Sound Of The Flamingos	1962	12.00	30.00
End LPS-316	(S)	The Sound Of The Flamingos	1962	16.00	40.00
Vee Jay LP-1052	(M)	The Flamingos Meet The Moonglows	1962	16.00	40.00
Constallation CS-3	(M)	The Flamingos	1964	8.00	20.00
Phillips 200206	(M)	Their Hits-Then And Now	1966	8.00	20.00
Phillips PHS-600206	(S)	Their Hits-Then And Now	1966	10.00	25.00
FLARES, THE					
Press PR-73001	(M)	Encore Of Foot Stompin' Hits	1961	6.00	15.00
Press PRS-83001	(S)	Encore Of Foot Stompin' Hits	1961	8.00	20.00
FLAT EARTH SOCIETY					
Fleetwood 3027	(S)	Waleeco	1968	100.00	200.00
FLEETWOOD MAC					
Also refer to Otis Spann.					
Epic BN-26402	(S)	Fleetwood Mac	1968	6.00	15.00
Epic BN-26446	(S)	English Rose	1969	6.00	15.00
Epic KE-30632	(S)	Black Magic Woman	1971	6.00	15.00
Reprise RS-6368	(S)	Then Play On (With "When You Say")	1969	8.00	20.00
Reprise RS-6408	(S)	Kiln House	1970	6.00	15.00
Reprise RS-6465	(S)	Future Games (Yellow cover)	1971	6.00	15.00
Reprise MS-2080	(S)	Bare Trees (With lyric sheet)	1972	6.00	15.00
Reprise MS-2158	(S)	Mystery To Me (With lyric sheet)	1973	5.00	12.00
Reprise MS-2138	(S)	Penguin	1973	5.00	12.00
Reprise MS-2196	(S)	Heroes Are Hard To Find	1974	5.00	12.00
Reprise MS-2225	(S)	Fleetwood Mac	1975	5.00	12.00
Mobile Fidelity 1-012	(S)	Fleetwood Mac	1978	14.00	35.00
Mobile Fidelity 1-119	(S)	Mirage		8.00	20.00
Nautilus 8	(S)	Rumours	1980	14.00	35.00

Label		Title	Year	VG+	NM
FLEETWOODS, THE					
Dolton BLP-2001	(M)	Mr. Blue	1959	16.00	40.00
Dolton BST-8001	(P)	Mr. Blue	1959	20.00	50.00
Dolton BLP-2002	(M)	The Fleetwoods	1960	12.00	30.00
Dolton BST-8002	(S)	The Fleetwoods	1960	16.00	40.00
Dolton BLP-2005	(M)	Softly	1961	8.00	20.00
Dolton BST-8005	(S)	Softly	1961	10.00	25.00
Dolton BLP-2007	(M)	Deep In A Dream	1961	8.00	20.00
Dolton BST-8007	(S)	Deep In A Dream	1961	10.00	25.00
Dolton BLP-2011	(M)	The Best Of The Oldies	1962	8.00	20.00
Dolton BST-8011	(S)	The Best Of The Oldies	1962	10.00	25.00
		(Dolton albums above have blue & silver labels.)			
Dolton BLP-2018	(M)	The Fleetwoods' Greatest Hits	1962	8.00	20.00
Dolton BST-8018	(P)	The Fleetwoods' Greatest Hits	1962	10.00	25.00
Dolton BLP-2025	(M)	Goodnight My Love	1963	8.00	20.00
Dolton BST-8025	(S)	Goodnight My Love	1963	10.00	25.00
Dolton BLP-2020	(M)	The Fleetwoods Sing For Lovers By Night	1963	8.00	20.00
Dolton BST-8020	(S)	The Fleetwoods Sing For Lovers By Night	1963	10.00	25.00
Dolton BLP-2030	(M)	Before And After	1965	8.00	20.00
Dolton BST-8030	(S)	Before And After	1965	10.00	25.00
Dolton BLP-2039	(M)	Folk Rock	1965	8.00	20.00
Dolton BST-8039	(S)	Folk Rock	1965	10.00	25.00
		(Dolton albums above have blue labels *with a color logo on the left side.)*			
FLEMING, RHONDA					
Columbia CL-1080	(M)	Rhonda	1958	12.00	30.00
FLEMONS, WADE					
Vee Jay LP-1011	(M)	Wade Flemons (Maroon label)	1959	30.00	60.00
FLIRTATIONS, THE					
Deram DES-18028	(S)	Nothing But A Heartache	1969	8.00	20.00
FLOYD, EDDIE					
Stax 714	(M)	Knock On Wood	1967	8.00	20.00
Stax S-714	(S)	Knock On Wood	1967	10.00	25.00
Stax STS-2002	(S)	I've Never Found A Girl	1968	8.00	20.00
Stax STS-2011	(S)	Rare Stamps	1969	6.00	15.00
Stax STS-2017	(S)	You've Got To Have Eddie	1969	6.00	15.00
FOLEY, RED					
Decca DL-5303 (10")	(M)	Souvenir Album	1951	30.00	60.00
Decca DL-5338 (10")	(M)	Lift Up Your Voice	1954	30.00	60.00
Decca DL-8298	(M)	Red And Ernie	1956	20.00	50.00
Decca DL-8294	(M)	Souvenir Album	1958	16.00	40.00
Decca DL-8296	(M)	Beyond The Sunset	1958	12.00	30.00
Decca DL-8767	(M)	He Walks With Thee	1958	12.00	30.00
Decca DL-8806	(M)	My Keepsake Album	1958	12.00	30.00
Decca DL-8847	(M)	Let's All Sing With Red Foley	1959	12.00	30.00
Decca DL7-8847	(S)	Let's All Sing With Red Foley	1959	14.00	35.00
Decca DL-8903	(M)	Let's All Sing To Him	1959	10.00	20.00
Decca DL7-8903	(S)	Let's All Sing To Him	1959	10.00	25.00
		(Decca albums above have black & silver labels.)			
Decca DL-4107	(M)	Red Foley's Golden Favorites	1961	10.00	25.00
Decca DL-4140	(M)	Company's Comin'	1961	10.00	25.00
Decca DL7-4140	(S)	Company's Comin'	1961	12.00	30.00
Decca DL-4198	(M)	Songs Of Devotion	1961	8.00	20.00
Decca DL7-4198	(S)	Songs Of Devotion	1961	10.00	25.00
Decca DL-4290	(M)	Dear Hearts And Gentle People	1962	8.00	20.00
Decca DL7-4290	(S)	Dear Hearts And Gentle People	1962	10.00	25.00
Decca DL-4341	(M)	The Red Foley Show	1963	6.00	15.00
Decca DL7-4341	(S)	The Red Foley Show	1963	8.00	20.00
Decca DXB-177	(M)	The Red Foley Story	1964	6.00	15.00
Decca DXSB7-177	(S)	The Red Foley Story	1964	8.00	20.00
Decca DL-4603	(M)	Songs Everybody Knows	1965	5.00	12.00
Decca DL7-4603	(S)	Songs Everybody Knows	1965	6.00	15.00
		(Decca albums above have black labels with *"Mfrd by Decca" beneath the rainbow)*			

Label		Title	Year	VG+	NM
FOLKSWINGERS, THE					
World Pacific T-1812	(M)	12 String Guitar	1963	4.00	10.00
World Pacific ST-1812	(S)	12 String Guitar	1963	5.00	12.00
World Pacific ST-1812	(S)	12 String Guitar (Red vinyl)	1963	8.00	20.00
World Pacific T-1814	(M)	12 String Guitar, Volume 2	1963	4.00	10.00
World Pacific ST-1814	(S)	12 String Guitar, Volume 2	1963	5.00	12.00
World Pacific WP-1846	(M)	Raga Rock	1966	4.00	10.00
World Pacific WPS-21846	(S)	Raga Rock	1966	5.00	12.00
FONTANA, WAYNE (& THE MINDBENDERS)					
Fontana MGF-27542	(M)	The Game Of Love	1965	10.00	25.00
Fontana SRF-67542	(E)	The Game Of Love	1965	8.00	20.00
MGM E-4459	(M)	Wayne Fontana	1967	5.00	12.00
MGM SE-4459	(S)	Wayne Fontana	1967	6.00	15.00
FONTANE SISTERS, THE					
Dot DLP-3004	(M)	The Fontane Sisters	1956	8.00	20.00
Dot DLP-3042	(M)	The Fontanes Sing	1957	8.00	20.00
Dot DLP-3531	(M)	Tips Of My Fingers	1963	6.00	15.00
Dot DLP-25531	(S)	Tips Of My Fingers	1963	8.00	20.00
FORBES, WALTER					
RCA LPM-2472	(M)	Ballads And Bluegrass	1962	5.00	12.00
RCA LSP-2472	(S)	Ballads And Bluegrass	1962	6.00	15.00
RCA LPM-2670	(M)	Folk Song Festival	1963	5.00	12.00
RCA LSP-2670	(S)	Folk Song Festival	1963	6.00	15.00
FORD, FRANKIE					
Ace LP-1005	(M)	Let's Take A Sea Cruise	1959	75.00	150.00
FORD, ROCKY					
Audio Lab AL-1561	(M)	A New Singing Star	1960	20.00	50.00
FOREIGNER					
Mobile Fidelity 1-052	(S)	Double Vision		10.00	25.00
FORTUNE, JOHNNY					
Park Avenue 401	(M)	Soul Surfer	1963	16.00	40.00
Park Avenue 401	(S)	Soul Surfer	1963	30.00	60.00
FORTUNES, THE					
Press PR7-3002	(M)	The Fortunes	1965	10.00	25.00
Press PRS-83002	(S)	The Fortunes	1965	12.00	30.00
World Pacific WPS-21904	(S)	That Same Old Feeling	1970	5.00	12.00
Capitol ST-647	(S)	Freedom	1971	5.00	12.00
Capitol ST-809	(S)	Here Comes That Rainy Day Feeling Again	1971	6.00	15.00
FORUM, THE					
Mira MLP-301	(M)	The River Is Wide	1967	5.00	12.00
Mira MLPS-3014	(P)	The River Is Wide	1967	6.00	15.00
FORTY-NINTH PARALLEL, THE					
Maverick MAS-7001	(S)	The Forty-Ninth Parallel	1969	50.00	100.00
FOUR ACES, THE					
Decca DL-5429 (10")	(M)	The Four Aces		16.00	40.00
Decca DL-8122	(M)	The Mood For Love	1956	12.00	30.00
Decca DL-8191	(M)	Sentimental Souvenirs/Merry Christmas	1956	12.00	30.00
Decca DL-8228	(M)	Heart And Soul	1956	12.00	30.00
Decca DL-8312	(M)	She Sees All The Hollywood Hits	1957	12.00	30.00
Decca DL-8424	(M)	Written On The Wind (Sdtk)	1957	16.00	40.00
Decca DL-8567	(M)	Shuffling Along	1958	12.00	30.00
Decca DL-8693	(M)	Hits From Hollywood	1958	12.00	30.00
Decca DL-8766	(M)	The Swingin' Aces	1958	10.00	25.00
Decca DL7-8766	(S)	The Swingin' Aces	1958	14.00	35.00
Decca DL-8855	(M)	Hits From Broadway	1959	10.00	25.00
Decca DL7-8855	(S)	Hits From Broadway	1959	14.00	35.00
Decca DL-8944	(M)	Beyond The Blue Horizon	1959	10.00	25.00
Decca DL7-8944	(S)	Beyond The Blue Horizon	1959	14.00	35.00

(Decca albums above have black & silver labels.)

Label		Title	Year	VG+	NM
Decca DL-4013	(M)	The Golden Hits Of The Four Aces		8.00	20.00
Decca DL7-4013	(S)	The Golden Hits Of The Four Aces		8.00	20.00
United Arts. UAL-3337	(M)	Record Oldies		6.00	15.00
United Arts. UAS-6337	(S)	Record Oldies		8.00	20.00

FOUR FRESHMEN, THE

Label		Title	Year	VG+	NM
Capitol T-522	(M)	Voices In Modern	1955	10.00	25.00
Capitol T-683	(M)	Four Freshmen And Five Trombones	1956	10.00	25.00
Capitol T-743	(M)	Freshmen Favorites	1956	10.00	25.00
Capitol T-763	(M)	Four Freshmen And Five Trumpets	1957	10.00	25.00
Capitol T-844	(M)	Four Freshmen And Five Saxes	1957	10.00	25.00
Capitol T-992	(M)	Voices In Latin	1958	10.00	25.00
Capitol T-1008	(M)	The Four Freshmen In Person	1958	6.00	15.00
Capitol ST-1008	(S)	The Four Freshmen In Person	1958	8.00	20.00
		(Capitol albums above have turquoise labels.)			
Capitol T-1074	(M)	Voices In Love	1958	6.00	15.00
Capitol ST-1074	(S)	Voices In Love	1958	8.00	20.00
Capitol T-1103	(M)	Freshmen Favorites, Volume 2	1959	6.00	15.00
Capitol ST-1103	(S)	Freshmen Favorites, Volume 2	1959	8.00	20.00
Capitol T-1189	(M)	Love Lost	1959	6.00	15.00
Capitol ST-1189	(S)	Love Lost	1959	8.00	20.00
Capitol T-1255	(M)	The Four Freshmen And Five Guitars	1960	6.00	15.00
Capitol ST-1255	(S)	The Four Freshmen And Five Guitars	1960	8.00	20.00
Capitol T-1295	(M)	Voices And Brass	1960	6.00	15.00
Capitol ST-1295	(S)	Voices And Brass	1960	8.00	20.00
Capitol T-1378	(M)	First Affair	1960	6.00	15.00
Capitol ST-1378	(S)	First Affair	1960	8.00	20.00
Capitol T-1485	(M)	Freshmen Year	1961	6.00	15.00
Capitol ST-1485	(S)	Freshmen Year	1961	8.00	20.00
Capitol T-1543	(M)	Voices In Fun	1961	6.00	15.00
Capitol ST-1543	(S)	Voices In Fun	1961	8.00	20.00
Capitol T-1640	(M)	The Best Of The Four Freshmen	1962	6.00	15.00
Capitol ST-1640	(S)	The Best Of The Four Freshmen	1962	8.00	20.00
Capitol T-1682	(M)	Stars In Our Eyes	1962	6.00	15.00
Capitol ST-1682	(S)	Stars In Our Eyes	1962	8.00	20.00
		(Capitol albums above have black labels with the Capitol logo on the left side.)			
Capitol T-1753	(M)	Swingers	1962	5.00	12.00
Capitol ST-1753	(S)	Swingers	1962	6.00	15.00
Capitol T-1860	(M)	The Four Freshmen In Person, Volume 2	1963	5.00	12.00
Capitol ST-1860	(S)	The Four Freshmen In Person, Volume 2	1963	6.00	15.00
Capitol T-1950	(M)	Got That Feelin'	1963	5.00	12.00
Capitol ST-1950	(S)	Got That Feelin'	1963	6.00	15.00
Capitol T-2067	(M)	Funny How Time Slips Away	1964	5.00	12.00
Capitol ST-2067	(S)	Funny How Time Slips Away	1964	6.00	15.00
Capitol T-2168	(M)	More Four Freshmen And Five Trombones	1964	5.00	12.00
Capitol ST-2168	(S)	More Four Freshmen And Five Trombones	1964	6.00	15.00
		(Capitol albums above have black labels with the Capitol logo on top.)			
Liberty LST-7563	(S)	Today Is Tomorrow	1968	6.00	15.00
Liberty LST-7590	(S)	In A Class By Themselves	1969	6.00	15.00

FOUR KNIGHTS, THE

Label		Title	Year	VG+	NM
Capitol H-345 (10")	(M)	Spotlight Songs	1953	75.00	150.00
Capitol T-345	(M)	Spotlight Songs	1956	30.00	60.00
Coral CRL-52221	(M)	The Four Knights		16.00	40.00
Coral CRL-57309	(M)	Million Dollar Baby	1960	12.00	30.00
Coral CRL7-57309	(S)	Million Dollar Baby	1960	16.00	40.00

FOUR LADS, THE

Label		Title	Year	VG+	NM
Columbia CL-6329 (10")	(M)	Stage Show		12.00	30.00
Columbia CL-2045 (10")	(M)	The Four Lads Sing Frank Loesser		12.00	30.00
Columbia CL-912	(M)	On The Sunny Side	1956	8.00	20.00
Columbia CL-950	(M)	The Stingiest Man In Town (Sdtk)	1956	16.00	40.00
Columbia CL-1235	(M)	The Four Lads' Greatest Hits	1958	8.00	20.00
Columbia CL-1???	(M)	Breezin' Along	1959	6.00	15.00
Columbia CS-8035	(S)	Breezin' Along	1959	8.00	20.00
Columbia CL-1111	(M)	Four On The Aisle	1959	6.00	15.00
Columbia CS-8047	(S)	Four On The Aisle	1959	8.00	20.00
Columbia CL-1299	(M)	The Four Lads Swing Along	1959	6.00	15.00
Columbia CS-8106	(S)	The Four Lads Swing Along	1959	8.00	20.00

Label		Title	Year	VG+	NM
Columbia CL-1407	(M)	High Spirits!	1959	6.00	15.00
Columbia CS-8203	(S)	High Spirits!	1959	8.00	20.00
Columbia CL-1502	(M)	Love Affair	1960	5.00	12.00
Columbia CS-8293	(S)	Love Affair	1960	6.00	15.00
Columbia CL-1550	(M)	Everything Goes	1960	5.00	12.00
Columbia CS-8350	(S)	Everything Goes	1960	6.00	15.00
		(Columbia albums above have six black "eye" logos on each label.)			
Kapp KL-1224	(M)	Twelve Hits	1961	5.00	12.00
Kapp KS-3224	(S)	Twelve Hits	1961	6.00	15.00
Kapp KL-1254	(M)	Dixieland Doin's	1961	5.00	12.00
Kapp KS-3254	(S)	Dixieland Doin's	1961	6.00	15.00
Dot DLP-3438	(M)	Hits Of The 60's	1962	5.00	12.00
Dot DLP-25438	(S)	Hits Of The 60's	1962	6.00	15.00
Dot DLP-3533	(M)	Oh, Happy Day	1963	5.00	12.00
Dot DLP-25533	(S)	Oh, Happy Day	1963	6.00	15.00
United Arts. UAL-3356	(M)	This Year's Top Movie Hits	1964	5.00	12.00
United Arts. UAS-6356	(S)	This Year's Top Movie Hits	1964	6.00	15.00
United Arts. UAL-3399	(M)	Songs Of World War I	1964	5.00	12.00
United Arts. UAS-6399	(S)	Songs Of World War I	1964	6.00	15.00

FOUR LOVERS, THE
Members Frankie Valli, Nick DeVito and Hank Majewski formed the Four Seasons.

Label		Title	Year	VG+	NM
RCA LPM-1317	(M)	Joyride	1956	300.00	500.00

FOUR PREPS, THE

Label		Title	Year	VG+	NM
Capitol T-994	(M)	The Four Preps (Turquoise label)	1958	10.00	25.00
Capitol T-1090	(M)	Things We Did Last Summer	1958	8.00	20.00
Capitol T-1216	(M)	Dancing And Dreaming	1959	6.00	15.00
Capitol ST-1216	(S)	Dancing And Dreaming	1959	8.00	20.00
Capitol T-1291	(M)	Down By The Station	1960	6.00	15.00
Capitol ST-1291	(S)	Down By The Station	1960	8.00	20.00
Capitol T-1566	(M)	Four Preps On Campus	1961	5.00	12.00
Capitol ST-1566	(S)	Four Preps On Campus	1961	6.00	15.00
Capitol T-1647	(M)	Campus Encore	1962	5.00	12.00
Capitol ST-1647	(S)	Campus Encore	1962	6.00	15.00
		(Capitol albums above have black labels with the Capitol logo on the left side.)			
Capitol T-1814	(M)	Campus Confidential	1963	5.00	12.00
Capitol ST-1814	(S)	Campus Confidential	1963	6.00	15.00
Capitol T-1976	(S)	Songs For A Campus Party	1963	5.00	12.00
Capitol ST-1976	(S)	Songs For A Campus Party	1963	6.00	15.00
Capitol T-2169	(S)	How To Succeed In Love	1964	5.00	12.00
Capitol ST-2169	(S)	How To Succeed In Love	1964	6.00	15.00
Capitol T-2708	(S)	The Best Of The Four Preps	1967	5.00	12.00
Capitol ST-2708	(S)	The Best Of The Four Preps	1967	6.00	15.00
		(Capitol albums above have black labels with the Capitol logo on top.)			

FOUR SEASONS, THE
Also refer to the Four Lovers and the Beatles.

Label		Title	Year	VG+	NM
Vee Jay LP-1053	(M)	Sherry And 11 Others	1962	10.00	25.00
Vee Jay SR-1053	(P)	Sherry And 11 Others	1962	12.00	30.00
Vee Jay LP-1055	(M)	Four Seasons' Greetings		12.00	30.00
Vee Jay SR-1055	(S)	Four Seasons' Greetings		14.00	35.00
Vee Jay LP-1056	(M)	Big Girls Don't Cry	1963	10.00	25.00
Vee Jay SR-1056	(P)	Big Girls Don't Cry	1963	12.00	30.00
Vee Jay LP-1059	(M)	Ain't That A Shame	1963	10.00	25.00
Vee Jay SR-1059	(P)	Ain't That A Shame	1963	12.00	30.00
Vee Jay LP-1065	(M)	Golden Hits Of The Four Seasons	1963	8.00	20.00
Vee Jay SR-1065	(P)	Golden Hits Of The Four Seasons	1963	10.00	25.00
Vee Jay LP-1082	(M)	Folk-Nanny	1964	8.00	20.00
Vee Jay SR-1082	(P)	Folk-Nanny	1964	10.00	25.00
Vee Jay LP-1082	(M)	Stay & Other Great Hits	1964	6.00	15.00
Vee Jay LP-1082	(P)	Stay & Other Great Hits	1964	8.00	20.00
Vee Jay LP-1088	(M)	More Golden Hits By The Four Seasons	1964	8.00	20.00
Vee Jay SR-1088	(P)	More Golden Hits By The Four Seasons	1964	10.00	25.00
		(Includes "Long Lonely Nights.")			
Vee Jay LP-1088	(M)	More Golden Hits By The Four Seasons	1964	6.00	15.00
Vee Jay SR-1088	(P)	More Golden Hits By The Four Seasons	1964	8.00	20.00
		(Includes "Apple Of My Eye.")			

Label		Title	Year	VG+	NM
Vee Jay LP-1121	(M)	We Love Girls	1965	8.00	20.00
Vee Jay SR-1121	(S)	We Love Girls	1965	10.00	25.00
Vee Jay LP-1136	(M)	More Great Hits Of 1964	1964	6.00	15.00
Vee Jay SR-1136	(P)	More Great Hits Of 1964	1964	8.00	20.00
Vee Jay LP-1154	(M)	Recorded Live On Stage	1965	8.00	20.00
Vee Jay SR-1154	(S)	Recorded Live On Stage	1965	10.00	25.00
Philips 200124	(M)	Dawn Go Away And 11 Other Great Songs	1964	6.00	15.00
Philips 600124	(S)	Dawn Go Away And 11 Other Great Songs	1964	8.00	20.00
Philips 200129	(M)	Born To Wander	1964	6.00	15.00
Philips 600129	(S)	Born To Wander	1964	8.00	20.00
Philips 200146	(M)	Rag Doll	1964	6.00	15.00
Philips 600146	(P)	Rag Doll	1964	8.00	20.00
Philips 200150	(M)	All The Song Hits Of The Four Seasons	1964	6.00	15.00
Philips 600150	(S)	All The Song Hits Of The Four Seasons	1964	8.00	20.00
Philips 200164	(M)	The Four Seasons Entertain You	1965	6.00	15.00
Philips 600164	(S)	The Four Seasons Entertain You	1965	8.00	20.00
Philips 200193	(M)	Big Hits By Bacharach, David & Dylan	1965	8.00	20.00
Philips 600193	(S)	Big Hits By Bacharach, David & Dylan	1965	10.00	25.00
		(The cover has a medieval motif.)			
Philips 200193	(M)	Big Hits By Bacharach, David & Dylan	1965	12.00	30.00
Philips 600193	(S)	Big Hits By Bacharach, David & Dylan	1965	14.00	35.00
		(The cover photos of the group.)			
Philips 200196	(M)	Gold Vault Of Hits	1965	5.00	12.00
Philips 600196	(S)	Gold Vault Of Hits	1965	6.00	15.00
Philips 200201	(M)	Working My Way Back To You	1966	6.00	15.00
Philips 600201	(S)	Working My Way Back To You	1966	8.00	20.00
Philips 200221	(M)	2nd Gold Vault Of Hits	1966	5.00	12.00
Philips 600221	(S)	2nd Gold Vault Of Hits	1966	6.00	15.00
Philips 200222	(M)	Lookin' Back	1966	6.00	15.00
Philips 600222	(S)	Lookin' Back	1966	8.00	20.00
Philips 200223	(M)	The Four Seasons' Christmas Album	1966	8.00	20.00
Philips 600223	(S)	The Four Seasons' Christmas Album	1966	10.00	25.00
Philips 200243	(M)	New Gold Hits	1967	6.00	15.00
Philips 600243	(S)	New Gold Hits	1967	8.00	20.00
Philips PHS-2-6501	(S)	Edizone D'Oro	1968	6.00	15.00
		(The "4" on the cover is red.)			
Philips PHS-2-6501	(S)	Edizone D'Oro	1968	10.00	25.00
		(The "4" on the cover is white.)			

FOUR TOPS, THE

Label		Title	Year	VG+	NM
Workshop 217	(M)	Jazz Impressions	1962	300.00	500.00
Motown 622	(M)	The Four Tops	1964	6.00	15.00
Motown MS-622	(S)	The Four Tops	1964	8.00	20.00
Motown 634	(M)	The Four Tops, No. 2	1964	6.00	15.00
Motown MS-634	(S)	The Four Tops, No. 2	1965	8.00	20.00
Motown 647	(M)	The Four Tops On Top	1966	6.00	15.00
Motown MS-647	(S)	The Four Tops On Top	1966	8.00	20.00
Motown 654	(M)	The Four Tops Live	1966	6.00	15.00
Motown MS-654	(S)	The Four Tops Live	1966	8.00	20.00
Motown 657	(M)	The Four Tops On Broadway	1967	5.00	12.00
Motown MS-657	(S)	The Four Tops On Broadway	1967	6.00	15.00
Motown 660	(M)	Reach Out	1967	5.00	12.00
Motown MS-660	(S)	Reach Out	1967	6.00	15.00
Motown 662	(M)	The Four Tops' Greatest Hits	1967	5.00	12.00
Motown MS-662	(S)	The Four Tops' Greatest Hits	1967	6.00	15.00

FOUR TUNES, THE

Label		Title	Year	VG+	NM
Jubilee LP-1039	(M)	12 X 4		35.00	70.00

FOWLEY, KIM

Label		Title	Year	VG+	NM
Tower T-5080	(M)	Love Is Alive And Well	1967	6.00	15.00
Tower ST-5080	(S)	Love Is Alive And Well	1967	8.00	20.00
Imperial LP-12413	(S)	Born To Be Wild	1968	8.00	20.00
Imperial LP-12423	(S)	Outrageous	1969	8.00	20.00
Imperial LP-12443	(S)	Good Clean Fun	1969	8.00	20.00

FOXX, INEZ & CHARLIE

Label		Title	Year	VG+	NM
Symbol SYM-4400	(M)	Mockingbird	1963	20.00	50.00
Sue LP-1037	(M)	Inez And Charlie Foxx	1965	10.00	25.00
Sue LP-1037	(S)	Inez And Charlie Foxx	1965	12.00	30.00

Label		Title	Year	VG+	NM
Dynamo 7000	(M)	Come By Here	1967	5.00	12.00
Dynamo 7000	(S)	Come By Here	1967	6.00	15.00
Dynamo 8002	(M)	Inez And Charlie Foxx's Greatest Hits	1967	5.00	12.00
Dynamo 8002	(S)	Inez And Charlie Foxx's Greatest Hits	1967	6.00	15.00

FRANCIS, CONNIE

Label		Title	Year	VG+	NM
MGM E-3686	(M)	Who's Sorry Now?	1958	16.00	40.00
MGM E-3761	(M)	The Exciting Connie Francis	1959	12.00	30.00
MGM SE-3761	(S)	The Exciting Connie Francis	1959	14.00	35.00
		(MGM albums above have yellow labels.)			
MGM E-3776	(M)	My Thanks To You	1959	10.00	25.00
MGM SE-3776	(S)	My Thanks To You	1959	12.00	30.00
MGM E-3791	(M)	Italian Favorites	1959	6.00	15.00
MGM SE-3791	(S)	Italian Favorites	1959	8.00	20.00
MGM E-3792	(M)	Christmas In My Heart	1959	10.00	25.00
MGM SE-3792	(S)	Christmas In My Heart	1959	12.00	30.00
MGM E-3793	(M)	Connie's Greatest Hits	1960	8.00	20.00
MGM SE-3793	(S)	Connie's Greatest Hits	1960	10.00	25.00
MGM E-3794	(M)	Rock 'N' Roll Million Sellers	1960	10.00	25.00
MGM SE-3794	(S)	Rock 'N' Roll Million Sellers	1960	12.00	30.00
MGM E-3795	(M)	Country And Western Golden Hits	1960	8.00	20.00
MGM SE-3795	(S)	Country And Western Golden Hits	1960	10.00	25.00
MGM E-3853	(M)	Spanish And Latin American Favorites	1960	5.00	12.00
MGM SE-3853	(S)	Spanish And Latin American Favorites	1960	6.00	15.00
MGM E-3869	(M)	Jewish Favorites	1961	5.00	12.00
MGM SE-3869	(S)	Jewish Favorites	1961	6.00	15.00
MGM E-3871	(M)	More Italian Favorites	1961	5.00	12.00
MGM SE-3871	(S)	More Italian Favorites	1961	6.00	15.00
MGM E-3893	(M)	Songs To A Swingin' Band	1961	8.00	20.00
MGM SE-3893	(S)	Songs To A Swingin' Band	1961	10.00	25.00
MGM E-3913	(M)	Connie Francis At The Copa	1961	6.00	15.00
MGM SE-3913	(S)	Connie Francis At The Copa	1961	8.00	20.00
MGM E-3942	(M)	More Greatest Hits	1961	6.00	15.00
MGM SE-3942	(S)	More Greatest Hits	1961	8.00	20.00
MGM E-3965	(M)	Never On Sunday	1961	6.00	15.00
MGM SE-3965	(S)	Never On Sunday	1961	8.00	20.00
MGM E-3969	(M)	Folk Song Favorites	1961	8.00	20.00
MGM SE-3969	(S)	Folk Song Favorites	1961	10.00	25.00
MGM E-4022	(M)	Do The Twist With Connie Francis	1962	8.00	20.00
MGM SE-4022	(S)	Do The Twist With Connie Francis	1962	10.00	25.00
MGM E-4048	(M)	Award Winning Motion Picture Hits	1962	6.00	15.00
MGMS E-4048	(S)	Award Winning Motion Picture Hits	1962	8.00	20.00
MGM E-4049	(M)	Second Hand Love And Other Hits	1962	6.00	15.00
MGM SE-4049	(S)	Second Hand Love And Other Hits	1962	8.00	20.00
MGM E-4079	(M)	Country Music Connie Style	1962	6.00	15.00
MGM SE-4079	(S)	Country Music Connie Style	1962	8.00	20.00
MGM E-4102	(M)	Modern Italian Hits	1963	5.00	12.00
MGM SE-4102	(S)	Modern Italian Hits	1963	6.00	15.00
MGM E-4123	(M)	Follow The Boys (Sdtk)	1963	5.00	12.00
MGM SE-4123	(S)	Follow The Boys (Sdtk)	1963	6.00	15.00
MGM E-4124	(M)	German Favorites	1963	5.00	12.00
MGM SE-4124	(S)	German Favorites	1963	6.00	15.00
MGM E-4145	(M)	Greatest American Waltzes	1963	5.00	12.00
MGM SE-4145	(S)	Greatest American Waltzes	1963	6.00	15.00
MGM E-4161	(M)	Mala Femmena	1963	5.00	12.00
MGM SE-4161	(S)	Mala Femmena	1963	6.00	15.00
MGM E-4167	(M)	The Very Best Of Connie Francis	1963	6.00	15.00
MGM SE-4167	(S)	The Very Best Of Connie Francis	1963	8.00	20.00
MGM E-4210	(M)	In The Summer Of His Years	1964	6.00	15.00
MGM SE-4210	(S)	In The Summer Of His Years	1964	8.00	20.00
MGM E-4229	(M)	Looking For Love (Sdtk)	1964	6.00	15.00
MGM SE-4229	(S)	Looking For Love (Sdtk)	1964	8.00	20.00
MGM E-4251	(M)	Great Country Favorites	1964	6.00	15.00
MGM SE-4251	(S)	Great Country Favorites	1964	8.00	20.00
		(With Hank Williams, Jr.)			
MGM E-4253	(M)	A New Kind Of Connie	1964	6.00	15.00
MGM SE-4253	(S)	A New Kind Of Connie	1964	8.00	20.00
MGM E-4294	(M)	Connie Francis Sings For Mama	1965	5.00	12.00
MGM SE-4294	(S)	Connie Francis Sings For Mama	1965	6.00	15.00
MGM E-4298	(M)	The All Time International Hits	1965	6.00	15.00
MGM SE-4298	(S)	The All Time International Hits	1965	8.00	20.00

Label		Title	Year	VG+	NM
MGM E-4334	(M)	When The Boys Meet The Girls (Sdtk)	1965	3.50	8.00
MGM SE-4334	(S)	When The Boys Meet The Girls (Sdtk)	1965	4.00	10.00
MGM E-4382	(M)	Movie Greats Of The 60's	1966	5.00	12.00
MGM SE-4382	(S)	Movie Greats Of The 60's	1966	6.00	15.00
MGM E-4411	(M)	Live At The Sahara In Las Vegas	1966	5.00	12.00
MGM SE-4411	(S)	Live At The Sahara In Las Vegas	1966	6.00	15.00
MGM E-4448	(M)	Love Italian Style	1967	5.00	12.00
MGM SE-4448	(S)	Love Italian Style	1967	6.00	15.00
MGM E-4472	(M)	Happiness	1967	5.00	12.00
MGM SE-4472	(S)	Happiness	1967	6.00	15.00
MGM E-4487	(M)	My Heart Cries For You	1967	5.00	12.00
MGM SE-4487	(S)	My Heart Cries For You	1967	6.00	15.00
		(MGM albums above have black labels.)			
MGM E-4522	(M)	Hawaii Connie	1968	6.00	15.00
MGM SE-4573	(S)	Connie And Clyde	1968	6.00	15.00
MGM E-4585	(M)	Connie Sings Bacharach & David	1968	6.00	15.00
MGM E-4637	(S)	The Wedding Cake	1969	6.00	15.00

FRANKLIN, ARETHA

Label		Title	Year	VG+	NM
Columbia CL-1612	(M)	Aretha	1961	8.00	20.00
Columbia CS-8412	(S)	Aretha	1961	10.00	25.00
Columbia CL-1761	(M)	The Electrifying Aretha Franklin	1962	8.00	20.00
Columbia CS-8561	(S)	The Electrifying Aretha Franklin	1962	10.00	25.00
Columbia CL-1876	(M)	The Tender... Swinging Aretha Franklin	1962	8.00	20.00
Columbia CS-8676	(S)	The Tender... Swinging Aretha Franklin	1962	10.00	25.00
		(Columbia albums above have six black "eye" logos on each label.)			
Columbia CL-2079	(M)	Laughing On The Outside	1963	6.00	15.00
Columbia CS-8879	(S)	Laughing On The Outside	1963	8.00	20.00
Columbia CL-2163	(M)	Unforgettable	1964	6.00	15.00
Columbia CS-8963	(S)	Unforgettable	1964	8.00	20.00
Columbia CL-2281	(M)	Runnin' Out Of Fools	1964	6.00	15.00
Columbia CS-9081	(S)	Runnin' Out Of Fools	1964	8.00	20.00
Columbia CL-2351	(M)	Yeah!!!	1965	6.00	15.00
Columbia CS-9151	(S)	Yeah!!!	1965	8.00	20.00
Columbia CL-2521	(M)	Soul Sister	1966	6.00	15.00
Columbia CS-9321	(S)	Soul Sister	1966	8.00	20.00
Columbia CL-2629	(M)	Take It Like You Give It	1967	5.00	12.00
Columbia CS-9429	(S)	Take It Like You Give It	1967	6.00	15.00
Columbia CL-2673	(M)	Aretha Franklin's Greatest Hits	1967	5.00	12.00
Columbia CS-9473	(S)	Aretha Franklin's Greatest Hits	1967	6.00	15.00
Columbia CL-2754	(M)	Take A Look	1967	5.00	12.00
Columbia CS-9554	(S)	Take A Look	1967	6.00	15.00
Columbia CS-9601	(S)	Aretha Franklin's Greatest Hits, Volume 2	1968	6.00	15.00
Columbia CS-9776	(S)	Soft And Beautiful	1969	6.00	15.00
		(Columbia albums above have "360 Sound" labels.)			
Atlantic 8139	(M)	I Never Loved A Man The Way I Love You	1967	6.00	15.00
Atlantic SD-8139	(S)	I Never Loved A Man The Way I Love You	1967	5.00	12.00
Atlantic 8150	(M)	Aretha Arrives	1967	6.00	15.00
Atlantic SD-8150	(S)	Aretha Arrives	1967	5.00	12.00
Atlantic SD-8176	(S)	Lady Soul	1968	5.00	12.00
Atlantic SD-8186	(S)	Aretha Now	1968	5.00	12.00
		(Stereo Atlantic albums above have green & blue labels.)			
Atlantic SD-8207	(S)	Aretha In Paris	1968	4.00	10.00
Atlantic SD-8212	(S)	Soul '69	1969	4.00	10.00
Atlantic QD-7205	(Q)	Live At The Fillmore West	1971	6.00	15.00
Atlantic QD	(Q)	The Best Of Aretha Franklin	1971	6.00	15.00

FRANKLIN, ERMA

Label		Title	Year	VG+	NM
Epic LN-3824	(S)	Her Name Is Erma	1962	5.00	12.00
Epic BN-619	(S)	Her Name Is Erma	1962	6.00	15.00

FRATERNITY OF MAN, THE

Label		Title	Year	VG+	NM
ABC S-647	(S)	The Fraternity Of Man	1968	8.00	20.00
Dot DLP-25955	(S)	Get It On	1969	8.00	20.00

FREAK SCENE

Label		Title	Year	VG+	NM
Columbia CL-2556	(M)	Psychedelic Soul	1967	8.00	20.00
Columbia CS-9356	(S)	Psychedelic Soul	1967	10.00	25.00

Label		Title	Year	VG+	NM
FREBERG, STAN					
Capitol T-732	(M)	Comedy Caravan		10.00	25.00
Capitol T-777	(M)	A Child's Garden Of Freberg		10.00	25.00
		(Capitol albums above have turquoise labels.)			
Capitol WBO-1035	(M)	The Best Of The Stan Freberg Show	1958	8.00	20.00
Capitol T-1242	(M)	Stan Freberg With The Original Cast	1959	8.00	20.00
Capitol T-1694	(M)	Face The Funnies	1962	8.00	20.00
Capitol W-1573	(M)	The United States Of America	1961	6.00	15.00
Capitol SW-1573	(S)	The United States Of America	1961	8.00	20.00
		(Capitol albums above have black labels with the Capitol logo on the left side.)			
Capitol T-1816	(M)	Madison Avenue Werewolf	1962	8.00	20.00
Capitol J-3264	(M)	Mickey Mouse's Birthday Party	1963	10.00	25.00
Capitol T-2020	(M)	The Best Of Stan Freberg	1964	8.00	20.00
Capitol T-2551	(M)	Underground Show #1	1966	6.00	15.00
Capitol ST-2551	(S)	Underground Show #1	1966	8.00	20.00
		(Capitol albums above have black labels with the Capitol logo on top.)			
FRED, JOHN, & HIS PLAYBOY BAND					
Paula LP-2191	(M)	John Fred And His Playboys	1966	5.00	12.00
Paula LPS-2191	(S)	John Fred And His Playboys	1966	6.00	15.00
Paula LP-2193	(M)	34:40 Of John Fred And His Playboys	1967	5.00	12.00
Paula LPS-2193	(S)	34:40 Of John Fred And His Playboys	1967	6.00	15.00
Paula LP-2197	(M)	Agnes English	1967	5.00	12.00
Paula LPS-2197	(S)	Agnes English	1967	6.00	15.00
Paula LPS-2197	(S)	Judy In Disguise With Glasses	1968	6.00	15.00
Paula LPS-2201	(S)	Permanently Stated	1968	5.00	12.00
FREDDIE & THE DREAMERS					
Tower T-5003	(M)	I'm Telling You Now	1965	8.00	20.00
Tower DT-5003	(E)	I'm Telling You Now	1965	6.00	15.00
Mercury MG-21017	(M)	Freddie And The Dreamers	1965	8.00	20.00
Mercury SR-61017	(E)	Freddie And The Dreamers	1965	6.00	15.00
Mercury MG-21026	(M)	Do The Freddie	1965	6.00	15.00
Mercury SR-61026	(S)	Do The Freddie	1965	8.00	20.00
Mercury MG-21031	(M)	Seaside Swingers (Sdtk)	1965	5.00	12.00
Mercury SR-61031	(S)	Seaside Swingers (Sdtk)	1965	6.00	15.00
Mercury MG-21053	(M)	Frantic Freddie	1965	5.00	12.00
Mercury SR-61053	(S)	Frantic Freddie	1965	6.00	15.00
Mercury MG-21061	(M)	Fun Lovin' Freddie	1966	5.00	12.00
Mercury SR-61061	(S)	Fun Lovin' Freddie	1966	6.00	15.00
Decca DL-4751	(M)	Out Of Sight (Sdtk)	1966	6.00	15.00
Decca DL7-4751	(S)	Out Of Sight (Sdtk)	1966	8.00	20.00
FREDRIC					
Forte 301	(S)	Phases And Faces	1968	150.00	250.00
FREE SPIRITS, THE					
ABC 593	(M)	Out Of Sight And Sound	1967	6.00	15.00
ABC S-593	(S)	Out Of Sight And Sound	1967	8.00	20.00
FREEBORNE					
Monitor MPS-607	(S)	Peak Impressions	1967	35.00	70.00
FREEMAN, BOBBY					
Jubilee JLP-1086	(S)	Do You Wanna Dance?	1959	20.00	50.00
Jubilee SDJLP-1086	(S)	Do You Wanna Dance?	1959	50.00	100.00
Jubilee JGM-5010	(M)	Twist With Bobby Freeman	1962	12.00	30.00
Autumn LP-102	(M)	C' Mon And S-W-I-M	1964	12.00	30.00
King 930	(M)	The Lovable Style Of Bobby Freeman	1965	16.00	40.00
Josie JM-4007	(M)	Get In The Swim With Bobby Freeman	1965	10.00	25.00
Josie JGS-4007	(E)	Get In The Swim With Bobby Freeman	1965	8.00	20.00
FREHLEY, ACE					
Casablanca NBLP-7121	(S)	Ace Frehley (With poster)	1978	6.00	15.00
Casablanca NBPIX-7121	(S)	Ace Frehley (Picture Disc)	1979	10.00	25.00
FRIAR TUCK					
Mercury MG-21111	(M)	Friar Tuck & His Psychedelic Guitar	1967	5.00	12.00
Mercury SR-61111	(S)	Friar Tuck & His Psychedelic Guitar	1967	6.00	15.00

Label		Title	Year	VG+	NM
FRIENDSOUND (BROTHERHOOD)					
RCA LSP-4114	(S)	Joyride	1969	6.00	15.00
FRIJID PINK					
Parrot PAS-71033	(S)	Frijid Pink	1970	6.00	15.00
Parrot PAS-71041	(S)	Frijid Pink Defrosted	1970	6.00	15.00
FRIZZELL, LEFTY					
Columbia HL-9019 (10")	(M)	The Songs Of Jimmie Rodgers	1951	30.00	60.00
Columbia HL-9021 (10")	(M)	Listen To Lefty	1952	30.00	60.00
Columbia CL-1342	(M)	The One And Only ("Eyes" logo label)	1959	20.00	50.00
Columbia CL-2169	(M)	Saginaw, Michigan	1964	14.00	35.00
Columbia CS-8969	(S)	Saginaw, Michigan	1964	16.00	40.00
Columbia CL-2386	(M)	The Sad Side Of Love	1965	14.00	35.00
Columbia CS-9186	(S)	The Sad Side Of Love	1965	16.00	40.00
Columbia CL-2488	(M)	Lefty Frizzell's Greatest Hits	1966	14.00	35.00
Columbia CS-9288	(S)	Lefty Frizzell's Greatest Hits	1966	16.00	40.00
Columbia CL-2772	(M)	Puttin' On	1967	14.00	35.00
Columbia CS-9572	(S)	Puttin' On	1967	16.00	40.00
		(Columbia albums above have "360 Sound" labels.)			
FROGGIE BEAVER					
Froggie Beaver 7301	(S)	From The Pond	1973	12.00	30.00
FROMAN, JANE					
Capitol T-309	(M)	With A Song In My Heart	1956	10.00	25.00
Capitol T-726	(M)	Faith		8.00	20.00
Capitol T-889	(M)	Songs At Sunset		8.00	20.00
FROST, THE					
Vanguard VSD-6520	(S)	Frost Music	1969	6.00	15.00
Vanguard VSD-6541	(S)	Rock And Roll Music	1969	6.00	15.00
Vanguard VSD-6556	(S)	Through The Eyes Of Music	1970	6.00	15.00
FROST, FRANK, & THE NIGHTHAWKS					
Phillips International 1975	(M)	Hey Boss Man!	1961	500.00	750.00
FROST, MAX, & THE TROOPERS					
Tower ST-5147	(S)	Shape Of Things To Come	1968	16.00	40.00
FRUMMOX					
Probe 4511	(S)	From Here To There	1969	6.00	15.00
FRUT					
Trash 1001	(S)	Keep On Truckin'	1971	8.00	20.00
FUGITIVES, THE					
Hideout 1001	(M)	The Fugitives At Dave's Hideout	1968	180.00	300.00
FUGITIVES, THE					
Westchester 1005	(S)	The Fugitives Said Goodbye	1969	35.00	70.00
FUGS, THE					
Broadside 304	(M)	Ballads Of Contemporary Protest	1966	35.00	70.00
ESP 1018	(M)	The Fugs First Album	1966	10.00	25.00
ESP 1028	(S)	The Fugs	1966	10.00	25.00
ESP 1038	(S)	Virgin Fugs: For Adults Minds Only	1967	10.00	25.00
ESP 2018	(S)	Fugs Four, Rounders Score	1967	10.00	25.00
Reprise RS-6280	(S)	Tenderness Junction	1967	8.00	20.00
Reprise RS-6305	(S)	It Crawled Into My Hand, Honest	1968	8.00	20.00
Reprise RS-6359	(S)	Belle Of Avenue A	1969	8.00	20.00
Reprise RS-6396	(S)	Golden Filth	1970	8.00	20.00
FULLER, JERRY					
Lin LP-100	(M)	Teenage Love	1960	10.00	25.00
FULLER, JESSE					
Cavalier 5006 (10")	(M)	Frisco Bound		40.00	80.00
Cavalier 6009	(M)	Frisco Bound		30.00	60.00

The Best Of The Stan Freberg Show. One of the most influential of all American comedians. Whereas other comedians brought their stage act into the studio and recorded it straight, Freberg was one of the first to utilize the special nature of the medium. His send-ups of "The Banana Boat Song" and "Heartbreak Hotel," both chart singles, are as brilliant as they are irreverent.

The Bobby Fuller Four, *KRLA King Of The Wheels.* Bobby Fuller's great "I Fought The Law" could have heralded a return to the type of texmex rockabilly popularized by Buddy Holly. Unfortunately, Fuller's early and mysterious death (ruled an accident, it has all the earmarks of a murder and a cover-up) put an end to the neo-rockabilly movement before it could get started. This album has been heavily counterfeited.

Label		Title	Year	VG+	NM
FULLER FOUR, BOBBY					
Mustang M-900	*(M)*	KRLA King Of The Wheels	1966	20.00	50.00
Mustang MS-900	*(S)*	KRLA King of The Wheels	1966	30.00	60.00
Mustang M-901	*(M)*	I Fought The Law	1966	12.00	30.00
Mustang MS-901	*(S)*	I Fought The Law	1966	16.00	40.00
FULSON, LOWELL (LOWELL FOLSOM)					
Chess 408	*(M)*	Hung Down Head		8.00	20.00
Kent KLP-5016	*(M)*	Lowell Fulson	1965	8.00	20.00
Kent KLP-5020	*(M)*	Lowell Fulson	1965	8.00	20.00
Kent KLP-520	*(M)*	The Tramp	1967	5.00	12.00
Kent KST-520	*(S)*	The Tramp	1967	6.00	15.00
Kent KST-531	*(S)*	Lowell Fulson Now	1969	5.00	12.00
FUN & GAMES					
Uni 73042	*(S)*	Elephant Candy	1968	6.00	15.00
FUNKADELIC (PARLIAMENT)					
Westbound 2000	*(S)*	Funkadelic	1970	6.00	15.00
Westbound 2001	*(S)*	Free Your Mind And Your Ass Will Follow	1970	6.00	15.00
Westbound 2007	*(S)*	Maggot Brain	1971	6.00	15.00
Westbound 2020	*(S)*	America Eats Its Young	1972	6.00	15.00
Westbound 2022	*(S)*	Cosmic Slop	1973	5.00	12.00
Westbound 1001	*(S)*	Standing On The Verge Of Getting It On	1974	5.00	12.00
Westbound 215	*(S)*	Let's Take It To The Stage	1975	5.00	12.00
Westbound 227	*(S)*	Tales Of Kidd Funkadelic	1976	5.00	12.00
FUSE					
Epic BN-26502	*(S)*	Fuse	1970	10.00	25.00

Label		Title	Year	VG+	NM
G.T.O.'S (GIRLS TOGETHER OUTRAGEOUSLY)					
Straight STS-1059	*(S)*	Permanent Damage (With booklet)	1969	35.00	70.00
Reprise RS-6390	*(S)*	Permanent Damage	1970	14.00	35.00
GALAHADS, THE					
Liberty LRP-3371	*(M)*	Galahads	1964	8.00	20.00
Liberty LST-7371	*(S)*	Galahads	1964	10.00	25.00
GALE, SUNNY					
RCA LPM-1277	*(M)*	Sunny And Blue	1956	10.00	25.00
GALS & PALS					
Fontana MGF-27538	*(M)*	The Gals And Pals	1965	6.00	15.00
Fontana SRS-67538	*(S)*	The Gals And Pals	1965	8.00	20.00
GAME					
Faithful Virtue 2003	*(S)*	Game	1969	8.00	20.00
GANDALF					
Capitol ST-121	*(S)*	Gandalf	1969	30.00	60.00
GANDALF THE GREY					
G.W.R. 7	*(S)*	The Grey Wizard Am I		75.00	150.00
GANT, CECIL					
Sound 601	*(M)*	The Incomparable Cecil Gant	1957	30.00	60.00
King 671	*(M)*	Cecil Gant		35.00	70.00

Label		Title	Year	VG+	NM
GANTS, THE					
Liberty LRP-3432	(M)	Road Runner	1965	8.00	20.00
Liberty LST-7432	(P)	Road Runner	1965	10.00	25.00
Liberty LRP-3455	(M)	The Gants Galore	1966	6.00	15.00
Liberty LST-7455	(S)	The Gants Galore	1966	8.00	20.00
Liberty LRP-3473	(M)	The Gants Again	1966	6.00	15.00
Liberty LST-7473	(S)	The Gants Again	1966	8.00	20.00
GARAGIOLA, JOE					
United Arts. UAS-6032	(S)	That Holler Guy	1973	6.00	15.00
GARBO, GRETA					
MGM E-4201	(M)	Garbo		16.00	40.00
GARCIA, JERRY					
Also refer to Howard Wales.					
MGM SE-4468	(S)	Zabriskie Point (Sdtk)	1970	6.00	15.00
Warners BS-2582	(S)	Garcia	1972	10.00	25.00
Round RX-102	(S)	Garcia	1974	8.00	20.00
Round RX-107	(S)	Reflections	1975	8.00	20.00
United Arts. LA565	(S)	Reflections	1976	6.00	15.00
GARDNER, DON, & DEE DEE FORD					
Fire LP-105	(M)	Need Your Lovin'	1962	50.00	100.00
Sue LP-1044	(M)	In Sweden	1965	14.00	35.00
GARLAND, JUDY					
MGM E-501 (10")	(M)	Tills The Clouds Roll By (Sdtk)	1950	30.00	60.00
MGM E-502 (10")	(M)	Easter Parade (Sdtk)	1950	50.00	100.00
MGM E-505 (10")	(M)	Words And Music (Sdtk)	1950	20.00	50.00
MGM E-519 (10")	(M)	Summer Stock (Sdtk)	1950	20.00	50.00
MGM E-21 (10")	(M)	The Pirate/Summer Stock (Sdtk)	1951	20.00	50.00
MGM E-82 (10")	(M)	Judy Garland Sings		16.00	40.00
MGM E-3149	(M)	If You Feel Like Singing, Sing	1955	16.00	40.00
MGM E-3227	(M)	Easter Parade (Sdtk)	1955	16.00	40.00
MGM E-3231	(M)	Tills The Clouds Roll By (Sdtk)	1955	16.00	40.00
MGM E-3232	(M)	In The Good Old Summertime (Sdtk)	1955	16.00	40.00
MGM E-3233	(M)	Words And Music (Sdtk)	1955	16.00	40.00
MGM E-3234	(M)	Summer Stock/The Pirate (Sdtk)	1955	16.00	40.00
Capitol T-676	(M)	Miss Show Business	1955	16.00	40.00
Capitol T-734	(M)	Judy	1956	16.00	40.00
Capitol T-835	(M)	Alone	1957	14.00	35.00
		(Capitol albums above have turquoise labels.)			
MGM E-3249	(M)	Judy Garland With The MGM Orchestra	1956	16.00	40.00
MGM E-3464	(M)	The Wizard Of Oz (Sdtk)	1956	16.00	40.00
Decca DL-8190	(M)	Judy Garland's Greatest Performances	1956	16.00	40.00
Decca DL-8387	(M)	The Wizard Of Oz	1957	16.00	40.00
Decca DL-8498	(M)	Meet Me In St. Louis (Sdtk)	1957	16.00	40.00
Decca DL-8498	(M)	The Harvey Girls (Sdtk)	1957	35.00	70.00
Columbia CL-1101	(M)	A Star Is Born (Sdtk)	1958	12.00	30.00
Capitol T-1036	(M)	In Love	1958	10.00	25.00
Capitol ST-1036	(S)	In Love	1958	14.00	35.00
MGM E-3770	(M)	Tills The Clouds Roll By (Sdtk)	1959	16.00	40.00
MGM E-3771	(M)	Words And Music/Good News (Sdtk)	1959	16.00	40.00
		(MGM albums above have yellow labels.)			
Capitol T-1118	(M)	Garland At The Grove	1959	10.00	25.00
Capitol ST-1118	(S)	Garland At The Grove	1959	14.00	35.00
Capitol T-1188	(M)	The Letter (With letter attached to cover)	1959	16.00	40.00
Capitol ST-1188	(S)	The Letter (With letter attached to cover)	1959	20.00	50.00
Capitol T-1467	(M)	That's Entertainment	1960	10.00	25.00
Capitol ST-1467	(S)	That's Entertainment	1960	12.00	30.00
Capitol WBO-1569	(M)	Judy At Carnegie Hall	1961	10.00	25.00
Capitol SWBO-1569	(S)	Judy At Carnegie Hall	1961	12.00	30.00
		(Capitol albums above have black labels with the Capitol logo on the left side.)			
Decca DL-4199	(M)	The Magic Of Judy Garland	1961	10.00	25.00
Colpix CP-507	(M)	Pepe (Sdtk)	1961	12.00	30.00
Colpix SCP-507	(S)	Pepe (Sdtk)	1961	12.00	30.00
Warners B-1479	(M)	Gay Purr-ee (Sdtk)	1962	8.00	20.00
Warners BS-1479	(S)	Gay Purr-ee (Sdtk)	1962	12.00	30.00
MGM E-3989	(M)	The Star Years		10.00	25.00

Label		Title	Year	VG+	NM
MGM E-3996	(M)	The Wizard Of Oz	1962	10.00	25.00
MGM SE-3996	(E)	The Wizard Of Oz	1962	10.00	25.00
MGM E-4005	(M)	The Hollywood Years		10.00	25.00
MGM E-4204	(M)	The Very Best Of Judy Garland		10.00	25.00
		(MGM albums above have black labels.)			
Capitol W-1710	(M)	The Garland Touch	1962	10.00	25.00
Capitol SW-1710	(S)	The Garland Touch	1962	12.00	30.00
Capitol W-1861	(M)	I Could Go On Singing (Sdtk)	1963	10.00	25.00
Capitol SW-1861	(S)	I Could Go On Singing (Sdtk)	1963	12.00	30.00
Capitol T-1941	(M)	Our Love Letter	1963	10.00	25.00
Capitol ST-1941	(S)	Our Love Letter	1963	12.00	30.00
Capitol T-1999	(M)	The Hits Of Judy Garland	1963	8.00	20.00
Capitol ST-1999	(S)	The Hits Of Judy Garland	1963	10.00	25.00
Columbia CL-1940	(M)	A Star Is Born (Sdtk)	1963	5.00	12.00
Columbia CS-8740	(E)	A Star Is Born (Sdtk)	1963	5.00	12.00
Capitol W-2062	(M)	Just For Openers	1964	8.00	20.00
Capitol DW-2062	(S)	Just For Openers	1964	10.00	25.00
Decca DXB-172	(M)	The Best Of Judy Garland	1964	6.00	15.00
Decca DXSB7-172	(S)	The Best Of Judy Garland	1964	8.00	20.00
Capitol TAO-2295	(M)	Live At The London Palladium	1965	6.00	15.00
Capitol STAO-2295	(S)	Live At The London Palladium	1965	8.00	20.00
Capitol STCL-2988	(S)	Deluxe Set	1967	16.00	40.00
		(Capitol albums above have black labels			
		with the Capitol logo on top.)			
ABC 620	(M)	At Home At The Palace	1967	8.00	20.00
ABC S-620	(S)	At Home At The Palace	1967	8.00	20.00
MGM SDP-1	(P)	Golden Years At M-G-M	1969	6.00	15.00
MGM GAS-113	(P)	Judy Garland	1970	6.00	15.00
Decca DL7-5150	(S)	Judy Garland's Greatest Hits	1970	6.00	15.00
Decca DL7-5	(E)	Collectors Items 1936-1945	1970	6.00	15.00
Mobile Fidelity 1-048	(S)	Live At The London Palladium		6.00	15.00

GAS MASK

Tonsil 4001	(S)	Gas Mask	1970	8.00	20.00

GATES, HEN, & HIS GATERS

Masterseal M-700	(M)	Let's Go Dancing To Rock And Roll		12.00	30.00

GATEWAY SINGERS, THE

Decca DL-8413	(M)	Puttin' On The Style	1958	8.00	20.00
Decca DL-8671	(M)	The Gateway Singers At The Hungry i	1958	8.00	20.00
Decca DL-8742	(M)	The Gateway Singers In Hi Fi	1958	8.00	20.00
Warners W-1295	(M)	The Gateway Singers On The Lot	1959	5.00	12.00
Warners WS-1295	(S)	The Gateway Singers On The Lot	1959	6.00	15.00
Warners W-1334	(M)	Wagons West	1969	5.00	12.00
Warners WS-1334	(S)	Wagons West	1969	6.00	15.00
MGM E-3905	(M)	Down In The Valley	1961	5.00	12.00
MGM SE-3905	(S)	Down In The Valley	1961	6.00	15.00
MGM E-4154	(M)	Hootenanny	1963	5.00	12.00
MGM SE-4154	(S)	Hootenanny	1963	6.00	15.00

GATEWAY TRIO, THE

Capitol T-1868	(M)	The Mad, Mad, Mad, Mad Gateway Trio		6.00	15.00
Capitol ST-1868	(S)	The Mad, Mad, Mad, Mad Gateway Trio		8.00	20.00
Capitol T-2184	(M)	The Gateway Trio		5.00	12.00
Capitol ST-2184	(S)	The Gateway Trio		6.00	15.00

GAUCHOS, THE

ABC-Paramount 506	(M)	The Gauchos Featuring Jim Dovel	1965	10.00	25.00
ABC-Paramount S-506	(S)	The Gauchos Featuring Jim Dovel	1965	12.00	30.00

GAYE, MARVIN
Also refer to Diana Ross and Mary Wells.

Tamla 221	(M)	Soulful Moods Of Marvin Gaye	1961	40.00	80.00
Tamla 239	(M)	That Stubborn Kind Of Fella	1963	40.00	80.00
Tamla 242	(M)	On Stage Recorded Live	1963	16.00	40.00
Tamla 251	(M)	When I'm Alone I Cry	1964	16.00	40.00
Tamla 258	(M)	How Sweet It Is To Be Loved By You	1965	12.00	30.00
Tamla TS-258	(S)	How Sweet It Is To Be Loved By You	1965	16.00	40.00
Tamla 259	(M)	Hello Broadway, This Is Marvin	1965	10.00	25.00
Tamla TS-259	(S)	Hello Broadway, This Is Marvin	1965	12.00	30.00

Label		Title	Year	VG+	NM
Tamla 261	(M)	Tribute To The Great Nat King Cole	1965	8.00	20.00
Tamla TS-261	(S)	Tribute To The Great Nat King Cole	1965	10.00	25.00
Tamla 266	(M)	Moods Of Marvin Gaye	1966	8.00	20.00
Tamla TS-266	(S)	Moods Of Marvin Gaye	1966	10.00	25.00
Tamla 270	(M)	Marvin Gaye And Kim Weston	1966	8.00	20.00
Tamla TS-270	(S)	Marvin Gaye And Kim Weston	1966	8.00	20.00
Tamla 278	(M)	Marvin Gaye's Greatest Hits, Volume 2	1967	6.00	15.00
Tamla TS-278	(S)	Marvin Gaye's Greatest Hits, Volume 2	1967	8.00	20.00
Tamla TS-285	(S)	In The Groove	1968	8.00	20.00
Tamla TS-285	(S)	I Heard It Through The Grapevine	1968	6.00	15.00
Tamla TS-292	(S)	M.P.G.	1969	6.00	15.00
Tamla TS-293	(S)	Marvin Gaye And His Girls	1969	5.00	12.00
Tamla TS-299	(S)	That's The Way Love Is	1970	6.00	15.00
Tamla TS-300	(S)	Marvin Gaye's Super Hits	1970	6.00	15.00

GAYE, MARVIN, & TAMI TERRELL

Label		Title	Year	VG+	NM
Tamla 277	(M)	United	1967	4.00	10.00
Tamla TS-277	(S)	United	1967	5.00	12.00
Tamla TS-284	(S)	You're All I Need	1968	5.00	12.00
Tamla TS-294	(S)	Easy	1969	5.00	12.00
Tamla TS-302	(S)	Greatest Hits	1970	4.00	10.00

GAYLE, CRYSTAL

Label		Title	Year	VG+	NM
Mobile Fidelity 1-043	(S)	We Must Believe In Magic		6.00	15.00

GAYLORDS, THE

Label		Title	Year	VG+	NM
Mercury MG-25198 (10")	(M)	By Request		14.00	35.00
Mercury MG-20075	(M)	Let's Have A Pizza Party		10.00	25.00
Mercury MG-20186	(M)	Italia		10.00	25.00
Wing MGW-12139	(M)	Italiano Favorites	1959	6.00	15.00
Mercury MG-20620	(M)	American Hits In Italian	1961	5.00	12.00
Mercury SR-60620	(S)	American Hits In Italian	1961	6.00	15.00
Mercury MG-20695	(M)	The Gaylords At The Shamrock	1962	5.00	12.00
Mercury SR-60695	(S)	The Gaylords At The Shamrock	1962	6.00	15.00
Mercury MG-20742	(M)	Party Style	1963	5.00	12.00
Mercury SR-60742	(S)	Party Style	1963	6.00	15.00

GEILS BAND, J.

Label		Title	Year	VG+	NM
Atlantic QD-7260	(Q)	Bloodshot	1973	6.00	15.00
Atlantic QD-7286	(Q)	Ladies Invited	1973	6.00	15.00
Atlantic QD-18107	(Q)	Nightmares	1974	6.00	15.00
Atlantic SD-7260	(S)	Bloodshot (Red vinyl)	1973	6.00	15.00
Nautilus NR-25	(S)	Love Stinks		8.00	20.00

GENE & DEBBIE

Label		Title	Year	VG+	NM
T.R.X. LPS-1001	(S)	Hear And Now	1968	10.00	25.00

GENESIS

Label		Title	Year	VG+	NM
Mercury SR-61175	(S)	In The Beginning (Red label)	1968	6.00	15.00

GENESIS

Label		Title	Year	VG+	NM
Impulse AS-9025	(S)	Trespass	1970	8.00	20.00
Famous Charisma 1052	(S)	Nursery Cryme (Pink label)	1972	5.00	12.00
Famous Charisma 1058	(S)	Foxtrot (Pink label)	1972	5.00	12.00
London PS-643	(S)	From Genesis To Revelation	1974	6.00	15.00
Buddah BDS-5659	(S)	The Best Of Genesis	1976	6.00	15.00
Mobile Fidelity 1-062	(S)	A Trick Of The Tail	1981	12.00	30.00

GENTLE GIANT

Label		Title	Year	VG+	NM
Vertigo VE-1005	(S)	Acquiring The Taste	1971	6.00	15.00

GENTLE SOUL

Label		Title	Year	VG+	NM
Epic BN-26374	(S)	Gentle Soul	1968	8.00	20.00

GENTRYS, THE

Label		Title	Year	VG+	NM
MGM E-4336	(M)	Keep On Dancing	1965	6.00	15.00
MGM SE-4336	(S)	Keep On Dancing	1965	8.00	20.00
MGM E-4346	(M)	Time	1966	5.00	12.00
MGM SE-4346	(S)	Time	1966	6.00	15.00
MGM GAS-127	(S)	The Gentrys	1966	5.00	12.00
Sun 117	(S)	The Gentrys	1970	8.00	20.00

Judy Garland, *Judy.* One of the most enigmatic entertainers in recent memory, Ms. Garland had been a star for MGM pictures and records for decades before signing with Capitol in the mid '50s. *Judy* was her second album for her new label.

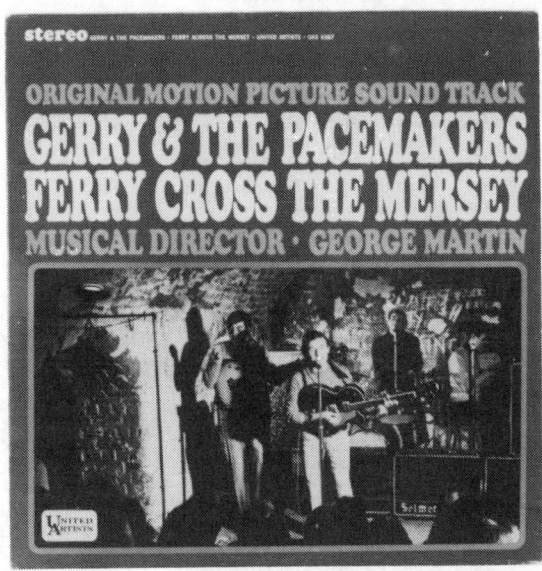

Gerry & The Pacemakers, *Ferry Cross the Mersey.* Rightfully a soundtrack to one of the better rock related films of all time, this is also one G&TP's better albums. Copies in anything resembling mint condition are increasingly difficult to find. Also features the George Martin Orchestra.

Label		Title	Year	VG+	NM
GEORDIE					
MGM SE-4903	(S)	Hope You Like It	1973	10.00	25.00
GEORGE, BARBARA					
A.F.O. 5001	(M)	I Know You Don't Love Me Anymore	1962	50.00	100.00
GERONIMO BLACK					
Uni 73132	(S)	Geronimo Black	1972	10.00	25.00
GERRY & THE PACEMAKERS					
Laurie LLP-2024	(M)	Don't Let The Sun Catch You Crying	1964	10.00	25.00
Laurie SLP-2024	(E)	Don't Let The Sun Catch You Crying	1964	8.00	20.00
Laurie LLP-2027	(M)	Second Album	1964	10.00	25.00
Laurie SLLP-2027	(E)	Second Album	1964	8.00	20.00
United Arts. UAL-3387	(M)	Ferry Across The Mersey (Sdtk)	1965	10.00	25.00
United Arts. UAS-6387	(S)	Ferry Across The Mersey (Sdtk)	1965	12.00	30.00
Laurie LLP-2030	(M)	I'll Be There	1964	10.00	25.00
Laurie SLLP-2030	(E)	I'll Be There	1964	8.00	20.00
Laurie LLP-2031	(M)	Gerry & The Pacemakers' Greatest Hits	1965	8.00	20.00
Laurie SLLP-2031	(E)	Gerry & The Pacemakers' Greatest Hits	1965	6.00	15.00
Laurie LLP-2037	(M)	Girl On A Swing	1967	10.00	25.00
Laurie SLP-2037	(E)	Girl On A Swing	1965	8.00	20.00
GHOULS, THE					
Capitol T-2215	(M)	Dracula's Deuce	1965	8.00	20.00
Capitol ST-2215	(S)	Dracula's Deuce	1965	10.00	25.00
GIANT CRAB					
Uni 73037	(S)	A Giant Crab Comes Forth	1968	6.00	15.00
Uni 73057	(S)	Cool It, Helios	1969	6.00	15.00
GIBB, ROBIN					
Atco SD-33-323	(S)	Robin's Reign	1970	6.00	15.00
GIBBS, GEORGIA					
Mercury MG-25175 (10")	(M)	Georgia Gibbs Sings Oldies		12.00	30.00
Mercury MG-25199 (10")	(M)	The Man That Got Away		12.00	30.00
Mercury MG-20071	(M)	Music And Memories		10.00	25.00
Mercury MG-20114	(M)	Song Favorites		10.00	25.00
Mercury MG-20170	(M)	Swingin' With Her Nibs		10.00	25.00
Coral CRL-56037	(M)	Ballin' The Jack		8.00	20.00
Coral CRL-57183	(M)	Her Nibs		8.00	20.00
Imperial LP-9264	(M)	Something's Gotta Give		6.00	15.00
Imperial LP-12264	(S)	Something's Gotta Give		8.00	20.00
Epic LN-24059	(M)	Georgia Gibbs' Greatest Hits		5.00	12.00
Epic BN-26059	(S)	Georgia Gibbs' Greatest Hits		6.00	15.00
Bell 6000	(M)	Call Me	1966	5.00	12.00
Bell 6000	(S)	Call Me	1966	6.00	15.00
GIBSON, DON					
Lion 70069	(M)	Songs By Don Gibson	1958	20.00	50.00
RCA LPM-1743	(M)	Oh Lonesome Me	1958	12.00	30.00
RCA LPM-1918	(M)	No One Stands Alone	1959	8.00	20.00
RCA LSP-1918	(S)	No One Stands Alone	1959	10.00	25.00
RCA LPM-2038	(M)	That Gibson Boy	1959	8.00	20.00
RCA LSP-2038	(S)	That Gibson Boy	1959	10.00	25.00
RCA LPM-2184	(M)	Look Who's Blue	1960	8.00	20.00
RCA LSP-2184	(S)	Look Who's Blue	1960	10.00	25.00
RCA LPM-2269	(M)	Sweet Dreams	1960	8.00	20.00
RCA LPM-2269	(S)	Sweet Dreams	1960	10.00	25.00
RCA LPM-2361	(M)	Girls, Guitars And Gibson	1961	6.00	15.00
RCA LSP-2361	(S)	Girls, Guitars And Gibson	1961	10.00	25.00
RCA LPM-2448	(M)	Some Favorites Of Mine	1962	6.00	15.00
RCA LSP-2448	(S)	Some Favorites Of Mine	1962	10.00	25.00
RCA LPM-2702	(M)	I Wrote A Song	1963	6.00	15.00
RCA LSP-2702	(S)	I Wrote A Song	1963	10.00	25.00
		(Mono RCA albums above have "Long Play" on the bottom of the label. Stereo albums have "Living Stereo" on the bottom.)			
RCA LPM-2878	(M)	God Walks These Hills	1964	6.00	15.00
RCA LSP-2878	(S)	God Walks These Hills	1964	8.00	20.00

Label		Title	Year	VG+	NM
RCA LPM-3376	(M)	The Best Of Don Gibson	1965	6.00	15.00
RCA LSP-3376	(S)	The Best Of Don Gibson	1965	8.00	20.00
RCA LPM-3470	(M)	Too Much Hurt	1965	6.00	15.00
RCA LSP-3470	(S)	Too Much Hurt	1965	8.00	20.00
RCA LPM-3594	(M)	Don Gibson With Spanish Guitar	1966	6.00	15.00
RCA LSP-3594	(S)	Don Gibson With Spanish Guitar	1966	8.00	20.00
RCA LPM-3680	(M)	Great Country Songs	1966	6.00	15.00
RCA LSP-3680	(S)	Great Country Songs	1966	8.00	20.00
RCA LPM-3843	(M)	All My Love	1967	6.00	15.00
RCA LSP-3843	(S)	All My Love	1967	8.00	20.00
RCA LSP-3974	(S)	The King Of Country Soul	1968	6.00	15.00
RCA LSP-4053	(S)	More Country Soul	1968	6.00	15.00
		(RCA albums above have black labels.)			

GIBSON, HARRY

Label		Title	Year	VG+	NM
Sutton SSU-313	(M)	Rockin' Rhythm		6.00	15.00

GIBSON, STEVE, & THE RED CAPS

Label		Title	Year	VG+	NM
Mercury MG-25116 (10")	(M)	Steve Gibson And The Red Caps		100.00	200.00

GILBERT, ANN

Label		Title	Year	VG+	NM
Vik 1090	(M)	In A Swingin' Mood		10.00	25.00
Groove 1004	(M)	The Many Moods Of Ann Gilbert		10.00	25.00

GILES, GILES & FRIPP

Label		Title	Year	VG+	NM
Deram DES-18019	(S)	Cheerful Insanity	1968	14.00	35.00

GILLESPIE, DARLENE

Label		Title	Year	VG+	NM
Disneyland WDL-3010	(M)	Darlene Of The Teens		20.00	50.00

GILLEY, MICKEY

Label		Title	Year	VG+	NM
Astro 101	(M)	Lonely Wine	1964	180.00	300.00

GILMER, JIMMY, & THE FIREBALLS

Label		Title	Year	VG+	NM
Dot DLP-3512	(M)	Torquay	1963	12.00	30.00
Dot DLP-25512	(S)	Torquay	1963	16.00	40.00
Dot DLP-3545	(M)	Sugar Shack	1963	10.00	25.00
Dot DLP-25545	(S)	Sugar Shack	1963	12.00	30.00
Dot DLP-3577	(M)	Buddy's Buddy	1964	16.00	40.00
Dot DLP-25577	(S)	Buddy's Buddy	1964	20.00	50.00
Dot DLP-3643	(M)	Lucky 'Leven	1965	8.00	20.00
Dot DLP-25643	(S)	Lucky 'Leven	1965	10.00	25.00
Dot DLP-3668	(M)	Folkbeat	1965	8.00	20.00
Dot DLP-25668	(S)	Folkbeat	1965	10.00	25.00
Dot DLP-3709	(M)	Campusology	1966	8.00	20.00
Dot DLP-25709	(S)	Campusology	1966	10.00	25.00
Dot DLP-25856	(P)	Firewater	1968	8.00	20.00

GINNY & GALLIONS

Label		Title	Year	VG+	NM
Downey DS-1003	(S)	Two Sides Of Ginny And Gallions	1964	14.00	35.00

GINSBERG, ALLEN

Label		Title	Year	VG+	NM
Fantasy 7006	(M)	Howl And Other Poems (Red vinyl)	1959	20.00	50.00
Atlantic 4001	(M)	Allen Ginsberg Reads Kaddish	1966	8.00	20.00
Forecast FVS-3083	(M)	Songs Of Innocence And Experience	1969	8.00	20.00

GLACIERS, THE

Label		Title	Year	VG+	NM
Mercury MG-20895	(M)	From Sea To Ski	1964	8.00	20.00
Mercury SR-60895	(S)	From Sea To Ski	1964	10.00	25.00

GLASER, TOMPALL (& THE GLASER BROTHERS)

Label		Title	Year	VG+	NM
Decca DL-4041	(M)	The Land-Folk Songs	1960	8.00	20.00
Decca DL7-4041	(S)	The Land-Folk Songs	1960	10.00	25.00
United Arts. UAL-3540	(M)	The Ballad Of Namu The Killer Whale	1966	6.00	15.00
United Arts. UAS-6540	(S)	The Ballad Of Namu The Killer Whale	1966	8.00	20.00

GLASS HARP, THE

Label		Title	Year	VG+	NM
Decca DL-75261	(S)	Glass Harp	1971	6.00	15.00
Decca DL-75306	(S)	Synergy	1971	6.00	15.00
Decca DL-75358	(S)	It Makes Me Glad	1972	6.00	15.00

Label		Title	Year	VG+	NM
GLEASON (ORCHESTRA), JACKIE					
Capitol H-352 (10")	(M)	Music For Lovers Only	1953	8.00	20.00
Capitol H-455 (10")	(M)	Music To Make You Misty	1954	8.00	20.00
Capitol T-475	(M)	Music For Lovers Only/To Make You Misty	1955	8.00	20.00
Capitol T-509	(M)	Music, Martinis And Memories	1955	6.00	15.00
Capitol T-511	(M)	And Awaaay We Go!	1955	6.00	15.00
Capitol T-570	(M)	Music To Remember Her	1955	6.00	15.00
Capitol T-568	(M)	Romantic Jazz	1955	6.00	15.00
Capitol T-627	(M)	Lonesome Echo	1955	6.00	15.00
Capitol T-632	(M)	Music To Change Her Mind	1956	6.00	15.00
Capitol T-717	(M)	Night Winds	1956	6.00	15.00
Capitol T-758	(M)	Merry Christmas	1956	6.00	15.00
Capitol T-816	(M)	Music For The Love Hours	1957	6.00	15.00
		(Capitol albums above have turquoise or grey labels with "Long Playing" on the bottom.)			
Capitol T-859	(M)	Velvet Brass	1957	6.00	15.00
Capitol T-905	(M)	Jackie Gleason Presents "Ooool"	1957	6.00	15.00
		(Capitol albums above have turquoise or grey labels with "Long Playing High Fidelity" on the bottom.)			
RCA LOC-1050	(M)	Take Me Along (Cast)	1959	12.00	30.00
RCA LSO-1050	(S)	Take Me Along (Cast)	1959	16.00	40.00
Capitol W-1754	(M)	Gigot (Sdtk)	1962	12.00	30.00
Capitol SW-1754	(S)	Gigot (Sdtk)	1962	16.00	40.00
Capitol T-1877	(M)	Movie Themes	1963	3.50	8.00
Capitol ST-1877	(S)	Movie Themes	1963	4.00	10.00
Capitol T-1978	(M)	Today's Romantic Hits	1963	3.50	8.00
Capitol ST-1978	(S)	Today's Romantic Hits	1963	4.00	10.00
Capitol T-2056	(M)	Today's Romantic Hits, Volume 2	1964	3.50	8.00
Capitol ST-2056	(S)	Today's Romantic Hits, Volume 2	1964	4.00	10.00
Capitol T-2409	(M)	Silk 'N' Brass	1966	3.50	8.00
Capitol ST-2409	(S)	Silk 'N' Brass	1966	4.00	10.00
Capitol T-2582	(M)	How Sweet It Is For Lovers	1966	3.50	8.00
Capitol ST-2582	(S)	How Sweet It Is For Lovers	1966	4.00	10.00
Capitol T-2684	(M)	A Taste Of Brass	1967	3.50	8.00
Capitol ST-2684	(S)	A Taste Of Brass	1967	4.00	10.00
		(Capitol albums above have black labels with the Capitol logo on top.)			
GLENN, LLOYD					
Alladin 808	(M)	Chica Boo		30.00	60.00
Alladin 808	(M)	Chica Boo (Red vinyl)		100.00	200.00
GLORY					
Avalanche LA148	(S)	Glory	1973	8.00	20.00
GNARLY, PHIL & THE TOUGH GUYS					
Flaming Pie 319	(S)	Philville	1987	4.00	10.00
GO-GOS, THE					
RCA LPM-2930	(M)	Swim With The Go-Go's	1964	8.00	20.00
RCA LSP-2930	(S)	Swim With The Go-Go's	1964	10.00	25.00
GODCHAUX, KEITH & DONNA					
Round RX-104	(S)	Keith And Donna	1975	10.00	25.00
GODZ, THE					
ESP 1037	(S)	Contact High With The Godz	1967	12.00	30.00
ESP 1047	(S)	Godz 2	1968	12.00	30.00
ESP 1077	(S)	Third Testament	1969	12.00	30.00
ESP 2017	(S)	Godzundheit	1970	12.00	30.00
GOLDBERG, BARRY					
Epic LN-24199	(M)	Blowing My Mind	1966	6.00	15.00
Epic BN-26199	(S)	Blowing My Mind	1966	8.00	20.00
GOLDEN DAWN					
International Arts. 4	(S)	Power Plant	1968	12.00	30.00
GOLDEN EARRING					
Capitol T-2823	(M)	Winter Harvest	1967	12.00	30.00
Capitol St-2823	(S)	Winter Harvest	1967	14.00	35.00
Capitol ST-164	(S)	Miracle Mirror	1969	12.00	30.00

Label		Title	Year	VG+	NM
Capitol ST-11315	(S)	Golden Earring	1974	5.00	12.00
Atlantic SD-8244	(S)	Eight Miles High	1969	8.00	20.00
Track 396	(S)	Moontan (Nude dancer on the cover)	1973	6.00	15.00

GOLDEN GATE QUARTET, THE

Columbia CL-6102 (10")	(M)	The Golden Gate Spirituals	1950	50.00	100.00
Mercury MG-25063 (10")	(M)	Spirituals		50.00	100.00
Camden CAL-308	(M)	The Golden Gate Quartet		10.00	25.00
Harmony HL-7018	(M)	That Golden Chariot		10.00	25.00

GOLDENROD

Chartmaker CSG-1101	(S)	Goldenrod		65.00	130.00

GOLDSBOTRO, BOBBY

United Arts. UAL-3358	(M)	The Bobby Goldsboro Album	1964	4.00	10.00
United Arts. UAS-6358	(S)	The Bobby Goldsboro Album	1964	5.00	12.00
United Arts. UAL-3381	(M)	I Can't Stop Loving You	1964	4.00	10.00
United Arts. UAS-6381	(S)	I Can't Stop Loving You	1964	5.00	12.00
United Arts. UAL-3425	(M)	Little Things	1965	4.00	10.00
United Arts. UAS-6425	(S)	Little Things	1965	5.00	12.00
United Arts. UAL-3471	(M)	Broomstick Cowboy	1966	3.50	8.00
United Arts. UAS-6471	(S)	Broomstick Cowboy	1966	4.00	10.00
United Arts. UAL-3486	(M)	It's Too Late	1966	3.50	8.00
United Arts. UAS-6486	(S)	It's Too Late	1966	4.00	10.00
United Arts. UAL-3552	(M)	Blue Autumn	1966	3.50	8.00
United Arts. UAS-6552	(S)	Blue Autumn	1966	4.00	10.00

GOLDTONES, THE

LaBrea L-8011	(M)	The Goldtones Featuring Randy Seol		12.00	30.00

GOLLIWOGS, THE (CREEDENCE CLEARWATER REVIVAL)

Fantasy F-9474	(S)	Pre-Creedence	1975	6.00	15.00

GOOD OLD BOYS, THE

Round 576	(S)	Pistol Packin' Mama	1976	6.00	15.00

GOOD RATS, THE

Kapp KS-3580	(S)	The Good Rats	1969	8.00	20.00

GOODIES, THE

Hip HIS-7002	(S)	Candy Coated Goodies	1969	10.00	25.00

GORE, CHARIE

Audio Lab AL-1526	(M)	The Country Gentleman	1959	20.00	50.00

GORE, LESLEY

Mercury MG-20805	(M)	I'll Cry If I Want To	1963	8.00	20.00
Mercury SR-60805	(S)	I'll Cry If I Want To	1963	10.00	25.00
Mercury MG-20849	(M)	Lesley Gore Sings Of Mixed Up Hearts	1963	6.00	15.00
Mercury SR-60849	(S)	Lesley Gore Sings Of Mixed Up Hearts	1963	8.00	20.00
Mercury MG-20901	(M)	Boys, Boys, Boys	1964	6.00	15.00
Mercury SR-60901	(S)	Boys, Boys, Boys	1964	8.00	20.00
Mercury MG-20943	(M)	Girl Talk	1964	6.00	15.00
Mercury SR-60943	(S)	Girl Talk	1964	8.00	20.00
Mercury MG-21024	(M)	The Golden Hits Of Lesley Gore	1965	5.00	12.00
Mercury SR-61024	(S)	The Golden Hits Of Lesley Gore	1965	6.00	15.00
Mercury MG-21042	(M)	My Town, My Guy And Me	1965	6.00	15.00
Mercury SR-61042	(S)	My Town, My Guy And Me	1965	8.00	20.00
Mercury MG-21066	(M)	Sings All About Love	1966	6.00	15.00
Mercury SR-61066	(S)	Sings All About Love	1966	8.00	20.00
Mercury MG-21120	(M)	California Nights	1967	6.00	15.00
Mercury SR-61120	(S)	California Nights	1967	8.00	20.00
Mercury SR-61185	(S)	The Golden Hits Of Lesley Gore, Volume 2	1968	8.00	20.00

GORME, EYDIE

Also refer to Steve Lawrence & Eydie Gorme.

ABC-Paramount 150	(M)	Eydie Gorme	1957	10.00	25.00
ABC-Paramount 192	(M)	Eydie Swings The Blues	1957	10.00	25.00
ABC-Paramount 218	(M)	Eydie Gorme Vamps The Roaring '20s	1958	10.00	25.00
ABC-Paramount 246	(M)	Eydie In Love	1958	10.00	25.00
ABC-Paramount 307	(M)	Eydie Gorme On Stage	1959	6.00	15.00
ABC-Paramount S-307	(S)	Eydie Gorme On Stage	1959	8.00	20.00

Label		Title	Year	VG+	NM
United Arts. UAL-3143	(M)	Come Sing With Me	1961	5.00	12.00
United Arts. UAS-6143	(S)	Come Sing With Me	1961	6.00	15.00
United Arts. UAL-3189	(M)	The Very Best Of Eydie Gorme	1962	5.00	12.00
United Arts. UAS-6189	(S)	The Very Best Of Eydie Gorme	1962	6.00	15.00
Columbia CL-2012	(M)	Blame It On The Bossa Nova	1963	5.00	12.00
Columbia CS-8812	(S)	Blame It On The Bossa Nova	1963	6.00	15.00
Columbia CL-2065	(M)	Let The Good Times Roll	1963	4.00	10.00
Columbia CS-8865	(S)	Let The Good Times Roll	1963	5.00	12.00

(Columbia albums above have "360 Sound" labels.)

GOSDIN BROTHERS, THE (VERN & REX GOSDIN)
Also refer to Gene Clark.

Capitol ST-2852	(S)	Sounds Of Goodbye	1968	8.00	20.00

GOULDMAN, GRAHAM

RCA LPM-3954	(S)	Graham Gouldman Thing	1968	16.00	40.00
RCA LSP-3954	(S)	Graham Gouldman Thing	1968	16.00	40.00

GRACIOUS

Capitol ST-602	(S)	Gracious	1970	10.00	25.00

GRAMMER, BILLY

Monument MLP-4000	(M)	Travelin' On	1961	10.00	25.00
Monument SLP-14000	(S)	Travelin' On	1961	14.00	35.00

GRAND FUNK RAILROAD

Capitol ST-307	(S)	On Time	1969	6.00	15.00
Capitol SKAO-406	(S)	Grand Funk	1969	6.00	15.00
Capitol SKAO-471	(S)	Closer To Home	1970	6.00	15.00
Capitol SWBB-633	(S)	Grand Funk/Live Album	1970	5.00	12.00
Capitol SW-764	(S)	Survival	1971	5.00	12.00
Capitol SW-853	(S)	E Pluribus Funk	1971	5.00	12.00

(Capitol albums above have green labels.)

GRANDMA'S ROCKERS

Fredlo 6727	(M)	Homemade Apple Pie	1967	240.00	400.00

GRANT, GOGI

Era 20001	(M)	Suddenly There's Gogi Grant		12.00	30.00
Era 20001	(M)	Suddenly There's Gogi Grant (Red vinyl)		30.00	60.00
Era EL-106	(M)	The Wayward Wind	1957	16.00	40.00
RCA LOC-1030	(M)	The Helen Morgan Story (Sdtk)	1957	20.00	50.00
RCA LPM-1716	(M)	Gigi (Studio Cast)	1958	10.00	25.00
RCA LPM-1717	(M)	Welcome To My Heart	1958	14.00	35.00
RCA LPM-1940	(M)	Torch Time		8.00	20.00
RCA LSP-1940	(S)	Torch Time		10.00	25.00
RCA LPM-1984	(M)	Kiss Me, Kate		8.00	20.00
RCA LSP-1984	(S)	Kiss Me, Kate		10.00	25.00
Liberty LRP-3144	(M)	If You Want To Get To Heaven, Shout		6.00	15.00
Liberty LST-7144	(S)	If You Want To Get To Heaven, Shout		8.00	20.00
Charter C-107	(S)	City Girl In The Country	1964	6.00	15.00
Charter CS-107	(M)	City Girl In The Country	1964	8.00	20.00

GRASS ROOTS, THE

Dunhill D-50011	(M)	Where Were You When I Needed You?	1966	8.00	20.00
Dunhill DS-50011	(S)	Where Were You When I Needed You?	1966	8.00	20.00
Dunhill D-50020	(M)	Let's Live For Today	1967	6.00	15.00
Dunhill DS-50020	(S)	Let's Live For Today	1967	6.00	15.00
Command QD-40013	(Q)	Their 16 Greatest Hits	1974	6.00	15.00

GRATEFUL DEAD, THE
Also refer to Ken Kesey.

Warners W-1689	(M)	The Grateful Dead (Gold label)	1967	16.00	40.00
Warners WS-1689	(S)	The Grateful Dead (Gold label)	1967	10.00	25.00
Warners WS-1749	(S)	Anthem Of The Sun (Purple cover)	1968	6.00	15.00
Warners WS-1790	(S)	Aoxomoxoa	1969	6.00	15.00
Warners WS-1830	(S)	Live/Dead (With booklet)	1969	8.00	20.00
Warners WS-1869	(S)	Workingman's Dead	1970	6.00	15.00

*(Warners albums above have green labels
with a "W7" logo on top.)*

MGM SE-4468	(S)	Zabriskie Point (Sdtk)	1970	10.00	25.00
Sunflower SUN-5001	(M)	Vintage Dead	1970	8.00	20.00

Label		Title	Year	VG+	NM
Warners WS-1893	(S)	American Beauty	1970	5.00	12.00
Sunflower SNF-5004	(M)	Historic Dead	1971	10.00	25.00
Warners WS-1749	(S)	Anthem Of The Sun (White cover)	1971	5.00	12.00
Warners WS-1790	(S)	Aoxomoxoa	1969	6.00	15.00
		(1749 and 1790 above are second pressings and have green labels with the "WB" logo and contain different mixes by Phil Lesh.)			
Warners WS-1935	(S)	The Grateful Dead	1971	10.00	25.00
		(Issued with a "Skull & Roses" sticker attached to the front.)			
Warners WS-1935	(S)	The Grateful Dead	1971	6.00	15.00
		(Without the "Skull & Roses" sticker on the front.)			
Pride PRD-0016	(M)	The History Of The Grateful Dead	1972	10.00	25.00
Warners WX-2668	(S)	Europe '72	1972	6.00	15.00
Warners BS-2721	(S)	History Of The Grateful Dead/Bear's Choice	1973	3.50	8.00
Grateful Dead GD-01	(S)	Wake Of The Flood	1973	6.00	15.00
		(The back cover has the crow in the right corner but does not list contributing artists.)			
Grateful Dead GD-01	(S)	Wake Of The Flood	1973	4.00	10.00
		(The back cover has the crow in the right corner and lists the contributing artists.)			
Warners B-2764	(S)	Skeletons From The Closet	1974	3.50	8.00
		(Warners albums above have green labels with a "WB" logo on top.)			
Grateful Dead GD-102	(S)	From The Mars Hotel	1974	10.00	25.00
		(Without a United Artists sticker on the jacket.)			
Grateful Dead GD-102	(S)	From The Mars Hotel	1974	6.00	15.00
		(With a United Artists sticker on the jacket.)			
Grateful Dead LA-494	(S)	Blues For Allah	1975	8.00	20.00
Grateful Dead LA-620	(S)	Steal Your Face	1976	8.00	20.00
Warners 2W-3091	(S)	What A Long Strange Trip It's Been	1977	5.00	12.00
		(Burbank/palm tree label.)			
Mobile Fidelity 1-014	(S)	American Beauty	1978	8.00	20.00
Arista AB-4198	(S)	Shakedown Street	1978	4.00	10.00
		(Black label with blue logo on top.)			
Direct Disk SD-16619	(S)	Terrapin Station	1979	20.00	50.00
Mobile Fidelity 1-172	(S)	From The Mars Hotel	1980	12.00	30.00

GRAY, DOBIE

Label		Title	Year	VG+	NM
Charger CHRM-2002	(M)	Dobie Gray Sings For In Crowders	1965	10.00	25.00
Charger CHRS-2002	(S)	Dobie Gray Sings For In Crowders	1965	16.00	40.00

GRAYSON, KATHRYN

Label		Title	Year	VG+	NM
MGM E-3257	(M)	Kathryn Grayson Sings		8.00	20.00

GREAT SOCIETY, THE

Label		Title	Year	VG+	NM
Columbia CS-9624	(S)	Conspicuous Only In It's Absence	1968	5.00	12.00
Columbia CS-9702	(S)	How It Was	1968	5.00	12.00
		(Columbia albums above have "360 Sound" labels.)			

GREAVES, R.B.

Label		Title	Year	VG+	NM
Atco SD-33-311	(S)	R.B. Greaves	1969	6.00	15.00

GREEK FOUNTAIN RIVER FRONT BAND, THE

Label		Title	Year	VG+	NM
Montel LLP-110	(M)	Takes Requests	1965	50.00	100.00

GREEN, AL

Label		Title	Year	VG+	NM
Hot Line 1500	(M)	Back Up Train	1967	10.00	25.00
Hot Line 1500	(S)	Back Up Train	1967	12.00	30.00

GREEN, PETER

Label		Title	Year	VG+	NM
Reprise RS-6436	(S)	The End Of The Game	1971	6.00	15.00

GREEN, ST. JOHN

Label		Title	Year	VG+	NM
Flick Disc FLS-45001	(S)	St. John Green	1968	18.00	20.00

GREEN BULLFROG

Label		Title	Year	VG+	NM
Decca DL-75269	(S)	Green Bullfrog	1971	10.00	25.00

GREEN RIVER BOYS FEATURING GLEN CAMPBELL, THE

Label		Title	Year	VG+	NM
Capitol T-1810	(M)	Big Bluegrass Special	1962	20.00	50.00
Capitol ST-1810	(S)	Big Bluegrass Special	1962	30.00	60.00

Label		Title	Year	VG+	NM
GREENE, BERNIE, & HIS STEREO MAD-MEN					
RCA LPM-1929	(M)	Musically Mad	1958	14.00	35.00
RCA LSP-1929	(S)	Musically Mad	1958	20.00	50.00
		(With a portrait of Alfred E. Neuman on the cover.)			
GREENE, DOD					
Blue Note 9001	(M)	My Hour Of Need	1962	8.00	20.00
Blue Note 89001	(S)	My Hour Of Need	1962	10.00	25.00
GREENWICH, ELLIE					
United Arts. UAS-6648	(S)	Composes, Produces And Sings	1968	8.00	20.00
Verve V6-5091	(S)	Let It Be Written, Let It Be Sung	1973	4.00	10.00
GREGG, BOBB, & HIS FRIENDS					
Epic LN-24051	(M)	Let's Stomp And Wild Weekend	1963	6.00	15.00
Epic BN-26051	(S)	Let's Stomp And Wild Weekend	1963	8.00	20.00
GRIFFIN, JAMES					
Reprise R-6091	(M)	Summer Holiday	1963	10.00	25.00
Reprise R9-6091	(S)	Summer Holiday	1963	12.00	30.00
GRIFFITH, ANDY					
Capitol T-962	(M)	Just For Laughs	1958	8.00	20.00
Capitol T-1105	(M)	The Blues And Old Time Songs	1959	8.00	20.00
Capitol T-1215	(M)	This Here Andy Griffith	1959	8.00	20.00
Capitol T-1611	(M)	The Andy Griffith Show	1961	6.00	15.00
Capitol ST-1611	(S)	The Andy Griffith Show	1961	8.00	20.00
Capitol T-2066	(M)	Andy And Cleopatra	1964	5.00	12.00
Capitol ST-2066	(S)	Andy And Cleopatra	1964	6.00	15.00
GRODECK WHIPPERJENNY					
People 3000	(S)	Grodeck Whipperjenny		20.00	50.00
GROOV-U					
Gateway GLP-3010	(M)	Groov-U On Campus		12.00	30.00
GROOVIE GOOLIES, THE					
RCA LSP-4420	(S)	The Groovie Goolies	1970	8.00	20.00
GROUNDHOGS, THE					
Cleve CH-82871	(S)	The Groundhogs With John Lee Hooker And John Mayall		12.00	30.00
World Pacific WPS-21892	(S)	Scratching The Surface	1968	8.00	20.00
Imperial LP-12452	(S)	Blues Obituary	1969	10.00	25.00
Liberty LST-7644	(S)	Thank Christ For The Bomb	1970	8.00	20.00
United Arts. UAS-5513	(S)	The Groundhogs Split	1971	6.00	15.00
United Arts. UAS-5570	(S)	Who Will Save The World	1972	6.00	15.00
United Arts. LA008	(S)	Hogwash	1973	6.00	15.00
United Arts. LA603	(S)	Crosscut Saw	1976	6.00	15.00
United Arts. LA680	(S)	Black Diamond	1976	6.00	15.00
GROUP, THE					
Bell 6038	(S)	The Group		8.00	20.00
GROUP, THE					
RCA LPM-2663	(M)	The Group	1963	8.00	20.00
RCA LSP-2663	(S)	The Group	1963	10.00	25.00
GROUP ONE					
RCA LPM-3524	(M)	Brothers Go To Mothers And Others	1966	6.00	15.00
RCA LST-3524	(S)	Brothers Go To Mothers And Others	1966	8.00	20.00
GROUP THERAPY					
RCA LSP-3976	(S)	People Get Ready For Group Therapy	1968	6.00	15.00
Philips PHS-600303	(S)	37 Minutes Of Group Therapy	1969	5.00	12.00
GROUPIES, THE					
Earth ELPS-1000	(S)	The Groupies		10.00	25.00
GROVE, BOBBY					
King 831	(M)	It Was For You	1963	10.00	25.00

Label		Title	Year	VG+	NM
GROWING CONCERN, THE					
Mainstream S-6108	(S)	Growing Concern	1968	8.00	20.00
GUARD, DAVE, & THE WHISKEYHILL SINGERS					
Capitol T-1728	(M)	Dave Guard & The Whiskeyhill Singers	1962	6.00	15.00
Capitol ST-1728	(S)	Dave Guard & The Whiskeyhill Singers	1962	8.00	20.00
GUESS WHO, THE					
Wand WDS-691	(E)	Born In Canada	1969	6.00	15.00
MGM SE-4645	(S)	The Guess Who	1969	5.00	12.00
RCA LSP-4141	(S)	Wheatfield Soul	1969	5.00	12.00
RCA LSP-4157	(S)	Canned Wheat	1969	5.00	12.00
RCA LSP-4779	(S)	Live At The Paramount, Seattle	1972	10.00	25.00
RCA APD1-0130	(Q)	Guess Who No. 10	1973	6.00	15.00
RCA APD1-0269	(Q)	The Best Of The Guess Who, Volume 2	1974	6.00	15.00
RCA APD1-0405	(Q)	Road Food	1974	6.00	15.00
		(RCA albums above have orange labels.)			
GUITAR, BONNIE					
Dot DLP-3069	(M)	Moonlight And Shadows	1957	12.00	30.00
Dot DLP-3151	(M)	Whispering Hope	1959	8.00	20.00
Dot DLP-25151	(S)	Whispering Hope	1959	10.00	25.00
Dot DLP-3335	(M)	Dark Moon	1962	8.00	20.00
Dot DLP-25335	(E)	Dark Moon	1962	5.00	12.00
Dot DLP-3696	(M)	Two Worlds	1966	5.00	12.00
Dot DLP-25696	(S)	Two Worlds	1966	6.00	15.00
Dot DLP-3737	(M)	Miss Bonnie Guitar	1966	5.00	12.00
Dot DLP-25737	(S)	Miss Bonnie Guitar	1966	6.00	15.00
Dot DLP-3746	(M)	Merry Christams From Bonnie Guitar	1966	5.00	12.00
Dot DLP-25746	(S)	Merry Christams From Bonnie Guitar	1966	6.00	15.00
Dot DLP-3793	(M)	Award Winner	1967	5.00	12.00
Dot DLP-25793	(S)	Award Winner	1967	6.00	15.00
GUITAR JR.					
Goldband 1085	(M)	Pick Me Up On Your Way Down	1960	10.00	25.00
GUITAR SLIM (LEE BAKER)					
Capitol ST-403	(S)	Broke And Hungry	1969	5.00	12.00
Specialty 2120	(S)	Things That I Used To Do		8.00	20.00
GUNTER, ARTHUR					
Excello 8017	(M)	Black And Blues		75.00	150.00
GUY, BUDDY					
Chess LP-409	(S)	I Was Walking Through The Woods		8.00	20.00
Vanguard VSD-79272	(S)	A Man And The Blues	1968	6.00	15.00
Vanguard VSD-79290	(S)	This Is Buddy Guy	1968	6.00	15.00
Chess LPS-1527	(S)	Left My Blues In San Francisco	1969	5.00	12.00
Blue Thumb 20	(S)	Buddy And The Juniors	1970	4.00	10.00
Blue Thumb 20	(S)	Buddy And The Juniors (Colored vinyl)	1970	8.00	20.00

Label		Title	Year	VG+	NM
H.P. LOVECRAFT					
Phillips PHM-200252	(M)	H. P. Lovecraft	1967	8.00	20.00
Phillips PHS-600252	(S)	H. P. Lovecraft	1967	10.00	25.00
Phillips PHS-600279	(S)	Lovecraft II	1968	10.00	25.00
Reprise RS-6419	(S)	Valley Of The Moon	1970	6.00	15.00
Mercury SRM-1-1031	(S)	We Love You	1976	6.00	15.00

Label		Title	Year	VG+	NM
HA' PENNYS, THE					
Fersch 1110	(M)	Love Is Not The Same	1968	150.00	250.00
HAGGARD, MERLE (& THE STRANGERS)					
Capitol T-2373	(M)	Strangers	1965	6.00	15.00
Capitol ST-2373	(S)	Strangers	1965	8.00	20.00
Capitol T-2453	(M)	Just Between The Two Of Us	1966	5.00	12.00
Capitol ST-2453	(S)	Just Between The Two Of Us	1966	6.00	15.00
		(With Bonnie Owens.)			
Capitol T-2585	(M)	Swinging Doors	1966	5.00	12.00
Capitol ST-2585	(S)	Swinging Doors	1966	6.00	15.00
Capitol T-2702	(M)	I'm A Lonesome Fugitive	1967	5.00	12.00
Capitol ST-2702	(S)	I'm A Lonesome Fugitive	1967	6.00	15.00
Capitol T-2789	(M)	Branded Man/I Threw Away The Rose	1967	5.00	12.00
Capitol ST-2789	(S)	Branded Man/I Threw Away The Rose	1967	6.00	15.00
Tower ST-5141	(S)	Killers Three (Sdtk)	1968	8.00	20.00
HAGGARD'S STRANGERS, MERLE					
Capitol ST-169	(S)	The Instrumental Sound Of The Strangers	1969	6.00	15.00
Capitol ST-445	(S)	Introducing My Friends, The Strangers	1970	6.00	15.00
Capitol ST-590	(S)	Gettin' To Know Merle Haggard's Strangers	1970	6.00	15.00
Capitol ST-796	(S)	Honky Tonkin'	1971	6.00	15.00
HALEY, BILL, & HIS COMETS					
Decca DL-5560 (10")	(M)	Shake, Rattle And Roll	1954	300.00	500.00
Decca DL-8225	(M)	Rock Around The Clock	1955	100.00	200.00
Decca DL-8315	(M)	He Digs Rock And Roll	1956	75.00	150.00
Decca DL-8345	(M)	Rock And Roll Stage Show	1956	75.00	150.00
Essex LP-202	(M)	Rock With Bill Haley And The Comets	1956	100.00	200.00
Trans World 202	(M)	Rock With Bill Haley And The Comets	1956	40.00	80.00
Somerset P-4600	(M)	Rock With Bill Haley And The Comets	1956	20.00	50.00
Decca DL-8569	(M)	Rockin' The Oldies	1957	40.00	80.00
Decca DL-8692	(M)	Rockin' Around The World	1957	40.00	80.00
Decca DL-8775	(M)	Rockin' The Joint	1958	40.00	80.00
Decca DL-8821	(M)	Bill Haley's Chicks	1959	35.00	70.00
Decca DL7-8821	(S)	Bill Haley's Chicks	1959	50.00	100.00
Decca DL-8964	(M)	Strictly Instrumental	1959	35.00	70.00
Decca DL7-8964	(S)	Strictly Instrumental	1959	50.00	100.00
		(Decca albums above have black & silver labels.)			
Warners W-1738	(M)	Bill Haley And The Comets	1960	12.00	30.00
Warners WS-1738	(S)	Bill Haley And The Comets	1960	16.00	40.00
Warners W-1391	(M)	Jukebox	1960	12.00	30.00
Warners WS-1391	(S)	Jukebox	1960	16.00	40.00
Roulette R-25174	(M)	Twistin' Knights At The Round Table	1962	12.00	30.00
Roulette RS-25174	(S)	Twistin' Knights At The Round Table	1962	16.00	40.00
Vocalion VL-3696	(M)	Bill Haley And The Comets	1965	10.00	25.00
Guest Star 1454	(M)	Bill Haley And The Comets Live	1965	10.00	25.00
Decca DL-5027	(M)	Bill Haley's Greatest Hits	1968	10.00	25.00
Decca DL7-5027	(S)	Bill Haley's Greatest Hits	1968	10.00	25.00
Kama Sutra KLPS-2104	(S)	Scrapbook/Live At The Bitter End	1970	10.00	25.00
Decca DXSE-7211	(P)	Bill Haley's Golden Hits	1972	6.00	15.00
HALFNELSON					
Bearsville BV-2048	(S)	Halfnelson	1972	8.00	20.00
HALL, CONNIE					
Decca DL-4217	(M)	Connie Hall	1962	5.00	12.00
Decca DL7-4217	(S)	Connie Hall	1962	6.00	15.00
HALL, DICKSON (DIXON HALL)					
MGM E-329 (10")	(M)	Outlaws Of The Old West	1954	10.00	25.00
MGM E-3263	(M)	Outlaws Of The Old West	1956	8.00	20.00
Kapp KL-1067	(M)	Fabulous Country Hits Way Out West	1957	8.00	20.00
Epic LN-3427	(M)	25 All-Time Country And Western Hits	1953	8.00	20.00
Kapp KL-1464	(M)	24 Fabulous Country Hits	1966	4.00	10.00
Kapp KS-3464	(S)	24 Fabulous Country Hits	1966	5.00	12.00
HALL, LARRY					
Strand SL-1005	(M)	Sandy	1960	20.00	50.00
Strand SL-1005	(E)	Sandy	1960	20.00	50.00

Label		Title	Year	VG+	NM
HALL & OATES					
Mobile Fidelity 1-069	(S)	Abandoned Luncheonette		6.00	15.00
HALLYDAY, JOHNNY					
Phillips 200019	(M)	America's Rockin' Hits	1961	16.00	40.00
Phillips PHS-600019	(S)	America's Rockin' Hits	1961	20.00	50.00
HALOS, THE					
Warwick W-2046	(M)	The Halos	1962	60.00	120.00
HAMILTON, FRANK					
Capitol T-2005	(M)	Sing A Song With The Kingston Trio	1964	6.00	15.00
Capitol ST-2005	(S)	Sing A Song With The Kingston Trio	1964	8.00	20.00
HAMILTON, RUSS					
Kapp KL-1076	(M)	Rainbow	1957	30.00	60.00
HAMILTON IV, GEORGE					
ABC-Paramount 220	(M)	George Hamilton IV On Campus	1958	10.00	25.00
ABC-Paramount S-220	(S)	George Hamilton IV On Campus	1958	12.00	30.00
ABC-Paramount 251	(M)	Sing Me A Sad Song	1958	10.00	25.00
ABC-Paramount S-251	(S)	Sing Me A Sad Song	1958	12.00	30.00
ABC-Paramount 461	(M)	Big Fifteen	1963	6.00	15.00
ABC-Paramount S-461	(S)	Big Fifteen	1963	8.00	20.00
RCA LPM-2373	(M)	To You And Yours From Me And Mine	1961	5.00	12.00
RCA LSP-2373	(S)	To You And Yours From Me And Mine	1961	6.00	15.00
RCA LPM-2778	(M)	Abilene	1963	6.00	15.00
RCA LSP-2778	(S)	Abilene	1963	8.00	20.00
RCA LPM-2972	(M)	Fort Worth, Dallas Or Houston	1964	5.00	12.00
RCA LSP-2972	(S)	Fort Worth, Dallas Or Houston	1964	6.00	15.00
RCA LPM-3371	(M)	Mister Sincerity	1965	5.00	12.00
RCA LSP-3371	(S)	Mister Sincerity	1965	6.00	15.00
RCA LPM-3510	(M)	Coast Country	1966	5.00	12.00
RCA LSP-3510	(S)	Coast Country	1966	6.00	15.00
RCA LPM-3601	(M)	Steel Rail Blues	1966	5.00	12.00
RCA LSP-3601	(S)	Steel Rail Blues	1966	6.00	15.00
RCA LPM-3752	(M)	Folk Country Classics	1967	4.00	10.00
RCA LSP-3752	(S)	Folk Country Classics	1967	5.00	12.00
RCA LPM-3854	(M)	Folksy	1967	4.00	10.00
RCA LSP-3854	(S)	Folksy	1967	5.00	12.00
RCA LSP-3962	(S)	The Gentle Sound Of George Hamilton IV	1968	4.00	10.00
RCA LSP-4006	(S)	George Hamilton IV	1968	4.00	10.00
		(RCA albums above have black labels.)			
HAMMER					
San Francisco SD-203	(S)	Hammer	1970	8.00	20.00
HAMMOND, JOHN					
Vanguard VRS-9153	(M)	Big City Blues	1964	5.00	12.00
Vanguard VSD-79153	(S)	Big City Blues	1964	6.00	15.00
Vanguard VRS-9178	(M)	So Many Roads	1966	5.00	12.00
Vanguard VSD-79178	(S)	So Many Roads	1966	6.00	15.00
Vanguard VRS-9198	(M)	Country Blues	1966	5.00	12.00
Vanguard VSD-79198	(S)	Country Blues	1966	6.00	15.00
Vanguard VRS-9245	(M)	Mirrors	1967	5.00	12.00
Vanguard VSD-79245	(S)	Mirrors	1967	6.00	15.00
Atlantic SD-8206	(S)	Sooner Or Later	1968	5.00	12.00
Atlantic SD-8152	(S)	I Can Tell	1968	5.00	12.00
Atlantic SD-8251	(S)	Southern Fried	1969	5.00	12.00
HANGMEN, THE					
Monument MLP-8077	(M)	Bitter Sweet	1967	6.00	15.00
Monument SLP-18077	(S)	Bitter Sweet	1967	8.00	20.00
HAPPENINGS, THE					
B.T. Puppy 1001	(M)	The Happenings	1966	8.00	20.00
B.T. Puppy S-1001	(S)	The Happenings	1966	10.00	25.00
B.T. Puppy 1002	(M)	Back To Back (With the Tokens)	1967	5.00	12.00
B.T. Puppy S-1002	(S)	Back To Back (With the Tokens)	1967	6.00	15.00
B.T. Puppy 1003	(M)	Psycle	1967	8.00	20.00
B.T. Puppy S-1003	(S)	Psycle	1967	10.00	25.00

Label		Title	Year	VG+	NM
B.T. Puppy S-1004	(S)	The Happenings' Golden Hits!	1968	16.00	40.00
Jubilee JGS-8028	(S)	Piece Of Mind	1969	8.00	20.00
Jubilee JGS-8030	(S)	The Happenings' Greatest Hits!	1969	8.00	20.00

HAPSHASH & THE COLOURED COAT

Imperial LP-12377	(S)	Hapshash And The Coloured Coat	1968	8.00	20.00
Imperial LP-12430	(S)	Western Flyer	1969	8.00	20.00

HARD WATER

Capitol ST-2954	(S)	Hard Water	1968	8.00	20.00

HARDTIMES, THE

World Pacific WP-1867	(M)	Blew Mind	1968	6.00	15.00
World Pacific WPS-21867	(S)	Blew Mind	1968	8.00	20.00

HARDY, FRANCOISE

Four Corners FC-4231	(M)	Francoise		8.00	20.00
Four Corners FCS-4231	(S)	Francoise		10.00	25.00
Four Corners FC-4238	(M)	Je Vous Aime		8.00	20.00
Four Corners FCS-4238	(S)	Je Vous Aime		10.00	25.00
Reprise RS-6290	(S)	Francoise Hardy	1968	10.00	25.00

HARDY BOYS, THE

RCA LSP-4217	(S)	Here Come The Hardy Boys	1969	5.00	12.00
RCA LSP-4315	(S)	Wheels	1970	5.00	12.00

HARPER, ROY

Sunset SLS-50373	(S)	Folkjokeopus	1969	10.00	25.00
Harvest SKAO-418	(S)	Flat, Baroque And Berserk	1970	5.00	12.00

HARPER, TONI

Verve V-2001	(M)	Toni	1956	12.00	30.00
RCA LPM-2092	(M)	Lady Lonely	1960	6.00	15.00
RCA LSP-2092	(S)	Lady Lonely	1960	8.00	20.00
RCA LPM-2253	(M)	Night Mood	1960	6.00	15.00
RCA LSP-2253	(S)	Night Mood	1960	8.00	20.00

HARPO, SLIM

Excello LP-8003	(M)	Raining In My Heart	1961	40.00	80.00
Excello LP-8005	(M)	Baby, Scratch My Back	1966	20.00	50.00
Excello LP-8008	(S)	Tip On In	1968	12.00	30.00
Excello LP-8010	(S)	The Best Of Slim Harpo	1969	12.00	30.00
Excello LP-8013	(M)	Slim Harpo Knew The Blues	1970	10.00	25.00

HARPTONES, THE

Musicnote M-8001	(M)	The Paragons Versus The Harptones	1964	14.00	35.00
Ambient Sound 37718	(S)	Love Needs	1982	4.00	10.00

HARRIS, EMMY LOU

Jubilee JGS-8031	(S)	Gliding Bird (Full color cover)		50.00	100.00
Mobile Fidelity 1-015	(S)	Quarter Moon In A Ten Cent Town		12.00	30.00

HARRIS, PEPPERMINT

Time 5	(M)	Peppermint Harris	1962	10.00	25.00

HARRIS, ROLF

Epic LN-24053	(M)	The Original Sun Arise	1963	6.00	15.00
Epic BN-26053	(S)	The Original Sun Arise	1963	8.00	20.00
Epic LN-24110	(M)	The Court Of King Caractacus	1964	5.00	12.00
Epic BN-26110	(S)	The Court Of King Caractacus	1964	6.00	15.00

HARRIS, WYNONIE

Aladdin 703 (10")	(M)	Party After Hours	1956	150.00	250.00
Aladdin 703 (10")	(M)	Party After Hours (Red vinyl)	1956	210.00	350.00
		(Features Amos Miburn & Prince Waterford.)			
King 607	(M)	Battle Of The Blues, Volume 1	1958	180.00	300.00
King 627	(M)	Battle Of The Blues, Volume 2	1959	180.00	300.00
		(King 607 and 627 also feature Roy Brown.)			
King 668	(M)	Battle Of The Blues, Volume 4	1960	400.00	600.00
		(Also features Roy Brown & Eddie Vinson.)			
King KS-1086	(E)	Good Rockin' Blues	1970	10.00	25.00

Label		Title	Year	VG+	NM
HARRISON, GEORGE					
Apple ST-3350	(S)	Wonderwall Music (With insert)	1969	8.00	20.00
Zapple ST-3358	(S)	Electronic Sound	1969	12.00	30.00
Apple STCH-639 (3 LPs)	(S)	All Things Must Pass	1970	8.00	20.00
		(With poster and custom inner sleeves.)			
Apple STCX-3385 (3 LPs)	(S)	The Concert For Bangla Desh	1972	8.00	20.00
		(Label reads "Mfg. by Apple Records.")			
Apple SMAS-3410	(S)	Living In The Material World (With insert)	1973	5.00	12.00
Apple SMAS-3418	(S)	Dark Horse (With insert)	1974	5.00	12.00
Apple SMAS-3420	(S)	Extra Texture	1975	5.00	12.00
HARRISON, WILBERT					
Sphere Sound SR-7000	(M)	Kansas City	1965	20.00	50.00
Sphere Sound SSR-7000	(E)	Kansas City	1965	16.00	40.00
Sue SSLP-8801	(S)	Let's Work Together	1970	10.00	25.00
Juggernaut ST-8803	(S)	Shoot You Full Of Love	1971	6.00	15.00
Buddah BDS-5092	(S)	Wilbert Harrison	1971	6.00	15.00
HARROW, NANCY					
Candid 8008	(M)	Wild Women Don't Have The Blues	1962	6.00	15.00
Candid 9008	(S)	Wild Women Don't Have The Blues	1962	8.00	20.00
Atlantic 8075	(M)	You Never Know	1963	6.00	15.00
Atlantic SD-8075	(S)	You Never Know	1963	8.00	20.00
HART, MICKEY					
Warners BS-2635	(S)	Rolling Thunder (With insert)	1972	12.00	30.00
HASSLES, THE					
United Arts. UAS-6631	(S)	The Hassles	1968	8.00	20.00
United Arts. UAS-6699	(S)	The Hour Of The Wolf	1969	8.00	20.00
HAWKINS, DALE					
Chess 1429	(M)	Suzie-Q	1958	210.00	350.00
Roulette R-25175	(M)	Let's All Twist	1962	35.00	70.00
Roulette SR-25175	(S)	Let's All Twist	1962	50.00	100.00
Bell 6036	(S)	L.A., Memphis And Tyler, Texas	1969	16.00	40.00
HAWKINS, HAWKSHAW					
King 587	(M)	Hawkshaw Hawkins	1958	16.00	40.00
King 592	(M)	Grand Ole Opry Favorites	1958	16.00	40.00
King 599	(M)	Hawkshaw Hawkins	1959	16.00	40.00
King 808	(M)	The All New Hawkshaw Hawkins	1963	10.00	25.00
King S-808	(S)	The All New Hawkshaw Hawkins	1963	12.00	30.00
King 858	(M)	Taken From Our Vaults, Volume 1	1963	8.00	20.00
King S-858	(P)	Taken From Our Vaults, Volume 1	1963	6.00	15.00
King 870	(M)	Taken From Our Vaults, Volume 2	1963	8.00	20.00
King S-870	(P)	Taken From Our Vaults, Volume 2	1963	6.00	15.00
King 873	(M)	Taken From Our Vaults, Volume 3	1963	8.00	20.00
King S-873	(P)	Taken From Our Vaults, Volume 3	1963	6.00	15.00
HAWKINS, JENNELL					
Amazon AM-1001	(M)	The Many Moods Of Jenny	1961	6.00	15.00
Amazon AS-1001	(S)	The Many Moods Of Jenny	1961	8.00	20.00
Amazon AM-1002	(M)	Moments To Remember	1962	6.00	15.00
Amazon AS-1002	(S)	Moments To Remember	1962	8.00	20.00
HAWKINS, RONNIE					
Roulette R-25078	(M)	Ronnie Hawkins	1959	35.00	70.00
Roulette SR-25078	(S)	Ronnie Hawkins	1959	50.00	100.00
Roulette SR-25078	(S)	Ronnie Hawkins (Red vinyl)	1959	150.00	250.00
Roulette R-25102	(M)	Mr. Dynamo	1960	35.00	70.00
Roulette SR-25102	(S)	Mr. Dynamo	1960	50.00	100.00
Roulette SR-25102	(S)	Mr. Dynamo (Red vinyl)	1960	150.00	250.00
Roulette R-25120	(M)	The Folk Ballads Of Ronnie Hawkins	1960	16.00	40.00
Roulette SR-25120	(S)	The Folk Ballads Of Ronnie Hawkins	1960	20.00	50.00
Roulette R-25137	(M)	The Songs Of Hank Williams	1960	16.00	40.00
Roulette SR-25137	(S)	The Songs Of Hank Williams	1960	20.00	50.00
Roulette SR-42045	(S)	The Best Of Ronnie Hawkins & His Band	1970	10.00	25.00
		(Features an early incarnation of The Band.)			

Emmy Lou Harris, *Gliding Bird.* Before being discovered by Gram Parsons; before signing with the Warner/Reprise conglomerate; before becoming one of the finest and most original vocalists in contemporary country music, there was *Gliding Bird.* The original is very rare and counterfeits do exist.

Joe Henderson, *Snap Your Fingers.* Joe Henderson scored big on the pop charts with the title tune (#8 in 1962) and then failed to reach similar heights of success.

Label		Title	Year	VG+	NM
HAWKINS, SCREAMIN' JAY					
Epic LN-3448	(M)	At Home With Screamin' Jay Hawkins	1956	180.00	300.00
Epic LN-3457	(M)	I Put A Spell On You	1957	100.00	200.00
Sounds Of Hawaii 5015	(S)	A Night At Forbidden City		20.00	50.00
Epic BN-26457	(E)	I Put A Spell On You	1969	20.00	50.00
Phillips PHS-600319	(S)	What That Is	1969	16.00	40.00
Phillips PHS-600336	(S)	Screamin' Jay Hawkins	1970	16.00	40.00
HAWKWIND					
United Arts. UAS-5519	(S)	In Search Of Space	1971	6.00	15.00
United Arts. UAS-5567	(S)	Hawkwind	1971	6.00	15.00
United Arts. LA001	(S)	Doremi Fasol Latido	1973	5.00	12.00
United Arts. LA120	(S)	Space Ritual Alive	1973	6.00	15.00
United Arts. LA328	(S)	Hall Of The Mountain Grill	1974	5.00	12.00
HAYDEN, WILLIE					
Dooto DTL-293	(M)	Blame It On The Blues	1960	16.00	40.00
HAYES, MARTHA					
Jubilee 1023	(M)	A Hayes Named Martha	1956	12.00	30.00
HAYMARKET SQUARE					
Chaparral 201	(S)	Magic Lantern	1968	150.00	250.00
HEAD					
Buddah BDS-5062	(S)	Head	1970	8.00	20.00
HEAD, JIM, & HIS DEL RAYS					
H.P. 22893	(M)	Hayden Proffitt Presents Jim Head	1963	16.00	40.00
H.P. 22893	(S)	Hayden Proffitt Presents Jim Head	1963	20.00	50.00
HEAD, ROY					
TNT 101	(M)	Roy Head And The Traits	1965	50.00	100.00
Scepter S-532	(M)	Treat Me Right	1965	10.00	25.00
Scepter SS-532	(S)	Treat Me Right	1965	12.00	30.00
HEAD SHOP, THE					
Epic BN-26476	(S)	The Head Shop	1969	14.00	35.00
HEADS, THE					
Liberty LST-7581	(S)	Heads Up	1968	8.00	20.00
HEART					
Mushroom MRS-5005	(S)	Dreamboat Annie	1976	6.00	15.00
Mushroom MRS-5008	(S)	Magazine	1977	8.00	20.00
		(With contractual dispute disclaimer on cover.)			
Nautilus 3	(S)	Dreamboat Annie	1979	10.00	25.00
Portrait HR-44799	(S)	Little Queen (1/2 speed)	1981	10.00	25.00
HEARTBEATS, THE					
Roulette R-25107	(M)	A Thousand Miles Away	1960	50.00	100.00
Roulette SR-25107	(E)	A Thousand Miles Away	1960	40.00	80.00
HEARTS & FLOWERS					
Capitol T-2762	(M)	Now Is The Time	1967	8.00	20.00
Capitol ST-2762	(S)	Now Is The Time	1967	10.00	25.00
Capitol ST-2868	(S)	Of Horses, Kids And Forgotten Women	1968	12.00	30.00
HEATHER BLACK					
American Playboy 1001	(S)	Heather Black		50.00	100.00
HEAVY BALLOON, THE					
Elephant EVS-104	(S)	Sixteen Ton		14.00	35.00
HEBB, BOBBY					
Phillips 200212	(M)	Sunny	1966	8.00	20.00
Phillips PHS-600212	(S)	Sunny	1966	10.00	25.00
Epic BN-26523	(S)	Love Games	1970	4.00	10.00
HELL, RICHARD, & THE VOIDOIDS					
Sire SR-6037	(S)	Blank Generation	1977	8.00	20.00

Label		Title	Year	VG+	NM
HELMS, BOBBY					
Decca DL-8638	(M)	To My Special Angel	1957	30.00	60.00
Columbia CL-2060	(M)	The Best Of Bobby Helms	1963	6.00	15.00
Columbia CS-8860	(S)	The Best Of Bobby Helms	1963	8.00	20.00
Kapp KL-13463	(M)	I'm The Man	1966	5.00	12.00
Kapp KS-3463	(M)	I'm The Man	1966	6.00	15.00
Kapp KL-1505	(S)	Sorry My Name Isn't Fred	1966	5.00	12.00
Kapp KS-3505	(S)	Sorry My Name Isn't Fred	1966	6.00	15.00
HELP					
Decca DL-75257	(S)	Help	1971	10.00	25.00
Decca DL-75304	(S)	Second Chance	1971	10.00	25.00
HENDERSON GROUP, BUGS					
Armadillo LP-78-1	(S)	The Bugs Henderson Group At Last		12.00	30.00
HENDERSON, JOE					
Todd MT-2701	(M)	Snap Your Fingers	1962	8.00	20.00
Todd ST-2701	(S)	Snap Your Fingers	1962	10.00	25.00
Capitol T-1765	(M)	You'd Be So Nice To Come Home To	1962	8.00	20.00
Capitol ST-1765	(S)	You'd Be So Nice To Come Home To	1962	10.00	25.00
Milestone 9040	(S)	Black Is The Color	1972	4.00	10.00
HENDRIX, JIMI					
Reprise R-6261	(M)	Are You Experienced?	1967	16.00	40.00
Reprise RS-6261	(P)	Are You Experienced?	1967	10.00	25.00
Capitol T-2856	(M)	Get That Feeling (With Curtis Knight)	1967	8.00	20.00
Capitol ST-2856	(S)	Get That Feeling (With Curtis Knight)	1967	8.00	20.00
Capitol ST-2894	(S)	Flashing (With Curtis Knight)	1968	6.00	15.00
Reprise R-6281	(M)	Axis: Bold As Love	1968	150.00	250.00
Reprise RS-6281	(S)	Axis: Bold As Love	1968	12.00	30.00
		(Reprise albums above have pink, gold and green riverboat labels.)			
Reprise 2RS-6307	(S)	Electric Ladyland	1968	10.00	25.00
Reprise MS-2025	(P)	Smash Hits (With poster)	1969	35.00	70.00
		(Poster is advertised on the cover.)			
Reprise MS-2025	(P)	Smash Hits	1969	10.00	25.00
		(Reprise albums above have brown and orange riverboat label.)			
Reprise MS-2029	(S)	Historic Performances At The Monterey International Pop Festival	1970	5.00	12.00
Capitol STAO-472	(S)	Band Of Gypsies (Green label)	1970	6.00	15.00
Capitol STAO8-472	(S)	Band Of Gypsies (Record club)	1970	8.00	20.00
Cotillion CT3-500	(S)	Woodstock (Sdtk)	1970	8.00	20.00
Cotillion CT2-400	(S)	Woodstock Two	1971	6.00	15.00
Maple 6004	(S)	Together With Lonnie Youngblood	1971	8.00	20.00
T-Neck TNS-3007	(S)	In The Beginning (With the Isley Brothers)	1971	5.00	12.00
Reprise MS-2034	(S)	The Cry Of Love	1971	4.00	10.00
Reprise MS-2040	(S)	Rainbow Bridge	1971	6.00	15.00
A.L.A. 1972	(S)	Friends From The Beginning (With Little Richard.)	1972	6.00	15.00
Reprise MS-2049	(S)	Jimi Hendrix In The West	1972	8.00	20.00
Reprise MS-2103	(S)	War Heroes	1972	8.00	20.00
Reprise MS-2204	(S)	Crash Landing	1975	5.00	12.00
Reprise MS-2229	(S)	Midnight Lightning	1975	5.00	12.00
		(Reprise albums above have brown riverboat labels.)			
Warners BSK-3335	(S)	Over The Edge (Sdtk)	1979	6.00	15.00
HENRI, ADRIAN, & ROGER MCGOUGH					
Epic LN-26336	(M)	The Incredible New Liverpool Scene	1967	8.00	20.00
Epic BN-24336	(S)	The Incredible New Liverpool Scene	1967	10.00	25.00
HENRY, CLARENCE "FROGMAN"					
Argo LP-4009	(M)	You Always Hurt The One You Love	1961	50.00	100.00
Roulette SR-42039	(S)	Alive And Well And Living In New Orleans	1969	8.00	20.00
HENSKE & YESTER (JUDY HENSKE & JERRY YESTER)					
Straight STS-1052	(S)	Farewell Aldebaran	1968	8.00	20.00
Reprise RS-6388	(S)	Farewell Aldebaran	1971	5.00	12.00

Label		Title	Year	VG+	NM
HERD, THE					
Fontana SRF-67579	(S)	Lookin Thru You	1968	10.00	25.00
HERMAN'S HERMITS					
MGM E-4282	(M)	Introducing Herman's Hermits	1965	6.00	15.00
MGM SE-4282	(E)	Introducing Herman's Hermits	1965	5.00	12.00
		(The front cover reads "Featuring I'm Into Something Good.")			
MGM E-4282	(M)	Introducing Herman's Hermits	1965	5.00	12.00
MGM SE-4282	(E)	Introducing Herman's Hermits	1965	4.00	10.00
		(The cover reads "Featuring Mrs. Brown You've Got A Lovely Daughter.")			
MGM E-4295	(M)	On Tour: Their Second Album	1965	2.50	6.00
MGM SE-4295	(E)	On Tour: Their Second Album	1965	2.00	5.00
MGM E-4315	(M)	The Best Of Herman's Hermits	1965	4.00	10.00
MGM SE-4315	(P)	The Best Of Herman's Hermits	1965	4.00	10.00
MGM E-4334	(M)	When The Boys Meet The Girls (Sdtk)	1965	3.50	8.00
MGM SE-4334	(S)	When The Boys Meet The Girls (Sdtk)	1966	4.00	10.00
MGM E-4342	(M)	Hold On! (Sdtk)	1966	2.00	5.00
MGM SE-4342	(S)	Hold On! (Sdtk)	1966	2.50	6.00
MGM E-4386	(M)	Both Sides Of Herman's Hermits	1966	2.50	6.00
MGM SE-4386	(P)	Both Sides Of Herman's Hermits	1966	2.00	5.00
MGM E-4416	(M)	The Best Of Herman's Hermits, Volume 2	1966	3.50	8.00
MGM SE-4416	(P)	The Best Of Herman's Hermits, Volume 2	1966	3.50	8.00
MGM E-4438	(M)	There's A Kind Of Hush	1967	2.50	6.00
MGM SE-4438	(E)	There's A Kind Of Hush	1967	2.00	5.00
MGM E-4478	(M)	Blaze	1967	2.00	5.00
MGM SE-4478	(S)	Blaze	1967	2.50	6.00
MGM E-4505	(M)	The Best Of Herman's Hermits, Volume 3	1967	4.00	10.00
MGM SE-4505	(P)	The Best Of Herman's Hermits, Volume 3	1967	4.00	10.00
MGM E-4548	(M)	Mrs. Brown You've Got A Lovely Daughter	1968	2.00	5.00
MGM SE-4548	(P)	Mrs. Brown You've Got A Lovely Daughter	1968	2.50	6.00
HERON, MIKE					
Elektra EKS-74093	(S)	Smiling Men With Bad Reputations	1971	6.00	15.00
HESTER, CARLOYN					
Columbia CL-1796	(M)	Carloyn Hester ("Eye" logo label)	1962	8.00	20.00
Columbia CS-8596	(S)	Carloyn Hester ("Eye" logo label)	1962	10.00	25.00
Columbia CL-2031	(M)	This Is My Living	1963	5.00	12.00
Columbia CS-8831	(S)	This Is My Living	1963	6.00	15.00
Dot DLP-3604	(M)	That's My Song	1964	5.00	12.00
Dot DLP-25604	(S)	That's My Song	1964	6.00	15.00
Dot DLP-3649	(M)	Carloyn Hester At The Town Hall	1965	5.00	12.00
Dot DLP-25649	(S)	Carloyn Hester At The Town Hall	1965	6.00	15.00
HI-LITES, THE					
Dandee DLP-206	(M)	For Your Precious Love		12.00	30.00
HI-LO'S, THE					
Also refer to Rosemary Clooney.					
Starlite 7005	(M)	Under Glass		10.00	25.00
Starlite 7006	(M)	Listen To The		10.00	25.00
Starlite 7007	(M)	The Hi-Lo's, I Presume		10.00	25.00
Starlite 7008	(M)	On Hand		10.00	25.00
Kapp KL-1027	(M)	The Hi-Lo's		8.00	20.00
Kapp KL-1184	(M)	Under Glass		8.00	20.00
Kapp KL-1194	(M)	On Hand		8.00	20.00
Omega 11	(S)	The Hi-Lo's In Stereo		8.00	20.00
Columbia CL-952	(M)	Suddenly It's The Hi-Lo's	1957	10.00	25.00
Columbia CL-1023	(M)	Now Hear This	1957	10.00	25.00
Columbia CL-1259	(M)	All That Jazz	1959	8.00	20.00
Columbia CS-8077	(S)	All That Jazz	1959	10.00	25.00
Columbia CL-1416	(M)	Broadway Playbill	1959	8.00	20.00
Columbia CS-8213	(S)	Broadway Playbill	1959	10.00	25.00
Columbia CL-1509	(M)	All Over The Place	1960	8.00	20.00
Columbia CS-8300	(S)	All Over The Place	1960	10.00	25.00
Columbia CL-1723	(M)	This Time It's Love	1962	6.00	15.00
Columbia CS-8523	(S)	This Time It's Love	1962	8.00	20.00
		(Columbia albums above have six black "eye" logos on each label.)			

Label		Title	Year	VG+	NM
HIBBLER, AL					
Score 4013	(M)	I Surrender, Dear		20.00	50.00
Marterry 601	(M)	Melodies By Al Hibbler		16.00	40.00
Argo	(M)	Melodies By Al Hibbler		12.00	30.00
Verve V-4000	(M)	Al Hibbler Sings Love Songs	1956	12.00	30.00
Atlantic 1251	(M)	After The Lights Go Down	1957	20.00	50.00
Decca DL-8328	(M)	Starring Al Hibbler	1957	14.00	35.00
Brunswick BL-54036	(M)	Al Hibbler With The Ellingtonians	1958	12.00	30.00
Decca DL-8420	(M)	Here's Hibbler	1958	14.00	35.00
Decca DL-8697	(M)	Torchy And Blue	1958	14.00	35.00
Decca DL-8757	(M)	Hits By Hibbler	1958	14.00	35.00
Decca DL-8862	(M)	Remember The Big Songs Of The Big Bands	1959	14.00	35.00
L.M.I. 10001	(M)	Al Hibbler With The Roland Hanna Trio		12.00	30.00
Reprise R-2005	(M)	Monday Every Day	1961	12.00	30.00
Reprise R9-2005	(S)	Monday Every Day	1961	14.00	35.00
Imperial LP-9185	(M)	Billie, Al Hibbler And The Blues	1962	14.00	35.00
Atlantic SD-1630	(S)	A Meeting Of The Times	1972		15.00
HICKMAN, DWAYNE					
Capitol T-1441	(M)	Dobie!		8.00	20.00
Capitol ST-1441	(S)	Dobie!		10.00	25.00
HIGGINS, CHUCK					
Dooto DL-223	(M)	Rock 'N' Roll Versus Rhythm 'N' Blues	1959	50.00	100.00
		(Also features Roy Milton.)			
Combo LP-300	(M)	Pachuko Hop (Nude woman on cover)	1960	100.00	200.00
Combo LP-300	(M)	Pachuko Hop (Higgins on cover)	1960	40.00	80.00
HIGH TIDE					
Liberty LST-7638	(S)	Sea Shanties	1969	8.00	20.00
HIGHTOWER, DEAN					
ABC-Paramount 312	(M)	Guitar-Twangy With A Beat	1959	12.00	30.00
ABC-Paramount S-312	(S)	Guitar-Twangy With A Beat	1959	16.00	40.00
HIGHTOWER, DONNA					
Capitol T-1133	(M)	Take One	1959	10.00	25.00
Capitol T-1273	(M)	Gee Baby, Ain't I Good To You?	1959	10.00	25.00
HILLMEN, THE					
Together STT-1012	(S)	The Hillmen	1970	16.00	40.00
HILLTOPPERS, THE					
Dot DLP-3003	(M)	Tops In Pops	1956	10.00	25.00
Dot DLP-3029	(M)	The Towering Hilltoppers	1957	10.00	25.00
Dot DLP-3073	(M)	The Hilltoppers	1958	10.00	25.00
HILLOW HAMMET					
House Of Fox 2	(S)	Hammer		18.00	45.00
HINSON, DON					
Capitol T-2219	(M)	Monster Dance Party	1964	5.00	12.00
Capitol ST-2219	(S)	Monster Dance Party	1964	6.00	15.00
HINTON, JOE					
Backbeat B-60	(M)	Funny How Time Slips Away	1965	8.00	20.00
Backbeat B-60	(S)	Funny How Time Slips Away	1965	10.00	25.00
HITCHCOCK, ALFRED					
Imperial LP-9052	(M)	Music To Be Murdered By		16.00	40.00
Imperial LP-12052	(S)	Music To Be Murdered By		20.00	50.00
HOBBITS, THE					
Decca DL-4290	(M)	Down To Middle Earth	1967	16.00	40.00
Decca DL-74290	(S)	Down To Middle Earth	1967	20.00	50.00
Decca DL-75009	(S)	Men And Doors	1968	8.00	20.00
HOFFMAN, ABBIE					
Big Toe 1	(M)	Wake Up, America!		10.00	25.00

Label		Title	Year	VG+	NM
HOGG, SMOKEY (ANDREW HOGG)					
Time 6	(M)	Smokey Hogg	1962	16.00	40.00
HOLDEN, RANDY					
Hobbit 5002	(S)	Population II	1968	50.00	100.00
HOLDEN, RON					
Donna DLP-2111	(M)	I Love You So	1960	30.00	60.00
Donna DLPS-2111	(S)	I Love You So	1960	40.00	80.00
HOLIDAY, BILLIE					
Commodore 20005 (10")	(M)	Billie Holiday, Volume 1	1950	30.00	60.00
Commodore 20006 (10")	(M)	Billie Holiday, Volume 2	1950	30.00	60.00
Columbia CL-2531 (10")	(M)	Ella, Lena And Billie	1950	30.00	60.00
Columbia CL-6129 (10")	(M)	Billie Holiday Sings	1950	30.00	60.00
Columbia CL-6163 (10")	(M)	Favorites	1950	30.00	60.00
Dale 25 (10")	(M)	Billie And Stan	1951	30.00	60.00
Decca DL-6345 (10")	(M)	Lover Man	1952	30.00	60.00
Clef 144 (10")	(M)	An Evening With Billie	1953	30.00	60.00
Clef 118 (10")	(M)	Favorites	1953	30.00	60.00
Clef 161 (10")	(M)	Favorites	1954	30.00	60.00
Clef 169 (10")	(M)	Jazz At The Philharmonic	1954	20.00	50.00
Clef 669	(M)	Music For Torching	1955	20.00	50.00
Clef 686	(M)	A Recital	1955	20.00	50.00
Clef 690	(M)	Solitude	1956	20.00	50.00
Clef 713	(M)	Velvet Moods	1956	20.00	50.00
Clef 718	(M)	Jazz Recital	1956	20.00	50.00
Clef 721	(M)	Lady Sings The Blues	1956	20.00	50.00
Columbia CL-637	(M)	Lady Day ("Eye" logo label)	1956	16.00	40.00
Jazztone 1209	(M)	Billie Holiday Sings	1956	16.00	40.00
Score LP-4014	(M)	Billie Holiday Sings The Blues	1957	16.00	40.00
Decca DL-8215	(M)	The Lady Sings	1956	16.00	40.00
Verve V-8026	(M)	Music For Torching	1957	16.00	40.00
Verve V-8027	(M)	A Recital	1957	16.00	40.00
Verve V-8074	(M)	Solitude	1957	16.00	40.00
Verve V-8096	(M)	Velvet Moods	1957	16.00	40.00
Verve V-8098	(M)	Jazz Recital	1957	16.00	40.00
Verve V-8099	(M)	Lady Sings The Blues	1957	16.00	40.00
Verve V-8197	(M)	Body And Soul	1957	16.00	40.00
Verve V-8234	(M)	Ella And Billie At Newport	1958	16.00	40.00
Columbia CL-1157	(M)	Lady In Satin ("Eye" logo label)	1958	16.00	40.00
Decca DL-8701	(M)	Blues Are Brewin'	1958	16.00	40.00
Decca DL-8702	(M)	Lover Man	1958	16.00	40.00
Decca DXB-161	(M)	The Billie Holiday Story	1959	16.00	40.00
MGM E-3764	(M)	Billie Holiday	1959	12.00	30.00
MGM SE-3764	(S)	Billie Holiday	1959	12.00	30.00
Columbia CL-1248	(M)	Lady In Satin	1959	8.00	20.00
Columbia CS-8048	(S)	Lady In Satin	1959	12.00	30.00
MGM E-3764	(M)	Billie Holiday	1959	16.00	40.00
Commodore 30008	(M)	Billie Holiday, Volume 2	1959	16.00	40.00
Commodore 30011	(M)	Billie Holiday, Volume 1	1959	16.00	40.00
Verve V-8257	(M)	Songs For Distingue' Lovers	1959	16.00	40.00
Verve VS-6021	(S)	Songs For Distingue' Lovers	1959	16.00	40.00
Verve V-8302	(M)	Stay With Me	1959	16.00	40.00
Verve V-8329	(M)	All Or Nothing At All	1959	12.00	30.00
Verve V-8338	(M)	The Unforgettable Lady Day	1960	16.00	40.00
		(Verve albums above have black labels with			
		"Verve Records, Inc." on the bottom.)			
Verve MGV-8410	(M)	The Essential Billie Holiday	1961	12.00	30.00
Columbia C3L-21 (3 LPs)	(M)	The Golden Years	1962	20.00	50.00
United Arts. UAL-14014	(M)	Lady Love	1962	10.00	25.00
United Arts. UAS-15014	(S)	Lady Love	1962	12.00	30.00
Imperial LP-9185	(M)	Billie Holiday, Al Hibbler And The Blues	1962	14.00	35.00
Ric 2001	(M)	Rare Live Recordings	1964	10.00	25.00
Mainstream 6000	(M)	The Commodore Recordings	1965	8.00	20.00
Mainstream 56000	(S)	The Commodore Recordings	1965	8.00	20.00
Mainstream 6022	(M)	Once Upon A Time	1965	8.00	20.00
Mainstream 56022	(S)	Once Upon A Time	1965	8.00	20.00
Decca DXB-161	(M)	The Billie Holiday Story	1965	6.00	15.00
Decca DXSB7-161	(E)	The Billie Holiday Story	1965	6.00	15.00
Columbia C3L-40	(M)	The Golden Years, Volume 2	1966	8.00	20.00

Label		Title	Year	VG+	NM
Columbia CL-2666	(M)	Billie Holiday's Greatest Hits	1967	6.00	15.00
Decca DL7-5040	(S)	Billie Holiday's Greatest Hits	1968	6.00	15.00

HOLLAND, EDDIE

Motown 604	(M)	Eddie Holland	1963	20.00	50.00

HOLLIES, THE
Also refer to the Everly Brothers.

Imperial LP-9265	(M)	Here I Go Again	1964	20.00	50.00
Imperial LP-12265	(E)	Here I Go Again	1964	16.00	40.00
Imperial LP-9299	(M)	Hear! Here!	1965	16.00	40.00
Imperial LP-12299	(E)	Hear! Here!	1965	12.00	30.00
Imperial LP-9312	(M)	The Hollies/Beat Group	1966	12.00	30.00
Imperial LP-12312	(E)	The Hollies/Beat Group	1966	8.00	20.00
Imperial LP-9330	(M)	Bus Stop	1966	6.00	15.00
Imperial LP-12330	(S)	Bus Stop	1966	8.00	20.00
Imperial LP-9339	(M)	Stop! Stop! Stop!	1967	6.00	15.00
Imperial LP-12339	(S)	Stop! Stop! Stop!	1967	8.00	20.00
Imperial LP-9350	(M)	The Hollies' Greatest Hits	1967	6.00	15.00
Imperial LP-12350	(P)	The Hollies' Greatest Hits	1967	6.00	15.00
United Arts. UAL-4148	(M)	After The Fox (Sdtk)	1966	6.00	15.00
United Arts. UAS-5148	(S)	After The Fox (Sdtk)	1966	8.00	20.00
Epic LN-24315	(M)	Evolution	1967	5.00	12.00
Epic BN-26315	(S)	Evolution	1967	6.00	15.00
Epic LN-24344	(M)	Dear Eloise/King Midas In Reverse	1967	5.00	12.00
Epic BN-26344	(S)	Dear Eloise/King Midas In Reverse	1967	6.00	15.00
Epic BN-26447	(S)	Words And Music By Bob Dylan	1969	5.00	12.00
Epic BN-26538	(S)	He Ain't Heavy, He's My Brother	1970	5.00	12.00
Epic KE-30255	(S)	Moving Finger	1971	5.00	12.00
Epic KE-30958	(S)	Distant Light	1972	4.00	10.00
Epic KE-31992	(S)	Romany	1972	4.00	10.00
		(Epic albums above have yellow labels.)			

HOLLOWAY, BRENDA

Tamla 257	(M)	Every Little Bit Hurts	1965	16.00	40.00

HOLLY, BUDDY (& THE CRICKETS)

Brunswick BL-54038	(M)	The "Chirping" Crickets	1957	180.00	300.00
Decca DL-8707	(M)	That'll Be The Day (Black label)	1958	300.00	500.00
Coral CRL-57210	(M)	Buddy Holly	1958	150.00	250.00
Coral CRL-57279	(M)	The Buddy Holly Story	1959	60.00	120.00
		(The print on the back cover is red & black.)			
Coral CRL-57326	(M)	The Buddy Holly Story, Volume 2	1959	50.00	100.00
Coral CRL-57405	(M)	Buddy Holly And The Crickets	1962	35.00	70.00
Coral CRL7-57405	(E)	Buddy Holly And The Crickets	1962	35.00	70.00
Coral CRL-57426	(M)	Reminiscing	1963	30.00	60.00
Coral CRL7-57426	(E)	Reminiscing	1963	30.00	60.00
		(Coral albums above have maroon labels.)			
Coral CRL-57450	(M)	Showcase	1964	30.00	60.00
Coral CRL7-57450	(E)	Showcase	1964	30.00	60.00
Coral CRL-57463	(M)	Holly In The Hills	1965	35.00	70.00
Coral CRL7-57463	(E)	Holly In The Hills	1965	30.00	60.00
Coral CXB-8	(M)	The Best Of Buddy Holly	1966	20.00	50.00
Coral CXSB-8	(E)	The Best Of Buddy Holly	1966	20.00	50.00
Coral CRL-57492	(M)	Buddy Holly's Greatest Hits	1967	20.00	50.00
Coral CRL7-57492	(E)	Buddy Holly's Greatest Hits	1967	20.00	50.00
Vocalion VL-3811	(M)	The Great Buddy Holly	1967	20.00	50.00
Vocalion VL7-3811	(S)	The Great Buddy Holly	1967	20.00	50.00
Coral CRL7-57504	(E)	Giant	1969	16.00	40.00
Vocalion VL7-3923	(E)	Good Rockin'	1971	50.00	100.00
Decca DXSE7-207	(P)	A Rock & Roll Collection	1972	8.00	20.00

HOLLYWOOD ARGYLES, THE

Lute L-9001	(M)	Ally Oop	1960	150.00	250.00

HOLLYWOOD PERSUADERS, THE

Original Sound 8874	(M)	Drums A Go-Go	1965	10.00	25.00
Original Sound S-8874	(S)	Drums A Go-Go	1965	12.00	30.00

HOLY MACKEREL

Reprise 6311	(S)	Holy Mackerel	1968	8.00	20.00

Label		Title	Year	VG+	NM
HOLY MODEL ROUNDERS, THE					
Prestige PR-7410	(M)	The Holy Model Rounders, Volume 1	1965	8.00	20.00
Prestige PRS-7451	(S)	The Holy Model Rounders, Volume 2	1967	8.00	20.00
Elektra EKS-74026	(S)	The Moray Eels Eats			
		The Holy Model Rounders	1968	8.00	20.00
ESP 1068	(S)	Indian War Whoop	1969	8.00	20.00
Metromedia MD-1039	(S)	Good Taste Is Timeless	1971	8.00	20.00
Rounder 3004	(S)	Alleged In Their Own Time	1972	6.00	15.00
Fantasy F-24711	(S)	Stampfel And Weber	1972	6.00	15.00
HOMBRES, THE					
Forecast FT-3036	(M)	Let It Out	1967	8.00	20.00
Forecast FTS-3036	(S)	Let It Out	1967	10.00	25.00
HOMER & JETHRO					
RCA LPM-3112 (10")	(M)	Homer & Jethro Fracture Frank Loesser	1953	20.00	50.00
RCA LPM-1412	(M)	Barefoot Ballads	1957	10.00	25.00
RCA LPM-1560	(M)	The Worst Of Homer & Jethro	1957	10.00	25.00
RCA LPM-1880	(M)	Life Can Be Miserable	1958	6.00	15.00
RCA LSP-1880	(S)	Life Can Be Miserable	1958	10.00	25.00
Audio Lab AL-1513	(M)	Musical Madness	1958	20.00	50.00
King 639	(M)	They Sure Are Corny	1959	14.00	35.00
RCA LPM-2181	(M)	At The Country Club	1960	5.00	12.00
RCA LSP-2181	(S)	At The Country Club	1960	8.00	20.00
RCA LPM-2286	(M)	Songs My Mother Never Sang	1961	5.00	12.00
RCA LSP-2286	(S)	Songs My Mother Never Sang	1961	8.00	20.00
RCA LPM-2455	(M)	Zany Songs Of The '30s	1962	5.00	12.00
RCA LSP-2455	(S)	Zany Songs Of The '30s	1962	8.00	20.00
RCA LPM-2459	(M)	Playing It Straight	1962	5.00	12.00
RCA LSP-2459	(S)	Playing It Straight	1962	8.00	20.00
RCA LPM-2492	(M)	At The Convention	1962	5.00	12.00
RCA LSP-2492	(S)	At The Convention	1962	8.00	20.00
King 848	(M)	Cornier Than Corn	1963	12.00	30.00
RCA LPM-2674	(M)	Homer & Jethro Go West	1963	5.00	12.00
RCA LSP-2674	(S)	Homer & Jethro Go West	1963	8.00	20.00
		(Mono RCA albums above have "Long Play" on the bottom of the label. Stereo albums have "Living Stereo" on the bottom.)			
HONDELLS, THE					
Mercury MG-20940	(M)	Go Little Honda	1964	10.00	25.00
Mercury SR-60940	(S)	Go Little Honda	1964	12.00	30.00
Mercury MG-20982	(M)	The Hondells	1965	10.00	25.00
Mercury SR-60982	(S)	The Hondells	1965	12.00	30.00
HONEY & THE BEES					
Josie JOS-4013	(S)	Honey And The Bees		6.00	15.00
HONEYCOMBS					
Interphon IN-88001	(M)	Here Are The Honeycombs	1964	12.00	30.00
Interphon IN-88001	(E)	Here Are The Honeycombs	1964	10.00	25.00
Vee Jay IN-88001	(M)	Here Are The Honeycombs	1964	16.00	40.00
Vee Jay IN-88001	(E)	Here Are The Honeycombs	1964	14.00	35.00
HOOKER, JOHN LEE					
Also refer to the Groundhogs.					
Vee Jay LP-1007	(M)	I'm John Lee Hooker (Maroon label)	1959	30.00	60.00
Vee Jay LP-1023	(M)	Travelin'	1960	16.00	40.00
Chess LP-1438	(M)	House Of The Blues	1960	16.00	40.00
Chess LP-1454	(M)	Plays And Sings The Blues	1961	16.00	40.00
King 727	(M)	John Lee Hooker Sings The Blues	1961	35.00	70.00
Fortune 3002	(M)	Big Maceo Merriweather & John Lee Hooker		20.00	50.00
Vee Jay LP-1033	(M)	The Folk Lore Of John Lee Hooker	1961	8.00	20.00
Vee Jay SR-1033	(S)	The Folk Lore Of John Lee Hooker	1961	10.00	25.00
Vee Jay LP-1043	(M)	Burnin'	1962	8.00	20.00
Vee Jay SR-1043	(S)	Burnin'	1962	10.00	25.00
Vee Jay LP-1049	(M)	The Best Of John Lee Hooker	1962	6.00	15.00
Vee Jay SR-1049	(S)	The Best Of John Lee Hooker	1962	8.00	20.00
Atco 33-151	(M)	Don't Turn Me From Your Door	1963	10.00	25.00
Atco SD-33-151	(S)	Don't Turn Me From Your Door	1963	12.00	30.00

The Hollies, *Here I Go Again.* Never the success in the U.S. they were elsewhere, the Hollies rank second only to the Beatles for singles chart success in the U.K. in the '60s. This album, essentially a hodge-podge of covers and originals, showcases the title track, an uptempo ballad with soaring vocals and strumming guitars, British beat at its best.

Ferlin Husky, *By Request.* Husky has been a consistent country recording artist since the '50s. His Capitol albums are marked by the same attention to detail, well-chosen material and expertly arranged performances that were the hallmark of that label's many fine country recordings of the '50s and '60s.

Label		Title	Year	VG+	NM
Vee Jay LP-1066	(M)	John Lee Hooker On Campus	1963	6.00	15.00
Vee Jay SR-1066	(S)	John Lee Hooker On Campus	1963	8.00	20.00
Vee Jay LP-1078	(M)	John Lee Hooker At Newport	1964	6.00	15.00
Vee Jay SR-1078	(S)	John Lee Hooker At Newport	1964	8.00	20.00
		(Vee Jay albums above have black rainbow labels.)			
Riverside 12838	(M)	Folk Blues		8.00	20.00
Folkways 3003	(M)	Seven Nights	1965	5.00	12.00
Folkways FTS-3003	(S)	Seven Nights	1965	6.00	15.00
Chess LP-1508	(M)	Real Folk Blues	1966	8.00	20.00
Chess LPS-1508	(S)	Real Folk Blues	1966	10.00	25.00
Impulse A-9103	(M)	It Serves Me Right To Suffer	1966	6.00	15.00
BluesWay BL-6002	(M)	Live At Cafe Au-Go-Go	1966	5.00	12.00
BluesWay BLS-6002	(S)	Live At Cafe Au-Go-Go	1966	6.00	15.00
BluesWay BLS-6012	(S)	Urban Blues	1968	5.00	12.00
BluesWay 6023	(S)	Simply The Truth	1969	5.00	12.00
Stax STS-2013	(S)	That's Where It's At	1969	5.00	12.00
Buddah BDS-4002	(S)	The Very Best Of John Lee Hooker	1969	5.00	12.00
Buddah BDS-7506	(S)	Big Band Blues	1969	5.00	12.00

HOPE, LYNN

Label		Title	Year	VG+	NM
Aladdin 707 (10")	(M)	Lynn Hope And His Tenor Sax		75.00	150.00
Aladdin 820	(M)	Lynn Hope		50.00	100.00
Score LP-4015	(M)	Tenderly		35.00	70.00

HOPKIN, MARY

Label		Title	Year	VG+	NM
Apple SW-3351	(S)	Postcard	1969	6.00	15.00
Apple SW-3351	(S)	Postcard (Record club)	1969	10.00	25.00
Apple SMAS-3381	(S)	Earth Song/Ocean Song	1969	4.00	10.00
Paramount PAS-5005	(S)	Where's Jack (Sdtk)	1969	6.00	15.00
American Int. STA-1042	(S)	Kidnapped (Sdtk)	1972	6.00	15.00
Apple SW-3395	(P)	Those Were The Days	1972	6.00	15.00

HOPKINS, LIGHTNIN'

Label		Title	Year	VG+	NM
Herald 1012	(M)	Lightnin' And The Blues	1960	150.00	250.00
Score 4022	(M)	Lightnin' Hopkins Strums The Blues	1960	75.00	150.00
Tradition TLP-1035	(M)	Country Blues	1960	16.00	40.00
Tradition TLP-1040	(M)	Autobiography In Blues	1960	16.00	40.00
Time 70004	(M)	Last Of The Great Blues Singers	1960	12.00	30.00
Bluesville BV-1019	(M)	Lightnin'	1961	12.00	30.00
Bluesville BV-1029	(M)	Last Night Blues	1961	12.00	30.00
Bluesville BV-1057	(M)	Walkin' This Road By Myself	1961	12.00	30.00
Fire 104	(M)	Mojo Hand	1962	50.00	100.00
Vee Jay LP-1044	(M)	Lightnin' Hopkins	1962	16.00	40.00
Time 1	(M)	Blues/Folk	1962	8.00	20.00
Time 3	(M)	Blues/Folk, Volume 2	1962	8.00	20.00
Verve V-8453	(M)	Fast Life Woman	1962	12.00	30.00
Imperial LP-9180	(M)	Lightnin' Hopkins On Stage	1962	12.00	30.00
Imperial LP-9211	(M)	Lightnin' Hopkins And The Blues	1962	12.00	30.00
Imperial LP-12211	(S)	Lightnin' Hopkins And The Blues	1962	16.00	40.00
Mt. Vernon 104	(M)	Nothin' But The Blues		8.00	20.00
Bluesville BV-1045	(M)	Blues In My Bottle	1963	10.00	25.00
Bluesville BV-1070	(M)	Smokes Like Lightnin'	1963	10.00	25.00
Bluesville BV-1073	(M)	Goin' Away	1964	10.00	25.00
Bluesville BV-1084	(M)	His Greatest Hits	1964	10.00	25.00
Bluesville BV-1986	(M)	Down Home Blues	1964	10.00	25.00
Prestige PR-7370	(M)	My Life In The Blues	1965	10.00	25.00
Folkways FV-9000	(M)	The Roots Of Lightnin' Hopkins	1965	6.00	15.00
Folkways FVS-9000	(S)	The Roots Of Lightnin' Hopkins	1965	8.00	20.00
Folkways FV-9022	(M)	Lightnin' Strikes	1965	6.00	15.00
Folkways FVS-9022	(S)	Lightnin' Strikes	1965	8.00	20.00
Folkways FV-3013	(M)	Something Blue	1967	6.00	15.00
Folkways FVS-3013	(S)	Something Blue	1967	6.00	15.00
Prestige PR-7377	(M)	Soul Blues	1966	6.00	15.00
Prestige PRS-7377	(S)	Soul Blues	1966	8.00	20.00
International Arts. 6	(S)	Free Form Patterns	1968	75.00	150.00
		(With a picture of Hopkins on the cover.)			
Vault 129	(S)	California Mudslide	1969	8.00	20.00
Poppy 60002	(S)	Lightnin'	1969	8.00	20.00

HORN, SHIRLEY

Label		Title	Year	VG+	NM
Stereocraft 16	(M)	Embers And Ashes	1961	8.00	20.00

Label		Title	Year	VG+	NM
Mercury MG-20761	(M)	Loads Of Love	1963	6.00	15.00
Mercury SR-60761	(S)	Loads Of Love	1963	8.00	20.00
Mercury MG-20835	(M)	Shirley Horn With Horns	1964	6.00	15.00
Mercury SR-60835	(S)	Shirley Horn With Horns	1964	8.00	20.00
ABC-Paramount 538	(M)	Travelin' Light	1965	6.00	15.00
ABC-Paramount S-538	(S)	Travelin' Light	1965	8.00	20.00

HORNE, LENA

Label		Title	Year	VG+	NM
Columbia CL-2531 (10")	(M)	Ella, Lena And Billie	1950	35.00	70.00
Jazztone 1262	(M)	Lena And Ivie		14.00	35.00
RCA LPM-1148	(M)	It's Love	1955	14.00	35.00
RCA LPM-1375	(M)	Stormy Weather	1956	14.00	35.00
RCA LOC-1028	(M)	Lena Horne At The Waldorf Astoria	1957	8.00	20.00
RCA LSO-1028	(S)	Lena Horne At The Waldorf Astoria	1957	12.00	30.00
RCA LOC-1036	(M)	Jamaica (Original Cast)	1957	10.00	25.00
RCA LSO-1036	(S)	Jamaica (Original Cast)	1957	16.00	40.00
RCA LPM-1879	(M)	Give The Lady What She Wants	1958	8.00	20.00
RCA LSP-1879	(S)	Give The Lady What She Wants	1958	12.00	30.00
RCA LPM-1895	(M)	Songs Of Burke And Van Heusen	1959	8.00	20.00
RCA LSP-1895	(S)	Songs Of Burke And Van Heusen	1959	12.00	30.00
RCA LOC-1507	(M)	Porgy And Bess (Studio Cast)	1959	6.00	15.00
RCA LSO-1507	(S)	Porgy And Bess (Studio Cast)	1959	10.00	25.00
RCA LPM-2364	(M)	Lena Horne At The Sands	1961	6.00	15.00
RCA LSP-2364	(S)	Lena Horne At The Sands	1961	10.00	25.00
RCA LPM-2465	(M)	On The Blue Side	1962	6.00	15.00
RCA LSP-2465	(S)	On The Blue Side	1962	10.00	25.00

(Mono RCA albums above have "Long Play"
on the bottom of the label. Stereo albums
have "Living Stereo" on the bottom.)

Label		Title	Year	VG+	NM
RCA LPM-2587	(M)	Lovely And Alive	1963	6.00	15.00
RCA LSP-2587	(S)	Lovely And Alive	1963	8.00	20.00
Charter CL-101	(M)	Lena Horne Sings Your Requests	1963	6.00	15.00
Charter CLS-101	(S)	Lena Horne Sings Your Requests	1963	8.00	20.00
Charter CL-106	(M)	Like Latin	1964	6.00	15.00
Charter CLS-106	(S)	Like Latin	1964	8.00	20.00
Movietone 71005	(M)	Once In A Lifetime		6.00	15.00
Movietone 72005	(S)	Once In A Lifetime		8.00	20.00
20th Century TF-4115	(M)	Here's Lena Now	1964	6.00	15.00
20th Century TFS-4115	(S)	Here's Lena Now	1964	8.00	20.00
RCA LOC-1103	(M)	Jamaica (Original Cast)	1965	6.00	15.00
RCA LSO-1103	(S)	Jamaica (Original Cast)	1965	8.00	20.00
United Arts. UAL-3433	(M)	Feelin' Good	1965	6.00	15.00
United Arts. UAS-6433	(S)	Feelin' Good	1965	8.00	20.00
United Arts. UAL-3470	(M)	Lena In Hollywood	1966	6.00	15.00
United Arts. UAS-6470	(S)	Lena In Hollywood	1966	8.00	20.00
United Arts. UAL-3496	(M)	Soul	1966	8.00	20.00
United Arts. UAS-6496	(S)	Soul	1966	8.00	20.00
Mobile Fidelity 1-094	(S)	A Lady And Her Music		6.00	15.00

HORNETS, THE

Label		Title	Year	VG+	NM
Liberty LRP-3348	(M)	Motorcycles U.S.A.	1963	5.00	12.00
Liberty LST-7348	(S)	Motorcycles U.S.A.	1963	6.00	15.00
Liberty LRP-3364	(M)	Big Drag Boats U.S.A.	1964	5.00	12.00
Liberty LST-7364	(S)	Big Drag Boats U.S.A.	1964	6.00	15.00

HORSES, THE

Label		Title	Year	VG+	NM
White Whale 7121	(S)	Horses	1970	8.00	20.00

HORTON, JOHNNY

Label		Title	Year	VG+	NM
Briar Int. 104	(M)	Done Rovin'		50.00	100.00
SESAC 1201	(M)	Free And Easy Songs	1959	75.00	150.00
Mercury MG-20478	(M)	The Fantastic Johnny Horton	1959	20.00	50.00
Columbia CL-1362	(M)	The Spectacular Johnny Horton	1960	8.00	20.00
Columbia CS-8167	(S)	The Spectacular Johnny Horton	1960	12.00	30.00
Columbia CL-1478	(M)	Johnny Horton Makes History	1960	8.00	20.00
Columbia CS-8269	(S)	Johnny Horton Makes History	1960	12.00	30.00
Columbia CL-1596	(M)	Greatest Hits (With bonus photo)	1961	10.00	25.00
Columbia CS-8396	(S)	Greatest Hits (With bonus photo)	1961	14.00	35.00

(Columbia albums above have six
black eye logos on each label.)

Label		Title	Year	VG+	NM
Columbia CL-1721	(M)	Honky-Tonk Man	1962	10.00	25.00
Columbia CS-8779	(E)	Honky-Tonk Man	1962	6.00	15.00
Dot DLP-3221	(M)	Johnny Horton	1962	12.00	30.00
Columbia CL-2299	(M)	I Can't Forget You	1965	8.00	20.00
Columbia CS-9099	(E)	I Can't Forget You	1965	5.00	12.00
Columbia CL-2566	(S)	Johnny Horton On Stage	1966	6.00	15.00
Columbia CS-9366	(S)	Johnny Horton On Stage	1966	8.00	20.00
Columbia CS-9940	(S)	Johnny Horton On The Road	1969	6.00	15.00
		(Columbia albums above have "360 Sound" labels.)			

HORTON, SHAKEY (WALTER HORTON)

Argo 4037	(M)	The Soul Of Blues Harmonica		40.00	80.00

HOT DOGGERS, THE

Epic LN-24054	(M)	Surfin' USA	1963	30.00	60.00
Epic BN-26054	(S)	Surfin' USA	1963	40.00	80.00

HOT POOP

Hot Poop 3072	(S)	Hot Poop Does Their Stuff	1975	20.00	50.00

HOT TUNA (JORMA KAUKONEN & JACK CASADY)

RCA LSP-4353	(S)	Hot Tuna Recorded Live	1970	6.00	15.00
RCA LSP-4550	(S)	First Pull Up, Then Pull Down	1971	5.00	12.00
Grunt BFD1-0820	(Q)	America's Choice	1975	6.00	15.00
Grunt BFD1-1238	(Q)	Yellow Fever	1975	6.00	15.00

HOTLEGS

Capitol ST-587	(S)	Hotlegs Thinks: School Stinks	1971	8.00	20.00

HOUR GLASS, THE

Liberty LRP-3536	(M)	The Hour Glass	1967	6.00	15.00
Liberty LST-7536	(S)	The Hour Glass	1967	8.00	20.00
Liberty LST-7555	(S)	The Power Of Love	1968	8.00	20.00

HOUSE, SON

Columbia CL-2417	(M)	Father Of The Folk Blues	1965	6.00	15.00
Columbia CS-9217	(S)	Father Of The Folk Blues	1965	8.00	20.00
Folkways 9035	(M)	Son House And J. D. Short	1966	6.00	15.00
Folkways 9035	(S)	Son House And J. D. Short	1966	8.00	20.00

HOUSTON, JOE

Combo LP-100	(M)	Where Is Joe?	1960	50.00	100.00
Combo LP-400	(M)	Rockin, At The Drive In	1960	50.00	100.00
Modern LMP-1206	(M)	Joe Houston Blows All Night Long	1960	14.00	35.00

HOUSTON, THELMA

Sheffield Lab 2	(S)	I've Got The Music In Me	1974	8.00	20.00

HOUSTON FEARLESS

Imperial LP-12421	(S)	Houston Fearless	1969	8.00	20.00

HOWARD, DAVE

Choreo 5	(M)	I Love Everybody	1961	10.00	25.00

HOWARD, HARLAN

Capitol T-1631	(M)	Harlan Howard Sings Harlan Howard	1961	10.00	25.00
Capitol ST-1631	(S)	Harlan Howard Sings Harlan Howard	1961	12.00	30.00
Monument MLP-8038	(M)	All-Time Favorite Country Songwriter	1965	8.00	20.00
Monument SLP-18038	(S)	All-Time Favorite Country Songwriter	1965	10.00	25.00
RCA LPM-3729	(M)	Mr. Songwriter	1967	6.00	15.00
RCA LSP-3729	(S)	Mr. Songwriter	1967	8.00	20.00
RCA LPM-3886	(M)	Down To Earth	1968	6.00	15.00
RCA LSP-3886	(S)	Down To Earth	1968	8.00	20.00

HOWLIN' WOLF, THE (CHESTER BURNETT)
Also refer to Bo Diddley.

Chess LP-1434	(M)	Moanin' In The Moonlight	1958	40.00	80.00
Chess LP-1469	(M)	Howlin' Wolf	1962	35.00	70.00
		(Chess albums above have black & silver labels.)			
Custom CM-2055	(M)	Big City Blues		8.00	20.00
Custom CS-2055	(S)	Big City Blues		8.00	20.00

Label		Title	Year	VG+	NM
Chess LP-1502	(M)	The Real Folk Blues	1966	20.00	50.00
Chess LP-1512	(M)	More Real Folk Blues	1967	20.00	50.00
		(Chess albums above have black labels with a color logo on top.)			
Kent KLP-526	(M)	Original Folk Blues	1967	6.00	15.00
Kent KST-526	(E)	Original Folk Blues	1967	5.00	12.00
Kent KST-527	(E)	Howlin' Wolf's Twenty Greatest R&B Hits		6.00	15.00
Kent KST-535	(E)	Underground Blues		6.00	15.00
Cadet 319	(S)	This Is Howlin' Wolf's New Album	1969	10.00	25.00
Chess LP-1540	(S)	Evil	1969	10.00	25.00
Chess 60016	(E)	Howlin' Wolf A.K.A. Chester Burnett	1972	10.00	25.00
Chess CH-50045	(M)	The Back Door Wolf	1974	10.00	25.00
Chess CH-60008	(S)	The London Sessions	1971	8.00	20.00
Chess CH-50015	(S)	Live And Cookin'	1972	6.00	15.00
		(Chess albums above have blue & white labels.)			

HUDSON, ROCK

Label		Title	Year	VG+	NM
Stanyan 10014	(S)	Rock Gently	1971	10.00	25.00

HUGHES, FREDDIE

Label		Title	Year	VG+	NM
Wand WD-664	(M)	Send My Baby Back	1965	5.00	12.00
Wand WDS-664	(S)	Send My Baby Back	1965	6.00	15.00

HUGHES, JIMMY

Label		Title	Year	VG+	NM
Vee Jay 1102	(M)	Steal Away	1965	5.00	12.00
Vee Jay SR-1102	(S)	Steal Away	1965	6.00	15.00
Atco 33-209	(M)	Why Not Tonight	1967	4.00	10.00
Atco SD-33-209	(S)	Why Not Tonight	1967	5.00	12.00

HULLABALOOS, THE

Label		Title	Year	VG+	NM
Roulette R-25297	(M)	England's Newest Singing Sensations	1965	10.00	25.00
Roulette SR-25297	(E)	England's Newest Singing Sensations	1965	8.00	20.00
Roulette R-25310	(M)	The Hullaballoos On Hullaballoo	1965	10.00	25.00
Roulette SR-25310	(S)	The Hullaballoos On Hullaballoo	1965	8.00	20.00

HUMAN BEINZ, THE

Label		Title	Year	VG+	NM
Gateway GLP-3012	(S)	Nobody But Me (With the Mammals)	1968	12.00	30.00
Capitol St-2906	(S)	Nobody But Me	1968	10.00	25.00
Capitol ST-2926	(S)	Evolutions	1968	8.00	20.00

HUMAN ZOO, THE

Label		Title	Year	VG+	NM
Accent 5-055	(S)	The Human Zoo	1969	20.00	50.00

HUNGER

Label		Title	Year	VG+	NM
Public 1006	(S)	Strickly From Hunger	1969	50.00	100.00

HUNT, TOMMY

Label		Title	Year	VG+	NM
Scepter 506	(M)	I Just Don't Know What To Do With Myself	1962	14.00	35.00
Scepter SS-506	(S)	I Just Don't Know What To Do With Myself	1962	16.00	40.00
Dynamo 8001	(M)	Tommy Hunt's Greatest Hits	1967	8.00	20.00
Dynamo 8001	(S)	Tommy Hunt's Greatest Hits	1967	10.00	25.00

HUNTER, IVORY JOE

Label		Title	Year	VG+	NM
MGM E-3488	(M)	I Get That Lonesome Feeling	1957	50.00	100.00
Sound 603	(M)	Ivory Joe Hunter	1957	50.00	100.00
King 605	(M)	16 Of His Greatest Hits	1958	75.00	150.00
Atlantic 8008	(M)	Ivory Joe Hunter (Black label)	1958	50.00	100.00
Atlantic 8015	(M)	Sings The Old And The New (Black label)	1958	50.00	100.00
Sage 603	(M)	Ivory Joe Hunter	1959	30.00	60.00
Goldisc 403	(M)	The Fabulous Ivory Joe Hunter	1961	20.00	50.00
Smash MGS-27037	(M)	Ivory Joe Hunter's Golden Hits	1963	10.00	25.00
Smash SRS-67037	(S)	Ivory Joe Hunter's Golden Hits	1963	14.00	35.00
Dot DLP-3569	(M)	This Is Ivory Joe Hunter	1964	10.00	25.00
Dot DLP-25569	(S)	This Is Ivory Joe Hunter	1964	12.00	30.00
Epic SE-30348	(S)	The Return Of Ivory Joe Hunter	1971	8.00	20.00
Everest 289	(S)	Ivory Joe Hunter	1974	4.00	10.00
Paramount PAS-6080	(S)	I've Always Been Country	1974	5.00	12.00
Lion L-70068	(M)	I Need You So		16.00	40.00
Strand 1123	(M)	The Artistry Of Ivory Joe Hunter		8.00	20.00

Label		Title	Year	VG+	NM
HUNTER, LURLEAN					
RCA LPM-1151	(M)	Lonesome Gal	1955	16.00	40.00
Vik 1061	(M)	Night Life	1956	12.00	30.00
Vik 1116	(M)	Stepping Out	1958	12.00	30.00
Atlantic 1344	(M)	Blue And Sentimental	1960	10.00	25.00
Atlantic SD-1344	(S)	Blue And Sentimental	1960	14.00	35.00
HUNTER, ROBERT					
Round RX-101	(S)	Tales Of The Great Rum Runners	1974	6.00	15.00
Round RX-105	(S)	Tiger Rose	1975	6.00	15.00
HUNTER, TAB					
RCA LOC-1047	(M)	Damn Yankees (Sdtk)	1958	12.00	30.00
Dot DLP-9001	(M)	Hans Brinker (Sdtk)	1958	10.00	25.00
Warners W-1221	(M)	Tab Hunter	1958	8.00	20.00
Warners WS-1221	(S)	Tab Hunter	1958	10.00	25.00
Warners W-1292	(M)	When I Fall In Love	1959	8.00	20.00
Warners WS-1292	(S)	When I Fall In Love	1959	10.00	25.00
Warners W-1367	(M)	R.F.D. Tab Hunter	1960	8.00	20.00
Warners WS-1367	(S)	R.F.D. Tab Hunter	1960	10.00	25.00
Dot DLP-3370	(M)	Young Love	1961	6.00	15.00
Dot DLP-25370	(S)	Young Love	1961	8.00	20.00
HUNTER MUSKETT					
Bradley 1003	(S)	Hunter Muskett	1969	20.00	50.00
HURT, MISSISSIPPI JOHN					
Vanguard VRS-9145	(M)	Blues At Newport	1965	8.00	20.00
Vanguard VSD-79145	(S)	Blues At Newport	1965	10.00	25.00
Vanguard VRS-9220	(M)	Mississippi John Hurt Today	1966	8.00	20.00
Vanguard VSD7-9220	(S)	Mississippi John Hurt Today	1966	10.00	25.00
Vanguard VRS-9248	(M)	The Immortal Mississippi John Hurt	1967	8.00	20.00
Vanguard VSD7-9248	(S)	The Immortal Mississippi John Hurt	1967	10.00	25.00
HURVITZ, SANDY					
Verve V6-5064	(S)	Sandy's Album Is Here At Last	1968	6.00	15.00
HUSKY, FERLIN (SIMON CRUM)					
Capitol T-718	(M)	Songs Of The Home And Heart	1956	16.00	40.00
Capitol T-880	(M)	Boulevard Of Broken Dreams	1957	14.00	35.00
Capitol T-976	(M)	Sittin' On A Rainbow	1959	12.00	30.00
		(Capitol albums above have turquoise labels.)			
King 647	(M)	Country Tunes Sung From The Heart	1959	14.00	35.00
King 728	(M)	Easy Livin'	1960	14.00	35.00
Capitol T-1204	(M)	Born To Lose	1959	10.00	25.00
Capitol T-1280	(M)	Ferlin's Favorites	1960	10.00	25.00
Capitol T-1383	(M)	Gone	1960	8.00	20.00
Capitol T-1546	(M)	Walkin' And Hummin'	1961	6.00	15.00
Capitol ST-1546	(S)	Walkin' And Hummin'	1961	8.00	20.00
Capitol T-1633	(M)	Memories Of Home	1961	6.00	15.00
Capitol ST-1633	(S)	Memories Of Home	1961	8.00	20.00
		(Capitol albums above have black labels with the Capitol logo on the side.)			
Capitol T-1720	(M)	Some Of My Favorites	1962	5.00	12.00
Capitol ST-1720	(S)	Some Of My Favorites	1962	6.00	15.00
Capitol T-1885	(M)	The Heart And Soul Of Ferlin Husky	1963	5.00	12.00
Capitol ST-1885	(S)	The Heart And Soul Of Ferlin Husky	1963	6.00	15.00
Capitol T-1991	(M)	The Hits Of Ferlin Husky	1963	8.00	20.00
Capitol DT-1991	(E)	The Hits Of Ferlin Husky	1963	5.00	12.00
Capitol T-2101	(M)	By Request	1964	5.00	12.00
Capitol ST-2101	(S)	By Request	1964	6.00	15.00
Capitol T-2305	(M)	True, True Lovin'	1965	5.00	12.00
Capitol ST-2305	(S)	True, True Lovin'	1965	6.00	15.00
Capitol T-2439	(M)	Songs Of Music City, U.S.A.	1966	5.00	12.00
Capitol ST-2439	(S)	Songs Of Music City, U.S.A.	1966	6.00	15.00
Capitol T-2548	(M)	I Could Sing All Night	1966	5.00	12.00
Capitol ST-2548	(S)	I Could Sing All Night	1966	6.00	15.00
Capitol T-2705	(M)	What Am I Gonna Do Now?	1967	5.00	12.00
Capitol ST-2705	(S)	What Am I Gonna Do Now?	1967	6.00	15.00
Capitol T-2793	(M)	Christmas All Year Long	1967	5.00	12.00
Capitol ST-2793	(S)	Christmas All Year Long	1967	6.00	15.00

Label		Title	Year	VG+	NM
Capitol ST-2870	(S)	Just For You	1968	5.00	12.00
Capitol ST 2913	(S)	Where No One Stands Alone	1968	5.00	12.00
		(Capitol albums above have black labels with the Capitol logo on top.)			

HUTTON, JUNE

| Capitol T-643 | (M) | Afterglow | | 8.00 | 20.00 |
| Venise 10017 | (M) | Dream | | 8.00 | 20.00 |

HYLAND, BRIAN

Kapp KL-1202	(M)	The Bashful Blonde	1960	10.00	25.00
Kapp KS-3202	(S)	The Bashful Blonde	1960	12.00	30.00
ABC-Paramount 400	(M)	Let Me Belong To You	1961	6.00	15.00
ABC-Paramount S-400	(S)	Let Me Belong To You	1961	8.00	20.00
ABC-Paramount 431	(M)	Sealed With A Kiss	1962	8.00	20.00
ABC-Paramount S-431	(P)	Sealed With A Kiss	1962	10.00	25.00
ABC-Paramount 463	(M)	Country Meets Folk	1964	6.00	15.00
ABC-Paramount S-463	(S)	Country Meets Folk	1964	8.00	20.00
Phillips PHM-200136	(M)	Here's To Our Love	1964	6.00	15.00
Phillips PHS-600136	(S)	Here's To Our Love	1964	8.00	20.00
Phillips PHM-200158	(M)	Rockin' Folk	1965	6.00	15.00
Phillips PHS-600158	(S)	Rockin, Folk	1965	8.00	20.00
Phillips PHM-200217	(M)	Joker Went Wild	1966	6.00	15.00
Phillips PHS-600217	(S)	Joker Went Wild	1966	8.00	20.00
Dot DLP-25926	(S)	Tragedy	1969	5.00	12.00
Dot DLP-25954	(S)	Stay And Love Me All Summer	1969	5.00	12.00

IAN & THE ZODIACS

| Phillips PHM-200176 | (M) | Ian And The Zodiacs | 1965 | 10.00 | 25.00 |
| Phillips PHS-600176 | (S) | Ian And The Zodiacs | 1965 | 12.00 | 30.00 |

ID, THE

| RCA LPM-3805 | (M) | The Inner Sounds Of The Id | 1967 | 8.00 | 20.00 |
| RCA LSP-3805 | (S) | The Inner Sounds Of The Id | 1967 | 10.00 | 25.00 |

ID, THE

| Aura 1000 | (S) | Where Are We Going? | 1976 | 12.00 | 30.00 |

IDLE RACE, THE
Features Jeff Lynne.

| Liberty LST-7603 | (S) | Birthday Party | 1969 | 10.00 | 25.00 |

IKETTES, THE

| Modern M-102 | (M) | Soul Hits | 1965 | 6.00 | 15.00 |
| Modern MST-102 | (S) | Soul Hits | 1965 | 8.00 | 20.00 |

ILL WIND

| ABC S-641 | (S) | Flashes | 1968 | 12.00 | 30.00 |

ILLUSTRATION

| Janus 3010 | (S) | Illustration | 1969 | 10.00 | 25.00 |

ILMO SMOKEHOUSE

| Beautiful Sound 3002 | (S) | Ilmo Smokehouse | 1971 | 14.00 | 35.00 |
| Roulette SR-3002 | (S) | Ilmo Smokehouse | 1971 | 6.00 | 15.00 |

Label		Title	Year	VG+	NM
IMPACS, THE					
King 886	(M)	Impact!	1964	16.00	40.00
King KS-886	(S)	Impact!	1964	20.00	50.00
King 916	(M)	Weekend With The Impacs	1964	16.00	40.00
King KS-916	(S)	Weekend With The Impacs	1964	20.00	50.00
IMPACTS, THE					
Del-Fi DFLP-1234	(M)	Wipe Out	1963	10.00	25.00
Del-Fi DFS-1234	(S)	Wipe Out	1963	12.00	30.00
IMPALA SYNDROME, THE					
Parallax 4002	(S)	The Impala Syndrome	1970	12.00	30.00
IMPALAS, THE					
Cub 8003	(M)	Sorry I Ran All The Way Home	1959	75.00	150.00
Cub S-8003	(S)	Sorry I Ran All The Way Home	1959	150.00	250.00
IMPRESSIONS, THE					
ABC-Paramount 450	(M)	The Impressions	1963	8.00	20.00
ABC-Paramount S-450	(S)	The Impressions	1963	10.00	25.00
ABC-Paramount 468	(M)	Never Ending Impressions	1964	6.00	15.00
ABC-Paramount S-468	(S)	Never Ending Impressions	1964	8.00	20.00
ABC-Paramount 493	(M)	Keep On Pushing	1964	6.00	15.00
ABC-Paramount S-493	(S)	Keep On Pushing	1964	8.00	20.00
ABC-Paramount 505	(M)	People Get Ready	1965	6.00	15.00
ABC-Paramount S-505	(S)	People Get Ready	1965	8.00	20.00
ABC-Paramount 515	(M)	The Impressions' Greatest Hits	1965	6.00	15.00
ABC-Paramount S-515	(S)	The Impressions' Greatest Hits	1965	8.00	20.00
ABC-Paramount 523	(M)	One By One	1965	5.00	12.00
ABC-Paramount S-523	(S)	One By One	1965	6.00	15.00
ABC-Paramount 545	(M)	Ridin' High	1966	5.00	12.00
ABC-Paramount S-545	(S)	Ridin' High	1966	6.00	15.00
ABC-Paramount 606	(M)	The Fabulous Impressions	1967	5.00	12.00
ABC-Paramount S-606	(S)	The Fabulous Impressions	1967	6.00	15.00
ABC-Paramount S-635	(S)	We're A Winner	1968	6.00	15.00
IN-SECT, THE					
Camden CAL-909	(M)	Introducing The In-Sect	1965	12.00	30.00
Camden CAS-909	(S)	Introducing The In-Sect	1965	16.00	40.00
INCREDIBLE STRING BAND, THE					
Elektra EKL-322	(M)	The Incredible String Band	1967	5.00	12.00
Elektra EKS7-322	(S)	The Incredible String Band	1967	6.00	15.00
Elektra EKL-4010	(M)	The 5,000 Spirits	1967	5.00	12.00
Elektra EKS7-4010	(S)	The 5,000 Spirits	1967	6.00	15.00
Elektra EKS-74021	(S)	The Hangman's Beautiful Daughter	1968	6.00	15.00
Elektra EKS7-4036	(S)	Wee Tam	1969	6.00	15.00
Elektra EKS7-4037	(S)	The Big Huge	1969	6.00	15.00
		(Elektra albums above have brown labels.)			
INGMANN, JORGEN					
Mercury MG-20200	(M)	Swinging Guitar	1956	10.00	25.00
Atco 33-130	(M)	Apache	1961	10.00	25.00
Atco SD-33-130	(S)	Apache	1961	12.00	30.00
Atco 33-139	(M)	The Many Guitars Of Jorgen Ingmann	1962	8.00	20.00
Atco SD-33-139	(S)	The Many Guitars Of Jorgen Ingmann	1962	10.00	25.00
INK SPOTS, THE					
Waldorf Music 144 (10")	(M)	Spirituals And Jubilees		14.00	35.00
Waldorf Music 152 (10")	(M)	Spirituals And Jubilees, Volume 2		14.00	35.00
Decca DL-5056 (10")	(M)	The Ink Spots, Volume 1		14.00	35.00
Decca DL-5071 (10")	(M)	The Ink Spots, Volume 2		14.00	35.00
Decca DL-8154	(M)	The Ink Spots		10.00	25.00
Decca DL-8232	(M)	Time Out For Tears		10.00	25.00
Decca DL-8768	(M)	Torch Time		10.00	25.00
King LP-535	(M)	Something Old, Something New	1958	16.00	40.00
King LP-642	(M)	Songs That Will Live Forever	1959	16.00	40.00
Grand LP-328	(M)	The Ink Spots' Greatest	1959	6.00	15.00
Grand LP-354	(M)	The Ink Spots' Greatest, Volume 2	1959	6.00	15.00
Verve V-6096	(M)	Favorites	1960	8.00	20.00
Verve VS-606	(S)	Favorites	1960	8.00	20.00

Label		Title	Year	VG+	NM
Crown CST-144	(E)	The Ink Spots' Greatest Hits (Red vinyl)		12.00	30.00
Crown CST-217	(S)	The Sensational Ink Spots (Red vinyl)		12.00	30.00
Mayfair 9685S	(S)	In The Spotlight (Yellow vinyl)		12.00	30.00
Vocalion VL-3606	(M)	Sincerely Yours	1964	6.00	15.00
Vocalion VL-3725	(M)	Lost In A Dream	1965	6.00	15.00
Vocalion VL7-3725	(S)	Lost In A Dream	1965	6.00	15.00
Decca DL-4297	(M)	Our Golden Favorites		6.00	15.00
Decca DXB-182	(M)	The Best Of The Ink Spots	1965	6.00	15.00
Decca DXSB7-182	(P)	The Best Of The Ink Spots	1965	6.00	15.00

INNOCENCE, THE

Label		Title	Year	VG+	NM
Kama Sutra KLP-8059	(M)	The Innocence	1967	5.00	12.00
Kama Sutra KLPS-8059	(S)	The Innocence	1967	8.00	20.00

INNOCENTS, THE; Refer to KATHY YOUNG & THE INNOCENTS

INSECT TRUST, THE

Label		Title	Year	VG+	NM
Capitol SKAO-109	(S)	The Insect Trust	1968	14.00	35.00
Atco SD-33-313	(S)	Hoboken Saturday Night	1970	14.00	35.00

INTERNATIONAL SUBMARINE BAND, THE

Label		Title	Year	VG+	NM
L.H.I. 12001	(S)	Safe At Home (Multi-color label)	1968	30.00	60.00

INTRIGUES, THE

Label		Title	Year	VG+	NM
Yew YS-777	(S)	In A Moment	1970	16.00	40.00

INTRUDERS, THE

Label		Title	Year	VG+	NM
Gamble 5001	(M)	The Intruders Are Together	1967	6.00	15.00
Gamble KZ-5001	(S)	The Intruders Are Together	1967	8.00	20.00
Gamble KZ-5004	(S)	Cowboys To Girls	1968	6.00	15.00
Gamble KZ-5005	(P)	The Intruders' Greatest Hits	1969	5.00	12.00
Gamble KZ-5008	(S)	When We Get Married	1970	4.00	10.00

INVADERS, THE

Label		Title	Year	VG+	NM
Justice JLP-125	(M)	On The Right Track		150.00	250.00

INVICTAS, THE

Label		Title	Year	VG+	NM
Sahara 101	(M)	The Invictas A-Go-Go	1965	30.00	60.00

IRON BUTTERFLY

Label		Title	Year	VG+	NM
Atco 33-227	(M)	Heavy	1967	8.00	20.00
Atco SD-33-227	(S)	Heavy	1967	6.00	15.00
Atco SD-33-245	(S)	The Savage Seven (Sdtk)	1968	6.00	15.00
Atco SD-33-250	(S)	In-A-Gadda-Da-Vida (Red & green label)	1968	6.00	15.00

ISLEY BROTHERS, THE

Label		Title	Year	VG+	NM
RCA LPM-2156	(M)	Shout!	1959	20.00	50.00
RCA LSP-2156	(S)	Shout!	1959	30.00	60.00
Wand WD-653	(M)	Twist And Shout	1962	12.00	30.00
Wand WDS-653	(S)	Twist And Shout	1962	16.00	40.00
United Arts. UAL-6313	(M)	The Famous Isley Brothers	1963	10.00	25.00
United Arts. UAS-6313	(S)	The Famous Isley Brothers	1963	12.00	30.00
Scepter SC-552	(M)	Take Some Time Out For The Isley Brothers	1966	6.00	15.00
Scepter SCS-552	(S)	Take Some Time Out For The Isley Brothers	1966	8.00	20.00
Tamla T-269	(M)	This Old Heart Of Mine	1966	6.00	15.00
Tamla TS-269	(S)	This Old Heart Of Mine	1966	8.00	20.00
Tamla 275	(M)	Soul On The Rocks	1967	5.00	12.00
Tamla TS-275	(S)	Soul On The Rocks	1967	6.00	15.00
Tamla TS-287	(S)	Doin' Their Thing	1969	5.00	12.00
T-Neck TNS-3007	(S)	In The Beginning (With Jimi Hendrix)	1971	5.00	12.00

ITALIAN ASPHALT & PAVEMENT CO., THE

Label		Title	Year	VG+	NM
Colossus 5000	(S)	Dupree's Gold	1970	6.00	15.00

IT'S A BEAUTIFUL DAY

Label		Title	Year	VG+	NM
Columbia CS-9768	(S)	It's A Beautiful Day ("360 Sound" label)	1969	12.00	30.00
Columbia CS-1058	(S)	Marrying Maiden	1970	8.00	20.00
Columbia C-30734	(S)	Choice Quality Stuff/Anytime	1971	6.00	15.00
Columbia KC-31338	(S)	Live At Carnegie Hall	1972	6.00	15.00
Columbia KC-32181	(S)	It's A Beautiful Day Today	1973	6.00	15.00
San Fran. Sound 11790	(S)	It's A Beautiful Day (1/2 speed)	1985	12.00	30.00

Label		Title	Year	VG+	NM
IVEYS, THE (BADFINGER)					
Apple SAPCOR-8S	(S)	Maybe Tomorrow	1968	**240.00**	**400.00**
		(This Italian release is listed due to the fact that it			
		has been heavily counterfeited and sold in the U.S.			
		as legitimate. The originals have green Apple labels			
		while the counterfeits have black labels.)			
IVORY, JACKIE					
Atco 33-178	(M)	Soul Discovery	1965	**8.00**	**20.00**
Atco SD-33-178	(S)	Soul Discovery	1965	**10.00**	**25.00**
IVORY LIBRARY					
Dairyland	(S)	Ivory Library	1985	**4.00**	**10.00**
IVY LEAGUE, THE					
Cameo C-2000	(M)	Tossing And Turning	1965	**8.00**	**20.00**
Cameo CS-2000	(S)	Tossing And Turning	1965	**10.00**	**25.00**

Label		Title	Year	VG+	NM
JACKS, THE					
R.P.M. LRP-3006	(M)	Jumpin' With The Jacks		**75.00**	**150.00**
Crown CLP-5021	(M)	The Jacks		**20.00**	**50.00**
JACKSON, BULL MOOSE					
Audio Lab 1524	(M)	Bull Moose Jackson		**50.00**	**100.00**
JACKSON, CHUCK					
Wand LP-650	(M)	I Don't Want To Cry	1961	**8.00**	**20.00**
Wand WDS-650	(S)	I Don't Want To Cry	1961	**10.00**	**25.00**
Wand LP-654	(M)	Any Day Now	1962	**8.00**	**20.00**
Wand WDS-654	(S)	Any Day Now	1962	**10.00**	**25.00**
Wand LP-655	(M)	Encore	1963	**8.00**	**20.00**
Wand WDS-655	(S)	Encore	1963	**10.00**	**25.00**
Wand LP-658	(M)	Chuck Jackson On Tour	1964	**6.00**	**15.00**
Wand WDS-658	(S)	Chuck Jackson On Tour	1964	**8.00**	**20.00**
Wand LP-667	(M)	Mr. Everything	1965	**6.00**	**15.00**
Wand WDS-667	(S)	Mr. Everything	1965	**8.00**	**20.00**
Wand LP-669	(M)	Saying Something (With Maxine Brown)	1965	**6.00**	**15.00**
Wand WDS-669	(S)	Saying Something (With Maxine Brown)	1965	**8.00**	**20.00**
Wand LP-673	(M)	A Tribute To Rhythm And Blues	1966	**6.00**	**15.00**
Wand WDS-673	(S)	A Tribute To Rhythm And Blues	1966	**8.00**	**20.00**
Wand LP-676	(M)	A Tribute To Rhythm And Blues, Volume 2	1966	**6.00**	**15.00**
Wand WDS-676	(S)	A Tribute To Rhythm And Blues, Volume 2	1966	**8.00**	**20.00**
Wand LP-678	(M)	Hold On, We're Coming	1966	**6.00**	**15.00**
Wand WDS-678	(S)	Hold On, We're Coming	1966	**8.00**	**20.00**
		(With Maxine Brown.)			
Wand LP-680	(M)	Dedicated To The King!!	1966	**8.00**	**20.00**
Wand WDS-680	(S)	Dedicated To The King!!	1966	**10.00**	**25.00**
Wand LP-682	(M)	The Early Show (With Tammi Terrell)	1967	**6.00**	**15.00**
Wand WDS-682	(S)	The Early Show (With Tammi Terrell)	1967	**8.00**	**20.00**
Wand LP-683	(M)	Chuck Jackson's Greatest Hits	1967	**5.00**	**12.00**
Wand WDS-683	(S)	Chuck Jackson's Greatest Hits	1967	**6.00**	**15.00**
Motown MS-667	(S)	Chuck Jackson Arrives	1968	**6.00**	**15.00**
Motown MS-687	(S)	Goin' Back To Chuck Jackson	1969	**5.00**	**12.00**
JACKSON, DEON					
Atco 33-188	(M)	Love Makes The World Go Round	1966	**8.00**	**20.00**
Atco SD-33-188	(S)	Love Makes The World Go Round	1966	**10.00**	**25.00**

Label		Title	Year	VG+	NM
JACKSON, J.J.					
Calla C-1101	(M)	But It's Alright/I Dig Girls	1967	6.00	15.00
Calla CS-1101	(S)	But It's Alright/I Dig Girls	1967	8.00	20.00
Congress 7000	(S)	Greatest Little Soul Band In The World	1968	8.00	20.00
Warners WS-1797	(S)	The Great J.J. Jackson	1969	5.00	12.00
JACKSON, JOE					
Mobile Fidelity 1-050	(S)	Night And Day		5.00	12.00
JACKSON, LIL' SON					
Imperial 9142	(M)	Rockin' And Rollin'	1961	60.00	120.00
JACKSON, MICHAEL					
Epic HE-47545	(S)	Off The Wall (1/2 speed)	1980	8.00	20.00
Epic HE-48112	(S)	Thriller (1/2 speed)	1982	12.00	30.00
JACKSON, STONEWALL					
Columbia CL-1391	(M)	The Dynamic Stonewall Jackson	1959	8.00	20.00
Columbia CS-8186	(S)	The Dynamic Stonewall Jackson	1959	12.00	30.00
Columbia CL-1770	(M)	Sadness In A Song	1962	8.00	20.00
Columbia CS-8570	(S)	Sadness In A Song	1962	10.00	25.00
		(Columbia albums above have six black "eye" logos on each label.)			
Columbia CL-2059	(M)	I Love A Song	1963	6.00	15.00
Columbia CS-8859	(S)	I Love A Song	1963	8.00	20.00
Columbia CL-2278	(M)	Trouble And Me	1965	6.00	15.00
Columbia CS-9078	(S)	Trouble And Me	1965	8.00	20.00
Columbia CL-2377	(M)	Stonewall Jackson's Greatest Hits	1965	5.00	12.00
Columbia CS-9177	(S)	Stonewall Jackson's Greatest Hits	1965	6.00	15.00
Columbia CL-2509	(M)	All's Fair In Love 'N' War	1966	5.00	12.00
Columbia CS-9309	(S)	All's Fair In Love 'N' War	1966	6.00	15.00
Columbia CL-2674	(M)	Help Stamp Out Loneliness	1967	5.00	12.00
Columbia CS-9474	(S)	Help Stamp Out Loneliness	1967	6.00	15.00
Columbia CL-2762	(M)	Stonewall Jackson Country	1967	5.00	12.00
Columbia CS-9562	(S)	Stonewall Jackson Country	1967	6.00	15.00
Columbia CL-2869	(M)	Nothing Takes The Place Of Loving You	1968	6.00	15.00
Columbia CS-9669	(S)	Nothing Takes The Place Of Loving You	1968	6.00	15.00
		(Columbia albums above have "360 Sound" labels.)			
JACKSON, WANDA (& THE PARTY TIMERS)					
Capitol T-1041	(M)	Wanda Jackson	1958	50.00	100.00
Capitol T-1384	(M)	Rockin' With Wanda!	1960	50.00	100.00
Capitol T-1511	(M)	There's A Party Goin' On	1961	50.00	100.00
Capitol ST-1511	(S)	There's A Party Goin' On	1961	60.00	120.00
Capitol T-1596	(M)	Right Or Wrong	1961	16.00	40.00
Capitol ST-1596	(S)	Right Or Wrong	1961	20.00	50.00
		(Capitol albums above have black labels with the Capitol logo on the left side.)			
Decca DL-4224	(M)	Lovin' Country Style	1962	20.00	50.00
Capitol T-1776	(M)	Wonderful Wanda	1962	8.00	20.00
Capitol ST-1776	(S)	Wonderful Wanda	1962	10.00	25.00
Capitol T-1911	(M)	Love Me Forever	1963	8.00	20.00
Capitol ST-1911	(S)	Love Me Forever	1963	10.00	25.00
Capitol T-2030	(M)	Two Sides Of Wanda Jackson	1964	14.00	35.00
Capitol ST-2030	(S)	Two Sides Of Wanda Jackson	1964	16.00	40.00
Capitol T-2306	(M)	Blues In My Heart	1964	10.00	25.00
Capitol ST-2306	(S)	Blues In My Heart	1964	12.00	30.00
Capitol T-2438	(M)	Wanda Jackson Sings Country Songs	1966	6.00	15.00
Capitol ST-2438	(S)	Wanda Jackson Sings Country Songs	1966	8.00	20.00
Capitol T-2606	(M)	Salutes The Country Music Hall Of Fame	1966	6.00	15.00
Capitol ST-2606	(S)	Salutes The Country Music Hall Of Fame	1966	8.00	20.00
Capitol T-2704	(M)	Reckless Love Affair	1967	5.00	12.00
Capitol ST-2704	(S)	Reckless Love Affair	1967	6.00	15.00
Capitol T-2812	(M)	You'll Always Have My Love	1967	5.00	12.00
Capitol ST-2812	(S)	You'll Always Have My Love	1967	6.00	15.00
Capitol T-2883	(M)	The Best Of Wanda Jackson	1967	5.00	12.00
Capitol ST-2883	(S)	The Best Of Wanda Jackson	1967	6.00	15.00
Capitol ST-2976	(S)	Cream Of The Crop	1968	6.00	15.00
		(Capitol albums above have black labels with the Capitol logo on top.)			

Two Sides Of Wanda Jackson. Ms Jackson was one of only a handful of female rockers on a major label in the '50s, recording several rockabilly-style singles and albums for Capitol. While these are highly sought-after collectibles, they did not fare all too well either with the pop or country audience, to which Wanda devoted her complete attention in the early '60s.

Michael Jackson, *Thriller.* While most of Michael's records have been so absurdly successful that it will be generations before the demand can match the existing supply and make them "collectible," the half-speed masters of this and *Off The Wall* are already hard to find.

Label		Title	Year	VG+	NM
JACKSON FIVE, THE (THE JACKSONS)					
Motown MS-700	(S)	Diana Ross Presents The Jackson Five	1969	6.00	15.00
Epic HE-46424	(S)	Triumph (1/2 speed)	1981	8.00	20.00
JACKSON HEIGHTS					
Mercury SR-61331	(S)	King Progress	1970	10.00	25.00
Verve V6-5089	(S)	Jackson Heights	1973	8.00	20.00
JACOBS, HANK					
Sue 1023	(M)	So Far Away	1964	12.00	30.00
JAGGER, MICK					
United Arts. UAS-5213	(S)	Ned Kelly (Sdtk)	1970	6.00	15.00
Warners BS-1846	(S)	Performance (Sdtk)	1970	8.00	20.00
JAIM					
Ethereal 1001	(S)	Prophesy Fulfilled	1970	20.00	50.00
JAMES, ELMORE					
Crown CLP-5168	(M)	Blues After Hours	1961	20.00	50.00
Kent KLP-5022	(M)	Original Folk Blues	1964	16.00	40.00
Kent KLP-9001	(M)	Anthology Of The Blues Legend		10.00	25.00
Kent KLP-9010	(M)	The Resurrection Of Elmore James		10.00	25.00
Sphere Sound 7002	(M)	The Sky Is Crying		14.00	35.00
Sphere Sound 7008	(M)	I Need You		14.00	35.00
Chess 1537	(S)	Whose Muddy Shoes	1969	10.00	25.00
Bell 6037	(S)	Elmore James	1969	10.00	25.00
United 7716	(S)	Blues In My Heart, Rhythm In My Soul	1969	4.00	10.00
United 7743	(M)	Original Folk Blues	1969	4.00	10.00
United 7787	(M)	The Resurrection Of Elmore James	1969	4.00	10.00
JAMES, ETTA					
Argo 4003	(M)	At Last	1961	10.00	25.00
Argo S-4003	(S)	At Last	1961	12.00	30.00
Argo 4011	(M)	The Second Time Around	1961	10.00	25.00
Argo S-4011	(S)	The Second Time Around	1961	12.00	30.00
Argo 4013	(M)	Etta James	1962	10.00	25.00
Argo S-4013	(S)	Etta James	1962	12.00	30.00
Argo 4018	(M)	Etta James Sings For Lovers	1962	10.00	25.00
Argo S-4018	(S)	Etta James Sings For Lovers	1962	12.00	30.00
Argo 4025	(M)	Top Ten	1963	8.00	20.00
Argo S-4025	(S)	Top Ten	1963	10.00	25.00
Argo 4032	(M)	Etta James Rocks The House	1964	8.00	20.00
Argo S-4032	(S)	Etta James Rocks The House	1964	10.00	25.00
Argo 4040	(M)	The Queen Of Soul	1965	8.00	20.00
Argo S-4040	(S)	The Queen Of Soul	1965	10.00	25.00
Kent 3002	(M)	Miss Etta James		6.00	15.00
Kent 3002	(M)	Miss Etta James (Red vinyl)		14.00	35.00
JAMES, JONI					
MGM E-234 (10")	(M)	Award Winning Album		16.00	40.00
MGM E-3328	(M)	In The Still Of The Night	1956	14.00	35.00
MGM E-3346	(M)	Award Winning Album	1956	14.00	35.00
MGM E-3468	(M)	Merry Christmas From Joni	1957	14.00	35.00
MGM E-3528	(M)	Give Us This Day	1958	14.00	35.00
		(MGM albums above have yellow labels.)			
MGM E-3739	(M)	Songs Of Hank Williams	1959	10.00	25.00
MGM SE-3739	(S)	Songs Of Hank Williams	1959	12.00	30.00
MGM E-3749	(M)	Irish Favorites	1959	8.00	20.00
MGM SE-3749	(S)	Irish Favorites	1959	10.00	25.00
MGM E-3755	(M)	100 Strings And Joni	1959	8.00	20.00
MGM SE-3755	(S)	100 Strings And Joni	1959	10.00	25.00
MGM E-3772	(M)	Joni James Swings Sweet	1959	8.00	20.00
MGM SE-3772	(S)	Joni James Swings Sweet	1959	10.00	25.00
MGM E-3800	(M)	Joni James At Carnegie Hall	1959	8.00	20.00
MGM SE-3800	(S)	Joni James At Carnegie Hall	1959	10.00	25.00
MGM E-3837	(M)	I'm In The Mood For Love	1960	6.00	15.00
MGM SE-3837	(S)	I'm In The Mood For Love	1960	8.00	20.00
MGM E-3839	(M)	100 Strings And Joni On Broadway	1960	6.00	15.00
MGM SE-3839	(S)	100 Strings And Joni On Broadway	1960	8.00	20.00

Label		Title	Year	VG+	NM
MGM E-3840	(M)	Joni James Sings Hollywood	1960	6.00	15.00
MGM SE-3840	(S)	Joni James Sings Hollywood	1960	8.00	20.00
MGM E-3885	(M)	More Joni Hits	1960	6.00	15.00
MGM SE-3885	(S)	More Joni Hits	1960	8.00	20.00
MGM E-3892	(M)	100 Voices, 100 Strings	1960	6.00	15.00
MGM SE-3892	(S)	100 Voices, 100 Strings	1960	8.00	20.00
MGM E-3958	(M)	Folk Songs By Joni James	1961	6.00	15.00
MGM SE-3958	(S)	Folk Songs By Joni James	1961	8.00	20.00
MGM E-3987	(M)	The Mood Is Swinging	1961	8.00	20.00
MGM SE-3987	(S)	The Mood Is Swinging	1961	10.00	25.00
MGM E-3990	(M)	The Mood Is Romance	1961	8.00	20.00
MGM SE-3990	(S)	The Mood Is Romance	1961	10.00	25.00
MGM E-3991	(M)	The Mood Is Blue	1961	8.00	20.00
MGM SE-3991	(S)	The Mood Is Blue	1961	10.00	25.00
MGM E-4053	(M)	I Feel A Song Comin' On	1962	8.00	20.00
MGM SE-4053	(S)	I Feel A Song Comin' On	1962	10.00	25.00
MGM E-4054	(M)	I'm Your Girl	1962	8.00	20.00
MGM SE-4054	(S)	I'm Your Girl	1962	10.00	25.00
MGM E-4088	(M)	After Hours	1962	8.00	20.00
MGM SE-4088	(S)	After Hours	1962	10.00	25.00
MGM E-4101	(M)	Country Girl Style	1962	8.00	20.00
MGM SE-4101	(S)	Country Girl Style	1962	10.00	25.00
MGM E-4151	(M)	The Very Best Of Joni James	1963	6.00	15.00
MGM SE-4151	(S)	The Very Best Of Joni James	1963	8.00	20.00
MGM E-4158	(M)	Something For The Boys	1963	6.00	15.00
MGM SE-4158	(S)	Something For The Boys	1963	8.00	20.00
MGM E-4182	(M)	Three O' Clock In The Morning	1963	6.00	15.00
MGM SE-4182	(S)	Three O' Clock In The Morning	1963	8.00	20.00
MGM E-4200	(M)	My Favorite Things	1963	6.00	15.00
MGM SE-4200	(S)	My Favorite Things	1963	8.00	20.00
MGM E-4248	(M)	Put On A Happy Face	1964	6.00	15.00
MGM SE-4248	(S)	Put On A Happy Face	1964	8.00	20.00
MGM E-4255	(M)	Joni James Sings The Gershwins	1964	6.00	15.00
MGM SE-4255	(S)	Joni James Sings The Gershwins	1964	8.00	20.00
MGM E-4263	(M)	Beyond The Reef	1964	6.00	15.00
MGM SE-4263	(S)	Beyond The Reef	1964	8.00	20.00
MGM E-4286	(M)	Bossa Nova Style	1965	6.00	15.00
MGM SE-4286	(S)	Bossa Nova Style	1965	8.00	20.00
		(MGM albums above have black labels.)			

JAMES, LEONARD

Label		Title	Year	VG+	NM
Decca DL-8772	(M)	Boppin' And A Strollin'	1958	20.00	50.00

JAMES, SKIP

Label		Title	Year	VG+	NM
Vanguard VSR-9219	(M)	Skip James Today!	1966	6.00	15.00
Vanguard VSD7-9219	(S)	Skip James Today!	1966	8.00	20.00
Vanguard VSD7-9273	(S)	Devil Got My Woman	1968	8.00	20.00

JAMES, SONNY

Label		Title	Year	VG+	NM
Capitol T-779	(M)	The Southern Gentleman	1957	12.00	30.00
Capitol T-867	(M)	Sonny	1957	10.00	25.00
Capitol T-988	(M)	Honey	1958	10.00	25.00
Capitol T-1178	(M)	This Is Sonny James	1959	10.00	25.00
		(Capitol albums above have turquoise labels.)			
Dot DLP-3462	(M)	Young Love	1962	6.00	15.00
Dot DLP-25462	(S)	Young Love	1962	8.00	20.00
Capitol T-2017	(M)	The Minute You're Gone	1964	5.00	12.00
Capitol ST-2017	(S)	The Minute You're Gone	1964	6.00	15.00
Capitol T-2209	(M)	You're The Only World I Know	1965	5.00	12.00
Capitol ST-2209	(S)	You're The Only World I Know	1965	6.00	15.00
Capitol T-2317	(M)	I'll Keep Holding On	1965	5.00	12.00
Capitol ST-2317	(S)	I'll Keep Holding On	1965	6.00	15.00
Capitol T-2415	(M)	Behind The Tear	1965	5.00	12.00
Capitol ST-2415	(S)	Behind The Tear	1965	6.00	15.00
Capitol T-2500	(M)	True Love's A Blessing	1966	5.00	12.00
Capitol ST-2500	(S)	True Love's A Blessing	1966	6.00	15.00
Capitol T-2561	(M)	Till The Last Leaf Shall Fall	1966	5.00	12.00
Capitol ST-2561	(S)	Till The Last Leaf Shall Fall	1966	6.00	15.00
Capitol T-2589	(M)	My Christmas Dream	1966	5.00	12.00
Capitol ST-2589	(S)	My Christmas Dream	1966	6.00	15.00

Label		Title	Year	VG+	NM
Capitol T-2615	(M)	The Best Of Sonny James	1966	5.00	12.00
Capitol ST-2615	(P)	The Best Of Sonny James	1966	6.00	15.00
Capitol T-2703	(M)	Need You	1967	5.00	12.00
Capitol ST-2703	(S)	Need You	1967	6.00	15.00
Capitol T-2788	(M)	I'll Never Find Another You	1967	5.00	12.00
Capitol ST-2788	(S)	I'll Never Find Another You	1967	6.00	15.00
Capitol ST-2884	(S)	A World Of Our Own	1968	5.00	12.00
Capitol ST-2937	(S)	Heaven Says Hello	1968	5.00	12.00
		(Capitol albums above have black labels with the Capitol logo on top.)			

JAMES, TOMMY (& THE SHONDELLS)

Label		Title	Year	VG+	NM
Roulette R-25336	(M)	Hanky Panky	1966	6.00	15.00
Roulette SR-25336	(S)	Hanky Panky	1966	8.00	20.00
Roulette R-25344	(M)	It's Only Love	1967	5.00	12.00
Roulette SR-25344	(S)	It's Only Love	1967	6.00	15.00
Roulette R-25353	(M)	I Think We're Alone Now	1967	5.00	12.00
Roulette SR-25353	(P)	I Think We're Alone Now (Photo cover)	1967	6.00	15.00
Roulette SR-25353	(P)	I Think We're Alone Now (Footprint cover)	1968	6.00	15.00
Roulette SR-25355	(P)	Something Special!	1968	5.00	12.00
Roulette SR-25357	(S)	Gettin' Together	1968	5.00	12.00
Roulette SR-42012	(P)	Mony Mony	1968	5.00	12.00
Roulette SR-42023	(S)	Crimson And Clover	1968	5.00	12.00

JAN & DEAN

Label		Title	Year	VG+	NM
Dore 101	(M)	Jan & Dean	1960	75.00	150.00
		(Issued with a bonus photo, priced separately below.)			
		Jan & Dean Bonus Photo		50.00	100.00
Liberty LRP-3248	(M)	Jan & Dean's Golden Hits	1962	12.00	30.00
Liberty LST-7248	(P)	Jan & Dean's Golden Hits	1962	12.00	30.00
Liberty LRP-3294	(M)	Jan & Dean Take Linda Surfing	1963	14.00	35.00
Liberty LST-7294	(S)	Jan & Dean Take Linda Surfing	1963	16.00	40.00
		(The Beach Boys provide instrumental and vocal backing on several tracks.)			
Liberty LRP-3314	(M)	Surf City	1963	10.00	25.00
Liberty LST-7314	(S)	Surf City	1963	12.00	30.00
Liberty LRP-3339	(M)	Drag City	1963	8.00	20.00
Liberty LST-7339	(S)	Drag City	1963	10.00	25.00
L-J 101	(M)	Jan And Dean With The Soul Surfers	1963	8.00	20.00
Liberty LRP-3361	(M)	Dead Man's Curve/New Girl In School	1964	8.00	20.00
Liberty LST-7361	(S)	Dead Man's Curve/New Girl In School	1964	10.00	25.00
Liberty LRP-3368	(M)	Ride The Wild Surf (Sdtk)	1964	12.00	30.00
Liberty LST-7368	(S)	Ride The Wild Surf (Sdtk)	1964	14.00	35.00
Liberty LRP-3377	(M)	Little Old Lady From Pasadena	1964	6.00	15.00
Liberty LST-7377	(S)	Little Old Lady From Pasadena	1964	8.00	20.00
Liberty LRP-3403	(M)	Command Performance	1965	8.00	20.00
Liberty LST-7403	(S)	Command Performance	1965	10.00	25.00
Liberty LRP-3414	(M)	Jan & Dean's Pop Symphony No.1	1965	16.00	40.00
Liberty LST-7414	(S)	Jan & Dean's Pop Symphony No.1	1965	20.00	50.00
Liberty LRP-3417	(M)	Jan & Dean's Golden Hits, Volume 2	1965	6.00	15.00
Liberty LST-7417	(S)	Jan & Dean's Golden Hits, Volume 2	1965	8.00	20.00
Liberty LRP-3431	(M)	Folk 'N' Roll	1965	6.00	15.00
Liberty LST-7431	(S)	Folk 'N' Roll	1965	8.00	20.00
Liberty LRP-3441	(M)	Filet Of Soul	1966	6.00	15.00
Liberty LST-7441	(S)	Filet Of Soul	1966	8.00	20.00
Liberty LRP-3444	(M)	Jan & Dean Meet Batman	1966	16.00	40.00
Liberty LST-7444	(S)	Jan & Dean Meet Batman	1966	20.00	50.00
Liberty LRP-3458	(M)	Popsicle	1966	8.00	20.00
Liberty LST-7458	(S)	Popsicle	1966	10.00	25.00
Liberty LRP-3460	(M)	Jan & Dean's Golden Hits, Volume 3	1966	8.00	20.00
Liberty LST-7460	(S)	Jan & Dean's Golden Hits, Volume 3	1966	8.00	20.00
Columbia CL-2661	(M)	Save For A Rainy Day	1967	----	----
Columbia CS-9461	(S)	Save For A Rainy Day	1967	----	----
		(Despite years of rumors, no copies of this album are known to exist.)			
J&D 101	(M)	Save For A Rainy Day	1967	75.00	150.00
United Arts. UAS-9961	(P)	The Jan And Dean Anthology Album	1971	6.00	15.00
United Arts. UA-341	(P)	Gotta Take That One Last Ride	1971	5.00	12.00
Deadman's Curve	(M)	Live At The Keystone Berkeley	1981	10.00	25.00
		(Original copies were issued in plain cardboard jackets with inserts.)			

Jan & Dean Take Linda Surfing. Their first album of original material for their new label, Liberty, this album features vocal and instrumental backing by the Beach Boys on both "Surfin'" and "Surfin' Safari." The title is a neat conceit based on their earlier hit.

The Fabulous Country Music Sound Of George Jones. The most distinctive country stylist of the past thirty years, George Jones' influence ranges far outside the country music field, embracing rock and soul singers alike. George has recorded prolifically for Starday, Mercury, United Artist, Musicor and, most recently, Epic, leaving a growing legacy that will take generations to fully appreciate.

Label		Title	Year	VG+	NM
JANIS, JOHNNY					
ABC-Paramount LP-140	(M)	For The First Time	1957	20.00	50.00
Columbia CL-1674	(M)	The Start Of Something New	1961	6.00	15.00
Columbia CS-8474	(S)	The Start Of Something New	1961	8.00	20.00
Monument M-8036	(M)	Once In A Blue Moon	1965	6.00	15.00
Monument SM-18036	(S)	Once In A Blue Moon	1965	8.00	20.00
JASPER WRAITH					
Sunflower SNF-5003	(S)	Jasper Wraith (With insert)	1971	10.00	25.00
JAY & THE AMERICANS					
United Arts. UAL-3222	(M)	She Cried	1962	8.00	20.00
United Arts. UAS-6222	(S)	She Cried	1962	10.00	25.00
United Arts. UAL-3300	(M)	At The Cafe Wha?	1963	8.00	20.00
United Arts. UAS-6300	(S)	At The Cafe Wha?	1963	10.00	25.00
United Arts. UAL-3407	(M)	Come A Little Bit Closer	1964	5.00	12.00
United Arts. UAS-6407	(S)	Come A Little Bit Closer	1964	6.00	15.00
United Arts. UAL-3417	(M)	Blockbusters	1965	5.00	12.00
United Arts. UAS-6417	(S)	Blockbusters	1965	6.00	15.00
United Arts. UAL-3453	(M)	Jay And The Americans' Greatest Hits	1965	5.00	12.00
United Arts. UAS-6453	(P)	Jay And The Americans' Greatest Hits	1965	6.00	15.00
United Arts. UAL-3474	(M)	Sunday And Me	1966	4.00	10.00
United Arts. UAS-6474	(S)	Sunday And Me	1966	5.00	12.00
United Arts. UAL-3534	(M)	Livin' Above Your Head	1966	4.00	10.00
United Arts. UAS-6534	(S)	Livin' Above Your Head	1966	5.00	12.00
United Arts. UAL-3555	(M)	Greatest Hits, Volume 2	1966	5.00	12.00
United Arts. UAS-6555	(S)	Greatest Hits, Volume 2	1966	6.00	15.00
Decca DL-4699	(M)	Wild, Wild Winter (Sdtk)	1966	6.00	15.00
Decca DL7-4699	(S)	Wild, Wild Winter (Sdtk)	1966	8.00	20.00
United Arts. UAL-3562	(M)	Try Some Of This	1967	4.00	10.00
United Arts. UAS-6562	(S)	Try Some Of This	1967	5.00	12.00
JAY & THE TECHNIQUES					
Smash MGS-27095	(M)	Apples, Peaches, Pumpkin Pie	1967	5.00	12.00
Smash SRS-67095	(S)	Apples, Peaches, Pumpkin Pie	1967	6.00	15.00
Smash SRS-67102	(S)	Love Lost And Found	1968	5.00	12.00
JAYNETTES, THE					
Tuff LP-13	(M)	Sally Go Round The Roses	1963	50.00	100.00
JEFFERSON, BLIND LEMON					
Riverside 1014 (10")	(M)	The Folk Blues Of Blind Lemon Jefferson		20.00	50.00
Riverside 1053 (10")	(M)	Penitentiary Blues		20.00	50.00
Riverside 125	(M)	Folk Blues Classics		14.00	35.00
Riverside 126	(M)	Blind Lemon		14.00	35.00
JEFFERSON, EDDIE					
Riverside 411	(M)	Letter From Home	1962	10.00	25.00
Riverside 9411	(S)	Letter From Home	1962	12.00	30.00
JEFFERSON AIRPLANE, THE					
RCA LPM-3584	(M)	The Jefferson Airplane Takes Off!	1966	75.00	150.00
RCA LSP-3584	(S)	The Jefferson Airplane Takes Off!	1966	75.00	150.00
		(Includes "Runnin' Round The World," which was deleted from all subsequent pressings. The price is a conservative estimate.)			
RCA LPM-3584	(M)	The Jefferson Airplane Takes Off!	1966	6.00	15.00
RCA LSP-3584	(S)	The Jefferson Airplane Takes Off!	1966	6.00	15.00
RCA LPM-3766	(M)	Surrealistic Pillow	1967	10.00	25.00
RCA LSP-3766	(S)	Surrealistic Pillow	1967	6.00	15.00
RCA LCO-1511	(M)	After Bathing At Baxter's	1967	8.00	20.00
RCA LOS-1511	(S)	After Bathing At Baxter's	1967	6.00	15.00
		(RCA albums above have black labels.)			
RCA LSP-4058	(S)	Crown Of Creation	1968	4.00	10.00
RCA LSP-4133	(S)	Bless Its Pointed Little Head	1969	6.00	15.00
RCA LSP-4238	(S)	Volunteers	1969	4.00	10.00
RCA LSP-4448	(S)	Blows Against The Empire	1970	4.00	10.00
RCA LSP-4448	(S)	Blows Against The Empire (Clear vinyl)	1970	50.00	100.00
		(RCA albums above have orange labels.)			
Cotillion CT3-500	(S)	Woodstock (Soundtrack)	1970	8.00	20.00
Cotillion CT2-400	(S)	Woodstock Two	1971	6.00	15.00

Label		Title	Year	VG+	NM
Grunt FTR-1001	(S)	Bark (Issued in a brown paper bag)	1971	6.00	15.00
Grunt FTR-1007	(S)	Long John Silver	1972	4.00	10.00
RCA APD1-0320	(Q)	Volunteers	1973	8.00	20.00

JEFFERSON STARSHIP, THE

Grunt BFD1-0717	(Q)	Dragonfly	1974	6.00	15.00
Grunt BFD1-0999	(Q)	Red Octopus	1975	6.00	15.00
Grunt BFD1-1557	(Q)	Spitfire	1976	6.00	15.00

JEFFREY, JOE

Wand WDS-686	(S)	My Pledge Of Love	1969	6.00	15.00

JELLY BEAN BANDITS, THE

Mainstream 56103	(M)	Jelly Bean Bandits	1967	8.00	20.00
Mainstream S-6103	(S)	Jelly Bean Bandits	1967	10.00	25.00

JENNINGS, WAYLON

Sounds 1001	(M)	Waylon Jennings At JD's	1964	75.00	150.00
RCA LPM-3523	(M)	Folk Country	1966	8.00	20.00
RCA LSP-3523	(S)	Folk Country	1966	10.00	25.00
RCA LPM-3620	(M)	Leavin' Town	1966	8.00	20.00
RCA LSP-3620	(S)	Leavin' Town	1966	10.00	25.00
RCA LPM-3660	(M)	Waylon Sings Ol' Harlan	1967	10.00	25.00
RCA LSP-3660	(S)	Waylon Sings Ol' Harlan	1967	12.00	30.00
RCA LPM-3736	(M)	Nashville Rebel (Sdtk)	1967	6.00	15.00
RCA LSP-3736	(S)	Nashville Rebel (Sdtk)	1967	6.00	15.00
RCA LPM-3825	(M)	Love Of The Common People	1967	5.00	12.00
RCA LSP-3825	(S)	Love Of The Common People	1967	6.00	15.00
RCA LSP-3918	(S)	Hangin' On	1968	6.00	15.00
RCA LSP-4023	(S)	Only The Greatest	1968	6.00	15.00
RCA LSP-4085	(S)	Jewels	1968	6.00	15.00
		(RCA albums above have black labels.)			

JENSEN, KRIS

Hickory MH-110	(M)	Torture	1962	20.00	50.00

JETHRO TULL

Reprise RS-6336	(S)	This Was	1969	8.00	20.00
Reprise RS-6360	(S)	Stand Up	1969	8.00	20.00
		(Fold-open cover has a cardboard stand-up of the group on the inside.)			
Reprise RS-6400	(S)	Benefit	1970	6.00	15.00
Reprise MS-2035	(S)	Aqualung	1971	6.00	15.00
Reprise MS-2072	(S)	Thick As A Brick (With booklet)	1972	6.00	15.00
Chrysalis MS-2106	(S)	Living In The Past (With booklet)	1972	6.00	15.00
Chrysalis CHR-1040	(S)	A Passion Play (With booklet)	1973	4.00	10.00
Chrysalis CH4-1044	(Q)	Aqualung	1973	10.00	25.00
Chrysalis CH4-1067	(Q)	War Child	1974	10.00	25.00
Mobile Fidelity 1-061	(S)	Aqualung	1980	30.00	60.00
Mobile Fidelity 1-092	(S)	The Broadsword And The Beast	1982	10.00	25.00

JIVE FIVE, THE

United Arts. UAL-3455	(M)	The Jive Five	1965	12.00	30.00
United Arts. UAS-6455	(S)	The Jive Five	1965	14.00	35.00
Ambient Sound 37717	(S)	Here We Are	1982	4.00	10.00

JOEL, BILLY

Family Prod. 2700	(S)	Cold Spring Harbor (Color label)	1971	20.00	50.00
Columbia CQ-32544	(Q)	Piano Man	1974	6.00	15.00
Columbia PCQ-33146	(Q)	Streetlife Serenade	1974	6.00	15.00
Columbia PCQ-33848	(Q)	Turnstiles	1976	6.00	15.00
Columbia HC-34987	(S)	The Stranger (1/2 speed)	1980	8.00	20.00
Columbia HC-45609	(S)	52nd Street (1/2 speed)	1981	8.00	20.00

JOHN, ELTON

Viking 105	(S)	Games, The (Sdtk)	1970	75.00	150.00
Uni 73090	(S)	Elton John (With booklet)	1970	6.00	15.00
Uni 93090	(S)	Elton John (With booklet)	1971	4.00	10.00
Uni 73096	(S)	Tumbleweed Connection (With booklet)	1971	6.00	15.00
Uni 93105	(S)	11-17-70	1971	5.00	12.00
Uni 93120	(S)	Madman Across The Water (With booklet)	1971	6.00	15.00

Label		Title	Year	VG+	NM
Uni 93135	(S)	Honky Chateau	1972	5.00	12.00
MCA 2100	(S)	Don't Shoot Me, I'm Only The Piano Player	1972	4.00	10.00
		(Solid black label with a lyric book.)			
Nautilus 10003	(S)	Goodbye Yellow Brick Road	1980	20.00	50.00

JOHN, LITTLE WILLIE

King 395-564	(M)	Fever (Brown Cover)	1956	50.00	100.00
King 395-596	(M)	Talk To Me	1958	40.00	80.00
King 603	(M)	Mister Little Willie John	1958	40.00	80.00
King 691	(M)	Action	1960	30.00	60.00
King 739	(M)	Sure Things	1961	20.00	50.00
King 767	(M)	The Sweet, The Hot, The Teenage Beat	1961	20.00	50.00
King 802	(M)	Come On And Join Little Willie John	1962	20.00	50.00
King 895	(M)	These Are My Favorite Songs	1964	20.00	50.00
King K-949	(M)	Little Willie Sings All Originals	1966	14.00	35.00
King KS-949	(S)	Little Willie Sings All Originals	1966	20.00	50.00
King KS-1081	(P)	Free At Last	1970	16.00	40.00
BluesWay 6069	(P)	Free At Last	1970	6.00	15.00

JOHN'S CHILDREN

White Whale WW-7128	(S)	Orgasm	1970	75.00	100.00

JOHNNIE & JOE

Ambient Sound 38345	(S)	Kingdom Of Love	1982	4.00	10.00

JOHNNY & JACK

RCA LPM-1587	(M)	The Tennessee Mountain Boys	1957	10.00	25.00
RCA LPM-2017	(M)	Hits By Johnny And Jack	1959	10.00	25.00
Decca DL-4308	(M)	Smiles And Tears	1962	5.00	12.00
Decca DL7-4308	(S)	Smiles And Tears	1962	6.00	15.00

JOHNNY & THE BLUE BEATS

Winsor R-1001	(M)	Smile		12.00	30.00
Winsor RL-1001	(S)	Smile		12.00	30.00

JOHNNY & THE HURRICANES

Warwick W-2007	(M)	Johnny & The Hurricanes	1959	40.00	80.00
Warwick WST-2007	(P)	Johnny & The Hurricanes	1959	50.00	100.00
Warwick W-2010	(M)	Stormsville	1960	30.00	60.00
Warwick WST-2010	(S)	Stormsville	1960	40.00	80.00
Big Top 12-1302	(M)	Big Sound Of Johnny & The Hurricanes	1960	30.00	60.00
Big Top ST-1302	(S)	Big Sound Of Johnny & The Hurricanes	1960	40.00	80.00
Atila 1030	(M)	Live At The Star Club	1962	35.00	70.00

JOHNSON, BETTY

Atlantic 8017	(M)	Betty Johnson	1958	8.00	20.00
Atlantic 8027	(M)	Songs You Heard When You Fell In Love	1959	8.00	20.00

JOHNSON, BLIND WILLIE

Folkways 3585	(M)	Blues	1957	16.00	40.00
Folkways 10	(M)	Blind Willie Johnson	1965	10.00	25.00

JOHNSON, BUBBER

King 395-569	(M)	Come Home	1957	40.00	80.00
King 624	(M)	Sings Sweet Love Songs	1959	30.00	60.00

JOHNSON, BUDDY

Wing MGW-12005	(M)	Rock 'N' Roll Stage Show	1956	16.00	40.00
Mercury MG-20072	(M)	Buddy Johnson Wails	1958	12.00	30.00
Mercury MG-20209	(M)	Rock 'N' Roll	1958	16.00	40.00
Mercury MG-20322	(M)	Walkin'	1958	12.00	30.00

JOHNSON, BUDDY & ELLA

Mercury MG-20347	(M)	Swing Me	1958	10.00	25.00
Roulette R-25085	(M)	Go Ahead And Rock And Roll	1959	12.00	30.00
Roulette SR-25085	(S)	Go Ahead And Rock And Roll	1959	16.00	40.00

JOHNSON, LONNIE

King 395-520	(M)	Lonesome Road		60.00	120.00
Bluesville BV-1007	(M)	Blues By Lonnie Johnson	1960	16.00	40.00
Bluesville BV-1011	(M)	Blues And Ballads	1960	16.00	40.00

Label		Title	Year	VG+	NM
Bluesville BV-1024	(M)	Losing Game	1961	16.00	40.00
Bluesville BV-1044	(M)	Idle Hours	1961	16.00	40.00
Bluesville BV-1054	(M)	Woman Blues	1963	14.00	35.00
Bluesville BV-1062	(M)	Another Night To Cry	1963	14.00	35.00
King K-958	(M)	Sings 24 Twelve Bar Blues	1966	8.00	20.00
King KS-958	(S)	Sings 24 Twelve Bar Blues	1966	10.00	25.00
Prestige 7724	(S)	Losing Game	1969	6.00	15.00
King KS-1083	(S)	Tomorrow Night	1970	6.00	15.00

JOHNSON, MARV

United Arts. UAL-3081	(M)	Marvelous Marv Johnson	1960	12.00	30.00
United Arts. UAS-6081	(S)	Marvelous Marv Johnson	1960	14.00	35.00
United Arts. UAL-3118	(M)	More Marv Johnson	1960	12.00	30.00
United Arts. UAS-6118	(S)	More Marv Johnson	1960	14.00	35.00
United Arts. UAL-3187	(M)	I Believe	1962	12.00	30.00
United Arts. UAS-6187	(S)	I Believe	1962	14.00	35.00

JOHNSON, PETE

Savoy MG-14018	(M)	Pete's Blues		14.00	35.00

JOHNSON, ROBERT

Columbia CL-1654	(M)	King Of The Delta Blues Singers	1961	12.00	30.00
		(The label has six "eye" logos on each side.)			
Columbia CL-30034	(M)	King Of The Delta Blues Singers, Volume 2	1970	5.00	12.00

JOHNSTON, BRUCE
Also refer to the Centurians.

Del-Fi DELP-1228	(M)	Surfer's Pajama Party	1963	20.00	50.00
Del-Fi DFST-1228	(S)	Surfer's Pajama Party	1963	30.00	60.00
Columbia CL-2057	(M)	Surfin' 'Round The World	1963	35.00	70.00
Columbia CS-8857	(S)	Surfin' 'Round The World	1963	50.00	100.00

JONES, BRIAN

Roll. Stones RSR-49100	(S)	Pipes Of Pan At Joujouka (With inserts)	1971	12.00	35.00

JONES, DAVY

Colpix CP-493	(M)	David Jones	1965	8.00	20.00
Colpix SCP-493	(S)	David Jones	1965	10.00	25.00
Bell 6067	(S)	Davy Jones	1971	6.00	15.00

JONES, ETTA

King 544	(M)	Etta Jones Sings	1958	20.00	50.00
King 707	(M)	Etta Jones Sings	1961	16.00	40.00
Prestige PRLP-7186	(M)	Don't Go To Strangers	1960	12.00	30.00
Prestige PRLP-7194	(M)	Something Nice	1961	12.00	30.00
Prestige PRLP-7204	(M)	So Warm	1961	12.00	30.00
Prestige PRLP-7214	(M)	From The Heart	1962	12.00	30.00
Prestige PRLP-7241	(M)	Lonely And Blue	1962	12.00	30.00
Prestige PRLP-7272	(M)	Love Shout	1963	12.00	30.00
Prestige PRLP-7284	(M)	Holler	1963	12.00	30.00
		(Prestige albums above have yellow labels.)			
Prestige PRLP-7186	(M)	Don't Go To Strangers	1965	8.00	20.00
Prestige PRLP-7194	(M)	Something Nice	1965	8.00	20.00
Prestige PRLP-7204	(M)	So Warm	1965	8.00	20.00
Prestige PRLP-7214	(M)	From The Heart	1965	8.00	20.00
Prestige PRLP-7241	(M)	Lonely And Blue	1965	8.00	20.00
Prestige PRLP-7272	(M)	Love Shout	1965	8.00	20.00
Prestige PRLP-7284	(M)	Holler	1965	8.00	20.00
		(Prestige albums above have blue labels.)			

JONES, GEORGE
Also refer to the Jones Boys.

Starday SLP-101	(M)	The Grand Ole Opry's New Star	1958	50.00	100.00
Starday SLP-125	(M)	The Crown Prince Of Country Music	1960	12.00	30.00
Starday SLP-150	(M)	His Greatest Hits	1962	10.00	25.00
Starday SLP-151	(M)	Fabulous Country Music Sound	1962	12.00	30.00
Starday SLP-335	(M)	George Jones	1965	6.00	15.00
Starday SLP-335	(S)	George Jones	1965	8.00	20.00
Starday SLP-344	(M)	Long Live King George	1965	6.00	15.00
Starday SLP-344	(S)	Long Live King George	1965	8.00	20.00
Starday SLP-366	(M)	The George Jones Story (With photo)	1966	12.00	30.00

Label		Title	Year	VG+	NM
Starday SLP-401	(M)	Song Book & Picture Album (With booklet)	1967	12.00	30.00
Starday SLP-401	(S)	Song Book & Picture Album (With booklet)	1967	12.00	30.00
Starday SLP-440	(S)	The Golden Country Hits Of George Jones	1969	4.00	10.00
Mercury MG-20306	(M)	14 Country Favorites	1958	16.00	40.00
Mercury MG-20462	(M)	Country Church Time	1959	16.00	40.00
Mercury MG-20477	(M)	White Lightning And Other Favorites	1959	16.00	40.00
Mercury MG-20257	(M)	George Jones Salutes Hank Williams	1960	10.00	25.00
Mercury SR-60257	(S)	George Jones Salutes Hank Williams	1960	14.00	35.00
Mercury MG-20621	(M)	George Jones' Greatest Hits	1961	4.00	10.00
Mercury SR-60621	(S)	George Jones' Greatest Hits	1961	10.00	25.00
Mercury MG-20624	(M)	Country And Western Hits	1961	8.00	20.00
Mercury SR-60624	(S)	Country And Western Hits	1961	10.00	25.00
Mercury MG-20694	(M)	From The Heart	1962	8.00	20.00
Mercury SR-60694	(S)	From The Heart	1962	10.00	25.00
Mercury MG-20747	(M)	Duets Country Style	1962	8.00	20.00
Mercury SR-60747	(S)	Duets Country Style	1962	10.00	25.00
		(With Margie Singleton.)			
Mercury MG-20793	(M)	The Novelty Side Of George Jones	1963	14.00	35.00
Mercury SR-60793	(S)	The Novelty Side Of George Jones	1963	16.00	40.00
Mercury MG-20836	(M)	The Ballad Side Of George Jones	1963	8.00	20.00
Mercury SR-60836	(S)	The Ballad Side Of George Jones	1963	10.00	25.00
		(Mercury albums above have black labels.)			
Mercury MG-20906	(M)	Blue And Lonesome	1964	8.00	20.00
Mercury SR-60906	(S)	Blue And Lonesome	1964	10.00	25.00
Mercury MG-20937	(M)	Country And Western #1 Male Singer	1964	8.00	20.00
Mercury SR-60937	(S)	Country And Western #1 Male Singer	1964	10.00	25.00
Mercury MG-20990	(M)	Heartaches And Tears	1965	8.00	20.00
Mercury SR-60990	(S)	Heartaches And Tears	1965	10.00	25.00
Mercury MG-21029	(M)	Singing The Blues	1965	8.00	20.00
Mercury SR-61029	(S)	Singing The Blues	1965	10.00	25.00
Mercury MG-21048	(M)	George Jones' Greatest Hits, Volume 2	1965	6.00	15.00
Mercury SR-61048	(S)	George Jones' Greatest Hits, Volume 2	1965	8.00	20.00
		(Mercury albums above have red labels.)			
United Arts. UAL-3193	(M)	The New Favorites Of George Jones	1962	6.00	15.00
United Arts. UAS-6193	(S)	The New Favorites Of George Jones	1962	8.00	20.00
United Arts. UAL-3218	(M)	The Hits Of His Country Cousins	1962	6.00	15.00
United Arts. UAS-6218	(S)	The Hits Of His Country Cousins	1962	8.00	20.00
United Arts. UAL-3219	(M)	Homecoming In Heaven	1962	6.00	15.00
United Arts. UAS-6219	(S)	Homecoming In Heaven	1962	8.00	20.00
United Arts. UAL-3220	(M)	My Favorites Of Hank Williams	1962	6.00	15.00
United Arts. UAS-6220	(S)	My Favorites Of Hank Williams	1962	8.00	20.00
United Arts. UAL-3221	(M)	George Jones Sings Bob Wills	1962	6.00	15.00
United Arts. UAS-6221	(S)	George Jones Sings Bob Wills	1962	8.00	20.00
United Arts. UAL-3270	(M)	I Wish Tonight Would Never End	1963	6.00	15.00
United Arts. UAS-6270	(S)	I Wish Tonight Would Never End	1963	8.00	20.00
United Arts. UAL-3291	(M)	The Best Of George Jones	1963	5.00	12.00
United Arts. UAS-6291	(S)	The Best Of George Jones	1963	6.00	15.00
United Arts. UAL-3301	(M)	What's In Our Hearts	1963	6.00	15.00
United Arts. UAS-6301	(S)	What's In Our Hearts	1963	8.00	20.00
		(With Melba Montgomery.)			
United Arts. UAL-3338	(M)	More New Favorites	1964	6.00	15.00
United Arts. UAS-6338	(S)	More New Favorites	1964	8.00	20.00
United Arts. UAL-3352	(M)	Bluegrass Hootenanny	1964	6.00	15.00
United Arts. UAS-6352	(S)	Bluegrass Hootenanny	1964	8.00	20.00
		(With Melba Montgomery.)			
United Arts. UAL-3364	(M)	George Jones Sings Like The Dickens	1964	8.00	20.00
United Arts. UAS-6364	(S)	George Jones Sings Like The Dickens	1964	10.00	25.00
United Arts. UAL-3388	(M)	I Get Lonely In A Hurry	1964	6.00	15.00
United Arts. UAS-6388	(S)	I Get Lonely In A Hurry	1964	8.00	20.00
United Arts. UAL-3408	(M)	Trouble In Mind	1965	6.00	15.00
United Arts. UAS-6408	(S)	Trouble In Mind	1965	8.00	20.00
United Arts. UAL-3422	(M)	The Race Is On	1965	5.00	12.00
United Arts. UAS-6422	(S)	The Race Is On	1965	6.00	15.00
United Arts. UAL-3442	(M)	King Of Broken Hearts	1965	6.00	15.00
United Arts. UAS-6442	(S)	King Of Broken Hearts	1965	8.00	20.00
United Arts. UAL-3457	(M)	The Great George Jones	1966	6.00	15.00
United Arts. UAS-6457	(S)	The Great George Jones	1966	8.00	20.00
United Arts. UAL-3472	(M)	Blue Moon Of Kentucky	1966	6.00	15.00
United Arts. UAS-6472	(S)	Blue Moon Of Kentucky	1966	6.00	15.00
		(With Melba Montgomery.)			

Label		Title	Year	VG+	NM
United Arts. UAL-3532	(M)	George Jones' Golden Hits, Volume 1	1966	5.00	12.00
United Arts. UAS-6532	(S)	George Jones' Golden Hits, Volume 1	1966	6.00	15.00
United Arts. UAL-3558	(M)	The Young George Jones	1967	5.00	12.00
United Arts. UAS-6558	(S)	The Young George Jones	1967	6.00	15.00
United Arts. UAL-3566	(M)	George Jones' Golden Hits, Volume 1	1967	5.00	12.00
United Arts. UAS-6566	(S)	George Jones' Golden Hits, Volume 1	1967	6.00	15.00
		(U.A. albums above have black labels.)			
Musicor M-2044	(M)	For The First Time! (With Gene Pitney)	1965	5.00	12.00
Musicor MS-3044	(S)	For The First Time! (With Gene Pitney)	1965	6.00	15.00
Musicor M-2044	(M)	Recorded In Nashville (With Gene Pitney)	1965	5.00	12.00
Musicor MS-3044	(S)	Recorded In Nashville (With Gene Pitney)	1965	6.00	15.00
Musicor M-2046	(M)	Mr. Country And Western	1965	6.00	15.00
Musicor MS-3046	(S)	Mr. Country And Western	1965	8.00	20.00
Musicor M-2060	(M)	New Country Hits	1965	6.00	15.00
Musicor MS-3060	(S)	New Country Hits	1965	8.00	20.00
Musicor M-2061	(M)	Old Brush Arbors	1966	6.00	15.00
Musicor MS-3061	(S)	Old Brush Arbors	1966	8.00	20.00
Musicor M-2065	(M)	It's Country Time Again (With Gene Pitney)	1965	5.00	12.00
Musicor MS-3065	(S)	It's Country Time Again (With Gene Pitney)	1965	6.00	15.00
Musicor M-2079	(M)	Famous Country Duets	1965	5.00	12.00
Musicor MS-3079	(S)	Famous Country Duets	1965	6.00	15.00
		(With Melba Montgomery and Gene Pitney.)			
Musicor M-2088	(M)	Love Bug	1966	6.00	15.00
Musicor MS-3088	(S)	Love Bug	1966	8.00	20.00
Musicor P2-5094	(M)	Country Heart	1966	8.00	20.00
Musicor P2S-5094	(S)	Country Heart	1966	10.00	25.00
Musicor M-2099	(M)	I'm A People	1966	5.00	12.00
Musicor MS-3099	(S)	I'm A People	1966	6.00	15.00
Musicor M-2106	(M)	We Found Heaven Right Here On Earth	1966	5.00	12.00
Musicor MS-3106	(S)	We Found Heaven Right Here On Earth	1966	6.00	15.00
Musicor M-2109	(M)	Close Together As You And Me	1966	5.00	12.00
Musicor MS-3109	(S)	Close Together As You And Me	1966	6.00	15.00
		(With Melba Montgomery.)			
Musicor M-2116	(M)	George Jones' Greatest Hits	1967	5.00	12.00
Musicor MS-3116	(S)	George Jones' Greatest Hits	1967	6.00	15.00
Musicor M-2119	(M)	Walk Through This World With Me	1967	5.00	12.00
Musicor MS-3119	(S)	Walk Through This World With Me	1967	6.00	15.00
Musicor M-2124	(M)	Cup Of Loneliness	1967	5.00	12.00
Musicor MS-3124	(S)	Cup Of Loneliness	1967	6.00	15.00
Musicor M-2127	(M)	Let's Get Together	1967	5.00	12.00
Musicor MS-3127	(S)	Let's Get Together	1967	6.00	15.00
		(With Melba Montgomery.)			
Musicor M-2128	(M)	Hits By George	1967	5.00	12.00
Musicor MS-3128	(S)	Hits By George	1967	6.00	15.00
Musicor MS-3149	(S)	The Songs Of Dallas Frazier	1968	5.00	12.00
Musicor MS-3158	(S)	If My Heart Had Windows	1968	5.00	12.00
Musicor MS-3159	(S)	The Musical Loves, Life And Sorrows Of America's Great Country Star	1968	8.00	20.00
Musicor MS-3169	(S)	My Country	1969	6.00	15.00
Musicor MS-3177	(S)	I'll Share My World With You	1969	5.00	12.00
Musicor MS-3181	(S)	Where Grass Won't Grow	1969	5.00	12.00
Musicor MS-3188	(S)	Will You Visit Me On Sunday?	1970	5.00	12.00
Musicor MS-3191	(S)	The Best Of George Jones	1970	5.00	12.00
Musicor MS-3194	(S)	With Love	1971	5.00	12.00
Musicor MS-3203	(S)	The Best Of Sacred Music	1971	5.00	12.00
Musicor MS-3204	(S)	The Great Songs Of Leon Payne	1971	5.00	12.00
		(Musicor albums above have black labels.)			

JONES, GRANPA

Label		Title	Year	VG+	NM
King 554	(M)	Granpa Jones Sings His Greatest Hits	1958	14.00	35.00
King 625	(M)	Strictly Country Tunes	1959	14.00	35.00
King 809	(M)	Rollin' Along With Granpa Jones	1963	12.00	30.00
King 822	(M)	16 Sacred Gospel Songs	1963	12.00	30.00
King 845	(M)	Do You Remember?	1963	12.00	30.00
King 888	(M)	The Other Side Of Granpa Jones	1964	10.00	25.00
King 1042	(M)	The Living Legend Of Country Music	1969	4.00	10.00
Decca DL-4364	(M)	An Evening With Granpa Jones	1963	8.00	20.00

JONES, JIMMY

Label		Title	Year	VG+	NM
MGM E-3847	(M)	Good Timin'	1960	20.00	50.00
MGM SE-3847	(S)	Good Timin'	1960	30.00	60.00

Label		Title	Year	VG+	NM
JONES, JOE					
Roulette R-25143	(M)	You Talk Too Much	1961	12.00	30.00
Roulette SR-25143	(S)	You Talk Too Much	1961	16.00	40.00
JONES, LINDA					
Loma 5907	(S)	Hypnotized	1967	10.00	25.00
Turbo 7007	(S)	Your Precious Love		10.00	25.00
JONES, SPIKE					
RCA LPM-18 (10")	(M)	Spike Jones Plays The Charleston	1949	50.00	100.00
RCA LPM-3054 (10")	(M)	Bottoms Up		35.00	70.00
RCA LPM-3128 (10")	(M)	Spike Jones Murders Carmen		35.00	70.00
Verve V-2021	(M)	Let's Sing A Song For Christmas		20.00	50.00
Verve V-4005	(M)	Dinner Music For People Who Aren't Very Hungry	1956	20.00	50.00
Verve V-8564	(M)	35 Reasons Why Christmas Can Be Fun	1958	14.00	35.00
Liberty LRP-3140	(M)	Omnibust	1959	16.00	40.00
Liberty LST-7140	(S)	Omnibust	1959	20.00	50.00
Liberty LST-7140	(S)	Omnibust (Red vinyl)	1959	40.00	80.00
Liberty LRP-3154	(M)	60 Years Of Music America Hates Best	1959	16.00	40.00
Liberty LST-7154	(S)	60 Years Of Music America Hates Best	1959	20.00	50.00
Warners B-1332	(M)	Spike Jones In Hi Fi	1960	12.00	30.00
Warners WS-1332	(S)	Spike Jones In Stereo	1960	16.00	40.00
RCA LPM-2224	(M)	Thank You, Music Lovers	1960	16.00	40.00
Liberty LRP-3338	(M)	Washington Square	1963	14.00	35.00
Liberty LST-7338	(S)	Washington Square	1963	14.00	35.00
Liberty LRP-3401	(M)	Hank Williams Hits	1965	10.00	25.00
Liberty LST-7401	(S)	Hank Williams Hits	1965	12.00	30.00
RCA LOC-3235	(M)	Spike Jones Is Murdering The Classics	1965	12.00	30.00
RCA LSC-3235	(E)	Spike Jones Is Murdering The Classics	1965	10.00	25.00
RCA LPM-3849	(M)	The Best Of Spike Jones	1967	10.00	25.00
RCA LSP-3849	(E)	The Best Of Spike Jones	1967	8.00	20.00
MGM SE-4731	(S)	Let's Sing A Song For Christmas	1970	8.00	20.00
JONES BOYS, THE (GEORGE JONES)					
Musicor M-2017	(M)	Country & Western Songbook	1964	6.00	15.00
Musicor MS-3017	(S)	Country & Western Songbook	1964	8.00	20.00
Musicor MS-3182	(S)	My Boys, The Jones Boys	1970	6.00	15.00
JORDAN, LOUIS					
Score 4007	(M)	Go Blow Your Horn		50.00	100.00
Mercury MG-20242	(M)	Somebody Up There Digs Me	1957	16.00	40.00
Mercury MG-20331	(M)	Man, We're Wailin'	1958	16.00	40.00
Decca DL-8551	(M)	Let The Good Times Roll	1958	16.00	40.00
MGM E-3641	(M)	Gigi (Sdtk)	1958	6.00	15.00
MGM SE-3641	(S)	Gigi (Sdtk)	1958	8.00	20.00
Capitol W-1301	(M)	Can-Can (Sdtk)	1960	6.00	15.00
Capitol SW-1301	(S)	Can-Can (Sdtk)	1960	8.00	20.00
Decca DL-5035	(M)	Louis Jordan's Greatest Hits		8.00	20.00
Decca DL7-9180	(S)	Red Sky At Morning (Sdtk)	1971	10.00	25.00
JORDANAIRES, THE					
RCA LPM-3081 (10")	(M)	Beautiful City	1953	16.00	40.00
Decca DL-8681	(M)	Peace In The Valley	1957	12.00	30.00
Capitol T-1011	(M)	Heavenly Spirit	1958	10.00	25.00
Capitol T-1167	(M)	Gloryland	1959	10.00	25.00
Capitol T-1311	(M)	Land Of Jordan	1960	8.00	20.00
Capitol ST-1311	(S)	Land Of Jordan	1960	10.00	25.00
Capitol T-1742	(M)	Spotlight On The Jordanaires	1962	8.00	20.00
Capitol ST-1742	(S)	Spotlight On The Jordanaires	1962	10.00	25.00
Capitol T-1559	(M)	To God Be The Glory	1961	8.00	20.00
Capitol ST-1559	(S)	To God Be The Glory	1961	10.00	25.00
Columbia CL-2214	(M)	This Land	1964	6.00	15.00
Columbia CS-9014	(S)	This Land	1964	8.00	20.00
Columbia CL-2458	(M)	Big Country Hits	1966	6.00	15.00
Columbia CS-9258	(S)	Big Country Hits	1966	8.00	20.00
JOSEFUS					
Hookah 330	(S)	Dead Man	1969	75.00	150.00
Mainstream 6127	(S)	Josefus	1970	16.00	40.00

Label		Title	Year	VG+	NM
JOSIE & THE PUSSYCATS					
Capitol ST-665	(S)	Josie And The Pussycats	1970	10.00	25.00
JOURNEY					
Columbia PCQ-33904	(Q)	Look Into The Future	1976	5.00	12.00
Columbia HC-46339	(S)	Departure (1/2 speed)	1981	6.00	15.00
Mobile Fidelity 1-144	(S)	Escape	1981	50.00	100.00
Columbia HC-47408	(S)	Escape (1/2 speed)	1981	8.00	20.00
Columbia HC-4912	(S)	Infinity (1/2 speed)	1981	6.00	15.00
Columbia HC-47998	(S)	Dream After Dream (1/2 speed)	1982	6.00	15.00
JOURNEYMEN, THE					
Capitol T-1629	(M)	The Journeymen	1961	8.00	20.00
Capitol ST-1629	(S)	The Journeymen	1961	10.00	25.00
Capitol T-1951	(M)	New Directions In Folk Music	1963	8.00	20.00
Capitol ST-1951	(S)	New Directions In Folk Music	1963	10.00	25.00
JOYFUL NOISE					
RCA LSP-3963	(S)	Joyful Noise	1968	6.00	15.00
JUICY LUCEY					
Atco SD-33-325	(S)	Juicy Lucy	1970	6.00	15.00
Atco SD-33-345	(S)	Lie Back And Enjoy It	1970	6.00	15.00
Atco SD-33-367	(S)	Get A Whiff Of This	1971	6.00	15.00
JULIAN, DON					
Amazon 1009	(M)	Greatest Oldies	1963	20.00	50.00
JULY					
Epic BN-26416	(S)	July	1969	30.00	60.00
JUST IV					
Liberty LRP-3340	(M)	First Twelve Sides	1964	5.00	12.00
Liberty LST-7340	(S)	First Twelve Sides	1964	6.00	15.00
JUSTIS, BILL					
Phillips International 1950	(M)	Cloud Nine	1959	100.00	200.00

Label		Title	Year	VG+	NM
K-DOE, ERNIE (ERNEST KADOR)					
Minit LP-0002	(M)	Mother-In-Law	1961	40.00	80.00
KAK					
Epic BN-26429	(S)	Kak	1969	40.00	80.00
KALEIDOSCOPE					
Epic LN-24304	(M)	Side Trips	1967	10.00	25.00
Epic BN-26304	(S)	Side Trips	1967	12.00	30.00
Epic LN-24333	(M)	A Beacon From Mars	1967	20.00	50.00
Epic BN-26333	(S)	A Beacon From Mars	1967	30.00	60.00
Epic BN-26467	(S)	Incredible Kaleidoscope	1969	10.00	25.00
Epic BN-26508	(S)	Bernice	1970	8.00	20.00
MGM SE-4468	(S)	Zabriskie Point (Soundtrack)	1970	10.00	25.00
Pacific Arts 102	(S)	When Scopes Collide	1978	4.00	10.00
KALEN, KITTY					
Mercury MG-25206 (10")	(M)	Pretty Kitty Kalen Sings		16.00	40.00
Decca DL-8397	(M)	It's A Lonesome Old Town	1958	12.00	30.00

Label		Title	Year	VG+	NM
Vocalion VL-3679	(M)	Little Things Mean A Lot	1959	10.00	25.00
Columbia CL-1404	(M)	If I Give My Heart To You	1960	6.00	15.00
Columbia CS-8204	(S)	If I Give My Heart To You	1960	8.00	20.00
Columbia CL-1662	(M)	Honky Tonk Angel	1961	6.00	15.00
Columbia CS-8462	(S)	Honky Tonk Angel	1961	8.00	20.00
RCA LPM-2640	(M)	My Coloring Book	1963	6.00	15.00
RCA LSP-2640	(S)	My Coloring Book	1963	8.00	20.00

KALIN TWINS, THE

Label		Title	Year	VG+	NM
Decca DL-8812	(M)	The Kalin Twins		30.00	60.00

KANSAS

Label		Title	Year	VG+	NM
Kirshner HZ-44224	(S)	Leftoverture (1/2 speed)	1981	10.00	25.00
Kirshner HZ-44929	(S)	Point Of Know Return (1/2 speed)	1981	10.00	25.00
Kirshner HZ-48002	(S)	Vinyl Confessions (1/2 speed)	1982	10.00	25.00

KARLOFF, BORIS

Label		Title	Year	VG+	NM
Mercury MG-20815	(M)	Tales Of The Frightened, Volume 1	1963	14.00	35.00
Mercury SR-60815	(S)	Tales Of The Frightened, Volume 1	1963	16.00	40.00
Mercury MG-20816	(M)	Tales Of The Frightened, Volume 2	1963	14.00	35.00
Mercury SR-60816	(S)	Tales Of The Frightened, Volume 2	1963	16.00	40.00
MGM E-901	(M)	How The Grinch Stole Christmas	1966	8.00	20.00
MGM SE-901	(S)	How The Grinch Stole Christmas	1966	10.00	25.00
Decca DL-4833	(M)	An Evening With Karloff And His Friends	1967	8.00	20.00
Decca DL7-4833	(S)	An Evening With Karloff And His Friends	1967	10.00	25.00

KATZ, FRED

Label		Title	Year	VG+	NM
Warners W-1277	(M)	Folk Songs For Far Out Folks	1959	5.00	12.00
Warners WS-1277	(S)	Folk Songs For Far Out Folks	1959	6.00	15.00

KAUFMANN, BOB

Label		Title	Year	VG+	NM
L.H.I. 12002	(S)	Trip Through A Blown Mind	1967	16.00	40.00

KAY, JOHN, & THE SPARROWS

Label		Title	Year	VG+	NM
Columbia CS-9758	(S)	John Kay & Sparrows ("360 Sound" label)	1970	8.00	20.00

KELLER, JERRY

Label		Title	Year	VG+	NM
Kapp KL-1178	(M)	Here Comes Jerry Keller	1960	8.00	20.00
Kapp KS-3178	(S)	Here Comes Jerry Keller	1960	10.00	25.00

KELLY, BEVERLY

Label		Title	Year	VG+	NM
Audio Fidelity 1874	(M)	Beverly Kelly Sings	1958	10.00	25.00
Audio Fidelity 5874	(S)	Beverly Kelly Sings	1958	12.00	30.00
Riverside 328	(M)	Love Locked Out	1959	10.00	25.00
Riverside 9328	(S)	Love Locked Out	1959	12.00	30.00
Riverside 345	(M)	Beverly Kelly In Person	1960	10.00	25.00
Riverside 9345	(S)	Beverly Kelly In Person	1960	12.00	30.00

KENNEDY, JERRY
Also refer to Tom & Jerry.

Label		Title	Year	VG+	NM
Smash MGS-27004	(M)	Dancing Guitars Rock Elvis' Hits	1962	8.00	20.00
Smash SRS-67004	(S)	Dancing Guitars Rock Elvis' Hits	1962	10.00	25.00
Smash MGS-27024	(M)	The Golden Standards	1963	5.00	12.00
Smash SRS-67024	(S)	The Golden Standards	1963	6.00	15.00
Smash MGS-27066	(M)	From Nashville To Soulville	1965	5.00	12.00
Smash SRS-67066	(S)	From Nashville To Soulville	1965	6.00	15.00

KENNY & THE KASUALS

Label		Title	Year	VG+	NM
Mark 5000	(M)	The Impact Sound	1966	240.00	400.00
Mark 6000	(M)	Teen Dreams (Red vinyl)	1978	100.00	200.00
Mark 7000	(S)	Garage Kings	1979	20.00	50.00

KENTUCKY COLONELS, THE

Label		Title	Year	VG+	NM
World Pacific T-1821	(M)	Appalachian Swing	1964	8.00	20.00
World Pacific ST-1821	(S)	Appalachian Swing	1964	10.00	25.00

KEROUAC, JACK

Label		Title	Year	VG+	NM
Dot DLP-3154	(M)	Poetry For The Beat Generation	1959	75.00	150.00
Hanover HML-5000	(M)	Poetry For The Beat Generation	1959	50.00	100.00
Hanover HML-5006	(M)	Blues And Haikus	1959	50.00	100.00
Verve MGV-15005	(M)	Readings On The Beat Generation	1959	50.00	100.00

Label		Title	Year	VG+	NM
KESEY, KEN					
Sound City 27690	(M)	The Acid Test (With the Grateful Dead)	1967	100.00	200.00
KICKSTANDS, THE					
Capitol T-2078	(M)	Black Boots And Bikes	1964	8.00	20.00
Capitol ST-2078	(S)	Black Boots And Bikes	1964	10.00	25.00
KILLING FLOOR					
Sire SES-97019	(S)	Killing Floor	1970	12.00	30.00
KING, ALBERT					
King 852	(M)	Big Blues	1963	35.00	70.00
Stax 723	(M)	Born Under A Bad Sign	1967	12.00	30.00
Stax 723	(S)	Born Under A Bad Sign	1967	14.00	35.00
Stax STS-2003	(S)	Live Wire/Blues Power	1968	6.00	15.00
King KS-1060	(S)	Travelin' To California	1969	8.00	20.00
Chess 1538	(S)	Door To Door (With Otis Rush)	1969	6.00	15.00
Atlantic SD-8213	(S)	King Of The Blues Guitar	1969	6.00	15.00
Stax STS-2010	(S)	Years Gone By	1970	5.00	12.00
Stax STS-2015	(S)	King Does The King's Thing	1970	5.00	12.00
Stax STS-2040	(S)	Love Joy	1971	5.00	12.00
Stax STS-3009	(S)	I'll Play The Blues For You	1972	5.00	12.00
Stax 5505	(S)	I Wanna Get Funky	1974	5.00	12.00
KING, B.B.					
Crown CLP-5063	(M)	The Blues	1960	6.00	15.00
Crown CLP-5115	(M)	B.B. King Wails	1960	6.00	15.00
Crown CST-147	(S)	B.B. King Wails	1960	6.00	15.00
Crown CST-147	(S)	B.B. King Wails (Red vinyl)	1960	12.00	30.00
Crown CLP-5119	(M)	B.B. King Sings Spirituals	1960	6.00	15.00
Crown CST-152	(M)	B.B. King Sings Spirituals	1960	6.00	15.00
Crown CST-152	(M)	B.B. King Sings Spirituals (Red vinyl)	1960	12.00	30.00
Crown CLP-5143	(M)	The Great B.B. King	1961	6.00	15.00
Crown CLP-5167	(M)	King Of The Blues	1961	6.00	15.00
Crown CST-195	(S)	King Of The Blues	1961	6.00	15.00
Crown CST-195	(S)	King Of The Blues (Red vinyl)	1961	12.00	30.00
Crown CLP-5188	(M)	My Kind Of Blues	1961	6.00	15.00
Crown CLP-5248	(M)	Twist With B.B. King	1962	6.00	15.00
Crown CLP-5286	(M)	Easy Listening Blues	1962	6.00	15.00
Crown CLP-5309	(M)	Blues In My Heart	1962	6.00	15.00
Crown CLP-5359	(M)	B.B. King	1963	6.00	15.00
Galaxy 202	(M)	The Best Of B.B. King	1963	6.00	15.00
Galaxy 8202	(S)	The Best Of B.B. King	1963	8.00	20.00
Custom CM-2049	(M)	I Love You So		4.00	10.00
Custom CM-2046	(M)	Blues For Me		4.00	10.00
Custom CM-2052	(M)	The Soul Of B.B. King		4.00	10.00
ABC-Paramount 456	(M)	Mr. Blues	1963	6.00	15.00
ABC-Paramount S-456	(S)	Mr. Blues	1963	8.00	20.00
ABC-Paramount 509	(M)	Live At The Regal	1965	6.00	15.00
ABC-Paramount S-509	(S)	Live At The Regal	1965	8.00	20.00
ABC-Paramount 528	(M)	Confessin' The Blues	1965	6.00	15.00
ABC-Paramount S-528	(S)	Confessin' The Blues	1965	8.00	20.00
Kent KLP-5012	(M)	Rock Me Baby	1964	5.00	12.00
Kent KST-512	(S)	Rock Me Baby	1964	6.00	15.00
Kent KLP-5013	(M)	Let Me Love You	1965	5.00	12.00
Kent KST-513	(S)	Let Me Love You	1965	6.00	15.00
Kent KLP-5015	(M)	B.B. King Live On Stage	1965	5.00	12.00
Kent KST-515	(S)	B.B. King Live On Stage	1965	6.00	15.00
Kent KLP-5016	(M)	The Soul Of B.B. King	1966	5.00	12.00
Kent KST-516	(S)	The Soul Of B.B. King	1966	6.00	15.00
Kent KLP-5021	(M)	The Jungle	1967	5.00	12.00
Kent KST-521	(S)	The Jungle	1967	6.00	15.00
BluesWay BL-6001	(S)	Blues Is King	1967	5.00	12.00
BluesWay BLS-6001	(S)	Blues Is King	1967	6.00	15.00
BluesWay BLS-6011	(S)	Blues On Top Of Blues	1968	5.00	12.00
BluesWay BLS-6016	(S)	Lucille	1968	5.00	12.00
BluesWay BLS-6022	(S)	His Best/The Electric B.B. King	1968	5.00	12.00
BluesWay BLS-6031	(S)	Live And Well	1969	4.00	10.00
BluesWay BLS-6037	(S)	Completely Well	1969	4.00	10.00
BluesWay BLS-6050	(S)	Back In The Alley	1970	4.00	10.00

King Crimson, *In The Court Of The Crimson King.* One of the most influential band's of the past twenty year, this, their most popular album, also ranks as one of the most collectible titles in the Mobile Fidelity catalog.

Jonathon King, *Or Then Again.* King's bittersweet ballad, "Everyone's Gone To The Moon," was one of the pop highlights of 1965, a year filled with wonderful pop creations. This album, like many on the Parrot label, received little attention and almost no sales.

Label		Title	Year	VG+	NM
KING, BEN E.					
Atco SD-33-133	(M)	Spanish Harlem	1961	14.00	35.00
Atco SD-33-133	(S)	Spanish Harlem	1961	20.00	50.00
Atco SD-33-137	(M)	Ben E. King Sings For Soulful Lovers	1962	12.00	30.00
Atco SD-33-137	(S)	Ben E. King Sings For Soulful Lovers	1962	16.00	40.00
Atco SD-33-142	(M)	Don't Play That Song	1962	12.00	30.00
Atco SD-33-142	(S)	Don't Play That Song	1962	16.00	40.00
Atco SD-33-165	(M)	Ben E. King's Greatest Hits	1964	10.00	25.00
Atco SD-33-165	(S)	Ben E. King's Greatest Hits	1964	12.00	30.00
Atco SD-33-174	(M)	Seven Letters	1965	10.00	25.00
Atco SD-33-174	(S)	Seven Letters	1965	12.00	30.00
KING, CAROLE					
Ode SP-77009	(S)	Tapestry (Textured cover)	1971	5.00	12.00
Ode SQ-88013	(Q)	Carole King Music	1971	5.00	12.00
Epic/Ode HE-44946	(S)	Tapestry (1/2 speed)	1980	10.00	25.00
KING, FREDDIE					
King 762	(M)	Freddie King Sings The Blues	1961	30.00	60.00
King 773	(M)	Let's Hide Away And Dance Away	1961	30.00	60.00
King 777	(M)	Boy-Girl-Boy	1962	20.00	50.00
King 821	(M)	Bossa Nova And Blues	1962	20.00	50.00
King 856	(M)	Freddie King Goes Surfin'	1963	16.00	40.00
King 856	(S)	Freddie King Goes Surfin'	1963	20.00	50.00
King 928	(M)	A Bonanza Of Instrumentals	1965	10.00	25.00
King 928	(S)	A Bonanza Of Instrumentals	1965	12.00	30.00
King 964	(M)	24 Vocals And Instrumentals	1966	10.00	25.00
King KS-1059	(S)	Hide Away	1969	6.00	15.00
Cotillion SD-9004	(S)	Freddie King Is A Blues Master	1969	5.00	12.00
Cotillion SD-9016	(S)	My Feeling For The Blues	1970	5.00	12.00
Shelter SW-8905	(S)	Getting Ready	1971	5.00	12.00
Shelter SW-8913	(S)	Texas Cannonball	1972	5.00	12.00
Shelter SW-8919	(S)	Woman Across The River	1973	5.00	12.00
KING, JONATHON					
Parrot PA-61013	(M)	Or Then Again	1967	8.00	20.00
Parrot PAS-71013	(P)	Or Then Again	1967	10.00	25.00
UK S-53101	(S)	Bubble Rock Is Here To Stay	1972	6.00	15.00
UK S-53104	(S)	Pandora's Box	1973	6.00	15.00
KING, MORGANA					
EmArcy MG-36079	(M)	For You, For Me, Forever More	1956	12.00	30.00
Mercury MG-20231	(M)	Morgana King Sings The Blues	1958	10.00	25.00
Camden CAL-543	(M)	The Greatest Songs Ever Swung	1959	8.00	20.00
United Arts. UAL-3020	(M)	Let Me Love You	1960	6.00	15.00
United Arts. UAS-6020	(S)	Let Me Love You	1960	8.00	20.00
United Arts. UAL-3028	(M)	Folk Songs Ala King	1960	6.00	15.00
United Arts. UAS-6028	(S)	Folk Songs Ala King	1960	8.00	20.00
Ascot ALM-13014	(M)	The Winter Of My Discontent	1965	6.00	15.00
Ascot ALM-13019	(S)	The End Of A Love Affair	1965	5.00	12.00
Ascot ALS-16019	(M)	The End Of A Love Affair	1965	6.00	15.00
Ascot ALM-13020	(M)	Everybody Loves Saturday Night	1965	5.00	12.00
Ascot ALS-16020	(S)	Everybody Loves Saturday Night	1965	6.00	15.00
Reprise R-6205	(M)	Wild Is Love	1966	5.00	12.00
Reprise RS-6205	(S)	Wild Is Love	1966	6.00	15.00
Reprise R-6257	(M)	Gemini Changes	1967	5.00	12.00
Reprise RS-6257	(S)	Gemini Changes	1967	6.00	15.00
KING, PEGGY					
Imperial LP-9026	(M)	Peggy King	1959	5.00	12.00
Imperial LP-12026	(S)	Peggy King	1959	6.00	15.00
KING CRIMSON					
Atlantic SD-8245	(S)	In The Court Of The Crimson King	1969	8.00	20.00
Atlantic SD-8266	(S)	In The Wake Of Poseidon	1970	5.00	12.00
Atlantic SD-8278	(S)	Lizard	1971	5.00	12.00
Atlantic SD-7212	(S)	Islands	1972	4.00	10.00
Atlantic SD-7263	(S)	Lark's Tongue In Aspic	1973	4.00	10.00
Atlantic SD-7298	(S)	Starless And Bible Black	1974	4.00	10.00
Mobile Fidelity 1-075	(S)	In The Court Of The Crimson King		16.00	40.00

Label		Title	Year	VG+	NM
KING CURTIS					
Also refer to the Shirelles.					
Atco 33-113	(M)	Have Tenor Sax, Will Blow	1959	10.00	25.00
Atco SD-33-113	(S)	Have Tenor Sax, Will Blow	1959	12.00	30.00
New Jazz 8237	(M)	The New Scene Of King Curtis	1960	8.00	20.00
Everest DBR-1121	(M)	Azure	1961	8.00	20.00
Tru-Sound TS-15009	(M)	Doin' The Dixie Twist	1962	6.00	15.00
Tru-Sound STS-15009	(S)	Doin' The Dixie Twist	1962	8.00	20.00
Tru-Sound TS-15008	(M)	It's Party Time	1962	6.00	15.00
Tru-Sound STS-15008	(S)	It's Party Time	1962	8.00	20.00
Capitol T-2095	(M)	Soul Serenade	1964	6.00	15.00
Capitol ST-2095	(S)	Soul Serenade	1964	8.00	20.00
Capitol T-2341	(M)	Hits Made Famous By Sam Cooke	1965	6.00	15.00
Capitol ST-2341	(S)	Hits Made Famous By Sam Cooke	1965	8.00	20.00
Atco 33-189	(M)	That Lovin' Feeling	1966	5.00	12.00
Atco SD-33-189	(S)	That Lovin' Feeling	1966	6.00	15.00
Atco 33-198	(M)	Live At Small's Paradise	1966	5.00	12.00
Atco SD-33-198	(S)	Live At Small's Paradise	1966	6.00	15.00
Atco 33-211	(M)	King Curtis Plays The Great Memphis Hits	1967	5.00	12.00
Atco SD-33-211	(S)	King Curtis Plays The Great Memphis Hits	1967	6.00	15.00
Atco 33-231	(M)	King Size Soul	1967	5.00	12.00
Atco SD-33-231	(S)	King Size Soul	1967	6.00	15.00
Atco SD-33-247	(S)	Sweet Soul	1968	6.00	15.00
Atco SD-33-266	(S)	The Best Of King Curtis	1968	5.00	12.00
Capitol ST-2858	(S)	The Best Of King Curtis	1968	6.00	15.00
Atco SD-33-293	(S)	Instant Groove	1969	5.00	12.00
Atco SD-33-338	(S)	Get Ready	1970	4.00	10.00
Atco SD-33-359	(S)	Live At Fillmore West	1971	4.00	10.00
Atco SD-33-385	(S)	Everybody's Talkin'	1972	4.00	10.00
KING PINS, THE					
King 865	(M)	It Won't Be This Way Always	1963	16.00	40.00
KINGDOM					
Speciality 2135	(S)	Kingdom	1970	20.00	50.00
KINGFISH					
Round RX-108	(S)	Kingfish	1976	6.00	15.00
KINGSMEN, THE					
Wand WD-657	(M)	The Kingsmen In Person	1964	8.00	20.00
Wand WDS-657	(S)	The Kingsmen In Person	1964	10.00	25.00
Wand WD-659	(M)	More Great Sounds	1964	8.00	20.00
Wand WDS-659	(S)	More Great Sounds	1964	10.00	25.00
		(With "Death Of An Angel.")			
Wand WD-659	(M)	More Great Sounds	1964	6.00	15.00
Wand WDS-659	(S)	More Great Sounds	1964	8.00	20.00
Wand WD-662	(M)	The Kingsmen, Volume 3	1965	6.00	15.00
Wand WDS-662	(S)	The Kingsmen, Volume 3	1965	8.00	20.00
Wand WD-670	(M)	The Kingsmen On Campus	1965	5.00	12.00
Wand WDS-670	(S)	The Kingsmen On Campus	1965	6.00	15.00
Wand WD-671	(M)	How To Stuff A Wild Bikini (Soundtrack)	1965	6.00	15.00
Wand S-671	(S)	How To Stuff A Wild Bikini (Soundtrack)	1965	8.00	20.00
Wand WD-674	(M)	15 Great Hits	1966	5.00	12.00
Wand WDS-674	(S)	15 Great Hits	1966	6.00	15.00
Wand WD-675	(M)	Up And Away	1966	5.00	12.00
Wand WDS-675	(S)	Up And Away	1966	6.00	15.00
Wand WD-681	(M)	The Kingsmen's Greatest Hits	1967	5.00	12.00
Wand WDS-681	(S)	The Kingsmen's Greatest Hits	1967	6.00	15.00
KINGSTON TRIO, THE					
Also refer to Frank Hamilton.					
Capitol T-996	(M)	The Kingston Trio (Turquoise label)	1958	12.00	30.00
Capitol T-1107	(M)	From The Hungry i	1959	10.00	25.00
Capitol ST-1183	(S)	Stereo Concert	1959	12.00	30.00
Capitol T-1199	(M)	The Kingston Trio At Large	1959	8.00	20.00
Capitol ST-1199	(S)	The Kingston Trio At Large	1959	10.00	25.00
Capitol T-1258	(M)	Here We Go Again	1959	8.00	20.00
Capitol ST-1258	(S)	Here We Go Again	1959	10.00	25.00
Capitol T-1352	(M)	Sold Out	1960	8.00	20.00
Capitol ST-1352	(S)	Sold Out	1960	10.00	25.00

Label		Title	Year	VG+	NM
Capitol T-1497	(M)	String Along	1960	8.00	20.00
Capitol ST-1497	(S)	String Along	1960	10.00	25.00
Capitol T-1446	(M)	The Last Month Of The Year	1960	8.00	20.00
Capitol ST-1446	(S)	The Last Month Of The Year	1960	10.00	25.00
Capitol T-1474	(M)	Make Way!	1961	8.00	20.00
Capitol ST-1474	(S)	Make Way!	1961	10.00	25.00
Capitol T-1564	(M)	Goin' Places	1961	8.00	20.00
Capitol ST-1564	(S)	Goin' Places	1961	10.00	25.00
Capitol DT-1612	(E)	Encores	1961	10.00	25.00
Capitol T-1642	(M)	Close Up	1961	8.00	20.00
Capitol ST-1642	(S)	Close Up	1961	10.00	25.00
		(Capitol albums above have black labels			
		with the Capitol logo on the left side.)			
Capitol T-1658	(M)	College Concert	1962	6.00	15.00
Capitol ST-1658	(S)	College Concert	1962	8.00	20.00
Capitol T-1705	(M)	Best Of The Kingston Trio	1962	5.00	12.00
Capitol ST-1705	(S)	Best Of The Kingston Trio	1962	6.00	15.00
Capitol T-1747	(M)	Something Special	1962	6.00	15.00
Capitol ST-1747	(S)	Something Special	1962	8.00	20.00
Capitol T-1809	(M)	New Frontier	1962	6.00	15.00
Capitol ST-1809	(S)	New Frontier	1962	8.00	20.00
Capitol T-1871	(M)	Kingston Trio #16	1963	6.00	15.00
Capitol ST-1871	(S)	Kingston Trio #16	1963	8.00	20.00
Capitol T-1935	(M)	Sunny Side!	1963	6.00	15.00
Capitol ST-1935	(S)	Sunny Side!	1963	8.00	20.00
Capitol T-2011	(M)	Time To Think	1963	8.00	20.00
Capitol ST-2011	(S)	Time To Think	1963	10.00	25.00
Capitol T-2081	(M)	Back In Town	1964	6.00	15.00
Capitol ST-2081	(S)	Back In Town	1964	8.00	20.00
Capitol TCL-2180	(M)	The Folk Era	1964	12.00	30.00
Capitol STCL-2180	(S)	The Folk Era	1964	16.00	40.00
Capitol T-2280	(M)	Best Of The Kingston Trio, Volume 2	1965	5.00	12.00
Capitol ST-2280	(S)	Best Of The Kingston Trio, Volume 2	1965	6.00	15.00
Capitol T-2614	(M)	Best Of The Kingston Trio, Volume 3	1966	5.00	12.00
Capitol ST-2614	(S)	Best Of The Kingston Trio, Volume 3	1966	6.00	15.00
		(Capitol albums above have black labels			
		with the Capitol logo on top.)			
Decca DL-4613	(M)	The Kingston Trio/Nick-Bob-John	1965	6.00	15.00
Decca DL7-4613	(S)	The Kingston Trio/Nick-Bob-John	1965	8.00	20.00
Decca DL-4656	(M)	Stay Awhile	1965	6.00	15.00
Decca DL7-4656	(S)	Stay Awhile	1965	8.00	20.00
Decca DL-4694	(M)	Somethin' Else	1965	6.00	15.00
Decca DL7-4694	(S)	Somethin' Else	1965	8.00	20.00
Decca DL-4758	(M)	Children In The Morning	1966	8.00	20.00
Decca DL7-4758	(S)	Children In The Morning	1966	10.00	25.00
Tetragrammaton 5101	(S)	Once Upon A Time	1969	10.00	25.00
Capitol DT-996	(E)	The Kingston Trio	1969	6.00	15.00
Nautilus NR-2	(S)	Aspen Gold (1/2 speed)	1979	14.00	35.00

KINKS, THE

Label		Title	Year	VG+	NM
Reprise R-6143	(M)	You Really Got Me	1965	16.00	40.00
Reprise RS-6143	(S)	You Really Got Me	1965	16.00	40.00
Reprise R-6158	(M)	Kinks Size	1965	16.00	40.00
Reprise RS-6158	(E)	Kinks Size	1965	12.00	30.00
Reprise R-6173	(M)	Kinda Kinks	1965	16.00	40.00
Reprise RS-6173	(E)	Kinda Kinks	1965	12.00	30.00
Reprise R-6185	(M)	Kinks' Kinkdom	1965	16.00	40.00
Reprise RS-6185	(E)	Kinks' Kinkdom	1965	12.00	30.00
Reprise R-6197	(M)	Kinks' Kontroversy	1966	16.00	40.00
Reprise RS-6197	(E)	Kinks' Kontroversy	1966	12.00	30.00
Reprise R-6217	(M)	The Kinks' Greatest Hits	1966	10.00	25.00
Reprise RS-6217	(E)	The Kinks' Greatest Hits	1966	8.00	20.00
Reprise R-6228	(M)	Face To Face	1967	12.00	30.00
Reprise RS-6228	(E)	Face To Face	1967	10.00	25.00
Reprise R-6260	(M)	Live Kinks	1967	10.00	25.00
Reprise RS-6260	(S)	Live Kinks	1967	8.00	20.00
Reprise RS-6279	(M)	Something Else By The Kinks	1968	12.00	30.00
Reprise RS-6279	(S)	Something Else By The Kinks	1968	10.00	25.00
		(Reprise albums above have pink,			
		gold & green steamboat labels.)			

Label		Title	Year	VG +	NM
Reprise RS-6327	(S)	The Kinks Are The Village Green Preservation Society	1969	6.00	15.00
Reprise RS-6366	(S)	Arthur	1969	8.00	20.00
		(Reprise albums above have brown & orange steamboat labels.)			
Reprise PRO-328	(P)	Then, Now And In Between Box	1969	240.00	400.00
		(Boxed includes a postcard, decal, bag of grass, letter, Union Jack pin, Kinks consumer guide, "God Save The Kinks" button; and an album.)			
Reprise PRO-328	(P)	Then, Now And In Between Album	1969	50.00	100.00
Reprise RS-6454	(P)	The Kink Kronikles	1972	4.00	10.00
Reprise MS-2172	(S)	The Great Lost Kinks Album	1973	14.00	35.00
RCA LSP-4644	(S)	Muswell Hillbillies	1971	4.00	10.00
RCA VPS-6065	(S)	Everybody's In Show Biz	1972	5.00	12.00
RCA LPL1-5002	(S)	Preservation, Act 1	1973	4.00	10.00
RCA CPL2-5040	(S)	Preservation, Act 2	1974	5.00	12.00
RCA APL1-5081	(S)	Soap Opera	1975	4.00	10.00
		(RCA albums above have orange labels.)			
Mobile Fidelity 1-070	(S)	Misfits	1981	5.00	12.00

KISS

Casablanca NBLP-9001	(S)	Kiss (Without "Kissin' Time")	1974	8.00	20.00
Casablanca NBLP-9001	(S)	Kiss (With "Kissin' Time")	1974	5.00	12.00
Casablanca NBLP-7006	(S)	Hotter Than Hell	1974	5.00	12.00
Casablanca NBLP-7016	(S)	Dressed To Kill	1975	5.00	12.00
Casablanca NBLP-7020	(S)	Alive!	1975	6.00	15.00
Casablanca NBLP-7025	(S)	Destroyer	1976	5.00	12.00
Casablanca NBLP-7032	(S)	Kiss The Originals (With inserts)	1976	20.00	50.00
Casablanca NBLP-7037	(S)	Rock And Roll Over	1976	4.00	10.00
Casablanca NBLP-7057	(S)	Love Gun	1977	4.00	10.00
Casablanca NBLP-7076	(S)	Alive II	1977	4.00	10.00
Casablanca NBLP-7100	(S)	Double Platinum	1978	4.00	10.00
Casablanca NBLP-7225	(S)	Unmasked	1979	4.00	10.00
Casablanca NBLP-7252	(S)	Dynasty	1980	5.00	12.00
Casablanca NBLP-7261	(S)	The Elder	1981	8.00	20.00
Casablanca NBLP-7270	(S)	Creatures Of The Night	1982	8.00	20.00

KIT KATS, THE

Jamie LPM-3029	(M)	It's Just A Matter Of Time	1966	12.00	30.00
Jamie LPS-3029	(E)	It's Just A Matter Of Time	1966	10.00	25.00
Jamie LPM-3032	(M)	Do Their Thing Live	1967	10.00	25.00
Jamie LPS-3032	(S)	Do Their Thing Live	1967	12.00	30.00

KITCHEN CINQ, THE

L.H.I. 12000	(S)	Everything But The Kitchen Cinq	1967	8.00	20.00

KITT, EARTHA

RCA LPM-1109	(M)	Down To Eartha	1955	14.00	35.00
RCA LPM-1183	(M)	That Bad Eartha	1955	14.00	35.00
RCA LPM-1300	(M)	Thursday's Child	1956	14.00	35.00
RCA LPM-1661	(M)	St. Louis Blues	1958	12.00	30.00
RCA LSP-1661	(S)	St. Louis Blues	1958	16.00	40.00
Kapp KL-1046	(M)	The Fabulous Eartha Kitt	1959	8.00	20.00
Kapp KS-346	(S)	The Fabulous Eartha Kitt	1959	10.00	25.00
Kapp KL-1192	(M)	Eartha Kitt Revisited	1960	8.00	20.00
Kapp KS-3192	(S)	Eartha Kitt Revisited	1960	10.00	25.00
MGM E-4009	(M)	Bad But Beautiful	1962	6.00	15.00
MGM SE-4009	(S)	Bad But Beautiful	1962	8.00	20.00

KLUGMAN, JACK, & TONY RANDALL

London XPS-903	(S)	The Odd Couple Sings	1973	6.00	15.00

KNICKERBOCKERS, THE

Challenge LP-12664	(M)	Sing And Sync Along With Lloyd Thaxton	1965	30.00	60.00
Challenge LP-621	(M)	Jerk And Twine Time	1965	30.00	60.00
Challenge CH-622	(M)	Lies	1966	12.00	30.00
Challenge CHS-622	(S)	Lies	1966	16.00	40.00
Decca DL-4751	(M)	Out Of Sight (Soundtrack)	1966	6.00	15.00
Decca DL7-4751	(S)	Out Of Sight (Soundtrack)	1966	8.00	20.00

Label		Title	Year	VG+	NM
KNIGHT, GLADYS, & THE PIPS					
Fury 1003	(M)	Letter Full Of Tears	1962	50.00	100.00
Sphere Sound 7006	(M)	Gladys Knight And The Pips		14.00	35.00
Maxx 3000	(M)	Gladys Knight And The Pips	1964	14.00	35.00
Soul 706	(M)	Everybody Needs Love	1967	5.00	12.00
Soul SS-706	(S)	Everybody Needs Love	1967	6.00	15.00
Soul SS-707	(S)	Feelin' Bluesy	1968	5.00	12.00
Bell 6013	(S)	Tastiest Hits	1968	6.00	15.00
Bell 1323	(S)	In The Beginning	1969	6.00	15.00
KNIGHT, SONNY					
Aura AR-3001	(M)	If You Want This Love	1964	6.00	15.00
Aura AS-3001	(S)	If You Want This Love	1964	8.00	20.00
KNIGHT, TERRY, & THE PACK					
Lucky Eleven 8000	(M)	Terry Knight And The Pack	1966	6.00	15.00
Lucky Eleven S-8000	(S)	Terry Knight And The Pack	1966	8.00	20.00
Cameo C-2007	(M)	Reflections	1967	6.00	15.00
Cameo C-2007	(S)	Reflections	1967	8.00	20.00
KNIGHTS, THE					
Capitol T-2189	(M)	Hot Rod High	1964	20.00	50.00
Capitol ST-2189	(S)	Hot Rod High	1964	30.00	60.00
KNIGHTS, THE					
Ace MG-200854	(M)	Across The Road	1966	75.00	150.00
Ace MG-201303	(M)	The Knights 1967	1967	65.00	130.00
KNOCKOUTS, THE					
Tribute 1202	(M)	Go Ape With The Knockouts	1964	20.00	50.00
KNOWBODY ELSE					
Hip HIS-7003	(S)	Knowbody Else	1969	8.00	20.00
KNOTTS, DON					
United Arts. UAL-4090	(M)	Don Knotts	1961	8.00	20.00
KNOX, BUDDY					
Roulette R-25003	(M)	Buddy Knox	1957	50.00	100.00
Roulette R-25048	(M)	Buddy Knox And Jimmy Bowen	1958	75.00	150.00
Liberty LRP-3251	(M)	Buddy Knox's Golden Hits	1962	12.00	30.00
Liberty LSP-7251	(P)	Buddy Knox's Golden Hits	1962	16.00	40.00
United Arts. UAS-6689	(S)	Gypsy Man	1969	10.00	25.00
KOALA, THE					
Capitol SKAO-176	(S)	The Koala	1969	8.00	20.00
KODAKS, THE					
Sphere Sound LP-7005	(M)	The Kodaks Versus The Starlites		50.00	100.00
KRAMER, BILLY J., & THE DAKOTAS					
Imperial LP-9267	(M)	Little Children	1964	10.00	25.00
Imperial LP-12267	(S)	Little Children	1964	12.00	30.00
		(Black label with stars on top.)			
Imperial LP-9273	(M)	I'll Keep You Satisfied	1964	8.00	20.00
Imperial LP-12273	(S)	I'll Keep You Satisfied	1964	10.00	25.00
Imperial LP-9291	(M)	Trains And Boats And Planes	1965	8.00	20.00
Imperial LP-12291	(S)	Trains And Boats And Planes	1965	10.00	25.00
KRAZY KATS, THE					
Damon 12478	(S)	Movin' Out		16.00	40.00
KUBAN, BOB					
Musicland 3500	(M)	Look Out For The Cheater	1966	8.00	20.00
Musicland SLP-3500	(S)	Look Out For The Cheater	1966	10.00	25.00
KUPFERBERG, TULI					
ESP 1035	(S)	No Deposit No Return (Gold vinyl)		16.00	40.00
ESP 1035	(S)	No Deposit No Return (With insert)		10.00	25.00

Label		Title	Year	VG+	NM
KUSTOM KINGS, THE					
Smash MGS-27051	(M)	Kustom City, U.S.A.	1964	14.00	35.00
Smash SRS-67051	(S)	Kustom City, U.S.A.	1964	16.00	40.00
KWESKIN, JIM, & THE JUG BAND					
Vanguard VRS-9163	(M)	Jug Band Music	1966	5.00	12.00
Vanguard VSD7-9163	(S)	Jug Band Music	1966	6.00	15.00
Vanguard VRS-9234	(M)	See Reverse Side For Title	1967	5.00	12.00
Vanguard VSD7-9234	(S)	See Reverse Side For Title	1967	6.00	15.00
Reprise R-6266	(M)	Garden Of Joy	1967	5.00	12.00
Reprise RS-6266	(S)	Garden Of Joy	1967	6.00	15.00

Label		Title	Year	VG+	NM
LaBELLE, PATTI, & THE BLUEBELLES					
Newtown 631	(M)	Apollo Presents The Bluebelles	1963	20.00	50.00
Newtown 632	(M)	Sleigh Bells, Jingle Bells And Blue Bells	1963	16.00	40.00
Parkway 7043	(M)	The Bluebelles On Stage	1965	16.00	40.00
Atlantic 8101	(M)	Dreamer	1965	10.00	25.00
Atlantic SD-8101	(S)	Dreamer	1965	12.00	30.00
Atlantic 8119	(M)	Over The Rainbow	1966	10.00	25.00
Atlantic SD-8119	(S)	Over The Rainbow	1966	12.00	30.00
LAINE, DENNY					
Capitol ST-11588	(S)	Holly Days (With Paul McCartney)	1977	8.00	20.00
LAINE, FRANKIE					
Also refer to Jo Stafford.					
Columbia CL-2504 (10")	(M)	Lover's Laine		14.00	35.00
Columbia CL-2548 (10")	(M)	One For My Baby		14.00	35.00
Columbia CL-2567 (10")	(M)	Guys And Dolls (Studio Cast)		14.00	35.00
Mercury MG-25007 (10")	(M)	Favorites		14.00	35.00
Mercury MG-20069	(M)	Songs By Frankie Laine	1955	14.00	35.00
Mercury MG-20080	(M)	That's My Desire	1955	14.00	35.00
Mercury MG-20083	(M)	Frankie Laine Sings For Us	1955	14.00	35.00
Mercury MG-20085	(M)	Concert Date	1955	14.00	35.00
Mercury MG-20105	(M)	With All My Heart	1955	14.00	35.00
Mercury MG-20587	(M)	Frankie Laine's Golden Hits	1960	10.00	25.00
Columbia CL-625	(M)	Command Performance	1956	14.00	35.00
Columbia CL-808	(M)	Jazz Spectacular	1956	14.00	35.00
Columbia CL-975	(M)	Rockin'	1957	14.00	35.00
Columbia CL-1116	(M)	Foreign Affair	1958	14.00	35.00
Columbia CL-1231	(M)	Frankie Laine's Greatest Hits	1959	12.00	30.00
Columbia CL-1224	(M)	Torchin'	1960	6.00	15.00
Columbia CS-8024	(S)	Torchin'	1960	8.00	20.00
Columbia CL-1287	(M)	Reunion In Rhythm	1961	6.00	15.00
Columbia CS-8087	(S)	Reunion In Rhythm	1961	8.00	20.00
Columbia CL-1319	(M)	You Are My Love	1961	6.00	15.00
Columbia CS-8119	(S)	You Are My Love	1961	8.00	20.00
Columbia CL-1388	(M)	Frankie Laine, Balladeer	1961	6.00	15.00
Columbia CS-8188	(S)	Frankie Laine, Balladeer	1961	8.00	20.00
Columbia CL-1615	(M)	Hell Bent For Leather!	1961	6.00	15.00
Columbia CS-8415	(S)	Hell Bent For Leather!	1961	8.00	20.00
Columbia CL-1696	(M)	Deuces Wild	1962	6.00	15.00
Columbia CS-8496	(S)	Deuces Wild	1962	8.00	20.00
		(Columbia albums above have six black "eye" logos on each label.)			
Columbia CL-1829	(M)	Call Of The Wild	1962	5.00	12.00
Columbia CS-8629	(S)	Call Of The Wild	1962	6.00	15.00

Label		Title	Year	VG+	NM
Columbia CL-1962	(M)	Wanderlust	1963	5.00	12.00
Columbia CS-8762	(S)	Wanderlust	1963	6.00	15.00
ABC 604	(M)	I'll Take Care Of Your Cares		5.00	12.00
ABC S-604	(S)	I'll Take Care Of Your Cares		6.00	15.00
ABC 608	(M)	I Want Someone To Love		5.00	12.00
ABC S-608	(S)	I Want Someone To Love		6.00	15.00
ABC 628	(M)	To Each His Own		5.00	12.00
ABC S-628	(S)	To Each His Own		6.00	15.00
Capitol T-2277	(M)	I Believe	1965	5.00	12.00
Capitol ST-2277	(S)	I Believe	1965	6.00	15.00
Tower T-5092	(M)	Memory Laine	1967	5.00	12.00
Tower ST-5092	(S)	Memory Laine	1967	6.00	15.00

LAMEGO, DANNY, & HIS JUMPIN' JACKS

Forget-Me-Not 105A	(M)	The Big Weekend	1964	20.00	50.00

LAMOUR, DOROTHY

Design 45	(M)	The Road To Romance		10.00	25.00

LANCE, MAJOR

OKeh OKM-12105	(M)	The Monkey Time	1963	8.00	20.00
OKeh OKS-14105	(S)	The Monkey Time	1963	10.00	25.00
OKeh OKM-12106	(M)	Um, Um, Um, Um, Um, Um	1964	8.00	20.00
OKeh OKS-14106	(S)	Um, Um, Um, Um, Um, Um	1964	10.00	25.00
OKeh OKM-12110	(M)	Major Lance's Greatest Hits	1965	6.00	15.00
OKeh OKS-14110	(P)	Major Lance's Greatest Hits	1965	8.00	20.00

LANGDON, DORY

Verve V-2101	(M)	Leprechauns Are Upon Me		8.00	20.00

LARKS, THE

Money LP-1102	(M)	The Jerk	1965	14.00	35.00
Money LP-1107	(M)	Soul Kaleidoscope	1966	8.00	20.00
Money MS-1107	(S)	Soul Kaleidoscope	1966	10.00	25.00
Money MY-1110	(M)	Superslick	1967	8.00	20.00
Money MS-1110	(S)	Superslick	1967	10.00	25.00

LaROSA, JULIUS

RCA LPM-1299	(M)	Julius LaRosa	1956	12.00	30.00
Cadence CLP-107	(M)	Julius LaRosa		10.00	25.00
Roulette R-25054	(M)	Love Songs A LaRosa	1959	8.00	20.00
Roulette SR-25054	(S)	Love Songs A LaRosa	1959	6.00	15.00
Roulette R-25083	(M)	On The Sunny Side	1960	8.00	20.00
Roulette SR-25083	(S)	On The Sunny Side	1960	6.00	15.00
Forum S-16012	(M)	Just Say I Love Her	1960	6.00	15.00
Forum SF-16012	(S)	Just Say I Love Her	1960	8.00	20.00
Kapp KL-1245	(M)	The New Julie LaRosa	1961	6.00	15.00
Kapp KS-3245	(S)	The New Julie LaRosa	1961	8.00	20.00
MGM E-4398	(M)	You're Gonna Hear From Me	1966	5.00	12.00
MGM SE-4398	(S)	You're Gonna Hear From Me	1966	6.00	15.00

LAST POETS, THE

Juggernaut 8802	(S)	Right On	1971	6.00	15.00
Douglas Z-30583	(S)	This Is Madness	1971	5.00	12.00
Douglas Z-30811	(S)	Last Poets	1971	5.00	12.00

LAST WORDS, THE

Atco SD-33-235	(S)	The Last Words	1968	6.00	15.00

LAUREN, ROD

RCA LPM-2176	(M)	I'm Rod Lauren	1961	10.00	25.00
RCA LSP-2176	(S)	I'm Rod Lauren	1961	12.00	30.00

LAURIE SISTERS, THE

Camden CAL-545	(M)	Hits Of The Great Girl Groups	1960	10.00	25.00
Camden CAS-545	(S)	Hits Of The Great Girl Groups	1960	12.00	30.00

LAWSON, DEE

Roulette R-52017	(M)	'Round Midnight	1958	16.00	40.00

Label		Title	Year	VG+	NM
LAZARUS					
Amazon 1001	(S)	Lazarus	1970	8.00	20.00
LEA, BARBARA					
Riverside 2518 (10")	(M)	A Woman In Love	1955	12.00	30.00
Prestige 7065	(M)	Barbara Lea	1956	12.00	30.00
Prestige 7100	(M)	Lea In Love	1957	12.00	30.00
LEADBELLY (HUDDIE LEDBETTER)					
Capitol H-369 (10")	(M)	Leadbelly		75.00	150.00
Allegro 4027 (10")		Sinful Songs		30.00	60.00
Folkways 4 (10")	(M)	Leadbelly	1950	8.00	20.00
Folkways 14 (10")	(M)	Leadbelly	1950	8.00	20.00
Folkways 24 (10")	(M)	Leadbelly	1950	8.00	20.00
Folkways 43 (10")	(M)	Leadbelly	1950	8.00	20.00
Folkways FP-241	(M)	Last Sessions		6.00	15.00
Folkways FP-242	(M)	Last Sessions		6.00	15.00
Folkways 2013 (10")	(M)	Huddie Ledbetter	1950	20.00	50.00
Folkways 2014 (10")	(M)	Rock Island Line	1951	20.00	50.00
Stinson SLP-17	(M)	Leadbelly Memorial, Volume 1	1962	6.00	15.00
Stinson SLP-19	(M)	Leadbelly Memorial, Volume 2	1962	6.00	15.00
Stinson SLP-39	(M)	Leadbelly Plays Parties	1962	6.00	15.00
Stinson SLP-41	(M)	Leadbelly Plays Parties, Volume 2	1962	6.00	15.00
Stinson SLP-48	(M)	Leadbelly Memorial, Volume 3	1962	6.00	15.00
Stinson SLP-48	(M)	Leadbelly Memorial, Volume 3 (Red vinyl)	1962	12.00	30.00
Stinson SLP-51	(M)	Leadbelly Memorial, Volume 4	1962	6.00	15.00
Folkways 2941	(M)	Last Sessions, Part 2	1963	8.00	20.00
Folkways 2941	(E)	Last Sessions, Part 2	1963	6.00	15.00
RCA LPV-505	(M)	Midnight Special	1964	10.00	25.00
Folkways FV-9001	(M)	Take This Hammer	1965	8.00	20.00
Folkways FVS-9001	(E)	Take This Hammer	1965	10.00	25.00
Folkways FV-9021	(M)	Keep Your Hands Off Her	1965	8.00	20.00
Folkways FVS-9021	(E)	Keep Your Hands Off Her	1965	6.00	15.00
Elektra EKL-301-2	(M)	Library Of Congress Recordings	1966	10.00	25.00
Folkways 3019	(M)	From The Last Sessions	1967	8.00	20.00
Folkways 3019	(E)	From The Last Sessions	1967	6.00	15.00
Folkways 31006	(E)	Leadbelly Sings Folk Songs	1968	6.00	15.00
Tradition 2093	(M)	Legend Of Leadbelly, Josh White And Sonny Terry	1969	6.00	15.00
LEARY, TIMOTHY					
Pixie CA-1069	(M)	L.S.D.	1966	20.00	50.00
ESP 1027	(M)	Turn On, Tune In, Drop Out	1966	12.00	30.00
Mercury MG-21131	(M)	Turn On, Tune In, Drop Out (Sdtk)	1967	10.00	25.00
Mercury SR-61131	(S)	Turn On, Tune In, Drop Out (Sdtk)	1967	12.00	30.00
Douglas 1	(M)	You Can Be Anyone This Time Around		16.00	40.00
LEATHERCOATED MINDS, THE					
Viva V-36003	(M)	Trip Down Sunset Strip	1967	16.00	40.00
Viva VS-36003	(S)	Trip Down Sunset Strip	1967	20.00	50.00
LEAVES, THE					
Mire 3005	(M)	Hey Joe	1966	10.00	25.00
Mire LPS-3005	(S)	Hey Joe	1966	12.00	30.00
Capitol T-2638	(M)	All The Good That's Happening	1967	8.00	20.00
Capitol ST-2638	(S)	All The Good That's Happening	1967	10.00	25.00
LED ZEPPELIN					
Atlantic SD-8216	(S)	Led Zeppelin	1968	50.00	100.00
		(Purple & brown label common to Atco.)			
Atlantic SD-8216	(S)	Led Zeppelin	1968	8.00	20.00
Atlantic SD-8236	(S)	Led Zeppelin II	1969	6.00	15.00
Cotillion ST-2638	(S)	Homer (Sdtk)	1970	6.00	15.00
Atlantic SD-7201	(S)	Led Zeppelin III	1970	6.00	15.00
Atlantic SD-7208	(S)	Led Zeppelin IV	1971	4.00	10.00
Atlantic SD-7255	(S)	Houses Of The Holy	1973	4.00	10.00
		(Atlantic albums above have green & orange labels with "1841 Broadway" on the bottom.)			
Mobile Fidelity 1-065	(S)	Led Zeppelin II	1980	16.00	40.00

Label		Title	Year	VG+	NM
LEE, BRENDA					
Decca DL-8873	(M)	Grandma, What Great Songs You Sang	1959	10.00	25.00
Decca DL7-8873	(S)	Grandma, What Great Songs You Sang	1959	16.00	40.00
Decca DL-4039	(M)	Brenda Lee	1960	10.00	25.00
Decca DL7-4039	(S)	Brenda Lee	1960	12.00	30.00
Decca DL-4082	(M)	This Is Brenda	1960	10.00	25.00
Decca DL7-4082	(S)	This Is Brenda	1960	12.00	30.00
Decca DL-4104	(M)	Emotions	1961	8.00	20.00
Decca DL7-4104	(S)	Emotions	1961	10.00	25.00
Decca DL-4176	(M)	All The Way	1961	8.00	20.00
Decca DL7-4176	(S)	All The Way	1961	10.00	25.00
Decca DL-4216	(M)	Sincerely, Brenda Lee	1962	8.00	20.00
Decca DL7-4216	(S)	Sincerely, Brenda Lee	1962	10.00	25.00
Decca DL-4326	(M)	That's All	1962	6.00	15.00
Decca DL7-4326	(S)	That's All	1962	8.00	20.00
Decca MG-9226	(M)	The Show For Christmas Seals	1962	10.00	25.00
Decca MG7-9226	(S)	The Show For Christmas Seals	1962	12.00	30.00
Decca DL-4370	(M)	All Alone Am I	1963	6.00	15.00
Decca DL7-4370	(S)	All Alone Am I	1963	8.00	20.00
Decca DL-4439	(M)	Let Me Sing	1963	6.00	15.00
Decca DL7-4439	(S)	Let Me Sing	1963	8.00	20.00
Decca DL-4509	(M)	By Request	1964	6.00	15.00
Decca DL7-4509	(S)	By Request	1964	8.00	20.00
Decca DL-4583	(M)	Merry Christmas From Brenda Lee	1964	6.00	15.00
Decca DL7-4583	(S)	Merry Christmas From Brenda Lee	1964	8.00	20.00
Decca DL-4626	(M)	Top Teen Hits	1965	6.00	15.00
Decca DL7-4626	(S)	Top Teen Hits	1965	8.00	20.00
Decca DL-4661	(M)	The Versatile Brenda Lee	1965	6.00	15.00
Decca DL7-4661	(S)	The Versatile Brenda Lee	1965	8.00	20.00
Decca DL-4684	(M)	Too Many Rivers	1965	6.00	15.00
Decca DL7-4684	(S)	Too Many Rivers	1965	8.00	20.00
Decca DL-4755	(M)	Bye, Bye Blues	1966	6.00	15.00
Decca DL7-4755	(S)	Bye, Bye Blues	1966	8.00	20.00
Decca DL-4757	(M)	Ten Golden Years (Fold-open cover)	1966	8.00	20.00
Decca DL7-4757	(S)	Ten Golden Years (Fold-open cover)	1966	10.00	25.00
Decca DL-4825	(M)	Coming On Strong	1966	5.00	12.00
Decca DL7-4825	(S)	Coming On Strong	1966	6.00	15.00
		(Decca albums above have black labels with			
		"Mfrd by Decca" beneath the rainbow.)			
LEE, JULIA					
Capitol H-228 (10")	(M)	Party Time	1952	40.00	80.00
Capitol T-228	(M)	Party Time	1955	30.00	60.00
LEE, MICHELE					
Columbia OL-5800	(M)	Bravo Giovanni! (Sdtk)	1962	12.00	30.00
Columbia OS-2200	(S)	Bravo Giovanni! (Sdtk)	1962	16.00	40.00
Columbia CL-2486	(M)	A Taste Of The Fantastic	1967	4.00	10.00
Columbia CS-9286	(S)	A Taste Of The Fantastic	1967	5.00	12.00
Columbia CS-9682	(S)	L. David Sloane	1968	5.00	12.00
LEE, PEGGY					
Decca DL-5482 (10")	(M)	Black Coffee	1953	16.00	40.00
Capitol H-155 (10")	(M)	Rendezvous	1952	14.00	35.00
Capitol H-204 (10")	(M)	My Best To You	1952	14.00	35.00
Decca DL-5539 (10")	(M)	Song In Intimate Style	1953	16.00	40.00
Decca DL-5557 (10")	(M)	The Lady And The Tramp (Sdtk)	1955	35.00	70.00
Decca DL-8083	(M)	White Christmas (Sdtk)	1955	16.00	40.00
Decca DL-8166	(M)	Songs From Pete Kelly's Blues (Sdtk)	1955	16.00	40.00
Decca DL-8358	(M)	Black Coffee	1956	12.00	30.00
Decca DL-8411	(M)	Dream Street	1956	12.00	30.00
Capitol T-386	(M)	Is That All There Is?	1956	10.00	25.00
Capitol T-864	(M)	The Man I Love	1956	10.00	25.00
Capitol T-975	(M)	Jump For Joy	1957	10.00	25.00
		(Capitol albums above have turquoise labels.)			
Decca DL-8462	(M)	The Lady And The Tramp (Sdtk)	1957	20.00	50.00
Decca DL-8591	(M)	Sea Shells	1958	12.00	30.00
Decca DL-8816	(M)	Miss Wonderful	1959	12.00	30.00
		(Decca albums above have black & silver labels)			
Capitol T-1049	(M)	Things Are Swingin'	1959	6.00	15.00
Capitol ST-1049	(S)	Things Are Swingin'	1959	8.00	20.00

Peggy Lee, *In The Name Of Love*. Ms. Lee's career has been a successful one, where she has triumphed as both a jazz and pop vocalist and contributed her legendary prowess to at least one classic animated film, "The Lady And The Tramp." Her albums have not received the attention from collectors they deserve.

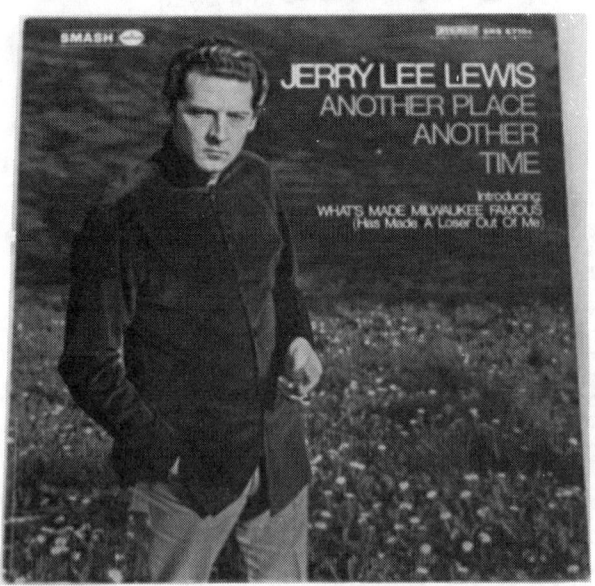

Jerry Lee Lewis, *Another Place, Another Time*. After struggling for years to overcome what must have appeared to have been insurmountable obstacles in his rock and roll career, Jerry Lee and Mercury staff producer Jerry Kennedy recorded a series of excellent country/western records. This album was titled after his first country Top Ten in 1968.

Label		Title	Year	VG+	NM
Capitol T-1131	(M)	I Like Men	1959	6.00	15.00
Capitol ST-1131	(S)	I Like Men	1959	8.00	20.00
Capitol T-1219	(M)	Beauty And The Beat	1960	6.00	15.00
Capitol ST-1219	(S)	Beauty And The Beat	1960	8.00	20.00
		(Capitol albums above have black labels with the Capitol logo on the left side.)			
Capitol T-1290	(M)	Latin Ala Lee!	1960	5.00	12.00
Capitol ST-1290	(S)	Latin Ala Lee!	1960	6.00	15.00
Capitol T-1366	(M)	All Aglow Again	1960	5.00	12.00
Capitol ST-1366	(S)	All Aglow Again	1960	6.00	15.00
Capitol T-1401	(M)	Pretty Eyes	1960	5.00	12.00
Capitol ST-1401	(S)	Pretty Eyes	1960	6.00	15.00
Capitol T-1423	(M)	Christmas Carousel	1960	5.00	12.00
Capitol ST-1423	(S)	Christmas Carousel	1960	6.00	15.00
Capitol T-1520	(M)	Basin Street East	1960	5.00	12.00
Capitol ST-1520	(S)	Basin Street East	1960	6.00	15.00
Capitol T-1671	(M)	Blue Cross Country	1961	5.00	12.00
Capitol ST-1671	(S)	Blue Cross Country	1961	6.00	15.00
Capitol T-1630	(M)	If You Go	1961	5.00	12.00
Capitol ST-1630	(S)	If You Go	1961	6.00	15.00
Capitol T-1743	(M)	Bewitching Lee	1962	5.00	12.00
Capitol ST-1743	(S)	Bewitching Lee	1962	6.00	15.00
Capitol T-1772	(M)	Sugar 'N' Spice	1962	5.00	12.00
Capitol ST-1772	(S)	Sugar 'N' Spice	1962	6.00	15.00
Capitol T-1850	(M)	Mink Jazz	1963	8.00	20.00
Capitol ST-1850	(S)	Mink Jazz	1963	10.00	25.00
Capitol T-1857	(M)	I'm A Woman	1963	5.00	12.00
Capitol ST-1857	(S)	I'm A Woman	1963	6.00	15.00
Capitol T-1969	(M)	In Love Again	1963	5.00	12.00
Capitol ST-1969	(S)	In Love Again	1963	6.00	15.00
Decca DL-4478	(M)	Lover	1964	5.00	12.00
Decca DL7-4478	(S)	Lover	1964	6.00	15.00
Decca DL-4461	(M)	The Fabulous Peggy Lee	1964	5.00	12.00
Decca DL7-4461	(S)	The Fabulous Peggy Lee	1964	6.00	15.00
Decca DXB-164	(M)	The Best Of Peggy Lee	1964	6.00	15.00
Decca DXSB7-164	(S)	The Best Of Peggy Lee	1964	8.00	20.00
Capitol T-2096	(M)	In The Name Of Love	1964	4.00	10.00
Capitol ST-2096	(S)	In The Name Of Love	1964	5.00	12.00
Capitol T-2320	(M)	Pass Me By	1965	4.00	10.00
Capitol ST-2320	(S)	Pass Me By	1965	5.00	12.00
Capitol T-2388	(M)	Then Was Then Now Is Now	1965	4.00	10.00
Capitol ST-2388	(S)	Then Was Then Now Is Now	1965	5.00	12.00
Capitol T-2475	(M)	Big Spender	1966	4.00	10.00
Capitol ST-2475	(S)	Big Spender	1966	5.00	12.00
Capitol T-2732	(M)	Extra Special	1967	4.00	10.00
Capitol ST-2732	(S)	Extra Special	1967	5.00	12.00
		(Capitol albums above have black labels with the Capitol logo on top.)			

LEE, PINKY

Decca DL-8421	(M)	The Surprise Party		14.00	35.00

LEFT BANKE, THE

Smash MGS-27088	(M)	Walk Away Renee/Pretty Ballerina	1967	14.00	35.00
Smash SRS-67088	(P)	Walk Away Renee/Pretty Ballerina	1967	16.00	40.00
Smash SRS-67113	(P)	Left Banke, Too	1968	16.00	40.00

LEGEND

Bell 6027	(S)	Legend	1969	6.00	15.00

LEGEND (DRAGONFLY)

Megaphone 101	(S)	Legend	1970	12.00	30.00

LEGENDS, THE

Ermine 101	(M)	The Legends Let Loose	1963	30.00	60.00
Capitol T-1925	(M)	The Legends Let Loose	1963	14.00	35.00
Capitol ST-1925	(S)	The Legends Let Loose	1963	16.00	40.00

LEHRER, TOM

Lehrer 101 (10")	(M)	Songs By Tom Lehrer		12.00	30.00
Lehrer 101	(M)	Songs By Tom Lehrer		8.00	20.00

Label		Title	Year	VG+	NM
Lehrer 102	(M)	More Songs By Tom Lehrer		8.00	20.00
Lehrer 102S	(S)	More Songs By Tom Lehrer		10.00	25.00
Lehrer 202	(M)	An Evening Wasted With Tom Lehrer		8.00	20.00
Lehrer 202S	(S)	An Evening Wasted With Tom Lehrer		10.00	25.00
Reprise R-6179	(M)	That Was The Year That Was	1965	5.00	12.00
Reprise RS-6179	(S)	That Was The Year That Was	1965	6.00	15.00
Reprise R-6199	(M)	An Evening Wasted With Tom Lehrer	1966	5.00	12.00
Reprise RS-6199	(S)	An Evening Wasted With Tom Lehrer	1966	6.00	15.00

LEIBER, JERRY

Kapp KL-1127	(M)	Scooby-Doo	1959	20.00	50.00

LEIBER & STOLLER BIG BAND

Atlantic 847	(M)	Yakety Yak	1960	10.00	25.00
Atlantic SD-847	(S)	Yakety Yak	1960	14.00	35.00

LEMMON, JACK

Epic LN-523	(M)	A Twist Of Lemmon	1959	8.00	20.00
Epic BN-523	(S)	A Twist Of Lemmon	1959	10.00	25.00
Capitol T-1943	(M)	Piano Selections From "Irma La Douce"	1963	8.00	20.00
Capitol ST-1943	(S)	Piano Selections From "Irma La Douce"	1963	10.00	25.00

LEMON PIPERS, THE

Buddah BD-5009	(M)	Green Tambourine	1968	5.00	12.00
Buddah BDS-5009	(S)	Green Tambourine	1968	6.00	15.00
Buddah BDS-5016	(S)	Jungle Marmalade	1968	5.00	12.00

LENNON, JOHN (PLASTIC ONO BAND)
Also refer to Nilsson.

Apple SW-3362	(S)	Live Peace In Toronto	1969	3.50	8.00
		(Apple label reads "Mfd. by Apple Records.")			
Apple SW-3362	(S)	Live Peace In Toronto	1969	16.00	40.00
		(Apple label reads "A Subsidiary of Capitol." With a calendar, priced separately below.)			
		Live Peace In Toronto Calendar	1969	3.50	8.00
Apple SW-3372	(S)	John Lennon/Plastic Ono Band	1970	6.00	15.00
Apple SW-3379	(S)	Imagine (With poster & postcard)	1971	10.00	25.00
Apple SW-3414	(S)	Mind Games	1973	6.00	15.00
Apple SW-3416	(S)	Walls And Bridges (With booklet)	1974	6.00	15.00
Apple SK-3419	(S)	Rock 'N' Roll	1975	6.00	15.00
Adam VIII LP-8018	(S)	The Great Rock and Roll Hits/Roots	1975	210.00	350.00
Apple SW-3421	(S)	Shaved Fish (With custom inner sleeve)	1975	5.00	12.00
Mobile Fidelity 1-153	(S)	Imagine	1984	5.00	12.00

LENNON, JOHN, & YOKO ONO

Apple T-5001	(S)	Two Virgins	1968	50.00	100.00
		(In a brown sleeve that opens on the right.)			
Zapple ST-3357	(S)	Life With The Lions	1969	10.00	25.00
Apple SMAX-3361	(S)	Wedding Album (Box)	1969	50.00	100.00
Apple SVBB-3392	(S)	Sometime In New York City	1972	12.00	30.00
		(Issued with a photo, a postcard & a petition.)			
Geffen GHS-2001	(S)	Double Fantasy	1980	6.00	15.00
		(Song titles are out of order on back cover.)			
Nautilus 47	(S)	Double Fantasy (With poster)	1980	16.00	40.00

LENOIR, J.B.

Chess 1410	(M)	Natural Man	1963	16.00	40.00

LESTER, KETTY

Era EL-108	(M)	Love Letters	1963	14.00	35.00
Era ES-108	(S)	Love Letters	1963	16.00	40.00
RCA LPM-2945	(M)	Soul Of Me	1964	6.00	15.00
RCA LSP-2945	(S)	Soul Of Me	1964	8.00	20.00
RCA LPM-3326	(M)	Where Is Love	1965	6.00	15.00
RCA LSP-3326	(S)	Where Is Love	1965	8.00	20.00
Tower T-5029	(M)	When A Woman Loves A Man	1967	6.00	15.00
Tower ST-5029	(S)	When A Woman Loves A Man	1967	6.00	15.00

LETTERMEN, THE

Capitol T-1669	(M)	A Song For Young Love	1962	4.00	10.00
Capitol ST-1669	(S)	A Song For Young Love	1962	5.00	12.00

Label		Title	Year	VG+	NM
Capitol T-1711	(M)	Once Upon A Time	1962	3.50	8.00
Capitol ST-1711	(S)	Once Upon A Time	1962	4.00	10.00
Capitol T-1761	(M)	Jim, Tony, Bob	1962	3.50	8.00
Capitol ST-1761	(S)	Jim, Tony, Bob	1962	4.00	10.00
Capitol T-1829	(M)	College Standards	1963	3.50	8.00
Capitol ST-1829	(S)	College Standards	1963	4.00	10.00
Capitol T-1936	(M)	The Lettermen In Concert	1963	3.50	8.00
Capitol ST-1936	(S)	The Lettermen In Concert	1963	4.00	10.00
Capitol T-2013	(M)	A Lettermen Kind Of Love	1964	3.50	8.00
Capitol ST-2013	(S)	A Lettermen Kind Of Love	1964	4.00	10.00
Capitol T-2083	(M)	The Lettermen Look At Love	1964	3.50	8.00
Capitol ST-2083	(S)	The Lettermen Look At Love	1964	4.00	10.00
Capitol T-2142	(M)	She Cried	1964	3.50	8.00
Capitol ST-2142	(S)	She Cried	1964	4.00	10.00
Capitol T-2270	(M)	Portrait Of My Love	1965	3.50	8.00
Capitol ST-2270	(S)	Portrait Of My Love	1965	4.00	10.00
Capitol T-2213	(M)	You'll Never Walk Alone	1965	3.50	8.00
Capitol ST-2213	(S)	You'll Never Walk Alone	1965	4.00	10.00
Capitol T-2359	(M)	The Hit Sounds Of The Lettermen	1965	3.50	8.00
Capitol ST-2359	(S)	The Hit Sounds Of The Lettermen	1965	4.00	10.00
Capitol T-2428	(M)	More Hit Sounds Of The Lettermen	1966	3.50	8.00
Capitol ST-2428	(S)	More Hit Sounds Of The Lettermen	1966	4.00	10.00
Capitol T-2496	(M)	A New Song For Young Love	1966	3.50	8.00
Capitol ST-2496	(S)	A New Song For Young Love	1966	4.00	10.00
Capitol T-2554	(M)	The Best Of The Lettermen	1966	2.50	6.00
Capitol ST-2554	(S)	The Best Of The Lettermen	1966	3.50	8.00
Capitol T-2587	(M)	For Christmas This Year	1966	2.50	6.00
Capitol ST-2587	(S)	For Christmas This Year	1966	3.50	8.00
Capitol T-2633	(M)	Warm	1967	2.50	6.00
Capitol ST-2633	(S)	Warm	1967	3.50	8.00
Capitol T-2711	(M)	Spring!!	1967	2.50	6.00
Capitol ST-2711	(S)	Spring!!	1967	3.50	8.00
Capitol T-2758	(M)	The Lettermen!! And Live!	1967	2.50	6.00
Capitol ST-2758	(S)	The Lettermen!! And Live!	1967	3.50	8.00
Capitol ST-2865	(S)	Goin' Out Of My Head	1968	3.50	8.00

LEWIS, BARBARA

Label		Title	Year	VG+	NM
Atlantic 8086	(M)	Hello Stranger	1963	10.00	25.00
Atlantic SD-8086	(S)	Hello Stranger	1963	14.00	35.00
Atlantic 8090	(M)	Snap Your Fingers	1964	10.00	25.00
Atlantic SD-8090	(S)	Snap Your Fingers	1964	12.00	30.00
Atlantic 8110	(M)	Baby, I'm Yours	1965	10.00	25.00
Atlantic SD-8110	(S)	Baby, I'm Yours	1965	12.00	30.00
Atlantic 8118	(M)	It's Magic	1966	8.00	20.00
Atlantic SD-8118	(S)	It's Magic	1966	10.00	25.00
Atlantic SD-8173	(S)	Workin' On A Groovy Thing	1968	8.00	20.00
Atlantic SD-8286	(S)	The Best Of Barbara Lewis	1971	6.00	15.00

LEWIS, BOBBY

Label		Title	Year	VG+	NM
Beltone 4000	(M)	Tossin' And Turnin'	1961	50.00	100.00

LEWIS, FURRY

Label		Title	Year	VG+	NM
Bluesville BV-1036	(M)	Back On My Feet Again	1961	14.00	35.00
Bluesville BVS-1036	(S)	Back On My Feet Again	1961	16.00	40.00
Prestige 7810	(S)	Back On My Feet Again	1970	5.00	12.00
Adelphi 1007	(S)	On The Road Again	1970	5.00	12.00
Ampex A-10140	(S)	Live At The Gaslight	1971	6.00	15.00

LEWIS, GARY (& THE PLAYBOYS)

Label		Title	Year	VG+	NM
Liberty LRP-3408	(M)	This Diamond Ring	1965	5.00	12.00
Liberty LST-7408	(S)	This Diamond Ring	1965	6.00	15.00
Liberty LRP-3419	(M)	A Session With Gary Lewis	1965	4.00	10.00
Liberty LST-7419	(S)	A Session With Gary Lewis	1965	5.00	12.00
Liberty LRP-3428	(M)	Everybody Loves A Clown	1965	4.00	10.00
Liberty LST-7428	(S)	Everybody Loves A Clown	1965	5.00	12.00
Liberty LRP-3435	(M)	She's Just My Style	1966	4.00	10.00
Liberty LST-7435	(S)	She's Just My Style	1966	5.00	12.00
Liberty LRP-3452	(M)	Hits Again!	1966	4.00	10.00
Liberty LST-7452	(S)	Hits Again!	1966	5.00	12.00
Decca DL-4751	(M)	Out Of Sight (Sdtk)	1966	6.00	15.00
Decca DL7-4751	(S)	Out Of Sight (Sdtk)	1966	8.00	20.00

Label		Title	Year	VG+	NM
Liberty LRP-3468	(M)	Gary Lewis' Golden Greats	1966	4.00	10.00
Liberty LST-7468	(S)	Gary Lewis' Golden Greats	1966	5.00	12.00
Liberty LRP-3487	(M)	You Don't Have To Paint Me A Picture	1967	3.50	8.00
Liberty LST-7487	(S)	You Don't Have To Paint Me A Picture	1967	4.00	10.00
Liberty LRP-3519	(M)	New Directions	1967	3.50	8.00
Liberty LST-7519	(S)	New Directions	1967	4.00	10.00
Liberty LRP-3524	(M)	Listen	1967	3.50	8.00
Liberty LST-7524	(S)	Listen	1967	4.00	10.00

LEWIS, JERRY

Label		Title	Year	VG+	NM
Decca DL-8410	(M)	Jerry Lewis Just Sings	1956	10.00	25.00
Decca DL-8936	(M)	Big Songs For Little People		6.00	15.00
Decca DL7-8936	(S)	Big Songs For Little People		8.00	20.00
Dot DLP-8001	(M)	Cinderfella (Sdtk)	1960	10.00	25.00
Dot DLP-38001	(S)	Cinderfella (Sdtk)	1960	14.00	35.00
Dot DLP-38001	(S)	Cinderfella (Sdtk on colored vinyl)	1960	30.00	60.00
Capitol J-3267	(M)	Nagger	1963	8.00	20.00

LEWIS, JERRY LEE

Label		Title	Year	VG+	NM
Sun SLP-1230	(M)	Jerry Lee Lewis	1958	60.00	120.00
Sun SLP-1265	(M)	Jerry Lee's Greatest	1961	75.00	150.00
Smash MGS-27040	(M)	The Golden Hits Of Jerry Lee Lewis	1964	8.00	20.00
Smash SRS-67040	(S)	The Golden Hits Of Jerry Lee Lewis	1964	10.00	25.00
Smash MGS-27056	(M)	The Greatest Live Show On Earth	1964	16.00	40.00
Smash SRS-67056	(S)	The Greatest Live Show On Earth	1964	20.00	50.00
Smash MGS-27063	(M)	The Return Of Rock	1965	10.00	25.00
Smash SRS-67063	(S)	The Return Of Rock	1965	12.00	30.00
Smash MGS-27071	(M)	Country Songs For City Folks	1965	6.00	15.00
Smash SRS-67071	(S)	Country Songs For City Folks	1965	8.00	20.00
Smash MGS-27079	(M)	Memphis Beat	1966	8.00	20.00
Smash SRS-67079	(S)	Memphis Beat	1966	10.00	25.00
Smash MGS-27086	(M)	By Request	1966	6.00	15.00
Smash SRS-67086	(S)	By Request	1966	8.00	20.00
Smash MGS-27097	(M)	Soul My Way	1967	8.00	20.00
Smash SRS-67097	(S)	Soul My Way	1967	10.00	25.00
Smash SRS-67014	(S)	Another Place, Another Time	1968	4.00	10.00
Smash SRS-67040	(S)	Golden Rock Hits	1968	4.00	10.00
Smash SRS-67040	(S)	The Golden Rock Hits Of Jerry Lee Lewis	1969	4.00	10.00
Smash SRS-67071	(S)	All Country	1969	4.00	10.00
Smash SRS-67112	(S)	She Still Comes Around	1968	4.00	10.00
Smash SRS-67117	(S)	Country Music Hall Of Fame Hits, Volume 1	1969	4.00	10.00
Smash SRS-67118	(S)	Country Music Hall Of Fame Hits, Volume 2	1969	4.00	10.00
Smash SRS-67126	(S)	Together (With Linda Gail Lewis)	1969	4.00	10.00
Smash SRS-67128	(S)	She Even Woke Me Up To Say Goodbye	1970	4.00	10.00
Smash SRS-67131	(S)	The Best Of Jerry Lee Lewis	1970	4.00	10.00
Wing MGW-12340	(M)	The Return Of Rock	1967	5.00	12.00
Wing SRW-16340	(S)	The Return Of Rock	1967	6.00	15.00
Wing SRW-16340	(S)	In Demand	1968	6.00	15.00
Wing SRW-16406	(S)	Unlimited	1968	6.00	15.00
Wibf PKW2-125	(S)	The Legend Of Jerry Lee Lewis	1969	6.00	15.00
Mercury SR-61278	(S)	Live At The International	1970	6.00	15.00
Mercury SR-61318	(S)	In Loving Memories	1971	4.00	10.00
Mercury SR-61323	(S)	There Must Be More To Love Than This	1971	4.00	10.00
Mercury SR-61343	(S)	Touching Home	1971	5.00	12.00
Mercury SR-61346	(S)	Would You Take Another Chance On Me	1971	5.00	12.00
Mercury SR-61366	(S)	Who's Gonna Play This Old Piano	1972	4.00	10.00
Mercury SRM-1-637	(S)	The Killer Rocks On	1972	6.00	15.00
Mercury SRM-1-677	(S)	Sometimes A Memory Ain't Enough	1973	3.50	8.00
Mercury SRM-1-690	(S)	Southern Roots	1973	3.50	8.00
Mercury SRM-1-710	(S)	I-40 Country	1974	6.00	15.00
Mercury SRM-2-803	(S)	The Session	1973	8.00	20.00
Mercury SRM-1-1030	(S)	Boogie Woogie Country Man	1975	3.50	8.00
Mercury SRM-1-1064	(S)	Odd Man In	1975	3.50	8.00
Mercury SRM-1-1109	(S)	Country Class	1976	3.50	8.00
Mercury SRM-1-5006	(S)	The Best Of Jerry Lee Lewis, Volume 2	1978	3.50	8.00
Mercury SRM-1-5004	(S)	Country Memories	1977	3.50	8.00
Mercury SRM-1-5010	(S)	Jerry Lee Lewis Keeps Rockin'	1978	3.50	8.00

LEWIS, MEADE LUX

Label		Title	Year	VG+	NM
Tops L-1533	(M)	Barrel House Piano		20.00	50.00
Riverside 9402	(M)	Blues Piano Artistry Of Meade Lux Lewis		20.00	50.00

Label		Title	Year	VG+	NM
ABC-Paramount 164	(M)	Out Of The Roaring '20s		8.00	20.00
ABC-Paramount S-164	(S)	Out Of The Roaring '20s		10.00	25.00

LEWIS, SMILEY

Imperial LP-9141	(M)	I Hear You Knocking	1961	100.00	200.00

LEWIS & CLARKE EXPEDITION

Colgems COL-105	(M)	The Lewis And Clarke Expedition	1967	6.00	15.00
Colgems COS-105	(S)	The Lewis And Clarke Expedition	1967	8.00	20.00

LIBERACE

Coral CRL-57346	(M)	Liberace At The Palladium	1961	5.00	12.00
Coral CRL7-57346	(S)	Liberace At The Palladium	1961	6.00	15.00
Coral CRL-57377	(M)	My Parade Of Golden Favorites	1961	5.00	12.00
Coral CRL7-57377	(S)	My Parade Of Golden Favorites	1961	6.00	15.00
Coral CRL-57392	(M)	As Time Goes By	1962	5.00	12.00
Coral CRL7-57392	(S)	As Time Goes By	1962	6.00	15.00
Dot DLP-3547	(M)	Mr. Showmanship	1963	5.00	12.00
Dot DLP-25547	(S)	Mr. Showmanship	1963	6.00	15.00
Dot DLP-3550	(M)	Christmas	1963	5.00	12.00
Dot DLP-25550	(S)	Christmas	1963	6.00	15.00
Dot DLP-3563	(M)	My Most Requested	1964	5.00	12.00
Dot DLP-25563	(S)	My Most Requested	1964	6.00	15.00
Dot DLP-3595	(M)	Liberace At The American	1964	5.00	12.00
Dot DLP-25595	(S)	Liberace At The American	1964	6.00	15.00
Coral CRL-57452	(M)	Golden Themes From Hollywood	1964	5.00	12.00
Coral CRL7-57452	(S)	Golden Themes From Hollywood	1964	6.00	15.00
Coral CXB-9	(M)	The Best Of Liberace	1965	6.00	15.00
Coral CXSB7-9	(S)	The Best Of Liberace	1965	8.00	20.00
Dot DLP-3816	(M)	Liberace Now	1967	5.00	12.00
Dot DLP-25816	(S)	Liberace Now	1967	6.00	15.00
Warners WS-1847	(S)	Brand New Me	1970	5.00	12.00

LIBERMAN, JEFFREY

Librah 1545	(S)	Jeffrey Liberman	1975	20.00	50.00
Librah 6969	(S)	Solitude Within	1975	20.00	50.00

LIGHTCRUST DOUGHBOYS, THE

Audio Lab 1525	(M)	The Lightcrust Doughboys		30.00	60.00

LIGHTFOOT, GORDON

U.A. UAL-3487	(M)	Lightfoot	1965	5.00	12.00
U.A. UAS-6487	(S)	Lightfoot	1965	6.00	15.00
U.A. UAL-3587	(M)	The Way I Feel	1967	5.00	12.00
U.A. UAS-6587	(S)	The Way I Feel	1967	6.00	15.00
Reprise MS4-2177	(Q)	Sundown	1974	6.00	15.00
Mobile Fidelity 1-018	(S)	Sundown		6.00	15.00
Reprise MS4-2206	(Q)	Cold On The Shoulder	1975	6.00	15.00

LIGHTNIN' SLIM

Excello 8000	(M)	Rooster Blues	1960	30.00	60.00
Excello 8004	(M)	Lightnin' Slim's Bell Ringer	1965	14.00	50.00
Excello S-8004	(S)	Lightnin' Slim's Bell Ringer	1965	16.00	40.00
Excello 8018	(S)	High And Low Down	1971	6.00	15.00
Excello 8023	(S)	London Gumbo	1972	6.00	15.00

LIMELITERS, THE

Elektra EKL-180	(M)	The Limeliters	1960	5.00	12.00
Elektra EKS7-180	(S)	The Limeliters	1960	6.00	15.00
RCA LPM-2272	(M)	Tonight: In Person	1961	4.00	10.00
RCA LSP-2272	(S)	Tonight: In Person	1961	6.00	15.00
RCA LPM-2393	(M)	The Slightly Fabulous Limeliters	1961	4.00	10.00
RCA LSP-2393	(S)	The Slightly Fabulous Limeliters	1961	6.00	15.00
RCA LPM-2445	(M)	Sing Out!	1962	4.00	10.00
RCA LSP-2445	(S)	Sing Out!	1962	6.00	15.00
RCA LPM-2512	(M)	Through Children's Eyes	1962	4.00	10.00
RCA LSP-2512	(S)	Through Children's Eyes	1962	6.00	15.00
RCA LPM-2547	(M)	Folk Matinee	1962	4.00	10.00
RCA LSP-2547	(S)	Folk Matinee	1962	6.00	15.00
RCA LPM-2588	(M)	Makin' A Joyful Noise	1963	4.00	10.00
RCA LSP-2588	(S)	Makin' A Joyful Noise	1963	6.00	15.00

Label		Title	Year	VG+	NM
RCA LPM-2609	(M)	Our Men In San Francisco	1963	4.00	10.00
RCA LSP-2609	(S)	Our Men In San Francisco	1963	6.00	15.00
RCA LPM-2671	(M)	Fourteen 14K Folk Songs	1963	4.00	10.00
RCA LSP-2671	(S)	Fourteen 14K Folk Songs	1963	6.00	15.00
RCA LPM-2844	(M)	More Of Everything	1964	4.00	10.00
RCA LSP-2844	(S)	More Of Everything	1964	5.00	12.00
RCA LPM-2889	(M)	The Best Of The Limeliters	1964	4.00	10.00
RCA LSP-2889	(S)	The Best Of The Limeliters	1964	5.00	12.00
RCA LPM-2906	(M)	Leave It To The Limeliters	1964	4.00	10.00
RCA LSP-2906	(S)	Leave It To The Limeliters	1964	5.00	12.00
RCA LPM-2907	(M)	London Concert	1965	4.00	10.00
RCA LSP-2907	(S)	London Concert	1965	5.00	12.00
RCA LPM-3385	(M)	The Limeliters Look At Love In Depth	1965	4.00	10.00
RCA LSP-3385	(S)	The Limeliters Look At Love In Depth	1965	5.00	12.00
RCA LSP-4100	(S)	The Original "Those Were The Days"	1968	4.00	10.00

LIMOUSINE

G.S.F 1002	(S)	Limousine	1972	6.00	15.00

LINCOLN, PHILAMORE

Epic BN-26497	(S)	More Wind Blew South	1970	6.00	15.00

LINCOLN STREET EXIT

Mainstream S-6126	(S)	Drive It	1970	8.00	20.00

LINDEN, KATHY

Felsted 7501	(M)	That Certain Boy		16.00	40.00

LIPSCOMB, MANCE

Reprise R-2012	(M)	Trouble In Mind	1961	10.00	25.00
Reprise R9-2012	(S)	Trouble In Mind	1961	12.00	30.00

LIPTON, PEGGY

Ode Z12-44006	(S)	Peggy Lipton	1968	6.00	15.00

LITE STORM

Beverly Hills 1135	(S)	Lite Storm Warning	1973	12.00	30.00

LITTER, THE

Warick UR-5M-1940	(M)	Distortions	1968	100.00	200.00
Hexagon HX-681	(S)	$100 Fine	1969	70.00	140.00
Probe CPLP-4504	(S)	Emerge	1969	12.00	30.00

LITTLE ANTHONY (& THE IMPERIALS)

End 303	(M)	We Are Little Anthony & The Imperials	1960	50.00	100.00
End 311	(M)	Shades Of The 40's	1960	35.00	70.00
DCP DC-3801	(M)	I'm On The Outside Looking In	1964	8.00	20.00
DCP DS-6801	(S)	I'm On The Outside Looking In	1964	10.00	25.00
DCP DC-3808	(M)	Goin' Out Of My Head	1965	8.00	20.00
DCP DS-6808	(S)	Goin' Out Of My Head	1965	10.00	25.00
DCP DC-3809	(M)	Best Of Little Anthony & The Imperials	1966	8.00	20.00
DCP DS-6809	(S)	Best Of Little Anthony & The Imperials	1966	10.00	25.00
Roulette R-25294	(M)	Greatest Hits	1965	6.00	15.00
Roulette SR-25294	(S)	Greatest Hits	1965	8.00	20.00
Veep VP-13510	(M)	I'm On The Outside Looking In	1966	5.00	12.00
Veep VPS-16510	(S)	I'm On The Outside Looking In	1966	6.00	15.00
Veep VP-13513	(M)	Payin' Our Dues	1966	5.00	12.00
Veep VPS-16513	(S)	Payin' Our Dues	1966	6.00	15.00
Veep VP-13514	(M)	Reflections	1967	5.00	12.00
Veep VPS-16514	(S)	Reflections	1967	6.00	15.00
Veep VP-13516	(M)	Movie Grabbers	1967	5.00	12.00
Veep VPS-16516	(S)	Movie Grabbers	1967	6.00	15.00
Veep VPS-16519	(S)	The Best Of Little Anthony, Volume 2	1968	6.00	15.00
U.A. UAS-6720	(S)	Out Of Sight, Out Of Mind	1969	6.00	15.00
U.A. LA026	(S)	Legendary Masters	1973	8.00	20.00

LITTLE BOY BLUES

Fontana MGF-27578	(M)	In The Woodland Of Weir	1967	10.00	25.00
Fontana SRF-67578	(S)	In The Woodland Of Weir	1967	12.00	30.00

Label		Title	Year	VG+	NM
LITTLE CAESAR & THE ROMANS					
Del-Fi DFLP-1218	(M)	Memories Of Those Oldies But Goodies	1961	20.00	50.00
LITTLE EVA (EVA BOYD)					
Dimension DLP-6000	(M)	L-L-L-L-Loco-Motion	1962	30.00	60.00
Dimension DLPS-6000	(E)	L-L-L-L-Loco-Motion	1962	50.00	100.00
LITTLE FEAT					
Mobile Fidelity 2-013	(S)	Waiting For Columbus	1978	12.00	30.00
LITTLE MILTON (MILTON CAMPBELL)					
Checker 2995	(M)	We're Gonna Make It	1965	14.00	35.00
		(Black or maroon label with silver print.)			
Checker 3002	(M)	Little Milton Sings Big Blues	1966	14.00	35.00
Checker 3011	(S)	Grits Ain't Groceries	1969	8.00	20.00
Checker 3012	(S)	If Walls Could Talk	1970	6.00	15.00
		(Checker albums above have blue labels.)			
LITTLE RICHARD (RICHARD PENNIMAN)					
Also refer to Canned Heat and Jimi Hendrix.					
Camden CAL-420	(M)	Little Richard	1956	50.00	100.00
Specialty 100	(M)	Here's Little Richard	1957	150.00	250.00
Specialty 2100	(M)	Here's Little Richard	1957	30.00	60.00
Specialty SP-2103	(M)	Little Richard	1957	30.00	60.00
Specialty SP-2104	(M)	The Fabulous Little Richard	1958	30.00	60.00
Mercury MG-20656	(M)	It's Real	1961	14.00	35.00
Mercury SR-60656	(S)	It's Real	1961	16.00	40.00
Crown CLP-5362	(M)	Little Richard Sings Freedom Songs	1963	8.00	20.00
Coral CRL-57446	(M)	Coming Home	1963	10.00	25.00
Coral CRL7-57446	(S)	Coming Home	1963	12.00	30.00
Specialty SP-2111	(M)	Little Richard's Biggest Hits	1963	16.00	40.00
Wing MGW-122288	(M)	King Of The Gospel Singers	1964	8.00	20.00
Wing SRW-162288	(S)	King Of The Gospel Singers	1964	10.00	25.00
20th Century FXG-5010	(M)	Little Richard Sings Gospel		6.00	15.00
20th Century SGM-5010	(S)	Little Richard Sings Gospel		8.00	20.00
Vee Jay LP-1107	(M)	Little Richard Is Back	1964	8.00	20.00
Vee Jay SR-1107	(S)	Little Richard Is Back	1964	10.00	25.00
Vee Jay LP-1124	(M)	Little Richard's Greatest Hits	1965	10.00	25.00
		(Vee Jay albums above have black labels with a "VJ" logo in brackets on top.)			
Modern 100	(M)	His Greatest Hits/Recorded Live		6.00	15.00
Modern 1000	(S)	His Greatest Hits/Recorded Live		6.00	15.00
Modern 103	(M)	The Wild And Frantic Little Richard		6.00	15.00
Modern 1003	(S)	The Wild And Frantic Little Richard		6.00	15.00
Vee Jay VJS-2-100	(S)	Little Richard's Gold		5.00	12.00
Dynasty DYS-730	(S)	Talkin' 'Bout Soul		6.00	15.00
Custom 2061	(M)	Little Richard Sings Spirituals		6.00	15.00
OKeh OKM-12121	(M)	Greatest Hits Recorded Live	1967	6.00	15.00
OKeh OKS-14121	(S)	Greatest Hits Recorded Live	1967	8.00	20.00
OKeh OKM-12117	(M)	The Explosive Little Richard	1967	6.00	15.00
OKeh OKS-14117	(S)	The Explosive Little Richard	1967	8.00	20.00
Specialty SP-2113	(E)	Grooviest 17 Original Hits	1968	6.00	15.00
Roulette RS-42007	(S)	Forever Yours	1968	6.00	15.00
Buddah BDS-7501	(S)	Little Richard	1969	8.00	20.00
Kama Sutra NSBS-2023	(S)	Little Richard	1970	8.00	20.00
Specialty SP-2136	(E)	Well Alright	1970	8.00	20.00
		(All Specialty albums above from 1957 through 1970 have black & gold labels.)			
Reprise RS-6406	(S)	The Rill Thing	1970	6.00	15.00
Reprise RS-6462	(S)	The King Of Rock And Roll	1971	6.00	15.00
Reprise MS-2051	(S)	Dollars (Sdtk)	1971	3.50	8.00
Reprise MS-2107	(S)	The Second Coming	1972	6.00	15.00
Epic EG-3042	(S)	Cast A Long Shadow	1971	6.00	15.00
Scepter 18020	(S)	The Best Of Little Richard	1971	6.00	15.00
Audio Encores 1002	(S)	Little Richard (Direct to disc)	1980	10.00	25.00
LITTLE WALTER					
Also refer to Bo Diddley.					
Chess LP-1428	(M)	The Best Of Little Walter	1963	30.00	60.00
Chess LPS-1535	(S)	Hate To See You Go	1969	6.00	15.00

Label		Title	Year	VG+	NM
LIVELY ONES, THE	,				
Del-Fi DFLP-1226	(M)	Surf-Rider	1963	10.00	25.00
Del-Fi DFST-1226	(S)	Surf-Rider	1963	12.00	35.00
Del-Fi DFLP-1231	(M)	Surf Drums	1963	10.00	25.00
Del-Fi DFST-1231	(S)	Surf Drums	1963	12.00	35.00
Del-Fi DFLP-1237	(M)	This Is Surf City	1963	10.00	25.00
Del-Fi DFST-1237	(S)	This Is Surf City	1963	12.00	35.00
Del-Fi DFLP-1238	(M)	Great Surf Hits	1963	10.00	25.00
Del-Fi DFST-1238	(S)	Great Surf Hits	1963	12.00	35.00
Del-Fi DFLP-1240	(M)	Surfin' South Of The Border	1964	10.00	25.00
Del-Fi DFST-1240	(S)	Surfin' South Of The Border	1964	12.00	35.00
MGM E-4449	(M)	Bugalu Party	1967	6.00	15.00
MGM SE-4449	(S)	Bugalu Party	1967	8.00	20.00
LIVERPOOLS BEATS, THE (THE BEATS)					
Rondo 2026	(M)	New Merseyside Sound	1964	16.00	40.00
LIVERPOOL FIVE, THE					
RCA LPM-3583	(M)	Arrive	1966	8.00	20.00
RCA LSP-3583	(S)	Arrive	1966	10.00	25.00
RCA LPM-3682	(M)	Out Of Sight	1967	8.00	20.00
RCA LSP-3682	(S)	Out Of Sight	1967	10.00	25.00
LIVERPOOL KIDS, THE					
Palace 777	(M)	Beatle Mash	1964	16.00	40.00
LIVERPOOL SCENE, THE					
Epic LN-24336	(M)	The Incredible New Liverpool Scene	1967	8.00	20.00
Epic BN-26336	(S)	The Incredible New Liverpool Scene	1967	10.00	25.00
RCA LSP-4189	(S)	Amazing Adventures	1969	6.00	15.00
RCA LSP-4267	(S)	Bread On The Night	1970	6.00	15.00
LIVERPOOLS, THE					
Wyncote 9001	(M)	Beatle-Mania In The U.S.A.	1964	16.00	40.00
Wyncote 9061	(M)	The Hit Sounds From England	1965	16.00	40.00
LIVIN' BLUES					
Dwarf 2003	(S)	Dutch Treat	1971	12.00	30.00
LOADING ZONE, THE					
Umbrella US-101	(S)	One For All	1968	30.00	60.00
RCA LSP-3959	(S)	The Loading Zone	1968	10.00	25.00
LOCHLIN, HANK					
RCA LPM-1673	(M)	Foreign Love	1958	12.00	30.00
RCA LPM-2291	(M)	Please Help Me, I'm Falling	1960	8.00	20.00
RCA LSP-2291	(S)	Please Help Me, I'm Falling	1960	10.00	25.00
King 672	(M)	The Best Of Hank Lochlin	1961	12.00	30.00
King 738	(M)	Encores	1961	12.00	30.00
RCA LPM-2464	(M)	Happy Journey	1962	8.00	20.00
RCA LSP-2464	(S)	Happy Journey	1962	10.00	25.00
RCA LPM-2597	(M)	A Tribute To Roy Acuff	1962	8.00	20.00
RCA LSP-2597	(S)	A Tribute To Roy Acuff	1962	10.00	25.00
RCA LPM-2680	(M)	The Ways Of Love	1963	8.00	20.00
RCA LSP-2680	(S)	The Ways Of Love	1963	10.00	25.00
		(Mono RCA albums above have "Long Play"			
		on the bottom of the label. Stereo albums			
		have "Living Stereo" on the bottom.)			
RCA LPM-2723	(M)	Three Country Gentlemen	1963	5.00	12.00
RCA LSP-2723	(S)	Three Country Gentlemen	1963	6.00	15.00
RCA LPM-2801	(M)	Irish Songs, Country Style	1964	6.00	15.00
RCA LSP-2801	(S)	Irish Songs, Country Style	1964	8.00	20.00
RCA LPM-2997	(M)	Hank Lochlin Sings Hank Williams	1964	6.00	15.00
RCA LSP-2997	(S)	Hank Lochlin Sings Hank Williams	1964	8.00	20.00
RCA LPM-3391	(M)	Hank Lochlin Sings Eddy Arnold	1965	6.00	15.00
RCA LSP-3391	(S)	Hank Lochlin Sings Eddy Arnold	1965	8.00	20.00
RCA LPM-3465	(M)	Once Over Lightly	1965	6.00	15.00
RCA LSP-3465	(S)	Once Over Lightly	1965	8.00	20.00
RCA LPM-3559	(M)	The Best Of Hank Lochlin	1966	6.00	15.00
RCA LSP-3559	(E)	The Best Of Hank Lochlin	1966	5.00	12.00

Label		Title	Year	VG+	NM
RCA LPM-3588	(M)	The Girls Get Prettier	1966	6.00	15.00
RCA LSP-3588	(S)	The Girls Get Prettier	1966	8.00	20.00
RCA LPM-3656	(M)	The Gloryland Way	1966	6.00	15.00
RCA LSP-3656	(S)	The Gloryland Way	1966	8.00	20.00
RCA LPM-3770	(M)	Send Me The Pillow You Dream On	1967	5.00	12.00
RCA LSP-3770	(S)	Send Me The Pillow You Dream On	1967	6.00	15.00
RCA LPM-3841	(M)	Nashville Women	1967	5.00	12.00
RCA LSP-3841	(S)	Nashville Women	1967	6.00	15.00
RCA LPM-3946	(M)	Country Hall Of Fame	1968	6.00	15.00
RCA LSP-3946	(S)	Country Hall Of Fame	1968	6.00	15.00
		(RCA albums above have black labels.)			

LOGGINS & MESSINA (KENNY LOGGINS & JIM MESSINA)

Columbia HC-44388	(S)	Best Of Friends (1/2 speed)	1982	6.00	15.00

LOGGINS, KENNY

Columbia HC-45387	(S)	Nightwatch (1/2 speed)	1981	6.00	15.00

LOGSDON, JIMMIE

King 843	(M)	Howdy, Neighbors	1963	12.00	30.00

LOLLIPOP SHOPPE, THE

Tower ST-5128	(S)	Angels From Hell (Sdtk)	1968	10.00	25.00
Uni 73019	(S)	The Lollipop Shoppe	1968	14.00	35.00

LOMAX, JACKIE

Apple ST-3354	(S)	Is This What You Want	1969	6.00	15.00

LONDON, JULIE

Liberty LRP-3006	(M)	Julie Is Her Name	1955	10.00	25.00
Liberty LRP-3012	(M)	Lonely Girl	1956	10.00	25.00
Liberty SL-9002	(M)	Calendar Girl	1956	14.00	35.00
Liberty LRP-3027	(M)	Julie Is Her Name	1957	10.00	25.00
Liberty LST-7027	(E)	Julie Is Her Name (Blue vinyl)	1957	20.00	50.00
Liberty LRP-3043	(M)	About The Blues	1957	10.00	25.00
Liberty LRP-3060	(M)	Make Love To Me	1957	10.00	25.00
Liberty LRP-3096	(M)	Julie	1957	10.00	25.00
Liberty LRP-3100	(M)	Julie Is Her Name, Volume 2	1958	10.00	25.00
Liberty LST-7100	(S)	Julie Is Her Name, Volume 2	1958	12.00	30.00
Liberty LRP-3105	(M)	London By Night	1958	10.00	25.00
Liberty LST-7105	(S)	London By Night	1958	12.00	30.00
Liberty LRP-3119	(M)	Swing Me An Old Song	1959	10.00	25.00
Liberty LST-7119	(S)	Swing Me An Old Song	1959	12.00	30.00
Liberty LRP-3130	(M)	Your Number Please	1959	10.00	25.00
Liberty LST-7130	(S)	Your Number Please	1959	12.00	30.00
		(Mono Liberty albums above have turquoise labels;			
		stereo albums have black & silver labels.)			
Liberty LRP-3152	(M)	Julie London At Home	1959	6.00	15.00
Liberty LST-7152	(S)	Julie London At Home	1959	8.00	20.00
Liberty LRP-3164	(M)	Around Midnight	1960	6.00	15.00
Liberty LST-7164	(S)	Around Midnight	1960	8.00	20.00
Liberty LRP-3171	(M)	Send For Me	1960	6.00	15.00
Liberty LST-7171	(S)	Send For Me	1960	8.00	20.00
Liberty LRP-3192	(M)	Whatever Julie Wants	1961	5.00	12.00
Liberty LST-7192	(S)	Whatever Julie Wants	1961	6.00	15.00
Liberty LRP-3203	(M)	Sophisticated Lady	1962	5.00	12.00
Liberty LST-7203	(S)	Sophisticated Lady	1962	6.00	15.00
Liberty LRP-3231	(M)	Love Letters	1962	5.00	12.00
Liberty LST-7231	(S)	Love Letters	1962	6.00	15.00
Liberty LRP-3278	(M)	Latin In A Satin Mood	1963	5.00	12.00
Liberty LST-7278	(S)	Latin In A Satin Mood	1963	6.00	15.00
Liberty LRP-3291	(M)	Golden Greats	1963	5.00	12.00
Liberty LST-7291	(S)	Golden Greats	1963	6.00	15.00
Liberty LRP-3300	(M)	The End Of The World	1963	5.00	12.00
Liberty LST-7300	(S)	The End Of The World	1963	6.00	15.00
Liberty LRP-3324	(M)	The Wonderful World Of Julie London	1963	5.00	12.00
Liberty LST-7324	(S)	The Wonderful World Of Julie London	1963	6.00	15.00
Liberty LRP-3342	(M)	Julie London	1964	4.00	10.00
Liberty LST-7342	(S)	Julie London	1964	5.00	12.00
Liberty LRP-3375	(M)	In Person At The Americana	1964	4.00	10.00
Liberty LST-7375	(S)	In Person At The Americana	1964	5.00	12.00

Label		Title	Year	VG+	NM
Liberty LRP-3392	(M)	Our Fair Lady	1965	4.00	10.00
Liberty LST-7392	(S)	Our Fair Lady	1965	5.00	12.00
Liberty LRP-3434	(M)	All Through The Night	1965	4.00	10.00
Liberty LST-7434	(S)	All Through The Night	1965	5.00	12.00
Liberty LRP-3478	(M)	For The Night People	1966	4.00	10.00
Liberty LST-7478	(S)	For The Night People	1966	5.00	12.00
		(Liberty albums above have black labels with a gold and white logo on the side.)			

LONDON, LAURIE

Capitol T-1016	(M)	Laurie London	1958	12.00	30.00

LONE RANGER, THE

Decca DL-8578	(M)	The Adventures Of The Lone Ranger		16.00	40.00

LONG, BARBARA

Savoy MG-12161	(M)	Soul	1961	10.00	25.00

LONGBRANCH PENNYWHISTLE

Amos AAS-7007	(S)	Longbranch/Pennywhistle	1969	16.00	40.00

LOOSE

Necturne 906	(S)	Freaky Billie, The Wheelie King	1970	12.00	30.00

LOPEZ, TRINI

King 863	(M)	Teenage Love Songs		10.00	25.00
King 877	(M)	More Of Trini Lopez		10.00	25.00

LORD SITAR

Capitol ST-3916	(S)	Lord Sitar	1968	10.00	25.00

LORD SUTCH

Cotillion SD-9015	(S)	Lord Sutch And His Heavy Friends	1972	12.00	30.00
Cotillion SD-9049	(S)	Hands Of Jack The Ripper	1972	10.00	25.00

LOREN, DONNA

Capitol T-2323	(M)	Beach Blanket Bingo	1965	10.00	25.00
Capitol ST-2323	(S)	Beach Blanket Bingo	1965	12.00	30.00

LOREN, SOPHIA

Columbia OL-6310	(M)	Sophia Loren In Rome		14.00	35.00
Columbia OS-2710	(S)	Sophia Loren In Rome		16.00	40.00
Angel 5910	(M)	Peter Sellers And Sophia Loren	1961	10.00	25.00
Angel 35910	(S)	Peter Sellers And Sophia Loren	1961	12.00	30.00
RCA Int. FOC-5	(M)	Boccaccio '70 (Sdtk)	1962	14.00	35.00
RCA Int. FSO-5	(S)	Boccaccio '70 (Sdtk)	1962	16.00	40.00

LOS BRAVOS

Press PR-73003	(M)	Black Is Black	1966	10.00	25.00
Press PAS-83003	(E)	Black Is Black	1966	10.00	25.00
Parrot PAS-71021	(S)	Bring A Little Lovin	1968	8.00	20.00

LOS LOBOS (LOS LOBOS DEL ESTE DE LOS ANGELES)

Pan American 101	(S)	Si Se Puede!	1976	50.00	100.00
New Vista 1001	(S)	Just Another Band From East L.A.	1978	75.00	150.00

LOST & FOUND

International Artists 3	(S)	Everybody's Here	1968	12.00	30.00
Tempo 7064	(S)	Number Two	1973	6.00	15.00

LOTHAR & THE HAND PEOPLE

Capitol ST-2997	(S)	Presenting Lothar & The Hand People	1968	12.00	30.00
Capitol ST-247	(S)	Space Hymn	1969	16.00	40.00

LOUDERMILK, JOHN D.

RCA LPM-2434	(M)	Language Of Love	1961	5.00	12.00
RCA LSP-2434	(S)	Language Of Love	1961	8.00	20.00
RCA LPM-2539	(M)	Twelve Sides Of Loudermilk	1962	5.00	12.00
RCA LSP-2539	(S)	Twelve Sides Of Loudermilk	1962	8.00	20.00
RCA LPM-3497	(M)	A Bizarre Collection Of... Unusual Songs	1965	5.00	12.00
RCA LSP-3497	(S)	A Bizarre Collection Of... Unusual Songs	1965	6.00	15.00

Label		Title	Year	VG+	NM
RCA LPM-3807	(M)	Suburban Attitudes In Country Verse	1967	5.00	12.00
RCA LSP-3807	(S)	Suburban Attitudes In Country Verse	1967	6.00	15.00
RCA LSP-4040	(S)	Country Love Songs	1968	5.00	12.00

LOUDON, DOROTHY

Coral CRL-57265	(M)	Live At The Blue Angel		6.00	15.00
Coral CRL7-57265	(S)	Live At The Blue Angel		8.00	20.00

LOUIE & THE LOVERS

Epic KE-30026	(S)	Rise	1970	6.00	15.00

LOUISIANA RED

Roulette R-25200	(M)	The Lowdown Back Porch Blues	1963	14.00	35.00
Atco SD-33-389	(S)	Louisiana Red Sings The Blues	1972	5.00	12.00

LOUVIN, CHARLIE

Capitol T-2208	(M)	Less And Less	1965	8.00	20.00
Capitol ST-2208	(S)	Less And Less	1965	10.00	25.00
Capitol T-2437	(M)	The Many Moods Of Charlie Louvin	1966	8.00	20.00
Capitol ST-2437	(S)	The Many Moods Of Charlie Louvin	1966	10.00	25.00
Capitol T-2482	(M)	Lonesome Is Me	1966	8.00	20.00
Capitol ST-2482	(S)	Lonesome Is Me	1966	10.00	25.00
Capitol T-2689	(M)	I'll Remember Always	1967	8.00	20.00
Capitol ST-2689	(S)	I'll Remember Always	1967	10.00	25.00
Capitol T-2787	(M)	I Forgot To Cry	1967	8.00	20.00
Capitol ST-2787	(S)	I Forgot To Cry	1967	10.00	25.00
Capitol ST-2958	(S)	Will You Visit Me On Sundays	1968	8.00	20.00

LOUVIN, IRA

Capitol T-2413	(M)	The Unforgettable Ira Louvin	1965	8.00	20.00
Capitol ST-2413	(S)	The Unforgettable Ira Louvin	1965	10.00	25.00

LOUVIN BROTHERS (CHARLIE & IRA LOUVIN)

MGM E-3426	(M)	The Louvin Brothers	1956	100.00	200.00
Capitol T-769	(M)	Tragic Songs Of Life	1956	50.00	100.00
Capitol T-825	(M)	Nearer My God To Thee	1957	40.00	80.00
Capitol T-910	(M)	Ira And Charlie	1958	40.00	80.00
		(Capitol albums above have turquoise labels.)			
Capitol T-1061	(M)	The Family Who Prays	1958	20.00	50.00
Capitol T-1106	(M)	Country Love Ballads	1959	20.00	50.00
Capitol T-1277	(M)	Satan Is Real	1960	20.00	50.00
Capitol T-1385	(M)	My Baby's Gone	1960	20.00	50.00
Capitol T-1449	(M)	A Tribute To The Delmore Brothers	1960	16.00	40.00
Capitol T-1547	(M)	Encore	1961	10.00	25.00
Capitol T-1616	(M)	Country Christmas	1961	8.00	20.00
Capitol ST-1616	(S)	Country Christmas	1961	10.00	25.00
		(Capitol albums above have black labels with the Capitol logo on the left side.)			
Capitol T-1721	(M)	Weapon Of Prayer	1962	8.00	20.00
Capitol ST-1721	(S)	Weapon Of Prayer	1962	10.00	25.00
Capitol T-1834	(M)	Keep Your Eyes On Jesus	1963	8.00	20.00
Capitol ST-1834	(S)	Keep Your Eyes On Jesus	1963	10.00	25.00
Capitol T-2091	(M)	Sing And Play Their Current Hits	1964	8.00	20.00
Capitol ST-2091	(S)	Sing And Play Their Current Hits	1964	10.00	25.00
Capitol T-2331	(M)	Thank God For My Christian Home	1965	6.00	15.00
Capitol ST-2331	(S)	Thank God For My Christian Home	1965	8.00	20.00
Capitol T-2827	(M)	The Great Roy Acuff Songs	1967	6.00	15.00
Capitol ST-2827	(S)	The Great Roy Acuff Songs	1967	8.00	20.00
		(Capitol albums above have black labels with the Capitol logo on top.)			

LOVE

Elektra EKL-4001	(M)	Love	1966	10.00	25.00
Elektra EKS-74001	(S)	Love (Brown label)	1966	6.00	15.00
Elektra EKL-4005	(M)	Da Capo	1966	10.00	25.00
Elektra EKS-74005	(S)	Da Capo (Brown label)	1966	6.00	15.00
Elektra EKL-4013	(M)	Forever Changes	1967	10.00	25.00
Elektra EKS-74013	(S)	Forever Changes (Brown label)	1967	6.00	15.00
Elektra EKS-74049	(S)	Four Sail	1969	5.00	12.00
Blue Thumb BTS-9000	(S)	Out Here	1969	5.00	12.00
Blue Thumb BTS-8822	(S)	False Start	1970	6.00	15.00

Label		Title	Year	VG+	NM
LOVE EXCHANGE, THE					
Tower ST-5115	(S)	The Love Exchange	1968	10.00	25.00
LOVE SCULPTURE					
Rare Earth RS-505	(S)	Blues Helping	1969	14.00	35.00
Parrot PAS-71035	(S)	Forms And Feeling	1970	10.00	25.00
LOVIN' SPOONFUL, THE					
Kama Sutra KLP-8050	(M)	Do You Believe In Magic?	1965	4.00	10.00
Kama Sutra KLPS-8050	(S)	Do You Believe In Magic?	1965	6.00	15.00
Kama Sutra KLP-8051	(M)	Daydream	1966	4.00	10.00
Kama Sutra KLPS-8051	(S)	Daydream	1966	6.00	15.00
Kama Sutra KLP-8053	(M)	What's Up, Tiger Lily? (Sdtk)	1966	4.00	10.00
Kama Sutra KLPS-8053	(S)	What's Up, Tiger Lily? (Sdtk)	1966	6.00	15.00
Kama Sutra KLP-8054	(M)	Hums Of The Lovin' Spoonful	1966	4.00	10.00
Kama Sutra KLPS-8054	(S)	Hums Of The Lovin' Spoonful	1966	6.00	15.00
Kama Sutra KLP-8056	(M)	The Best Of The Lovin' Spoonful	1967	4.00	10.00
Kama Sutra KLPS-8056	(S)	The Best Of The Lovin' Spoonful	1967	5.00	12.00
Kama Sutra KLP-8058	(M)	You're A Big Boy, Now	1967	4.00	10.00
Kama Sutra KLPS-8058	(S)	You're A Big Boy, Now	1967	5.00	12.00
Kama Sutra KLPS-8061	(S)	Everything Playing	1968	5.00	12.00
Kama Sutra KLPS-8064	(S)	The Best Of The Lovin' Spoonful, Volume 2	1968	5.00	12.00
Kama Sutra KOPS-750-2	(S)	24 Karat Hits	1968	6.00	15.00
Kama Sutra KLPS-8073	(S)	Revelations: Revolution '69	1969	5.00	12.00
LOWE, JIM					
Dot DLP-3051	(M)	Songs They Sang Behind The Green Door	1957	50.00	100.00
Dot DLP-3114	(M)	Wicked Women	1958	40.00	80.00
Mercury MG-20246	(M)	The Door Of Fame		16.00	40.00
LOWE & STRAUSS					
Riverside RS-7541	(M)	Folk Music For People Who Hate Folk Music	1963	5.00	12.00
Riverside RS9-7541	(S)	Folk Music For People Who Hate Folk Music	1963	6.00	15.00
LUCAS, NICK					
Decca DL-8653	(M)	Painting The Clouds With Sunshine	1957	12.00	30.00
LULU (MARIE LAWRIE)					
Fontana MGF-18030	(M)	To Sir With Love (Sdtk)	1967	5.00	12.00
Fontana SRF-67569	(S)	To Sir With Love (Sdtk)	1967	6.00	15.00
Epic LN-24339	(M)	To Sir With Love	1967	6.00	15.00
Epic BN-26339	(S)	To Sir With Love	1967	8.00	20.00
Parrot PA-61016	(M)	From Lulu With Love	1967	6.00	15.00
Parrot PAS-71016	(S)	From Lulu With Love	1967	8.00	20.00
LUMAN, BOB					
Warners W-1396	(M)	Let's Think About Livin'	1960	12.00	30.00
Warners WS-1396	(S)	Let's Think About Livin'	1960	30.00	60.00
Hickory 124	(M)	Livin' Lovin' Sounds	1965	5.00	12.00
Hickory 124	(S)	Livin' Lovin' Sounds	1965	6.00	15.00
LUTCHER, NELLIE					
Capitol H-232 (10")	(M)	Real Gone		20.00	50.00
Capitol T-232	(M)	Real Gone		16.00	40.00
Epic 1108 (10")	(M)	Whee! Nellie		20.00	50.00
Liberty LRP-3014	(M)	Our New Nellie		10.00	25.00
LYMON, FRANKIE, & THE TEENAGERS					
Gee GLP-701	(M)	The Teenagers (Red Label)	1957	180.00	300.00
Roulette R-25013	(M)	The Teenagers At The London Palladium	1958	100.00	200.00
Roulette R-25036	(M)	Rock And Roll	1958	100.00	200.00
Roulette R-25250	(M)	Jerry Blavatt Presents The Teenagers	1964	50.00	100.00
LYNN, BARBARA					
Jamie JLP-3023	(M)	You'll Lose A Good Thing	1962	10.00	25.00
Jamie JLPS-70-3023	(S)	You'll Lose A Good Thing	1962	14.00	35.00
Jamie JLP-3026	(M)	Sister Of Soul	1964	6.00	15.00
Jamie JLPS-3026	(S)	Sister Of Soul	1964	8.00	20.00
Atlantic SD-8171	(S)	Here Is Barbara Lynn	1968	6.00	15.00

Label		Title	Year	VG+	NM
LYNN, DONNA					
Capitol T-2085	(M)	Java Jones	1964	6.00	15.00
Capitol ST-2085	(S)	Java Jones	1964	8.00	20.00
LYNN, LORETTA					
Decca DL-4457	(M)	Loretta Lynn Sings	1963	16.00	40.00
Decca DL7-4457	(S)	Loretta Lynn Sings	1963	20.00	50.00
Decca DL-4541	(M)	Before I'm Over You	1964	12.00	30.00
Decca DL7-4541	(S)	Before I'm Over You	1964	16.00	40.00
Decca DL-4620	(M)	Songs From My Heart	1965	12.00	30.00
Decca DL7-4620	(S)	Songs From My Heart	1965	16.00	40.00
Decca DL-4639	(M)	Mr & Mrs Used To Be (With Ernest Tubb)	1965	10.00	25.00
Decca DL7-4639	(S)	Mr & Mrs Used To Be (With Ernest Tubb)	1965	12.00	30.00
Decca DL-4665	(M)	Blue Kentucky Girl	1965	12.00	30.00
Decca DL7-4665	(S)	Blue Kentucky Girl	1965	16.00	40.00
Decca DL-4695	(M)	Hymns	1965	8.00	20.00
Decca DL7-4695	(S)	Hymns	1965	10.00	25.00
Decca DL-4744	(M)	I Like 'Em Country	1966	8.00	20.00
Decca DL7-4744	(S)	I Like 'Em Country	1966	10.00	25.00
Decca DL-4872	(M)	Singin' Again (With Ernest Tubb)	1967	6.00	15.00
Decca DL7-4872	(S)	Singin' Again (With Ernest Tubb)	1967	8.00	20.00
Decca DL-4783	(M)	You Ain't Woman Enough	1966	8.00	20.00
Decca DL7-4783	(S)	You Ain't Woman Enough	1966	10.00	25.00
Decca DL-4817	(M)	A Country Christmas	1966	8.00	20.00
Decca DL7-4817	(S)	A Country Christmas	1966	10.00	25.00
		(Decca albums above have black labels with			
		"Mfrd. by Decca" beneath the rainbow.)			
Decca DL-4842	(M)	Don't Come Home Drinkin'	1967	6.00	15.00
Decca DL7-4842	(S)	Don't Come Home Drinkin'	1967	8.00	20.00
Decca DL-4930	(M)	Singin' With Feelin'	1967	6.00	15.00
Decca DL7-4930	(S)	Singin' With Feelin'	1967	6.00	15.00
Decca DL7-4928	(S)	Who Says God Is Dead?	1968	6.00	15.00
Decca DL7-4997	(S)	Fist City	1968	6.00	15.00
Decca DL7-5000	(S)	Loretta Lynn's Greatest Hits	1968	6.00	15.00
Decca DL7-5084	(S)	Your Squaw Is On The Warpath	1969	6.00	15.00
Decca DL7-5113	(S)	A Woman Of The World	1969	6.00	15.00
Decca DL7-5115	(S)	If We Put Our Heads Together	1969	6.00	15.00
		(With Ernest Tubb.)			
Decca DL7-5163	(S)	Wings Upon Your Horns	1970	6.00	15.00
Decca DL7-5198	(S)	Loretta Lynn Writes 'Em And Sings 'Em	1970	5.00	12.00
Decca DL7-5253	(S)	Coal Miner's Daughter	1971	5.00	12.00
Decca DL7-5282	(S)	I Wanna Be Free	1971	5.00	12.00
Decca DL7-5310	(S)	You're Lookin' At Country	1971	5.00	12.00
Decca DL7-5334	(S)	One's On The Way	1972	5.00	12.00
Decca DL7-5351	(S)	God Bless America Again	1972	5.00	12.00
Decca DL7-5381	(S)	Here I Am Again	1972	5.00	12.00

MC-5, THE (THE MOTOR CITY FIVE)					
Elektra EKS-74042	(S)	Kick Out The Jams (With liner notes)	1969	12.00	30.00
Elektra EKS-74042	(S)	Kick Out The Jams (Without liner notes)	1969	14.00	35.00
Atlantic SD-8247	(S)	Back In The U.S.A.	1970	12.00	30.00
Atlantic SD-8285	(S)	High Time	1971	16.00	40.00
MABON, WILLIE (& HIS COMBO)					
Chess 1439	(M)	Willie Mabon		40.00	80.00

Label		Title	Year	VG+	NM
MACDONALD, JEANETTE, & NELSON EDDY					
RCA Victor LPM-1738	(M)	Favorites In Hi-Fi	1959	8.00	20.00
MACK, LONNIE					
Fraternity SF-1014	(M)	The Wham Of That Memphis Man	1963	12.00	30.00
Fraternity SSF-1014	(S)	The Wham Of That Memphis Man	1963	30.00	60.00
Elektra EKS-74050	(S)	Whatever's Right	1969	8.00	20.00
Elektra EKS-74040	(S)	Glad I'm In The Band	1969	8.00	20.00
Elektra EKS-74077	(M)	For Collectors Only	1970	8.00	20.00
Elektra EKS-74012	(S)	The Hills Of Indiana	1971	8.00	20.00
MacKENZIE, GISELE					
Vik 1055	(M)	Gisele MacKenzie		10.00	25.00
Vik 1075	(M)	Mam' Selle Giselle		10.00	25.00
RCA LPM-1790	(M)	Gisele	1958	8.00	20.00
RCA LPM-2006	(M)	Christmas With Gisele	1969	8.00	20.00
MacRAE, GORDON					
Also refer to Jo Stafford.					
Capitol T-423	(M)	Memory Songs (With Jo Stafford)		10.00	25.00
Capitol T-537	(M)	Romantic Ballads		8.00	20.00
Capitol T-681	(M)	Operetta Favorites		8.00	20.00
Capitol T-765	(M)	The Best Things In Life Are Free		8.00	20.00
Capitol T-834	(M)	Cowboy's Lament		8.00	20.00
Capitol T-875	(M)	Motion Picture Soundstage		8.00	20.00
Capitol T-980	(M)	Gordon MacRae In Concert		8.00	20.00
Capitol T-1050	(M)	This Is Gordon MacRae		8.00	20.00
MAD LADS, THE					
Volt 414	(M)	The Mad Lads In Action	1966	6.00	15.00
Volt 414	(S)	The Mad Lads In Action	1966	8.00	20.00
MAD RIVER					
Capitol ST-2985	(S)	Mad River	1968	16.00	40.00
Capitol ST-185	(S)	Paradise Bar And Grill	1969	16.00	40.00
MADDOX, ROSE					
Columbia CL-1159	(M)	Precious Memories	1958	16.00	40.00
Capitol T-1312	(M)	The One Rose	1960	8.00	20.00
Capitol ST-1312	(S)	The One Rose	1960	10.00	25.00
Capitol T-1437	(M)	Glorybound Train	1960	8.00	20.00
Capitol ST-1437	(S)	Glorybound Train	1960	10.00	25.00
Capitol T-1548	(M)	A Big Bouquet Of Roses	1961	8.00	20.00
Capitol ST-1548	(S)	A Big Bouquet Of Roses	1961	10.00	25.00
Capitol T-1779	(M)	Rose Maddox Sing Bluegrass	1962	10.00	25.00
Capitol ST-1779	(S)	Rose Maddox Sing Bluegrass	1962	12.00	30.00
Capitol T-1993	(M)	Alone With You	1963	8.00	20.00
Capitol ST-1993	(S)	Alone With You	1963	10.00	25.00
MADDOX BROTHERS & ROSE					
King 669	(M)	A Collection Of Standard Sacred Songs	1956	30.00	60.00
King 677	(M)	The Maddox Brothers And Rose	1961	20.00	50.00
King 752	(M)	I'll Write Your Name In The Sand	1961	20.00	50.00
MAESTRO, JOHNNY					
Buddah BDS-5091	(P)	The Johnny Maestro Story (With inserts)	1971	16.00	40.00
MAGIC					
Armadillo 8031	(S)	Enclosed	1970	75.00	150.00
MAHAL, TAJ					
Columbia CS-9579	(S)	Taj Mahal	1968	8.00	20.00
Columbia CS-9698	(S)	Natch'l Blues	1969	8.00	20.00
Columbia 18	(S)	Giant Step	1969	6.00	15.00
		(Columbia albums above have "360 Sound" labels.)			
MAHOGANY RUSH					
Nine 936	(S)	Maxoom	1972	20.00	50.00
20th Century S-451	(S)	Child Of Nolvelty	1973	6.00	15.00
20th Century S-463	(S)	Maxoom	1975	6.00	15.00
20th Century S-482	(S)	Strange Universe	1975	6.00	15.00

Label		Title	Year	VG+	NM
MAIN ATTRACTION, THE					
Tower ST-5177	(S)	And Now	1968	8.00	20.00
MAINER, J. E.					
King 666	(M)	Good Ole Mountain Music	1960	12.00	30.00
King 765	(M)	Variety Album	1961	12.00	30.00
MAINER, WADE					
King 769	(M)	Soulful Sacred Songs	1961	12.00	30.00
MAJIC SHIP					
Bel Ami BA-711	(S)	Majic Ship	1968	150.00	250.00
MAJORS, THE					
Imperial LP-9222	(M)	Meet The Majors	1963	12.00	30.00
Imperial LP-12222	(P)	Meet The Majors	1963	14.00	35.00
MAKEBA, MIRIAM					
RCA LPM-2267	(M)	Miriam Makeba	1960	6.00	15.00
RCA LSP-2267	(S)	Miriam Makeba	1960	8.00	20.00
Kapp KL-1274	(M)	The Many Voices Of Miriam Makeba	1962	5.00	12.00
Kapp KS-3274	(S)	The Many Voices Of Miriam Makeba	1962	6.00	15.00
RCA LPM-2750	(M)	The World Of Miriam Makeba	1963	5.00	12.00
RCA LSP-2750	(S)	The World Of Miriam Makeba	1963	6.00	15.00
RCA LPM-2845	(M)	The Voice Of Africa	1964	5.00	12.00
RCA LSP-2845	(S)	The Voice Of Africa	1964	6.00	15.00
RCA LPM-3321	(M)	Makeba Sings	1965	5.00	12.00
RCA LSP-3321	(S)	Makeba Sings	1965	6.00	15.00
RCA LPM-3512	(M)	The Magic Of Makeba	1966	5.00	12.00
RCA LSP-3512	(S)	The Magic Of Makeba	1966	6.00	15.00
		(RCA albums above have black labels.)			
Mercury MG-21082	(M)	The Magnificent Miriam Makeba	1966	5.00	12.00
Mercury SR-61082	(S)	The Magnificent Miriam Makeba	1966	6.00	15.00
Mercury MG-261095	(M)	All About Miriam	1966	5.00	12.00
Mercury SR-61095	(S)	All About Miriam	1966	6.00	15.00
Reprise R-6253	(M)	Miriam Makeba In Concert!	1967	5.00	12.00
Reprise RS-6253	(S)	Miriam Makeba In Concert!	1967	6.00	15.00
Reprise R-6274	(M)	Pata Pata	1967	5.00	12.00
Reprise RS-6274	(S)	Pata Pata	1967	6.00	15.00
Reprise RS-6381	(S)	Keep Me In Mind	1970	5.00	12.00
MAMAS & THE PAPAS, THE					
Dunhill D-50006	(M)	If You Can Believe Your Eyes And Ears	1966	10.00	25.00
Dunhill DS-50006	(S)	If You Can Believe Your Eyes And Ears	1966	12.00	30.00
		(With the toilet on the cover clearly visible.)			
Dunhill D-50006	(M)	If You Can Believe Your Eyes And Ears	1966	5.00	12.00
Dunhill DS-50006	(S)	If You Can Believe Your Eyes And Ears	1966	6.00	15.00
		(With the toilet on the cover concealed.)			
Dunhill DS-50006	(S)	If You Can Believe Your Eyes And Ears	1966	10.00	25.00
		(Record club release with a black border along the bottom of the cover.)			
Dunhill D-50010	(M)	The Mamas And The Papas	1966	5.00	12.00
Dunhill DS-50010	(S)	The Mamas And The Papas	1966	6.00	15.00
Dunhill D-50014	(M)	The Mamas And The Papas Deliver	1967	5.00	12.00
Dunhill DS-50014	(S)	The Mamas And The Papas Deliver	1967	6.00	15.00
		(Dunhill albums above have black labels with "Dist. by ABC-Paramount" on the bottom.)			
Dunhill D-50025	(M)	Farewell To The First Golden Era	1967	6.00	15.00
Dunhill DS-50025	(S)	Farewell To The First Golden Era	1967	5.00	12.00
Dunhill DS-50031	(S)	The Papas And The Mamas	1968	6.00	15.00
		(Dunhill albums above have black labels with "A Subsidiary of ABC Records" on the bottom.)			
MANCHESTER, MELLISA					
Mobile Fidelity 1-028	(S)	Mellisa Manchester		8.00	20.00
MANCINI, HENRY					
RCA LPM-1956	(M)	Music From "Peter Gunn"	1959	5.00	12.00
RCA LSP-1956	(S)	Music From "Peter Gunn"	1959	8.00	20.00
RCA LPM-2040	(M)	More Music From "Peter Gunn"	1959	5.00	12.00
RCA LSP-2040	(S)	More Music From "Peter Gunn"	1959	8.00	20.00

Label		Title	Year	VG+	NM
RCA LPM-2198	(M)	Music From Mr. Lucky (Sdtk)	1960	5.00	12.00
RCA LSP-2198	(S)	Music From Mr. Lucky (Sdtk)	1960	8.00	20.00
RCA LPM-2258	(M)	Combo! The Original "Peter Gunn"	1961	5.00	12.00
RCA LPM-2258	(S)	Combo! The Original "Peter Gunn"	1961	8.00	20.00
RCA LPM-2360	(M)	Mr. Lucky Goes Latin	1961	5.00	12.00
RCA LSP-2360	(S)	Mr. Lucky Goes Latin	1961	8.00	20.00
RCA LPM-2362	(M)	Breakfast At Tiffany's (Sdtk)	1961	5.00	12.00
RCA LSP-2362	(S)	Breakfast At Tiffany's (Sdtk)	1961	8.00	20.00
RCA LPM-2442	(M)	Experiment In Terror (Sdtk)	1962	10.00	25.00
RCA LSP-2442	(S)	Experiment In Terror (Sdtk)	1962	12.00	30.00
		(The cover has Lee Remick being kidnapped.)			
RCA LPM-2442	(M)	Experiment In Terror (Sdtk)	1962	5.00	12.00
RCA LSP-2442	(S)	Experiment In Terror (Sdtk)	1962	8.00	20.00
		(The cover depicts two mannequins.)			
RCA LPM-2559	(M)	Hatari! (Sdtk)	1962	5.00	12.00
RCA LSP-2559	(S)	Hatari! (Sdtk)	1962	8.00	20.00
		(Mono RCA albums above have "Long Play" on the bottom of the label. Stereo albums have "Living Stereo" on the bottom.)			
RCA LPM-2755	(M)	Charade (Sdtk)	1963	4.00	10.00
RCA LSP-2755	(S)	Charade (Sdtk)	1963	5.00	12.00
RCA LPM-2795	(M)	The Pink Panther (Sdtk)	1964	4.00	10.00
RCA LSP-2795	(S)	The Pink Panther (Sdtk)	1964	5.00	12.00
RCA LPM-3402	(M)	The Great Race (Sdtk)	1965	5.00	12.00
RCA LSP-3402	(S)	The Great Race (Sdtk)	1965	6.00	15.00
RCA LPM-3623	(M)	Arabesque (Sdtk)	1966	5.00	12.00
RCA LSP-3623	(S)	Arabesque (Sdtk)	1966	6.00	15.00
RCA LPM-3648	(M)	What Did You Do In The War, Daddy? (Sdtk)	1966	5.00	12.00
RCA LSP-3648	(S)	What Did You Do In The War, Daddy? (Sdtk)	1966	6.00	15.00
RCA LPM-3802	(M)	Two For The Road (Sdtk)	1967	5.00	12.00
RCA LSP-3802	(S)	Two For The Road (Sdtk)	1967	6.00	15.00
RCA LPM-3840	(M)	Gunn (Sdtk)	1967	5.00	12.00
RCA LSP-3840	(S)	Gunn (Sdtk)	1967	6.00	15.00
RCA LPM-3997	(M)	The Party (Sdtk)	1968	6.00	15.00
RCA LSP-3997	(S)	The Party (Sdtk)	1968	6.00	15.00
		(RCA albums above have black labels.)			
RCA APD1-0098	(Q)	Brass, Ivory And Strings	1973	4.00	10.00
RCA APD1-1025	(Q)	Symphonic Soul	1975	4.00	10.00

MANDRAKE MEMORIAL

Label		Title	Year	VG+	NM
Poppy PYS-40,002	(S)	Mandrake Memorial	1968	6.00	15.00
Poppy PYS-40,003	(S)	Medium	1969	6.00	15.00
Poppy PYS-40,006	(S)	Puzzle	1970	6.00	15.00

MANFRED MANN

Label		Title	Year	VG+	NM
Ascot ALM-13015	(M)	The Manfred Mann Album	1964	10.00	25.00
Ascot ALS-16015	(S)	The Manfred Mann Album	1964	12.00	30.00
Ascot ALM-13018	(M)	The Five Faces Of Manfred Mann	1965	8.00	20.00
Ascot ALS-16018	(S)	The Five Faces Of Manfred Mann	1965	10.00	25.00
Ascot ALM-13021	(M)	My Little Red Book Of Winners	1965	10.00	25.00
Ascot ALS-16021	(S)	My Little Red Book Of Winners	1965	12.00	30.00
Ascot ALM-13024	(M)	Mann Made	1966	8.00	20.00
Ascot ALS-16024	(S)	Mann Made	1966	10.00	25.00
United Arts. UAL-4128	(M)	What's New, Pussycat? (Sdtk)	1965	4.00	10.00
United Arts. UAS-5128	(S)	What's New, Pussycat? (Sdtk)	1965	5.00	12.00
United Arts. UAL-3549	(M)	Pretty Flamingo	1966	6.00	15.00
United Arts. UAS-6549	(S)	Pretty Flamingo	1966	8.00	20.00
United Arts. UAL-3551	(M)	Manfred Mann's Greatest Hits	1966	6.00	15.00
United Arts. UAS-6551	(P)	Manfred Mann's Greatest Hits	1966	8.00	20.00
United Arts. UAS-5177	(S)	Charge Of The Light Brigade (Sdtk)	1968	5.00	12.00
Mercury SR-61168	(S)	The Mighty Quinn	1968	8.00	20.00

MANHATTAN TRANSFER, THE

Label		Title	Year	VG+	NM
Mobile Fidelity 1-022	(S)	Live	1978	8.00	20.00

MANHATTANS, THE

Label		Title	Year	VG+	NM
Carnival CLPS-201	(S)	Dedicated To You		6.00	15.00
Carnival CLPS-202	(S)	For You And Yours		6.00	15.00
Deluxe DLP-12000	(S)	With These Hands	1970	6.00	15.00
Deluxe DLP-12004	(S)	A Million To One	1972	6.00	15.00
Columbia PCQ-34450	(Q)	It Feels So Good	1977	5.00	12.00

Label		Title	Year	VG+	NM
MANILOW, BARRY					
Bell 1129	(S)	Barry Manilow	1972	6.00	15.00
Bell 1314	(S)	Barry Manilow II	1973	6.00	15.00
Arista AQ-4016	(Q)	Barry Manilow II	1974	10.00	25.00
Arista AQ-6060	(Q)	Tryin' To Get That Feeling	1975	10.00	25.00
Mobile Fidelity 1-097	(S)	I		5.00	12.00
MANN, BARRY					
ABC-Paramount 399	(M)	Who Put The Bomp	1963	16.00	40.00
ABC-Paramount S-399	(S)	Who Put The Bomp	1963	20.00	50.00
MANN, CARL					
Phillips International 1960	(M)	Like Mann	1960	300.00	500.00
MANSFIELD, JAYNE					
20th Century	(M)	Jayne Mansfield Busts Up Las Vegas		14.00	35.00
MGM E-4204	(M)	Shakespeare, Tchaikovsky And Me	1964	8.00	20.00
MGM SE-4204	(S)	Shakespeare, Tchaikovsky And Me	1964	10.00	25.00
MANSON, CHARLES					
Awareness 22145	(M)	Lie	1970	50.00	100.00
MAPHIS, JOE					
Columbia CL-1005	(M)	Fire On The Strings ("Eye" logo label)	1957	20.00	50.00
MAPHIS, JOE & ROSE LEE					
Capitol T-1778	(M)	With The Blue Ridge Mountain Boys	1962	8.00	20.00
Capitol ST-1778	(S)	With The Blue Ridge Mountain Boys	1962	10.00	25.00
Starday SLP-286	(S)	Mr. And Mrs. Country Music	1964	8.00	20.00
MAPHIS, ROSE LEE					
Columbia CL-1598	(M)	Rose Lee Maphis ("Eye" logo label)	1961	6.00	15.00
Columbia CS-8398	(S)	Rose Lee Maphis ("Eye" logo label)	1961	8.00	20.00
MAR-KEYS, THE					
Also refer to Booker T. & The MG's.					
Atlantic 8055	(M)	Last Night	1961	8.00	20.00
Atlantic SD-8055	(E)	Last Night	1961	10.00	25.00
Atlantic 8062	(M)	Do The Pop-Eye With The Mar-Kays	1962	8.00	20.00
Atlantic SD-8062	(S)	Do The Pop-Eye With The Mar-Keys	1962	10.00	25.00
MARATHONS, THE					
Arvee A-428	(M)	Peanut Butter	1961	50.00	100.00
MARBLE PHROGG, THE					
Derrick 8868	(S)	The Marble Phrogg	1968	300.00	500.00
MARCELS, THE					
Colpix CP-416	(M)	Blue Moon (Gold Label)	1961	50.00	100.00
MARCH, LITTLE PEGGY					
RCA LPM-2732	(M)	I Will Follow Him	1963	10.00	25.00
RCA LSP-2732	(S)	I Will Follow Him	1963	14.00	35.00
RCA LPM-3408	(M)	In Our Fashion	1965	14.00	35.00
RCA LSP-3408	(S)	In Our Fashion	1965	16.00	45.00
RCA LSP-3883	(S)	No Foolin'	1968	10.00	25.00
MARCHAN, BOBBY					
Sphere Sound SSR-7004	(M)	There's Something On Your Mind	1964	20.00	50.00
MARESCA, ERNIE					
Seville SV-77001	(M)	Shout! Shout! Knock Yourself Out	1962	12.00	30.00
Seville 87001	(S)	Shout! Shout! Knock Yourself Out	1962	16.00	40.00
MARKETTS, THE					
Liberty LRP-3226	(M)	Surfer's Stomp	1962	10.00	25.00
Liberty LST-7226	(S)	Surfer's Stomp	1962	12.00	30.00
Liberty LRP-3226	(M)	The Surfing Scene	1963	8.00	20.00
Liberty LST-7226	(S)	The Surfing Scene	1963	10.00	25.00
Warners T-1509	(M)	Take To Wheels	1963	6.00	15.00
Warners ST-1509	(S)	Take To Wheels	1963	8.00	20.00

Peggy March & Bennie Thomas, *In Our Fashion.* Little Peggy, best known for her #1 hit in 1963, the pre-feminist "I Will Follow Him," released three albums on RCA. Oddly, each is rather difficult to find; even more odd is the fact that the stereo versions are extremely scare. This, her third album, recorded with Bennie Thomas, is the rarest and regularly appears on the want-lists of '60s pop collectors.

Guy Marks, *Loving You Has Made Me Bananas.* The wacky novelty title tune, a mish-mash of old vaudevillian cliches, came out of left field in the spring of 1968, scoring very highly on a number of prominent regional charts. The album's cover adequately sums up its contents.

Label		Title	Year	VG+	NM
Warners T-1537	(M)	Out Of Limits	1964	6.00	15.00
Warners ST-1537	(S)	Out Of Limits	1964	8.00	20.00
Warners T-1642	(M)	Batman Theme	1966	6.00	15.00
Warners ST-1642	(S)	Batman Theme	1966	8.00	20.00
World Pacific T-1870	(M)	Sun Power	1967	4.00	10.00
World Pacific ST-1870	(S)	Sun Power	1967	5.00	12.00
Mercury SRM-1-679	(S)	AM, FM, Etc	1973	4.00	10.00

MARKLEY

Forward 1007	(S)	Markley: A Group	1969	12.00	30.00

MARKS, GUY

ABC 648	(M)	Loving You Has Made Me Bananas	1967	5.00	12.00
ABC S-648	(S)	Loving You Has Made Me Bananas	1967	6.00	15.00

MARLEY, BOB, & THE WAILERS

Island SW-9256	(S)	Burnin'	1975	6.00	15.00
Island SW-9329	(S)	Catch A Fire	1975	16.00	40.00
		(Cigarette lighter cover opens on the side)			
Island SW-9329	(S)	Catch A Fire	1975	4.00	10.00
Island SW-9281	(S)	Natty Dread	1975	4.00	10.00
Island SW-9376	(S)	Bob Marley Live	1976	4.00	10.00
Island SW-9383	(S)	Rastaman Vibrations	1976	4.00	10.00
		(Island albums above have black labels with an "i" on the bottom.)			

MARSHALL, JACK

Capitol T-1939	(M)	My Son The Surf Nut	1963	6.00	15.00
Capitol ST-1939	(S)	My Son The Surf Nut	1963	8.00	20.00

MARTHA & THE VANDELLAS

Gordy 902	(M)	Come And Get These Memories	1963	20.00	50.00
Gordy GS-902	(S)	Come And Get These Memories	1963	30.00	60.00
Gordy 907	(M)	Heat Wave	1963	14.00	35.00
Gordy GS-907	(S)	Heat Wave	1963	16.00	40.00
Gordy 915	(M)	Dance Party	1965	8.00	20.00
Gordy GS-915	(S)	Dance Party	1965	10.00	25.00
Gordy 917	(M)	Martha And The Vandellas' Greatest Hits	1966	5.00	12.00
Gordy GS-917	(S)	Martha And The Vandellas' Greatest Hits	1966	6.00	15.00
Gordy 920	(M)	Watchout!	1967	5.00	12.00
Gordy GS-920	(S)	Watchout!	1967	6.00	15.00
Gordy 925	(M)	Martha And The Vandellas' Live!	1967	5.00	12.00
Gordy GS-925	(S)	Martha And The Vandellas' Live!	1967	6.00	15.00
Gordy GS-926	(S)	Ridin' High	1968	4.00	10.00
Gordy GS-944	(S)	Sugar 'N Spice	1969	4.00	10.00
Gordy GS-952	(S)	Natural Resources	1970	4.00	10.00
Gordy GS-958	(S)	Black Magic	1972	4.00	10.00

MARTIN, DEAN

Capitol L-401 (10")	(M)	The Stooge (Sdtk)	1952	16.00	40.00
Capitol T-401	(M)	The Stooge (Sdtk)	1956	12.00	30.00
Capitol T-576	(M)	Swingin' Down Yonder		12.00	30.00
Capitol T-849	(M)	Pretty Baby		12.00	30.00
Capitol T-1047	(M)	This Is Martin		12.00	30.00
		(Capitol albums above have turquoise labels.)			
Capitol T-1150	(M)	Sleep Warm	1959	6.00	15.00
Capitol ST-1150	(S)	Sleep Warm	1959	8.00	20.00
Capitol T-1285	(M)	Winter Romance	1959	6.00	15.00
Capitol ST-1285	(S)	Winter Romance	1959	8.00	20.00
Capitol W-1435	(M)	Bells Are Ringing (Sdtk)	1960	6.00	15.00
Capitol SW-1435	(S)	Bells Are Ringing (Sdtk)	1960	8.00	20.00
Capitol T-1442	(M)	This Time I'm Swingin'	1961	6.00	15.00
Capitol ST-1442	(S)	This Time I'm Swingin'	1961	8.00	20.00
Capitol W-1580	(M)	Dean Martin	1961	6.00	15.00
Capitol SW-1580	(S)	Dean Martin	1961	8.00	20.00
Capitol T-1659	(M)	Dino	1962	6.00	15.00
Capitol ST-1659	(S)	Dino	1962	8.00	20.00
		(Capitol albums above have black labels with the Capitol logo on the left side.)			
Capitol T-2212	(M)	Hey Brother, Pour The Wine	1964	5.00	12.00
Capitol DT-2212	(E)	Hey Brother, Pour The Wine	1964	4.00	10.00

Label		Title	Year	VG+	NM
Capitol T-2297	(M)	Dean Martin Sings, Sinatra Conducts	1965	6.00	15.00
Capitol ST-2297	(S)	Dean Martin Sings, Sinatra Conducts	1965	8.00	20.00
Capitol T-2333	(M)	Southern Style	1965	5.00	12.00
Capitol DT-2333	(E)	Southern Style	1965	4.00	10.00
Capitol TT-2343	(M)	Holiday Cheer	1965	4.00	10.00
Capitol STT-2343	(S)	Holiday Cheer	1965	5.00	12.00
Tower T-5006	(M)	Lush Years	1965	3.50	8.00
Tower ST-5006	(S)	Lush Years	1965	4.00	10.00
Tower T-5018	(M)	Relaxin'	1966	3.50	8.00
Tower ST-5018	(S)	Relaxin'	1966	4.00	10.00
Tower T-5036	(M)	Happy In Love	1966	3.50	8.00
Tower ST-5036	(S)	Happy In Love	1966	4.00	10.00
Capitol T-2601	(M)	The Best Of Dean Martin	1966	4.00	10.00
Capitol DT-2601	(E)	The Best Of Dean Martin	1966	3.50	8.00
Capitol TCL-2815	(M)	Deluxe Set	1967	8.00	20.00
Capitol DTCL-2815	(E)	Deluxe Set	1967	6.00	15.00
Capitol DT-2941	(E)	Favorites	1968	4.00	10.00
		(Capitol albums above have black labels with the Capitol logo on top.)			
Reprise R-6021	(M)	French Style	1962	3.50	8.00
Reprise RS-6021	(S)	French Style	1962	4.00	10.00
Reprise R-6054	(M)	Dino Latino	1963	3.50	8.00
Reprise RS-6054	(S)	Dino Latino	1963	4.00	10.00
Reprise R-6061	(M)	Country Style	1963	3.50	8.00
Reprise RS-6061	(S)	Country Style	1963	4.00	10.00
Reprise R-6085	(M)	Dean "Tex" Martin Rides Again	1963	3.50	8.00
Reprise RS-6085	(S)	Dean "Tex" Martin Rides Again	1963	4.00	10.00
Reprise R-6123	(M)	Dream With Dean	1964	2.50	6.00
Reprise RS-6123	(S)	Dream With Dean	1964	3.50	8.00
Reprise R-6130	(M)	Everybody Loves Somebody	1964	2.50	6.00
Reprise RS-6130	(S)	Everybody Loves Somebody	1964	3.50	8.00
Reprise R-6140	(M)	The Door Is Still Open To My Heart	1964	2.50	6.00
Reprise RS-6140	(S)	The Door Is Still Open To My Heart	1964	3.50	8.00
Reprise R-6146	(M)	Dean Martin Hits Again	1965	2.50	6.00
Reprise RS-6146	(S)	Dean Martin Hits Again	1965	3.50	8.00
Reprise R-6170	(M)	Remember Me I'm The One Who Loves You	1965	2.50	6.00
Reprise RS-6170	(S)	Remember Me I'm The One Who Loves You	1965	3.50	8.00
Reprise R-6181	(M)	Houston	1965	2.50	6.00
Reprise RS-6181	(S)	Houston	1965	3.50	8.00
Reprise R-6201	(M)	Somewhere There's A Someone	1966	2.50	6.00
Reprise RS-6201	(S)	Somewhere There's A Someone	1966	3.50	8.00
Reprise R-6211	(M)	Songs From The Silencers	1966	2.50	6.00
Reprise RS-6211	(S)	Songs From The Silencers	1966	3.50	8.00
Reprise R-6213	(M)	The Hit Sound Of Dean Martin	1966	2.00	5.00
Reprise RS-6213	(S)	The Hit Sound Of Dean Martin	1966	2.50	6.00
Reprise R-6222	(M)	Christmas Album	1966	2.00	5.00
Reprise RS-6222	(S)	Christmas Album	1966	2.50	6.00
Reprise R-6233	(M)	The Dean Martin TV Show	1966	2.00	5.00
Reprise RS-6233	(S)	The Dean Martin TV Show	1966	2.50	6.00
Reprise R-6242	(M)	Happiness Is Dean Martin	1967	2.00	5.00
Reprise RS-6242	(S)	Happiness Is Dean Martin	1967	2.50	6.00
Reprise R-6250	(M)	Welcome To My World	1967	2.00	5.00
Reprise RS-6250	(S)	Welcome To My World	1967	2.50	6.00
		(Reprise albums above have pink, gold & green steamboat labels.)			
Reprise RS-6301	(S)	Dean Martin's Greatest Hits! Volume 1	1968	2.00	5.00
Reprise RS-6320	(S)	Dean Martin's Greatest Hits! Volume 2	1968	2.00	5.00
Reprise RS-6330	(S)	Gentle On My Mind	1969	2.00	5.00
Reprise RS-6338	(S)	I Take A Lot Of Pride In What I Am	1969	2.00	5.00
Reprise RS-6403	(S)	My Woman, My Woman, My Wife	1970	2.00	5.00
Reprise RS-6428	(S)	For The Good Times	1971	2.00	5.00
Reprise MS-2053	(S)	Dino	1972	2.00	5.00

MARTIN, GEORGE (& HIS ORCHESTRA)

Mr. Martin was the "fifth" Beatle, producer of all of their work, 1962-1969.

United Arts. UAL-3377	(M)	Off The Beatle Track	1964	16.00	40.00
United Arts. UAS-6377	(S)	Off The Beatle Track	1964	20.00	50.00
United Arts. UAL-3366	(M)	A Hard Day's Night (Sdtk)	1964	20.00	50.00
United Arts. UAL-3366	(P)	A Hard Day's Night (Sdtk)	1964	16.00	40.00
United Arts. UAL-3383	(M)	A Hard Day's Night	1964	12.00	30.00
United Arts. UAS-6383	(S)	A Hard Day's Night	1964	14.00	35.00

Label		Title	Year	VG+	NM
United Arts. UAL-3387	(M)	Ferry Cross The Mersey (Sdtk)	1965	12.00	30.00
United Arts. UAS-6387	(S)	Ferry Cross The Mersey (Sdtk)	1965	14.00	35.00
United Arts. UAL-3420	(M)	George Martin	1965	10.00	25.00
United Arts. UAS-6420	(S)	George Martin	1965	12.00	30.00
United Arts. UAL-3448	(M)	George Martin Plays "Help"	1965	12.00	30.00
United Arts. UAS-6448	(S)	George Martin Plays "Help"	1965	14.00	35.00
United Arts. UAL-3539	(M)	George Martin Salutes The Beatle Girls	1966	12.00	30.00
United Arts. UAS-6539	(S)	George Martin Salutes The Beatle Girls	1966	14.00	35.00
United Arts. UAL-3647	(M)	London By George	1967	8.00	20.00
United Arts. UAS-6647	(S)	London By George	1967	10.00	25.00
Apple SW-153	(P)	Yellow Submarine (Sdtk)	1968	6.00	15.00
United Arts. LA100	(S)	Live And Let Die (Sdtk)	1973	6.00	15.00

MARVELETTES, THE

Label		Title	Year	VG+	NM
Tamla 228	(M)	Please Mr. Postman	1961	50.00	100.00
Tamla 229	(M)	The Marvelettes Sing	1962	35.00	70.00
Tamla 231	(M)	Playboy	1962	30.00	60.00
Tamla 237	(M)	The Marvelous Marvelettes	1963	20.00	50.00
Tamla 243	(M)	On Stage	1963	16.00	40.00
Tamla 253	(M)	The Marvelettes' Greatest Hits	1966	6.00	15.00
Tamla TS-253	(S)	The Marvelettes' Greatest Hits	1966	8.00	20.00
Tamla 274	(M)	The Marvelettes	1967	5.00	12.00
Tamla TS-274	(S)	The Marvelettes	1967	6.00	15.00
Tamla TS-286	(S)	Sophisticated Soul	1968	5.00	12.00
Tamla TS-288	(S)	The Marvelettes In Full Bloom	1969	5.00	12.00
Tamla TS-305	(S)	Return Of The Marvelettes	1970	5.00	12.00

MARX, GROUCHO

Label		Title	Year	VG+	NM
Decca DL-5405 (10")	(M)	Hooray For Captain Spaulding		100.00	200.00
A&M SP-3515	(M)	An Evening With Groucho	1972	6.00	15.00
A&M SP-3515	(M)	An Evening With Groucho (Picture disc)	1972	16.00	40.00

MARX, HARPO

Label		Title	Year	VG+	NM
Mercury MG-20232	(M)	Harpo In Hi-Fi		16.00	40.00
Mercury SR-60232	(M)	Harpo In Hi-Fi		20.00	50.00
RCA LPM-2720	(M)	Harp By Harpo	1963	14.00	35.00
RCA LSP-2720	(S)	Harp By Harpo	1963	16.00	40.00

MARX BROTHERS, THE (GROUCHO, HARPO & ZEPPO MARX)

Label		Title	Year	VG+	NM
Decca DL7-9168	(E)	The Marx Brothers	1969	8.00	20.00

MASKED MARAUDERS, THE

Label		Title	Year	VG+	NM
Reprise RS-6378	(S)	The Masked Marauders	1969	6.00	15.00

MASON, BARBARA

Label		Title	Year	VG+	NM
Arctic ALP-1000	(M)	Yes, I'm Ready	1965	6.00	15.00
Arctic ALPS-1000	(S)	Yes, I'm Ready	1965	8.00	20.00
Arctic ALPS-1004	(S)	Oh, How It Hurts	1968	6.00	15.00

MASON, DAVE

Label		Title	Year	VG+	NM
Blue Thumb BTS-19	(S)	All Together (Multi-colored vinyl)	1970	10.00	25.00
Blue Thumb BTS-19	(S)	All Together	1970	6.00	15.00
Blue Thumb BTS-25	(S)	Dave Mason And Cass Elliot	1969	5.00	12.00
Columbia PCQ-31721	(Q)	It's Like You Never Left	1974	5.00	12.00
Columbia PCQ-33096	(Q)	Dave Mason	1974	5.00	12.00
Columbia PCQ-33698	(Q)	Split Coconut	1976	5.00	12.00

MASON, LINDA

Label		Title	Year	VG+	NM
RIC R-1005	(M)	How Many Seas Must A White Dove Sail?	1964	6.00	15.00

MASON PROFITT

Label		Title	Year	VG+	NM
Happy Tiger HT-1009	(S)	Wanted! Mason Profitt	1970	6.00	15.00
Happy Tiger HT-1019	(S)	Movin' Toward Happiness	1971	6.00	15.00

MATCHBOX WHOOPEE BAND, CAPTAIN

Label		Title	Year	VG+	NM
ESP 3009	(S)	Smoke Dreams	1973	6.00	15.00

MATHIS, JOHNNY

Label		Title	Year	VG+	NM
Columbia CL-887	(M)	Johnny Mathis	1957	14.00	35.00
Columbia CL-1028	(M)	Wonderful, Wonderful	1957	14.00	35.00
Columbia CL-1078	(M)	Warm	1957	14.00	35.00

Label		Title	Year	VG+	NM
Columbia CL-1090	(M)	Wild Is The Wind (Sdtk)	1957	20.00	50.00
Columbia CL-1119	(M)	Good Night, Dear Lord	1958	14.00	35.00
Columbia CL-1133	(M)	Johnny's Greatest Hits	1958	14.00	35.00
Columbia CL-1165	(M)	Swing Softly	1958	14.00	35.00
Columbia CL-1194	(M)	A Certain Smile (Sdtk)	1958	16.00	40.00
Columbia CL-1195	(M)	Merry Christmas	1958	14.00	35.00
Columbia CL-1270	(M)	Open Fire, Two Guitars	1959	14.00	35.00
Columbia CL-1344	(M)	More Johnny's Greatest Hits	1959	10.00	25.00
Columbia CL-1351	(M)	Heavenly	1959	6.00	15.00
Columbia CS-8152	(S)	Heavenly	1959	8.00	20.00
Columbia CL-1419	(M)	Faithfully	1960	6.00	15.00
Columbia CS-8219	(S)	Faithfully	1960	8.00	20.00
Columbia CL-1526	(M)	Johnny's Moods	1960	6.00	15.00
Columbia CS-8326	(S)	Johnny's Moods	1960	8.00	20.00
Columbia C2L-803	(M)	The Rhythms And Ballads Of Broadway	1960	8.00	20.00
Columbia C2S-803	(S)	The Rhythms And Ballads Of Broadway	1960	10.00	25.00
Columbia CL-1623	(M)	I'll Buy You A Star	1961	5.00	12.00
Columbia CS-8423	(S)	I'll Buy You A Star	1961	6.00	15.00
Columbia CL-1644	(M)	Portrait Of Johnny	1961	5.00	12.00
Columbia CS-8444	(S)	Portrait Of Johnny	1961	6.00	15.00
		(With a bonus portrait, priced separately below.)			
		Portrait Of Johnny Bonus Portrait	1961	6.00	15.00
Columbia CL-1711	(M)	Live It Up!	1962	5.00	12.00
Columbia CS-8511	(S)	Live It Up!	1962	6.00	15.00
		(Columbia albums above have six			
		black "eye" logos on each label.)			
Columbia CL-1834	(M)	Johnny's Greatest Hits	1962	6.00	15.00
Columbia CS-8634	(E)	Johnny's Greatest Hits	1962	4.00	10.00
Columbia CL-1915	(M)	Rapture	1962	3.50	8.00
Columbia CS-8715	(S)	Rapture	1962	4.00	10.00
Columbia CL-2016	(M)	Johnny's Newest Hits	1963	4.00	10.00
Columbia CS-8816	(S)	Johnny's Newest Hits	1963	5.00	12.00
Columbia CL-2044	(M)	Johnny	1963	3.50	8.00
Columbia CS-8844	(S)	Johnny	1963	4.00	10.00
Columbia CL-2098	(M)	Romantically	1963	3.50	8.00
Columbia CS-8898	(S)	Romantically	1963	4.00	10.00
Columbia CL-2143	(M)	I'll Search My Heart And Other Great Hits	1964	3.50	8.00
Columbia CS-8943	(S)	I'll Search My Heart And Other Great Hits	1964	4.00	10.00
Columbia C2L-834	(M)	The Great Years	1964	3.50	8.00
Columbia C2S-834	(S)	The Great Years	1964	4.00	10.00
Columbia CL-2223	(M)	The Ballads Of Broadway	1964	3.50	8.00
Columbia CS-9023	(S)	The Ballads Of Broadway	1964	4.00	10.00
Columbia CL-2224	(M)	The Rhythms Of Broadway	1964	3.50	8.00
Columbia CS-9024	(S)	The Rhythms Of Broadway	1964	4.00	10.00
Columbia CL-2246	(E)	Wonderful! Wonderful!	1964	4.00	10.00
Columbia CS-9046	(E)	Wonderful! Wonderful!	1964	3.50	8.00
		(Columbia albums above have "360 Sound" labels.)			
Mercury MG-20837	(M)	The Sound Of Christmas	1964	4.00	12.00
Mercury SR-60837	(S)	The Sound Of Christmas	1964	5.00	15.00
Mercury MG-20890	(M)	Tender Is The Night	1964	4.00	12.00
Mercury SR-60890	(S)	Tender Is The Night	1964	5.00	15.00
Mercury MG-20913	(M)	The Wonderful World Of Make Believe	1964	4.00	12.00
Mercury SR-60913	(S)	The Wonderful World Of Make Believe	1964	5.00	15.00
Mercury MG-20942	(M)	This Is Love	1964	4.00	12.00
Mercury SR-60942	(S)	This Is Love	1964	5.00	15.00
Mercury MG-20988	(M)	Johnny Mathis Ole	1964	4.00	12.00
Mercury SR-60988	(S)	Johnny Mathis Ole	1964	5.00	15.00
Mercury MG-20991	(M)	Love Is Everything	1965	4.00	12.00
Mercury SR-60991	(S)	Love Is Everything	1965	5.00	15.00
Mercury MG-21041	(M)	The Sweetheart Tree	1965	4.00	12.00
Mercury SR-61041	(S)	The Sweetheart Tree	1965	5.00	15.00
Mercury MG-21073	(M)	The Shadow Of Your Smile	1966	4.00	12.00
Mercury SR-61073	(S)	The Shadow Of Your Smile	1966	5.00	15.00
Mercury MG-21091	(M)	So Nice	1966	4.00	12.00
Mercury SR-61091	(S)	So Nice	1966	5.00	15.00
Mercury MG-21107	(M)	Johnny Mathis Sings	1967	4.00	12.00
Mercury SR-61107	(S)	Johnny Mathis Sings	1967	5.00	15.00
MGM E-4446	(M)	The Biggest Bundle Of Them All (Sdtk)	1967	5.00	12.00
MGM SE-4446	(S)	The Biggest Bundle Of Them All (Sdtk)	1967	6.00	15.00
Columbia CL-2726	(M)	Up, Up And Away	1967	2.50	6.00
Columbia CS-9526	(S)	Up, Up And Away	1967	3.50	8.00

Label		Title	Year	VG+	NM
Columbia CL-2837	(M)	Love Is Blue	1968	2.50	6.00
Columbia CS-9637	(S)	Love Is Blue	1968	3.50	8.00
Columbia CS-2905	(M)	Those Were The Days	1968	2.50	6.00
Columbia CS-9705	(S)	Those Were The Days	1968	3.50	8.00
Columbia CS-9871	(S)	People	1969	3.50	8.00
Columbia CS-9872	(S)	The Impossible Dream	1969	3.50	8.00
Columbia CS-9909	(S)	Romeo And Juliet	1969	3.50	8.00
		(Columbia albums above have "360 Sound" labels.)			
Columbia CQ-30740	(Q)	You've Got A Friend	1971	4.00	12.00
Columbia CQ-30979	(Q)	Johnny Mathis In Person	1972	6.00	15.00
Columbia CQ-31626	(Q)	Song Sung Blue	1972	4.00	12.00
Columbia CQ-32114	(Q)	Me And Mrs Jones	1973	4.00	12.00
Columbia CQ-32435	(Q)	I'm Coming Home	1973	4.00	12.00
Columbia CQ-33420	(Q)	When Will I See You Again	1975	4.00	12.00
Mobile Fidelity 1-171	(S)	Heavenly		6.00	15.00

MAUDS, THE

Label		Title	Year	VG+	NM
Mercury MG-21135	(M)	The Mauds Hold On	1967	5.00	12.00
Mercury SR-61135	(S)	The Mauds Hold On	1967	6.00	15.00

MAXWELL, DIANE

Label		Title	Year	VG+	NM
Challenge CHL-607	(M)	Almost Seventeen	1959	10.00	25.00
Challenge CHS-2501	(S)	Almost Seventeen	1959	12.00	30.00

MAY, BILLY

Label		Title	Year	VG+	NM
Capitol T-562	(M)	Sorta May	1955	8.00	20.00

MAYALL, JOHN (JOHN MAYALL'S BLUESBREAKERS)
Also refer to the Groundhogs.

Label		Title	Year	VG+	NM
London LL-3492	(M)	Blues Breakers With Eric Clapton	1967	6.00	15.00
London PS-492	(S)	Blues Breakers With Eric Clapton	1967	8.00	20.00
London LL-3502	(M)	A Hard Road	1967	5.00	12.00
London PS-502	(S)	A Hard Road	1967	6.00	15.00
London PS-529	(S)	Crusade	1968	6.00	15.00
London PS-534	(S)	The Blues Alone	1968	5.00	12.00
London PS-537	(S)	Bare Wires	1968	5.00	12.00
London PS-545	(S)	Blues From Laurel Canyon	1969	5.00	12.00

MAYER, NATHANIEL

Label		Title	Year	VG+	NM
Fortune 8014	(M)	Going Back To The Village Of Love	1964	14.00	35.00

MAZE

Label		Title	Year	VG+	NM
M.T.A. 5012	(S)	Armageddon	1971	20.00	50.00

McAULIFF, LEON (& HIS CIMMARON BOYS)

Label		Title	Year	VG+	NM
Dot DLP-3139	(M)	Take Off	1958	10.00	25.00
ABC-Paramount 394	(M)	Cozy Inn	1961	8.00	20.00
ABC-Paramount S-394	(S)	Cozy Inn	1961	10.00	25.00
Capitol T-2016	(M)	The Dancin'est Band Around	1964	5.00	12.00
Capitol ST-2016	(S)	The Dancin'est Band Around	1964	6.00	15.00
Capitol T-2148	(M)	Everybody Dance! Everybody Swing!	1964	5.00	12.00
Capitol ST-2148	(S)	Everybody Dance! Everybody Swing!	1964	6.00	15.00

McCALL, MARY ANN

Label		Title	Year	VG+	NM
Discovery 3011 (10")	(M)	Mary Ann McCall Sings		8.00	20.00
Regent 6040	(M)	Easy Living		6.00	15.00
Jubilee 1078	(M)	Detour To The Moon		6.00	15.00
Coral CRL-56276	(M)	Melancholy Baby		6.00	15.00

McCARTNEY, PAUL (& WINGS)
Also refer to Denny Laine and Percy Thrillington.

Label		Title	Year	VG+	NM
London 76007	(M)	The Family Way (Sdtk)	1967	20.00	50.00
London 82007	(S)	The Family Way (Sdtk)	1967	35.00	70.00
Apple STAO-3363	(S)	McCartney	1970	6.00	15.00
		(Label reads "Mfd. by Apple" on the bottom.)			
Apple STAO-3363	(S)	McCartney	1970	16.00	40.00
		(Apple label with Capitol logo on the bottom.)			
Apple SMAS-3375	(S)	Ram	1971	6.00	15.00
		(Label reads "Mfd. by Apple" on the bottom.)			
Apple SMAS-3375	(S)	Ram	1971	12.00	30.00
		(Apple label with Capitol logo on the bottom.)			

Manfred Mann, *Pretty Flamingo*. All of the Manfred Mann albums contain excellent British r&b. This is probably their most commercial and, consequently, over-looked effort. The model on the cover is the quintessence of mid '60s mod for young femmes.

Johnny Mathis, *The Shadow Of Your Smile*. After placing five singles and fourteen albums in the Top Ten for Columbia between 1957 and 1963, Johnny signed a lucrative contract with Mercury, where his hits dried up. (*The Shadow Of Your Smile* was his sole Top Ten for his new label.) Consequently, his Mercury albums are hard to find, although they have usually taken second fiddle to the earlier Columbia albums with collectors.

Label		Title	Year	VG+	NM
Apple SMAS-3375	(S)	Ram	1971	10.00	25.00
		(With unsliced Apple label on both sides.)			
Apple SW-3386	(S)	Wild Life	1971	6.00	15.00
Apple SMAL-3409	(S)	Red Rose Speedway	1971	6.00	15.00
Apple SO-3415	(S)	Band On The Run (With poster)	1973	6.00	15.00
United Arts. LA100	(S)	Live And Let Die (Sdtk)	1973	6.00	15.00
Capitol SMAS-3363	(S)	McCartney	1975	8.00	20.00
Capitol SMAS-3375	(S)	Ram	1975	8.00	20.00
Capitol SW-3386	(S)	Wild Life	1975	8.00	20.00
Capitol SMAL-3409	(S)	Red Rose Speedway	1975	8.00	20.00
Capitol SO-3415	(S)	Band On The Run (With poster)	1975	6.00	15.00
Capitol SMAS-11419	(S)	Venus And Mars (With four inserts)	1975	6.00	15.00
Capitol SW-11525	(S)	Wings At The Speed Of Sound	1976	4.00	10.00
Capitol SWCO-11593	(S)	Wings Over America (With poster)	1976	8.00	20.00
Capitol SW-11777	(S)	London Town (With poster)	1978	4.00	10.00
Capitol SEAX-11901	(S)	Band On The Run (Picture disc)	1978	10.00	25.00
Capitol S00-11905	(S)	Wings' Greatest (With poster)	1978	4.00	10.00
		(Capitol albums above have black & silver labels.)			
Columbia HC-36482	(S)	Band On The Run (1/2 speed with poster)	1981	16.00	40.00

McCOYS, THE

Label		Title	Year	VG+	NM
Bang BLP-212	(M)	Hang On Sloopy	1965	8.00	20.00
Bang BLPS-212	(P)	Hang On Sloopy	1965	10.00	25.00
Bang BLP-213	(M)	You Make Me Feel So Good	1966	8.00	20.00
Bang BLPS-213	(S)	You Make Me Feel So Good	1966	10.00	25.00
Mercury SR-61163	(S)	Infinite McCoys	1968	6.00	15.00
Mercury SR-61207	(S)	Human Ball	1969	6.00	15.00

McCRACKLIN, JIMMY

Label		Title	Year	VG+	NM
Chess 1464	(M)	Jimmy McCracklin Sings	1961	20.00	50.00
Stax 8506	(M)	I Just Gotta Know	1963	16.00	40.00
Imperial LP-9285	(M)	Every Night, Every Day	1965	8.00	20.00
Imperial LP-12285	(S)	Every Night, Every Day	1965	10.00	25.00
Imperial LP-9297	(M)	Think	1965	8.00	20.00
Imperial LP-12297	(S)	Think	1965	10.00	25.00
Imperial LP-9306	(M)	My Answer	1966	8.00	20.00
Imperial LP-12306	(S)	My Answer	1966	10.00	25.00
Imperial 9316	(M)	New Soul Of Jimmy McCracklin	1966	8.00	20.00
Imperial LP-12316	(S)	New Soul Of Jimmy McCracklin	1966	10.00	25.00
Minit LP-4009	(M)	The Best Of Jimmy McCracklin	1967	5.00	12.00
Minit LP-24009	(S)	The Best Of Jimmy McCracklin	1967	6.00	15.00
Minit LP-24011	(S)	Let's Get Together	1968	6.00	15.00
Minit 24017	(S)	Stinger Man	1969	6.00	15.00

McDANIELS, GENE

Label		Title	Year	VG+	NM
Liberty LRP-3146	(M)	In Times Like These	1960	8.00	20.00
Liberty LST-7146	(S)	In Times Like These	1960	10.00	25.00
Liberty LRP-3175	(M)	Sometimes I'm Happy, Sometimes I'm Blue	1960	8.00	20.00
Liberty LST-7175	(S)	Sometimes I'm Happy, Sometimes I'm Blue	1960	10.00	25.00
Liberty LRP-3191	(M)	100 Lbs. Of Clay	1961	8.00	20.00
Liberty LST-7191	(S)	100 Lbs. Of Clay	1961	10.00	25.00
Liberty LRP-3204	(M)	Gene McDaniels Sings Movie Memories	1962	6.00	15.00
Liberty LST-7204	(S)	Gene McDaniels Sings Movie Memories	1962	8.00	20.00
Liberty LRP-3215	(M)	Tower Of Strength	1962	8.00	20.00
Liberty LST-7215	(S)	Tower Of Strength	1962	10.00	25.00
Liberty LRP-3258	(M)	Hit After Hit	1962	6.00	15.00
Liberty LST-7258	(S)	Hit After Hit	1962	8.00	20.00
Liberty LRP-3275	(M)	Spanish Lace	1963	8.00	20.00
Liberty LST-7275	(S)	Spanish Lace	1963	10.00	25.00
Liberty LRP-3311	(M)	The Wonderful Word Of Gene McDaniels	1963	6.00	15.00
Liberty LST-7311	(S)	The Wonderful Word Of Gene McDaniels	1963	8.00	20.00

McDONALD, "COUNTRY" JOE

Label		Title	Year	VG+	NM
Mobile Fidelity 1-056	(S)	Paradise With An Ocean View	1980	6.00	15.00

McDONALD, MICHAEL

Label		Title	Year	VG+	NM
Mobile Fidelity 1-149	(S)	If That's What It Takes		5.00	12.00

McDONALD, KATHY

Label		Title	Year	VG+	NM
Capitol ST-11224	(S)	Insane Asylum	1974	8.00	20.00

Label		Title	Year	VG+	NM
McDONALD, SKEETS					
Capitol T-1040	(M)	Goin' Steady With The Blues	1958	16.00	40.00
Capitol T-1179	(M)	The Country's Best	1959	14.00	35.00
Columbia CL-2170	(M)	Call Me Skeets!	1964	6.00	15.00
Columbia CS-8970	(S)	Call Me Skeets!	1964	8.00	20.00
McDOWELL, "MISSISSIPPI" FRED					
Capitol 409	(S)	I Do Not Play No Rock 'N' Roll	1969	8.00	20.00
Sire 97018	(S)	Mississippi Fred McDowell In London	1970	6.00	15.00
Everest 253	(S)	Mississippi Fred McDowell	1971	5.00	12.00
McDUFF, BROTHER JACK					
Prestige 7259	(M)	Screamin'	1963	6.00	15.00
Prestige 7274	(S)	Live!	1963	6.00	15.00
McGHEE, BROWNIE					
Also refer to Sonny Terry & Brownie McGhee.					
Folkways 2030 (10")	(M)	Blues		12.00	30.00
Folkways 2421	(M)	Blues Of America		10.00	25.00
Folkways 3557	(M)	Blues		10.00	25.00
Sharp 2003	(M)	Brownie McGhee		20.00	50.00
Smash MGS-27067	(M)	Brownie McGhee At The Bunkhouse	1965	10.00	25.00
McGHEE, STICKS, & JOHN LEE HOOKER					
Audio Lab AL-1520	(M)	Highway Of Blues	1959	35.00	70.00
McGUIRE, BARRY					
Dunhill D-50003	(M)	Eve Of Destruction	1966	6.00	15.00
Dunhill DS-50003	(S)	Eve Of Destruction	1966	8.00	20.00
McGUIRE SISTERS, THE					
Coral CRL-56123 (10")	(M)	By Request	1955	10.00	25.00
Coral CRL-57097	(M)	Children's Holiday		8.00	20.00
Coral CRL-57026	(M)	Do You Remember When?		8.00	20.00
Coral CRL-57033	(M)	He		8.00	20.00
Coral CRL-57052	(M)	Sincerely		8.00	20.00
Coral CRL-57134	(M)	Teenage Party		8.00	20.00
Coral CRL-57145	(M)	When The Lights Are Low		8.00	20.00
Coral CRL-57180	(M)	Musical Magic		8.00	20.00
Coral CRL-57217	(M)	Sugartime	1958	8.00	20.00
Coral CRL-57225	(M)	Greetings From The McGuire Sisters		8.00	20.00
Coral CRL-57349	(M)	Our Golden Favorites		8.00	20.00
Coral CRL-57296	(M)	May You Always	1959	6.00	15.00
Coral CRL7-57296	(S)	May You Always	1959	8.00	20.00
Coral CRL-57303	(M)	In Harmony With Him		6.00	15.00
Coral CRL7-57303	(S)	In Harmony With Him		8.00	20.00
Coral CRL-57337	(M)	His And Her's		6.00	15.00
Coral CRL7-57337	(S)	His And Her's		8.00	20.00
Coral CRL-57385	(M)	Just For Old Times Sake		6.00	15.00
Coral CRL7-57385	(S)	Just For Old Times Sake		8.00	20.00
Coral CRL-57398	(M)	Subways Are For Sleeping		6.00	15.00
Coral CRL7-57398	(S)	Subways Are For Sleeping		8.00	20.00
Coral CRL-57415	(M)	Songs Everybody Knows	1962	6.00	15.00
Coral CRL7-57415	(S)	Songs Everybody Knows	1962	8.00	20.00
		(Coral albums above have maroon & silver labels.)			
Coral CRL-57443	(M)	Showcase	1964	5.00	12.00
Coral CRL7-57443	(S)	Showcase	1964	6.00	15.00
Coral CXB-6	(M)	The Best Of The McGuire Sisters	1966	5.00	12.00
Coral CXSB7-6	(S)	The Best Of The McGuire Sisters	1966	6.00	15.00
ABC 530	(S)	The McGuire Sisters Today	1966	5.00	12.00
ABC S-530	(S)	The McGuire Sisters Today	1966	6.00	15.00
McKUEN, ROD					
Decca DL-8714	(M)	Summer Love (Sdtk)	1958	16.00	40.00
Decca DL-8882	(M)	Anywhere I Wander	1958	6.00	15.00
Decca DL7-8882	(S)	Anywhere I Wander	1958	6.00	15.00
Decca DL-8946	(M)	Alone After Dark	1958	6.00	15.00
Decca DL7-8946	(S)	Alone After Dark	1958	6.00	15.00
		(Decca albums above have black & silver labels.)			
Hi Fi R-419	(M)	Beatsville		4.00	10.00
Hi Fi SR-419	(S)	Beatsville		5.00	12.00

Label		Title	Year	VG+	NM
Jubilee J-5013	(M)	Mr. Oliver Twist	1962	4.00	10.00
Jubilee SJ-5013	(S)	Mr. Oliver Twist	1962	5.00	12.00
Horizon T-1612	(M)	New Sounds In Folk Music	1963	4.00	10.00
Horizon ST-1612	(S)	New Sounds In Folk Music	1963	5.00	12.00
In 1003	(M)	Seasons In The Sun	1964	4.00	10.00
In S-1003	(S)	Seasons In The Sun	1964	5.00	12.00
Capitol T-2079	(M)	Rod McKuen Sings Rod McKuen	1964	4.00	10.00
Capitol ST-2079	(S)	Rod McKuen Sings Rod McKuen	1964	5.00	12.00
RCA LPM-3424	(M)	Rod McKuen Sings His Own	1965	4.00	10.00
RCA LSP-3424	(S)	Rod McKuen Sings His Own	1965	5.00	12.00
RCA LPM-3508	(M)	The Loner	1966	4.00	10.00
RCA LSP-3508	(S)	The Loner	1966	5.00	12.00
RCA LPM-3635	(M)	Other Kinds Of Songs	1966	4.00	10.00
RCA LSP-3635	(S)	Other Kinds Of Songs	1966	5.00	12.00
RCA LPM-3786	(M)	Through European Windows	1967	3.50	8.00
RCA LSP-3786	(S)	Through European Windows	1967	4.00	10.00
Liberty LRP-3537	(M)	Something Beyond	1967	3.50	8.00
Liberty LST-7537	(S)	Something Beyond	1967	4.00	10.00
Tradition 2063	(M)	A San Francisco Hippie Trip	1967	8.00	20.00
Kapp KL-1538	(M)	In A Lonely Place	1967	3.50	8.00
Kapp KS-3538	(S)	In A Lonely Place	1967	4.00	10.00
Stanyan 001	(M)	Rod McKuen In Concert	1967	3.50	8.00
Stanyan 001	(S)	Rod McKuen In Concert	1967	3.50	8.00
Stanyan 003	(M)	Seasons In The Sun	1967	3.50	8.00
Stanyan 003	(S)	Seasons In The Sun	1967	3.50	8.00
Stanyan 004	(M)	Seasons In The Sun, Volume 2	1967	3.50	8.00
Stanyan 004	(S)	Seasons In The Sun, Volume 2	1967	3.50	8.00
RCA LPM-3863	(M)	Listen To The Warm	1968	3.50	8.00
RCA LSP-3863	(S)	Listen To The Warm	1968	3.50	8.00
RCA LSP-4010	(S)	Single Man	1968	2.50	6.00
		(RCA albums above have black labels.)			
20th Century 4202	(S)	Joanna (Sdtk)	1968	5.00	12.00
Epic BN-26370	(S)	In Search Of Eros	1968	3.50	8.00
Everest 3208	(S)	Desire Has No Special Time	1968	3.50	8.00
Everest 3267	(S)	Life Is	1969	3.50	8.00
Decca DL7-4969	(S)	Very Warm	1968	3.50	8.00
Decca DL7-5078	(S)	Bits And Pieces	1969	3.50	8.00
Columbia OS-3350	(S)	Me, Natalie (Sdtk)	1969	5.00	12.00
20th Century 4207	(S)	The Prime Of Miss Jean Brodie (Sdtk)	1969	4.00	10.00
Warners WS-1772	(S)	Greatest Hits Of Rod McKuen	1969	2.50	6.00
Warners WS-1794	(S)	Rod McKuen At Carnegie Hall	1969	3.50	8.00
Warners WS-1837	(S)	New Ballads	1970	2.50	6.00
		(Warner albums above have green labels with a "W7" logo on top.)			
Buena Vista STER-5004	(S)	Scandalous John (Sdtk)	1971	4.00	10.00
Warners WS-1894	(S)	Pastorale	1971	3.50	8.00
Warners WS-1947	(S)	Grand Tour	1971	3.50	8.00
Warners BS-2622	(S)	Winter		2.50	6.00
Warners BS-2707	(S)	Summer	1972	2.00	5.00
Warners BS4-2707	(Q)	Summer		4.00	10.00
Warners BS-2638	(S)	Odyssey	1972	2.50	6.00
Warners BS-2688	(S)	Rod McKuen's Greatest Hits, Volume 3	1972	2.50	6.00
Warners BS-2731	(S)	Back To Carnegie Hall	1973	3.50	8.00
Stanyan 9010	(S)	McKuen Conducts McKuen	1972	2.50	6.00
Stanyan 5016	(S)	Live In London	1972	2.50	6.00
Stanyan 5040	(S)	Goodtime Music	1972	2.50	6.00
Stanyan 5042	(S)	Grand Tour, Volume 2	1972	2.50	6.00
Stanyan 5046	(S)	Seasons In The Sun, Volumes 1 & 2	1972	3.50	8.00
Stanyan 5047	(S)	Pastures Green	1972	2.50	6.00
Stanyan 4014	(S)	The Borrowers (Sdtk)	1974	4.00	10.00

McLAIN, DENNY

Capitol ST-204	(S)	Denny McLain In Las Vegas	1969	10.00	25.00

McLUHAN, MARSHALL

Columbia CL-2701	(M)	The Medium Is The Message	1967	8.00	20.00
Columbia CS-9501	(S)	The Medium Is The Message	1967	10.00	25.00

McNAIR, BARBARA

Warners W-1541	(M)	I Enjoy Being A Girl	1964	5.00	12.00
Warners WS-1541	(S)	I Enjoy Being A Girl	1964	6.00	15.00

Label		Title	Year	VG+	NM
Warners W-1570	(M)	Livin' End	1964	5.00	12.00
Warners WS-1570	(S)	Livin' End	1964	6.00	15.00
Motown 644	(M)	Where I Am	1966	5.00	12.00
Motown S-644	(S)	Where I Am	1966	6.00	15.00
Motown S-680	(S)	The Real Barbara McNair	1969	5.00	12.00

McNEELY, BIG JAY

Label		Title	Year	VG+	NM
Federal 295-96 (10")	(M)	Big Jay McNeely	1954	100.00	200.00
Savoy MG-15045 (10")	(M)	A Rhythm And Blues Concert	1955	75.00	150.00
Federal LP-395-530	(M)	Big Jay McNeely In 3-D	1956	75.00	150.00
King 650	(M)	Big Jay McNeely In 3-D	1959	35.00	70.00
Warners W-1523	(M)	Big Jay McNeely	1963	12.00	30.00
Warners WS-1523	(S)	Big Jay McNeely	1963	16.00	40.00

McPHATTER, CLYDE
Also refer to Billy Ward & The Dominoes and the Drifters.

Label		Title	Year	VG+	NM
Atlantic 8024	(M)	Love Ballads (Black label)	1958	75.00	150.00
Atlantic 8031	(M)	Clyde (Black label)	1959	50.00	100.00
MGM E-3775	(M)	Let's Start Over Again	1959	16.00	40.00
MGM SE-3775	(S)	Let's Start Over Again	1959	20.00	50.00
MGM E-3866	(M)	Clyde McPhatter's Greatest Hits	1960	16.00	40.00
MGM SE-3866	(S)	Clyde McPhatter's Greatest Hits	1960	20.00	50.00
Mercury MG-20597	(M)	Ta Ta	1960	10.00	25.00
Mercury SR-60597	(S)	Ta Ta	1960	12.00	30.00
Mercury MG-20655	(M)	Golden Blues Hits	1962	10.00	25.00
Mercury SR-60655	(S)	Golden Blues Hits	1962	12.00	30.00
Mercury MG-20711	(M)	Lover Please	1962	10.00	25.00
Mercury SR-60711	(S)	Lover Please	1962	12.00	30.00
Mercury MG-20750	(M)	Rhythm And Soul	1962	10.00	25.00
Mercury SR-60750	(S)	Rhythm And Soul	1962	12.00	30.00
Atlantic 8077	(M)	The Best Of Clyde McPhatter	1963	16.00	40.00
Mercury MG-20783	(M)	Clyde McPhatter's Greatest Hits	1963	10.00	25.00
Mercury SR-60783	(S)	Clyde McPhatter's Greatest Hits	1963	12.00	30.00
Mercury MG-20902	(M)	Songs Of The Big City	1964	10.00	25.00
Mercury SR-60902	(S)	Songs Of The Big City	1964	12.00	30.00
Mercury MG-20915	(M)	Live At The Apollo	1964	10.00	25.00
Mercury SR-60915	(S)	Live At The Apollo	1964	12.00	30.00
Decca DL7-5231	(S)	Welcome Home	1970	6.00	15.00

McRAE, CARMEN
Also refer to Sammy Davis, Jr.

Label		Title	Year	VG+	NM
Bethlehem 1023 (10")	(M)	Carmen McRae	1954	16.00	40.00
Decca DL-8173	(M)	By Special Request	1955	12.00	30.00
Decca DL-8267	(M)	Torchy	1955	12.00	30.00
Decca DL-8347	(M)	Blue Moon	1956	16.00	40.00
Decca DL-8583	(M)	After Glow	1957	12.00	30.00
Decca DL-8662	(M)	Mad About The Man	1957	16.00	40.00
Decca DL-8738	(M)	Carmen For Cool Ones	1958	12.00	30.00
Decca DL-8815	(M)	Birds Of A Feather	1958	16.00	40.00
Kapp KL-1117	(M)	Book Of Ballads	1958	8.00	20.00
Kapp KS-3001	(S)	Book Of Ballads	1960	6.00	15.00
Kapp KL-1018	(M)	When You're Away	1959	8.00	20.00
Kapp KS-3018	(S)	When You're Away	1960	6.00	15.00
Kapp KL-1169	(M)	Something To Swing About	1959	8.00	20.00
Kapp KS-3053	(S)	Something To Swing About	1960	6.00	15.00
Kapp KL-1541	(M)	This Is Carmen McRae		5.00	12.00
Kapp KS-3541	(S)	This Is Carmen McRae		6.00	15.00
Columbia CL-1609	(M)	Tonight's The Night	1961	5.00	12.00
Columbia CS-8409	(S)	Tonight's The Night	1961	6.00	15.00
Columbia CL-1730	(M)	Lover Man	1962	5.00	12.00
Columbia CS-8530	(S)	Lover Man	1962	6.00	15.00
Columbia CL-1943	(M)	Something Wonderful	1962	5.00	12.00
Columbia CS-8743	(S)	Something Wonderful	1962	6.00	15.00
Time 52104	(M)	Live At Sugar Hill	1963	5.00	12.00
Time 2104	(S)	Live At Sugar Hill	1963	6.00	15.00
Focus 334	(M)	Bittersweet	1965	5.00	12.00
Focus 334	(S)	Bittersweet	1965	6.00	15.00
Mainstream 56028	(M)	Second To None	1966	5.00	12.00
Mainstream 6028	(S)	Second To None	1966	6.00	15.00
Mainstream 56044	(M)	Haven't We Met?	1965	5.00	12.00
Mainstream 6044	(S)	Haven't We Met?	1965	6.00	15.00

Label		Title	Year	VG+	NM
McTELL, "BLIND" WILLIE					
Melodeon 7323	(M)	1940	1956	20.00	50.00
Bluesville BV-1040	(M)	Last Session	1962	6.00	15.00
MEAT LOAF					
Epic E99-34974	(S)	Bat Out Of Hell (Pictude disc)	1979	6.00	15.00
Epic HE-44974	(S)	Bat Out Of Hell (1/2 speed)	1981	6.00	15.00
MECKI MARK MEN, THE					
Limelight LS-86054	(S)	The Mecki Mark Men	1968	8.00	20.00
Limelight LS-86068	(S)	Running In The Summer Night	1969	8.00	20.00
MEDIUM					
Gamma GS-503	(S)	Medium		10.00	25.00
MELLANCAMP COUGAR, JOHN (JOHN COUGAR)					
MCA 2225	(S)	Chestnut Street Incident	1977	10.00	25.00
MELLO-LARKS, THE					
Camden CAL-530	(M)	Just For A Lark	1959	14.00	35.00
MELLOKINGS, THE					
Herald H-1013	(M)	Tonight-Tonight	1960	100.00	200.00
MEMPHIS SLIM (PETER CHATMAN)					
Also refer to Willie Dixon.					
Vee Jay VJLP-1012	(M)	Memphis Slim At The Gate Of The Horn	1959	30.00	60.00
Chess LP-1455	(M)	Memphis Slim	1961	20.00	50.00
United Arts. UAL-3137	(M)	Broken Soul Blues	1961	10.00	25.00
United Arts. UAS-6137	(S)	Broken Soul Blues	1961	12.00	30.00
Bluesville BV-1018	(M)	Just Blues	1961	10.00	25.00
Bluesville BVS-1018	(S)	Just Blues	1961	12.00	30.00
Candid 9023	(M)	Tribute To Big Bill Broonzy	1961	16.00	40.00
Candid 9023	(S)	Tribute To Big Bill Broonzy	1961	20.00	50.00
Candid 9024	(M)	Memphis Slim, U.S.A.	1962	16.00	40.00
Candid 9024	(S)	Memphis Slim, U.S.A.	1962	20.00	50.00
Bluesville BV-1031	(M)	No Strain	1962	8.00	20.00
Bluesville BVS-1031	(S)	No Strain	1962	10.00	25.00
Bluesville BV-1053	(M)	All Kinds Of Blues	1963	8.00	20.00
Bluesville BVS-1053	(S)	All Kinds Of Blues	1963	10.00	25.00
Battle BM-6118	(M)	Alone With My Friends	1963	10.00	25.00
Bluesville BV-1075	(M)	Steady Rollin' Blues	1964	8.00	20.00
Bluesville BVS-1075	(S)	Steady Rollin' Blues	1964	10.00	25.00
King LP-885	(M)	Memphis Slim	1964	10.00	25.00
Chess 1510	(M)	Real Folk Blues	1966	16.00	40.00
Scepter SM-535	(M)	Self Portrait	1966	10.00	25.00
Strand SLS-1046	(S)	The World's Foremost Blues Singer		8.00	20.00
Jubilee 8003	(S)	Legend Of The Blues	1967	6.00	15.00
Everest 215	(S)	Memphis Slim	1968	6.00	15.00
Buddah BDS-7505	(S)	Mother Earth	1969	6.00	15.00
King KS-1082	(S)	Messin' Around With The Blues	1970	6.00	15.00
Jewell 5004	(S)	Born With The Blues	1971	4.00	10.00
Warners WS-1899	(S)	Blue Memphis	1971	6.00	15.00
Warners BS-2646	(S)	South Side Reunion	1972	5.00	12.00
MEMPHIS WILLIE B.					
Bluesville BV-1034	(M)	Introducing Memphis Willie B.	1961	6.00	15.00
Bluesville BVS-1034	(S)	Introducing Memphis Willie B.	1961	8.00	20.00
MENDES, SERGIO					
Mobile Fdelity 1-118	(S)	Brazil '66		5.00	12.00
MERCER, MABEL					
Atlantic 1213	(M)	Mabel Mercer Sings Cole Porter		10.00	25.00
Atlantic 1244	(M)	Midnight At Mabel Mercer's		10.00	25.00
MERKIN					
Windi 1004	(S)	Music From Merkin Manor	1969	75.00	150.00
MERRILL, HELEN					
EmArcy MC-36006	(M)	Helen Merrill	1955	12.00	30.00

Label		Title	Year	VG+	NM
EmArcy MC-36057	(M)	Helen Merrill With Strings	1956	12.00	30.00
EmArcy MC-36078	(M)	Dream Of You	1956	12.00	30.00
EmArcy MC-36107	(M)	Merrill At Midnight	1956	12.00	30.00
EmArcy MC-36134	(M)	The Nearness Of You	1957	12.00	30.00
Atco 33-112	(M)	American Country Songs	1959	6.00	15.00
Atco SD-33-112	(S)	American Country Songs	1959	8.00	20.00
Metrojazz 1010	(M)	You've Got A Date With The Blues	1959	10.00	25.00
Mainstream 56014	(M)	The Artistry Of Helen Merrill	1965	5.00	12.00
Mainstréam 6014	(S)	The Artistry Of Helen Merrill	1965	6.00	15.00

MERRIWEATHER, BIG MACEO

Fortune 3002	(M)	Big Maceo Merriweather & John Lee Hooker		20.00	50.00

MERRY-GO-ROUND, THE

A&M 4132	(M)	The Merry-Go-Round	1967	8.00	20.00
A&M SP-4132	(S)	The Merry-Go-Round	1967	10.00	25.00

MERRYWEATHER (NEIL MERRYWEATHER)

Capitol SKAO-220	(S)	Merryweather	1969	5.00	12.00
Capitol STBB-278	(S)	Word Of Mouth	1969	6.00	15.00
RCA LSP-4442	(S)	Ivar Avenue Reunion	1970	6.00	15.00
RCA LSP-4485	(S)	Vacuum Cleaner	1971	5.00	12.00
Kent KST-546	(S)	Neil Merryweather And The Boers	1972	8.00	20.00

MERSEYBEATS, THE

ARC International 834	(M)	Englands Best Sellers	1964	16.00	40.00

MERSEYBOYS, THE

Vee Jay VJ-1101	(M)	15 Greatest Songs Of The Beatles	1964	16.00	40.00
Vee Jay VJS-1101	(S)	15 Greatest Songs Of The Beatles	1964	20.00	50.00

MESMERIZING EYE, THE

Smash MGS-27090	(M)	Psychedelia/A Musical Light Show	1967	10.00	25.00

MESSINA, JIM

Audio Fidelity DF-7037	(M)	The Dragsters	1964	10.00	25.00
Audio Fidelity DFS-7037	(S)	The Dragsters	1964	12.00	30.00

METERS, THE

Josie JOS-4010	(S)	The Meters	1969	6.00	15.00
Josie JOS-4011	(S)	Look-Ka Py Py	1970	6.00	15.00
Josie JOS-4012	(S)	Struttin'	1970	6.00	15.00

METRONOMES, THE

Strand 3002	(M)	The Standard Hits		12.00	30.00
Strand S-3002	(S)	The Standard Hits		16.00	40.00

METROTONES, THE

Columbia 6341 (10")	(M)	Tops In Rock And Roll	1955	100.00	200.00

MICKEY & SYLVIA (MICKEY BAKER & SLVIA VANDERPOOL)

Vik LX-1102	(M)	New Sounds	1958	75.00	150.00
Camden CAL-863	(M)	Love Is Strange	1965	20.00	50.00

MIGHTY BABY

Head LPS-025	(S)	Mighty Baby	1969	12.00	30.00

MILBURN, AMOS

Aladdin 703 (10")	(M)	Party After Hours (Red vinyl)	1956	300.00	500.00
Aladdin 703 (10")	(M)	Party After Hours	1956	150.00	250.00
		(Features Wynonie Harris & Prince Waterford.)			
Aladdin 704 (10")	(M)	Rockin' The Boogie (Red vinyl)	1956	240.00	400.00
Aladdin 704 (10")	(M)	Rockin' The Boogie	1956	180.00	300.00
Aladdin 810	(M)	Rockin' The Boogie	1958	100.00	200.00
Score LP-4012	(M)	Let's Have A Party		75.00	150.00
Imperial A-9176	(M)	Million Sellers	1962	40.00	80.00
Motown 608	(M)	The Blues Boss	1963	75.00	150.00

MILES, LIZZIE

Cook 1182	(M)	Moans And Blues	1956	12.00	30.00
Cook 1183	(M)	Hot Songs	1956	12.00	30.00

Label		Title	Year	VG+	NM
Cook 1184	(M)	Torchy Lullabies	1956	12.00	30.00
Cook 11815	(M)	Clambake On Bourbon St.	1957	12.00	30.00

MILKWOOD

| Paramount PAS-6046 | (S) | Hows The Weather? | 1973 | 12.00 | 30.00 |

MILLENIUM

| Columbia CS-9663 | (S) | Millennium Begin | 1968 | 8.00 | 20.00 |

MILLER, FRANKIE

Starday SLP-134	(M)	Country Music's New Star	1961	10.00	25.00
Starday SLP-199	(M)	The True Country Style Of Frankie Miller	1962	8.00	20.00
Audio Lab 1562	(M)	The Fine Country Singing Of Frankie Miller	1963	20.00	50.00
Starday SLP-338	(M)	Backland Farmer	1965	8.00	20.00

MILLER, JODY

Capitol T-1913	(M)	Wednesday's Child Is Full Of Woe	1963	5.00	12.00
Capitol ST-1913	(S)	Wednesday's Child Is Full Of Woe	1963	6.00	15.00
Capitol T-2349	(M)	Queen Of The House	1965	5.00	12.00
Capitol ST-2349	(S)	Queen Of The House	1965	6.00	15.00
Capitol T-2414	(M)	Home Of The Brave	1965	5.00	12.00
Capitol ST-2414	(S)	Home Of The Brave	1965	6.00	15.00
Capitol T-2446	(M)	The Great Hits Of Buck Owens	1966	4.00	10.00
Capitol ST-2446	(S)	The Great Hits Of Buck Owens	1966	5.00	12.00
Capitol ST-2996	(S)	The Nashville Sound Of Jody Miller	1969	4.00	10.00

MILLER, MRS. (ELVA MILLER)

Capitol T-2494	(M)	Mrs. Miller's Greatest Hits	1966	5.00	12.00
Capitol ST-2494	(S)	Mrs. Miller's Greatest Hits	1966	6.00	15.00
Capitol T-2579	(M)	Will Success Spoil Mrs. Miller?	1966	5.00	12.00
Capitol ST-2579	(S)	Will Success Spoil Mrs. Miller?	1966	6.00	15.00
Capitol T-2734	(M)	The Country Soul Of Mrs. Miller	1967	5.00	12.00
Capitol ST-2734	(S)	The Country Soul Of Mrs. Miller	1967	6.00	15.00
Amaret 5000	(S)	Mrs. Miller Does Her Thing	1969	5.00	12.00

MILLER, NED

Fabor FLP-1001	(M)	From A Jack To A King (Colored vinyl)	1963	40.00	80.00
Fabor FLP-1001	(M)	From A Jack To A King	1963	16.00	40.00
Capitol T-2330	(M)	Ned Miller Sings The Songs Of Ned Miller	1965	6.00	15.00
Capitol ST-2330	(S)	Ned Miller Sings The Songs Of Ned Miller	1965	8.00	20.00
Capitol T-2414	(M)	The Best Of Ned Miller	1966	5.00	12.00
Capitol ST-2414	(S)	The Best Of Ned Miller	1966	6.00	15.00
Capitol T-2586	(M)	Teardrop Lane	1967	5.00	12.00
Capitol ST-2586	(S)	Teardrop Lane	1967	6.00	15.00
Capitol ST-2914	(S)	In The Name Of Love	1968	6.00	15.00

MILLER, STEVE (STEVE MILLER BLUES BAND)
Also refer to Chuck Berry.

United Arts. UAS-5185	(S)	Revolution (Sdtk)	1968	6.00	15.00
Capitol SKAO-2920	(S)	Children Of The Future (Black label)	1968	6.00	15.00
Capitol ST-2984	(S)	Sailor (Black label)	1968	6.00	15.00
Capitol ST-184	(S)	Brave New World (Black label)	1969	5.00	12.00
Mobile Fidelity 1-021	(S)	Fly Like An Eagle	1976	10.00	25.00

MILLS, HAYLEY

Disneyland ST-1960	(M)	Pollyanna (Sdtk)	1960	10.00	25.00
Buena Vista BV-3309	(M)	The Parent Trap (Sdtk)	1961	6.00	15.00
Buena Vista STER-3309	(S)	The Parent Trap (Sdtk)	1961	10.00	25.00
Disneyland ST-3916	(M)	In Search Of The Castaways (Sdtk)	1962	6.00	15.00
Disneyland ST-3916	(S)	In Search Of The Castaways (Sdtk)	1962	10.00	25.00
Buena Vista BV-3311	(M)	Let's Get Together		6.00	15.00
Buena Vista STER-3311	(S)	Let's Get Together		8.00	20.00
MGM E-4025	(M)	Summer Magic (Sdtk)	1963	8.00	20.00
MGM SE-4025	(S)	Summer Magic (Sdtk)	1963	10.00	25.00
Buena Vista BV-3508	(M)	Annette And Hayley Mills		50.00	100.00
Mainstream 56090	(M)	Gypsy Girl (Sdtk)	1966	6.00	15.00
Mainstream 6090	(S)	Gypsy Girl (Sdtk)	1966	8.00	20.00

MILLS BROTHERS, THE

| Decca DL-5102 (10") | (M) | Souvenir Album | | 14.00 | 35.00 |
| Decca DL-5337 (10") | (M) | Wonderful Words | | 14.00 | 35.00 |

Label		Title	Year	VG+	NM
Decca DL-5506 (10")	(M)	Meet The Mills Brothers		14.00	35.00
Decca DL-5509 (10")	(M)	Louis Armstrong And The Mills Brothers		14.00	35.00
Decca DL-8148	(M)	Souvenir Album		10.00	25.00
Decca DL-8209	(M)	Singin' And Swingin'		10.00	25.00
Decca DL-8219	(M)	Memory Lane		10.00	25.00
Decca DL-8491	(M)	One Dozen Roses		10.00	25.00
Decca DL-8664	(M)	The Mills Brothers In Hi-Fi		10.00	25.00
Decca DL-8827	(M)	Glow With The Mills Brothers		10.00	25.00
Decca DL-8890	(M)	Barber Shop Harmony		10.00	25.00
Decca DL-8892	(M)	Harmonizin' With The Mills Brothers		10.00	25.00
Decca DXB-193	(M)	The Best Of The Mills Brothers		10.00	25.00
Decca DXSB7-193	(P)	The Best Of The Mills Brothers		10.00	25.00
		(Decca albums above have black & silver labels.)			
Dot DLP-3103	(M)	Mmmm, The Mills Brothers	1958	6.00	15.00
Dot DLP-25103	(S)	Mmmm, The Mills Brothers	1958	8.00	20.00
Dot DLP-3157	(M)	The Mills Brothers' Greatest Hits	1958	6.00	15.00
Dot DLP-25157	(S)	The Mills Brothers' Greatest Hits	1958	8.00	20.00
Dot DLP-3208	(M)	Great Barbershop Hits	1959	6.00	15.00
Dot DLP-25208	(S)	Great Barbershop Hits	1959	8.00	20.00
Dot DLP-3232	(M)	Merry Christmas	1959	6.00	15.00
Dot DLP-25232	(S)	Merry Christmas	1959	8.00	20.00
Dot DLP-3237	(M)	The Mills Brothers Sing	1960	6.00	15.00
Dot DLP-25237	(S)	The Mills Brothers Sing	1960	8.00	20.00
Dot DLP-3338	(M)	Yellow Bird	1961	6.00	15.00
Dot DLP-25338	(S)	Yellow Bird	1961	8.00	20.00
Dot DLP-3363	(M)	San Antonio Rose	1961	6.00	15.00
Dot DLP-25363	(S)	San Antonio Rose	1961	8.00	20.00
Dot DLP-3368	(M)	Great Hawaiian Hits	1961	6.00	15.00
Dot DLP-25368	(S)	Great Hawaiian Hits	1961	8.00	20.00
Dot DLP-3465	(M)	The Beer Barrel Polka And Other Hits	1962	5.00	12.00
Dot DLP-25465	(S)	The Beer Barrel Polka And Other Hits	1962	6.00	15.00
Dot DLP-3508	(M)	The End Of The World	1963	5.00	12.00
Dot DLP-25508	(S)	The End Of The World	1963	6.00	15.00
Dot DLP-3565	(M)	Gems By The Mills Brothers	1964	5.00	12.00
Dot DLP-25565	(S)	Gems By The Mills Brothers	1964	6.00	15.00
Dot DLP-3568	(M)	Hymns We Love	1964	5.00	12.00
Dot DLP-25568	(S)	Hymns We Love	1964	6.00	15.00
Dot DLP-3592	(M)	Say Si Si And Other Great Latin Hits	1964	5.00	12.00
Dot DLP-25592	(S)	Say Si Si And Other Great Latin Hits	1964	6.00	15.00
Hamilton HL-12116	(M)	The Mills Brothers Sing For You	1964	5.00	12.00
Hamilton HS-12116	(S)	The Mills Brothers Sing For You	1964	5.00	12.00
Dot DLP-3652	(M)	Ten Years Of Hits 1954-1964	1965	5.00	12.00
Dot DLP-25652	(S)	Ten Years Of Hits 1954-1964	1965	6.00	15.00
Dot DLP-3699	(M)	These Are The Mills Brothers	1966	5.00	12.00
Dot DLP-25699	(S)	These Are The Mills Brothers	1966	6.00	15.00
Dot DLP-3744	(M)	That Country Feeling	1966	5.00	12.00
Dot DLP-25744	(S)	That Country Feeling	1966	6.00	15.00
Dot DLP-3783	(M)	The Mills Brothers Live	1967	5.00	12.00
Dot DLP-25783	(S)	The Mills Brothers Live	1967	6.00	15.00
Dot DLP-25809	(S)	Fortuosity	1968	6.00	15.00
Dot DLP-25838	(S)	The Board Of Directors	1968	6.00	15.00
Dot DLP-25872	(S)	My Shy Violet	1968	6.00	15.00
Dot DLP-25927	(S)	Dream	1969	6.00	15.00

MILTON, ROY

Label		Title	Year	VG+	NM
Dooto DL-223	(M)	Rock 'N' Roll Versus Rhythm And Blues	1959	50.00	100.00
		(Also features Chuck Higgins.)			
Kent 554	(M)	The Great Roy Milton	1963	20.00	50.00

MIMMS, GARNET, & THE ENCHANTERS

Label		Title	Year	VG+	NM
United Arts. UAL-3305	(M)	Cry Baby And 11 Other Hits	1963	8.00	20.00
United Arts. UAS-6305	(M)	Cry Baby And 11 Other Hits	1963	10.00	25.00
United Arts. UAL-3396	(S)	As Long As I Have You		6.00	15.00
United Arts. UAS-6396	(S)	As Long As I Have You		8.00	20.00
United Arts. UAL-3498	(S)	I'll Take Good Care Of You		6.00	15.00
United Arts. UAS-6498	(S)	I'll Take Good Care Of You		8.00	20.00

MIND GARAGE

Label		Title	Year	VG+	NM
RCA LSP-4218	(S)	Mind Garage	1969	6.00	15.00
RCA LSP-4319	(S)	Mind Garage Again!	1970	6.00	15.00

Label		Title	Year	VG+	NM
MINDBENDERS, THE					
Refer to Wayne Fontana.					
Fontana MGF-27554	(M)	A Groovy Kind Of Love	1966	10.00	25.00
Fontana SRF-67554	(E)	A Groovy Kind Of Love	1966	8.00	20.00
Fontana MGF-18030	(M)	To Sir With Love (Sdtk)	1967	6.00	15.00
Fontana SRF-67569	(S)	To Sir With Love (Sdtk)	1967	8.00	20.00
MIND-EXPANDERS, THE					
Dot DLP-3773	(M)	What's Happening	1967	60.00	120.00
Dot DLP-25773	(S)	What's Happening	1967	10.00	25.00
MINEO, SAL					
Columbia CL-1117	(M)	Aladdin (Sdtk)	1958	35.00	70.00
Epic LN-3405	(M)	Sal	1958	30.00	60.00
MINNELLI, LIZA					
Cadence CE-4012	(M)	Best Foot Forward (Original Cast)	1963	10.00	25.00
Cadence CLP-24012	(S)	Best Foot Forward (Original Cast)	1963	12.00	30.00
Capitol T-2174	(M)	Liza! Liza!	1964	6.00	15.00
Capitol ST-2174	(S)	Liza! Liza!	1964	8.00	20.00
Capitol T-2271	(M)	It Amazes Me	1965	6.00	15.00
Capitol ST-2271	(S)	It Amazes Me	1965	8.00	20.00
ABC-Paramount 536	(M)	The Dangerous Christmas Of Red Riding Hood (Sdtk)	1965	10.00	25.00
ABC-Paramount S-536	(S)	The Dangerous Christmas Of Red Riding Hood (Sdtk)	1965	12.00	30.00
Capitol TAO-2295	(M)	Live At The London Palladium	1965	8.00	20.00
Capitol STAO-2295	(S)	Live At The London Palladium	1965	10.00	25.00
RCA LOC-1111	(M)	Flora The Red Menace (Sdtk)	1965	8.00	20.00
RCA LSO-1111	(S)	Flora The Red Menace (Sdtk)	1965	10.00	25.00
Capitol T-2448	(M)	There Is A Time	1966	6.00	15.00
Capitol ST-2448	(S)	There Is A Time	1966	8.00	20.00
Columbia CQ-32149	(Q)	The Singer	1973	6.00	15.00
MINT TATTOO					
Dot DLP-25918	(S)	Mint Tattoo	1969	8.00	20.00
MR. GASSER & THE WEIRDOS					
Also refer to the Superstocks.					
Capitol T-2010	(M)	Hot Rod Hootenanny	1963	10.00	25.00
Capitol ST-2010	(S)	Hot Rod Hootenanny	1963	12.00	30.00
Capitol T-2057	(M)	Rods N' Ratfinks	1963	10.00	25.00
Capitol ST-2057	(S)	Rods N' Ratfinks	1963	12.00	30.00
Capitol T-2114	(M)	Surfink!	1964	12.00	30.00
Capitol ST-2114	(S)	Surfink!	1964	14.00	35.00
		(Includes a bonus single by the Super Stocks.)			
MITCHELL, GUY					
Columbia CL-6231 (10")	(M)	Songs Of Open Spaces		14.00	35.00
Columbia CL-1211	(M)	A Guy In Love	1959	12.00	30.00
Columbia CS-8011	(S)	A Guy In Love	1959	16.00	40.00
Columbia CL-1226	(M)	Guy Mitchell's Greatest Hits		14.00	35.00
Columbia CS-8026	(E)	Guy Mitchell's Greatest Hits		10.00	25.00
Columbia CL-1552	(M)	Sunshine Guitar	1960	10.00	25.00
Columbia CS-8352	(S)	Sunshine Guitar	1960	12.00	30.00
MITCHELL, JONI					
Asylum EQ-10001	(Q)	Court And Spark	1974	6.00	15.00
Nautilus 11	(S)	Court And Spark		10.00	25.00
MITCHELL, WILLIE					
Hi HL-32010	(M)	Sunrise Serenade	1963	6.00	15.00
Hi SHL-32010	(S)	Sunrise Serenade	1963	8.00	20.00
Hi HL-32021	(M)	Hold It	1964	5.00	12.00
Hi SHL-32021	(S)	Hold It	1964	6.00	15.00
Hi HL-32026	(M)	It's Dance Time	1965	5.00	12.00
Hi SHL-32026	(S)	It's Dance Time	1965	6.00	15.00
Hi HL-32029	(M)	Driving Beat	1966	5.00	12.00
Hi SHL-32029	(S)	Driving Beat	1966	6.00	15.00
Hi HL-32034	(M)	Hit Sound Of Willie Mitchell	1967	5.00	12.00
Hi SHL-32034	(S)	Hit Sound Of Willie Mitchell	1967	6.00	15.00

Label		Title	Year	VG+	NM
Hi HL-32039	(M)	Ooh Baby, You Turn Me On	1967	5.00	12.00
Hi HL-32039	(S)	Ooh Baby, You Turn Me On	1967	6.00	15.00

MITCHELL TRIO, CHAD

Label		Title	Year	VG+	NM
Kapp KL-1262	(M)	Mighty Day On Campus	1962	5.00	12.00
Kapp KS-3262	(S)	Mighty Day On Campus	1962	6.00	15.00
Kapp KL-1281	(M)	At The Bitter End	1962	5.00	12.00
Kapp KS-3281	(S)	At The Bitter End	1962	6.00	15.00
Kapp KL-1313	(M)	Blowin' In The Wind	1963	5.00	12.00
Kapp KS-3313	(S)	Blowin' In The Wind	1963	6.00	15.00
Kapp KL-1334	(M)	The Best Of The Chad Mitchell Trio	1963	5.00	12.00
Kapp KS-3334	(S)	The Best Of The Chad Mitchell Trio	1963	6.00	15.00
Colpix CP-411	(M)	The Chad Mitchell Trio Arrives	1963	5.00	12.00
Colpix SCP-411	(S)	The Chad Mitchell Trio Arrives	1963	6.00	15.00
Colpix CP-463	(M)	In Concert	1964	5.00	12.00
Colpix SCP-463	(S)	In Concert	1964	6.00	15.00
Mercury MG-20838	(M)	Singin' Our Mind	1963	4.00	10.00
Mercury SR-60838	(S)	Singin' Our Mind	1963	5.00	12.00
Mercury MG-20891	(M)	Reflecting	1964	4.00	10.00
Mercury SR-60891	(S)	Reflecting	1964	5.00	12.00
Mercury MG-20944	(M)	The Slightly Irreverent Mitchell Trio	1964	4.00	10.00
Mercury SR-60944	(S)	The Slightly Irreverent Mitchell Trio	1964	5.00	12.00
Mercury MG-20992	(M)	Typical American Boys	1965	4.00	10.00
Mercury SR-60992	(S)	Typical American Boys	1965	5.00	12.00
Mercury MG-21049	(M)	That's The Way It's Gonna Be	1965	4.00	10.00
Mercury SR-61049	(S)	That's The Way It's Gonna Be	1965	5.00	12.00
Mercury MG-21067	(M)	Violets Of Dawn	1966	4.00	10.00
Mercury SR-61067	(S)	Violets Of Dawn	1966	5.00	12.00

MITCHUM, ROBERT

Label		Title	Year	VG+	NM
Capitol T-853	(M)	Calypso Is Like So		20.00	50.00
Monument MLP-8086	(M)	That Man, Robert Mitchum, Sings	1967	8.00	20.00
Monument SLP-18086	(S)	That Man, Robert Mitchum, Sings	1967	10.00	25.00

MIXTURES, THE

Label		Title	Year	VG+	NM
Linda 3301	(M)	Stompin' At The Rainbow	1962	20.00	50.00

MOBY GRAPE

Label		Title	Year	VG+	NM
Columbia CL-2698	(M)	Moby Grape (With poster)	1967	12.00	30.00
Columbia CS-9498	(S)	Moby Grape (With poster)	1967	12.00	30.00
		(Both the cover and poster show Don Stephenson holding a washboard and "giving the finger.")			
Columbia CL-2698	(M)	Moby Grape (With poster)	1967	8.00	20.00
Columbia CS-9498	(S)	Moby Grape (With poster)	1967	8.00	20.00
		(Both the cover and poster have Stephenson's offending finger airbrushed out.)			
Columbia CS-9613	(S)	Wow/Grape Jam	1968	8.00	20.00
Columbia CS-9696	(S)	Moby Grape '69	1969	6.00	15.00
Columbia CS-9912	(S)	Truly Fine Citizen	1969	6.00	15.00
Columbia AS-341098	(S)	Great Grape	1972	4.00	10.00
Reprise RS-6460	(S)	20 Granite Creek	1971	5.00	12.00
San Fran. Sound 04805	(S)	Moby Grape (1/2 speed)	1983	6.00	15.00
San Fran. Sound 04801	(S)	Wow/Grape Jam (1/2 speed)	1983	8.00	20.00

MODERN FOLK QUARTET, THE

Label		Title	Year	VG+	NM
Warners W-1511	(M)	MFQ	1963	6.00	15.00
Warners WS-1511	(S)	MFQ	1963	8.00	20.00
Warners W-1519	(M)	Palm Springs Weekend (Sdtk)	1963	8.00	20.00
Warners WS-1519	(S)	Palm Springs Weekend (Sdtk)	1963	10.00	25.00
Warners W-1546	(M)	Changes	1964	5.00	12.00
Warners WS-1546	(S)	Changes	1964	6.00	15.00

MODERN LOVERS, THE: *Refer to* JONATHAN RICHMAN

MODUGNO, DOMENICO

Label		Title	Year	VG+	NM
Decca DL-8808	(M)	Nel Blu Dipinti Blu		12.00	30.00
Decca DL-4133	(M)	Viva Italia	1961	8.00	20.00

MONKEES, THE

Label		Title	Year	VG+	NM
Colgems COM-101	(M)	The Monkees (With "Papa Jean's Blues")	1966	10.00	25.00
Colgems COS-101	(S)	The Monkees (With "Papa Jean's Blues")	1966	12.00	30.00

Label		Title	Year	VG+	NM
Colgems COM-101	(M)	The Monkees (With "Papa Gene's Blues")	1966	8.00	20.00
Colgems COS-101	(S)	The Monkees (With "Papa Gene's Blues")	1966	10.00	25.00
Colgems COM-102	(M)	More Of The Monkees	1967	8.00	20.00
Colgems COS-102	(S)	More Of The Monkees	1967	10.00	25.00
Colgems COM-103	(M)	Headquarters	1967	14.00	35.00
Colgems COS-103	(S)	Headquarters	1967	16.00	40.00
		(Back cover has a photo of two bearded Monkees.)			
Colgems COM-103	(M)	Headquarters	1967	8.00	20.00
Colgems COS-103	(S)	Headquarters	1967	10.00	25.00
		(The back cover has a photo without the beards.)			
Colgems COM-104	(M)	Pisces, Aquarius, Capricorn & Jones	1967	8.00	20.00
Colgems COS-104	(S)	Pisces, Aquarius, Capricorn & Jones	1967	10.00	25.00
		(Colgems albums above have "TM of Colgems Records" on top of the label and do not have an "RE" on the front cover.)			
Colgems COM-109	(M)	The Birds, The Bees And The Monkees	1968	16.00	40.00
Colgems COS-109	(S)	The Birds, The Bees And The Monkees	1968	10.00	25.00
Colgems COSO-5008	(S)	Head	1968	16.00	40.00
Colgems COS-113	(S)	Instant Replay	1969	12.00	30.00
Colgems COS-115	(S)	The Monkees' Greatest Hits	1969	12.00	30.00
Colgems COS-117	(S)	The Monkees Present	1969	12.00	30.00
Colgems COS-119	(S)	Changes	1970	30.00	60.00
Colgems SCOS-1001	(S)	A Barrel Full Of Monkees	1971	20.00	50.00
RCA PRS-329	(S)	The Monkees' Golden Hits	1972	16.00	40.00
Bell 6081	(S)	Refocus	1973	20.00	50.00
Arista AL-4089	(S)	The Monkees' Greatest Hits	1976	10.00	25.00

MONRO, MATT

Label		Title	Year	VG+	NM
Warwick 2045	(M)	My Kind Of Girl	1961	6.00	15.00
Liberty LRP-3240	(M)	Matt Monro	1962	5.00	12.00
Liberty LST-7240	(S)	Matt Monro	1962	6.00	15.00
United Arts. UAL-4114	(M)	From Russia With Love (Sdtk)	1964	4.00	10.00
United Arts. UAS-5114	(S)	From Russia With Love (Sdtk)	1964	5.00	12.00
Liberty LRP-3356	(M)	From Russia With Love	1964	4.00	10.00
Liberty LST-7356	(S)	From Russia With Love	1964	5.00	12.00
Liberty LRP-3402	(M)	Walk Away	1965	4.00	10.00
Liberty LST-7402	(S)	Walk Away	1965	5.00	12.00
Liberty LRP-3423	(M)	All My Loving	1965	4.00	10.00
Liberty LST-7423	(S)	All My Loving	1965	5.00	12.00
Liberty LRP-3437	(M)	Yesterday	1966	4.00	10.00
Liberty LST-7437	(S)	Yesterday	1966	5.00	12.00
Liberty LRP-3459	(M)	Matt Monro's Best	1966	4.00	10.00
Liberty LST-7459	(S)	Matt Monro's Best	1966	5.00	12.00
MGM E-4368	(M)	Born Free (Sdtk)	1966	4.00	10.00
MGM SE-4368	(S)	Born Free (Sdtk)	1966	5.00	12.00
Columbia OL-6660	(M)	The Quiller Memorandum (Sdtk)	1966	10.00	25.00
Columbia OS-3060	(S)	The Quiller Memorandum (Sdtk)	1966	12.00	30.00
Capitol T-2730	(M)	Invitation To The Movies/Born Free	1967	4.00	10.00
Capitol ST-2730	(S)	Invitation To The Movies/Born Free	1967	5.00	12.00
Decca DL-9160	(M)	A Matter Of Innocence (Sdtk)	1968	6.00	15.00
Decca DL7-9160	(S)	A Matter Of Innocence (Sdtk)	1968	6.00	15.00
Colgems COSO-5009	(S)	The Southern Star (Sdtk)	1969	8.00	20.00
Paramount PAS-5007	(S)	The Italian Job (Sdtk)	1969	4.00	10.00
Capitol SKAO-152	(S)	The Best Of Matt Monro	1969	4.00	10.00

MONROE, BILL (& HIS BLUEGRASS BOYS)

Label		Title	Year	VG+	NM
Decca DL-8731	(M)	Knee Deep In Bluegrass	1958	12.00	30.00
Decca DL7-8731	(S)	Knee Deep In Bluegrass	1958	14.00	35.00
Decca DL-8769	(M)	I Saw The Light	1959	12.00	30.00
Decca DL7-8769	(S)	I Saw The Light	1959	14.00	35.00
		(Decca albums above have black & silver labels.)			
Decca DL-4080	(M)	Mr. Bluegrass	1960	12.00	30.00
Decca DL7-4080	(S)	Mr. Bluegrass	1960	14.00	35.00
Harmony HL-7290	(M)	The Great Bill Monroe	1961	8.00	20.00
Decca DL-4266	(M)	Bluegrass Ramble	1962	8.00	20.00
Decca DL7-4266	(S)	Bluegrass Ramble	1962	10.00	25.00
Decca DL-4327	(M)	My All Time Country Favorites	1962	8.00	20.00
Decca DL7-4327	(S)	My All Time Country Favorites	1962	10.00	25.00
Camden CAL-719	(M)	Father Of Bluegrass Music	1962	8.00	20.00
Camden CAL-774	(M)	Early Bluegrass	1963	8.00	20.00

Label		Title	Year	VG+	NM
Decca DL-4382	(M)	Bluegrass Special	1963	8.00	20.00
Decca DL7-4382	(S)	Bluegrass Special	1963	10.00	25.00
Decca DL-4537	(M)	I'll Meet You In Church Sunday Morning	1964	6.00	15.00
Decca DL7-4537	(S)	I'll Meet You In Church Sunday Morning	1964	8.00	20.00
Vocalion VL-3702	(M)	Bill Monroe Sings Country Songs	1964	6.00	15.00
Harmony HL-7315	(M)	Bill Monroe's Best	1964	6.00	15.00
Harmony HL-7338	(M)	Original Blue Grass Sound	1965	6.00	15.00
Decca DL-4601	(M)	Bluegrass Instrumentals	1965	6.00	15.00
Decca DL7-4601	(S)	Bluegrass Instrumentals	1965	8.00	20.00
Decca DL-4780	(M)	The High Lonesome Sound Of Bill Monroe	1966	6.00	15.00
Decca DL7-4780	(S)	The High Lonesome Sound Of Bill Monroe	1966	8.00	20.00
		(Decca albums above have black labels with			
		"Mfd by Decca" beneath the rainbow.)			
Decca DL-4896	(M)	Bluegrass Time	1967	6.00	15.00
Decca DL7-4896	(S)	Bluegrass Time	1967	8.00	20.00
Decca DL7-5010	(E)	Bill Monroe's Greatest Hits	1968	4.00	10.00
Decca DL7-5135	(S)	A Voice From On High	1969	6.00	15.00
Decca DL7-5213	(S)	Kentucky Bluegrass	1970	6.00	15.00
Decca DL7-5281	(S)	Country Music Hall Of Fame	1971	6.00	15.00
Decca DL7-5348	(S)	Uncle Pen	1972	6.00	15.00

MONROE, MARILYN

Label		Title	Year	VG+	NM
MGM E-208 (10")	(M)	Gentlemen Prefer Blondes (Sdtk)	1953	50.00	100.00
MGM E-3231	(M)	Gentlemen Prefer Blondes (Sdtk)	1955	20.00	50.00
United Arts. UAL-4030	(M)	Some Like It Hot (Sdtk)	1959	14.00	35.00
United Arts. UAS-5030	(S)	Some Like It Hot (Sdtk)	1959	20.00	50.00
Columbia CL-1527	(M)	Let's Make Love (Sdtk)	1960	16.00	40.00
Columbia CS-8327	(S)	Let's Make Love (Sdtk)	1960	20.00	50.00
20th Century FXG-5000	(M)	Marilyn (With poster)	1959	50.00	100.00
20th Century SXG-5000	(E)	Marilyn (With poster)	1959	40.00	80.00
Ascot ALM-13008	(M)	Marilyn Monroe		16.00	40.00
Ascot ALS-16008	(S)	Marilyn Monroe		20.00	50.00
Ascot US-13500	(M)	Some Like It Hot (Sdtk)	1964	6.00	15.00
Ascot US-16500	(S)	Some Like It Hot (Sdtk)	1964	8.00	20.00
Movietone 72016	(M)	The Unforgettable Marilyn Monroe	1967	10.00	25.00
Movietone 72016	(S)	The Unforgettable Marilyn Monroe	1967	12.00	30.00

MONTAGE

Label		Title	Year	VG+	NM
Laurie SLP-2049	(S)	Montage	1969	6.00	15.00

MONTANA, PATSY

Label		Title	Year	VG+	NM
Sims LP-122	(M)	The New Sound Of Patsy Montana	1964	10.00	25.00

MONTANA, SLIM (WILF CARTER)

Label		Title	Year	VG+	NM
Decca DL-8917	(M)	I'm Ragged But I'm Right	1959	16.00	40.00
Camden CAL-527	(M)	Wilf Carter/Montana Slim	1959	10.00	25.00
Decca DL-4092	(S)	The Dynamite Trail	1960	16.00	40.00
Camden CAL-668	(M)	Reminiscin'	1962	6.00	15.00
Starday SLP-300	(M)	Wilf Carter As Montana Slim	1964	8.00	20.00
Starday SLP-300	(E)	Wilf Carter As Montana Slim	1964	5.00	12.00
Camden CAL-846	(M)	32 Wonderful Years	1965	6.00	15.00

MONTENEGRO, HUGO, & HIS ORCHESTRA

Label		Title	Year	VG+	NM
RCA LPM-3475	(M)	Music From The Man From U.N.C.L.E.	1966	6.00	15.00
RCA LSP-3475	(S)	Music From The Man From U.N.C.L.E.	1966	8.00	20.00
RCA LPM-3574	(M)	More Music From			
		"The Man From U.N.C.L.E."	1966	6.00	15.00
RCA LSP-3574	(S)	More Music From			
		"The Man From U.N.C.L.E."	1966	8.00	20.00

MONTEZ, CHRIS

Label		Title	Year	VG+	NM
Monogram M-100	(M)	Let's Dance And Have Some Kinda' Fun!!!	1963	35.00	70.00
A&M LP-115	(M)	The More I See You/Call Me	1966	8.00	20.00
A&M SP-4115	(P)	The More I See You/Call Me	1966	10.00	25.00
A&M LP-120	(M)	Time After Time	1966	6.00	15.00
A&M SP-4120	(S)	Time After Time	1966	8.00	20.00
A&M LP-128	(M)	Foolin' Around	1967	6.00	15.00
A&M SP-4128	(S)	Foolin' Around	1967	8.00	20.00
A&M LP-157	(M)	Watch What Happens	1967	6.00	15.00
A&M SP-4157	(S)	Watch What Happens	1967	8.00	20.00

Label		Title	Year	VG+	NM
MONTGOMERY, "LITTLE BROTHER"					
Riverside 403	(M)	Southside Blues	1960	10.00	25.00
Bluesville BV-1012	(M)	Tasty Blues	1965	6.00	15.00
MONTGOMERY, MARIAN					
Capitol T-1884	(M)	Swings For Winners And Losers	1963	5.00	12.00
Capitol ST-1884	(S)	Swings For Winners And Losers	1963	6.00	15.00
Capitol T-1982	(M)	Let There Be Marian Montgomery	1963	5.00	12.00
Capitol ST-1982	(S)	Let There Be Marian Montgomery	1963	6.00	15.00
MONTGOMERY, MELBA					
Also refer to George Jones and Gene Pitney.					
United Arts. UAL-3341	(M)	#1 Country & Western Girl Singer	1964	5.00	12.00
United Arts. UAS-6341	(S)	#1 Country & Western Girl Singer	1964	6.00	15.00
United Arts. UAL-3369	(M)	Down Home	1964	5.00	12.00
United Arts. UAS-6369	(S)	Down Home	1964	6.00	15.00
United Arts. UAL-3391	(M)	I Can't Get Used To Being Lonely	1964	5.00	12.00
United Arts. UAS-6391	(S)	I Can't Get Used To Being Lonely	1964	6.00	15.00
Musicor M-2074	(M)	Country Girl	1966	4.00	10.00
Musicor MS-3074	(S)	Country Girl	1966	5.00	12.00
Musicor M-2097	(M)	The Hallelujah Road	1966	4.00	10.00
Musicor MS-3097	(S)	The Hallelujah Road	1966	5.00	12.00
Musicor M-2113	(M)	Melba Toast	1966	4.00	10.00
Musicor MS-3113	(S)	Melba Toast	1966	5.00	12.00
Musicor M-2114	(M)	Don't Keep Me Lonely Too Long	1966	4.00	10.00
Musicor MS-3114	(S)	Don't Keep Me Lonely Too Long	1966	5.00	12.00
Musicor M-2129	(M)	I'm Just Living	1967	4.00	10.00
Musicor MS-3129	(S)	I'm Just Living	1967	5.00	12.00
MOODY, CLYDE					
King 891	(M)	The Best Of Clyde Moody	1964	14.00	35.00
MOODY BLUES, THE					
London LL-3428	(M)	Go Now/Moody Blues #1	1965	12.00	30.00
London (E) PS-428	(E)	Go Now/Moody Blues #1	1965	8.00	20.00
Mobile Fidelity 1-042	(S)	Days Of Future Passed		8.00	20.00
Mobile Fidelity 1-151	(S)	Seventh Sojourn		6.00	15.00
Nautilus 21	(S)	On The Threshold Of A Dream		8.00	20.00
MOON, KEITH					
MCA 2136	(S)	Two Sides Of The Moon	1975	8.00	20.00
MOONGLOWS, THE					
Chess LP-1425	(M)	Rock, Rock, Rock (Sdtk)	1958	50.00	100.00
Chess LP-1430	(M)	Look It's The Moonglows	1959	75.00	150.00
Chess 1471	(M)	The Best Of Bobby Lester & The Moonglows	1962	50.00	100.00
Vee Jay LP-1052	(M)	The Flamingos Meet The Moonglows		20.00	50.00
Constellation CS-2	(M)	The Moonglows/Collectors Showcase	1964	12.00	30.00
RCA LSP-4722	(S)	The Return Of The Moonglows	1972	6.00	15.00
MOORE, BOBBY, & THE RHYTHM ACES					
Checker LP-3000	(M)	Searching For My Love	1966	6.00	15.00
Checker LPS-3000	(E)	Searching For My Love	1966	6.00	15.00
MOORE, DEBBY					
Top Rank TR-301	(M)	Debby Moore	1959	12.00	30.00
MOORE, GATEMOUTH					
King 684	(M)	I'm A Fool To Care	1960	300.00	500.00
MOORE, LATTIE					
Audio Lab AL-1555	(M)	The Best Of Lattie Moore	1960	20.00	50.00
Audio Lab AL-1573	(M)	Country Side	1962	20.00	50.00
MOORE, MARILYN					
Bethlehem 73	(M)	Moody	1957	12.00	30.00
MOORE, SCOTTY					
Epic LN-24103	(M)	The Guitar That Changed The World	1964	16.00	40.00
Epic BN-26103	(S)	The Guitar That Changed The World	1964	20.00	50.00

Label		Title	Year	VG+	NM
MORENO, RITA					
Strand 1039	(M)	Rita Moreno Sings		10.00	25.00
Wynne 103	(M)	Warm, Wonderful And Wild		10.00	25.00
MORGAN, GEORGE					
Columbia CL-1044	(M)	Morgan, By George	1957	12.00	30.00
Columbia CL-1831	(M)	Golden Memories	1961	6.00	15.00
Columbia CS-8431	(S)	Golden Memories	1961	8.00	20.00
Columbia CL-2111	(M)	Tender Lovin' Care	1964	5.00	12.00
Columbia CS-8911	(S)	Tender Lovin' Care	1964	6.00	15.00
Columbia CL-2197	(M)	Slippin' Around	1964	5.00	12.00
Columbia CS-8997	(S)	Slippin' Around	1964	6.00	15.00
Columbia CL-2333	(M)	Red Roses For A Blue Lady	1965	5.00	12.00
Columbia CS-9133	(S)	Red Roses For A Blue Lady	1965	6.00	15.00
MORGAN, JANE					
Kapp KL-1023	(M)	Jane Morgan		8.00	20.00
Kapp KL-1066	(M)	Fascination	1957	8.00	20.00
Kapp KL-1098	(M)	Jane Morgan		8.00	20.00
Kapp KL-1105	(M)	The Day The Rain Came		8.00	20.00
Kapp KL-1129	(M)	Jane In Spain		8.00	20.00
Kapp KL-1191	(M)	Ballads Of Lady Jane		5.00	12.00
Kapp KS-3191	(S)	Ballads Of Lady Jane		6.00	15.00
Kapp KL-1239	(M)	Second Time Around	1961	5.00	12.00
Kapp KS-3239	(S)	Second Time Around	1961	6.00	15.00
Kapp KL-1246	(M)	The Great Golden Hits	1961	5.00	12.00
Kapp KS-3246	(S)	The Great Golden Hits	1961	6.00	15.00
Kapp KL-1247	(M)	Big Hits From Broadway	1961	5.00	12.00
Kapp KS-3247	(S)	Big Hits From Broadway	1961	6.00	15.00
Kapp KL-1250	(M)	Love Makes The World Go 'Round	1961	5.00	12.00
Kapp KS-3250	(S)	Love Makes The World Go 'Round	1961	6.00	15.00
Kapp KL-1268	(M)	Jane Morgan At The Cocoanut Grove	1962	5.00	12.00
Kapp KS-3268	(S)	Jane Morgan At The Cocoanut Grove	1962	6.00	15.00
Kapp KL-1296	(M)	What Now My Love	1962	5.00	12.00
Kapp KS-3296	(S)	What Now My Love	1962	5.00	12.00
Kapp KL-1329	(M)	Jane Morgan's Greatest Hits		5.00	12.00
Kapp KS-3329	(S)	Jane Morgan's Greatest Hits		5.00	12.00
Epic LN-24211	(M)	Fresh Flavor	1966	4.00	10.00
Epic BN-26211	(S)	Fresh Flavor	1966	5.00	12.00
Colpix CP-497	(M)	The Jane Morgan Album	1966	5.00	12.00
Colpix SCP-497	(S)	The Jane Morgan Album	1966	6.00	15.00
MORGEN (STEVE MORGEN)					
Probe CPLP-4507	(M)	Morgen (With poster)	1969	20.00	50.00
MOREL, TERRY					
Bethlehem 47	(M)	Songs Of A Woman In Love	1955	16.00	40.00
MORNING					
Vault 138	(S)	Morning	1970	8.00	20.00
MORNING DEW					
Roulette R-41045	(M)	Morning Dew	1967	14.00	35.00
Roulette RS-41045	(S)	Morning Dew	1967	16.00	40.00
MORNING GLORY					
Fontana MGF-27573	(M)	Two Suns Worth	1967	5.00	12.00
Fontana SRF-67573	(S)	Two Suns Worth	1967	6.00	15.00
Toya 2001	(S)	Growing	1972	10.00	25.00
MORRICONE, ENNIO					
Epic LN-24126	(M)	Malamondo (Sdtk)	1964	12.00	30.00
Epic BN-26126	(S)	Malamondo (Sdtk)	1964	16.00	40.00
United Arts. UAL-3608	(M)	For A Few Dollars More (Sdtk)	1967	5.00	12.00
United Arts. UAS-6608	(S)	For A Few Dollars More (Sdtk)	1967	6.00	15.00
United Arts. UAL-4171	(M)	The Battle Of Algiers (Sdtk)	1967	6.00	15.00
United Arts. UAS-5171	(S)	The Battle Of Algiers (Sdtk)	1967	8.00	20.00
United Arts. UAL-4172	(M)	The Good, The Bad And The Ugly (Sdtk)	1968	5.00	12.00
United Arts. UAS-5172	(S)	The Good, The Bad And The Ugly (Sdtk)	1968	6.00	15.00
MGM E-4565	(M)	Guns For San Sebastian (Sdtk)	1968	10.00	25.00
MGM SE-4565	(S)	Guns For San Sebastian (Sdtk)	1968	12.00	30.00

Label		Title	Year	VG+	NM
20th Century TFS-4209	(S)	The Sicilian Clan (Sdtk)	1970	12.00	30.00
Kapp KRS-5512	(S)	Two Mules For Sister Sara (Sdtk)	1970	16.00	40.00
Capitol SW-642	(S)	The Bird With The Crystal Plumage (Sdtk)	1970	16.00	40.00
United Arts. LA303	(S)	Burn (Sdtk)	1970	8.00	20.00
Bell 1105	(S)	The Burglars (Sdtk)	1971	10.00	25.00
Paramount PAS-6019	(S)	The Red Tent (Sdtk)	1971	8.00	20.00
RCA LSP-4612	(S)	Sacco And Vanzetti (Sdtk)	1971	8.00	20.00
RCA LSP-4736	(S)	Once Upon A Time In The West (Sdtk)	1972	6.00	15.00
United Arts. UAS-5521	(S)	Duck, You Sucker (Sdtk)	1972	10.00	25.00

MORRISEY, PAT

Label		Title	Year	VG+	NM
Mercury MG-20197	(M)	I'm Pat Morrisey, I Sing	1956	16.00	40.00

MORRISON, VAN

Label		Title	Year	VG+	NM
Bang BLP-218	(M)	Blowin' Your Mind (Red & white label)	1967	12.00	30.00
Bang BLPS-218	(S)	Blowin' Your Mind (Red & white label)	1967	12.00	30.00
Bang BLPS-222	(S)	The Best Of Van Morrison	1970	8.00	20.00
Bang BLPS-400	(S)	T.B. Sheets	1973	6.00	15.00
Nautilus	(S)	Moondance (Superdisk)	1981	12.00	30.00

MORSE, ELLA MAE

Label		Title	Year	VG+	NM
Capitol H-513 (10")	(M)	Barrelhouse Boogie And The Blues		50.00	100.00
Capitol T-513	(M)	Barrelhouse Boogie And The Blues		20.00	50.00
Capitol T-898	(M)	Morse Code		14.00	35.00
Capitol T-1802	(M)	Hits Of Ella Mae Morse And Freddie Slack		14.00	35.00

MOSS, GENE

Label		Title	Year	VG+	NM
RCA LPM-2977	(M)	Dracula's Greatest Hits	1964	5.00	12.00
RCA LSP-2977	(S)	Dracula's Greatest Hits	1964	6.00	15.00

MOTHERS OF INVENTION, THE: *Refer to* **FRANK ZAPPA**

MOTT THE HOOPLE (MOTT)

Label		Title	Year	VG+	NM
Atlantic SD-8272	(S)	Mad Shadows	1970	5.00	12.00
Atlantic SD-8258	(S)	Mott The Hoople	1970	5.00	12.00
Atlantic SD-8284	(S)	Wildlife	1971	5.00	12.00
Atlantic SD-8304	(S)	Brain Capers	1972	5.00	12.00
Columbia PCQ-32871	(Q)	The Hoople	1974	8.00	20.00

MOUNTAIN

Label		Title	Year	VG+	NM
Columbia CQ-32079	(Q)	The Best Of Mountain	1973	6.00	15.00
Columbia CQ-33088	(Q)	Avalanche	1974	6.00	15.00

MOUNTAIN BUS

Label		Title	Year	VG+	NM
Good 101	(S)	Sundance	1971	40.00	80.00

MOUSEKETEERS, THE

Label		Title	Year	VG+	NM
Disneyland T-3918	(M)	How To Be A Mouseketeer	1962	10.00	25.00
Disneyland ST-3918	(S)	How To Be A Mouseketeer	1962	14.00	35.00

MOVE, THE

Label		Title	Year	VG+	NM
A&M SP-4259	(S)	Shazam	1969	10.00	25.00
Capitol ST-658	(S)	Looking On	1971	8.00	20.00
Capitol ST-811	(S)	Message From The Country	1971	8.00	20.00

MOVING SIDEWALKS, THE

Label		Title	Year	VG+	NM
Tantara 6919	(S)	Flash	1968	75.00	150.00

MU (MERRELL FANKHAUSER)

Label		Title	Year	VG+	NM
R.T.V. 300	(S)	Mu (With insert)	1972	35.00	70.00

MUDDY WATERS (McKINLEY MORGANFIELD)
Also refer to Bo Diddley.

Label		Title	Year	VG+	NM
Chess LP-1427	(M)	The Best Of Muddy Waters	1957	30.00	60.00
Chess LP-1444	(M)	Muddy Waters Sings Big Bill	1960	20.00	50.00
Chess LP-1449	(M)	Muddy Waters At Newport	1963	20.00	50.00
Chess LP-1483	(M)	Folk Singer	1964	16.00	40.00
Chess LP-1501	(M)	The Real Folk Blues Of Muddy Waters	1965	14.00	35.00
Chess LPS-1501	(S)	The Real Folk Blues Of Muddy Waters	1965	20.00	50.00
Chess LP-1507	(M)	Muddy, Brass And Blues	1966	14.00	35.00
Chess LPS-1507	(S)	Muddy, Brass And Blues	1966	20.00	50.00

Label		Title	Year	VG+	NM
Chess LP-1511	(M)	More Real Folk Blues	1966	14.00	35.00
Chess LPS-1511	(S)	More Real Folk Blues	1966	20.00	50.00
Chess LP-1533	(M)	Blues From Big Bill's Copacabana		12.00	30.00
Chess LPS-1533	(S)	Blues From Big Bill's Copacabana		14.00	35.00
Cadet Concept 314	(S)	Electric Mud	1968	8.00	20.00
Cadet Concept 320	(S)	After The Rain	1969	8.00	20.00
Chess LPS-1539	(S)	Sail On	1969	10.00	25.00
Chess LPS-127	(S)	Fathers And Sons	1969	12.00	30.00
Chess LPS-1553	(S)	They Call Me Muddy Waters	1971	6.00	15.00
Chess 2CH-60006	(S)	McKinley Morganfield AKA Muddy Waters	1971	6.00	15.00
Chess CH-50012	(S)	Muddy Waters Live	1972	5.00	12.00
Chess CH-60013	(S)	The London Sessions	1972	6.00	15.00
Chess CH-50023	(S)	Can't Get No Grindin'	1973	5.00	12.00
Chess CH-60026	(S)	London Revisited	1974	5.00	12.00
Chess CH-60031	(S)	Unk In Funk	1974	5.00	12.00

MUGWUMPS, THE

Warners W-1697	(M)	The Mugwumps	1967	6.00	15.00
Warners WS-1697	(S)	The Mugwumps	1967	8.00	20.00

MULLICAN, MOON

Coral CRL-57235	(M)	Moon Over Mullican	1958	150.00	250.00
King 555	(M)	His All-Time Greatest Hits	1958	35.00	70.00
King 628	(M)	16 Of His Favorite Tunes	1959	35.00	70.00
King 681	(M)	The Many Moods Of Moon Mullican	1960	35.00	70.00
Sterling ST-601	(M)	I'll Sail My Ship Alone		20.00	50.00
Audio Lab AL-1568	(M)	Instrumentals	1962	40.00	80.00
Starday SLP-267	(M)	Mister Piano Man	1964	10.00	25.00
King 937	(M)	24 Of His Favorite Tunes	1965	10.00	25.00
Starday SLP-398	(M)	The Unforgettable Moon Mullican	1967	6.00	15.00

MUNSTERS, THE

Decca DL-4588	(M)	The Munsters		16.00	40.00
Decca DL7-4588	(S)	The Munsters		20.00	50.00

MURPHY, MARK

Decca DL-8390	(M)	Meet Mark Murphy	1956	12.00	30.00
Decca DL-8632	(M)	Let Yourself Go	1958	12.00	30.00
Capitol T-1177	(M)	This Could Be The Start Of Something	1959	8.00	20.00
Capitol ST-1177	(S)	This Could Be The Start Of Something	1959	10.00	25.00
Capitol T-1299	(M)	Hip Parade	1960	6.00	15.00
Capitol ST-1299	(S)	Hip Parade	1960	8.00	20.00
Capitol T-1458	(M)	Playing The Field	1960	6.00	15.00
Capitol ST-1458	(S)	Playing The Field	1960	8.00	20.00
Riverside 395	(M)	Rah!	1961	6.00	15.00
Riverside 395	(S)	Rah!	1961	8.00	20.00
Riverside 441	(M)	That's How I Love The Blues	1962	5.00	12.00
Riverside 441	(S)	That's How I Love The Blues	1962	6.00	15.00
Fontana MGF-27537	(M)	A Swingin' Singin' Affair	1965	5.00	12.00
Fontana SRF-67537	(S)	A Swingin' Singin' Affair	1965	6.00	15.00

MURPHY, ROSE

Royale 1835 (10")	(M)	Rose Murphy And Quartette		12.00	30.00
Verve V-2070	(M)	Not Cha-Cha, But Chi-Chi		8.00	20.00
United Arts. UAL-12025	(M)	Jazz, Joy And Happiness		6.00	15.00
United Arts. UAS-15025	(S)	Jazz, Joy And Happiness		8.00	20.00

MUSIC EMPORIUM, THE

Sentinal 1000	(S)	The Music Emporium	1969	150.00	250.00

MUSIC EXPLOSION, THE

Laurie LLP-2040	(M)	A Little Bit O' Soul	1967	8.00	20.00
Laurie SLLP-2040	(S)	A Little Bit O' Soul	1967	10.00	25.00

MUSIC MACHINE, THE (BONNIWELL'S MUSIC MACHINE)

Original Sound 5015	(M)	Turn On The Music Machine	1966	16.00	40.00
Original Sound 8875	(S)	Turn On The Music Machine	1966	20.00	50.00

MUSTANGS, THE

Providence PLP-001	(M)	Dartell Stomp	1963	16.00	40.00

The Hit Sound Of Dean Martin. While Dino enjoyed his most consistent chart success with Reprise in the mid '60s, it is his earlier, Capitol work that collectors seek. His Reprise work, singles and albums such as this one are often found in the bargain bins of many used record stores.

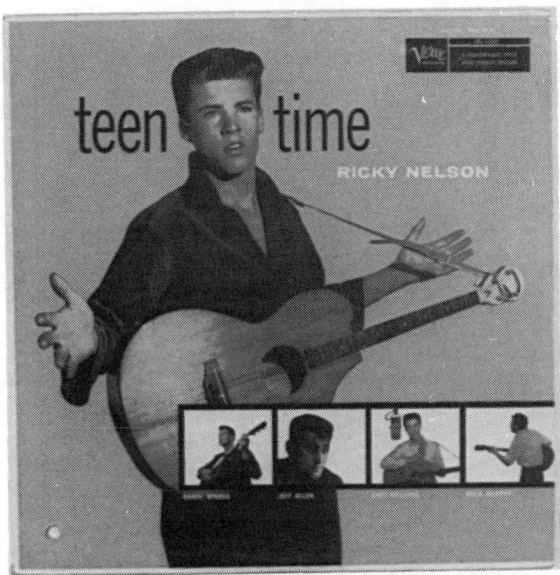

Ricky Nelson, *Teen Time.* Actually a various artists album that gathers several singles from Verve artists, this is generally regarded by collectors as Nelson's first album, as it includes all three of his first hits: "A Teenager's Romance," "I'm Walking" and "You're My One And Only Love." The great shot of the young Ricky on the cover adds to its desirability.

Label		Title	Year	VG+	NM
MYERS, DAVE, & THE SURFTONES					
Del-Fi DFLP-1239	(M)	Hangin' Twenty	1963	10.00	25.00
Del-Fi DFST-1239	(S)	Hangin' Twenty	1963	12.00	30.00
Carole CAR-8002	(M)	Greatest Racing Themes	1967	8.00	20.00
Carole CARS-8002	(S)	Greatest Racing Themes	1967	10.00	25.00
MYSTIC ASTROLOGIC CRYSTAL BAND, THE					
Carole 8001	(M)	Mystic Astrologic Crystal Band	1967	5.00	12.00
Carole S-8001	(S)	Mystic Astrologic Crystal Band	1967	6.00	15.00
Carole S-8003	(S)	Clip Out, Put On Book	1968	6.00	15.00
MYSTIC MOODS ORCHESTRA, THE					
Mobile Fidelity 1-001	(S)	Emotions		16.00	40.00
Mobile Fidelity 1-002	(S)	Cosmic Force		16.00	40.00
Mobile Fidelity 1-003	(S)	Stormy Weekend		16.00	40.00
MYSTIC NUMBER NATIONAL BANK, THE					
Probe CPLPS-4501	(S)	The Mystic Number National Bank	1969	6.00	15.00
MYSTIC SIVA					
V.O. 19713	(S)	Mystic Siva	1970	100.00	200.00

Label		Title	Year	VG+	NM
NRBQ (THE NEW RHYTHM & BLUES QUINTET)					
Columbia CS-9858	(S)	NRBQ ("360 Sound" label)	1969	6.00	15.00
Columbia CS-9981	(S)	Boppin' The Blues ("360 Sound" label)	1969	6.00	15.00
Kama Sutra KSBS-2045	(S)	Scraps	1972	5.00	12.00
Kama Sutra KSBS-2065	(S)	Workshop	1973	5.00	12.00
Annuit Coeptis 1001	(S)	Scraps/Workshop	1976	6.00	15.00
Red Rooster 101	(S)	All Hopped Up	1977	4.00	10.00
Mercury SRM-1-3712	(S)	NRBQ At Yankee Stadium	1978	4.00	10.00
NAGLE, RON					
Warners WS-1902	(S)	Bad Rice	1970	8.00	20.00
NAPOLEON XIV (JERRY SAMUELS)					
Warners W-1661	(M)	They're Coming To Take Me Away Ha Ha	1966	40.00	80.00
Warners WS-1661	(S)	They're Coming To Take Me Away Ha Ha	1966	50.00	100.00
NASHVILLE TEENS, THE					
London LL-3407	(M)	Tobacco Road	1964	35.00	70.00
London PS-407	(E)	Tobacco Road	1964	30.00	60.00
NAZZ					
SGC 5001	(S)	Nazz	1968	16.00	40.00
SGC 5002	(S)	Nazz Nazz	1969	30.00	60.00
SGC 5002	(S)	Nazz Nazz (Red vinyl)	1969	16.00	40.00
		(Orange & red label with a blue SGC logo.)			
SGC 5002	(S)	Nazz Nazz (Red vinyl)	1969	50.00	100.00
		(Orange & red label with a purple SGC logo.)			
SGC 5004	(S)	Nazz III	1971	16.00	40.00
NEIGHB'RHOOD CHILDR'N, THE					
Acta 38005	(S)	The Neighb'rhood Childr'n	1968	12.00	30.00
NELSON, OZZIE & HARRIET					
Imperial LP-9049	(M)	The Ozzie And Harriet Show		20.00	50.00

Label		Title	Year	VG+	NM
NELSON, RICK					
Verve V-2083	(M)	Teen Time	1957	100.00	200.00
Imperial LP-9048	(M)	Ricky	1957	30.00	60.00
Imperial LP-9050	(M)	Ricky Nelson	1958	20.00	50.00
Imperial LP-9061	(M)	Ricky Sings Again	1959	20.00	50.00
Imperial LP-9030	(M)	Songs By Ricky	1959	16.00	40.00
Imperial LP-12030	(S)	Songs By Ricky	1959	30.00	60.00
Imperial LP-9059	(M)	More Songs By Ricky	1960	16.00	40.00
Imperial LP-12059	(S)	More Songs By Ricky	1960	30.00	60.00
Imperial LP-12059	(S)	More Songs By Ricky (Blue vinyl)	1960	150.00	250.00
		(Issued with a poster, priced separately below.)			
		More Songs By Ricky Bonus Poster		20.00	50.00
Imperial LP-9152	(M)	Rick Is 21	1961	14.00	35.00
Imperial LP-12152	(S)	Rick Is 21	1961	20.00	50.00
Imperial LP-9082	(M)	Album Seven By Rick	1962	14.00	35.00
Imperial LP-12082	(S)	Album Seven By Rick	1962	20.00	50.00
Imperial LP-9218	(M)	Best Sellers By Rick Nelson	1963	12.00	30.00
Imperial LP-12218	(E)	Best Sellers By Rick Nelson	1963	10.00	25.00
Imperial LP-9223	(M)	It's Up To You	1963	12.00	30.00
Imperial LP-12223	(E)	It's Up To You	1963	10.00	25.00
Imperial LP-9232	(M)	Rick Nelson's Million Sellers	1963	12.00	30.00
Imperial LP-12232	(E)	Rick Nelson's Million Sellers	1963	10.00	25.00
Imperial LP-9244	(M)	A Long Vacation	1963	12.00	30.00
Imperial LP-12244	(E)	A Long Vacation	1963	10.00	25.00
Imperial LP-9251	(M)	Rick Nelson Sings For You	1964	12.00	30.00
Imperial LP-12251	(E)	Rick Nelson Sings For You	1964	10.00	25.00
		(Mono Imperial albums above have black labels with stars on top. Stereo albums have black & silver labels.)			
Decca DL-4419	(M)	For Your Sweet Love	1963	8.00	20.00
Decca DL7-4419	(S)	For Your Sweet Love	1963	12.00	30.00
Decca DL-4479	(M)	Rick Nelson Sings For You	1963	8.00	20.00
Decca DL7-4479	(S)	Rick Nelson Sings For You	1963	12.00	30.00
Decca DL-4559	(M)	The Very Thought Of You	1964	8.00	20.00
Decca DL7-4559	(S)	The Very Thought Of You	1964	12.00	30.00
Decca DL-4608	(M)	Spotlight On Rick	1964	8.00	20.00
Decca DL7-4608	(S)	Spotlight On Rick	1964	12.00	30.00
Decca DL-4660	(M)	Best Always	1965	8.00	20.00
Decca DL7-4660	(S)	Best Always	1965	12.00	30.00
Decca DL-4678	(M)	Love And Kisses	1965	8.00	20.00
Decca DL7-4678	(S)	Love And Kisses	1965	12.00	30.00
Sunset SUM-4118	(M)	Ricky Nelson	1966	6.00	15.00
Sunset SUS-5118	(P)	Ricky Nelson	1966	8.00	20.00
Decca DL-4779	(M)	Bright Lights And Country Music	1966	10.00	25.00
Decca DL7-4779	(S)	Bright Lights And Country Music	1966	12.00	30.00
Decca DL-4827	(M)	Country Fever	1967	10.00	25.00
Decca DL7-4827	(S)	Country Fever	1967	12.00	30.00
Decca DL-4836	(M)	On The Flip Side (Sdtk)	1967	8.00	20.00
Decca DL7-4836	(S)	On The Flip Side (Sdtk)	1967	10.00	25.00
		(Decca albums above have black labels with "Mfrd by Decca" beneath the rainbow.)			
Decca DL-4944	(M)	Another Side Of Rick	1967	10.00	25.00
Decca DL7-4944	(S)	Another Side Of Rick	1967	12.00	30.00
Decca DL7-5014	(S)	Perspective	1968	8.00	20.00
Sunset SUS-5205	(S)	I Need You	1968	6.00	15.00
Decca DL7-5162	(S)	Rick Nelson In Concert (Fold-open cover)	1970	6.00	15.00
Decca DL7-5236	(S)	Rick Sings Nelson (With poster)	1970	8.00	20.00
United Arts. UAS-960	(M)	Legendary Masters (Brown label)	1971	8.00	20.00
Decca DL7-5297	(S)	Rudy The Fifth	1971	6.00	15.00
Decca DL7-5391	(S)	Garden Party	1972	5.00	12.00
MCA 2-4004	(S)	Rick Nelson Country	1973	8.00	20.00
MCA 383	(S)	Windfall	1974	4.00	10.00
Epic KE-34420	(S)	Intakes	1977	4.00	10.00
Epic 3E-36868	(S)	Four You	1981	4.00	10.00
MCA 1517	(S)	The Decca Years	1982	2.50	6.00
NELSON, WILLIE					
Liberty LRP-3238	(M)	And Then I Wrote	1962	12.00	30.00
Liberty LST-7238	(S)	And Then I Wrote	1962	14.00	35.00
Liberty LRP-3308	(M)	Here's Willie Nelson	1963	12.00	30.00
Liberty LST-7308	(S)	Here's Willie Nelson	1963	14.00	35.00

Label		Title	Year	VG+	NM
RCA LPM-3418	(M)	Country Willie: His Own Songs	1965	6.00	15.00
RCA LSP-3418	(S)	Country Willie: His Own Songs	1965	8.00	20.00
RCA LPM-3528	(M)	Country Favorites, Willie Nelson Style	1966	6.00	15.00
RCA LSP-3528	(S)	Country Favorites, Willie Nelson Style	1966	8.00	20.00
RCA LPM-3659	(M)	Live Country Music Concert	1966	5.00	12.00
RCA LSP-3659	(S)	Live Country Music Concert	1966	6.00	15.00
RCA LPM-3748	(M)	Make Way For Willie Nelson	1967	5.00	12.00
RCA LSP-3748	(S)	Make Way For Willie Nelson	1967	6.00	15.00
RCA LPM-3858	(M)	The Party's Over	1967	5.00	12.00
RCA LSP-3858	(S)	The Party's Over	1967	6.00	15.00
RCA LPM-3937	(M)	Texas In My Soul	1968	6.00	15.00
RCA LSP-3937	(S)	Texas In My Soul	1968	6.00	15.00
		(RCA albums above have black labels.)			
Columbia HC-45305	(S)	Stardust (1/2 speed)	1981	8.00	20.00
Columbia HC-47951	(S)	Always On My Mind (1/2 speed)	1982	8.00	20.00
Columbia HC-48248	(S)	Tougher Than Leather (1/2 speed)	1983	8.00	20.00

NEP-TUNES, THE

Label		Title	Year	VG+	NM
Family FLP-552	(M)	Surfer's Holiday	1963	12.00	30.00
Family SFLP-552	(S)	Surfer's Holiday	1963	16.00	40.00

NESMITH, MICHAEL

Label		Title	Year	VG+	NM
RCA LSP-4371	(S)	Magnetic South	1970	8.00	20.00
RCA LSP-4415	(S)	Loose Salute	1970	8.00	20.00
RCA LSP-4497	(S)	Nevada Fighter	1971	8.00	20.00
RCA LSP-4563	(S)	Tantamount To Treason	1971	8.00	20.00
RCA LSP-4696	(S)	And The Hits Just Keep On Comin'	1972	8.00	20.00
Pacific Arts 7-101	(S)	The Prison (Box with booklet)	1978	16.00	40.00
Pacific Arts 7-101	(S)	The Prison (Standard cover)	1978	5.00	12.00
Pacific Arts 7-106	(S)	Michael Nesmith Compilation	1978	5.00	12.00
Pacific Arts 7-107	(S)	From A Radio Engine To The Photon Wing	1978	5.00	12.00
Pacific Arts 7-116	(S)	And The Hits Just Keep On Comin'	1978	5.00	12.00
Pacific Arts 7-117	(S)	Pretty Much Your Standard Ranch Stash	1978	5.00	12.00
Pacific Arts 7-118	(S)	Live At The Palais	1978	5.00	12.00
Pacific Arts 7-130	(S)	Infinite Rider On The Big Dogma	1979	5.00	12.00

NEVILLE, ARON

Label		Title	Year	VG+	NM
Par-Lo LP-1	(M)	Tell It Like It Is	1967	10.00	25.00
Par-Lo LP-1	(S)	Tell It Like It Is	1967	16.00	40.00
Minit LP-40007	(M)	Like It 'Tis	1967	10.00	25.00
Minit LP-40007	(E)	Like It 'Tis	1967	8.00	20.00

NEW COLONY SIX, THE

Label		Title	Year	VG+	NM
Sentar LP-101	(M)	Breakthrough	1966	150.00	250.00
Sentar ST-3001	(M)	Colonization	1967	8.00	20.00
Sentar SST-3001	(S)	Colonization	1967	10.00	25.00

NEW DIMENSIONS, THE

Label		Title	Year	VG+	NM
Sutton 331	(M)	Dueces And Eights	1963	8.00	20.00
Sutton SSU-331	(S)	Dueces And Eights	1963	10.00	25.00
Sutton 332	(M)	Surf 'N' Bongos	1963	8.00	20.00
Sutton SSU-332	(S)	Surf 'N' Bongos	1963	10.00	25.00
Sutton 336	(M)	Soul Surf	1964	8.00	20.00
Sutton SSU-336	(S)	Soul Surf	1964	10.00	25.00

NEW TWEEDY BROTHERS, THE

Label		Title	Year	VG+	NM
Ridon 234	(S)	The New Tweedy Brothers		300.00	500.00

NEW YORK DOLLS, THE

Label		Title	Year	VG+	NM
Mercury SRM-1-675	(S)	New York Dolls	1973	10.00	25.00
Mercury SRM-1-1001	(S)	Too Much, Too Soon	1974	10.00	25.00
		(Both albums above have custom dolls labels.)			

NEWBEATS, THE

Label		Title	Year	VG+	NM
Hickory LP-120	(M)	Bread And Butter	1964	16.00	40.00
Hickory LPS-120	(S)	Bread And Butter	1964	50.00	100.00
Hickory LP-122	(M)	Big Beat Sounds By The Newbeats	1965	12.00	30.00
Hickory LPS-122	(S)	Big Beat Sounds By The Newbeats	1965	16.00	40.00
Hickory LP-128	(M)	Run Baby Run	1965	12.00	30.00
Hickory LPS-128	(S)	Run Baby Run	1965	16.00	40.00

Label		Title	Year	VG+	NM
NEWTON-JOHN, OLIVIA					
Uni 73117	(S)	If Not For You	1971	16.00	40.00
Mobile Fidelity 1-040	(S)	Totally Hot	1981	5.00	12.00
NICHOLS, MIKE, & ELAINE MAY					
Mercury MG-20376	(M)	Improvisations To Music	1959	12.00	30.00
Mercury OCM-2200	(M)	An Evening With Mike Nichols & Elaine May	1960	6.00	15.00
Mercury OCM-2200	(S)	An Evening With Mike Nichols & Elaine May	1960	8.00	20.00
Mercury MG-20680	(M)	Examine Doctors	1962	5.00	12.00
Mercury SR-60680	(S)	Examine Doctors	1962	6.00	15.00
Mercury MG-20997	(M)	The Best Of Mike Nichols & Elaine May	1965	5.00	12.00
Mercury SR-60997	(S)	The Best Of Mike Nichols & Elaine May	1965	6.00	15.00
NICKS, STEVIE					
Also refer to Buckingham/Nicks.					
Mobile Fidelity 1-121	(S)	Bella Donna	1982	8.00	20.00
NICO					
Also refer to the Velvet Underground.					
Verve V-5032	(M)	Chelsea Girl	1967	8.00	20.00
Verve V6-5032	(S)	Chelsea Girl	1967	10.00	25.00
Elektra EKS-74029	(S)	The Marble Index	1968	8.00	20.00
Reprise RS-6424	(S)	Desert Shore	1970	8.00	20.00
Island ILPS-9311	(S)	The End	1975	6.00	15.00
NIGHT CAPS, THE					
Vandan 8124	(M)	Wine, Wine, Wine	1961	50.00	100.00
NIGHT OWLS, THE					
Valmor 79	(M)	Twisting The Oldies	1962	20.00	50.00
NIGHT SHADOWS, THE					
Hottrax 1414	(S)	The Square Root Of Two	1968	100.00	200.00
Hottrax 1430	(S)	Live At The Spot	1981	6.00	15.00
NIGHTCAPS, THE					
Vandan VRLP-8124	(M)	Wine, Wine, Wine		35.00	70.00
NIGHTCRAWLERS, THE					
Kapp KL-1520	(M)	The Little Black Egg	1967	16.00	40.00
Kapp KS-3520	(E)	The Little Black Egg	1967	12.00	30.00
NIGHTHAWKS, THE					
Aladdin 101	(M)	Rock And Roll		75.00	150.00
NIELSEN, GERTRUDE					
Decca DL-5138 (10")	(M)	Gertrude Nielsen		10.00	25.00
NILSSON (HARRY NILSSON)					
Tower T-5095	(M)	Spotlight On Nilsson	1967	5.00	12.00
Tower DT-5095	(E)	Spotlight On Nilsson	1967	4.00	10.00
RCA LPM-3874	(M)	Pandemonium Shadow Show	1967	4.00	10.00
RCA LSP-3874	(S)	Pandemonium Shadow Show	1967	5.00	12.00
RCA LPM-3956	(M)	Aerial Ballet	1967	4.00	10.00
RCA LSP-3956	(S)	Aerial Ballet	1967	5.00	12.00
		(RCA albums above have black labels.)			
RCA LSO-1152	(S)	Skidoo (Sdtk)	1968	8.00	20.00
RCA LSP-4289	(S)	Nilsson Sings Newman	1969	4.00	10.00
RCA LSPX-1003	(S)	The Point	1971	4.00	10.00
RCA LSP-4417	(S)	The Point (Fold-open cover with booklet)	1971	5.00	12.00
Rapple ABL1-0220	(S)	Son Of Dracula (Sdtk)	1974	4.00	10.00
RCA CPL1-0570	(S)	Pussy Cats (With John Lennon)	1974	4.00	10.00
RCA APD1-0570	(Q)	Pussy Cats (With John Lennon)	1974	6.00	15.00
		(RCA albums above have orange labels.)			
RCA APD1-0817	(Q)	Duit On Mon Dei	1975	4.00	10.00
RCA APD1-1031	(Q)	Sandman	1976	4.00	10.00
NIMOY, LEONARD					
Dot DLP-3794	(M)	Mr. Spock's Music From Outer Space	1967	14.00	35.00
Dot DLP-25794	(S)	Mr. Spock's Music From Outer Space	1967	16.00	40.00
Dot DLP-25835	(S)	Two Sides Of Leonard Nimoy	1968	10.00	25.00

Label		Title	Year	VG+	NM
Dot DLP-25883	(S)	The Way I Feel		10.00	25.00
Dot DLP-25910	(S)	The Touch Of Leonard Nimoy	1969	10.00	25.00
Dot DLP-25966	(S)	The New World Of Leonard Nimoy	1969	10.00	25.00
Paramount 1030	(S)	Outer Space/Inner Mind		12.00	30.00

NIRVANA

Bell 6015	(S)	The Story Of Simon Simopath	1968	8.00	20.00
Bell 6024	(S)	All Of Us	1969	6.00	15.00
Metromedia 1018	(S)	Nirvana	1970	6.00	15.00

NITTY GRITTY DIRT BAND, THE (THE DIRT BAND)

Liberty LRP-3501	(M)	The Nitty Gritty Dirt Band	1967	5.00	12.00
Liberty LST-7501	(S)	The Nitty Gritty Dirt Band	1967	6.00	15.00
Liberty LRP-3516	(M)	Ricochet	1967	6.00	15.00
Liberty LST-7516	(S)	Ricochet	1967	8.00	20.00
Liberty LST-7540	(S)	Rare Junk	1968	8.00	20.00
Liberty LST-7611	(S)	Alive	1969	8.00	20.00
Liberty LST-7642	(S)	Uncle Charlie And His Dog Teddy	1970	6.00	15.00

NITZSCHE, JACK

Reprise R-6101	(M)	The Lonely Surfer	1963	10.00	25.00
Reprise RS-6101	(S)	The Lonely Surfer	1963	12.00	30.00
Reprise R-6115	(M)	Dance To The Hits Of The Beatles	1964	10.00	25.00
Reprise RS-6115	(S)	Dance To The Hits Of The Beatles	1964	12.00	30.00
Reprise R-6200	(M)	Chopin '66	1966	6.00	15.00
Reprise RS-6200	(S)	Chopin '66	1966	8.00	20.00
Reprise MS-2092	(S)	St. Giles Cripplegate	1972	8.00	20.00

NOBLES, CLIFF, & COMPANY

Phil L.A. Of Soul 4001	(S)	The Horse	1968	12.00	30.00

NOLAND, TERRY

Brunswick BL-54041	(M)	Terry Noland	1958	100.00	200.00

NORDINE, KEN

Decca DL-8550	(M)	Concert In The Sky	1957	16.00	40.00
Dot DLP-3075	(M)	Word Jazz	1958	14.00	35.00
Dot DLP-3096	(M)	Son Of Word Jazz	1958	12.00	30.00
Dot DLP-25096	(S)	Son Of Word Jazz	1958	14.00	35.00
Dot DLP-3115	(M)	Love Words	1958	10.00	25.00
Dot DLP-25115	(S)	Love Words	1958	12.00	30.00
Dot DLP-3142	(M)	My Baby	1958	10.00	25.00
Dot DLP-25142	(S)	My Baby	1958	12.00	30.00
Dot DLP-3196	(M)	Next!	1959	10.00	25.00
Dot DLP-25196	(S)	Next!	1959	12.00	30.00
Dot DLP-3301	(M)	Word Jazz, Volume 2	1960	10.00	25.00
Dot DLP-25301	(S)	Word Jazz, Volume 2	1960	12.00	30.00
Philips 200224	(M)	Colors		8.00	20.00
Philips 600224	(S)	Colors		10.00	25.00
Philips 200258	(M)	Twink		8.00	20.00
Philips 600258	(S)	Twink		10.00	25.00
Dot DLP-25880	(S)	Classic Collection/Best Of Word Jazz	1968	10.00	25.00
Blue Thumb 33	(M)	How Are Things In Your Town?	1969	6.00	15.00

NORMA JEAN
Also refer to Porter Wagoner.

RCA LPM-2961	(M)	Let's Go All The Way	1964	5.00	12.00
RCA LSP-2961	(S)	Let's Go All The Way	1964	6.00	15.00
RCA LPM-3449	(M)	Pretty Miss Norma Jean	1965	5.00	12.00
RCA LSP-3449	(S)	Pretty Miss Norma Jean	1965	6.00	15.00
RCA LPM-3541	(M)	Please Don't Hurt Me	1966	5.00	12.00
RCA LSP-3541	(S)	Please Don't Hurt Me	1966	6.00	15.00
RCA LPM-3664	(M)	A Tribute To Kitty Wells	1966	5.00	12.00
RCA LSP-3664	(S)	A Tribute To Kitty Wells	1966	6.00	15.00
RCA LPM-3700	(M)	Norma Jean Sings Porter Wagoner	1967	5.00	12.00
RCA LSP-3700	(S)	Norma Jean Sings Porter Wagoner	1967	6.00	15.00
RCA LPM-3836	(M)	Jackson Ain't A Very Big Town	1967	5.00	12.00
RCA LSP-3836	(S)	Jackson Ain't A Very Big Town	1967	6.00	15.00
RCA LPM-3910	(M)	Heaven's Just A Prayer Away	1968	5.00	12.00
RCA LSP-3910	(S)	Heaven's Just A Prayer Away	1968	6.00	15.00

(RCA albums above have black labels.)

Label		Title	Year	VG+	NM
NORMAN, LARRY					
Capitol ST-446	(S)	Upon This Rock	1970	12.00	30.00
One Way JC-7937	(S)	Street Level	1970	10.00	25.00
One Way JC-900	(S)	Bootleg	1971	10.00	25.00
MGM SE-4942	(S)	So Long Ago/The Garden	1973	12.00	30.00
Solid Rock SRA-2001	(S)	In Another Land		6.00	15.00
Street Level 8885	(S)	Only Visiting This Planet		6.00	15.00
Sunrise AB-777	(S)	Streams Of White Light		6.00	15.00
Impac HWS-3121	(S)	Upon This Rock		6.00	15.00
NOTES FROM THE UNDERGROUND					
Vanguard VSD-6502	(S)	Notes From The Underground	1970	6.00	15.00
NUTTY SQUIRRELS, THE					
Hanover HML-8014	(M)	The Nutty Squirrels	1960	10.00	25.00
Columbia CL-1589	(M)	Bird Watching	1961	6.00	15.00
Columbia CS-8389	(S)	Bird Watching	1961	8.00	20.00
MGM E-4272	(M)	A Hard Day's Night	1964	8.00	20.00
MGM SE-4272	(S)	A Hard Day's Night	1964	10.00	25.00

Label		Title	Year	VG+	NM
O' BRIEN, HUGH					
ABC 203	(M)	Wyatt Earp Sings	1957	20.00	50.00
O' DAY, ANITA					
Advance 8 (10")	(M)	Specials	1951	16.00	40.00
Coral CRL-56073	(M)	Singin' And Swingin'	1953	14.00	35.00
Clef 130	(M)	Collate	1953	14.00	35.00
Norgan 30 (10")	(M)	Anita O' Day	1954	16.00	40.00
Norgan 1049	(M)	Anita O' Day Sings Jazz	1955	14.00	35.00
Norgan 1057	(M)	An Evening With Anita O' Day	1956	14.00	35.00
Verve V-2000	(M)	Anita	1956	12.00	30.00
Verve V-2043	(M)	Pick Yourself Up	1956	12.00	30.00
Verve V-2049	(M)	The Lady Is A Tramp	1956	12.00	30.00
Verve V-2050	(M)	An Evening With Anita O' Day	1956	12.00	30.00
Verve V-8259	(M)	Anita Sings The Most	1958	12.00	30.00
Verve V-8283	(M)	Anita O' Day Sings The Winners	1958	10.00	25.00
Verve VS-6002	(S)	Anita O' Day Sings The Winners	1958	12.00	30.00
Verve V-2113	(M)	Anita O' Day At Mr. Kelly's	1958	10.00	25.00
Verve VS-6043	(S)	Anita O' Day At Mr. Kelly's	1958	12.00	30.00
Verve V-2118	(M)	Anita O' Day Swings Cole Porter	1959	10.00	25.00
Verve VS-6059	(S)	Anita O' Day Swings Cole Porter	1959	12.00	30.00
Verve V-8312	(M)	Cool Heat	1959	10.00	25.00
Verve VS-6046	(S)	Cool Heat	1959	12.00	30.00
Verve V-2141	(M)	Anita O' Day Swings Rodgers And Hart	1959	12.00	30.00
Verve V-2145	(M)	Waiter, Make Mine Blues	1960	10.00	25.00
Verve V6-2145	(S)	Waiter, Make Mine Blues	1960	12.00	30.00
Verve V-2157	(M)	Trav'lin' Light	1961	8.00	20.00
Verve V6-2157	(S)	Trav'lin' Light	1961	10.00	25.00
Verve V-8442	(M)	All The Sad Young Men	1961	8.00	20.00
Verve V6-8442	(S)	All The Sad Young Men	1961	10.00	25.00
		(Verve albums above have black labels with "Verve Records, Inc" on the bottom.)			
Verve V-8472	(M)	Time For Two	1962	6.00	15.00
Verve V6-8472	(S)	Time For Two	1962	8.00	20.00
Verve V-8483	(M)	That Is Anita	1962	6.00	15.00
Verve V6-8483	(E)	That Is Anita	1962	5.00	12.00

Label		Title	Year	VG+	NM
Verve V-8514	(M)	Anita O' Day And The Three Sounds	1963	6.00	15.00
Verve V6-8514	(S)	Anita O' Day And The Three Sounds	1963	8.00	20.00
Verve V-8572	(M)	Incomparable Anita O' Day	1964	6.00	15.00
Verve V6-8572	(S)	Incomparable Anita O' Day	1964	8.00	20.00

O' DELL, MAC

Label		Title	Year	VG+	NM
Audio Lab AL-1544	(M)	Hymns For The Country Folk	1960	20.00	50.00

O' JAYS, THE

Label		Title	Year	VG+	NM
Imperial LP-9290	(M)	Comin' Through	1965	8.00	20.00
Imperial LP-12290	(S)	Comin' Through	1965	10.00	25.00
Minit LP-40008	(S)	Soul Sounds		6.00	15.00
Bell 6014	(S)	Back On Top	1968	6.00	15.00

O' LAY, RUTH

Label		Title	Year	VG+	NM
EmArcy 36125	(M)	O' Lay	1958	12.00	30.00
Mercury MG-20390	(M)	Easy Living	1959	10.00	25.00
Mercury SR-60390	(S)	Easy Living	1959	12.00	30.00
United Arts. UAL-3115	(M)	Ruth O' Lay In Person	1960	8.00	20.00
United Arts. UAL-6115	(S)	Ruth O' Lay In Person	1960	10.00	25.00
Everest 5218	(M)	O' Lay! OK!	1963	6.00	15.00
Everest 1218	(S)	O' Lay! OK!	1963	8.00	20.00

OBOLER, ARCH

Label		Title	Year	VG+	NM
Capitol T-1763	(M)	Drop Dead! An Exercise In Horror	1962	5.00	12.00
Capitol ST-1763	(S)	Drop Dead! An Exercise In Horror	1962	6.00	15.00

OCHS, PHIL

Label		Title	Year	VG+	NM
Elektra EKL-269	(M)	All The News That's Fit To Sing	1964	8.00	20.00
Elektra EKS7-269	(S)	All The News That's Fit To Sing	1964	10.00	25.00
Elektra EKL-287	(M)	I Ain't Marching Anymore	1965	8.00	20.00
Elektra EKS7-287	(S)	I Ain't Marching Anymore	1965	10.00	25.00
Elektra EKL-310	(M)	Phil Ochs In Concert	1965	8.00	20.00
Elektra EKS7-310	(S)	Phil Ochs In Concert	1965	10.00	25.00
A&M SLP-133	(M)	Pleasures Of The Harbor	1967	5.00	12.00
A&M SP-4133	(S)	Pleasures Of The Harbor	1967	6.00	15.00
A&M SP-4148	(S)	Tape From California	1968	6.00	15.00
A&M SP-4181	(S)	Rehearsals For Retirement	1969	6.00	15.00
A&M SP-4253	(S)	Phil Ochs' Greatest Hits	1970	6.00	15.00
		(A&M albums above have brown labels.)			

ODETTA

Label		Title	Year	VG+	NM
Vanguard VRS-2046	(M)	My Eyes Have Seen		5.00	12.00
Vanguard VSD7-2046	(S)	My Eyes Have Seen		6.00	15.00
Vanguard VRS-2057	(M)	Ballads For Americans		5.00	12.00
Vanguard VSD7-2057	(S)	Ballads For Americans		6.00	15.00
Vanguard VRS-2072	(M)	Odetta At Carnegie Hall		5.00	12.00
Vanguard VSD7-2072	(S)	Odetta At Carnegie Hall		6.00	15.00
Vanguard VRS-2079	(M)	Christmas Spirituals	1960	5.00	12.00
Vanguard VSD7-2079	(S)	Christmas Spirituals	1960	6.00	15.00
Riverside RLP-417	(M)	Odetta And The Blues	1962	6.00	15.00
Riverside RLP9-417	(S)	Odetta And The Blues	1962	8.00	20.00
Vanguard VRS-2109	(M)	Odetta At Town Hall	1962	5.00	12.00
Vanguard VSD7-2109	(S)	Odetta At Town Hall	1962	6.00	15.00
Vanguard VRS-2153	(M)	One Grain Of Sand	1963	5.00	12.00
Vanguard VSD7-2153	(S)	One Grain Of Sand	1963	6.00	15.00
RCA LPM-2573	(M)	Sometimes I Feel Like Crying	1962	4.00	10.00
RCA LSP-2573	(S)	Sometimes I Feel Like Crying	1962	5.00	12.00
RCA LPM-2643	(M)	Odetta Sings Folk Songs	1963	5.00	12.00
RCA LSP-2643	(S)	Odetta Sings Folk Songs	1963	6.00	15.00
RCA LPM-2792	(M)	It's A Mighty World	1964	4.00	10.00
RCA LSP-2792	(S)	It's A Mighty World	1964	5.00	12.00
RCA LPM-2923	(M)	Odetta Sings Of Many Things	1964	4.00	10.00
RCA LSP-2923	(S)	Odetta Sings Of Many Things	1964	5.00	12.00
RCA LPM-3324	(M)	Odetta Sings Dylan	1965	6.00	15.00
RCA LSP-3324	(S)	Odetta Sings Dylan	1965	8.00	20.00
RCA LPM-3457	(M)	Odetta In Japan	1966	4.00	10.00
RCA LSP-3457	(S)	Odetta In Japan	1966	5.00	12.00
		(RCA albums above have black labels.)			
Vanguard VRS-3003	(M)	Odetta At Carnegie Hall	1967	4.00	10.00
Vanguard VSD7-3003	(S)	Odetta At Carnegie Hall	1967	5.00	12.00

The Nashville Teens, *Tobacco Road.* Scoring with the great "Tobacco Road" in 1965, this unsung British beat group recorded one fine album before disbanding and providing other more successful groups with key members.

Olivia Newton-John, *If Not For You.* Before becoming the most successful white female vocalist of the past fiteen years, Olivia Newton-John scored a mild Top Forty hit with the title tune of this, her first American album, on the now defunt Uni label.

Label		Title	Year	VG+	NM
OHIO EXPRESS, THE					
Cameo CS-20,000	(S)	Beg, Borrow And Steal	1968	10.00	25.00
OHIO PLAYERS, THE					
Capitol ST-192	(S)	Observations In Time	1969	6.00	15.00
OLDHAM ORCHESTRA, ANDREW					
London LL-3457	(M)	The Rolling Stones Songbook	1965	16.00	40.00
London PS-457	(S)	The Rolling Stones Songbook	1965	20.00	50.00
Parrot PA-61003	(M)	East Meets West	1965	12.00	30.00
Parrot PAS-71003	(S)	East Meets West	1965	16.00	40.00
OLENN, JOHNNY					
Liberty LRP-3029	(M)	Just Rollin' With Johnny Olenn	1958	75.00	150.00
OLIVER & THE TWISTERS					
Colpix CP-423	(M)	Look Who's Twistin' Everybody	1961	16.00	40.00
OLYMPICS, THE					
Arvee A-423	(M)	Doin' The Hully Gully	1960	50.00	100.00
Arvee A-424	(M)	Dance By The Light Of The Moon	1961	35.00	70.00
Arvee A-429	(M)	Party Time	1961	35.00	70.00
Tri-Disc 1001	(M)	Do The Bounce	1963	16.00	40.00
Tri-Disc 1001	(S)	Do The Bounce	1963	20.00	50.00
Mirwood M-7003	(M)	Something Old, Something New	1966	12.00	30.00
Mirwood MS-7003	(S)	Something Old, Something New	1966	16.00	40.00
Post 8000	(M)	The Olympics Sing		6.00	15.00
ONES, THE					
Ashwood House 1105	(S)	The Ones		100.00	200.00
ONO, YOKO					
Also refer to John Lennon.					
Apple SW-3373	(S)	Plastic Ono Band	1971	6.00	15.00
Apple SVBB-3380	(S)	Fly (With insert)	1971	6.00	15.00
Apple SVBB-3399	(S)	Approximately Infinite Universe	1972	8.00	20.00
Apple SW-3412	(S)	Feeling The Space	1973	4.00	10.00
ORANG-UTAH					
Bell 6054	(S)	Orang-Utah	1971	8.00	20.00
ORBACH, JEFF					
MGM E-4056	(M)	Off Broadway		6.00	15.00
MGM SE-4056	(S)	Off Broadway		8.00	20.00
ORBISON, ROY					
Sun LP-1260	(M)	Roy Orbison At The Rockhouse	1961	100.00	200.00
Monument M-4002	(M)	Lonely And Blue	1961	35.00	70.00
Monument SM-14002	(S)	Lonely And Blue	1961	50.00	100.00
Monument M-4007	(M)	Crying	1962	35.00	70.00
Monument SM-14007	(S)	Crying	1962	50.00	100.00
Monument M-4009	(M)	Roy Orbison's Greatest Hits	1962	12.00	30.00
Monument SM-14009	(S)	Roy Orbison's Greatest Hits	1962	16.00	40.00
Monument MLP-8000	(M)	Roy Orbison's Greatest Hits	1963	6.00	15.00
Monument SLP-18000	(S)	Roy Orbison's Greatest Hits	1963	8.00	20.00
Monument MLP-8003	(M)	In Dreams	1963	16.00	40.00
Monument SLP-18003	(S)	In Dreams	1963	30.00	60.00
Monument MLP-8023	(M)	Early Orbison	1964	8.00	20.00
Monument SLP-18023	(S)	Early Orbison	1964	12.00	30.00
Monument MLP-8024	(M)	More Of Roy Orbison's Greatest Hits	1964	10.00	25.00
Monument SLP-18024	(S)	More Of Roy Orbison's Greatest Hits	1964	12.00	30.00
Camden CAL-820	(M)	Special Delivery	1964	10.00	25.00
Camden CAS-820	(E)	Special Delivery	1964	6.00	15.00
Monument MLP-8035	(M)	Orbisongs	1965	6.00	15.00
Monument SLP-18035	(S)	Orbisongs	1965	8.00	20.00
MGM E-4308	(M)	There Is Only One Roy Orbison	1965	5.00	12.00
MGM SE-4308	(S)	There Is Only One Roy Orbison	1965	6.00	15.00
MGM E-4322	(M)	The Orbison Way	1966	5.00	12.00
MGM SE-4322	(S)	The Orbison Way	1966	6.00	15.00
MGM E-4379	(M)	The Classic Roy Orbison	1966	5.00	12.00
MGM SE-4379	(S)	The Classic Roy Orbison	1966	6.00	15.00

The Osmond Brothers, *Songs We Sang On The Andy Williams Show.* Regulars on Andy's variety show in the early '60s, this was the cornerstone to the pop dynasty that would place thirty singles in the Top Forty between 1971 and 1978.

Roy Orbison, *Lonely And Blue.* While Roy's singles sold consistently in the six figures, his albums, like so many singles artists of the time, often failed to even dent the charts. Consequently they are rare and in great demand. Also, Orbison's early Monument albums, including this, his first for the label, are considered state of the art in regards to the stereo recording technique.

Label		Title	Year	VG+	NM
Monument MLP-8045	(M)	The Very Best Of Roy Orbison	1966	5.00	12.00
Monument SLP-18045	(P)	The Very Best Of Roy Orbison	1966	6.00	15.00
MGM E-4424	(M)	Roy Orbison Sings Don Gibson	1967	5.00	12.00
MGM SE-4424	(S)	Roy Orbison Sings Don Gibson	1967	6.00	15.00
MGM E-4475	(M)	The Fastest Guitar Alive (Sdtk)	1967	6.00	15.00
MGM SE-4475	(S)	The Fastest Guitar Alive (Sdtk)	1967	8.00	20.00
MGM E-4514	(M)	Cry Softly, Lonely One	1967	5.00	12.00
MGM SE-4514	(S)	Cry Softly, Lonely One	1967	6.00	15.00
MGM SE-4636	(S)	Roy Orbison's Many Moods	1969	6.00	15.00
MGM SE-4659	(S)	The Great Songs Of Roy Orbison	1970	6.00	15.00
MGM SE-4683	(S)	Hank Williams The Roy Orbison Way	1970	8.00	20.00
MGM 1SE-21	(S)	Zigzag (Sdtk)	1970	6.00	15.00
Monument KZG-31484	(P)	The All-Time Greatest Hits Of Roy Orbison	1972	8.00	20.00
MGM SE-4835	(S)	Roy Orbison Sings	1972	5.00	12.00
MGM SE-4867	(S)	Memphis	1972	5.00	12.00
MGM SE-4934	(S)	Milestones	1973	5.00	12.00
Mercury SRM-1-1045	(S)	I'm Still In Love With You	1975	5.00	12.00
Monument MG-7600	(S)	Regeneration	1976	5.00	12.00
Asylum 6E-198	(S)	Laminar Flow	1979	4.00	10.00

ORCHIDS, THE

Roulette R-25169	(M)	Twistin' At The Roundtable	1962	6.00	15.00
Roulette SR-25169	(S)	Twistin' At The Roundtable	1962	8.00	20.00

ORIOLES, THE: *Refer to* SONNY TIL

ORION, P.J., & THE MAGNATES

Magnate 122459	(M)	P.J. Orion And The Magnates		16.00	40.00

ORLANDO, TONY

Epic LN-611	(M)	Bless You And 11 Other Great Hits	1961	12.00	30.00
Epic BN-611	(S)	Bless You And 11 Other Great Hits	1961	16.00	40.00

ORLONS, THE

Cameo C-1020	(M)	The Wah Watusi	1962	16.00	40.00
Cameo C-1033	(M)	All The Hits	1962	14.00	35.00
Cameo C-1041	(M)	South Street	1963	16.00	40.00
Cameo C-1054	(M)	Not Me	1963	14.00	35.00
Cameo C-1061	(M)	Biggest Hits	1963	14.00	35.00
Cameo C-1067	(M)	Golden Hits Of The Orlons & The Dovells	1963	14.00	35.00
Cameo C-1073	(M)	Down Memory Lane	1963	14.00	35.00

ORPHAN EGG

Carole CARS-8004	(S)	Orphan Egg	1968	10.00	25.00

ORPHEUS

MGM SE-4524	(S)	Orpheus	1968	6.00	15.00
MGM SE-4569	(S)	Ascending	1968	5.00	12.00
MGM SE-4599	(S)	Joyful	1969	5.00	12.00

OSBORNE, MARY

Warwick 2004	(M)	A Girl And Her Guitar	1961	12.00	30.00

OSMOND BROTHERS, THE

MGM E-4146	(M)	Songs We Sang On The Andy Williams Show	1963	5.00	12.00
MGM SE-4146	(S)	Songs We Sang On The Andy Williams Show	1963	6.00	15.00
MGM E-4187	(M)	We Sing You A Merry Christmas	1963	5.00	12.00
MGM SE-4187	(S)	We Sing You A Merry Christmas	1963	6.00	15.00
MGM E-4235	(M)	All-Time Hymn Favorites	1964	5.00	12.00
MGM SE-4235	(S)	All-Time Hymn Favorites	1964	6.00	15.00
MGM E-4291	(M)	The New Sound Of The Osmond Brothers	1965	5.00	12.00
MGM SE-4291	(S)	The New Sound Of The Osmond Brothers	1965	6.00	15.00

OSMOSIS

RCA LSP-4369	(S)	Osmosis	1970	6.00	15.00

OSWALD, LEE HARVEY

Truth 22-65	(M)	Lee Harvey Oswald Speaks	1967	10.00	25.00
Inca 1001	(M)	Self Portrait In Red	1967	10.00	25.00

Label		Title	Year	VG+	NM
OTHER HALF, THE					
Acta A-38004	(S)	The Other Half	1968	12.00	30.00
OTIS, JOHNNY					
Dig 103	(M)	Mel Williams And Johnny Otis	1955	50.00	100.00
Dig 104	(M)	Rock And Roll Hit Parade, Volume 1	1957	100.00	200.00
Capitol T-940	(M)	The Johnny Otis Show	1958	50.00	100.00
Kent KST-534	(S)	Cold Shot		10.00	25.00
Epic BN-26524	(S)	Cuttin' Up	1970	8.00	20.00
Epic EG-30473	(S)	Live At Monterey	1971	8.00	20.00
OUTSIDERS, THE					
Capitol T-2501	(M)	Time Won't Let Me	1966	6.00	15.00
Capitol ST-2501	(S)	Time Won't Let Me	1966	8.00	20.00
Capitol T-2568	(M)	Album #2	1966	6.00	15.00
Capitol ST-2568	(P)	Album #2	1966	8.00	20.00
Capitol T-2636	(M)	Outsiders In	1967	6.00	15.00
Capitol ST-2636	(S)	Outsiders In	1967	8.00	20.00
Capitol T-2745	(M)	Happening Live	1967	6.00	15.00
Capitol ST-2745	(S)	Happening Live	1967	8.00	20.00
OWENS, BONNIE (& THE STRANGERS)					
Also refer to Merle Haggard.					
Capitol T-2403	(M)	Don't Take Advantage Of Me	1965	5.00	12.00
Capitol ST-2403	(S)	Don't Take Advantage Of Me	1965	6.00	15.00
Capitol T-2660	(M)	All Of Me Belongs To You	1967	5.00	12.00
Capitol ST-2660	(S)	All Of Me Belongs To You	1967	6.00	15.00
Capitol T-2760	(M)	Your Tender Loving Care	1967	5.00	12.00
Capitol ST-2760	(S)	Your Tender Loving Care	1967	6.00	15.00
Capitol ST-2861	(S)	Somewhere Between	1968	5.00	12.00
Tower ST-5141	(S)	Killers Three (Sdtk)	1968	8.00	20.00
OWENS, BUCK (& THE BUCKAROOS)					
Capitol T-1482	(M)	Buck Owens Sings Harlan Howard	1961	10.00	25.00
Capitol ST-1482	(S)	Buck Owens Sings Harlan Howard	1961	12.00	30.00
Capitol T-1489	(M)	Under Your Spell Again	1961	8.00	20.00
Capitol DT-1489	(E)	Under Your Spell Again	1961	10.00	25.00
Starday SLP-172	(M)	Fabulous Country Music Sound	1962	8.00	20.00
Capitol T-1777	(M)	You're For Me	1962	6.00	15.00
Capitol ST-1777	(S)	You're For Me	1962	8.00	20.00
Capitol T-1879	(M)	On The Bandstand	1963	6.00	15.00
Capitol ST-1879	(S)	On The Bandstand	1963	8.00	20.00
Capitol T-1989	(M)	Buck Owens Sings Tommy Collins	1963	6.00	15.00
Capitol ST-1989	(S)	Buck Owens Sings Tommy Collins	1963	8.00	20.00
Capitol T-2105	(M)	The Best Of Buck Owens	1964	5.00	12.00
Capitol ST-2105	(S)	The Best Of Buck Owens	1964	6.00	15.00
Capitol T-2135	(M)	Together Again	1964	5.00	12.00
Capitol ST-2135	(S)	Together Again	1964	6.00	15.00
Capitol T-2186	(M)	I Don't Care	1964	5.00	12.00
Capitol ST-2186	(S)	I Don't Care	1964	6.00	15.00
Capitol T-2283	(M)	I've Got A Tiger By The Tail	1965	5.00	12.00
Capitol ST-2283	(S)	I've Got A Tiger By The Tail	1965	6.00	15.00
Capitol T-2353	(M)	Before You Go	1965	5.00	12.00
Capitol ST-2353	(S)	Before You Go	1965	6.00	15.00
Capitol T-2367	(M)	The Instrumental Hits	1965	5.00	12.00
Capitol ST-2367	(S)	The Instrumental Hits	1965	6.00	15.00
Capitol T-2396	(M)	Christmas With Buck Owens	1965	5.00	12.00
Capitol ST-2396	(S)	Christmas With Buck Owens	1965	6.00	15.00
Capitol T-2443	(M)	Roll Out The Red Carpet	1966	5.00	12.00
Capitol ST-2443	(S)	Roll Out The Red Carpet	1966	6.00	15.00
Capitol T-2497	(M)	Dust On Mother's Bible	1966	5.00	12.00
Capitol ST-2497	(S)	Dust On Mother's Bible	1966	6.00	15.00
Capitol T-2556	(M)	Carnegie Hall Concert	1966	5.00	12.00
Capitol ST-2556	(S)	Carnegie Hall Concert	1966	6.00	15.00
Capitol T-2640	(M)	Open Up Your Heart	1967	5.00	12.00
Capitol ST-2640	(S)	Open Up Your Heart	1967	6.00	15.00
Capitol T-2715	(M)	Buck Owens & His Buckaroos In Japan	1967	5.00	12.00
Capitol ST-2715	(S)	Buck Owens & His Buckaroos In Japan	1967	6.00	15.00
Capitol T-2760	(M)	Your Tender Loving Care	1967	5.00	12.00
Capitol ST-2760	(S)	Your Tender Loving Care	1967	6.00	15.00
Capitol ST-2841	(S)	It Takes People Like You	1968	6.00	15.00

Label		Title	Year	VG+	NM
Capitol ST-2902	(S)	A Night On The Town	1968	6.00	15.00
Capitol ST-2962	(S)	Sweet Rosie Jones	1968	6.00	15.00
Capitol ST-2977	(S)	Christmas Shopping	1968	6.00	15.00
Capitol ST-2994	(S)	The Guitar Player	1968	6.00	15.00
		(Capitol albums above have black labels with the Capitol logo on top.)			

PABLO CRUISE

Mobile Fidelity 1-029	(S)	A Place In The Sun		5.00	12.00

PAGE, PATTI

Label		Title	Year	VG+	NM
EmArcy 36074	(M)	In The Land Of Hi Fi	1956	10.00	25.00
EmArcy 36116	(M)	The East Side		10.00	25.00
EmArcy 36136	(M)	The West Side		10.00	25.00
Mercury MG-20010	(M)	Let's Get Away From It All	1955	10.00	25.00
Mercury MG-20011	(M)	I've Heard That Song Before	1955	10.00	25.00
Mercury MG-20025	(M)	Patti Page On Camera	1955	10.00	25.00
Mercury MG-20037	(M)	Three Little Words	1955	10.00	25.00
Mercury MG-20049	(M)	The Waltz Queen	1955	10.00	25.00
Mercury MG-20059	(M)	Indiscretion	1955	10.00	25.00
Mercury MG-20076	(M)	Romance On The Range	1955	10.00	25.00
Mercury MG-20081	(M)	I'll Remember April	1956	10.00	25.00
Mercury MG-20095	(M)	Page I	1956	10.00	25.00
Mercury MG-20096	(M)	Page II	1956	10.00	25.00
Mercury MG-20097	(M)	Page III	1956	10.00	25.00
Mercury MG-20097	(M)	Page III	1956	10.00	25.00
Mercury MG-20098	(M)	You Go To My Head	1956	10.00	25.00
Mercury MG-20099	(M)	Music For Two In Love	1956	10.00	25.00
Mercury MG-20100	(M)	The Voices Of Patti Page	1956	10.00	25.00
Mercury MG-20101	(M)	Page IV	1956	10.00	25.00
Mercury MG-20102	(M)	My Song	1956	10.00	25.00
Mercury MG-20114	(M)	The East Side	1956	10.00	25.00
Mercury MG-20226	(M)	Manhattan Tower	1956	10.00	25.00
Mercury MG-20233	(M)	Just A Closer Walk With Thee	1957	10.00	25.00
Mercury MG-20260	(M)	Sings And Stars In "Elmer Gantry"	1960	10.00	25.00
Mercury MG-20495	(M)	Patti Page's Golden Hits	1961	6.00	15.00
Mercury SR-60495	(S)	Patti Page's Golden Hits	1961	6.00	15.00
Mercury MG-20615	(M)	Country And Western Golden Hits	1961	5.00	12.00
Mercury SR-60615	(S)	Country And Western Golden Hits	1961	6.00	15.00
Mercury MG-20689	(M)	Go On Home	1962	5.00	12.00
Mercury SR-60689	(S)	Go On Home	1962	6.00	15.00
Mercury MG-20712	(M)	Golden Hits Of The Boys	1962	5.00	12.00
Mercury SR-60712	(S)	Golden Hits Of The Boys	1962	6.00	15.00
Mercury MG-20758	(M)	Patti Page On Stage	1963	5.00	12.00
Mercury SR-60758	(S)	Patti Page On Stage	1963	6.00	15.00
Mercury MG-20794	(M)	Patti Page's Golden Hits, Volume 2	1963	5.00	12.00
Mercury SR-60794	(S)	Patti Page's Golden Hits, Volume 2	1963	6.00	15.00
Mercury MG-20909	(M)	Blue Dream Street	1964	5.00	12.00
Mercury SR-60909	(S)	Blue Dream Street	1964	6.00	15.00
Mercury MG-20952	(M)	The Nearness Of You	1964	5.00	12.00
Mercury SR-60952	(S)	The Nearness Of You	1964	6.00	15.00
		(Mercury albums above have black & silver labels.)			

PAISLEYS, THE

Audio City 70	(S)	Cosmic Mind At Play		50.00	100.00

Label		Title	Year	VG+	NM
PARAGONS, THE					
Jubilee JLP-1098	(M)	Paragons Meet The Jesters	1959	35.00	70.00
Jubilee JLP-1098	(M)	Paragons Meet The Jesters (Colored vinyl)	1959	100.00	200.00
Musicnote M-8001	(M)	The Paragons Versus The Harptones	1964	14.00	35.00
PARIS, JACKIE					
EmArcy MC-36095	(M)	Songs By Jackie Paris		10.00	25.00
Brunswick BL-54019	(M)	Skylark		12.00	30.00
Time 70009	(M)	Jackie Paris Sings The Lyrics Of Ira Gershwin		12.00	30.00
East/West 4002	(M)	The Jackie Paris Sound		14.00	35.00
Impulse 17	(M)	The Song Is Paris		8.00	20.00
Impulse 17	(S)	The Song Is Paris		10.00	25.00
PARKER, FESS					
Columbia CL-576 (10")	(M)	TV Sweethearts		16.00	40.00
Columbia CL-666 (10")	(M)	Davy Crockett		16.00	40.00
Disneyland WDA-3007	(M)	Three Adventures Of Davy Crockett		10.00	25.00
Disneyland WDA-3602	(M)	Yarns And Songs		10.00	25.00
Disneyland 1336	(M)	Cowboy And Indian Songs		6.00	15.00
RCA LPM-2973	(M)	Fess Parker Sings	1964	8.00	20.00
RCA LSP-2973	(S)	Fess Parker Sings	1964	10.00	25.00
PARKER, LITTLE JUNIOR					
Duke DLP-76	(M)	Driving Wheel	1962	20.00	50.00
Mercury MG-21101	(M)	Like It Is	1967	6.00	15.00
Mercury SR-61101	(S)	Like It Is	1967	8.00	20.00
Minit 24024	(S)	Blues Man	1969	6.00	15.00
Blue Rock SRB-64004	(S)	Honey-Drippin' Blues	1969	6.00	15.00
Capitol ST-64	(S)	The Outside Man	1970	5.00	12.00
Capitol ST-569	(S)	Dudes Doin' Business	1971	5.00	12.00
PARKER, ROBERT					
Nola LP-1001	(M)	Barefootin'	1966	10.00	25.00
Nola LP-1001	(S)	Barefootin'	1966	12.00	30.00
PARKS, VAN DYKE					
Warners WS-2727	(S)	Song Cycle (Gold Label)	1968	6.00	15.00
Warners BS-2589	(S)	Discover America	1972	6.00	15.00
Warners BS-2878	(S)	Clang Of The Yankee Reaper	1975	6.00	15.00
PARLIAMENT (FUNKADELIC)					
Invictus 7302	(S)	Osmium	1970	6.00	15.00
Casablanca NBLP-9003	(S)	Up For The Down Stroke	1974	4.00	10.00
Casablanca NBLP-7014	(S)	Chocolate City	1975	4.00	10.00
Casablanca NBLP-7034	(S)	Clones Of Dr. Funkenstein	1976	4.00	10.00
Casablanca NBLP-7053	(S)	Parliament Live/Funk Earth Tour	1977	4.00	10.00
Casablanca NBLP-7084	(S)	Funkentelechy Vs. The Placebo Syndrome	1977	4.00	10.00
Casablanca NBLP-7125	(S)	Motor Booty Affair	1978	4.00	10.00
Casablanca NBLP-7125	(S)	Motor Booty Affair (Picture Disc)	1979	5.00	12.00
Casablanca NBLP-7146	(S)	Invasion Of The Body Snatchers	1979	4.00	10.00
Casablanca NBLP-7195	(S)	Gloryhallastoopid	1979	4.00	10.00
Casablanca NBLP-7249	(S)	Trombipulation	1980	4.00	10.00
PARSONS PROJECT, ALAN					
Mobile Fidelity 1-084	(S)	I, Robot		6.00	15.00
Mobile Fidelity 1-084	(S)	I, Robot (UHQR)		16.00	40.00
Mobile Fidelity 1-175	(S)	The Best Of The Alan Parsons Project		5.00	12.00
PARTON, DOLLY					
Also refer to Porter Wagoner.					
Monument MLP-8085	(M)	Hello, I'm Dolly	1967	8.00	20.00
Monument SLP-18085	(S)	Hello, I'm Dolly	1967	10.00	25.00
Starday SLP-429	(E)	Dolly Parton And George Jones	1968	8.00	20.00
RCA LPM-3949	(M)	Just Because I'm A Woman	1968	5.00	12.00
RCA LSP-3949	(S)	Just Because I'm A Woman	1968	6.00	15.00
		(Black label with Nipper on top.)			
PARTRIDGE FAMILY, THE					
Bell 6050	(S)	Album	1970	5.00	12.00
Bell 6059	(S)	Up To Date	1971	4.00	10.00
Bell 6064	(S)	Sound Magazine	1971	4.00	10.00

Label		Title	Year	VG+	NM
Bell 6066	(S)	A Christmas Card (With card)	1971	5.00	12.00
Bell 6072	(S)	Family Shopping Bag	1972	4.00	10.00
Bell 1107	(S)	At Home With Their Greatest Hits	1972	4.00	10.00
Bell 1111	(S)	The Family Notebook	1972	4.00	10.00
Bell 1122	(S)	Crossword Puzzle	1973	4.00	10.00
Bell 1137	(S)	Family Bulletin Board	1973	4.00	10.00
Bell 1319	(S)	The World Of The Partridge Family	1974	5.00	12.00

PASCAL, NIK: *Refer to* **NIK PASCAL RAICEVIC**

PASSING FANCY, A

Label		Title	Year	VG+	NM
Boo 6801	(S)	A Passing Fancy		75.00	150.00

PASTEL SIX, THE

Label		Title	Year	VG+	NM
Zen 1001	(M)	Cinnamon Cinder	1963	16.00	40.00
Mark 56 MLP-511	(M)	Golden Oldies	1963	14.00	35.00

PATTON, JIMMY

Label		Title	Year	VG+	NM
Moon 101	(M)	Make Room For The Blues		20.00	50.00
Sims 127	(M)	Blue Darlin'	1965	20.00	50.00

PAUL & PAULA

Label		Title	Year	VG+	NM
Phillips PHM-200078	(M)	Paul And Paula Sing For Young Lovers	1963	6.00	15.00
Phillips PHS-600078	(S)	Paul And Paula Sing For Young Lovers	1963	8.00	20.00
Phillips PHM-200089	(M)	We Go Together	1963	6.00	15.00
Phillips PHS-600089	(S)	We Go Together	1963	8.00	20.00
Phillips PHM-200101	(M)	Holiday For Teens	1963	6.00	15.00
Phillips PHS-600101	(S)	Holiday For Teens	1963	8.00	20.00

PAUL, LES, & MARY FORD

Label		Title	Year	VG+	NM
Capitol H-226 (10")	(M)	New Sound, Volume 1		20.00	50.00
Capitol H-286 (10")	(M)	New Sound, Volume 2		20.00	50.00
Capitol H-356 (10")	(M)	Bye Bye Blues		20.00	50.00
Capitol T-226	(M)	New Sound, Volume 1		16.00	40.00
Capitol T-286	(M)	New Sound, Volume 2		16.00	40.00
Capitol T-356	(M)	Bye Bye Blues		16.00	40.00
Capitol T-416	(M)	The Hitmakers		12.00	30.00
Capitol T-577	(M)	Les And Mary		12.00	30.00
Capitol T-802	(M)	Time To Dream		12.00	30.00
Capitol T-1476	(M)	The Hits Of Les And Mary	1960	10.00	25.00
Columbia CL-1276	(M)	Lover's Luau	1959	8.00	20.00
Columbia CL-1688	(M)	Warm And Wonderful	1962	6.00	15.00
Columbia CS-8488	(S)	Warm And Wonderful	1962	8.00	20.00
Columbia CL-1821	(M)	Bouquet Of Roses	1962	6.00	15.00
Columbia CS-8621	(S)	Bouquet Of Roses	1962	8.00	20.00
Columbia CL-1928	(M)	Swingin' South	1963	6.00	15.00
Columbia CS-8728	(S)	Swingin' South	1963	8.00	20.00

PAYNE, LEON

Label		Title	Year	VG+	NM
Starday SLP-231	(M)	Leon Payne	1963	10.00	25.00
Starday SLP-236	(M)	Americana	1963	10.00	25.00

PEACHES & HERB

Label		Title	Year	VG+	NM
Date TE-3004	(M)	Let's Fall In Love	1967	5.00	12.00
Date TES-4004	(S)	Let's Fall In Love	1967	6.00	15.00
Date TE-3005	(M)	For Your Love	1967	5.00	12.00
Date TES-4005	(S)	For Your Love	1967	6.00	15.00
Date TES-4007	(S)	Peaches And Herbs' Golden Duets	1968	5.00	12.00
Date TES-4012	(S)	Peaches And Herbs' Greatest Hits	1968	5.00	12.00

PEANUT BUTTER CONSPIRACY, THE

Label		Title	Year	VG+	NM
Challenge 2000	(M)	For Children Of All Ages	1968	10.00	25.00
Columbia CL-2654	(M)	Peanut Butter Conspiracy Is Spreading	1967	5.00	12.00
Columbia CS-9495	(S)	Peanut Butter Conspiracy Is Spreading	1967	6.00	15.00
Columbia CS-9590	(S)	The Great Conspiracy	1968	6.00	15.00

PEARLS BEFORE SWINE

Label		Title	Year	VG+	NM
ESP 1054	(M)	One Nation Under Ground	1967	8.00	20.00
ESP 1054	(S)	One Nation Under Ground (Brown cover)	1967	10.00	25.00
ESP 1054	(S)	One Nation Under Ground (Color cover)	1967	8.00	20.00
ESP 1075	(S)	Balaklava	1968	8.00	20.00

Label		Title	Year	VG+	NM
Reprise MS-6364	(S)	These Things Too	1969	6.00	15.00
Reprise MS-6405	(S)	The Use Of Ashes	1970	6.00	15.00
Reprise MS-6442	(S)	City Of Gold	1971	6.00	15.00
Reprise MS-6467	(S)	Beautiful Lies You Could Live In	1971	6.00	15.00

PEDICIN, MIKE

| Apollo LP-484 | (M) | Musical Medicine | 1957 | 50.00 | 100.00 |

PEEL, DAVID (& THE LOWER EAST SIDE)

Elektra EKS-74032	(S)	Have A Marijuana	1968	10.00	25.00
Elektra EKS-74069	(S)	The American Revolution	1970	8.00	20.00
Apple SW-3391	(S)	The Pope Smokes Dope	1972	20.00	50.00

PEELS, THE

| Karate 5402 | (M) | Juanita Banana | 1966 | 20.00 | 50.00 |

PENETRATION

| Kigher Key 33071 | (S) | An Aquarian Symphony | 1974 | 50.00 | 100.00 |

PENGUINS, THE

| Dooto DTL-242 | (M) | The Cool Cool Penguins (Yellow & red label) | 1959 | 100.00 | 200.00 |

PEOPLE

Capitol ST-2924	(S)	I Love You	1968	20.00	50.00
Capitol ST-151	(S)	Both Sides Of People	1969	20.00	50.00
Paramount PAS-5013	(S)	There Are People And There Are People	1970	16.00	40.00

PEPPER, JIM

| Embryo SD-7312 | (S) | Pepper's Pow Wow | | 20.00 | 50.00 |

PEPPERMINT TROLLEY COMPANY, THE

| Acta A-38007 | (S) | The Peppermint Trolley Company | 1968 | 6.00 | 15.00 |

PERKINS, CARL

Sun LP-1225	(M)	The Dance Album Of Carl Perkins	1957	240.00	400.00
Columbia CL-1234	(M)	Whole Lotta Shakin' ("Eyes" logo label)	1958	100.00	200.00
Sun LP-1225	(M)	Teen Beat/The Best Of Carl Perkins	1961	150.00	250.00
Sun 112	(M)	Blue Suede Shoes	1969	4.00	10.00
Columbia CS-9833	(S)	Carl Perkins' Greatest Hits	1969	6.00	15.00
Columbia CS-9931	(S)	On Top	1969	6.00	15.00
Columbia CS-9981	(S)	Boppin' The Blues (With NRBQ)	1970	6.00	15.00
		(Columbia albums above have "360 Sound" labels.)			

PERKINS, TONY

RCA LPM-1679	(M)	From My Heart	1958	8.00	20.00
RCA LPM-1853	(M)	On A Rainy Afternoon	1958	8.00	20.00
Epic LN-3394	(M)	Tony Perkins		8.00	20.00

PERRINE, PEP

| Hideout 1003 | (M) | Pep Perrine Live And In Person | | 100.00 | 200.00 |

PERSUADERS, THE

| Saturn SAT-5000 | (M) | Surfer's Nightmare | 1963 | 35.00 | 70.00 |
| Saturn SATS-5000 | (S) | Surfer's Nightmare | 1963 | 50.00 | 100.00 |

PERSUASIONS, THE

Straight 6394	(S)	Acappella	1970	12.00	30.00
Capitol ST-791	(S)	We Came To Play	1971	8.00	20.00
Capitol ST-872	(S)	Street Corner Symphony	1972	8.00	20.00
Capitol ST-11101	(S)	Spread The Word	1972	6.00	15.00

PETER, PAUL & MARY
Peter Yarrow, Paul Stookey & Mary Travers.

Warners W-1473	(M)	Peter, Paul And Mary Moving	1962	5.00	12.00
Warners WS-1473	(S)	Peter, Paul And Mary Moving	1962	6.00	15.00
Warners W-1449	(M)	Peter, Paul And Mary	1962	5.00	12.00
Warners WS-1449	(S)	Peter, Paul And Mary	1962	6.00	15.00
Warners W-1507	(M)	Peter, Paul And Mary In The Wind	1963	5.00	12.00
Warners WS-1507	(S)	Peter, Paul And Mary In The Wind	1963	6.00	15.00
Warners W2-1555	(M)	In Concert	1964	5.00	12.00
Warners W2S-1555	(S)	In Concert	1964	6.00	15.00

Label		Title	Year	VG+	NM
Warners W-1589	(M)	A Song Will Rise	1965	5.00	12.00
Warners WS-1589	(S)	A Song Will Rise	1965	6.00	15.00
Warners W-1615	(M)	See What Tomorrow Brings	1965	5.00	12.00
Warners WS-1615	(S)	See What Tomorrow Brings	1965	6.00	15.00
		(Warner albums above have grey labels.)			
Warners W-1648	(M)	The Peter, Paul And Mary Album	1966	4.00	10.00
Warners WS-1648	(S)	The Peter, Paul And Mary Album	1966	5.00	12.00
Warners W-1700	(M)	Album 1700	1967	4.00	10.00
Warners WS-1700	(S)	Album 1700	1967	5.00	12.00
		(Warner albums above have gold labels.)			

PETER & GORDON (PETER ASHER & GORDON WALLER)

Label		Title	Year	VG+	NM
Capitol T-2115	(M)	A World Without Love	1964	5.00	12.00
Capitol ST-2115	(S)	A World Without Love	1964	6.00	15.00
Capitol T-2220	(M)	I Don't Want To See You Again	1964	5.00	12.00
Capitol ST-2220	(S)	I Don't Want To See You Again	1964	6.00	15.00
Capitol T-2324	(M)	I Go To Pieces	1965	5.00	12.00
Capitol ST-2324	(S)	I Go To Pieces	1965	6.00	15.00
Capitol T-2368	(M)	True Love Ways	1965	6.00	15.00
Capitol ST-2368	(S)	True Love Ways	1965	8.00	20.00
Capitol T-2430	(M)	The Hits Of Nashville	1966	6.00	15.00
Capitol ST-2430	(S)	The Hits Of Nashville	1966	8.00	20.00
Capitol T-2477	(M)	Woman	1966	5.00	12.00
Capitol ST-2477	(S)	Woman	1966	6.00	15.00
Capitol T-2549	(M)	The Best Of Peter And Gordon	1966	4.00	10.00
Capitol ST-2549	(S)	The Best Of Peter And Gordon	1966	5.00	12.00
Capitol T-2664	(M)	Lady Godiva	1967	5.00	12.00
Capitol ST-2664	(S)	Lady Godiva	1967	6.00	15.00
Capitol T-2729	(M)	A Knight In Rusty Armour	1967	5.00	12.00
Capitol ST-2729	(S)	A Knight In Rusty Armour	1967	6.00	15.00
Capitol T-2747	(M)	In London For Tea	1967	6.00	15.00
Capitol ST-2747	(S)	In London For Tea	1967	8.00	20.00
Capitol T-2882	(M)	Hot, Cold And Custard	1968	6.00	15.00
Capitol ST-2882	(S)	Hot, Cold And Custard	1968	8.00	20.00

PETERSEN, PAUL

Label		Title	Year	VG+	NM
Colpix CP-429	(M)	Lollipops And Roses	1962	8.00	20.00
Colpix SCP-429	(S)	Lollipops And Roses	1962	10.00	25.00
Colpix CP-442	(M)	My Dad	1963	6.00	15.00
Colpix SCP-442	(S)	My Dad	1963	8.00	20.00

PETERSON, RAY

Label		Title	Year	VG+	NM
RCA LPM-2297	(M)	Tell Laura I Love Her	1960	30.00	60.00
RCA LSP-2297	(S)	Tell Laura I Love Her	1960	40.00	80.00
MGM E-4250	(M)	The Very Best Of Ray Peterson	1964	10.00	25.00
MGM SE-4250	(S)	The Very Best Of Ray Peterson	1964	12.00	30.00
MGM E-4277	(M)	The Other Side Of Ray Peterson	1965	10.00	25.00
MGM SE-4277	(S)	The Other Side Of Ray Peterson	1965	12.00	30.00
Uni 73078	(S)	The Best Of Ray Peterson	1969	8.00	20.00
Decca DL7-5307	(S)	Ray Peterson Country	1971	8.00	20.00

PETTY TRIO, NORMAN

Label		Title	Year	VG+	NM
Columbia CL-1092	(M)	Moondreams	1958	50.00	100.00
Vik 1073	(M)	Corsage	1959	16.00	40.00
Top Rank RS-639	(S)	Petty For Your Thoughts	1960	14.00	35.00

PHANTOM, THE

Label		Title	Year	VG+	NM
Capitol ST-11313	(S)	The Phantom's Divine Comedy	1974	10.00	25.00

PHILLIPS, ESTHER (LITTLE ESTHER)

Label		Title	Year	VG+	NM
King LP-622	(M)	Memory Lane	1956	660.00	1,000.00
Lenox 227	(M)	Release Me	1962	20.00	50.00
Atlantic 8102	(M)	And I Love Him	1965	8.00	20.00
Atlantic SD-8102	(S)	And I Love Him	1965	10.00	25.00
Atlantic 8122	(M)	Esther	1966	8.00	20.00
Atlantic SD-8122	(S)	Esther	1966	10.00	25.00
Atlantic 8130	(M)	The Country Side Of Esther Phillips	1966	8.00	20.00
Atlantic SD-8130	(S)	The Country Side Of Esther Phillips	1966	10.00	25.00
Atlantic SD-1565	(S)	Burnin'	1970	6.00	15.00

Label		Title	Year	VG+	NM
PHILLIPS, WARREN, & THE ROCKETS					
Parrot PAS-71044	(S)	Rocked Out	1970	8.00	20.00
PHLUPH					
Verve V6-5054	(S)	Phluph	1968	6.00	15.00
PIANO RED					
Groove 1001	(M)	Jump Man, Jump		100.00	200.00
Groove 1002	(M)	Piano Red In Concert		100.00	200.00
PICKETT, BOBBY "BORIS" (& THE CRYPT KICKERS)					
Garpax GP-67001	(M)	The Monster Mash	1962	20.00	50.00
Garpax SGP-67001	(S)	The Monster Mash	1962	35.00	70.00
Parrott XPAS-71063	(E)	The Original Monster Mash	1973	6.00	15.00
PICKETT, WILSON					
Double-L DL-2300	(M)	It's Too Late	1963	12.00	30.00
Double-L SDL-8300	(M)	It's Too Late	1963	16.00	40.00
Atlantic 8114	(M)	In The Midnight Hour	1965	10.00	25.00
Atlantic SD-8114	(S)	In The Midnight Hour	1965	12.00	30.00
Atlantic 8129	(M)	The Exciting Wilson Pickett	1966	8.00	20.00
Atlantic SD-8129	(S)	The Exciting Wilson Pickett	1966	10.00	25.00
Atlantic 8138	(M)	The Wicked Pickett	1967	8.00	20.00
Atlantic SD-8138	(S)	The Wicked Pickett	1967	10.00	25.00
Atlantic 8145	(M)	The Sound Of Wilson Pickett	1967	8.00	20.00
Atlantic SD-8145	(S)	The Sound Of Wilson Pickett	1967	10.00	25.00
Atlantic 8151	(M)	The Best Of Wilson Pickett	1967	6.00	15.00
Atlantic SD-8151	(E)	The Best Of Wilson Pickett	1967	6.00	15.00
Atlantic SD-8175	(S)	I'm In Love	1968	6.00	15.00
Atlantic SD-8183	(S)	Midnight Mover	1968	6.00	15.00
Atlantic SD-8215	(S)	Hey Jude	1869	5.00	12.00
Atlantic SD-8250	(S)	Right On	1970	5.00	12.00
Atlantic SD-8270	(S)	Wilson Pickett In Philadelphia	1970	5.00	12.00
Atlantic SD-8290	(S)	The Best Of Wilson Pickett, Volume 2	1971	5.00	12.00
Atlantic SD-8300	(S)	Don't Knock My Love	1971	5.00	12.00
Atlantic SD-2501	(P)	Wilson Pickett's Greatest Hits	1973	5.00	12.00
PIERCE, WEBB					
Decca DL-5536 (10")	(M)	That Wondering Boy	1953	20.00	50.00
Decca DL-8129	(M)	Webb Pierce	1955	16.00	40.00
Decca DL-8295	(M)	That Wondering Boy	1956	16.00	40.00
Decca DL-8728	(M)	Just Imagination	1957	16.00	40.00
Decca DL-8889	(M)	Bound For The Kingdom	1959	8.00	20.00
Decca DL7-8889	(S)	Bound For The Kingdom	1959	10.00	25.00
Decca DL-8899	(M)	Webb!	1959	8.00	20.00
Decca DL7-8899	(S)	Webb!	1959	10.00	25.00
		(Decca albums above have black & silver labels.)			
King 648	(M)	The One And Only Webb Pierce	1959	12.00	30.00
Decca DL-4015	(M)	Webb With A Beat	1960	6.00	15.00
Decca DL7-4015	(S)	Webb With A Beat	1960	8.00	20.00
Decca DL-4079	(M)	Walking The Streets	1960	6.00	15.00
Decca DL7-4079	(S)	Walking The Streets	1960	8.00	20.00
Decca DL-4110	(M)	Golden Favorites	1961	6.00	15.00
Decca DL7-4110	(E)	Golden Favorites	1961	4.00	10.00
Decca DL-4144	(M)	Fallen Angel	1961	5.00	12.00
Decca DL7-4144	(S)	Fallen Angel	1961	6.00	15.00
Decca DL-4218	(M)	Hideaway Heart	1962	5.00	12.00
Decca DL7-4218	(S)	Hideaway Heart	1962	6.00	15.00
Decca DL-4294	(M)	Cross Country	1962	5.00	12.00
Decca DL7-4294	(S)	Cross Country	1962	6.00	15.00
Decca DL-4358	(M)	I've Got A New Heartache	1963	5.00	12.00
Decca DL7-4358	(S)	I've Got A New Heartache	1963	6.00	15.00
Decca DL-4384	(M)	Bow Thy Head	1963	5.00	12.00
Decca DL7-4384	(S)	Bow Thy Head	1963	6.00	15.00
Decca DXB-181	(M)	The Webb Pierce Story (With booklet)	1964	8.00	20.00
Decca DXSB7-181	(S)	The Webb Pierce Story (With booklet)	1964	10.00	25.00
Decca DL-4486	(M)	Sands Of Gold	1964	5.00	12.00
Decca DL7-4486	(S)	Sands Of Gold	1964	6.00	15.00
Decca DL-4604	(M)	Memory No. 1	1965	5.00	12.00
Decca DL7-4604	(S)	Memory No. 1	1965	6.00	15.00

Label		Title	Year	VG+	NM
Decca DL-4659	(M)	Country Music Time	1965	5.00	12.00
Decca DL7-4659	(S)	Country Music Time	1965	6.00	15.00
Decca DL-4739	(M)	Sweet Memories	1966	5.00	12.00
Decca DL7-4739	(S)	Sweet Memories	1966	6.00	15.00
Decca DL-4782	(M)	Webb's Choice	1966	5.00	12.00
Decca DL7-4782	(S)	Webb's Choice	1966	6.00	15.00
		(Decca albums above have black labels with "Mfrd by Decca" beneath the rainbow.)			

PIKE, PETE

Audio Lab AL-1559	(M)	Pete Pike	1960	20.00	50.00

PINK FLOYD

Tower T-5093	(M)	Piper At The Gates Of Dawn	1967	16.00	40.00
Tower ST-5093	(S)	Piper At The Gates Of Dawn (Orange label)	1967	14.00	35.00
Tower ST-5131	(S)	A Saucerful Of Secrets (Orange label)	1968	14.00	35.00
Tower ST-5169	(S)	More (Sdtk)	1968	10.00	25.00
Harvest 388	(S)	Ummagumma	1969	10.00	25.00
		(The cover has a copy of "Ummagumma" leaning against the wall behind the seated figure.)			
MGM SE-4468	(S)	Zabriskie Point (Sdtk)	1970	6.00	15.00
Harvest SMAS-382	(S)	Atom Heart Mother	1970	8.00	20.00
Harvest SW-759	(S)	Relics	1971	5.00	12.00
Harvest SMAS-832	(S)	Meddle	1971	4.00	10.00
Harvest ST-11078	(S)	Obscured By Clouds	1972	4.00	10.00
Harvest SMAS-11163	(S)	The Dark Side Of The Moon	1973	4.00	10.00
Harvest SABB-11257	(S)	Nice Pair	1973	3.50	8.00
Columbia PC-33453	(S)	Wish You Were Here	1975	4.00	10.00
Columbia PCQ-33453	(Q)	Wish You Were Here	1975	16.00	40.00
Columbia PCQ-34474	(Q)	Animals	1977	16.00	40.00
Mobile Fidelity 1-017	(S)	The Dark Side Of The Moon	1977	10.00	25.00
Capitol SEAX-11902	(S)	The Dark Side Of The Moon (Picture disc)	1978	12.00	30.00
Mobile Fidelity 1-027	(S)	The Dark Side Of The Moon (UHQR)	1982	100.00	200.00
Columbia HC-43453	(S)	Wish You Were Here (1/2 speed)	1982	12.00	30.00
Columbia H2C-46183	(S)	The Wall (1/2 speed)	1983	40.00	80.00
Columbia HG-47680	(S)	Collection Of Great Dance Songs (1/2 speed)	1983	12.00	30.00

PIPKINS, THE

Capitol ST-483	(S)	Gimme Dat Ding	1970	6.00	15.00

PIRANHAS, THE

Custom Fidelity 1452	(S)	Somethin' Fishy	1969	75.00	150.00

PITNEY, GENE

Musicor MM-2001	(M)	The Many Sides Of Gene Pitney	1962	5.00	12.00
Musicor MS-3001	(S)	The Many Sides Of Gene Pitney	1962	6.00	15.00
Musicor MM-2003	(M)	Only Love Can Break A Heart	1962	5.00	12.00
Musicor MS-3003	(S)	Only Love Can Break A Heart	1962	6.00	15.00
Musicor MM-2004	(M)	Gene Pitney Sings Just For You	1963	5.00	12.00
Musicor MS-3004	(S)	Gene Pitney Sings Just For You	1963	6.00	15.00
Musicor MM-2005	(M)	World-Wide Winners	1963	5.00	12.00
Musicor MS-3005	(S)	World-Wide Winners	1963	6.00	15.00
Musicor MM-2006	(M)	Blue Gene	1963	5.00	12.00
Musicor MS-3006	(S)	Blue Gene	1963	6.00	15.00
Musicor MM-2007	(M)	The Fair Young Ladies Of Folkland	1964	6.00	15.00
Musicor MS-3007	(S)	The Fair Young Ladies Of Folkland	1964	8.00	20.00
Musicor MM-2008	(M)	Gene Pitney's Big Sixteen	1964	4.00	10.00
Musicor MS-3008	(S)	Gene Pitney's Big Sixteen	1964	5.00	12.00
Musicor MM-2015	(M)	Gene Italiano	1964	4.00	10.00
Musicor MS-3015	(S)	Gene Italiano	1964	5.00	12.00
Musicor MM-2019	(M)	It Hurts To Be In Love	1964	4.00	10.00
Musicor MS-3019	(S)	It Hurts To Be In Love	1964	5.00	12.00
Musicor MM-2043	(M)	Big Sixteen, Volume 2	1965	4.00	10.00
Musicor MS-3043	(S)	Big Sixteen, Volume 2	1965	5.00	12.00
Musicor M-2044	(M)	For The First Time! (With George Jones)	1965	5.00	12.00
Musicor MS-3044	(S)	For The First Time! (With George Jones)	1965	6.00	15.00
Musicor M-2044	(M)	Recorded In Nashville (With George Jones)	1965	5.00	12.00
Musicor MS-3044	(S)	Recorded In Nashville (With George Jones)	1965	6.00	15.00
Musicor MM-2056	(M)	I Must Be Seeing Things	1965	4.00	10.00
Musicor MS-3056	(S)	I Must Be Seeing Things	1965	5.00	12.00

Label		Title	Year	VG+	NM
Musicor M-2065	(M)	It's Country Time Again!	1965	5.00	12.00
Musicor MS-3065	(S)	It's Country Time Again!	1965	6.00	15.00
		(With George Jones.)			
Musicor MM-2069	(M)	Looking Through The Eyes Of Love	1965	4.00	10.00
Musicor MS-3069	(S)	Looking Through The Eyes Of Love	1965	5.00	12.00
Musicor MM-2072	(M)	Gene Pitney Espanol	1965	4.00	10.00
Musicor MS-3072	(S)	Gene Pitney Espanol	1965	5.00	12.00
Musicor M-2077	(M)	Being Together (With Melba Montgomery)	1966	5.00	12.00
Musicor MS-3077	(S)	Being Together (With Melba Montgomery)	1966	6.00	15.00
Musicor M-2079	(M)	Famous Country Duets	1965	5.00	12.00
Musicor MS-3079	(S)	Famous Country Duets	1965	6.00	15.00
		(With Melba Montgomery and George Jones.)			
Musicor MM-2085	(M)	Big Sixteen, Volume 3	1966	4.00	10.00
Musicor MS-3085	(S)	Big Sixteen, Volume 3	1966	5.00	12.00
Musicor MM-2095	(M)	Backstage I'm Lonely	1966	4.00	10.00
Musicor MS-3095	(S)	Backstage I'm Lonely	1966	5.00	12.00
Musicor MM-2100	(M)	Messumo Mi Puo Giudicare	1966	4.00	10.00
Musicor MS-3100	(S)	Messumo Mi Puo Giudicare	1966	5.00	12.00
Musicor MM-2101	(M)	The Gene Pitney Show	1966	4.00	10.00
Musicor MS-3101	(S)	The Gene Pitney Show	1966	5.00	12.00
Musicor MM-2102	(M)	Greatest Hits Of All Time	1966	4.00	10.00
Musicor MS-3102	(S)	Greatest Hits Of All Time	1966	5.00	12.00
Musicor MM-2104	(M)	The Country Side Of Gene Pitney	1966	4.00	10.00
Musicor MS-3104	(S)	The Country Side Of Gene Pitney	1966	5.00	12.00
Musicor MM-2108	(M)	Young And Warm And Wonderful	1966	4.00	10.00
Musicor MS-3108	(S)	Young And Warm And Wonderful	1966	5.00	12.00
Musicor MM-2117	(M)	Just One Smile	1967	4.00	10.00
Musicor MS-3117	(S)	Just One Smile	1967	5.00	12.00
Musicor MM-2134	(M)	Golden Greats	1967	4.00	10.00
Musicor MS-3134	(S)	Golden Greats	1967	5.00	12.00
Musicor M2S-3148	(S)	The Gene Pitney Story	1968	6.00	15.00
Musicor MS-3161	(S)	Gene Pitney Sings Burt Bacharach	1968	4.00	10.00
Musicor MS-3164	(S)	She's A Heartbreaker	1968	5.00	12.00
Musicor P2S-5025	(S)	This Is Gene Pitney	1968	5.00	12.00
Musicor MS-3174	(S)	The Greatest Hits Of Gene Pitney	1969	4.00	10.00
Musicor MS-3183	(S)	This Is Gene Pitney	1970	4.00	10.00
Musicor MS-3206	(S)	Ten Years After	1971	4.00	10.00
PIXIES THREE, THE					
Mercury MG-20912	(M)	Party With The Pixies Three	1964	40.00	80.00
Mercury SR-60912	(P)	Party With The Pixies Three	1964	50.00	100.00
PLANT & SEE					
White Whale S-7120	(S)	Plant And See	1969	8.00	20.00
PLATTERS, THE					
Federal 395-549	(M)	The Platters	1955	300.00	500.00
King LP-549	(M)	The Platters	1956	180.00	300.00
Mercury MG-20146	(M)	The Platters	1956	50.00	100.00
Mercury MG-20216	(M)	The Platters, Volume 2	1956	30.00	60.00
Mercury MG-20298	(M)	Flying Platters	1957	20.00	50.00
Mercury MG-20366	(M)	Flying Platters Around The World	1959	12.00	30.00
Mercury SR-60043	(S)	Flying Platters Around The World	1959	16.00	40.00
Mercury MG-20410	(M)	Remember When?	1959	12.00	30.00
Mercury SR-60087	(S)	Remember When?	1959	16.00	40.00
Mercury MG-20472	(M)	Encore Of Golden Hits	1960	8.00	20.00
Mercury SR-60243	(S)	Encore Of Golden Hits	1960	10.00	25.00
Mercury MG-20481	(M)	Reflections	1960	8.00	20.00
Mercury SR-60160	(S)	Reflections	1960	10.00	25.00
Mercury MG-20589	(M)	The Platters	1960	8.00	20.00
Mercury SR-60254	(S)	The Platters	1960	10.00	25.00
Mercury MG-20591	(M)	More Encore Of Golden Hits	1960	6.00	15.00
Mercury SR-60252	(S)	More Encore Of Golden Hits	1960	8.00	20.00
Mercury MG-20669	(M)	The Platters Sing For The Lonely	1962	6.00	15.00
Mercury SR-60669	(S)	The Platters Sing For The Lonely	1962	8.00	20.00
Mercury MG-20693	(M)	Encore Of Golden Hits Of The Groups	1962	6.00	15.00
Mercury SR-60693	(S)	Encore Of Golden Hits Of The Groups	1962	8.00	20.00
Mercury MG-20759	(M)	Moonlight Memories	1963	6.00	15.00
Mercury SR-60759	(S)	Moonlight Memories	1963	8.00	20.00
Mercury MG-20782	(M)	The Platters Sing All The Movie Hits	1963	6.00	15.00
Mercury SR-60782	(S)	The Platters Sing All The Movie Hits	1963	8.00	20.00

Webb Pierce, *Sweet Memories.* Another country singer who has enjoyed three decades of success and whose Decca recordings are starting to receive the attention of collectors.

The Pipkins, *Gimme Dat Ding!* A novelty hit with an irresistible rhythm, this album came and went, with customers seeming oblivious to the hit single within and the great cover art without.

Label		Title	Year	VG+	NM
Mercury MG-20808	(M)	The Platters Sing Latino	1963	6.00	15.00
Mercury SR-60808	(S)	The Platters Sing Latino	1963	8.00	20.00
Mercury MG-20841	(M)	Christmas With The Platters	1963	6.00	15.00
Mercury SR-60841	(S)	Christmas With The Platters	1963	8.00	20.00
		(Mercury albums above have black & silver labels.)			

PLAYBACKS, THE

Round LP-1111	(M)	Greatest Of The Latest		20.00	50.00

POCO

Epic BN-26460	(S)	Pickin' Up The Pieces (Yellow Label)	1969	5.00	12.00
Epic EQ-30209	(Q)	Deliverin'	1971	5.00	12.00
Epic EQ-32354	(Q)	Crazy Eyes	1973	5.00	12.00
Epic PEQ-33192	(Q)	Cantamos	1974	5.00	12.00
Mobile Fidelity 1-020	(S)	Legend	1978	5.00	12.00

PONTY, JEAN LUC

World Pacific 20172	(S)	King Kong/Ponty Plays Zappa	1970	8.00	20.00

POOLE, BRIAN, & THE TREMELOES

Audio Fidelity 2151	(M)	Brian Poole Is Here	1966	8.00	20.00
Audio Fidelity 6151	(S)	Brian Poole Is Here	1966	10.00	25.00
Audio Fidelity 2177	(M)	The Tremeloes Are Here	1967	8.00	20.00
Audio Fidelity 6177	(S)	The Tremeloes Are Here	1967	10.00	25.00

POWELL, JANE

MGM E-530 (10")	(M)	Two Weeks With Love (Sdtk)	1950	20.00	50.00
MGM E-86 (10")	(M)	Rich, Young And Pretty (Sdtk)	1951	20.00	50.00
Capitol L-485 (10")	(M)	Three Sailors And A Girl (Sdtk)	1953	20.00	50.00
Columbia CL-2034 (10")	(M)	Romance		10.00	25.00
Columbia CL-2045 (10")	(M)	A Date With Jane Powell		10.00	25.00
Mercury MG-25202	(M)	Athena (Sdtk)	1954	50.00	100.00
MGM E-3233	(M)	Two Weeks With Love (Sdtk)	1955	12.00	30.00
MGM E-3236	(M)	Rich, Young And Pretty (Sdtk)	1955	12.00	30.00
Columbia CL-4148	(M)	Alice In Wonderland		8.00	20.00
Verve V-2023	(M)	Can't We Be Friends?		6.00	15.00

PREMIERS, THE

Warners W-1565	(M)	Farmer John	1964	10.00	25.00
Warners WS-1565	(S)	Farmer John	1964	14.00	35.00

PRESLEY, ELVIS

Due to the staggering number of re-issues of Elvis' records, the following label breakdown is provided. This should always be referred to when evaluating first pressings.

Monaural: LPM-1254 through 2697 have black labels with "Long 33 1/3 Play" on the bottom. LPM-2756 through 2999 have black labels with "Mono" on the bottom. LPM-3338 through 3989 have black labels with "Monaural" on the bottom.

Stereo: LSP-2231 through 2999 have black labels with "Living Stereo" on the bottom. LPM-3338 through 3989 have black labels with "Stereo" on the bottom. LPM-4088 through LSP-4460 (including LPM-6401) have orange labels and were originally pressed on thick, non-flexible vinyl. Camden CAS-2304 through 2428 have blue labels and were also pressed on thick, non-flexible vinyl. Re-issues of RCA and Camden titles with identical orange and blue labels on flexivble vinyl are worth 50-60% of the non-flexible prices.

LSP-4530 through CPM1-0818 (including LPM-6402) have orange labels on flexible vinyl. Camden CALX-2472 through CAS-2611 have blue labels on flexible vinyl. From 1975 on the labels are noted individually .

RCA LPM-1254	(M)	Elvis Presley	1956	75.00	150.00
		(With "Elvis" in light pink letters on the cover.)			
RCA LPM-1254	(M)	Elvis Presley	1956	50.00	100.00
		(With "Elvis" in dark pink letters on the cover.)			
RCA LPM-1382	(M)	Elvis	1956	75.00	150.00
		(With ads for other albums on back cover.)			
RCA LPM-1382	(M)	Elvis	1956	50.00	100.00
		(Without the ads on back cover.)			
RCA LPM-1382	(M)	Elvis	1956	150.00	250.00
		(The label prefixes each track with "Band 1" through "Band 6.")			

Label		Title	Year	VG+	NM
RCA LPM-1382	(M)	Elvis	1956	660.00	1,000.00
		(Contains an alternate take of "Old Shep." Copies with the matrix number ending with either "17S" or "19S" may or may not have the rare track; listening is required. In the first verse of the the rare version, Elvis sings "we were both... full of fun," pausing between "both" and "full.")			
RCA LPM-1515	(M)	Loving You (Sdtk)	1957	60.00	120.00
RCA LOC-1035	(M)	Elvis' Christmas Album	1957	240.00	400.00
RCA LPM-1707	(M)	Elvis' Golden Records	1958	60.00	120.00
		(The title on the front cover is in blue print.)			
RCA LPM-1884	(M)	King Creole (Sdtk)	1958	60.00	120.00
		King Creole Bonus Photo	1958	60.00	120.00
RCA LPM-1951	(M)	Elvis' Christmas Album	1958	50.00	100.00
RCA LPM-1990	(M)	For LP Fans Only	1959	75.00	150.00
RCA LPM-2011	(M)	A Date With Elvis	1959	100.00	200.00
		(Fold-open cover with a sticker on front listing the song titles within.)			
RCA LPM-2011	(M)	A Date With Elvis	1959	50.00	100.00
		(Fold-open cover with the song titles printed on the front.)			
RCA LPM-2075	(M)	Elvis' Gold Records, Volume 2	1960	50.00	100.00
RCA LPM-2231	(M)	Elvis Is Back!	1960	6.00	120.00
RCA LSP-2231	(S)	Elvis Is Back!	1960	75.00	150.00
		(Fold-open cover with a sticker on front listing the song titles within.)			
RCA LPM-2231	(M)	Elvis Is Back!	1960	40.00	80.00
RCA LSP-2231	(S)	Elvis Is Back!	1960	50.00	100.00
		(Fold-open cover with the song titles printed on the front.)			
RCA LPM-2256	(M)	G.I. Blues (Sdtk)	1960	16.00	40.00
RCA LSP-2256	(S)	G.I. Blues (Sdtk)	1960	30.00	60.00
RCA LPM-2328	(M)	His Hand In Mine	1961	20.00	50.00
RCA LSP-2328	(S)	His Hand In Mine	1961	35.00	70.00
RCA LPM-2370	(M)	Something For Everybody	1961	20.00	50.00
RCA LSP-2370	(S)	Something For Everybody	1961	35.00	70.00
RCA LPM-2426	(M)	Blue Hawaii (Sdtk)	1961	16.00	40.00
RCA LSP-2426	(S)	Blue Hawaii (Sdtk)	1961	30.00	60.00
RCA LPM-2426	(M)	Blue Hawaii (Sdtk)	1962	45.00	90.00
RCA LSP-2426	(S)	Blue Hawaii (Sdtk)	1962	50.00	100.00
		(With a sticker on the cover that reads "Contains the Twist Special.")			
RCA LPM-2523	(M)	Pot Luck With Elvis	1962	30.00	60.00
RCA LSP-2523	(S)	Pot Luck With Elvis	1962	40.00	80.00
RCA LPM-2621	(M)	Girls! Girls! Girls! (Sdtk)	1962	16.00	40.00
RCA LSP-2621	(S)	Girls! Girls! Girls! (Sdtk)	1962	30.00	60.00
		Girls! Girls! Girls! Bonus calendar	1962	40.00	80.00
RCA LPM-2697	(M)	It Happened At The World's Fair (Sdtk)	1963	20.00	50.00
RCA LSP-2697	(S)	It Happened At The World's Fair (Sdtk)	1963	30.00	60.00
		It Happened At The World's Fair Bonus Photo	1963	75.00	150.00
RCA LPM-2756	(M)	Fun In Acapulco (Sdtk)	1963	16.00	40.00
RCA LSP-2756	(S)	Fun In Acapulco (Sdtk)	1963	20.00	50.00
RCA LPM-2765	(M)	Elvis' Golden Records, Volume 3	1963	16.00	40.00
RCA LSP-2765	(S)	Elvis' Golden Records, Volume 3	1963	20.00	50.00
		Elvis' Golden Records, Volume 3 Bonus Book	1963	20.00	50.00
RCA LPM-2894	(M)	Kissin' Cousins (Sdtk)	1964	16.00	40.00
RCA LSP-2894	(S)	Kissin' Cousins (Sdtk)	1964	20.00	50.00
		(With a small black & white photo on the cover.)			
RCA LPM-2894	(M)	Kissin' Cousins (Sdtk)	1964	45.00	90.00
RCA LSP-2894	(S)	Kissin' Cousins (Sdtk)	1964	50.00	100.00
		(Without the black & white photo on the cover.)			
RCA LPM-2999	(M)	Roustabout (Sdtk)	1964	20.00	50.00
RCA LSP-2999	(S)	Roustabout (Sdtk)	1964	240.00	400.00
		(Black label with "Living Stereo" on the bottom.)			
RCA LSP-2999	(S)	Roustabout (Sdtk)	1964	20.00	50.00
		(Black label with "Stereo" on the bottom.)			
RCA LPM-3338	(M)	Girl Happy (Sdtk)	1965	16.00	40.00
RCA LSP-3338	(S)	Girl Happy (Sdtk)	1965	20.00	50.00

Label		Title	Year	VG+	NM
RCA LPM-3450	(M)	Elvis For Everyone	1965	16.00	40.00
RCA LSP-3450	(P)	Elvis For Everyone	1965	20.00	50.00
RCA LPM-3468	(M)	Harum Scarum (Sdtk)	1965	16.00	40.00
RCA LSP-3468	(S)	Harum Scarum (Sdtk)	1965	16.00	40.00
		Harum Scarum Bonus Photo	1965	14.00	35.00
RCA LPM-3553	(M)	Frankie And Johnny (Sdtk)	1966	16.00	40.00
RCA LSP-3553	(S)	Frankie And Johnny (Sdtk)	1966	16.00	40.00
		Frankie And Johnny Bonus Photo	1966	14.00	35.00
RCA LPM-3643	(M)	Paradise Hawaiian Style (Sdtk)	1966	16.00	40.00
RCA LSP-3643	(S)	Paradise Hawaiian Style (Sdtk)	1966	16.00	40.00
RCA LPM-3702	(M)	Spinout (Sdtk)	1966	16.00	40.00
RCA LSP-3702	(S)	Spinout (Sdtk)	1966	16.00	40.00
		Spinout Bonus Photo	1966	14.00	35.00
RCA LPM-3758	(M)	How Great Thou Art	1967	20.00	50.00
RCA LSP-3758	(S)	How Great Thou Art	1967	16.00	40.00
RCA LPM-3787	(M)	Double Trouble (Sdtk)	1967	20.00	50.00
RCA LSP-3787	(S)	Double Trouble (Sdtk)	1967	16.00	40.00
		(The cover has a printed announcement for the bonus photo.)			
		Double Trouble Bonus Photo	1967	14.00	35.00
RCA LPM-3893	(M)	Clambake (Sdtk)	1967	75.00	150.00
RCA LSP-3893	(S)	Clambake (Sdtk)	1967	16.00	40.00
		Clambake Bonus Photo	1967	14.00	35.00
RCA LPM-3921	(M)	Elvis' Gold Records, Volume 4	1968	400.00	600.00
RCA LSP-3921	(S)	Elvis' Gold Records, Volume 4	1968	16.00	40.00
		Elvis' Gold Records, Volume 4 Bonus Photo	1968	50.00	100.00
RCA LPM-3989	(M)	Speedway (Sdtk with Nancy Sinatra)	1968	530.00	800.00
RCA LSP-3989	(S)	Speedway (Sdtk with Nancy Sinatra)	1968	16.00	40.00
		Speedway Bonus Photo	1968	20.00	50.00
RCA PRS-279	(P)	Singer Presents Elvis	1968	10.00	25.00
		Singer Presents Elvis Bonus Photo	1968	10.00	25.00
RCA LPM-4088	(M)	Elvis/NBC TV Special	1968	10.00	25.00
Camden CAS-2304	(P)	Elvis Sings Flaming Star	1969	8.00	20.00
RCA LSP-4155	(S)	From Elvis In Memphis	1969	10.00	25.00
		From Elvis In Memphis Bonus Photo	1969	10.00	25.00
RCA LSP-6020	(S)	From Memphis To Vegas	1969	14.00	35.00
		From Memphis To Vegas Bonus Photo	1969	10.00	25.00
		(Issued with two photos; the price is for either one.)			
Camden CAS-2408	(P)	Let's Be Friends	1970	8.00	20.00
RCA LSP-4362	(S)	On Stage-February, 1970	1970	10.00	25.00
RCA LPM-6401	(M)	Worldwide 50 Gold Award Hits	1970	30.00	60.00
		Worldwide 50 Gold Award Hits Bonus Book	1970	10.00	25.00
Camden CAS-2440	(S)	Almost In Love	1970	8.00	20.00
Camden CAL-2428	(P)	Elvis' Christmas Album	1970	8.00	20.00
RCA LSP-4428	(S)	Elvis In Person At The International Hotel	1970	10.00	25.00
RCA LSP-4429	(S)	Back In Memphis	1970	10.00	25.00
RCA LSP-4445	(S)	That's The Way It Is	1970	10.00	25.00
RCA LSP-4460	(S)	Elvis Country	1971	10.00	25.00
		Elvis Country Bonus Photo	1971	8.00	20.00
Camden CALX-2472	(P)	You'll Never Walk Alone	1971	6.00	15.00
RCA LSP-4530	(S)	Love Letters From Elvis	1971	20.00	50.00
		(Orange label. The cover has the RCA logo on top.)			
RCA LSP-4530	(S)	Love Letters From Elvis	1971	10.00	25.00
		(Orange label. The cover has the RCA logo in the lower right corner.)			
Camden CAL-2518	(P)	C' Mon Everybody	1971	6.00	15.00
RCA LPM-6402	(M)	The Other Sides	1971	16.00	40.00
		The Other Sides Bonus Poster	1971	46.00	15.00
		The Other Sides Bonus Envelope	1971	5.00	12.00
		(Small envelope with a piece from Elvis' wardrobe.)			
Camden CAL-2533	(P)	I Got Lucky	1971	6.00	15.00
RCA LSP-4579	(S)	The Wonderful World Of Christmas	1971	14.00	35.00
		The Wonderful World Of Christmas Bonus Photo	1971	8.00	20.00
RCA LSP-4671	(S)	Elvis Now	1972	10.00	25.00
RCA LSP-4690	(S)	He Touched Me	1972	10.00	25.00
Camden CAS-2567	(S)	Elvis Sings The Hits From His Movies	1972	6.00	15.00
RCA LSP-4776	(S)	Elvis At Madison Square Garden	1972	6.00	15.00
Camden CAS-2595	(S)	Elvis Sings Burning Love	1972	10.00	25.00
		(The front cover has a star for the bonus photo.)			
		Elvis Sings Burning Love Bonus Photo	1972	20.00	50.00

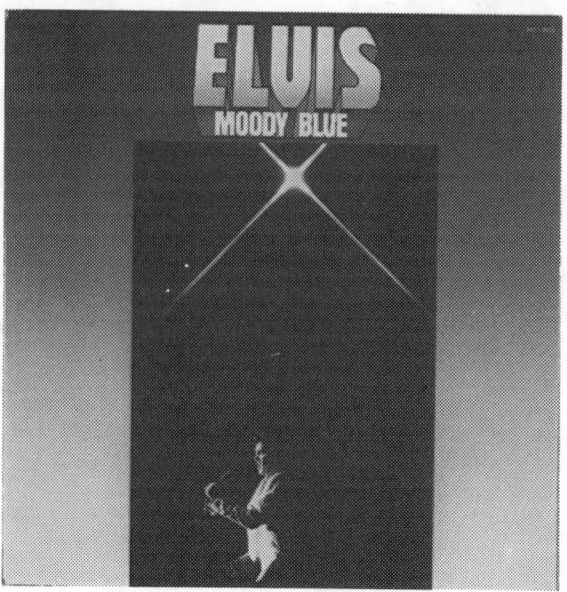

Elvis Presley, *Moody Blue*. Originally issued on blue vinyl (250,000 were initially pressed), RCA had switched to black vinyl shortly before Elvis' untimely death. They did an about face and went back to the blue, which went on to sell millions of copies. The black vinyl version with the original catalog number, AFL1-2428, is one of the rarest albums of the late '70s.

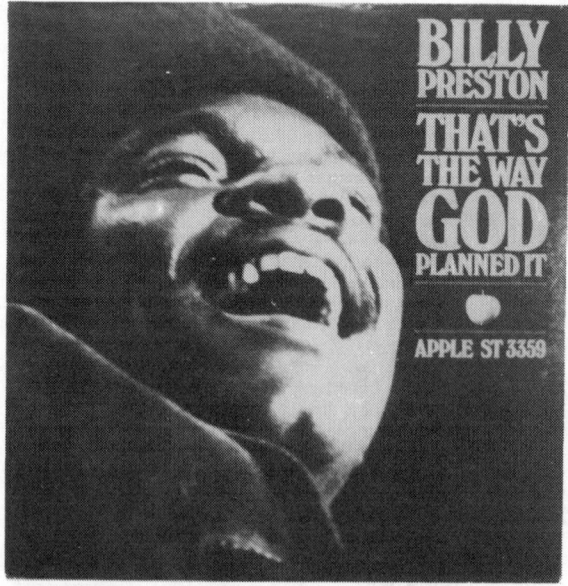

Billy Preston, *That's The Way God Planned It*. This, the original cover, was rather quickly recalled and replaced with another one featuring multiple images of Preston. This ranks as one of the most collectible Apple albums.

Label		Title	Year	VG+	NM
Camden CAS-2611	(P)	Separate Ways	1973	6.00	15.00
		Separate Ways Bonus Photo	1973	5.00	12.00
RCA VPSX-6089	(Q)	Aloha From Hawaii Via Satellite	1973	14.00	35.00
		(Red/orange label.)			
RCA VPSX-6089	(Q)	Aloha From Hawaii Via Satellite	1973	1,000.00	1,500.00
		(Red/orange label. The cover has a sticker for "Chicken of the Sea" tuna fish.)			
RCA DPL2-0056	(E)	Elvis (Brown label)	1973	12.00	30.00
RCA APL1-0283	(S)	Elvis	1973	16.00	40.00
RCA APL1-0388	(S)	Raised On Rock	1973	10.00	25.00
RCA CPL1-0341	(P)	A Legendary Performer, Volume 1	1974	6.00	15.00
		(Antique black label with a "window" cover.)			
RCA CPL1-0475	(S)	Good Times	1974	10.00	25.00
RCA APD1-0606	(Q)	Live On Stage In Memphis	1974	100.00	200.00
RCA CPL1-0606	(S)	Live On Stage In Memphis	1974	8.00	20.00
		(Both albums above have orange labels.)			
RCA R-213690	(M)	Worldwide Gold Award Hits, Parts 1 & 2	1974	14.00	35.00
Boxcar	(M)	Having Fun On Stage	1974	75.00	150.00
RCA CPM1-0818	(M)	Having Fun On Stage	1974	8.00	20.00
RCA APD1-0873	(Q)	Promised Land (Orange label)	1975	75.00	150.00
RCA APD1-0873	(Q)	Promised Land (Black label)	1976	30.00	60.00
RCA APL1-0873	(S)	Promised Land (Orange label)	1975	20.00	50.00
RCA APL1-0873	(S)	Promised Land (Brown label)	1975	6.00	15.00
RCA ANL1-0971	(P)	Pure Gold (Orange label)	1975	6.00	15.00
RCA APD1-1039	(Q)	Elvis Today (Orange label)	1975	75.00	150.00
RCA APD1-1039	(Q)	Elvis Today (Black label)	1976	30.00	60.00
RCA APL1-1039	(S)	Elvis Today (Orange label)	1975	20.00	50.00
RCA APL1-1039	(S)	Elvis Today (Brown label)	1975	6.00	15.00
RCA DPL2-0168	(P)	Elvis In Hollywood (Blue label)	1975	10.00	25.00
		Elvis In Hollywood Bonus Book	1975	4.00	10.00
RCA CPL1-1349	(P)	A Legendary Performer, Volume 2	1976	6.00	15.00
		(Antique black label with a "window" cover.)			
RCA APM1-1675	(M)	The Sun Sessions (Brown label)	1976	8.00	20.00
RCA APL1-1506	(S)	From Elvis Presley Boulevard (Brown label)		8.00	20.00
RCA APL1-2274	(P)	Welcome To My World	1977	4.00	10.00
RCA AFL1-2428	(S)	Moody Blue (Blue vinyl)	1977	3.50	8.00
RCA AFL1-2428	(S)	Moody Blue (Black vinyl)	1977	100.00	200.00
RCA APL2-2587	(S)	Elvis In Concert (Blue label)	1977	6.00	15.00
Mobile Fidelity 1-059	(S)	From Elvis In Memphis		6.00	15.00
PRESTON, BILLY					
Vee Jay 1123	(M)	The Most Exciting Organ Ever	1965	6.00	15.00
Vee Jay 1123	(S)	The Most Exciting Organ Ever	1965	8.00	20.00
Exodus EX-304	(M)	Early Hits Of 1965	1965	5.00	12.00
Exodus EX-304	(S)	Early Hits Of 1965	1965	6.00	15.00
Capitol T-2532	(M)	Wildest Organ In Town	1966	5.00	12.00
Capitol ST-2532	(S)	Wildest Organ In Town	1966	6.00	15.00
Buddah BDS-7502	(S)	Billy Preston	1969	5.00	12.00
Apple ST-3359	(S)	That's The Way God Planned It	1969	20.00	50.00
		(With a close-up of Preston's face on the cover.)			
Apple ST-3359	(S)	That's The Way God Planned It	1969	8.00	20.00
		(With multiple images of Preston on the cover.)			
Apple ST-3370	(S)	Encouraging Words	1970	5.00	12.00
PRESTON, JOHNNY					
Mercury MG-20592	(M)	Running Bear	1960	20.00	50.00
Mercury SR-60250	(P)	Running Bear	1960	30.00	60.00
Mercury MG-20609	(M)	Come Rock With Me	1961	16.00	40.00
Mercury SR-60609	(P)	Come Rock With Me	1961	20.00	50.00
PRETENDERS, THE					
Nautilus 38	(S)	The Pretenders		10.00	25.00
PRETTY THINGS, THE					
Fontana MGF-27544	(M)	The Pretty Things	1966	20.00	50.00
Fontana SRF-67544	(S)	The Pretty Things	1966	30.00	60.00
Rare Earth RS-506	(S)	S.F. Sorrow	1969	16.00	40.00
Rare Earth RS-515	(S)	Parachute	1970	6.00	15.00
Sire SASH-3713	(S)	The Vintage Years	1976	6.00	15.00
Rare Earth R-459	(S)	Real Pretty	1976	6.00	15.00

The Pretenders. While the original band members have passed on (or, in two cases, passed away) and left the band as Chrissie Hynde's backup group, this album sums up their claim as one of the best groups of the last ten years. This half-speed mastered version is increasingly difficult to find.

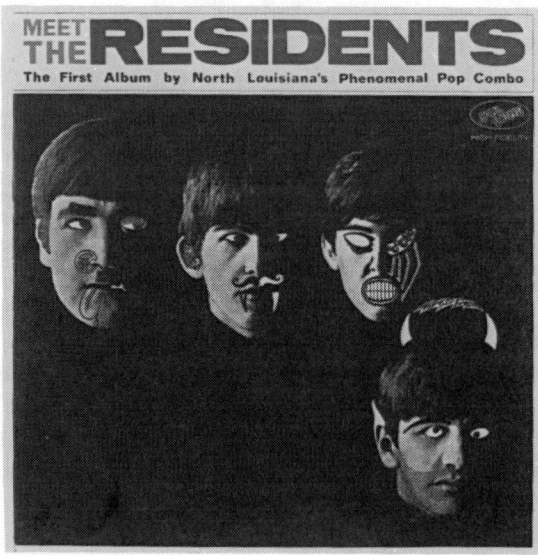

The Residents, *Meet The Residents.* America's #1 underground band. After the threat of a lawsuit from Capitol Records (another in a long line of legal actions that betray American corporations' complete lack of humor), the Resident first album was forced to undergo a complete facelift. It is now back in print with the compact disc release.

Label		Title	Year	VG+	NM
PRICE, ALAN					
Parrot PAS-71018	(S)	The Price Is Right	1968	6.00	15.00
PRICE, LLOYD					
Specialty SP-2105	(M)	Lloyd Price	1959	20.00	50.00
ABC-Paramount 277	(M)	The Exciting Lloyd Price	1959	12.00	30.00
ABC-Paramount S-277	(S)	The Exciting Lloyd Price	1959	16.00	40.00
ABC-Paramount 297	(M)	Mr. Personality	1959	12.00	30.00
ABC-Paramount S-297	(S)	Mr. Personality	1959	16.00	40.00
ABC-Paramount 315	(M)	Mr. Personality Sings The Blues	1960	12.00	30.00
ABC-Paramount S-315	(S)	Mr. Personality Sings The Blues	1960	16.00	40.00
ABC-Paramount 324	(M)	Mr. Personality's Big 15	1960	12.00	30.00
ABC-Paramount S-324	(E)	Mr. Personality's Big 15	1960	10.00	25.00
ABC-Paramount 346	(M)	The Fantastic Lloyd Price	1960	12.00	30.00
ABC-Paramount S-346	(E)	The Fantastic Lloyd Price	1960	10.00	25.00
ABC-Paramount 366	(M)	Lloyd Price Sings The Million Sellers	1961	10.00	25.00
ABC-Paramount S-366	(S)	Lloyd Price Sings The Million Sellers	1961	12.00	30.00
ABC-Paramount 382	(M)	Cookin' With Lloyd Price	1961	10.00	25.00
ABC-Paramount S-382	(S)	Cookin' With Lloyd Price	1961	12.00	30.00
Double-L D-2301	(M)	The Lloyd Price Orchestra	1963	8.00	20.00
Double-L SDL-8301	(S)	The Lloyd Price Orchestra	1963	10.00	25.00
Double-L D-2303	(M)	Misty	1963	8.00	20.00
Double-L SDL-8303	(S)	Misty	1963	10.00	25.00
Monument MLP-8032	(M)	Lloyd Swings For Sammy	1965	8.00	20.00
Monument SMP-18032	(S)	Lloyd Swings For Sammy	1965	10.00	25.00
Jad 1002	(S)	Lloyd Price Now		6.00	15.00
ABC-Paramount X-763	(P)	Lloyd Price's 16 Greatest Hits	1972	4.00	10.00
ABC-Paramount 30006	(P)	The ABC Collection	1976	4.00	10.00
PRICE, RAY					
Columbia CL-1015	(M)	Ray Price Sings Heart Songs	1957	12.00	30.00
Columbia CL-1148	(M)	Take To Your Heart	1958	10.00	25.00
Columbia CL-1494	(M)	Faith	1960	6.00	15.00
Columbia CS-8285	(S)	Faith	1960	8.00	20.00
Columbia CL-1566	(M)	Ray Price's Greatest Hits	1961	8.00	20.00
Columbia CL-1758	(M)	San Antonio Rose	1962	6.00	15.00
Columbia CS-8556	(S)	San Antonio Rose	1962	8.00	20.00
		(Columbia albums above have six black "eye" logos on each label.)			
Columbia CL-1971	(M)	Night Life	1963	5.00	12.00
Columbia CS-8771	(S)	Night Life	1963	6.00	15.00
Columbia CL-1976	(M)	Greatest Western Hits, Volume 1	1963	5.00	12.00
Columbia CS-8776	(S)	Greatest Western Hits, Volume 1	1963	6.00	15.00
Columbia CL-2189	(M)	Love Life	1964	5.00	12.00
Columbia CS-8989	(S)	Love Life	1964	6.00	15.00
Columbia CL-2289	(M)	Burning Memories	1965	5.00	12.00
Columbia CS-9089	(S)	Burning Memories	1965	6.00	15.00
Columbia CL-2339	(M)	Western Strings	1965	5.00	12.00
Columbia CS-9139	(S)	Western Strings	1965	6.00	15.00
Columbia CL-2382	(M)	The Other Woman	1965	5.00	12.00
Columbia CS-9182	(S)	The Other Woman	1965	6.00	15.00
Columbia CL-2528	(M)	Another Bridge To Burn	1966	4.00	10.00
Columbia CS-9328	(S)	Another Bridge To Burn	1966	5.00	12.00
Columbia CL-2606	(M)	Touch My Heart	1967	4.00	10.00
Columbia CS-9406	(S)	Touch My Heart	1967	5.00	12.00
Columbia CL-2670	(M)	Ray Price's Greatest Hits, Volume 2	1967	4.00	10.00
Columbia CS-9470	(S)	Ray Price's Greatest Hits, Volume 2	1967	5.00	12.00
Columbia CL-2677	(M)	Danny Boy	1967	4.00	10.00
Columbia CS-9477	(S)	Danny Boy	1967	5.00	12.00
Columbia CL-2806	(M)	Take Me As I Am	1968	5.00	12.00
Columbia CS-9606	(S)	Take Me As I Am	1968	5.00	12.00
Columbia CS-9733	(S)	She Wears My Ring	1968	5.00	12.00
Columbia CS-9822	(S)	Sweetheart Of The Year	1969	5.00	12.00
Columbia CS-9861	(S)	Ray Price's Christmas Album	1969	5.00	12.00
Columbia CS-9918	(S)	You Wouldn't Know Love	1970	5.00	12.00
		(Columbia albums above have "360 Sound" labels.)			
PRICE, RUTH					
Kapp KL-1006	(M)	My Name Is Ruth Price, I Sing	1958	12.00	30.00
Kapp KL-1054	(S)	The Party's Over	1958	12.00	30.00
Roost 2217	(M)	Ruth Price Sings	1958	10.00	25.00

Label		Title	Year	VG+	NM
Contemporary 3590	(M)	Ruth Price At The Manne-Hole	1961	6.00	15.00
Contemporary 7590	(S)	Ruth Price At The Manne-Hole	1961	8.00	20.00
Ave 54	(M)	Live And Beautiful	1963	8.00	20.00

PRICE, VINCENT

Columbia ML-5668	(M)	America The Beautiful	1961	8.00	20.00
Capitol SWBB-342	(S)	Witchcraft/Magic	1969	6.00	15.00

PRIMA, LOUIS

Rondo 842	(M)	Louis Prima	1959	16.00	40.00
Capitol T-1132	(M)	Strictly Prima	1959	16.00	40.00
Dot DLP-3352	(M)	Wonderland By Night	1960	10.00	25.00
Dot DLP-25352	(S)	Wonderland By Night	1960	12.00	30.00
Dot DLP-3410	(M)	Doin' The Twist	1961	10.00	25.00
Dot DLP-25410	(S)	Doin' The Twist	1961	12.00	30.00
Capitol T-1723	(M)	The Wildest Comes Home	1962	10.00	25.00
Capitol ST-1723	(S)	The Wildest Comes Home	1962	12.00	30.00

PRIMA, LOUIS, & KEELY SMITH

Capitol T-1160	(M)	Hey Boy, Hey Girl (Sdtk)	1959	16.00	40.00
Dot DLP-3210	(M)	Louis And Keely	1959	10.00	25.00
Dot DLP-25210	(S)	Louis And Keely	1959	12.00	30.00
Dot DLP-3263	(M)	Together	1960	10.00	25.00
Dot DLP-25263	(S)	Together	1960	12.00	30.00
Capitol T-1531	(M)	The Hits Of Louis And Keely	1961	12.00	30.00

PRINCE BUSTER

RCA LPM-3792	(M)	Ten Commandments	1967	8.00	20.00
RCA LSP-3792	(S)	Ten Commandments	1967	10.00	25.00

PRINZ, FREDDIE

Columbia PC-33562	(S)	Looking Good		6.00	15.00

PROBY, P.J.

Liberty LRP-3406	(M)	Go Go P.J. Proby	1965	6.00	15.00
Liberty LST-7406	(S)	Go Go P.J. Proby	1965	8.00	20.00
Liberty LRP-3421	(M)	P.J. Proby	1965	6.00	15.00
Liberty LST-7421	(S)	P.J. Proby	1965	8.00	20.00
Liberty LRP-3497	(M)	Enigma	1967	5.00	12.00
Liberty LST-7497	(S)	Enigma	1967	6.00	15.00
Liberty LRP-3515	(M)	Phenomenon	1967	5.00	12.00
Liberty LST-7515	(S)	Phenomenon	1967	6.00	15.00
Liberty LST-7561	(S)	What's Wrong With My World?	1968	6.00	15.00

PROCOL HARUM

Deram DE-16008	(M)	Procol Harum	1967	12.00	30.00
Deram DES-18008	(E)	Procol Harum	1967	6.00	15.00

PROCTOR, PHIL, & PETER BERGMAN

Columbia KC-32199	(S)	TV Or Not TV	1973	4.00	10.00

PROVINE, DOROTHY

Warners W-1394	(M)	The Roaring '20's	1961	6.00	15.00
Warners WS-1394	(S)	The Roaring '20's	1961	8.00	20.00
Warners W-1419	(M)	The Vamp Of The Roaring '20's	1961	6.00	15.00
Warners WS-1419	(S)	The Vamp Of The Roaring '20's	1961	8.00	20.00

PRYSOCK, ARTHUR

Old Town LP-102	(M)	I Worry About You	1962	10.00	25.00
Old Town LP-2004	(M)	Arthur Prysock Sings Only For You	1962	6.00	15.00
Old Town LP-2005	(M)	Coast To Coast	1963	6.00	15.00
Old Town LP-2006	(M)	Portrait	1963	6.00	15.00
Old Town LP-2007	(M)	Everlasting Songs For Everlasting Lovers	1964	6.00	15.00
Old Town LP-2008	(M)	Intimately Your's	1964	6.00	15.00
Old Town LP-2009	(M)	Double Header	1965	6.00	15.00
Old Town LP-2010	(M)	In A Mood	1965	6.00	15.00
Decca DL-4581	(M)	Strictly Sentimental	1965	5.00	12.00
Decca DL7-4581	(S)	Strictly Sentimental	1965	6.00	15.00
Decca DL-4628	(M)	Showcase	1965	5.00	12.00
Decca DL7-4628	(S)	Showcase	1965	6.00	15.00

Label		Title	Year	VG+	NM
PRYSOCK, RED					
Mercury MG-20086	(M)	Rock 'N' Roll	1955	20.00	50.00
Mercury MG-20106	(M)	Battle Royal	1956	14.00	35.00
Mercury MG-20188	(M)	Swing Softly Red	1956	14.00	35.00
Mercury MG-20211	(M)	Fruit Boots	1957	14.00	35.00
Mercury MG-20307	(M)	The Beat	1959	8.00	20.00
Mercury SR-60307	(S)	The Beat	1959	10.00	25.00
PUGSLEY MUNION					
J&S SLP-0001	(S)	Just Like You		35.00	70.00
PURIFY, JAMES & BOBBY					
Bell 6003	(M)	James And Bobby Purify	1967	5.00	12.00
Bell 6003	(S)	James And Bobby Purify	1967	6.00	15.00
Bell 6010	(M)	The Pure Sound Of The Purifys	1967	5.00	12.00
Bell 6010	(S)	The Pure Sound Of The Purifys	1967	6.00	15.00
PYRAMIDS, THE					
Best LPM-1001	(M)	Penetration	1964	40.00	80.00
Best BRS-36501	(E)	Penetration	1964	30.00	60.00

Label		Title	Year	VG+	NM
QUEEN					
Elektra EQ-5064	(Q)	Queen	1973	6.00	15.00
Mobile Fidelity 1-067	(S)	Night At The Opera	1980	6.00	15.00
QUESTION MARK & THE MYSTERIANS					
Cameo C-2004	(M)	96 Tears	1966	12.00	30.00
Cameo CS-2004	(E)	96 Tears	1966	10.00	25.00
Cameo C-2006	(M)	Action	1967	12.00	30.00
Cameo SC-2006	(E)	Action	1967	10.00	25.00
QUICKSILVER MESSENGER SERVICE (QUICKSILVER)					
United Arts. UAS-5185	(S)	Revolution (Sdtk)	1968	6.00	15.00
Capitol ST-2904	(S)	Quicksilver Messenger Service (Black label)	1968	8.00	20.00
Capitol ST-120	(S)	Happy Trails (Black label.)	1969	6.00	15.00

Label		Title	Year	VG+	NM
R.E.O. SPEEDWAGON					
Epic HE-45082	(S)	You Can Tune A Piano (1/2 speed)	1982	6.00	15.00
RABBLE, THE					
Transworld 6700	(M)	The Rabble Album	1966	30.00	60.00

Label		Title	Year	VG+	NM
RAEBURN, BOYD					
Columbia CL-1073	(M)	Teen Rock (Eyes logo label)	1957	16.00	40.00
RAFFERTY, GERRY					
Mobile Fidelity 1-058	(S)	City To City		6.00	15.00
RAICEVIC, NIK PASCAL					
Narco 102	(S)	Beyond The End Eternity	1971	6.00	15.00
Narco 666	(S)	Sixth Ear	1972	6.00	15.00
Narco 321	(S)	Magnetic Web	1973	6.00	15.00
Narco 123	(S)	Zero Gravity	1975	6.00	15.00
RAIDERS, THE					
Liberty LRP-3225	(M)	Twistin' The Country Classics	1962	6.00	15.00
Liberty LST-7225	(M)	Twistin' The Country Classics	1962	8.00	20.00
RAINDROPS, THE					
Jubilee J-5023	(M)	The Raindrops	1963	12.00	30.00
Jubilee SJ-5023	(S)	The Raindrops	1963	16.00	40.00
RAINWATER, MARVIN					
MGM E-3534	(M)	Songs By Marvin Rainwater	1957	30.00	60.00
MGM E-3721	(M)	With A Heart, With A Beat	1958	30.00	60.00
MGM E-4046	(M)	Gonna Find Me A Bluebird	1962	20.00	50.00
RAINY DAZE					
Uni 3002	(M)	That Acapulco Gold	1967	5.00	12.00
Uni 73002	(S)	That Acapulco Gold	1967	6.00	15.00
RAM, BUCK					
Mercury MG-20392	(M)	The Magic Touch	1960	8.00	20.00
Mercury SR-60067	(S)	The Magic Touch	1960	10.00	25.00
RAMBEAU, EDDIE					
DynoVoice 9001	(M)	Concrete And Clay	1965	6.00	15.00
DynoVoice DS-9001	(S)	Concrete And Clay	1965	8.00	20.00
RAMBLERS THREE, THE					
MGM E-4072	(M)	Make Way For The Ramblers Three	1962	6.00	15.00
RAMJET, RODGER					
Camden CAL-1075	(M)	Rodger Ramjet & The American Eagles	1966	6.00	15.00
Camden CAS-1075	(S)	Rodger Ramjet & The American Eagles	1966	8.00	20.00
RAMONES, THE					
Sire SRK-7520	(S)	The Ramones	1976	6.00	15.00
Sire SRK-7528	(S)	Leave Home (With "Carbona Not Glue.")	1977	6.00	15.00
RANDALL, TONY					
Mercury MG-21178	(M)	Warm And Wavery	1967	5.00	12.00
Mercury SR-61178	(S)	Warm And Wavery	1967	6.00	15.00
RANDAZZO, TEDDY					
Vik LX-1121	(M)	I'm Confessin'		16.00	40.00
ABC 352	(M)	Journey To Love	1961	12.00	30.00
ABC S-352	(S)	Journey To Love	1961	14.00	35.00
ABC 421	(M)	Teddy Randazzo Twists	1962	12.00	30.00
ABC S-421	(S)	Teddy Randazzo Twists	1962	14.00	35.00
Roulette R-25168	(M)	Hey, Let's Twist (Sdtk)	1962	12.00	30.00
Colpix CP-445	(M)	Big Wide World	1963	10.00	25.00
Colpix SCP-445	(S)	Big Wide World	1963	14.00	35.00
RANDY & THE RAINBOWS					
Ambient Sound 37715	(S)	C'Mon Let's Go	1982	4.00	10.00
RAPP, TOM					
Reprise MS-2069	(S)	Tom Rapp	1972	6.00	15.00
RARE BIRD					
Probe 24-4514	(S)	Rare Bird	1970	6.00	15.00

Label		Title	Year	VG+	NM
RASCALS: *Refer to* **YOUNG RASCALS**					
RASPBERRIES, THE					
Capitol ST-11036	(S)	Raspberries	1972	6.00	15.00
Capitol ST-11123	(S)	Fresh Raspberries	1972	8.00	20.00
Capitol SMAS-11220	(S)	Side Three	1973	8.00	20.00
Capitol ST-11329	(S)	Starting Over	1974	6.00	15.00
RATTLES, THE					
Mercury MG-20994	(M)	The Searchers Meet The Rattles	1965	16.00	40.00
Mercury SR-60994	(S)	The Searchers Meet The Rattles	1965	20.00	50.00
Mercury MG-21127	(M)	The Rattles' Greatest Hits	1967	14.00	35.00
Mercury SR-61127	(M)	The Rattles' Greatest Hits	1967	16.00	40.00
RAVENS, THE					
Regent MG-6062	(M)	Write Me A Letter (Green label)		50.00	100.00
RAW					
Coral CRL7-57515	(S)	Raw Holly	1971	12.00	30.00
RAY, JAMES					
Caprice LP-1002	(M)	If You Gotta Make A Fool Of Somebody	1962	12.00	30.00
Caprice SLP-1002	(S)	If You Gotta Make A Fool Of Somebody	1962	16.00	40.00
RAY, JOHNNY					
Columbia CL-2510 (10")	(M)	I Cry For You	1960	12.00	30.00
Columbia CL-6199 (10")	(M)	Johnny Ray		12.00	30.00
Columbia CL-961	(M)	The Big Beat	1957	10.00	25.00
Columbia CL-1225	(M)	'Til Morning	1959	10.00	25.00
Columbia CL-1227	(M)	Johnny Ray's Greatest Hits	1959	10.00	25.00
Columbia CL-1380	(M)	On The Trail	1959	10.00	25.00
		(Columbia albums above have "360 Sound" labels.)			
Epic LN-1120	(M)	Johnny Ray		8.00	20.00
Liberty LRP-3221	(M)	Johnny Ray	1962	6.00	15.00
Liberty LST-7221	(S)	Johnny Ray	1962	8.00	20.00
REDD, VI					
United Arts. UAL-14106	(M)	Bird Call	1962	8.00	20.00
United Arts. UAS-15106	(S)	Bird Call	1962	10.00	25.00
Atco 33-157	(M)	Lady Soul	1963	8.00	20.00
Atco SD-33-157	(S)	Lady Soul	1963	10.00	25.00
REDDING, OTIS					
Atco SD-33-161	(M)	Pain In My Heart	1964	16.00	40.00
Atco SD-33-161	(S)	Pain In My Heart	1964	20.00	50.00
Volt 411	(M)	Soul Ballads	1965	12.00	30.00
Volt S-411	(S)	Soul Ballads	1965	16.00	40.00
Volt 412	(M)	Otis Blue	1965	10.00	25.00
Volt S-412	(S)	Otis Blue	1965	12.00	30.00
Volt 413	(M)	The Soul Album	1966	10.00	25.00
Volt S-413	(S)	The Soul Album	1966	12.00	30.00
Volt 415	(M)	Dictionary Of Soul	1966	10.00	25.00
Volt S-415	(S)	Dictionary Of Soul	1966	12.00	30.00
Volt 416	(M)	Live In Europe	1967	10.00	25.00
Volt S-416	(S)	Live In Europe	1967	12.00	30.00
Volt 418	(M)	The History Of Otis Redding	1967	10.00	25.00
Volt S-418	(P)	The History Of Otis Redding	1967	12.00	30.00
Stax 716	(M)	The King And Queen (With Carla Thomas)	1967	10.00	25.00
Stax S-716	(S)	The King And Queen (With Carla Thomas)	1967	12.00	30.00
Volt S-419	(S)	Dock Of The Bay	1968	12.00	30.00
Atco SD-33-252	(S)	The Immortal Otis Redding	1968	10.00	25.00
Atco SD-33-265	(S)	In Person At The Whiskey A Go-Go	1968	10.00	25.00
Atco SD-33-288	(S)	The Dock Of The Bay	1968	10.00	25.00
Atco SD-33-289	(S)	Love Man	1969	10.00	25.00
Atco SD-33-333	(S)	Tell The Truth	1970	10.00	25.00
Atco SD-2-801	(S)	The Best Of Otis Redding	1972	6.00	15.00
REED, JIMMY					
Vee Jay LP-1004	(M)	I'm Jimmy Reed (Maroon label)	1958	50.00	100.00
Vee Jay LP-1008	(M)	Rockin' With Reed (Maroon label)	1959	40.00	80.00
Vee Jay LP-1022	(M)	Found Love	1960	16.00	40.00

Label		Title	Year	VG+	NM
Vee Jay LP-1025	(M)	Now Appearing	1960	16.00	40.00
Vee Jay 2LP-1035	(M)	Jimmy Reed At Carnegie Hall	1961	12.00	30.00
Vee Jay 2SR-1035	(P)	Jimmy Reed At Carnegie Hall	1961	16.00	40.00
Vee Jay LP-1039	(M)	The Best Of Jimmy Reed	1962	12.00	30.00
Vee Jay SR-1039	(P)	The Best Of Jimmy Reed	1962	16.00	40.00
Vee Jay LP-1050	(M)	Just Jimmy Reed	1962	12.00	30.00
		(Vee Jay albums above have black rainbow labels with a Vee Jay logo in an oval.)			
Vee Jay LP-1067	(M)	T'Ain't No Big Thing	1963	10.00	25.00
Vee Jay LP-1072	(M)	The Best Of The Blues	1963	10.00	25.00
Vee Jay LP-1073	(M)	The 12 String Guitar Blues	1963	10.00	25.00
Vee Jay SR-1073	(S)	The 12 String Guitar Blues	1963	12.00	30.00
Vee Jay LP-1080	(M)	More Of The Best Of Jimmy Reed	1964	10.00	25.00
Vee Jay SR-1080	(S)	More Of The Best Of Jimmy Reed	1964	12.00	30.00
Vee Jay LP-1095	(M)	Jimmy Reed At Soul City	1964	10.00	25.00
Vee Jay VJ-8501	(M)	The Legend, The Man	1965	10.00	25.00
Vee Jay VJS-8501	(S)	The Legend, The Man	1965	12.00	30.00
		(Vee Jay albums above have black rainbow labels with a "VJ" logo in brackets.)			
BluesWay BL-6004	(M)	The New Jimmy Reed Album	1967	5.00	12.00
BluesWay BLS-6004	(S)	The New Jimmy Reed Album	1967	6.00	15.00
BluesWay BL-6009	(M)	Soulin'	1967	5.00	12.00
BluesWay BLS-6009	(S)	Soulin'	1967	6.00	15.00
BluesWay BLS-6013	(S)	Big Boss Man	1968	5.00	12.00
BluesWay BLS-6024	(S)	Down In Virginia	1969	5.00	12.00
BluesWay BLS-6054	(S)	I Ain't From Chicago	1973	4.00	10.00

REED, LOU

Label		Title	Year	VG+	NM
RCA LSP-4701	(S)	Lou Reed (Orange label)	1972	6.00	15.00
RCA LSP-4807	(S)	Transformer (Orange label)	1972	5.00	12.00
RCA APL1-0207	(S)	Berlin (Orange label with booklet)	1973	5.00	12.00
RCA	(S)	Metal Machine Music		12.00	30.00
RCA	(Q)	Metal Machine Music		20.00	50.00

REED, LULU

Label		Title	Year	VG+	NM
King 604	(M)	Blue And Moody	1959	180.00	300.00

REESE, DELLA

Label		Title	Year	VG+	NM
Jubilee JLP-1026	(M)	Melancholy Baby	1957	10.00	25.00
Jubilee JLP-1071	(M)	A Date With Della Reese	1958	6.00	15.00
Jubilee SDJLP-1071	(S)	A Date With Della Reese	1958	10.00	25.00
Jubilee JLP-1083	(M)	Amen		6.00	15.00
Jubilee SDJLP-1083	(S)	Amen		10.00	25.00
Jubilee JLP-1095	(M)	The Story Of The Blues	1958	6.00	15.00
Jubilee SDJLP-1095	(S)	The Story Of The Blues	1958	10.00	25.00
Jubilee JLP-1109	(M)	What Do You Know About Love?	1959	6.00	15.00
Jubilee SDJLP-1109	(S)	What Do You Know About Love?	1959	10.00	25.00
Jubilee JLP-1116	(M)	And That Reminds Me	1959	6.00	15.00
Jubilee SDJLP-1116	(S)	And That Reminds Me	1959	8.00	20.00
RCA LPM-2157	(M)	Della	1960	6.00	15.00
RCA LSP-2157	(S)	Della	1960	8.00	20.00
RCA LPM-2204	(M)	Della By Starlight	1960	5.00	12.00
RCA LSP-2204	(S)	Della By Starlight	1960	6.00	15.00
RCA LPM-2280	(M)	Della Della Cha-Cha-Cha	1961	5.00	12.00
RCA LSP-2280	(S)	Della Della Cha-Cha-Cha	1961	6.00	15.00
RCA LPM-2391	(M)	Special Delivery	1961	5.00	12.00
RCA LSP-2391	(S)	Special Delivery	1961	6.00	15.00
RCA LPM-2419	(M)	Classic Della	1961	5.00	12.00
RCA LSP-2419	(S)	Classic Della	1961	6.00	15.00
RCA LPM-2568	(M)	Della Reese On Stage	1962	5.00	12.00
RCA LSP-2568	(S)	Della Reese On Stage	1962	6.00	15.00
		(Mono RCA albums above have "Long Play" on the bottom of the label. Stereo albums have "Living Stereo" on the bottom.)			

REEVES, JIM

Label		Title	Year	VG+	NM
Abbott LP-5001	(M)	Jim Reeves Sings	1956	400.00	600.00
RCA LPM-1256	(M)	Singing Down The Lane	1956	50.00	100.00
RCA LPM-1410	(M)	Jimbo	1957	30.00	60.00
RCA LPM-1576	(M)	Jim Reeves	1957	20.00	50.00
RCA LPM-1685	(M)	Girls I Have Known	1958	16.00	40.00

The Best Of Jim Reeves. Released in the wake of Reeve's untimely death in a plane crash in July 1964, this was his only Top Ten album on the Pop Charts, eventually earning an RIAA Gold Record.

Paul Revere And The Raiders, *In The Beginning.* Released at the height of their mid '60s popularity, this album was, in fact, a repackaging of their earlier (and ridiculously rare) eponymous album on Sande. The stereo affect is electronically created and usually commands a bit less than the mono.

Label		Title	Year	VG+	NM
RCA LPM-1950	(M)	God Be With You	1958	12.00	30.00
RCA LSP-1950	(S)	God Be With You	1958	16.00	40.00
RCA LPM-2001	(M)	Songs To Warm Your Heart	1959	12.00	30.00
RCA LSP-2001	(S)	Songs To Warm Your Heart	1959	14.00	35.00
RCA LPM-2216	(M)	The Intimate Jim Reeves	1960	8.00	20.00
RCA LSP-2216	(S)	The Intimate Jim Reeves	1960	10.00	25.00
RCA LPM-2223	(M)	He'll Have To Go	1960	8.00	20.00
RCA LSP-2223	(S)	He'll Have To Go	1960	10.00	25.00
RCA LPM-2284	(M)	Tall Tales And Short Tempers	1961	8.00	20.00
RCA LSP-2284	(S)	Tall Tales And Short Tempers	1961	10.00	25.00
RCA LPM-2339	(M)	Talkin' To Your Heart	1961	8.00	20.00
RCA LSP-2339	(S)	Talkin' To Your Heart	1961	10.00	25.00
RCA LPM-2487	(M)	A Touch Of Velvet	1962	6.00	15.00
RCA LSP-2487	(S)	A Touch Of Velvet	1962	8.00	20.00
RCA LPM-2552	(M)	We Thank Thee	1962	6.00	15.00
RCA LSP-2552	(S)	We Thank Thee	1962	8.00	20.00
RCA LPM-2605	(M)	Gentleman Jim	1963	6.00	15.00
RCA LSP-2605	(S)	Gentleman Jim	1963	8.00	20.00
RCA LPM-2704	(M)	The International Jim Reeves	1963	6.00	15.00
RCA LSP-2704	(S)	The International Jim Reeves	1963	8.00	20.00
		(Mono RCA albums above have "Long Play"			
		on the bottom of the label. Stereo albums			
		have "Living Stereo" on the bottom.)			
RCA LPM-2758	(M)	Twelve Songs Of Christmas	1963	5.00	12.00
RCA LSP-2758	(S)	Twelve Songs Of Christmas	1963	6.00	15.00
RCA LPM-2780	(M)	Kimberley Jim (Sdtk)	1964	6.00	15.00
RCA LSP-2780	(S)	Kimberley Jim (Sdtk)	1964	8.00	20.00
RCA LPM-2854	(M)	Moonlight And Roses	1964	5.00	12.00
RCA LSP-2854	(S)	Moonlight And Roses	1964	6.00	15.00
RCA LPM-2890	(M)	The Best Of Jim Reeves	1964	5.00	12.00
RCA LSP-2890	(P)	The Best Of Jim Reeves	1964	6.00	15.00
RCA LPM-2968	(M)	The Jim Reeves Way	1965	5.00	12.00
RCA LSP-2968	(S)	The Jim Reeves Way	1965	6.00	15.00
RCA LPM-3427	(M)	Up Through The Years	1965	5.00	12.00
RCA LSP-3427	(S)	Up Through The Years	1965	6.00	15.00
RCA LPM-3482	(M)	The Best Of Jim Reeves, Volume 2	1966	5.00	12.00
RCA LSP-3482	(P)	The Best Of Jim Reeves, Volume 2	1966	6.00	15.00
RCA LPM-3542	(M)	Distant Drums	1966	5.00	12.00
RCA LSP-3542	(S)	Distant Drums	1966	6.00	15.00
RCA LPM-3709	(M)	Your's Sincerely, Jim Reeves	1966	5.00	12.00
RCA LSP-3709	(S)	Your's Sincerely, Jim Reeves	1966	6.00	15.00
RCA LPM-3793	(M)	The Blue Side Of Lonesome	1967	5.00	12.00
RCA LSP-3793	(S)	The Blue Side Of Lonesome	1967	6.00	15.00
RCA LPM-3903	(M)	My Cathedral	1967	5.00	12.00
RCA LSP-3903	(S)	My Cathedral	1967	6.00	15.00
RCA LPM-3987	(M)	A Touch Of Sadness	1968	10.00	25.00
RCA LSP-3987	(S)	A Touch Of Sadness	1968	5.00	12.00
RCA LSP-4062	(S)	Jim Reeves On Stage	1968	5.00	12.00
		(The RCA albums above have black labels.)			

REFLECTIONS, THE

Golden World 300	(M)	Just Like Romeo And Juliet	1964	30.00	60.00

REGENTS, THE

Gee GLP-708	(M)	Barbara Ann	1961	40.00	80.00
Gee SGLP-708	(S)	Barbara Ann	1961	50.00	100.00
Capitol KAO-2153	(M)	Live At The AM/PM Discotheque	1964	16.00	40.00
Capitol SKAO-2153	(S)	Live At The AM/PM Discotheque	1964	20.00	50.00

REMAINS, THE

Epic LN-24214	(M)	The Remains	1966	40.00	80.00
Epic BN-26214	(S)	The Remains	1966	50.00	100.00

RENAISSANCE

Mobile Fidelity 1-099	(S)	Scheherezade		8.00	20.00

RENAY, DIANE

20th Century TF-3133	(M)	Navy Blue	1964	14.00	35.00
20th Century TFS-3133	(P)	Navy Blue	1964	16.00	40.00

Label		Title	Year	VG+	NM
REPARATA & THE DELRONS					
World Artists 2006	(M)	Whenever A Teenager Cries	1965	12.00	30.00
World Artists 3006	(S)	Whenever A Teenager Cries	1965	16.00	40.00
RESIDENTS, THE					
Ralph RR-0274	(S)	Meet The Residents	1974	75.00	150.00
		(The cover is a graphically adjusted duplication			
		of Capitol 2047, "Meet The Beatles.")			
Ralph RR-1075	(S)	Third Reich 'N' Roll	1976	20.00	50.00
		(Cover reads "First Pressing-1,000 Copies.")			
Ralph RR-1276	(S)	Fingerprince	1976	20.00	50.00
		(Cover states "First Pressing December 1976.")			
Ralph RR-0278	(S)	Duck Stab/Buster And Glen	1978	4.00	10.00
Ralph RR-1174	(S)	Not Available (Maroon & purple label)	1978	10.00	25.00
Ralph ESK-7906	(S)	Eskimo (White vinyl)	1980	10.00	25.00
Ralph ESK-7906	(S)	Eskimo	1980	4.00	10.00
Ralph RZ-8006	(S)	Diskomo	1980	6.00	15.00
Ralph RZ-8052	(S)	Commercial Album	1980	6.00	15.00
		(Back cover has incorrect song listings.)			
Ralph RZ-8052	(S)	Commercial Album	1980	4.00	10.00
		(Back cover has correct song listings.)			
Ralph RZ-8152	(S)	Mark Of The Mole (Brown vinyl)	1981	16.00	40.00
Ralph RZ-8152	(S)	Mark Of The Mole	1981	4.00	10.00
Ralph RZ-8522	(S)	Intermission	1982	4.00	10.00
Ralph ESK-7906	(S)	Eskimo (Picture disc)	1983	4.00	10.00
Ralph RZ-0001	(S)	The Mole Show	1983	12.00	30.00
Ralph RZ-0001	(S)	The Mole Show (Picture disc)	1983	12.00	30.00
Ralph RZ-8402	(S)	George And James	1984	16.00	40.00
Ralph RZ-8402	(S)	George And James (Clear vinyl)	1984	10.00	25.00
Ralph RZ-8452	(S)	Vileness Fats (Red vinyl)	1984	10.00	25.00
Ralph RR-0677	(S)	Meet The Residents (Picture disc)	1985	10.00	25.00
Episode ED-21	(S)	Census Taker (Sdtk)	1985	20.00	50.00
RESTIVO, JOHNNY					
RCA LPM-2149	(M)	Oh, Johnny	1959	16.00	40.00
RCA LSP-2149	(S)	Oh, Johnny	1959	20.00	50.00
REVELS, THE					
Impact LPM-1	(M)	Revels On A Rampage	1964	50.00	100.00
REVENGERS, THE					
Metro M-565	(M)	Batman And Other Supermen	1966	6.00	15.00
Metro MS-565	(S)	Batman And Other Supermen	1966	8.00	20.00
REVERE, PAUL, & THE RAIDERS					
Gardena G-1000	(M)	Like Long Hair	1961	150.00	250.00
Sande 1001	(M)	Paul Revere & The Raiders	1962	210.00	350.00
Columbia CL-2307	(M)	Here They Come	1965	8.00	20.00
Columbia CS-9107	(P)	Here They Come	1965	10.00	25.00
		(The back cover has short liner notes.)			
Columbia CL-2307	(M)	Here They Come	1965	6.00	15.00
Columbia CS-9107	(P)	Here They Come	1965	8.00	20.00
		(The back cover has lengthy liner notes.)			
Jerden JRL-7004	(M)	In The Beginning	1966	12.00	30.00
Jerden JRS-7004	(E)	In The Beginning	1966	8.00	20.00
Columbia CL-2451	(M)	Just Like Us	1966	6.00	15.00
Columbia CS-9251	(P)	Just Like Us	1966	8.00	20.00
Columbia CL-2508	(M)	Midnight Ride	1966	6.00	15.00
Columbia CS-9308	(P)	Midnight Ride	1966	8.00	20.00
Columbia CL-2595	(M)	The Spirit Of '67	1966	5.00	12.00
Columbia CS-9395	(P)	The Spirit Of '67	1966	6.00	15.00
Columbia KCL-2662	(M)	Greatest Hits (With booklet)	1967	5.00	12.00
Columbia KCS-9462	(P)	Greatest Hits (With booklet)	1967	6.00	15.00
Columbia CL-2721	(M)	Revolution	1967	5.00	12.00
Columbia CS-9521	(P)	Revolution	1967	6.00	15.00
Columbia CL-2755	(M)	Christmas Past And Present	1967	8.00	20.00
Columbia CS-9555	(S)	Christmas Past And Present	1967	10.00	25.00
Columbia CL-2805	(M)	Goin' To Memphis	1968	4.00	10.00
Columbia CS-9605	(S)	Goin' To Memphis	1968	4.00	10.00
Columbia CS-9665	(S)	Something Happening	1968	6.00	15.00
Columbia CS-9753	(S)	Hard 'N Heavy (Black & white cover)	1969	6.00	15.00

Label		Title	Year	VG+	NM
Columbia CS-9753	(S)	Hard 'N Heavy (Color cover)	1969	4.00	10.00
Columbia CS-9905	(S)	Alias Pink Puzz	1969	6.00	15.00
Columbia CS-9964	(S)	Collage	1970	3.50	8.00
		(Columbia albums above have "360 Sound" labels.)			
Sears SPS-439	(E)	Paul Revere & The Raiders	1970	50.00	100.00

REXROTH, KENNETH

Label		Title	Year	VG+	NM
Fantasy 700-8	(M)	Poetry & Jazz At The Blackhawk (Red vinyl)		16.00	40.00

REYNOLDS, DEBBIE

Label		Title	Year	VG+	NM
MGM E-530 (10")	(M)	Two Weeks With Love (Sdtk)	1950	20.00	50.00
MGM E-190 (10")	(M)	I Love Melvin (Sdtk)	1953	30.00	60.00
Mercury MG-25202	(M)	Athena (Sdtk)	1954	50.00	100.00
MGM E-3233	(M)	Two Weeks With Love (Sdtk)	1955	12.00	30.00
RCA LPM-1339	(M)	A Bundle Of Joy (Sdtk)	1956	30.00	60.00
Coral CRL-57159	(M)	Tammy And The Bachelor (Sdtk)	1957	20.00	50.00
Columbia CL-1337	(M)	Say One For Me (Sdtk)	1959	12.00	30.00
Columbia CS-8137	(S)	Say One For Me (Sdtk)	1959	20.00	50.00
Dot DLP-3191	(M)	Debbie	1959	5.00	12.00
Dot DLP-25191	(S)	Debbie	1959	6.00	15.00
Dot DLP-3295	(M)	Am I That Easy To Forget	1960	5.00	12.00
Dot DLP-25295	(S)	Am I That Easy To Forget	1960	6.00	15.00
Dot DLP-25295	(S)	Am I That Easy To Forget (Blue vinyl)	1960	12.00	30.00
Dot DLP-3298	(M)	Fine And Dandy	1960	5.00	12.00
Dot DLP-25298	(S)	Fine And Dandy	1960	6.00	15.00
Dot DLP-3492	(M)	Tammy	1963	5.00	12.00
Dot DLP-25492	(S)	Tammy	1963	6.00	15.00
MGM 1E-5	(M)	How The West Was Won (Sdtk)	1963	5.00	12.00
MGM S1E-5	(S)	How The West Was Won (Sdtk)	1963	6.00	15.00
MGM E-4232	(M)	The Unsinkable Molly Brown (Sdtk)	1964	5.00	12.00
MGM SE-4232	(S)	The Unsinkable Molly Brown (Sdtk)	1964	6.00	15.00
MGM 1E-7	(M)	The Singing Nun (Sdtk)	1966	5.00	12.00
MGM S1E-7	(S)	The Singing Nun (Sdtk)	1966	6.00	15.00
MGM 2E-43	(M)	Hit The Deck		5.00	12.00
MGM 2SE-43	(S)	Hit The Deck		6.00	15.00

REYS, RITA

Label		Title	Year	VG+	NM
Columbia CL-903	(M)	The Cool Sound Of Rita Reys		12.00	30.00
Epic LN-3522	(M)	Her Name Is Rita Reys		8.00	20.00
Dawn 1125	(M)	New Voices		8.00	20.00

RHYTHM ROCKERS, THE

Label		Title	Year	VG+	NM
Challenge CHL-617	(M)	Soul Surfin'	1963	12.00	30.00

RICH, CHARLIE

Label		Title	Year	VG+	NM
Philips International 1970	(M)	Lonely Weekends	1960	240.00	400.00
Groove G-1000	(M)	Charlie Rich	1964	10.00	25.00
Groove GS-1000	(S)	Charlie Rich	1964	14.00	35.00
RCA LPM-3352	(M)	That's Rich	1965	8.00	20.00
RCA LSP-3352	(S)	That's Rich	1965	10.00	25.00
RCA LPM-3537	(M)	Big Boss Man	1966	8.00	20.00
RCA LSP-3537	(S)	Big Boss Man	1966	10.00	25.00
Smash MGS-27070	(M)	The Many Sides Of Charlie Rich	1965	6.00	15.00
Smash SRS-67070	(S)	The Many Sides Of Charlie Rich	1965	8.00	20.00
Smash MGS-27078	(M)	The Best Years	1966	6.00	15.00
Smash SRS-67078	(S)	The Best Years	1966	8.00	20.00
Hi HL-32037	(M)	Charlie Rich Sings Country And Western	1967	5.00	12.00
Hi SHL-32037	(S)	Charlie Rich Sings Country And Western	1967	6.00	15.00
Epic EQ-31933	(Q)	The Best Of Charlie Rich	1972	5.00	12.00
Epic EQ-32247	(Q)	Behind Closed Doors	1973	5.00	12.00
Epic EQ-32531	(Q)	Very Special Love Songs	1974	5.00	12.00
Epic PEQ-33250	(Q)	The Silver Fox	1974	5.00	12.00
Epic PEQ-33455	(Q)	Every Time You Touch Me	1975	5.00	12.00

RICHARD, CLIFF (& THE SHADOWS)

Label		Title	Year	VG+	NM
ABC-Paramount 321	(M)	Cliff Sings	1960	12.00	30.00
ABC-Paramount S-321	(S)	Cliff Sings	1960	16.00	40.00
ABC-Paramount 391	(M)	Listen To Cliff	1961	12.00	30.00
ABC-Paramount S-391	(S)	Listen To Cliff	1961	16.00	40.00
Dot DLP-3474	(M)	Wonderful To Be Young (Sdtk)	1962	6.00	15.00
Dot DLP-25474	(S)	Wonderful To Be Young (Sdtk)	1962	8.00	20.00

Label		Title	Year	VG+	NM
Epic LN-24063	(M)	Summer Holiday (Sdtk)	1963	8.00	20.00
Epic BN-26063	(S)	Summer Holiday (Sdtk)	1963	10.00	25.00
Epic LN-24089	(M)	It's All In The Game	1964	8.00	20.00
Epic BN-26089	(S)	It's All In The Game	1964	10.00	25.00
Epic LN-24115	(M)	Cliff Richard In Spain	1964	8.00	20.00
Epic BN-26115	(S)	Cliff Richard In Spain	1964	10.00	25.00
Epic LN-24145	(M)	Swinger's Paradise (Sdtk)	1965	6.00	15.00
Epic BN-26145	(S)	Swinger's Paradise (Sdtk)	1965	8.00	20.00

RICHARDS, ANN

Label		Title	Year	VG+	NM
Capitol T-1087	(M)	I'm Shooting High	1958	10.00	25.00
Capitol T-1406	(M)	The Many Moods Of Ann Richards	1960	6.00	15.00
Capitol ST-1406	(S)	The Many Moods Of Ann Richards	1960	8.00	20.00
Capitol T-1495	(M)	Too Much	1961	6.00	15.00
Capitol ST-1495	(S)	Too Much	1961	8.00	20.00
Atco 33-136	(M)	Ann, Man!	1961	6.00	15.00
Atco SD-33-136	(S)	Ann, Man!	1961	8.00	20.00

RICHMAN, JONATHAN, & THE MODERN LOVERS

Label		Title	Year	VG+	NM
Home Of The Hits 1910	(S)	The Modern Lovers	1975	20.00	50.00
Bezerkley JBX-0048	(S)	Jonathan Richman & The Modern Lovers	1976	12.00	30.00
Bezerkley BZ-0050	(S)	The Modern Lovers	1976	16.00	40.00
Bezerkley JBZ-0053	(S)	Rock 'N' Roll With The Modern Lovers	1977	8.00	20.00
Bezerkley JBZ-0055	(S)	Modern Lovers Live	1978	8.00	20.00
Bezerkley BZ-0060	(S)	Back In Your Life	1979	8.00	20.00
Mohawk SCALP-0002	(S)	The Original Modern Lovers	1981	8.00	20.00
Bomp 4021	(S)	The Original Modern Lovers	1981	4.00	10.00
Sire 23939	(S)	Jonathan Sings!	1983	6.00	15.00

RICKS, JIMMY

Label		Title	Year	VG+	NM
Signature 1032	(M)	Jimmy Ricks	1961	8.00	20.00
Mainstream 56050	(M)	Vibrations	1965	5.00	12.00
Mainstream 6050	(S)	Vibrations	1965	6.00	15.00
Jubilee 8021	(M)	Tell Her You Love Her	1969	5.00	12.00

RIGHTEOUS BROTHERS, THE (BILL MEDLEY & BOBBY HATFIELD)

Label		Title	Year	VG+	NM
Moonglow 1001	(M)	Right Now!	1963	5.00	12.00
Moonglow S-1001	(S)	Right Now!	1963	6.00	15.00
Moonglow 1002	(M)	Some Blue-Eyed Soul	1964	5.00	12.00
Moonglow S-1002	(S)	Some Blue-Eyed Soul	1964	6.00	15.00
Moonglow 1003	(M)	This Is New!	1965	5.00	12.00
Moonglow S-1003	(S)	This Is New!	1965	6.00	15.00
Moonglow 1004	(M)	The Best Of The Righteous Brothers	1966	5.00	12.00
Moonglow S-1004	(S)	The Best Of The Righteous Brothers	1966	6.00	15.00
Philles PHLP-4007	(M)	You've Lost That Loving Feelin'	1965	6.00	15.00
Philles PHLP-ST-4007	(P)	You've Lost That Loving Feelin'	1965	8.00	20.00
Philles PHLP-4008	(M)	Just Once In My Life	1965	5.00	12.00
Philles PHLP-ST-4008	(P)	Just Once In My Life	1965	6.00	15.00
Philles PHLP-4009	(M)	Back To Back	1966	4.00	10.00
Philles PHLP-ST-4009	(P)	Back To Back	1966	5.00	12.00
HBR HLP-8500	(M)	A Swingin' Summer (Sdtk)	1966	12.00	30.00
HBR HST-8500	(S)	A Swingin' Summer (Sdtk)	1966	16.00	40.00
Verve V-5001	(M)	Soul And Inspiration	1966	5.00	12.00
Verve V6-5001	(S)	Soul And Inspiration	1966	6.00	15.00
Verve V-5004	(M)	Go Ahead And Cry	1966	4.00	10.00
Verve V6-5004	(S)	Go Ahead And Cry	1966	5.00	12.00
Verve V-5010	(M)	Sayin' Somethin'	1967	4.00	10.00
Verve V6-5010	(S)	Sayin' Somethin'	1967	5.00	12.00
Verve V-5020	(M)	The Righteous Brothers' Greatest Hits	1967	4.00	10.00
Verve V6-5020	(P)	The Righteous Brothers' Greatest Hits	1967	5.00	12.00
Verve V-5031	(M)	Souled Out	1967	4.00	10.00
Verve V6-5031	(S)	Souled Out	1967	5.00	12.00

RISERS, THE

Label		Title	Year	VG+	NM
Imperial LP-9269	(M)	She's A Bad Motorcycle	1964	6.00	15.00
Imperial LP-12269	(S)	She's A Bad Motorcycle	1964	8.00	20.00

RISING STORM, THE

Label		Title	Year	VG+	NM
Remnant BBA-3571	(M)	Calm Before The Rising Storm	1968	300.00	500.00

Label		Title	Year	VG+	NM
RITTER, TEX					
Capitol H-4004 (10")	(M)	Cowboy Favorites		30.00	60.00
Capitol T-971	(M)	Songs From The Western Screen	1958	20.00	50.00
		(Turquoise label.)			
Capitol T-1100	(M)	Psalms	1959	12.00	30.00
Capitol T-1292	(M)	Blood On The Saddle	1960	8.00	20.00
Capitol ST-1292	(S)	Blood On The Saddle	1960	10.00	25.00
Capitol W-1562	(M)	The Lincoln Hymns	1961	8.00	20.00
Capitol SW-1562	(S)	The Lincoln Hymns	1961	10.00	25.00
Capitol T-1623	(M)	Hillbilly Heaven	1961	8.00	20.00
Capitol ST-1623	(S)	Hillbilly Heaven	1961	10.00	25.00
		(Capitol albums above have black labels			
		with the Capitol logo on the left side.)			
Capitol T-1757	(M)	Stan Kenton/Tex Ritter	1962	6.00	15.00
Capitol ST-1757	(S)	Stan Kenton/Tex Ritter	1962	8.00	20.00
Capitol T-1910	(M)	Border Affair	1963	6.00	15.00
Capitol ST-1910	(S)	Border Affair	1963	8.00	20.00
Capitol T-2402	(M)	The Friendly Voice Of Tex Ritter	1965	6.00	15.00
Capitol ST-2402	(S)	The Friendly Voice Of Tex Ritter	1965	8.00	20.00
Capitol T-2595	(M)	The Best Of Tex Ritter	1966	5.00	12.00
Capitol ST-2595	(S)	The Best Of Tex Ritter	1966	6.00	15.00
Capitol T-2743	(M)	Sweet Land Of Liberty	1967	5.00	12.00
Capitol ST-2743	(S)	Sweet Land Of Liberty	1967	6.00	15.00
Capitol T-2786	(M)	Just Beyond The Moon	1967	5.00	12.00
Capitol ST-2786	(S)	Just Beyond The Moon	1967	6.00	15.00
MGM E-4506	(M)	What Am I Bid? (Sdtk)	1967	5.00	12.00
MGM SE-4506	(S)	What Am I Bid? (Sdtk)	1967	6.00	15.00
Capitol ST-2890	(S)	Bump Tiddil Dee Bum Bum!	1968	6.00	15.00
Capitol ST-2974	(S)	Tex Ritter's Wild West	1968	6.00	15.00
Capitol ST-213	(S)	Chuck Wagon Days	1969	5.00	12.00
		(Capitol albums above have black labels			
		with the Capitol logo on top.)			
RIVERS, JOHNNY					
Capitol T-2161	(M)	The Sensational Johnny Rivers	1964	5.00	12.00
Capitol ST-2161	(S)	The Sensational Johnny Rivers	1964	6.00	15.00
United Arts. UAL-3386	(M)	Go Johnny, Go	1964	4.00	10.00
United Arts. UAS-6386	(S)	Go Johnny, Go	1964	5.00	12.00
Imperial LP-9264	(M)	Johnny Rivers At The Whiskey A-Go-Go	1964	4.00	10.00
Imperial LP-12264	(S)	Johnny Rivers At The Whiskey A-Go-Go	1964	5.00	12.00
Imperial LP-9274	(M)	Here We A-Go-Go Again	1964	4.00	10.00
Imperial LP-12274	(S)	Here We A-Go-Go Again	1964	5.00	12.00
Imperial LP-9280	(M)	Johnny Rivers In Action	1965	4.00	10.00
Imperial LP-12280	(S)	Johnny Rivers In Action	1965	5.00	12.00
Imperial LP-9284	(M)	Meanwhile Back At The Whiskey A-Go-Go	1965	4.00	10.00
Imperial LP-12284	(S)	Meanwhile Back At The Whiskey A-Go-Go	1965	5.00	12.00
Imperial LP-9293	(M)	Johnny Rivers Rocks The Folk	1965	4.00	10.00
Imperial LP-12293	(S)	Johnny Rivers Rocks The Folk	1965	5.00	12.00
Imperial LP-9307	(M)	And I Know You Wanna Dance	1966	4.00	10.00
Imperial LP-12307	(S)	And I Know You Wanna Dance	1966	5.00	12.00
Imperial LP-9324	(M)	Johnny Rivers' Golden Hits	1966	4.00	10.00
Imperial LP-12324	(S)	Johnny Rivers' Golden Hits	1966	5.00	12.00
Imperial LP-9334	(M)	Changes	1966	3.50	8.00
Imperial LP-12334	(S)	Changes	1966	5.00	12.00
Imperial LP-9341	(M)	Rewind	1967	3.50	8.00
Imperial LP-12341	(S)	Rewind	1967	5.00	12.00
Imperial LP-12372	(S)	Realization	1968	3.50	8.00
Imperial LP-12427	(S)	A Touch Of Gold	1969	3.50	8.00
Imperial LP-16001	(S)	Slim Slo Rider	1969	3.50	8.00
RIVERS, MAVIS					
Capitol T-1408	(M)	The Simple Life	1960	5.00	12.00
Capitol ST-1408	(S)	The Simple Life	1960	6.00	15.00
Reprise R-2002	(M)	Mavis	1961	5.00	12.00
Reprise R9-2002	(S)	Mavis	1961	6.00	15.00
Reprise R-2009	(M)	Swing Along	1961	5.00	12.00
Reprise R9-2009	(S)	Swing Along	1961	6.00	15.00
Reprise R-6074	(M)	Mavis Rivers Meets Shorty Rogers	1962	5.00	12.00
Reprise RS-6074	(S)	Mavis Rivers Meets Shorty Rogers	1962	6.00	15.00
Vee Jay LP-1132	(M)	We Remember Mildred Bailey	1964	5.00	12.00
Vee Jay LPS-1132	(S)	We Remember Mildred Bailey	1964	6.00	15.00

Label		Title	Year	VG+	NM
RIVERAS, THE					
Riviera 701	(M)	Campus Party	1964	20.00	50.00
U.S.A. 102	(M)	Let's Have A Party	1964	20.00	50.00
RIVINGTONS, THE					
Liberty LRP-3282	(M)	Doin' The Bird	1963	20.00	50.00
Liberty LST-7282	(S)	Doin' The Bird	1963	30.00	60.00
ROAD RUNNERS, THE					
London LL-3381	(M)	The New Mustang	1964	6.00	15.00
London PS-381	(M)	The New Mustang	1964	8.00	20.00
ROBBINS, MARTY					
Columbia CL-2544 (10")	(M)	Carl, Lefty And Marty	1956	100.00	200.00
Columbia CL-2601 (10")	(M)	Rock 'N Roll 'N Robbins	1956	400.00	600.00
Columbia CL-976	(M)	The Song Of Robbins	1957	20.00	50.00
Columbia CL-1087	(M)	Song Of The Islands	1957	20.00	50.00
Columbia CL-1189	(M)	Marty Robbins	1958	16.00	40.00
Columbia CL-1325	(M)	Marty's Greatest Hits	1959	12.00	30.00
Columbia CL-1358	(M)	Gunfighter Ballads And Trail Songs	1959	8.00	20.00
Columbia CS-8158	(S)	Gunfighter Ballads And Trail Songs	1959	10.00	25.00
Columbia CL-1472	(M)	More Gunfighter Ballads And Trail Songs	1960	8.00	20.00
Columbia CS-8272	(S)	More Gunfighter Ballads And Trail Songs	1960	10.00	25.00
Columbia CL-1558	(M)	The Alamo (Sdtk)	1960	8.00	20.00
Columbia CS-8358	(S)	The Alamo (Sdtk)	1960	10.00	25.00
Columbia CL-1635	(M)	More Greatest Hits	1961	8.00	20.00
Columbia CS-8435	(S)	More Greatest Hits	1961	10.00	25.00
Columbia CL-1666	(M)	Just A Little Sentimental	1961	8.00	20.00
Columbia CS-8466	(S)	Just A Little Sentimental	1961	6.00	15.00
		(Columbia albums above have six black "eye" logos on each label.)			
Columbia CL-1801	(M)	Marty After Midnight	1962	8.00	20.00
Columbia CS-8601	(S)	Marty After Midnight	1962	10.00	25.00
Columbia CL-1855	(M)	Portrait Of Marty (With bonus photo)	1962	10.00	25.00
Columbia CS-8655	(S)	Portrait Of Marty (With bonus photo)	1962	12.00	30.00
Columbia CL-1918	(M)	Devil Woman	1962	6.00	15.00
Columbia CS-8718	(S)	Devil Woman	1962	8.00	20.00
Columbia CL-2040	(M)	Hawaii's Calling Me	1963	8.00	20.00
Columbia CS-8840	(S)	Hawaii's Calling Me	1963	10.00	25.00
Columbia CL-2072	(M)	Return Of The Gunfighter	1963	6.00	15.00
Columbia CS-8872	(S)	Return Of The Gunfighter	1963	8.00	20.00
Columbia CL-2176	(M)	Island Woman	1964	8.00	20.00
Columbia CS-8976	(S)	Island Woman	1964	10.00	25.00
Columbia CL-2220	(M)	R.F.D. Marty Robbins	1964	6.00	15.00
Columbia CS-9020	(S)	R.F.D. Marty Robbins	1964	8.00	20.00
Columbia CL-2304	(M)	Turn The Lights Down Low	1965	6.00	15.00
Columbia CS-9104	(S)	Turn The Lights Down Low	1965	8.00	20.00
Columbia CL-2448	(M)	What God Has Done	1965	6.00	15.00
Columbia CS-9248	(S)	What God Has Done	1965	8.00	20.00
Columbia CL-2527	(M)	The Drifter	1966	6.00	15.00
Columbia CS-9327	(S)	The Drifter	1966	8.00	20.00
Columbia DL-237	(M)	Saddle Tramp	1966	6.00	15.00
Columbia DS-237	(S)	Saddle Tramp	1966	8.00	20.00
Columbia CL-2621	(M)	The Song Of Robbins	1967	10.00	25.00
Columbia CS-9421	(E)	The Song Of Robbins	1967	8.00	20.00
Columbia CL-2625	(M)	Song Of The Islands	1967	10.00	25.00
Columbia CS-9425	(E)	Song Of The Islands	1967	8.00	20.00
Columbia CL-2645	(M)	My Kind Of Country	1967	6.00	15.00
Columbia CS-9445	(S)	My Kind Of Country	1967	8.00	20.00
Columbia CL-2725	(M)	Tonight Carmen	1967	6.00	15.00
Columbia CS-9525	(S)	Tonight Carmen	1967	8.00	20.00
Columbia CL-2735	(M)	Christmas With Marty Robbins	1967	6.00	15.00
Columbia CS-9535	(S)	Christmas With Marty Robbins	1967	8.00	20.00
Columbia CL-2817	(M)	By The Time I Get To Phoenix	1968	8.00	20.00
Columbia CS-9617	(S)	By The Time I Get To Phoenix	1968	8.00	20.00
Columbia CS-9725	(S)	I Walk Alone	1968	6.00	15.00
Columbia CS-9811	(S)	It's A Sin	1969	6.00	15.00
Columbia STS-2016	(E)	The Heart Of Marty Robbins	1969	12.00	30.00
Columbia GP-15	(S)	Marty's Country	1969	6.00	15.00
Columbia CS-9978	(S)	My Woman, My Woman, My Wife	1970	6.00	15.00
		(Columbia albums above have "360 Sound" labels.)			

Christmas With Marty Robbins. Arguably the most collectible of modern country singers, Marty's albums have long been collected by non-country fans. Several of his albums from the late '60s and early '70s sold poorly and are consequently rather difficult to find.

The Immortal Otis Redding. A great career cut short by a tragic accident. While this album was issued only in stereo to the public, it was mixed down to mono for radio play. These promotional mono copies are growing in demand with collectors of '60s music.

Label		Title	Year	VG+	NM
ROBBS, THE					
Mercury MG-21130	(M)	The Robbs	1967	6.00	15.00
Mercury SR-61130	(S)	The Robbs	1967	8.00	20.00
ROBERTSON, DON					
RCA LPM-3348	(M)	Heart On My Sleeve	1965	5.00	12.00
RCA LSP-3348	(S)	Heart On My Sleeve	1965	6.00	15.00
ROBINS, THE					
Whippet WLP-703	(M)	Rock 'N' Roll With The Robins		150.00	250.00
ROBINSON, FLOYD					
RCA LPM-2162	(M)	Floyd Robinson	1960	8.00	20.00
RCA LSP-2162	(S)	Floyd Robinson	1960	10.00	25.00
ROBINSON, SMOKEY, & THE MIRACLES					
Tamla 220	(M)	Hi! We're The Miracles	1961	75.00	150.00
Tamla 223	(M)	Cookin' With The Miracles	1962	60.00	120.00
Tamla 224	(M)	Shop Around	1962	60.00	120.00
Tamla 230	(M)	I'll Try Something New	1962	60.00	120.00
Tamla 236	(M)	Christmas With The Miracles	1963	60.00	120.00
Tamla 238	(M)	The Fabulous Miracles	1963	35.00	70.00
Tamla 238	(M)	You've Really Got A Hold On Me	1963	35.00	70.00
Tamla 241	(M)	The Miracles On Stage	1963	35.00	70.00
Tamla 245	(M)	Doin' Mickey's Monkey	1963	35.00	70.00
Tamla T-2245	(S)	Doin' Mickey's Monkey	1963	50.00	100.00
Tamla 254	(M)	Greatest Hits From The Beginning	1965	14.00	35.00
Tamla T-2254	(E)	Greatest Hits From The Beginning	1965	8.00	20.00
Tamla 267	(M)	Going To A Go-Go	1965	6.00	15.00
Tamla T-2267	(S)	Going To A Go-Go	1965	8.00	20.00
Motown MT-630	(M)	Nothing But A Man (Sdtk)	1965	8.00	20.00
Motown S-630	(S)	Nothing But A Man (Sdtk)	1965	10.00	25.00
Tamla 271	(M)	Away We A Go-Go	1966	6.00	15.00
Tamla T-2271	(S)	Away We A Go-Go	1966	8.00	20.00
Tamla 276	(M)	Make It Happen	1967	6.00	15.00
Tamla T-276	(S)	Make It Happen	1967	8.00	20.00
Tamla 276	(M)	Tears Of A Clown	1970	6.00	15.00
Tamla T-280	(S)	Greatest Hits, Volume 2	1968	5.00	12.00
Tamla T-289	(S)	Live!	1969	5.00	12.00
Tamla T-290	(S)	Special Occasion	1968	5.00	12.00
Tamla T-295	(S)	Time Out	1969	5.00	12.00
Tamla T-297	(S)	Four In Blue	1969	5.00	12.00
Tamla T-301	(S)	What Love Has Joined Together	1970	5.00	12.00
Tamla T-306	(S)	A Pocketful Of Miracles	1970	5.00	12.00
Tamla T-307	(S)	The Season For Miracles	1970	5.00	12.00
Tamla T-312	(S)	One Dozen Roses	1971	5.00	12.00
Tamla T-318	(S)	Flying High Together	1972	5.00	12.00
Tamla T-302	(S)	The Miracles 1957-1972	1973	5.00	12.00
ROBINSON, SUGAR RAY					
Continental 16009	(S)	I'm Still Swinging		10.00	25.00
ROCHE, BETTY					
Bethlehem 64	(M)	Take The A Train	1956	12.00	30.00
Prestige 7187	(M)	Singin' And Swingin'	1960	10.00	25.00
Prestige S-7187	(S)	Singin' And Swingin'	1960	12.00	30.00
Prestige 7198	(M)	Lightly And Politely	1961	10.00	25.00
Prestige S-7198	(S)	Lightly And Politely	1961	12.00	30.00
ROCK-A-TEENS, THE					
Roulette R-25109	(M)	Woo-Hoo	1960	40.00	80.00
Roulette SR-25109	(P)	Woo-Hoo	1960	50.00	100.00
ROCKETS, THE					
White Whale S-7116	(S)	The Rockets	1968	8.00	20.00
ROCKIN' FOO					
Hobbit HB-5001	(S)	Rockin' Foo	1969	8.00	20.00
ROCKIN' REBELS, THE					
Swan SLP-509	(M)	Wild Weekend	1962	50.00	100.00

Label		Title	Year	VG+	NM
ROCKY FELLERS, THE					
Scepter SP-512	(M)	Killer Joe	1963	6.00	15.00
Scepter SPS-512	(S)	Killer Joe	1963	8.00	20.00
ROD & THE COBRAS					
Somerset 20500	(M)	At A Drag Race At Surf City	1963	8.00	20.00
Somerset 20500	(S)	At A Drag Race At Surf City	1963	10.00	25.00
RODERICK, JUDY					
Columbia CL-2153	(M)	Ain't Nothin' But The Blues	1964	5.00	12.00
Columbia CS-8953	(S)	Ain't Nothin' But The Blues	1964	6.00	15.00
Vanguard VRS-9197	(M)	Woman Blue	1964	5.00	12.00
Vanguard VSD7-9197	(S)	Woman Blue	1964	6.00	15.00
RODGERS, JIMMIE					
RCA LPT-3037 (10")	(M)	Memorial Album, Volume 1	1952	20.00	50.00
RCA LPT-3038 (10")	(M)	Memorial Album, Volume 2	1952	20.00	50.00
RCA LPT-3039 (10")	(M)	Memorial Album, Volume 3	1952	20.00	50.00
RCA LPT-3073 (10")	(M)	Travelin' Blues	1952	20.00	50.00
RCA LPM-1232	(M)	Never No Mo' Blues/Memorial Album	1955	14.00	35.00
RCA LPM-1640	(M)	Train Whistle Blues	1957	14.00	35.00
RCA LPM-2112	(M)	My Rough And Rowdy Ways	1960	10.00	25.00
RCA LPM-2213	(M)	Jimmie The Kid	1961	10.00	25.00
RCA LPM-2531	(M)	Country Music Hall Of Fame	1962	10.00	25.00
RCA LPM-2634	(M)	The Short But Brilliant Life Of Jimmie Rodgers	1963	10.00	25.00
		(RCA albums above have "Long Play" on the bottom of the labels.)			
RCA LPM-2865	(M)	My Time Ain't Long	1964	10.00	25.00
RCA LPM-3315	(M)	Best Of The Legendary Jimmie Rodgers	1965	10.00	25.00
RCA LSP-3315	(E)	Best Of The Legendary Jimmie Rodgers	1965	6.00	15.00
		(RCA albums above have black labels.)			
RODGERS, JIMMIE					
Roulette R-25020	(M)	Folk Songs And Readings	1958	8.00	20.00
Roulette R-25026	(M)	The Long Hot Summer (Sdtk)	1958	16.00	40.00
Roulette R-25033	(M)	Number One Ballads	1958	8.00	20.00
Roulette R-25042	(M)	Jimmie Rodgers Sings Folk Songs	1958	8.00	20.00
Roulette R-25057	(M)	His Golden Year	1959	8.00	20.00
Roulette R-25071	(M)	TV Favorites	1959	5.00	12.00
Roulette SR-25071	(S)	TV Favorites	1959	6.00	15.00
Roulette R-25081	(M)	Twilight On The Trail	1959	5.00	12.00
Roulette SR-25081	(S)	Twilight On The Trail	1959	6.00	15.00
Roulette R-25095	(M)	It's Christmas Once Again	1959	5.00	12.00
Roulette SR-25095	(S)	It's Christmas Once Again	1959	6.00	15.00
Roulette R-25103	(M)	When The Spirit Moves You	1960	5.00	12.00
Roulette SR-25103	(S)	When The Spirit Moves You	1960	6.00	15.00
Roulette R-25128	(M)	At Home With Jimmie Rodgers	1960	5.00	12.00
Roulette SR-25128	(S)	At Home With Jimmie Rodgers	1960	6.00	15.00
Roulette R-25150	(M)	The Folk Song World Of Jimmie Rodgers	1961	5.00	12.00
Roulette SR-25150	(S)	The Folk Song World Of Jimmie Rodgers	1961	6.00	15.00
Roulette R-25160	(M)	The Best Of Jimmie Rodgers Folk Songs	1961	5.00	12.00
Roulette SR-25160	(S)	The Best Of Jimmie Rodgers Folk Songs	1961	6.00	15.00
Roulette R-25179	(M)	15 Million Sellers	1962	5.00	12.00
Roulette SR-25179	(S)	15 Million Sellers	1962	6.00	15.00
Roulette R-25199	(M)	Folk Songs	1963	5.00	12.00
Roulette SR-25199	(S)	Folk Songs	1963	6.00	15.00
ROE, TOMMY					
ABC-Paramount 432	(M)	Sheila	1962	8.00	20.00
ABC-Paramount S-432	(S)	Sheila	1962	10.00	25.00
ABC-Paramount 467	(M)	Something For Everybody	1964	6.00	15.00
ABC-Paramount S-467	(S)	Something For Everybody	1964	8.00	20.00
ABC-Paramount 575	(M)	Sweet Pea	1966	5.00	12.00
ABC-Paramount S-575	(S)	Sweet Pea	1966	6.00	15.00
ABC-Paramount 594	(M)	It's Now Winter's Day	1967	4.00	10.00
ABC-Paramount S-594	(S)	It's Now Winter's Day	1967	5.00	12.00
ABC-Paramount 610	(M)	Phantasy	1967	4.00	10.00
ABC-Paramount S-610	(S)	Phantasy	1967	5.00	12.00
ABC-Paramount S-683	(S)	Dizzy	1969	4.00	10.00

Label		Title	Year	VG+	NM
ROGERS, EILEEN					
Columbia CL-1229	(M)	Blue Swing		5.00	12.00
Columbia CS-8029	(S)	Blue Swing		6.00	15.00
ROGERS, GINGER					
Decca DL-5040 (10")	(M)	Alice In Wonderland		14.00	35.00
ROGERS, KENNY					
Mobile Fidelity 1-044	(S)	The Gambler		5.00	12.00
Mobile Fidelity 1-049	(S)	Greatest Hits		5.00	12.00
ROGERS, ROY (& DALE EVANS)					
RCA LPT-3041 (10")	(M)	Roy Rogers Souvenir Album	1952	20.00	50.00
RCA LPT-3168 (10")	(M)	Hymns Of Faith	1954	16.00	40.00
RCA LPM-1439	(M)	Sweet Hour Of Prayer	1957	12.00	30.00
Bluebird LBY-1022	(M)	Jesus Loves Me	1959	10.00	25.00
Capitol T-1745	(M)	The Bible Tells Me So	1962	10.00	25.00
Capitol ST-1745	(S)	The Bible Tells Me So	1962	10.00	25.00
Camden CAL-1054	(M)	Pecos Bill	1964	6.00	15.00
Camden CAL-1074	(M)	Lore Of The West	1966	6.00	15.00
Capitol T-2818	(M)	Christmas Is Always	1967	8.00	20.00
Capitol ST-2818	(S)	Christmas Is Always	1967	8.00	20.00
Camden CAL-1097	(M)	Peter Cottontail And His Friends	1968	6.00	15.00
Capitol ST-594	(S)	The Country Side Of Roy Rogers	1970	6.00	15.00
Capitol ST-785	(S)	A Man From Duck Run	1971	6.00	15.00
Capitol ST-11020	(S)	Take A Little Love And Pass It On	1972	5.00	12.00
ROLLING STONES, THE					
London LL-3375	(M)	The Rolling Stones	1964	100.00	200.00
		(Maroon label with "London/ffrr" in a box at the top. Issued with a bonus photo, which is advertised in the lower left corner of the cover.)			
London PS-3375	(M)	The Rolling Stones	1964	12.00	30.00
London PS-375	(E)	The Rolling Stones	1964	6.00	15.00
London LL-3402	(M)	12 X 5 (Blue vinyl)	1964	--	--
		(Recently discovered, there are no transactions from which to determine a value.)			
London LL-3402	(M)	12 X 5	1964	12.00	30.00
London PS-402	(E)	12 X 5	1964	6.00	15.00
London LL-3420	(M)	The Rolling Stones, Now!	1965	12.00	30.00
London PS-420	(E)	The Rolling Stones, Now!	1965	6.00	15.00
London LL-3429	(M)	Out Of Our Heads	1965	12.00	30.00
London PS-429	(E)	Out Of Our Heads	1965	6.00	15.00
		(Mono London albums above have maroon labels; stereo albums have blue labels. "London" is in silver script on top and is not enclosed in a box.)			
I.N.S. Radio 1003	(M)	It's Here Luv!! The Ed Rudy Interview	1965	50.00	100.00
London LL-4451	(M)	December's Children	1965	10.00	25.00
London PS-451	(E)	December's Children	1965	4.00	10.00
London NP-1	(M)	Big Hits/High Tide And Green Grass	1966	10.00	25.00
London NP NPS-1	(E)	Big Hits/High Tide And Green Grass	1966	4.00	10.00
London LL-3476	(M)	Aftermath	1966	10.00	25.00
London PS-476	(S)	Aftermath	1966	4.00	10.00
London LL-4493	(M)	Got Live If You Want It	1966	10.00	25.00
London PS-493	(P)	Got Live If You Want It	1966	4.00	10.00
London LL-499	(M)	Between The Buttons	1967	10.00	25.00
London PS-499	(S)	Between The Buttons	1967	4.00	10.00
London LL-509	(M)	Flowers	1967	10.00	25.00
London PS-509	(P)	Flowers	1967	4.00	10.00
London NP-2	(M)	Their Satanic Majesties Request (3-D cover)	1967	75.00	150.00
London NPS-2	(E)	Their Satanic Majesties Request (3-D cover)	1967	8.00	20.00
London PS-539	(S)	Beggar's Banquet	1968	4.00	10.00
London NPS-3	(P)	Through The Past, Darkly	1969	6.00	15.00
London NPS-4	(S)	Let It Bleed (With poster)	1969	10.00	25.00
London NPS-5	(S)	Get Your Ya-Ya's Out!	1970	6.00	15.00
		(London albums above have the "London" logo enclosed in a box at the top of the label. Stereo labels are a very deep blue and silver; later pressings tend to a more faded look.)			
ABKCO ANA-1	(P)	Metamorphosis	1975	6.00	15.00

Label		Title	Year	VG+	NM
Mobile Fidelity 1-060	(S)	Sticky Fingers	1980	10.00	25.00
Mobile Fidelity 1-087	(S)	Some Girls	1982	8.00	20.00
Mobile Fidelity	(P)	The Rolling Stones (11 LPs)	1984	75.00	150.00

ROMEOS, THE

Mark II 1001	(M)	Precious Memories	1967	10.00	25.00

ROMNEY, HUGH "WAVY GRAVY"

World Pacific WP-1805	(M)	Third Stream Humor	1962	10.00	25.00

RONETTES, THE

Philles PHLP-4006	(M)	Presenting The Fabulous Ronettes	1964	65.00	130.00
Philles PHLP-ST-4006	(S)	Presenting The Fabulous Ronettes	1964	100.00	200.00

RONNY & THE DAYTONAS

Mala 4001	(M)	G.T.O.	1964	16.00	40.00
Mala 4002	(M)	Sandy	1964	16.00	40.00
Mala 4002-S	(S)	Sandy	1964	16.00	40.00

RONNIE & THE POMONA CASUALS

Donna 2112	(M)	Everybody Jerk	1965	8.00	20.00

RONSTADT, LINDA

Capitol ST-208	(S)	Hand Sown (Green label)	1969	6.00	15.00
Capitol ST-407	(S)	Silk Purse (Green label)	1970	6.00	15.00
Capitol SMAS-635	(S)	Linda Ronstadt	1972	6.00	15.00
Mobile Fidelity 1-158	(S)	What's New?		5.00	12.00

RONSTADT, LINDA, & THE STONE PONEYS

Capitol T-2666	(M)	The Stone Poneys	1967	8.00	20.00
Capitol ST-2666	(S)	The Stone Poneys	1967	10.00	25.00
Capitol T-2763	(M)	Evergreen	1967	10.00	25.00
Capitol ST-2763	(S)	Evergreen	1967	12.00	30.00
Capitol ST-2863	(S)	Volume Three	1968	16.00	40.00

ROOFTOP SINGERS, THE

Vanguard VRS-2136	(M)	Walk Right In	1963	5.00	12.00
Vanguard VSD7-2136	(S)	Walk Right In	1963	6.00	15.00
Vanguard VRS-9134	(M)	Goodtime	1964	4.00	10.00
Vanguard VSD7-9134	(S)	Goodtime	1964	5.00	12.00
Vanguard VRS-9190	(M)	Rainy River	1965	4.00	10.00
Vanguard VSD7-9190	(S)	Rainy River	1965	5.00	12.00

ROSIE HAMLIN

Brunswick BL-54102	(M)	Lonely Blue Nights	1961	50.00	100.00
Brunswick BL7-54102	(S)	Lonely Blue Nights	1961	75.00	150.00

ROSS, JOE E.

Roulette R-25281	(M)	Love Songs From A Cop	1964	5.00	12.00
Roulette SR-25281	(S)	Love Songs From A Cop	1964	6.00	15.00

ROXY MUSIC

Reprise MS-2114	(S)	Roxy Music	1972	8.00	20.00
Reprise BS-2969	(S)	For Your Pleasure	1973	8.00	20.00
Atlantic SD-7045	(S)	Stranded	1974	6.00	15.00
Atco SD-33-106	(S)	Country Life	1975	8.00	20.00
		(Fold-open cover has several young ladies rather scantily clad.)			

ROYAL, BILLY JOE

Columbia CL-2403	(M)	Down In The Boondocks	1965	6.00	15.00
Columbia CS-9203	(S)	Down In The Boondocks	1965	8.00	20.00
Columbia CL-2781	(M)	Billy Joe Royal	1967	6.00	15.00
Columbia CS-9581	(S)	Billy Joe Royal	1967	8.00	20.00
Columbia CS-9974	(S)	Cherry Hill Park	1969	6.00	15.00

ROYAL GUARDSMEN, THE

Laurie LLP-2038	(S)	Snoopy Vs. The Red Baron	1967	8.00	20.00
Laurie SLLP-2038	(S)	Snoopy Vs. The Red Baron	1967	10.00	25.00
Laurie LLP-2039	(S)	The Return Of The Red Baron	1967	6.00	15.00
Laurie SLLP-2039	(S)	The Return Of The Red Baron	1967	8.00	20.00

Label		Title	Year	VG+	NM
Laurie LLP-2042	(S)	Snoopy And His Friends	1967	6.00	15.00
Laurie SLLP-2042	(S)	Snoopy And His Friends	1967	8.00	20.00
Laurie SLLP-2046	(S)	Snoopy For President	1968	8.00	20.00

ROYAL JOKERS, THE

Dawn 1119	(M)	Rock And Roll Spectacular		20.00	50.00

ROYAL PLAYBOYS, THE

Waldorf 33-136 (10")	(M)	Spirituals And Jubilees		16.00	40.00

ROYALETTES, THE

MGM E-4332	(M)	It's Gonna Take A Miracle	1965	6.00	15.00
MGM SE-4332	(S)	It's Gonna Take A Miracle	1965	8.00	20.00
MGM E-4366	(M)	The Elegant Sound Of The Royalettes	1966	6.00	15.00
MGM SE-4366	(S)	The Elegant Sound Of The Royalettes	1966	8.00	20.00

RUBBER MEMORY

R.P.C. 69401	(M)	Welcome	1966	16.00	40.00

RUBY & THE ROMANTICS

Kapp KL-1323	(M)	Our Day Will Come	1963	6.00	15.00
Kapp KS-3323	(S)	Our Day Will Come	1963	8.00	20.00
Kapp KL-1341	(M)	Till Then	1963	6.00	15.00
Kapp KS-3341	(S)	Till Then	1963	8.00	20.00
Kapp KL-1458	(M)	Greatest Hits Album	1966	5.00	12.00
Kapp KS-3458	(S)	Greatest Hits Album	1966	6.00	15.00
Kapp KL-1526	(M)	Ruby And The Romantics	1967	5.00	12.00
Kapp KS-3526	(S)	Ruby And The Romantics	1967	6.00	15.00
ABC S-638	(S)	More Than Yesterday	1968	6.00	15.00

RUMBLERS, THE

Downey 1001	(M)	Boss!	1963	16.00	40.00
Downey S-1001	(S)	Boss!	1963	20.00	50.00
Dot DLP-3509	(M)	Boss!	1963	10.00	25.00
Dot DLP-25509	(S)	Boss!	1963	12.00	30.00

RUNDGREN, TODD

Ampex 10105	(S)	Runt	1970	14.00	35.00
Ampex 10116	(S)	The Ballad Of Todd Rundgren	1971	14.00	35.00

RUSHING, JIMMY

Vanguard 8011 (10")	(M)	Going To Chicago	1954	16.00	40.00
Vanguard 8505	(M)	Listen To The Blues	1955	12.00	30.00
Vanguard 8513	(M)	If This Ain't The Blues	1957	12.00	30.00
Vanguard 8518	(M)	Going To Chicago	1957	12.00	30.00
Vanguard VDS-2008	(M)	If This Ain't The Blues	1958	12.00	30.00
Jazztone 1244	(M)	Listen To The Blues	1957	10.00	25.00
Columbia CL-963	(M)	The Jazz Odyssey Of James Rushing, Esq.	1957	12.00	30.00
Columbia CL-1152	(M)	Little Jimmy Rushing And The Big Brass	1958	6.00	15.00
Columbia CS-8060	(S)	Little Jimmy Rushing And The Big Brass	1958	8.00	20.00
Columbia CL-1401	(M)	Rushing Lullabies	1959	6.00	15.00
Columbia CS-8196	(S)	Rushing Lullabies	1959	8.00	20.00
Audio Lab 1512	(M)	Two Shades Of Blue	1959	16.00	40.00
Columbia CL-1553	(M)	Brubeck And Rushing	1960	6.00	15.00
Columbia CS-8353	(S)	Brubeck And Rushing	1960	8.00	20.00
Columbia CL-1605	(M)	Jimmy Rushing And The Smith Girls	1961	6.00	15.00
Columbia CS-8405	(S)	Jimmy Rushing And The Smith Girls	1961	8.00	20.00
		(Columbia albums above have six			
		black "eye" logos on each label.)			
Colpix CLP-446	(M)	Five Feet Of Soul	1963	6.00	15.00
Colpix SCP-446	(S)	Five Feet Of Soul	1963	6.00	15.00
BluesWay BL-3005	(M)	Everyday I Have The Blues	1967	5.00	12.00
BluesWay BLS-6005	(S)	Everyday I Have The Blues	1967	6.00	15.00
BluesWay BLS-6107	(S)	Livin' The Blues	1968	6.00	15.00

RUSSELL, JANE

MGM E-208 (10")	(M)	Gentlemen Prefer Blondes (Sdtk)	1953	50.00	100.00
MGM E-3231	(M)	Gentlemen Prefer Blondes (Sdtk)	1955	20.00	50.00

RUTLES, THE

Warners H-3151	(S)	Meet The Rutles (With booklet)	1978	5.00	12.00

Label		Title	Year	VG+	NM
RYAN, CHARLIE					
King 751	(M)	Hot Rod	1961	20.00	50.00
RYDELL, BOBBY					
Cameo C-1006	(M)	We Got Love	1959	12.00	30.00
Cameo C-1007	(M)	Bobby Sings	1960	12.00	30.00
Cameo C-1009	(M)	Biggest Hits (Fold-open cover with insert)	1961	12.00	30.00
Cameo C-1010	(M)	Bobby Rydell Salutes The Great Ones	1961	10.00	25.00
Cameo C-1011	(M)	Rydell At The Copa	1961	8.00	20.00
Cameo C-1013	(M)	Bobby Rydell/Chubby Checker	1961	10.00	25.00
Cameo C-1019	(M)	All The Hits	1962	8.00	20.00
Cameo C-1028	(M)	Biggest Hits, Volume 2	1962	8.00	20.00
Cameo C-1040	(M)	All The Hits, Volume 2	1963	8.00	20.00
Cameo C-1043	(M)	Bye Bye Birdie	1963	8.00	20.00
Cameo C-1055	(M)	Wild (Wood) Days	1963	8.00	20.00
Cameo CS-1055	(S)	Wild (Wood) Days	1963	10.00	25.00
Cameo C-1070	(M)	The Top Hits Of '63	1964	6.00	15.00
Cameo CS-1070	(S)	The Top Hits Of '63	1964	8.00	20.00
Cameo C-1080	(M)	Forget Him	1964	6.00	15.00
Cameo CS-1080	(S)	Forget Him	1964	8.00	20.00
Cameo C-2001	(M)	16 Golden Hits	1965	6.00	15.00
Cameo CS-2001	(E)	16 Golden Hits	1965	8.00	20.00
Cameo C-4017	(M)	An Era Reborn		6.00	15.00
Cameo CS-4017	(S)	An Era Reborn		8.00	20.00
Capitol T-2281	(M)	Somebody Loves You	1965	5.00	12.00
Capitol ST-2281	(S)	Somebody Loves You	1965	6.00	15.00
RYDER, MITCH (& THE DETROIT WHEELS)					
New Voice 2000	(M)	Take A Ride	1966	8.00	20.00
New Voice S-2000	(S)	Take A Ride	1966	10.00	25.00
New Voice 2002	(M)	Breakout!!!	1966	8.00	20.00
New Voice S-2002	(S)	Breakout!!!	1966	10.00	25.00
New Voice 2003	(M)	Sock It To Me!	1967	8.00	20.00
New Voice S-2003	(S)	Sock It To Me!	1967	10.00	25.00
New Voice 2004	(M)	All Mitch Ryder Hits!	1967	6.00	15.00
New Voice S-2004	(S)	All Mitch Ryder Hits!	1967	8.00	20.00
DynoVoice 1901	(M)	What Now My Love	1967	4.00	10.00
DynoVoice 31901	(S)	What Now My Love	1967	5.00	12.00
New Voice S-2005	(S)	Mitch Ryder Sings The Hits	1968	8.00	20.00

Label		Title	Year	VG+	NM
SRC					
Capitol ST-2991	(S)	SRC	1968	8.00	20.00
Capitol ST-134	(S)	Milestones	1969	8.00	20.00
Capitol SKAO-273	(S)	Travellers Tale	1970	8.00	20.00
SACRED MUSHROOM, THE					
Parallax P-4001	(S)	The Sacred Mushroom	1969	35.00	70.00
SAGITTARIUS					
Columbia CS-9644	(S)	Present Tense	1968	8.00	20.00
Together STT-1002	(S)	The Blue Marble	1969	12.00	30.00
ST. CLAIRE, BETTY					
Jubilee 15 (10")	(M)	Mal McHusick Plays/Betty St. Claire Sings		12.00	30.00
Jubilee 23 (10")	(M)	Cool And Clearer	1954	12.00	30.00
Jubilee 1011	(M)	What Is There To Say?	1956	12.00	30.00
Secco 456	(M)	Betty St. Claire At Basin Street East	1960	8.00	20.00

The Sandals, *The Endless Summer*. Originally recorded as The Sandells, this group turned in a memorable soundtrack to one of the most successful cult movies of all time. In this case the cult is *real* surfers and the music is both appropriate and timeless.

The Supremes Sing Holland, Dozier, Holland. While it is the stars of Motown who caught the public's eye, it was the writers, the producers and the musicians who caught their imagination, and no one was more successful than the Holland-Dozier-Holland team.

Label		Title	Year	VG+	NM
ST. LOUIS, JIMMY					
Bluesville BV-1028	(M)	Goin' Down Slow	1961	8.00	20.00
ST. PETERS, CRISPIAN					
Jamie JLPM-3027	(M)	The Pied Piper	1966	8.00	20.00
Jamie JLPS-3027	(E)	The Pied Piper	1966	6.00	15.00
SAKAMOTO, KYU					
Capitol Int. T-10349	(M)	Sukiyaki	1963	10.00	25.00
Capitol Int. DT-10349	(E)	Sukiyaki	1963	8.00	20.00
SALES, SOUPY					
Reprise R-6010	(M)	The Soupy Sales Show	1961	10.00	25.00
Reprise R9-6010	(S)	The Soupy Sales Show	1961	12.00	30.00
ABC 503	(M)	Spy With A Pie	1965	8.00	20.00
ABC S-503	(S)	Spy With A Pie	1965	10.00	25.00
ABC 517	(M)	Soupy Sez Do The Mouse	1965	8.00	20.00
ABC S-517	(S)	Soupy Sez Do The Mouse	1965	10.00	25.00
SAM & DAVE (SAM MOORE & DAVE PRATER)					
Roulette R-25323	(M)	Sam And Dave	1966	8.00	20.00
Roulette SR-25323	(S)	Sam And Dave	1966	10.00	25.00
Stax 708	(M)	Hold On I'm Comin'	1966	8.00	20.00
Stax 708	(S)	Hold On I'm Comin'	1966	10.00	25.00
Stax 712	(M)	Double Dynamite	1966	8.00	20.00
Stax 712	(S)	Double Dynamite	1966	10.00	25.00
Stax 725	(M)	Soul Men	1967	8.00	20.00
Stax 725	(S)	Soul Men	1967	10.00	25.00
Atlantic SD-8205	(S)	I Thank You	1968	8.00	20.00
Atlantic SD-8218	(S)	The Best Of Sam And Dave	1969	6.00	15.00
SAM THE SHAM & THE PHARAOHS					
MGM E-4297	(M)	Wooly Bully	1965	10.00	25.00
MGM SE-4297	(S)	Wooly Bully	1965	12.00	30.00
MGM E-4314	(M)	Their Second Album	1965	8.00	20.00
MGM SE-4314	(S)	Their Second Album	1965	10.00	25.00
MGM E-4334	(M)	When The Boys Meet The Girls (Sdtk)	1965	3.50	8.00
MGM SE-4334	(S)	When The Boys Meet The Girls (Sdtk)	1965	4.00	10.00
MGM E-4347	(M)	On Tour	1966	8.00	20.00
MGM SE-4347	(S)	On Tour	1966	10.00	25.00
MGM E-4407	(M)	Lil' Red Riding Hood	1966	10.00	25.00
MGM SE-4407	(S)	Lil' Red Riding Hood	1966	12.00	30.00
MGM E-4422	(M)	The Best Of Sam The Sham	1967	6.00	15.00
MGM SE-4422	(S)	The Best Of Sam The Sham	1967	8.00	20.00
MGM E-4479	(M)	Nefertiti	1967	6.00	15.00
MGM SE-4479	(S)	Nefertiti	1967	8.00	20.00
MGM SE-4479	(S)	Sam The Sham Revue	1968	6.00	15.00
MGM SE-4526	(S)	Ten Of Pentacles	1968	6.00	15.00
SANDELLS, THE (THE SANDALS)					
World Pacific 1818	(M)	Scramblers	1964	8.00	20.00
World Pacific ST-1818	(S)	Scramblers	1964	10.00	25.00
World Pacific ST-1818	(S)	Scramblers (Red vinyl)	1964	20.00	50.00
World Pacific WP-1832	(M)	The Endless Summer (Sdtk)	1966	6.00	15.00
World Pacific ST-1832	(S)	The Endless Summer (Sdtk)	1966	8.00	20.00
World Pacific WPS-21884	(S)	The Last Of The Ski Bums (Sdtk)	1969	6.00	15.00
SANDERS, ED					
Reprise RS-6374	(S)	Sanders' Truckstop	1969	8.00	20.00
Reprise MS-2105	(S)	Beer Cans On The Moon	1973	8.00	20.00
SANDERS, FELICIA					
Columbia CL-654	(M)	Felicia Sanders At The Blue Angel		8.00	20.00
Decca DL-8762	(M)	That Certain Feeling		6.00	15.00
Decca DL7-8762	(S)	That Certain Feeling		8.00	20.00
Time 70002	(M)	I Wish You Love	1960	6.00	15.00
Time 2007	(M)	The Songs Of Kurt Weill		6.00	15.00
Time 52007	(S)	The Songs Of Kurt Weill		8.00	20.00
Time 2110	(M)	Felicia Sanders	1964	5.00	12.00
Time 52110	(S)	Felicia Sanders	1964	6.00	15.00

Label		Title	Year	VG+	NM
SANDS, TOMMY					
Capitol T-848	(M)	Steady Date With Tommy Sands	1957	14.00	35.00
Capitol T-929	(M)	Sing Boy Sing (Sdtk)	1958	16.00	40.00
Capitol T-1081	(M)	Sands Storm	1959	10.00	25.00
Capitol T-1109	(M)	Teenage Rock	1959	12.00	30.00
Capitol T-1123	(M)	This Thing Called Love	1959	8.00	20.00
Capitol ST-1123	(S)	This Thing Called Love	1959	10.00	25.00
Capitol T-1239	(M)	When I'm Thinking Of You	1960	8.00	20.00
Capitol ST-1239	(S)	When I'm Thinking Of You	1960	10.00	25.00
Capitol T-1364	(M)	Sands At The Sands	1960	8.00	20.00
Capitol ST-1364	(S)	Sands At The Sands	1960	10.00	25.00
Capitol T-1426	(M)	Dream With Me	1961	8.00	20.00
Capitol ST-1426	(S)	Dream With Me	1961	10.00	25.00
Buena Vista BV-3309	(M)	The Parent Trap (Sdtk)	1961	8.00	20.00
Buena Vista BVS-3309	(S)	The Parent Trap (Sdtk)	1961	12.00	30.00
Buena Vista BV-4022	(M)	Babes In Toyland (Sdtk)	1961	14.00	35.00
Buena Vista BVS-4022	(S)	Babes In Toyland (Sdtk)	1961	18.00	45.00
SANTANA					
Columbia CS-9781	(S)	Santana ("360 Sound" label)	1969	5.00	12.00
Cotillion CT3-500	(S)	Woodstock (Sdtk)	1970	8.00	20.00
Columbia KC-30130	(S)	Abraxas (With poster)	1970	5.00	12.00
Columbia CQ-30130	(Q)	Abraxas	1974	5.00	12.00
Columbia CQ-31610	(Q)	Caravanserai	1974	5.00	12.00
Columbia PCQ-32445	(Q)	Welcome	1974	5.00	12.00
Columbia PCQ-32900	(Q)	Illuminations	1974	5.00	12.00
Columbia PCQ-32964	(Q)	Santana	1974	5.00	12.00
Columbia PCQ-33050	(Q)	Greatest Hits	1974	5.00	12.00
Columbia PCQ-33135	(Q)	Borboletta	1974	5.00	12.00
Columbia PCQ-33576	(Q)	Amigos	1976	5.00	12.00
Columbia PCQ-34423	(Q)	Festival	1977	5.00	12.00
Columbia HC-40130	(S)	Abraxas (1/2 speed)	1981	6.00	15.00
Columbia HC-47158	(S)	Zebop (1/2 speed)	1981	6.00	15.00
SANTO & JOHNNY (SANTO & JOHNNY FARINA)					
Canadian Am. 1001	(M)	Santo & Johnny	1959	20.00	50.00
Canadian Am. 1002	(M)	Encore	1960	12.00	30.00
Canadian Am. S-1002	(S)	Encore	1960	16.00	40.00
Canadian Am. 1004	(M)	Hawaii	1961	12.00	30.00
Canadian Am. S-1004	(S)	Hawaii	1961	16.00	40.00
Canadian Am. 1006	(M)	Come On In	1962	12.00	30.00
Canadian Am. S-1006	(S)	Come On In	1962	16.00	40.00
Canadian Am. 1011	(M)	Off Shore	1963	12.00	30.00
Canadian Am. S-1011	(S)	Off Shore	1963	16.00	40.00
Canadian Am. 1014	(M)	In The Still Of The Night	1963	12.00	30.00
Canadian Am. S-1014	(S)	In The Still Of The Night	1963	16.00	40.00
Canadian Am. 1016	(M)	Wish You Were Here	1964	12.00	30.00
Canadian Am. S-1016	(S)	Wish You Were Here	1964	16.00	40.00
Canadian Am. 1017	(M)	The Beatles' Greatest Hits	1964	16.00	40.00
Canadian Am. S-1017	(S)	The Beatles' Greatest Hits	1964	20.00	50.00
Canadian Am. 1018	(M)	Mucho	1965	10.00	25.00
Canadian Am. S-1018	(S)	Mucho	1965	14.00	35.00
Imperial LP-9363	(M)	Brilliant Guitar Sounds	1967	6.00	15.00
Imperial LP-12363	(S)	Brilliant Guitar Sounds	1967	8.00	20.00
Imperial LP-12366	(S)	Golden Guitars	1968	8.00	20.00
Imperial LP-12418	(S)	On The Road Again	1968	8.00	20.00
SAPPHIRES, THE					
Swan LP-513	(M)	Who Do You Love	1964	35.00	70.00
SAPPHIRE THINKERS, THE					
Hobbit HB-5003	(S)	From Within	1969	8.00	20.00
SATAN & THE DE-CIPLES					
Goldband 7750	(S)	Underground	1969	100.00	200.00
SATINS FOUR, THE, & THE CINNAMON ANGELS					
B.T. Puppy S-1010	(S)	Mixed Soul	1970	12.00	30.00
SAUVAGE, KATHERINE					
Epic LN-3489	(M)	The Songs Of Kurt Weill		8.00	20.00

Label		Title	Year	VG+	NM
SAVAGE SONS OF YO HO WA, THE					
Higher Key 3306	(S)	The Savage Sons Of Yo Ho Wa		50.00	100.00
Higher Key 3309	(S)	I'm Gonna Take You Home		50.00	100.00
SAVAGES, THE					
Drone	(M)	Live And Wild		100.00	200.00
SAXONS, THE					
Mirrosonic AS-1017	(M)	Love Minus Zero	1966	20.00	50.00
SCAFFOLD					
Bell 6018	(S)	Thank U Very Much	1968	6.00	15.00
SCAGGS, BOZ					
Columbia HC-43920	(S)	Silk Degrees (1/2 speed)	1980	6.00	15.00
SCAMPS, THE					
Project 8002	(M)	Teen Dance And Sing Along Party	1962	16.00	40.00
SCHILLER, LAWRENCE					
Capitol TAO-2574	(M)	L.S.D.	1966	6.00	15.00
Capitol STAO-2574	(S)	L.S.D.	1966	8.00	20.00
Capitol KAO-2630	(M)	Why Did Lenny Bruce Die?	1967	8.00	20.00
Capitol SKAO-2630	(S)	Why Did Lenny Bruce Die?	1967	10.00	25.00
Capitol KAO-2652	(M)	Homosexuality In The American Male	1967	6.00	15.00
Capitol SKAO-2652	(S)	Homosexuality In The American Male	1967	8.00	20.00
SCHOOLBOYS, THE					
Palace 778	(M)	Beatle Mania	1964	16.00	40.00
SCORPION					
Tower ST-5171	(S)	Scorpion	1969	5.00	12.00
SCOTT, BOBBY					
Bethlehem 1004 (10")	(M)	Great Scott	1954	16.00	40.00
Bethlehem 1009 (10")	(M)	The Compositions, Volume 1	1954	16.00	40.00
Bethlehem 1029 (10")	(M)	The Compositions, Volume 2	1954	16.00	40.00
Bethlehem 8	(M)	The Compositions	1955	16.00	40.00
ABC-Paramount 102	(M)	Scott Free	1956	10.00	25.00
ABC-Paramount 148	(M)	Bobby Scott And Two Horns	1957	10.00	25.00
Atlantic 1341	(M)	The Complete Musician	1960	8.00	20.00
Atlantic SD-1341	(S)	The Complete Musician	1960	10.00	25.00
Atlantic 1355	(M)	A Taste Of Honey	1960	8.00	20.00
Atlantic SD-1355	(S)	A Taste Of Honey	1960	10.00	25.00
Mercury MG-20701	(M)	Joyful Noises	1962	6.00	15.00
Mercury SR-60701	(S)	Joyful Noises	1962	8.00	20.00
Mercury MG-20767	(M)	When The Feeling Hits You	1963	8.00	20.00
Mercury SR-60767	(S)	When The Feeling Hits You	1963	10.00	25.00
Mercury MG-20854	(M)	108 Pounds Of Heartache	1963	6.00	15.00
Mercury SR-60854	(S)	108 Pounds Of Heartache	1963	8.00	20.00
SCOTT, CLIFORD					
World Pacific T-1811	(M)	The Big Ones		5.00	12.00
World Pacific ST-1811	(S)	The Big Ones		6.00	15.00
World Pacific ST-1811	(S)	The Big Ones (Green vinyl)		16.00	40.00
SCOTT, FREDDIE					
Colpix CP-461	(M)	Freddie Scott Sings (Gold Label)	1964	8.00	20.00
Colpix SCP-461	(S)	Freddie Scott Sings (Gold Label)	1964	10.00	25.00
Columbia CL-2258	(M)	Everything I Have Is Yours	1964	6.00	15.00
Columbia CS-9058	(S)	Everything I Have Is Yours	1964	8.00	20.00
Columbia CL-2660	(M)	Lonely Man	1967	5.00	12.00
Columbia CS-9460	(S)	Lonely Man	1967	6.00	15.00
Shout SLP-501	(M)	Are You Lonely For Me	1967	5.00	12.00
Shout SLPS-501	(S)	Are You Lonely For Me	1967	6.00	15.00
SCOTT, JACK					
Carlton LP-12-107	(M)	Jack Scott	1958	50.00	100.00
Carlton STLP-12-107	(S)	Jack Scott	1958	75.00	150.00
Carlton LP-12-122	(M)	What Am I Living For	1958	50.00	100.00
Carlton STLP-12-122	(S)	What Am I Living For	1958	75.00	150.00

Label		Title	Year	VG+	NM
Top Rank RM-319	(M)	I Remember Hank Williams	1960	50.00	100.00
Top Rank RS-619	(S)	I Remember Hank Williams	1960	75.00	150.00
Top Rank RM-326	(M)	What In The World's Come Over You?	1960	50.00	100.00
Top Rank RS-626	(S)	What In The World's Come Over You?	1960	75.00	150.00
Top Rank RM-348	(M)	The Spirit Moves Me	1961	50.00	100.00
Top Rank RS-648	(S)	The Spirit Moves Me	1961	75.00	150.00
Capitol T-2035	(M)	Burning Bridges	1964	35.00	70.00
Capitol ST-2035	(S)	Burning Bridges (Black label)	1964	50.00	100.00

SCOTT, JIMMY

Label		Title	Year	VG+	NM
Savoy MG-12027	(M)	Very Truly Yours	1957	10.00	25.00
Savoy MG-14003	(M)	If You Only Knew	1958	10.00	25.00
Savoy MG-12150	(M)	The Fabulous Songs Of Jimmy Scott	1959	8.00	20.00
Savoy MGS-12150	(S)	The Fabulous Songs Of Jimmy Scott	1959	10.00	25.00
		(Savoy albums above have maroon labels.)			

SCOTT, LINDA

Label		Title	Year	VG+	NM
Canadian Am. 1005	(M)	Starlight, Starbright	1961	16.00	40.00
Canadian Am. S-1005	(S)	Starlight, Starbright	1961	20.00	50.00
Canadian Am. 1007	(M)	Great Scott!! Her Greatest Hits	1962	16.00	40.00
Canadian Am. S -1007	(S)	Great Scott!! Her Greatest Hits	1962	20.00	50.00
Congress 3001	(M)	Linda	1962	12.00	30.00
Congress S-3001	(S)	Linda	1962	16.00	40.00
Kapp KL-1424	(M)	Hey, Look At Me Now	1965	10.00	25.00
Kapp KS-3424	(S)	Hey, Look At Me Now	1965	12.00	30.00

SCOTT, LIZABETH

Label		Title	Year	VG+	NM
Vik 1130	(M)	Lizabeth		12.00	30.00

SEA, JOHNNY

Label		Title	Year	VG+	NM
Philips 200-139	(M)	World Of A Country Boy	1964	6.00	15.00
Philips 600-139	(S)	World Of A Country Boy	1964	8.00	20.00
Philips 200-194	(M)	Live At The Bitter End	1965	6.00	15.00
Philips 600-194	(S)	Live At The Bitter End	1965	8.00	20.00
Warners B-1659	(M)	Day For Decision	1966	5.00	12.00
Warners BS-1659	(S)	Day For Decision	1966	6.00	15.00
MGM E-4506	(M)	What Am I Bid? (Sdtk)	1967	5.00	12.00
MGM SE-4506	(S)	What Am I Bid? (Sdtk)	1967	6.00	15.00

SEARCHERS, THE

Label		Title	Year	VG+	NM
Mercury MG-20914	(M)	Hear! Hear!	1964	12.00	30.00
Mercury SR-60914	(S)	Hear! Hear!	1964	16.00	40.00
Mercury MG-20994	(M)	The Searchers Meet The Rattles	1965	16.00	40.00
Mercury SR-60994	(S)	The Searchers Meet The Rattles	1965	20.00	50.00
Kapp KL-1363	(M)	Meet The Searchers	1964	10.00	25.00
Kapp KS-3363	(S)	Meet The Searchers	1964	14.00	35.00
Kapp KL-1409	(M)	This Is Us	1964	10.00	25.00
Kapp KS-3409	(S)	This Is Us	1964	14.00	35.00
Kapp KL-1412	(M)	The New Searchers LP	1965	10.00	25.00
Kapp KS-3412	(S)	The New Searchers LP	1965	14.00	35.00
Kapp KL-1449	(M)	The Searchers No. 4	1965	8.00	20.00
Kapp KS-3449	(S)	The Searchers No. 4	1965	12.00	30.00
Kapp KL-1477	(M)	Take Me For What I'm Worth	1966	10.00	25.00
Kapp KS-3477	(S)	Take Me For What I'm Worth	1966	14.00	35.00

SEDAKA, NEIL

Label		Title	Year	VG+	NM
RCA LPM-2035	(M)	Rock With Sedaka	1959	20.00	50.00
RCA LSP-2035	(S)	Rock With Sedaka	1959	30.00	60.00
RCA LPM-2317	(M)	Circulate	1960	12.00	30.00
RCA LSP-2317	(S)	Circulate	1960	16.00	40.00
RCA LPM-2421	(M)	Little Devil And His Other Hits	1961	12.00	30.00
RCA LSP-2421	(S)	Little Devil And His Other Hits	1961	16.00	40.00
RCA LPM-2627	(M)	Neil Sedaka Sings His Greatest Hits	1962	10.00	25.00
RCA LSP-2627	(S)	Neil Sedaka Sings His Greatest Hits	1962	14.00	35.00
		(Mono RCA albums above have "Long Play" on the bottom of the label. Stereo albums have "Living Stereo" on the bottom.)			
Vernon 518	(M)	Neil Sedaka With The Tokens	1963	8.00	20.00
Kirshner KES-111	(S)	Emergence	1971	4.00	10.00
Kirshner KES-117	(S)	Solitaire	1972	4.00	10.00

Label		Title	Year	VG+	NM
SEEDS, THE					
GNP/Crescendo 2023	(M)	The Seeds	1966	6.00	15.00
GNP/Crescendo S-2023	(S)	The Seeds	1966	4.00	10.00
GNP/Crescendo 2033	(M)	A Web Of Sound	1966	6.00	15.00
GNP/Crescendo S-2033	(S)	A Web Of Sound	1966	4.00	10.00
GNP/Crescendo 2038	(M)	Future	1967	6.00	15.00
GNP/Crescendo S-2038	(S)	Future	1967	4.00	10.00
GNP/Crescendo 2040	(M)	Full Spoon of Seedy Blues	1967	6.00	15.00
GNP/Crescendo S-2040	(S)	Full Spoon of Seedy Blues	1967	4.00	10.00
GNP/Crescendo 2043	(M)	Raw And Alive	1967	6.00	15.00
GNP/Crescendo S-2043	(S)	Raw And Alive	1967	4.00	10.00
Sidewalk ST-5913	(S)	Psych-Out (Sdtk)	1968	10.00	25.00
		(GNP albums above have red labels.)			
SEEGER, PETE					
Also refer to Big Bill Broonzy.					
Columbia CL-1101	(M)	We Shall Overcome	1958	8.00	20.00
Columbia CL-1648	(M)	Story Songs	1961	8.00	20.00
Columbia CS-8448	(S)	Story Songs	1961	8.00	20.00
Columbia CL-1916	(M)	In Person At The Bitter End	1962	6.00	15.00
Columbia CS-8716	(S)	In Person At The Bitter End	1962	8.00	20.00
Everest 2414	(M)	Pete Seeger And Sonny Terry		8.00	20.00
Everest 2451	(M)	Pete Seeger At The Village Gate		6.00	15.00
Philips PHM-2-300	(M)	The Story Of The Nativity	1963	6.00	15.00
Columbia CL-1947	(M)	Children's Concert At Town Hall	1963	5.00	12.00
Columbia CS-8747	(S)	Children's Concert At Town Hall	1963	6.00	15.00
Columbia CL-2257	(M)	I Can See A New Day	1964	5.00	12.00
Columbia CS-9057	(S)	I Can See A New Day	1964	6.00	15.00
Capitol W-2172	(M)	Folk Songs By Pete Seeger	1964	6.00	15.00
Prestige PR-7375	(M)	Folk Songs With Pete Seeger	1965	6.00	15.00
Columbia CL-2334	(M)	Strangers And Cousins	1965	5.00	12.00
Columbia CS-9134	(S)	Strangers And Cousins	1965	6.00	15.00
Columbia CL-2432	(M)	God Bless The Grass	1965	5.00	12.00
Columbia CS-9232	(S)	God Bless The Grass	1965	6.00	15.00
Columbia CL-2503	(M)	Dangerous Songs	1966	5.00	12.00
Columbia CS-9303	(S)	Dangerous Songs	1966	6.00	15.00
Capitol T-2718	(M)	Freight Train	1967	6.00	15.00
Capitol DT-2718	(E)	Freight Train	1967	4.00	10.00
Columbia CL-2616	(M)	Pete Seeger's Greatest Hits	1967	4.00	10.00
Columbia CS-9416	(S)	Pete Seeger's Greatest Hits	1967	5.00	12.00
Columbia CL-2705	(M)	Waist Deep In The Big Muddy	1967	4.00	10.00
Columbia CS-9505	(S)	Waist Deep In The Big Muddy	1967	5.00	12.00
Columbia CS-9717	(S)	Pete Seeger Now	1968	5.00	12.00
SEGER, BOB					
Palladium P-1006	(S)	Smokin' O.P.'s	1972	12.00	30.00
Reprise MS-2109	(S)	Smokin' O.P.'s	1972	8.00	20.00
Reprise MS-2126	(S)	Back In '72	1973	8.00	20.00
Reprise MS-2184	(S)	Seven	1974	8.00	20.00
Capitol ST-172	(S)	Ramblin' Gamblin' Man	1969	10.00	25.00
Capitol ST-236	(S)	Noah	1969	16.00	40.00
Capitol SKAO-499	(S)	Mongrel (Fold-open cover)	1970	10.00	25.00
Capitol ST-731	(S)	Brand New Morning	1971	16.00	40.00
Mobile Fidelity 1-034	(S)	Night Moves	1980	10.00	25.00
Mobile Fidelity 1-127	(S)	Against The Wind	1983	5.00	12.00
SELAH JUBILEE QUARTET, THE					
Remington 1023 (10")	(M)	Spirituals		20.00	50.00
SELLERS, BROTHER JOHN					
Monitor 505	(M)	Big Beat Up The River (With Mickey Baker)		16.00	40.00
SELLERS, PETER					
Angel 35884	(M)	The Best Of Peter Sellers	1960	6.00	15.00
Angel 35884	(S)	The Best Of Peter Sellers	1960	8.00	20.00
Angel 35910	(M)	Peter Sellers And Sophia Loren	1961	10.00	25.00
Angel 35910	(S)	Peter Sellers And Sophia Loren	1961	12.00	30.00
United Arts. UAL-4148	(M)	After The Fox (Sdtk)	1966	6.00	15.00
United Arts. UAS-5148	(S)	After The Fox (Sdtk)	1966	8.00	20.00
Warners W-1711	(M)	The Bobo (Sdtk)	1967	5.00	12.00
Warners WS-1711	(S)	The Bobo (Sdtk)	1967	6.00	15.00

Label		Title	Year	VG+	NM
SENSATIONS, THE					
Argo LP-4022	(M)	Let Me In	1963	30.00	60.00
SENTINALS, THE					
Del-Fi LP-1232	(M)	Big Surf	1963	8.00	20.00
Del-Fi ST-1232	(S)	Big Surf	1963	10.00	25.00
Del-Fi LP-1241	(M)	Surfer Girl	1963	8.00	20.00
Del-Fi ST-1241	(S)	Surfer Girl	1963	10.00	25.00
Sutton SU-338	(M)	Vegas Go-Go	1964	10.00	25.00
SERPENT POWER, THE					
Vanguard VSD-79252	(S)	The Serpent Power	1967	8.00	20.00
SEVEN BLENDS, THE					
Roulette R-5172	(M)	At The Miami Beach Peppermint Lounge	1962	5.00	12.00
Roulette SR-2-5172	(S)	At The Miami Beach Peppermint Lounge	1962	6.00	15.00
SEVENTH SONS, THE					
ESP 1078	(S)	The Seventh Sons		8.00	20.00
SEVILLE, DAVID (ROSS BAGDASARIAN)					
Liberty LRP-3073	(M)	The Music Of David Seville	1957	20.00	50.00
Liberty LRP-3092	(M)	The Witch Doctor	1958	20.00	50.00
SEX PISTOLS, THE					
Warners BSK-3147	(S)	Never Mind The Bollocks	1977	6.00	15.00
		(With custom label and inner sleeve.)			
SHACKLEFORDS, THE					
Mercury MG-20806	(M)	You Ain't Heard Nothing Yet	1963	5.00	12.00
Mercury SR-60806	(S)	You Ain't Heard Nothing Yet	1963	6.00	15.00
Capitol T-2450	(M)	The Shacklefords	1966	4.00	10.00
Capitol ST-2450	(S)	The Shacklefords	1966	5.00	12.00
SHADES OF BLUE, THE					
Impact IM-101	(M)	Happiness Is The Shades Of Blue	1966	10.00	25.00
Impact IM-1001	(S)	Happiness Is The Shades Of Blue	1966	14.00	35.00
SHADOWS, THE					
Also refer to Cliff Richard & The Shadows.					
Atlantic 8089	(M)	Surfing With The Shadows	1963	12.00	30.00
Atlantic SD-8089	(S)	Surfing With The Shadows	1963	14.00	35.00
Atlantic 8097	(M)	The Shadows Know	1964	10.00	25.00
Atlantic SD-8097	(S)	The Shadows Know	1964	12.00	30.00
SHADOWS OF KNIGHT, THE					
Dunwich 666	(M)	Gloria	1966	16.00	40.00
Dunwich S-666	(S)	Gloria	1966	20.00	50.00
Dunwich 667	(M)	Back Door Men	1966	16.00	40.00
Dunwich S-667	(S)	Back Door Men	1966	20.00	50.00
Super K SKS-6002	(S)	The Shadows Of Knight	1969	8.00	20.00
SHAGGS, THE					
Third World 3001	(S)	Philosophy Of The World		100.00	200.00
SHAKERS, THE					
Audio Fidelity 2155	(M)	The Break It All	1966	14.00	35.00
Audio Fidelity S-2155	(S)	The Break It All	1966	16.00	40.00
SHANGRI-LAS, THE					
Red Bird 20-101	(M)	Leader Of The Pack	1965	50.00	100.00
Red Bird 20-104	(M)	I Can Never Go Home Anymore	1965	50.00	100.00
Red Bird 20-104	(M)	The Shangri-Las '65	1965	35.00	70.00
Mercury MG-21099	(M)	The Shangri-Las' Golden Hits	1966	16.00	40.00
Mercury SR-61099	(P)	The Shangri-Las' Golden Hits	1966	20.00	50.00
Post 4000	(S)	The Shangri-Las Sing		10.00	25.00
SHANKAR, L.					
Zappa SRZ-1-1602	(S)	Touch Me There	1979	5.00	12.00

Label		Title	Year	VG+	NM
SHANNON, DEL					
Big Top 12-3003	(M)	Runaway	1961	35.00	70.00
Big Top S-12-3003	(S)	Runaway	1961	240.00	400.00
Big Top 12-1308	(M)	Little Town Flirt	1963	20.00	50.00
Big Top S-12-1308	(S)	Little Town Flirt	1963	50.00	100.00
Amy 8003	(M)	Handy Man	1964	16.00	40.00
Amy S-8003	(S)	Handy Man	1964	20.00	50.00
Amy 8004	(M)	Del Shannon Sings Hank Williams	1965	16.00	40.00
Amy S-8004	(S)	Del Shannon Sings Hank Williams	1965	20.00	50.00
Amy 8006	(M)	1,661 Seconds	1965	20.00	50.00
Amy S-8006	(S)	1,661 Seconds	1965	35.00	70.00
Liberty LRP-3453	(M)	This Is My Bag	1966	6.00	15.00
Liberty LRP-3453	(S)	This Is My Bag	1966	8.00	20.00
Liberty LRP-3479	(M)	Total Commitment	1966	6.00	15.00
Liberty LRP-3479	(S)	Total Commitment	1966	8.00	20.00
Liberty LST-7539	(S)	Further Adventures Of Charles Westover	1968	8.00	20.00
Dot DLP-3834	(M)	The Best Of Del Shannon	1967	8.00	20.00
Dot DLP-3834	(E)	The Best Of Del Shannon	1967	6.00	15.00
Post 9000	(E)	Del Shannon Sings		6.00	15.00
United Arts. LA151	(S)	Live In England	1973	6.00	15.00
Sire 3708	(P)	The Vintage Years	1975	8.00	20.00
SHANNON, HUGH					
Atlantic 406 (10")	(M)	Hugh Shannon Sings		20.00	50.00
SHAPIRO, HELEN					
Epic LN-24075	(M)	A Teenager In Love	1963	6.00	15.00
Epic BN-26075	(S)	A Teenager In Love	1963	8.00	20.00
SHARKEY					
Fireworks 1234	(S)	Signposts	1975	6.00	15.00
SHARP, DEE DEE					
Cameo C-1018	(M)	It's Mashed Potato Time	1962	12.00	30.00
Cameo C-1022	(M)	Songs Of Faith	1962	10.00	25.00
Cameo C-1032	(M)	All The Hits	1962	8.00	20.00
Cameo SC-1032	(S)	All The Hits	1962	12.00	30.00
Cameo C-1050	(M)	Do The Bird	1963	8.00	20.00
Cameo SC-1050	(S)	Do The Bird	1963	12.00	30.00
Cameo C-1062	(M)	Biggest Hits	1963	10.00	25.00
Cameo C-1074	(M)	Down Memory Lane	1963	10.00	25.00
Cameo C-2002	(M)	18 Golden Hits		8.00	20.00
Cameo SC-2002	(S)	18 Golden Hits		12.00	30.00
SHATNER, WILLIAM					
Decca DL7-5043	(S)	Transformed Man	1968	10.00	25.00
SHAW, SANDIE					
Reprise R-6166	(M)	Sandi Shaw	1965	8.00	20.00
Reprise RS-6166	(S)	Sandi Shaw	1965	10.00	25.00
Reprise R-6191	(M)	Me	1966	8.00	20.00
Reprise RS-6191	(S)	Me	1966	10.00	25.00
SHELTON, ROSCOE					
Excello 8002	(M)	Roscoe Shelton	1961	35.00	70.00
Sound Stage 7500	(S)	Music In His Soul, Soul In His Music		6.00	15.00
SHEP & THE LIMELITES					
Hull 1001	(M)	Our Anniversary	1962	180.00	300.00
Roulette R-25350	(M)	Our Anniversary	1967	20.00	50.00
SHEPARD, JEAN (& THE SECOND FIDDLES)					
Capitol T-728	(M)	Songs Of A Love Affair (Turquoise label)	1956	16.00	40.00
Capitol T-1126	(M)	Lonesome Love	1959	10.00	25.00
Capitol T-1253	(M)	This Is Jean Shepard	1959	10.00	25.00
Capitol T-1525	(M)	Got You On My Mind	1961	6.00	15.00
Capitol ST-1525	(S)	Got You On My Mind	1961	10.00	25.00
Capitol T-1663	(M)	Heartaches And Tears	1962	6.00	15.00
Capitol ST-1663	(S)	Heartaches And Tears	1962	10.00	25.00
		(Capitol albums above have black labels with the Capitol logo on the left side.)			

Label		Title	Year	VG+	NM
Capitol T-1922	(M)	The Best Of Jean Shepard	1963	5.00	12.00
Capitol ST-1922	(P)	The Best Of Jean Shepard	1963	6.00	15.00
Capitol T-2187	(M)	Lighthearted And Blue	1964	5.00	12.00
Capitol ST-2187	(S)	Lighthearted And Blue	1964	6.00	15.00
Capitol T-2416	(M)	It's A Man Everytime	1965	5.00	12.00
Capitol ST-2416	(S)	It's A Man Everytime	1965	6.00	15.00
Capitol T-2537	(M)	I'll Take The Dog	1966	5.00	12.00
Capitol ST-2537	(S)	I'll Take The Dog	1966	6.00	15.00
Capitol T-2547	(M)	Many Happy Hangovers	1966	5.00	12.00
Capitol ST-2547	(S)	Many Happy Hangovers	1966	6.00	15.00
Capitol T-2690	(M)	Heart, We Did All That We Could	1967	5.00	12.00
Capitol ST-2690	(S)	Heart, We Did All That We Could	1967	6.00	15.00
Capitol T-2765	(M)	Your Forevers Don't Last Very Long	1967	5.00	12.00
Capitol ST-2765	(S)	Your Forevers Don't Last Very Long	1967	6.00	15.00
Capitol ST-2871	(S)	Heart To Heart	1968	5.00	12.00
Capitol ST-2966	(S)	A Real Good Woman	1968	5.00	12.00
		(Capitol albums above have black labels with the Capitol logo on top.)			

SHEPPARDS, THE

Label		Title	Year	VG+	NM
Constellation CS-4	(M)	The Sheppards	1964	20.00	50.00

SHERMAN, ALLAN

Label		Title	Year	VG+	NM
Warners W-1475	(M)	My Son, The Folk Singer	1962	5.00	12.00
Warners WS-1475	(S)	My Son, The Folk Singer	1962	6.00	15.00
Warners W-1487	(M)	My Son, The Celebrity	1963	5.00	12.00
Warners WS-1487	(S)	My Son, The Celebrity	1963	6.00	15.00
Warners W-1501	(M)	My Son, The Nut	1963	5.00	12.00
Warners WS-1501	(S)	My Son, The Nut	1963	6.00	15.00
Warners W-1539	(M)	Allan In Wonderland	1964	5.00	12.00
Warners WS-1539	(S)	Allan In Wonderland	1964	6.00	15.00
Warners W-1569	(M)	For Swingin' Lovers Only	1964	5.00	12.00
Warners WS-1569	(S)	For Swingin' Lovers Only	1964	6.00	15.00
Warners W-1604	(M)	My Name Is Allan	1965	5.00	12.00
Warners WS-1604	(S)	My Name Is Allan	1965	6.00	15.00
		(Warner albums above have grey labels.)			

SHERRYS, THE

Label		Title	Year	VG+	NM
Guyden GLP-503	(M)	At The Hop With The Sherry's	1962	50.00	100.00

SHIP, THE

Label		Title	Year	VG+	NM
Elektra EKS7-5036	(S)	The Ship	1972	6.00	15.00

SHIRELLES, THE

Label		Title	Year	VG+	NM
Scepter S-501	(M)	Tonight's The Night	1961	20.00	50.00
Scepter SPS-501	(S)	Tonight's The Night	1961	30.00	60.00
Scepter S-502	(M)	The Shirelles Sing To Trumpets & Strings	1961	12.00	30.00
Scepter SPS-502	(S)	The Shirelles Sing To Trumpets & Strings	1961	16.00	40.00
Scepter S-504	(M)	Baby It's You	1962	16.00	40.00
Scepter SPS-504	(S)	Baby It's You	1962	20.00	50.00
Scepter S-505	(M)	A Twist Party (With King Curtis)	1962	16.00	40.00
Scepter SPS-505	(S)	A Twist Party (With King Curtis)	1962	20.00	50.00
Scepter S-507	(M)	The Shirelles' Greatest Hits	1963	12.00	30.00
Scepter SPS-507	(S)	The Shirelles' Greatest Hits	1963	16.00	40.00
Scepter S-511	(M)	Foolish Little Girl	1963	12.00	30.00
Scepter SPS-511	(S)	Foolish Little Girl	1963	16.00	40.00
Scepter S-514	(M)	It's A Mad, Mad, Mad, Mad, World	1963	10.00	25.00
Scepter SPS-514	(S)	It's A Mad, Mad, Mad, Mad, World	1963	14.00	35.00
Scepter S-516	(M)	The Shirelles Sing The Golden Oldies	1964	10.00	25.00
Scepter SPS-516	(S)	The Shirelles Sing The Golden Oldies	1964	14.00	35.00
Scepter S-560	(M)	The Shirelles' Greatest Hits, Volume 2	1967	8.00	20.00
Scepter SPS-560	(S)	The Shirelles' Greatest Hits, Volume 2	1967	10.00	25.00
Scepter S-562	(M)	Spontaneous Combustion	1967	8.00	20.00
Scepter SPS-562	(S)	Spontaneous Combustion	1967	10.00	25.00
Scepter SPS-2-599	(S)	Remember When	1972	6.00	15.00
Pricewise P-4001	(M)	Swing The Most		10.00	25.00
Pricewise P-4002	(M)	Here And Now		10.00	25.00

SHIRLEY & LEE (SHIRLEY GOODMAN & LEONARD LEE)

Label		Title	Year	VG+	NM
Aladdin 807	(M)	Let The Good Times Roll	1956	180.00	300.00
Score SLP-4023	(M)	Let The Good Times Roll	1957	50.00	100.00

The Shocking Blue. This Dutch group burst onto the American charts in early 1970 with "Venus," a now classic tune that was propelled forward by Pete Townsend-like guitar chords. While they were never able to duplicate their initial success here, they retained a loyal European following for years.

The Simon Sisters, *Cuddlebug.* Years before achieving fame as one of rock's sexiest vocalists, Carly Simon and sister Lucy teamed up and recorded several albums of children's music. This, their second for Kapp in 1964, is still fun to listen to and has a great cover to match. Possibly the rarest Carly Simon album.

Label		Title	Year	VG+	NM
Warwick 2028	(M)	Let The Good Times Roll	1961	35.00	70.00
Warwick WST-2028	(S)	Let The Good Times Roll	1961	50.00	100.00
Imperial A-9179	(M)	Let the Good Times Roll	1962	35.00	70.00
United Arts. LA026-G2	(S)	Legendary Masters	1974	10.00	25.00

SHIVA'S HEADBAND

Armadillo	(S)	Coming To A Head	1969	20.00	50.00
Capitol ST-538	(S)	Take Me To The Mountains	1970	10.00	25.00
Ape 1001	(S)	Psychedelic Yesterday	1981	10.00	25.00

SHOCKING BLUE, THE

Colossus CS-1000	(P)	The Shocking Blue	1970	8.00	20.00

SHONDELLS, THE

La Louisianne 109	(M)	The Shondells At The Saturday Hop	1964	40.00	80.00

SHORE, DINAH

Columbia CL-6105 (10")	(M)	S' Wonderful		16.00	40.00
RCA LOC-1000	(M)	Call Me Madam (Original Cast)	1950	50.00	100.00
RCA LPM-39 (10")	(M)	Two Tickets To Broadway (Sdtk)	1951	20.00	50.00
RCA LPM-3006 (10")	(M)	Aaron Slick From Punkin Crick (Sdtk)	1952	50.00	100.00
RCA LPM-3130 (10")	(M)	Dinah Shore Sings The Blues		10.00	25.00
RCA LPM-3214 (10")	(M)	The Dinah Shore TV Show		12.00	30.00
RCA LPM-1154	(M)	Holding Hands At Midnight	1955	14.00	35.00
RCA LPM-1214	(M)	Bouquet Of Blues	1956	10.00	25.00
RCA LPM-1719	(M)	Moments Like These	1958	10.00	25.00
Capitol T-1247	(M)	Dinah, Yes Indeed	1959	6.00	15.00
Capitol ST-1247	(S)	Dinah, Yes Indeed	1959	8.00	20.00
Capitol T-1296	(M)	Somebody Loves Me	1959	6.00	15.00
Capitol ST-1296	(S)	Somebody Loves Me	1959	8.00	20.00
Capitol T-1354	(M)	Dinah Sings Some Blues With Red	1960	6.00	15.00
Capitol ST-1354	(S)	Dinah Sings Some Blues With Red	1960	8.00	20.00
Capitol T-1422	(M)	Dinah Sings/Previn Plays	1960	6.00	15.00
Capitol ST-1422	(S)	Dinah Sings/Previn Plays	1960	8.00	20.00
Capitol T-1655	(M)	Dinah Down Home	1962	5.00	12.00
Capitol ST-1655	(S)	Dinah Down Home	1962	6.00	15.00
Capitol T-1704	(M)	Fabulous Hits Newly Recorded	1962	5.00	12.00
Capitol ST-1704	(S)	Fabulous Hits Newly Recorded	1962	6.00	15.00
		(Capitol albums above have black labels with the Capitol logo on the left side.)			

SHORT, BOBBY

Atlantic 606 (10")	(M)	Bobby Short Loves Cole Porter	1952	20.00	50.00

SIDEKICKS, THE

RCA LPM-3712	(M)	Fifi The Flea	1966	6.00	15.00
RCA LSP-3712	(S)	Fifi The Flea	1966	8.00	20.00

SIEGEL-SCHWALL BAND, THE

Vanguard VRS-9235	(M)	The Siegal-Schwall Band	1966	5.00	12.00
Vanguard VSD7-9235	(S)	The Siegal-Schwall Band	1966	6.00	15.00
Vanguard VRS-9249	(M)	Say	1967	5.00	12.00
Vanguard VSD7-9249	(S)	Say	1967	6.00	15.00
Vanguard VSD-79289	(S)	Shake!	1968	5.00	12.00

SIGLER, BUNNY

Parkway P-50000	(M)	Let The Good Times Roll	1967	8.00	20.00
Parkway PS-50000	(S)	Let The Good Times Roll	1967	10.00	25.00

SIGNATURES, THE

Whippet 702	(M)	Their Voices And Instruments	1957	12.00	30.00
Warners W-1250	(M)	The Signatures Sing In	1959	10.00	25.00
Warners W-1353	(M)	Prepare To Flip!	1959	10.00	25.00

SILHOUETTES, THE

Goodway GLP-100	(M)	Get A Job		75.00	150.00

SILKIE, THE

Fontana MGF-27548	(M)	You've Got To Hide Your Love Away	1965	10.00	25.00
Fontana SRF-67548	(E)	You've Got To Hide Your Love Away	1965	8.00	20.00
		(Full color cover.)			

Label		Title	Year	VG+	NM
Fontana MGF-27548	(M)	You've Got To Hide Your Love Away	1965	8.00	20.00
Fontana SRF-67548	(E)	You've Got To Hide Your Love Away *(Violet tone cover.)*	1965	6.00	15.00
SILLY SURFERS, THE					
Mercury MG-20977	(M)	Sounds Of The Silly Surfers	1965	6.00	15.00
Mercury SR-60977	(S)	Sounds Of The Silly Surfers	1965	8.00	20.00
SILVERSTEIN, SHEL					
Elektra EKL-176	(M)	Hairy Jazz	1959	10.00	25.00
Elektra EKS7-176	(S)	Hairy Jazz	1959	12.00	30.00
Atlantic 8072	(M)	Inside Folk Songs	1963	6.00	15.00
Atlantic SD-8072	(S)	Inside Folk Songs	1963	8.00	20.00
Cadet LP-4052	(M)	I'm So Good I Don't Have To Brag	1965	5.00	12.00
Cadet LPS-4052	(S)	I'm So Good I Don't Have To Brag	1965	6.00	15.00
Cadet LP-4054	(M)	Drain My Brain	1966	5.00	12.00
Cadet LPS-4054	(S)	Drain My Brain	1966	6.00	15.00
SIMMONS, GENE					
Casablanca NBLP-7120	(S)	Gene Simmons (With poster)	1978	6.00	15.00
Casablanca NBPIX-7120	(S)	Gene Simmons (Picture Disc)	1979	10.00	25.00
SIMMONS, JEFF					
Straight STS-1057	(S)	Lucille Has Messed My Mind Up	1969	16.00	40.00
Reprise 1057	(S)	Lucille Has Messed My Mind Up	1970	10.00	20.00
SIMMONS, JUMPIN' GENE					
Hi HL-12018	(M)	Jumpin' Gene Simmons	1964	8.00	20.00
Hi SHL-32018	(S)	Jumpin' Gene Simmons	1964	10.00	25.00
SIMON, PAUL					
Columbia CQ-30750	(Q)	Paul Simon	1973	5.00	12.00
Columbia PCQ-33540	(Q)	Still Crazy After All These Years	1975	5.00	12.00
Columbia HC-43540	(S)	Still Crazy After All These Years (1/2 speed)	1981	6.00	15.00
Columbia HC-45032	(S)	Greatest Hits, Etc. (1/2 speed)	1981	6.00	15.00
SIMON & GARFUNKEL (PAUL SIMON & ART GARFUNKEL)					
Columbia CL-2249	(M)	Wednesday Morning, 3 A.M.	1964	6.00	15.00
Columbia CS-9049	(S)	Wednesday Morning, 3 A.M.	1964	5.00	12.00
Columbia CL-2469	(M)	The Sounds Of Silence	1966	6.00	15.00
Columbia CS-9269	(S)	The Sounds Of Silence	1966	5.00	12.00
Columbia CL-2563	(M)	Parsley, Sage, Rosemary And Thyme	1966	6.00	15.00
Columbia CS-9363	(S)	Parsley, Sage, Rosemary And Thyme	1966	5.00	12.00
Pickwick SPC-3059	(S)	The Hit Sounds Of Simon And Garfunkel	1966	12.00	30.00
Columbia OS-3180	(S)	The Graduate (Sdtk)	1968	5.00	12.00
Columbia KCS-9529	(S)	Bookends	1968	5.00	12.00
Sears 435	(S)	Simon And Garfunkel	1969	10.00	25.00
Columbia CS-9914	(S)	Bridge Over Troubled Water	1971	4.00	10.00
		(Columbia albums above have "360 Sound" labels.)			
Columbia CQ-30995	(Q)	Bridge Over Troubled Water	1971	6.00	15.00
Columbia HC-41350	(S)	Greatest Hits (1/2 speed)	1981	6.00	15.00
Columbia HC-49914	(S)	Bridge Over Troubled Water (1/2 speed)	1981	6.00	15.00
Mobile Fidelity 1-173	(S)	Bridge Over Troubled Water	1981	5.00	12.00
SIMON SISTERS, THE (CARLY & LUCY SIMON)					
Kapp KL-1359	(M)	The Simon Sisters	1964	8.00	20.00
Kapp KS-3359	(S)	The Simon Sisters	1964	10.00	25.00
Kapp KL-1397	(M)	Cuddlebug	1964	8.00	20.00
Kapp KS-3397	(S)	Cuddlebug	1964	10.00	25.00
Columbia CC-24506	(S)	The Lobster Quadrille (With booklet)	1969	6.00	15.00
SIMONE, NINA					
Bethlehem BCP-6028	(M)	Little Girl Blue	1959	8.00	20.00
Bethlehem BCP-6041	(M)	Nina Simone And Her Friends	1959	6.00	15.00
Bethlehem BCP-6028	(M)	The Original Nina Simone	1961	6.00	15.00
Bethlehem BCPS-6028	(E)	The Original Nina Simone	1961	5.00	12.00
Colpix CP-407	(M)	The Amazing Nina Simone	1959	5.00	12.00
Colpix SCP-407	(S)	The Amazing Nina Simone	1959	6.00	15.00
Colpix CP-409	(M)	Nina At Town Hall	1959	5.00	12.00
Colpix SCP-409	(S)	Nina At Town Hall	1959	6.00	15.00

Frank Sinatra, *The Voice*. The chairman of the board. The finest, most influential white popular vocalist of the post-war years. The first truly successful album artist — by some accounts, the most successful album artist (in terms of chart action) of all time. Sinatra's Columbia and Capitol albums remain, like the bulk of his output, under-appreciated in the collector's market.

Alexander Spence, *Oar,* Alexander "Skip" Spence was the original drummer for the Jefferson Airplane, a position he did not want to fill and jumped ship to help form Moby Grape. *Oar,* his only solo work, is an idiosyncratic display of Spence's many talents and is among the rarest late '60s commercial releases on the Columbia label.

Label		Title	Year	VG+	NM
Colpix CP-412	(M)	Nina Simone At Newport	1960	5.00	12.00
Colpix SCP-412	(S)	Nina Simone At Newport	1960	6.00	15.00
Colpix CP-419	(M)	Forbidden Fruit	1961	5.00	12.00
Colpix SCP-419	(S)	Forbidden Fruit	1961	6.00	15.00
Colpix CP-421	(M)	Nina Simone At The Village Gate	1961	5.00	12.00
Colpix SCP-421	(S)	Nina Simone At The Village Gate	1961	6.00	15.00
Colpix CP-425	(M)	Nina Simone Sings Ellington	1962	5.00	12.00
Colpix SCP-425	(S)	Nina Simone Sings Ellington	1962	6.00	15.00
Colpix CP-443	(M)	Nina's Choice	1963	5.00	12.00
Colpix SCP-443	(S)	Nina's Choice	1963	6.00	15.00
Colpix CP-455	(M)	Nina Simone At Carnegie Hall	1963	5.00	12.00
Colpix SCP-455	(S)	Nina Simone At Carnegie Hall	1963	6.00	15.00
Colpix CP-465	(M)	Folksy Nina	1964	5.00	12.00
Colpix SCP-465	(S)	Folksy Nina	1964	6.00	15.00
Colpix CP-496	(M)	Nina With Strings	1966	5.00	12.00
Colpix SCP-496	(S)	Nina With Strings	1966	6.00	15.00
Philips 200135	(M)	Nina Simone In Concert	1964	4.00	10.00
Philips 600135	(S)	Nina Simone In Concert	1964	5.00	12.00
Philips 200148	(M)	Blues: Ballads	1964	4.00	10.00
Philips 600148	(S)	Blues: Ballads	1964	5.00	12.00
Philips 200172	(M)	I Put A Spell On You	1965	4.00	10.00
Philips 600172	(S)	I Put A Spell On You	1965	5.00	12.00
Philips 200187	(M)	Pastel Blues	1965	4.00	10.00
Philips 600187	(S)	Pastel Blues	1965	5.00	12.00
Philips 200202	(M)	Let It All Out	1966	4.00	10.00
Philips 600202	(S)	Let It All Out	1966	5.00	12.00
Philips 200207	(M)	Wild Is The Wind	1966	4.00	10.00
Philips 600207	(S)	Wild Is The Wind	1966	5.00	12.00
Philips 200219	(M)	The High Priestess Of Soul	1967	4.00	10.00
Philips 600219	(S)	The High Priestess Of Soul	1967	5.00	12.00
RCA LPM-3789	(M)	Nina Simone Sings The Blues	1966	4.00	10.00
RCA LSP-3789	(S)	Nina Simone Sings The Blues	1966	5.00	12.00
RCA LPM-3837	(M)	Silk And Soul	1967	4.00	10.00
RCA LSP-3837	(S)	Silk And Soul	1967	5.00	12.00
RCA LSP-4065	(S)	Nuff Said	1968	4.00	10.00
RCA LSP-4248	(S)	Black Gold	1970	4.00	10.00
RCA LSP-4347	(S)	The Best Of Nina Simone	1970	4.00	10.00
RCA LSP-4536	(S)	Here Comes The Sun	1972	4.00	10.00

SIMPSON, FRANK

Label		Title	Year	VG+	NM
Audio Lab 1552	(M)	Four Star Hits	1960	20.00	50.00

SIMS, FRANKIE LEE

Label		Title	Year	VG+	NM
Specialty SPS-2124	(S)	Lucy Mae Blues		8.00	20.00

SIN SAY SHUNS, THE

Label		Title	Year	VG+	NM
Venett V-940	(M)	I'll Be There		8.00	20.00
Venett VS-940	(S)	I'll Be There		10.00	25.00

SINATRA, FRANK

Label		Title	Year	VG+	NM
Columbia CL-6001 (10")	(M)	The Voice Of Sinatra		10.00	25.00
Columbia CL-6019 (10")	(M)	Christmas Songs By Sinatra		10.00	25.00
Columbia CL-6059 (10")	(M)	Frankly Sentimental Sinatra		10.00	25.00
Columbia CL-6087 (10")	(M)	Songs By Sinatra, Volume 1		10.00	25.00
Columbia CL-6096 (10")	(M)	Dedicated To You		10.00	25.00
Columbia CL-6143 (10")	(M)	Sing And Dance With Sinatra		10.00	25.00
Columbia CL-6268 (10")	(M)	New Orleans (With Jo Stafford)		10.00	25.00
Columbia CL-6290 (10")	(M)	I've Got A Crush On You		10.00	25.00
Columbia CL-6339 (10")	(M)	Young At Heart (Sdtk with Doris Day)	1955	10.00	25.00
Columbia ML-4271 (10")	(M)	Conducts The Music Of Alex Wilder	1955	12.00	30.00
Columbia CL-606	(M)	Frankie	1955	8.00	20.00
		(Columbia albums above have red labels with "Long LP Playing" on the bottom.)			
Columbia CL-743	(M)	The Voice	1955	6.00	15.00
Columbia CL-884	(M)	Conducts The Music Of Alec Wilder	1956	8.00	20.00
Columbia CL-902	(M)	That Old Feeling	1956	6.00	15.00
Columbia CL-953	(M)	Adventures Of The Heart	1957	6.00	15.00
Columbia CL-1032	(M)	Christmas Dreaming	1957	6.00	15.00
Columbia C2L-6	(M)	The Frank Sinatra Story	1958	6.00	15.00
Columbia CL-1136	(M)	Put Your Dreams Away	1958	6.00	15.00
Columbia CL-1241	(M)	Love Is A Kick	1958	6.00	15.00

Label		Title	Year	VG+	NM
Columbia CL-1297	(M)	The Broadway Kick	1959	6.00	15.00
Columbia CL-1359	(M)	Come Back To Sorrento	1959	6.00	15.00
Columbia CL-1448	(M)	Reflections	1960	6.00	15.00
Columbia C2L-6	(M)	The Frank Sinatra Story In Music		6.00	15.00
		(Columbia albums above have six			
		black "eye" logos on each label.)			
Columbia CL-2474	(M)	Greatest Hits/The Early Years	1965	6.00	15.00
Columbia CL-2521	(M)	Get Happy	1966	6.00	15.00
Columbia CL-2539	(M)	I've Got A Crush On You	1966	6.00	15.00
Columbia CL-2542	(M)	Christmas With Sinatra	1966	6.00	15.00
Columbia C3L-42	(M)	The Essential Frank Sinatra	1966	8.00	20.00
Columbia CL-2572	(M)	Greatest Hits/The Early Years, Volume 2	1967	4.00	10.00
Columbia CL-2739	(M)	The Essential Frank Sinatra, Volume 1	1967	4.00	10.00
Columbia CL-2740	(M)	The Essential Frank Sinatra, Volume 2	1967	6.00	15.00
Columbia CL-2741	(M)	The Essential Frank Sinatra, Volume 3	1967	6.00	15.00
Columbia CL-2913	(M)	Frank Sinatra In Hollywood 1943-1949	1968	6.00	15.00
		(Columbia albums above have "360 Sound" labels.)			
Capitol H-528 (10")	(M)	Swing Easy	1954	10.00	25.00
Capitol H-488 (10")	(M)	Songs For Young Lovers	1954	10.00	25.00
Capitol H-581 (10")	(M)	In The Wee Small Hours	1955	10.00	25.00
Capitol W-581	(M)	In The Wee Small Hours	1955	8.00	20.00
Capitol W-587	(M)	Swing Easy/Songs For Young Lovers	1955	8.00	20.00
Capitol W-653	(M)	Songs For Swingin' Lovers	1956	8.00	20.00
Capitol W-735	(M)	Conducts Tone Poems Of Color	1956	8.00	20.00
Capitol W-750	(M)	High Society (Sdtk)	1956	6.00	15.00
Capitol T-768	(M)	This Is Sinatra	1956	6.00	15.00
Capitol W-789	(M)	Close To You	1957	6.00	15.00
Capitol W-803	(M)	A Swingin' Affair	1957	6.00	15.00
Capitol SW-803	(S)	A Swingin' Affair	1957	6.00	15.00
		(Capitol albums above have turquoise or grey			
		labels with "Long Playing" on the bottom.)			
Capitol W-855	(M)	Where Are You	1957	6.00	15.00
Capitol W-894	(M)	A Jolly Christmas From Frank Sinatra	1957	10.00	25.00
Capitol W-912	(M)	Pal Joey (Sdtk)	1957	8.00	20.00
Capitol W-920	(M)	Come Fly With Me	1958	6.00	15.00
Capitol SW-920	(S)	Come Fly With Me	1958	6.00	15.00
Capitol W-982	(M)	This Is Sinatra, Volume 2	1958	6.00	15.00
		(Capitol albums above have turquoise or grey labels			
		with "Long Playing High Fidelity" on the bottom.)			
Capitol W-1053	(M)	Frank Sinatra Sings For Only The Lonely	1958	6.00	15.00
Capitol SW-1053	(S)	Frank Sinatra Sings For Only The Lonely	1958	6.00	15.00
Capitol W-1069	(M)	Come Dance With Me!	1959	6.00	15.00
Capitol SW-1069	(S)	Come Dance With Me!	1959	6.00	15.00
Capitol W-1164	(M)	Look To Your Heart	1959	6.00	15.00
Capitol W-1221	(M)	No One Cares	1959	6.00	15.00
Capitol SW-1221	(S)	No One Cares	1959	6.00	15.00
Capitol W-1301	(M)	Can-Can (Sdtk)	1960	6.00	15.00
Capitol SW-1301	(S)	Can-Can (Sdtk)	1960	8.00	20.00
Capitol W-1417	(M)	Nice 'N' Easy	1960	5.00	12.00
Capitol SW-1417	(S)	Nice 'N' Easy	1960	6.00	15.00
Capitol W-1429	(M)	Swing Easy	1960	6.00	15.00
Capitol W-1432	(M)	Songs For Young Lovers	1960	6.00	15.00
Capitol W-1491	(M)	Sinatra's Swingin' Session!!!	1961	5.00	12.00
Capitol SW-1491	(S)	Sinatra's Swingin' Session!!!	1961	6.00	15.00
Capitol W-1538	(M)	All The Way	1961	5.00	12.00
Capitol SW-1538	(S)	All The Way	1961	6.00	15.00
Capitol W-1594	(M)	Come Swing With Me!	1961	5.00	12.00
Capitol SW-1594	(S)	Come Swing With Me!	1961	6.00	15.00
Capitol W-1676	(M)	Point Of No Return	1962	5.00	12.00
Capitol SW-1676	(S)	Point Of No Return	1962	6.00	15.00
		(Capitol albums above have black labels			
		with the Capitol logo on the left side.)			
Capitol W-1729	(M)	Sinatra Sings Of Love And Things	1962	5.00	12.00
Capitol SW-1729	(S)	Sinatra Sings Of Love And Things	1962	6.00	15.00
Capitol WCO-1762	(M)	The Great Years		6.00	15.00
Capitol W-1825	(M)	Frank Sinatra Sings Rodgers And Hart	1963	6.00	15.00
Capitol DW-1825	(E)	Frank Sinatra Sings Rodgers And Hart	1963	5.00	12.00
Capitol T-1919	(M)	Tell Her You Love Her	1963	6.00	15.00
Capitol DT-1919	(E)	Tell Her You Love Her	1963	5.00	12.00
Capitol W-1984	(M)	The Select Johnny Mercer	1963	6.00	15.00
Capitol DW-1984	(E)	The Select Johnny Mercer	1963	5.00	12.00

Label		Title	Year	VG+	NM
Capitol T-2036	(M)	The Great Hits Of Frank Sinatra	1964	6.00	15.00
Capitol DT-2036	(E)	The Great Hits Of Frank Sinatra	1964	5.00	12.00
Capitol W-2301	(M)	The Select Cole Porter	1965	6.00	15.00
Capitol DW-2301	(E)	The Select Cole Porter	1965	5.00	12.00
Capitol T-2602	(M)	Forever Frank	1966	6.00	15.00
Capitol DT-2602	(E)	Forever Frank	1966	5.00	12.00
Capitol T-2700	(M)	The Movie Songs	1967	6.00	15.00
Capitol DT-2700	(E)	The Movie Songs	1967	5.00	12.00
Capitol STFL-2814	(M)	Deluxe Set	1968	12.00	30.00
		(Capitol albums above have black labels with the Capitol logo on top.)			
Capitol DWBB-254	(E)	Close-Up	1969	5.00	12.00
Capitol DKAO-374	(E)	Frank Sinatra's Greatest	1969	4.00	10.00
Colpix CP-516	(M)	The Victors (Sdtk)	1963	6.00	15.00
Colpix SCP-516	(S)	The Victors (Sdtk)	1963	8.00	20.00
Reprise F-1001	(M)	Ring-A-Ding-Ding!	1961	5.00	12.00
Reprise FS-1001	(S)	Ring-A-Ding-Ding!	1961	6.00	15.00
Reprise F-1002	(M)	Sinatra Swings	1961	5.00	12.00
Reprise FS-1002	(S)	Sinatra Swings	1961	6.00	15.00
Reprise F-1003	(M)	I Remember Tommy	1961	5.00	12.00
Reprise FS-1003	(S)	I Remember Tommy	1961	6.00	15.00
Reprise F-1004	(M)	Sinatra And Strings	1962	5.00	12.00
Reprise FS-1004	(S)	Sinatra And Strings	1962	6.00	15.00
Reprise F-1005	(M)	Sinatra And Swingin' Brass	1962	5.00	12.00
Reprise FS-1005	(S)	Sinatra And Swingin' Brass	1962	6.00	15.00
Reprise F-1007	(M)	All Alone	1962	5.00	12.00
Reprise FS-1007	(S)	All Alone	1962	6.00	15.00
Reprise R-6045	(M)	Conducts Music From Pictures	1962	6.00	15.00
Reprise R9-6045	(S)	Conducts Music From Pictures	1962	8.00	20.00
Reprise F-1008	(M)	Sinatra-Basie	1963	4.00	10.00
Reprise FS-1008	(S)	Sinatra-Basie	1963	5.00	12.00
Reprise F-1009	(M)	The Concert Sinatra	1963	4.00	10.00
Reprise FS-1009	(S)	The Concert Sinatra	1963	5.00	12.00
Reprise F-1010	(M)	Sinatra's Sinatra	1963	4.00	10.00
Reprise FS-1010	(S)	Sinatra's Sinatra	1963	5.00	12.00
Reprise R-6071	(M)	Come Blow Your Horn (Sdtk)	1963	6.00	15.00
Reprise R9-6071	(S)	Come Blow Your Horn (Sdtk)	1963	8.00	20.00
Reprise R-6116	(M)	Greatest Hits From The Greatest Films	1964	5.00	12.00
Reprise RS-6116	(S)	Greatest Hits From The Greatest Films	1964	6.00	15.00
Reprise F-1011	(M)	Days Of Wine And Roses	1964	4.00	10.00
Reprise FS-1011	(S)	Days Of Wine And Roses	1964	5.00	12.00
Reprise F-1012	(M)	It Might As Well Be Swing	1964	4.00	10.00
Reprise FS-1012	(S)	It Might As Well Be Swing	1964	5.00	12.00
Reprise F-1013	(M)	Softly, As I Leave You	1964	4.00	10.00
Reprise FS-1013	(S)	Softly, As I Leave You	1964	5.00	12.00
Reprise R-6167	(M)	Sinatra '65	1965	4.00	10.00
Reprise RS-6167	(S)	Sinatra '65	1965	5.00	12.00
Reprise F-1014	(M)	September Of My Years	1965	4.00	10.00
Reprise FS-1014	(S)	September Of My Years	1965	5.00	12.00
Reprise F-1015	(M)	My Kind Of Broadway	1965	4.00	10.00
Reprise FS-1015	(S)	My Kind Of Broadway	1965	5.00	12.00
Reprise 2F-1016	(M)	A Man And His Music	1965	6.00	15.00
Reprise 2FS-1016	(S)	A Man And His Music	1965	8.00	20.00
Reprise F-1017	(M)	Strangers In The Night	1966	4.00	10.00
Reprise FS-1017	(S)	Strangers In The Night	1966	6.00	15.00
Reprise F-1018	(M)	Moonlight Sinatra	1966	5.00	12.00
Reprise FS-1018	(S)	Moonlight Sinatra	1966	6.00	15.00
Reprise 2F-1019	(M)	Sinatra At The Sands	1966	5.00	12.00
Reprise 2FS-1019	(S)	Sinatra At The Sands	1966	6.00	15.00
Reprise F-1020	(M)	That's Life	1966	4.00	10.00
Reprise FS-1020	(S)	That's Life	1966	5.00	12.00
Reprise F-1021	(M)	Francis Albert Sinatra And Antonio Carlos Jobim	1967	5.00	12.00
Reprise FS-1021	(S)	Francis Albert Sinatr And Antonio Carlos Jobim	1967	6.00	15.00
Reprise F-1022	(M)	Frank Sinatra/The World We Knew	1967	4.00	10.00
Reprise FS-1022	(S)	Frank Sinatra/The World We Knew	1967	5.00	12.00
Reprise F-1023	(M)	Frank Sinatra And Frank And Nancy	1967	5.00	12.00
Reprise FS-1023	(S)	Frank Sinatra And Frank And Nancy	1967	6.00	15.00
Reprise FS-1024	(S)	Francis A. And Edward K.	1968	6.00	15.00
		(Reprise albums above have pink & green labels.)			

Label		Title	Year	VG+	NM
Reprise FS-1026	(S)	The Sinatra Family Wish You A Merry Christmas (With Nancy Sinatra)	1968	5.00	12.00
Reprise FS4-1029	(Q)	My Way	1973	6.00	15.00
Reprise FS-1031	(S)	Watertown	1970	4.00	10.00
Reprise FS4-2155	(Q)	Ol' Blue Eyes Is Back	1973	6.00	15.00
Reprise FS4-2195	(Q)	Some Nice Things I've Missed	1974	6.00	15.00
Mobile Fidelity 1-086	(S)	Nice 'N' Easy		5.00	12.00
Mobile Fidelity	(P)	Sinatra (16 LPs)		100.00	200.00

SINATRA, FRANK, & TOMMY DORSEY

Label		Title	Year	VG+	NM
RCA LPT-3063 (10")	(M)	Fabulous Frankie		10.00	25.00
RCA LPV-583	(M)	This Love of Mine		10.00	25.00
RCA LPM-1569	(M)	Frankie And Tommy	1957	10.00	25.00
RCA LPM-1632	(M)	We Three	1957	10.00	25.00
		(RCA albums have "Long Play" on the bottom of the label.)			

SINATRA, NANCY
Also refer to Elvis Presley and Frank Sinatra.

Label		Title	Year	VG+	NM
Reprise R-6202	(M)	Boots	1966	6.00	15.00
Reprise RS-6202	(S)	Boots	1966	8.00	20.00
Reprise R-6207	(M)	How Does That Grab You?	1966	5.00	12.00
Reprise RS-6207	(S)	How Does That Grab You?	1966	6.00	15.00
Reprise R-6221	(M)	Nancy In London	1966	3.50	8.00
Reprise RS-6221	(S)	Nancy In London	1966	4.00	10.00
Reprise R-6239	(M)	Sugar	1966	3.50	8.00
Reprise RS-6239	(S)	Sugar	1966	4.00	10.00
Reprise R-6251	(M)	Country, My Way	1967	3.50	8.00
Reprise RS-6251	(S)	Country, My Way	1967	4.00	10.00
Reprise R-6277	(M)	Movin' With Nancy	1968	4.00	10.00
Reprise RS-6277	(S)	Movin' With Nancy	1968	4.00	10.00
Reprise RS-6273	(S)	Nancy And Lee (With Lee Hazlewood)	1968	4.00	10.00
Reprise RS-6333	(S)	Nancy	1969	4.00	10.00
Reprise RS-6409	(S)	Nancy's Greatest Hits	1970	5.00	12.00
United Artists UAL-4155	(M)	You Only Live Twice (Sdtk)	1967	5.00	12.00
United Artists UAS-5155	(S)	You Only Live Twice (Sdtk)	1967	6.00	15.00
RCA LSP-4645	(S)	Nancy And Lee Again (With Lee Hazlewood)	1972	4.00	10.00
RCA LSP-4774	(S)	Woman	1972	4.00	10.00
Elektra 5E-549	(S)	Mel And Nancy (With Mel Tillis)	1981	4.00	10.00

SIR DOUGLAS QUINTET, THE (DOUG SAHM)

Label		Title	Year	VG+	NM
Tribe TR-37001	(M)	The Best Of The Sir Douglas Quintet	1966	12.00	30.00
Tribe TRS-47001	(S)	The Best Of The Sir Douglas Quintet	1966	12.00	30.00
Smash SRS-67108	(S)	Honkey Blues	1968	10.00	25.00
Smash SRS-67115	(S)	Mendocino	1969	8.00	20.00
Smash SRS-67130	(S)	Together After Five	1970	8.00	20.00
Philips PHS-600-344	(S)	1+1+1=4	1970	8.00	20.00
Philips PHS-600-353	(S)	The Return Of Doug Saldana	1971	10.00	25.00
Mercury SRM-1-655	(S)	Rough Edges	1972	8.00	20.00
Atlantic SD-7254	(S)	Doug Sahm And Band	1973	4.00	10.00
Atlantic SD-7267	(S)	Texas Tornado	1973	4.00	10.00
Warners BS-2810	(S)	Groover's Paradise	1974	8.00	20.00
Dot 2057	(S)	Texas Rock For Country Rollers	1976	6.00	15.00

SIR LORD BALTIMORE

Label		Title	Year	VG+	NM
Mercury SR-61328	(S)	Kingdom Come	1970	5.00	12.00
Mercury SRM-1-613	(S)	Sir Lord Baltimore	1971	5.00	12.00

SKELTON, RED

Label		Title	Year	VG+	NM
Liberty LRP-3425	(M)	Red Skelton Conducts	1965	5.00	12.00
Liberty LST-7425	(S)	Red Skelton Conducts	1965	6.00	15.00
Liberty LRP-3477	(M)	Music From The Heart	1966	5.00	12.00
Liberty LST-7477	(S)	Music From The Heart	1966	6.00	15.00

SKINNER, JIMMIE

Label		Title	Year	VG+	NM
Mercury MG-20352	(M)	Songs That Make The Juke Box Play	1957	16.00	40.00
Decca DL-4132	(E)	Country Singer	1961	8.00	20.00
Decca DL7-4132	(E)	Country Singer	1961	6.00	15.00
Mercury MG-20700	(M)	Jimmie Skinner Sings Jimmie Rodgers	1962	5.00	12.00
Mercury SR-60700	(S)	Jimmie Skinner Sings Jimmie Rodgers	1962	6.00	15.00

Label		Title	Year	VG+	NM
SKIP & THE CREATIONS					
Justice	(S)	Mobam		150.00	250.00
SKULL SNAPS, THE					
G.S.F. 1011	(S)	The Skull Snaps	1973	6.00	15.00
SKUNKS, THE					
Teen Town 101	(S)	Gettin' Started		20.00	50.00
SKYLARKS, THE					
Decca DL-8083	(M)	White Christmas (Sdtk)	1950	16.00	40.00
SKYLINERS, THE					
Calico LP-3000	(M)	The Skyliners	1959	100.00	200.00
Original Sound 8873	(M)	Since I Don't Have You	1963	12.00	30.00
Original Sound S-8873	(P)	Since I Don't Have You	1963	16.00	40.00
Kama Sutra KSBS-2026	(S)	Once Upon A Time	1971	6.00	15.00
SLACK, FREDDIE					
Wing MGW-60003 (10")	(M)	Boogie Woogie On The 88		20.00	50.00
SLEDGE, PERCY					
Atlantic 8125	(M)	When A Man Loves A Woman	1966	10.00	25.00
Atlantic SD-8125	(S)	When A Man Loves A Woman	1966	12.00	30.00
Atlantic 8132	(M)	Warm And Tender Soul	1966	10.00	25.00
Atlantic SD-8132	(S)	Warm And Tender Soul	1966	12.00	30.00
Atlantic 8146	(M)	The Percy Sledge Way	1967	8.00	20.00
Atlantic SD-8146	(S)	The Percy Sledge Way	1967	10.00	25.00
Atlantic SD-8180	(S)	Take Time To Know Her	1968	10.00	25.00
Atlantic SD-8210	(S)	The Best Of Percy Sledge	1969	6.00	15.00
SLEEPY HOLLOW					
Family Productions 2708	(S)	Sleepy Hollow	1973	6.00	15.00
SLOAN, P.F.					
Dunhill D-50004	(M)	Songs Of Our Times	1965	5.00	12.00
Dunhill D-50004	(S)	Songs Of Our Times	1965	6.00	15.00
Dunhill D-50007	(S)	Twelve More Times	1966	5.00	12.00
Dunhill D-50007	(S)	Twelve More Times	1966	6.00	15.00
SLY & THE FAMILY STONE (SLY)					
Epic LN-24324	(M)	A Whole New Thing	1967	8.00	20.00
Epic BN-26324	(S)	A Whole New Thing	1967	8.00	20.00
Epic LN-24371	(M)	Dance To The Music	1968	6.00	15.00
Epic BN-26371	(S)	Dance To The Music	1968	6.00	15.00
Epic BN-26397	(S)	Life	1968	5.00	12.00
Epic BN-26456	(S)	Stand!	1969	5.00	12.00
Epic KE-30333	(S)	Life	1970	4.00	10.00
Cotillion CT3-500	(S)	Woodstock (Sdtk)	1970	8.00	20.00
Epic KE-30325	(P)	Greatest Hits	1970	4.00	10.00
Epic KE-30986	(S)	There's A Riot Goin' On	1971	4.00	10.00
		(Epic albums above have yellow labels.)			
Epic EQ-30325	(Q)	Greatest Hits	1973	20.00	50.00
Epic PEQ-32930	(Q)	Small Talk	1974	6.00	15.00
Epic PEQ-33835	(Q)	High On You	1975	6.00	15.00
SMALL FACES, THE (THE FACES)					
Immediate Z12-52-002	(S)	There Are But Four Small Faces	1968	10.00	25.00
Immediate Z12-52-008	(S)	Ogden's Nut Gone Flake (Round Cover)	1968	10.00	25.00
Warners WS-1851	(S)	First Step	1970	5.00	12.00
Warners WS-1892	(S)	Long Player	1971	4.00	10.00
Warners BS-2574	(S)	A Nod Is As Good As A Wink	1971	4.00	10.00
Pride 0001	(S)	Early Faces	1972	4.00	10.00
Pride 0014	(S)	The History Of The Small Faces	1973	4.00	10.00
Immediate 4225	(S)	Ogden's Nut Gone Flake	1973	5.00	12.00
Warners BS-2665	(S)	Ooh La La	1973	4.00	10.00
Sire 3709	(S)	The Immediate Story		5.00	12.00
SMALL, MILLIE					
Smash MGS-27055	(M)	My Boy Lollipop	1964	12.00	30.00
Smash SRS-67055	(E)	My Boy Lollipop	1964	10.00	25.00

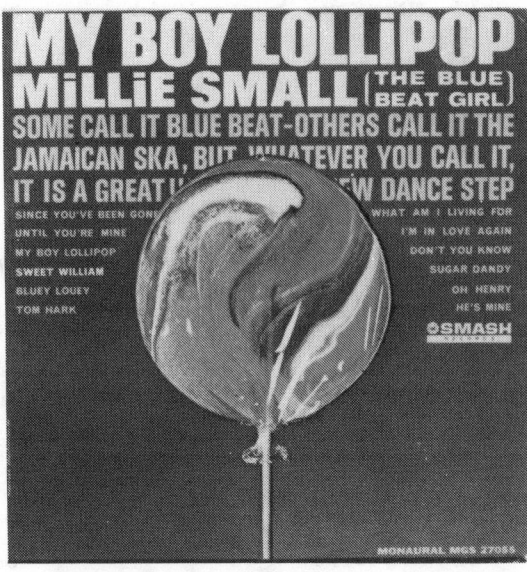

Millie Small, *My Boy Lollipop.* The Jamaican rhythm, known under a variety of terms, including ska and rock steady, slowly developed into what is now known as reggae. Millie Small's hit (#2 in 1964) was the first successful foray into the U.S. charts by that music.

Joanie Sommers, *Behind Closed Doors At A Recording Session.* An interesting package, this box contains one album with Ms. Sommers working out a recording in detail and a sheet of technical information on the process. Very rare.

Label		Title	Year	VG+	NM
SMART SET, THE					
Warners W-1203	(M)	A New Experience In Vocal Styles	1958	8.00	20.00
SMILE					
Pickwick SPC-3288	(S)	Smile	1973	12.00	30.00
SMITH, ARTHUR					
MGM E-236 (10")	(M)	Foolish Questions		20.00	50.00
MGM E-533 (10")	(M)	Fingers On Fire		20.00	50.00
MGM E-3301 (10")	(M)	Specials		20.00	50.00
MGM E-3525	(M)	Fingers On Fire		16.00	40.00
SMITH, BOB					
Kent KST-551	(S)	The Visit	1969	30.00	60.00
SMITH, BUSTER					
Atlantic 1323	(M)	The Legendary Buster Smith	1960	12.00	30.00
SMITH, CARL					
Columbia HL-9023 (10")	(M)	Sentimental Songs		14.00	35.00
Columbia HL-9026 (10")	(M)	Softly And Tenderly		14.00	35.00
Columbia HL-2579 (10")	(M)	Carl Smith	1956	14.00	35.00
Columbia CL-959	(M)	Sunday Down South	1957	8.00	20.00
Columbia CL-1022	(M)	Smith's The Name	1957	8.00	20.00
Columbia CL-1172	(M)	Let's Live A Little	1958	8.00	20.00
Columbia CL-1532	(M)	The Carl Smith Touch	1960	5.00	12.00
Columbia CS-8332	(S)	The Carl Smith Touch	1960	8.00	20.00
Columbia CL-1740	(M)	Easy To Please	1962	5.00	12.00
Columbia CS-8540	(S)	Easy To Please	1962	8.00	20.00
		(Columbia albums above have six black "eye" logos on each label.)			
Columbia CL-1937	(M)	Carl Smith's Greatest Hits	1962	6.00	15.00
Columbia CS-8737	(P)	Carl Smith's Greatest Hits	1962	6.00	15.00
Columbia CL-2091	(M)	Tall, Tall Gentleman	1963	5.00	12.00
Columbia CS-8891	(S)	Tall, Tall Gentleman	1963	6.00	15.00
Columbia CL-2173	(M)	There Stands The Glass	1964	4.00	10.00
Columbia CS-8973	(S)	There Stands The Glass	1964	5.00	12.00
Columbia CL-2293	(M)	I Want To Live And Love	1965	4.00	10.00
Columbia CS-9093	(S)	I Want To Live And Love	1965	5.00	12.00
Columbia CL-2358	(M)	Kisses Don't Lie	1965	4.00	10.00
Columbia CS-9158	(S)	Kisses Don't Lie	1965	5.00	12.00
Columbia CL-2501	(M)	Man With A Plan	1966	4.00	10.00
Columbia CS-9301	(S)	Man With A Plan	1966	5.00	12.00
Columbia CL-2610	(M)	The Country Gentleman	1967	4.00	10.00
Columbia CS-9410	(S)	The Country Gentleman	1967	5.00	12.00
Columbia CL-2687	(M)	The Country Gentleman Sings	1967	4.00	10.00
Columbia CS-9487	(S)	The Country Gentleman Sings	1967	5.00	12.00
		(Columbia albums above have "360 Sound" labels.)			
SMITH, "GUITAR BOOGIE"					
Dot DLP-5600	(M)	Original Guitar Boogie	1964	8.00	20.00
SMITH, HUEY "PIANO"					
Ace LP-1004	(M)	Having A Good Time	1959	50.00	100.00
Ace LP-1015	(M)	For Dancing	1961	50.00	100.00
Ace LP-1027	(M)	Twas The Night Before Christmas	1962	40.00	80.00
Ace LP-2021	(M)	Rock 'N' Roll Revival		40.00	80.00
SMITH, KEELY					
Also refer to Louis Prima.					
Capitol W-914	(M)	I Wish You Love (Turquoise label)	1957	8.00	20.00
Capitol T-1073	(M)	Politely	1958	6.00	15.00
Capitol ST-1073	(S)	Politely	1958	8.00	20.00
Capitol T-1145	(M)	Swingin' Pretty	1959	6.00	15.00
Capitol ST-1145	(S)	Swingin' Pretty	1959	8.00	20.00
		(Capitol albums above have black labels with the Capitol logo on the left side.)			
Dot DLP-3415	(M)	Because You're Mine		5.00	12.00
Dot DLP-25415	(S)	Because You're Mine		6.00	15.00
Dot DLP-3421	(M)	Be My Love		5.00	12.00
Dot DLP-25421	(S)	Be My Love		6.00	15.00

Label		Title	Year	VG+	NM
Dot DLP-3423	(M)	Twist With Keely Smith	1962	5.00	12.00
Dot DLP-25423	(S)	Twist With Keely Smith	1962	6.00	15.00
Reprise R-6086	(M)	Little Girl Blue, Little Girl New	1963	5.00	12.00
Reprise R9-6086	(S)	Little Girl Blue, Little Girl New	1963	6.00	15.00
Reprise R-6142	(M)	The Lennon-McCartney Songbook	1964	5.00	12.00
Reprise R9-6142	(S)	The Lennon McCartney Songbook	1964	6.00	15.00

SMITH, OSBORNE

Argo 4000	(M)	Eyes Of Love	1960	8.00	20.00

SMITH, RAY

Judd JLPA-701	(M)	Travelin' With Ray	1960	75.00	150.00
T 56062	(M)	The Best Of Ray Smith		10.00	25.00
Columbia CL-1937	(M)	Greatest Hits	1963	8.00	20.00
Columbia CS-8737	(S)	Greatest Hits ("360 Sound" label)	1963	10.00	25.00

SMITH, ROGER

Warners W-1305	(M)	Beach Romance	1959	6.00	15.00
Warners WS-1305	(S)	Beach Romance	1959	8.00	20.00

SMITH, TAB

United LP-001 (10")	(M)	Music Styled By Tab Smith		50.00	100.00
United LP-003 (10")	(M)	Red, Hot And Cool Blues		50.00	100.00

SMITH, WARREN

Liberty LRP-3199	(M)	The First Country Collection	1961	16.00	40.00
Liberty LST-7199	(S)	The First Country Collection	1961	20.00	50.00

SMOKE, THE

Sidewalk ST-5912	(S)	The Smoke	1968	12.00	30.00

SMOKE, THE

Uni 73052	(S)	The Smoke	1969	6.00	15.00
Uni 73065	(S)	At Georges Coffee Shop	1970	6.00	15.00

SMOKEY BABE

Bluesville BV-1063	(M)	Blues Of Smokey Babe	1963	6.00	15.00
Folk-Lyric FL-108	(M)	Smokey Babe		6.00	15.00

SMOTHERS, SMOKEY

King 779	(M)	The Backporch Blues	1962	100.00	200.00

SMOTHERS BROTHERS, THE (DICK & TOM SMOTHERS)

Mercury MG-20611	(M)	Songs And Comedy		4.00	10.00
Mercury SR-60611	(S)	Songs And Comedy		5.00	12.00
Mercury MG-20675	(M)	The Two Sides Of The Smothers Brothers	1962	4.00	10.00
Mercury SR-60675	(S)	The Two Sides Of The Smothers Brothers	1962	5.00	12.00
Mercury MG-20777	(M)	Think Ethnic!	1963	4.00	10.00
Mercury SR-60777	(S)	Think Ethnic!	1963	5.00	12.00
		(Mercury albums above have black & silver labels.)			
Mercury MG-20862	(M)	Curb You Tongue, Knave!	1963	3.50	8.00
Mercury SR-60862	(S)	Curb You Tongue, Knave!	1963	4.00	10.00
Mercury MG-20904	(M)	It Must Have Been Something I Said	1964	3.50	8.00
Mercury SR-60904	(S)	It Must Have Been Something I Said	1964	4.00	10.00
Mercury MG-20948	(M)	Tour De Farce: American History	1964	3.50	8.00
Mercury SR-60948	(S)	Tour De Farce: American History	1964	4.00	10.00
Mercury MG-20989	(M)	Aesop's Fables	1965	3.50	8.00
Mercury SR-60989	(S)	Aesop's Fables	1965	4.00	10.00
Mercury MG-21051	(M)	Mom Always Liked You Best!	1965	3.50	8.00
Mercury SR-61051	(S)	Mom Always Liked You Best!	1965	4.00	10.00
Mercury MG-21064	(M)	The Smothers Brothers Play It Straight	1965	3.50	8.00
Mercury SR-61064	(S)	The Smothers Brothers Play It Straight	1965	4.00	10.00
Mercury MG-21089	(M)	Golden Hits, Volume 2	1966	3.50	8.00
Mercury SR-61089	(S)	Golden Hits, Volume 2	1966	4.00	10.00

SNAKEFINGER

Ralph SN-7909	(S)	Chewing Hides The Sound		4.00	10.00
Ralph SN-8053	(S)	Green Pastures		4.00	10.00
Ralph SN-8203	(S)	Manual Of Errors		4.00	10.00

Label		Title	Year	VG+	NM
SNOW, HANK					
RCA LPT-3026 (10")	(M)	Country Classics	1952	30.00	60.00
RCA LPT-3070 (10")	(M)	Hank Snow Sings	1952	30.00	60.00
RCA LPT-3131 (10")	(M)	Hank Snow Salutes Jimmie Rodgers	1953	30.00	60.00
RCA LPT-3267 (10")	(M)	Hank Snow's Country Guitar	1954	30.00	60.00
RCA LPM-1113	(M)	Just Keep A-Movin'	1955	20.00	50.00
RCA LPM-1156	(M)	Old Doc Brown And Other Narrations	1955	30.00	60.00
RCA LPM-1233	(M)	Country Classics	1955	20.00	50.00
RCA LPM-1419	(M)	Country And Western Jamboree	1957	20.00	50.00
RCA LPM-1435	(M)	Hank Snow's Country Guitar	1957	20.00	50.00
RCA LPM-1638	(M)	Hank Snow Sings Sacred Songs	1958	16.00	40.00
RCA LPM-1861	(M)	When Tragedy Struck	1958	16.00	40.00
RCA LPM-2043	(M)	Hank Snow Sings Jimmie Rodgers Songs	1959	12.00	30.00
RCA LSP-2043	(S)	Hank Snow Sings Jimmie Rodgers Songs	1959	16.00	40.00
RCA LPM-2285	(M)	Souvenirs	1961	12.00	30.00
RCA LSP-2285	(S)	Souvenirs	1961	14.00	35.00
RCA LPM-2458	(M)	Big Country Hits	1961	12.00	30.00
RCA LSP-2458	(S)	Big Country Hits	1961	14.00	35.00
RCA LPM-2580	(M)	Together Again	1962	10.00	25.00
RCA LSP-2580	(S)	Together Again	1962	12.00	30.00
RCA LPM-2675	(M)	I've Been Everywhere	1963	10.00	25.00
RCA LSP-2675	(S)	I've Been Everywhere	1963	12.00	30.00
RCA LPM-2705	(M)	Railroad Man	1963	8.00	20.00
RCA LSP-2705	(S)	Railroad Man	1963	10.00	25.00
		(Mono RCA albums above have "Long Play"			
		on the bottom of the label. Stereo albums			
		have "Living Stereo" on the bottom.)			
RCA LPM-2723	(M)	Three Country Gentlemen	1963	5.00	12.00
RCA LSP-2723	(S)	Three Country Gentlemen	1963	6.00	15.00
RCA LPM-2812	(M)	More Hank Snow Souvenirs	1964	6.00	15.00
RCA LSP-2812	(S)	More Hank Snow Souvenirs	1964	8.00	20.00
RCA LPM-2901	(M)	Songs Of Tragedy	1964	6.00	15.00
RCA LSP-2901	(S)	Songs Of Tragedy	1964	8.00	20.00
RCA LPM-2952	(M)	Reminiscing (With Chet Atkins)	1964	6.00	15.00
RCA LSP-2952	(S)	Reminiscing (With Chet Atkins)	1964	8.00	20.00
RCA LPM-3317	(M)	Your Favorite Country Hits	1965	6.00	15.00
RCA LSP-3317	(S)	Your Favorite Country Hits	1965	8.00	20.00
RCA LPM-3378	(M)	Gloryland March	1965	6.00	15.00
RCA LSP-3378	(S)	Gloryland March	1965	8.00	20.00
RCA LPM-3471	(M)	Heartbreak Trail	1965	6.00	15.00
RCA LSP-3471	(S)	Heartbreak Trail	1965	8.00	20.00
RCA LPM-3478	(M)	The Best Of Hank Snow	1966	6.00	15.00
RCA LSP-3478	(S)	The Best Of Hank Snow	1966	6.00	15.00
RCA LPM-3548	(M)	The Guitar Stylings Of Hank Snow	1966	6.00	15.00
RCA LSP-3548	(S)	The Guitar Stylings Of Hank Snow	1966	8.00	20.00
RCA LPM-3595	(M)	Gospel Train	1966	6.00	15.00
RCA LSP-3595	(S)	Gospel Train	1966	8.00	20.00
RCA LPM-6014	(M)	This Is My Story	1966	6.00	15.00
RCA LSP-6014	(S)	This Is My Story	1966	8.00	20.00
RCA LPM-3737	(M)	Snow In Hawaii	1967	6.00	15.00
RCA LSP-3737	(S)	Snow In Hawaii	1967	8.00	20.00
RCA LPM-3826	(M)	Christmas With Hank Snow	1967	6.00	15.00
RCA LSP-3826	(S)	Christmas With Hank Snow	1967	8.00	20.00
RCA LPM-3857	(M)	Spanish Fireball	1967	6.00	15.00
RCA LSP-3857	(S)	Spanish Fireball	1967	8.00	20.00
RCA LPM-3965	(M)	Hits, Hits And More Hits	1968	8.00	20.00
RCA LSP-3965	(S)	Hits, Hits And More Hits	1968	8.00	20.00
RCA LSP-4032	(S)	Tales Of The Yukon	1968	6.00	15.00
		(RCA albums above have black labels.)			
SOFT MACHINE, THE					
Probe 4500	(S)	The Soft Machine (Movable parts cover)	1968	10.00	25.00
Probe 4500	(S)	The Soft Machine (Standard Cover)	1969	6.00	15.00
Probe 4505	(S)	Soft Machine, Volume 2	1969	6.00	15.00
SOMMERS, JOANIE					
Warners W-1346	(M)	Positively The Most	1960	8.00	20.00
Warners WS-1346	(S)	Positively The Most	1960	10.00	25.00
Warners B-1348	(M)	Behind Closed Doors			
		At A Recording Session	1960	10.00	25.00
		(Boxed set; one album with a booklet.)			

Label		Title	Year	VG+	NM
Warners W-1412	(M)	The Voice Of The 60's	1961	8.00	20.00
Warners WS-1412	(S)	The Voice Of The 60's	1961	10.00	25.00
Warners W-1436	(M)	For Those Who Think Young	1962	8.00	20.00
Warners WS-1436	(S)	For Those Who Think Young	1962	10.00	25.00
Warners W-1470	(M)	Johnny Get Angry	1962	10.00	25.00
Warners WS-1470	(S)	Johnny Get Angry	1962	12.00	30.00
Warners W-1474	(M)	Let's Talk About Love	1962	8.00	20.00
Warners WS-1474	(S)	Let's Talk About Love	1962	10.00	25.00
Decca DL7-9119	(M)	The Lively Set (Sdtk)	1964	8.00	20.00
Decca DL-9119	(S)	The Lively Set (Sdtk)	1964	10.00	25.00
Warners W-1504	(M)	Sommer's Seasons	1964	8.00	20.00
Warners WS-1504	(S)	Sommer's Seasons	1964	10.00	25.00
Warners W-1575	(M)	Softly, The Brazilian Sound	1965	8.00	20.00
Warners WS-1575	(S)	Softly, The Brazilian Sound	1965	10.00	25.00
Columbia CL-2495	(M)	Come Alive	1966	6.00	15.00
Columbia CS-9295	(S)	Come Alive	1966	8.00	20.00
Decca DL-4836	(M)	On The Flip Side (Sdtk)	1967	8.00	20.00
Decca DL7-4836	(S)	On The Flip Side (Sdtk)	1967	10.00	25.00

SONICS, THE

Label		Title	Year	VG+	NM
Etiquette ALB-02	(M)	Merry Christmas (With the Wailers)		100.00	200.00
Etiquette LP-024	(M)	Here Are The Sonics!!!	1965	50.00	100.00
Etiquette LP-027	(M)	The Sonics Boom	1966	40.00	80.00
Etiquette LPS-027	(E)	The Sonics Boom	1966	35.00	70.00
Jerden JRL-7007	(M)	Introducing The Sonics	1967	40.00	80.00
Buckshot BSR-001	(S)	Explosives	1974	16.00	40.00
First American 7715	(S)	Original Northwest Punk	1977	6.00	15.00
First American 7719	(S)	Unreleased	1981	6.00	15.00
First American 7779	(S)	Fire And Ice	1983	4.00	10.00

SONNY & CHER

Label		Title	Year	VG+	NM
RCA LPM-3441	(M)	Wild On The Beach (Sdtk)	1965	6.00	15.00
RCA LSP-3441	(S)	Wild On The Beach (Sdtk)	1965	8.00	20.00
Reprise R-6177	(M)	Baby Don't Go	1965	6.00	15.00
Reprise RS-6177	(S)	Baby Don't Go	1965	8.00	20.00
Atco 33-177	(M)	Look At Us	1965	6.00	15.00
Atco SD-33-177	(S)	Look At Us	1965	8.00	20.00
Atco 33-183	(M)	The Wondrous World Of Sonny & Cher	1966	4.00	10.00
Atco SD-33-183	(S)	The Wondrous World Of Sonny & Cher	1966	5.00	12.00
Atco 33-203	(M)	In Case You're In Love	1967	4.00	10.00
Atco SD-33-203	(S)	In Case You're In Love	1967	5.00	12.00
Atco 33-214	(M)	Good Times (Sdtk)	1967	4.00	10.00
Atco SD-33-214	(S)	Good Times (Sdtk)	1967	5.00	12.00
Atco 33-219	(M)	The Best Of Sonny & Cher	1967	4.00	10.00
Atco SD-33-219	(S)	The Best Of Sonny & Cher	1967	5.00	12.00

SONNY & THE CASCADES

Label		Title	Year	VG+	NM
Columbia CL-2172	(M)	Exciting New Liverpool Sound	1964	12.00	30.00

SONNY & THE DEMONS

Label		Title	Year	VG+	NM
United Arts. UAL-3316	(M)	Drag Kings	1964	5.00	12.00
United Arts. UAS-6316	(S)	Drag Kings	1964	6.00	15.00

SONNY TERRY
Also refer to Leadbelly and Pete Seeger.

Label		Title	Year	VG+	NM
Elektra 14 (10")	(M)	Folk Blues		10.00	25.00
Folkways 35 (10")	(M)	Harmonica		10.00	25.00
Folkways 2006 (10")	(M)	Washboard Band		10.00	25.00
Folkways 2035 (10")	(M)	Harmoniica		10.00	25.00
Folkways 2327 (10")	(M)	Blues And Folk Songs		10.00	25.00
Stinson 55 (10")	(M)	Blues		10.00	25.00
Everest 206	(S)	Sonny Terry		12.00	30.00
Fantasy 3254	(M)	Sonny Terry		12.00	30.00
Riverside 12-644	(M)	Sonny Terry and His Mouth Harp		12.00	30.00
Roulette R-25074	(M)	Folk Songs		12.00	30.00
Washington W-702	(M)	Talkin' 'Bout The Blues	1961	16.00	40.00
Bluesville BV-1025	(M)	Sonny's Story	1961	14.00	35.00
Bluesville BV-1059	(M)	Sonny Is King	1963	12.00	30.00
Brut 6002	(S)	The Book Of Numbers (Sdtk)	1973	4.00	10.00

Label		Title	Year	VG+	NM
SONNY TERRY & BROWNIE McGHEE					
Also refer to Big Bill Broonzy.					
Savoy MG-14019	(M)	Back Country Blues		30.00	60.00
Columbia OL-5240	(M)	Simply Heavenly (Original Cast)	1957	16.00	40.00
Folkways F6-3557	(M)	Blues	1959	16.00	40.00
Roulette R-25074	(M)	The Folk Songs Of Sonny & Brownie	1959	16.00	40.00
World Pacific WP-1294	(M)	Blues Is A Story	1960	12.00	30.00
World Pacific WPS-1294	(S)	Blues Is A Story	1960	14.00	35.00
World Pacific WP-1296	(M)	Way Down South Summit Meetin'	1960	12.00	30.00
World Pacific WPS-1296	(S)	Way Down South Summit Meetin'	1960	14.00	35.00
Bluesville BV-1002	(M)	Down Home Blues	1960	12.00	30.00
Bluesville BVS-1002	(S)	Down Home Blues	1960	14.00	35.00
Bluesville BV-1005	(M)	Blues & Folk	1960	12.00	30.00
Bluesville BVS-1005	(S)	Blues & Folk	1960	14.00	35.00
Bluesville BV-1020	(M)	Blues All Around My Head	1961	12.00	30.00
Bluesville BVS-1020	(S)	Blues All Around My Head	1961	14.00	35.00
Bluesville BV-1033	(M)	Blues In My Soul	1961	12.00	30.00
Bluesville BVS-1033	(S)	Blues In My Soul	1961	14.00	35.00
Verve V6-3008	(M)	Blues Is My Companion	1961	12.00	30.00
Verve V6-3008	(S)	Blues Is My Companion	1961	14.00	35.00
Folkways F-2421	(M)	Traditional Blues, Volume 1	1961	12.00	30.00
Folkways FS-2422	(M)	Traditional Blues, Volume 2	1961	12.00	30.00
Fantasy F-3254	(M)	Sonny Terry & Brownie McGhee	1961	12.00	30.00
Fantasy F-3254	(M)	Sonny Terry & Brownie McGhee (Red vinyl)	1961	30.00	60.00
Fantasy F-3296	(M)	Just A Closer Walk With Thee	1962	12.00	30.00
Fantasy F-3296	(M)	Just A Closer Walk With Thee (Red vinyl)	1962	30.00	60.00
Fantasy F-8091	(M)	Sonny & Brownie At Sugar Hill	1962	12.00	30.00
Fantasy F-8091	(M)	Sonny & Brownie At Sugar Hill (Blue vinyl)	1962	30.00	60.00
Fantasy F-3317	(M)	Blues & Shouts	1962	12.00	30.00
Fantasy F-3317	(M)	Blues & Shouts (Red vinyl)	1962	30.00	60.00
Bluesville BV-1042	(M)	Brownie's Blues	1962	10.00	25.00
Bluesville BVS-1042	(S)	Brownie's Blues	1962	12.00	30.00
Bluesville BV-1058	(M)	At The 2nd Fret	1962	12.00	30.00
Folkways FV-9019	(M)	Guitar Highway	1965	8.00	20.00
Folkways FVS-9019	(S)	Guitar Highway	1965	10.00	25.00
Mainstream MS-6049	(M)	Hometown Blues	1965	8.00	20.00
Mainstream MS-6049	(S)	Hometown Blues	1965	10.00	25.00
Everest 242	(S)	Brownie McGhee & Sonny Terry	1969	6.00	15.00
Prestige 7715	(S)	Best Of Sonny Terry & Brownie McGhee	1969	6.00	15.00
Fontana SGF-67599	(S)	Where The Blues Begin	1969	8.00	20.00
BluesWay 6028	(S)	Long Way From Home	1969	6.00	15.00
BluesWay 6059	(S)	I Couldn't Believe My Eyes	1973	6.00	15.00
Olympic 7108	(S)	Hootin' & Hollerin'	1973	4.00	10.00
Savoy 12218	(S)	Down Home Blues	1973	4.00	10.00
A&M SP-34379	(S)	Sonny & Brownie	1973	5.00	12.00
Fantasy 24708	(S)	Back To New Orleans	1972	6.00	15.00
SONS OF THE PIONEERS, THE					
RCA LPM-3032 (10")	(M)	Cowboy Classics	1952	30.00	60.00
RCA LPM-3095 (10")	(M)	Cowboy Hymns And Spirituals	1952	30.00	60.00
RCA LPM-3162 (10")	(M)	Western Classics	1953	30.00	60.00
RCA LPM-1130	(M)	Favorite Cowboy Songs	1955	10.00	25.00
RCA LPM-1431	(M)	How Great Thou Art	1957	10.00	25.00
RCA LPM-1483	(M)	One Man's Songs	1957	10.00	25.00
RCA LPM-2118	(M)	Cool Water	1959	5.00	12.00
RCA LSP-2118	(S)	Cool Water	1959	6.00	15.00
RCA LPM-2356	(M)	Lure Of The West	1961	5.00	12.00
RCA LSP-2356	(S)	Lure Of The West	1961	6.00	15.00
RCA LPM-2456	(M)	Tumbleweed Trails	1962	5.00	12.00
RCA LSP-2456	(S)	Tumbleweed Trails	1962	6.00	15.00
RCA LPM-2603	(M)	Our Men Out West	1963	5.00	12.00
RCA LSP-2603	(S)	Our Men Out West	1963	6.00	15.00
RCA LPM-2652	(M)	Hymns Of The Cowboy	1963	5.00	12.00
RCA LSP-2652	(S)	Hymns Of The Cowboy	1963	6.00	15.00
		(Mono RCA albums above have "Long Play" on the bottom of the label. Stereo albums have "Living Stereo" on the bottom.)			
SOPHOMORES, THE					
Seeco CELP-451	(M)	The Sophomores		20.00	50.00

Label		Title	Year	VG+	NM
SOPWITH CAMEL, THE					
Kama Sutra KLP-8060	(M)	The Sopwith Camel	1967	8.00	20.00
Kama Sutra KLPS-8060	(S)	The Sopwith Camel	1967	10.00	25.00
Kama Sutra KSBS-2063	(S)	The Sopwith Camel In Hello, Hello	1973	8.00	20.00
Reprise MS-2108	(S)	The Miraculous Hump Returns	1973	6.00	15.00
SOUL, JIMMY					
S.P.Q.R. E-16001	(M)	If You Wanna Be Happy	1963	20.00	50.00
Spinorama 123	(M)	Jimmy Soul And The Belmonts	1963	8.00	20.00
SOUL SISTERS, THE					
Sue LP-1022	(M)	I Can't Stand It	1964	12.00	30.00
SOUL SURVIVORS, THE					
Crimson LP-502	(M)	When The Whistle Blows Anything Goes	1967	6.00	15.00
Crimson LP-502	(P)	When The Whistle Blows Anything Goes	1967	6.00	15.00
Atco SD-33-277	(S)	Take Another Look	1969	5.00	12.00
SOUND FOUNDATION					
Smobro 9001	(S)	Sound Foundation	1971	5.00	12.00
SOUP					
Arf Arm 1	(S)	Soup	1970	20.00	50.00
		(Issued with an insert in lieu of a cover.)			
Big Tree 2007	(S)	The Soup Album	1971	6.00	15.00
SOUTH 40					
Metrobeat MBS-1000	(S)	Live At The Someplace Else		8.00	20.00
SOUTHERN, JERI					
Decca DL-5331 (10")	(M)	Warm		12.00	30.00
Decca DL-8214	(M)	You Better Go Now		10.00	25.00
Decca DL-8394	(M)	When Your Heart's On Fire		10.00	25.00
Decca DL-8472	(M)	Jeri Southern Gently Jumps		10.00	25.00
Decca DL-8745	(M)	Prelude To A Kiss		10.00	25.00
Decca DL-8761	(M)	Southern Hospitality		10.00	25.00
Capitol T-1278	(M)	Jeri Southern At The Crescendo		10.00	25.00
Capitol T-1173	(M)	Jeri Southern Meets Cole Porter		10.00	25.00
Roulette R-25010	(M)	Southern Breeze		6.00	15.00
Roulette SR-25010	(S)	Southern Breeze		8.00	20.00
Roulette R-25016	(M)	Jeri Southern Meets Johnny Smith		6.00	15.00
Roulette SR-25016	(S)	Jeri Southern Meets Johnny Smith		8.00	20.00
Roulette R-25039	(M)	Coffee, Cigarettes And Memories		6.00	15.00
Roulette SR-25039	(S)	Coffee, Cigarettes And Memories		8.00	20.00
SOUTHWEST F.O.B.					
Hip HIS-7001	(S)	Smell Of Incense	1969	12.00	30.00
SOUTHWIND					
Venture VTS-4002	(S)	Southwind	1969	5.00	12.00
Blue Thumb BTS-13	(S)	Ready To Ride	1969	5.00	12.00
Blue Thumb BTS-26	(S)	What A Place To Land	1970	5.00	12.00
SOVINE, RED					
MGM E-3465	(M)	Red Sovine	1957	12.00	30.00
Starday SLP-132	(M)	The One And Only Red Sovine	1961	8.00	20.00
Starday SLP-197	(M)	The Golden Country Ballads Of The 1960s	1962	6.00	15.00
Decca DL-4445	(M)	Red Sovine	1964	6.00	15.00
Decca DL7-4445	(S)	Red Sovine	1964	8.00	20.00
Decca DL-4736	(M)	Country Music Time	1966	5.00	12.00
Decca DL7-4736	(S)	Country Music Time	1966	6.00	15.00
SOXX, BOBB B., & THE BLUE JEANS					
Philles PHLP-4002	(M)	Zip A Dee Doo Dah	1963	75.00	150.00
SPACE					
Hand 5167	(S)	Space	1969	10.00	25.00
SPACEMEN, THE					
Roulette MG-25275	(M)	Rockin' In The 25th Century	1964	6.00	15.00
Roulette SR-25275	(S)	Rockin' In The 25th Century	1964	8.00	20.00

Phil Spector's Christmas Album. One of the most re-released albums in pop history. Originally issued on Spector's Philles label in 1963, it remained out of print until revived on Apple for the 1972 holiday season and again by Warners in 1975. Each of the above was in mono only. Then in 1981, this version, on Columbia's Pavillion subsidiary, appeared in glorious wide channel stereo... only to be withdrawn.

April Stevens, *Teach Me Tiger.* Before teaming up with Phil Spector associate Nino Tempo, Ms. Stevens issued two solo albums, one on the long defunct and highly collectible Audio Lab label and this, her one and only for Imperial. Great cover.

Label		Title	Year	VG+	NM
Roulette MG-25322	(M)	Music For Batman And Robin	1966	10.00	25.00
Roulette SR-25322	(S)	Music For Batman And Robin	1966	12.00	30.00
SPANDAU BALLET					
Mobile Fidelity 1-152	(S)	True		5.00	12.00
SPANIELS, THE					
Vee Jay LP-1002	(M)	Goodnite, It's Time To Go (Maroon Label)	1958	180.00	300.00
Vee Jay LP-1024	(M)	The Spaniels	1960	75.00	150.00
SPANN, OTIS					
Candid CJS-9001	(S)	Otis Spann Is The Blues	1960	35.00	70.00
BluesWay BLS-6003	(S)	The Blues Is Where It's At	1967	8.00	20.00
BluesWay BLS-6013	(S)	The Bottom Of The Blues	1968	8.00	20.00
London PS-543	(S)	Raw Blues	1968	5.00	12.00
London PS-551	(S)	Cracked Spanner Head	1969	5.00	12.00
Prestige 7719	(S)	The Blues Never Die	1969	4.00	10.00
Vanguard VDS-6514	(S)	Cryin' Time	1970	4.00	10.00
SPANN, OTIS, & FLEETWOOD MAC					
Blue Horizon BH-4802	(S)	The Biggest Thing Since Colossus	1970	8.00	20.00
Blue Horizon BH-4803	(S)	Blues Jam In Chicago	1970	8.00	20.00
SPARKS, RANDY					
Verve V-2103	(M)	Randy Sparks	1959	10.00	25.00
Verve V-2126	(M)	Walkin' The Low Road	1960	8.00	20.00
Verve V-2143	(M)	Randy Sparks Three	1960	8.00	20.00
Verve VS-2143	(S)	Randy Sparks Three	1960	10.00	25.00
SPARROWS, THE					
Elkay 3009	(M)	The Mersey Sound	1964	12.00	30.00
SPAT					
ABC-Paramount 502	(M)	Cookin' With The Spats	1965	6.00	15.00
ABC-Paramount S-502	(S)	Cookin' With The Spats	1965	8.00	20.00
SPEAR, ROGER RUSKIN					
United Arts. LA097	(S)	Electric Shocks	1973	6.00	15.00
SPECTOR, PHIL					
Philles PHLP-4004	(M)	Philles Records Presents Today's Hits	1963	50.00	100.00
Philles PHLP-4005	(M)	A Christmas Gift For You (Blue label)	1963	35.00	70.00
Philles PHLP-4005	(M)	A Christmas Gift For You (Yellow label)	1964	14.00	35.00
Apple SMAS-3410	(M)	Phil Spector's Christmas Album	1972	10.00	25.00
Warner Spector 9103	(M)	Phil Spector's Christmas Album	1975	5.00	12.00
Warner Spector 9104	(P)	Phil Spector's Twenty Greatest Hits	1977	8.00	20.00
Pavillion PZ-37686	(S)	Phil Spector's Christmas Album	1981	10.00	25.00
		(The above albums are all compilations of Spector's various productions.)			
SPELLBINDERS, THE					
Columbia CL-2814	(M)	The Magic Of The Spellbinders	1966	6.00	15.00
Columbia CS-9314	(S)	The Magic Of The Spellbinders	1966	8.00	20.00
SPENCE, ALEXANDER "SKIP"					
Columbia CS-9831	(S)	Oar	1969	14.00	35.00
SPENCER, JEREMY					
Columbia KC-31990	(S)	Jeremy Spencer And The Children	1971	6.00	15.00
SPIDERS, THE					
Imperial LP-9140	(M)	I Didn't Wanna Do It	1961	100.00	200.00
SPIDERS FROM MARS, THE					
Pye 12125	(S)	The Spiders From Mars	1976	6.00	15.00
SPINNERS, THE					
Time 52092	(M)	Party-My Pad	1963	20.00	50.00
Motown 639	(M)	The Original Spinners	1967	6.00	15.00
Motown 639	(S)	The Original Spinners	1967	8.00	20.00
V.I.P. 405	(S)	The Second Time Around	1970	4.00	10.00

Label		Title	Year	VG+	NM
SPIRIT					
Ode Z12-44004	(S)	Spirit	1968	8.00	20.00
Ode Z12-44014	(S)	The Family That Plays Together	1968	8.00	20.00
Ode Z12-44016	(S)	Clear Spirit	1969	8.00	20.00
Epic KE-30267	(S)	Twelve Dreams Of Dr. Sardonicus	1970	6.00	15.00
Epic KE-31175	(S)	Feedback	1972	5.00	12.00
Epic KEG-31457	(S)	Spirit	1972	5.00	12.00
Epic KE-31461	(S)	The Family That Plays Together	1972	5.00	12.00
		(Epic albums above have yellow labels.)			
SPOKESMEN, THE					
Decca DL-4712	(M)	Dawn Of Correction	1965	8.00	20.00
Decca DL-74712	(S)	Dawn Of Correction	1965	10.00	25.00
SPOONER					
Mountain Rail. 8005	(S)	Every Corner Dance	1982	5.00	12.00
Boat 1004	(S)	Wildest Dreams	1984	4.00	10.00
SPRING					
Marilyn and Diane Rovell of the Honeys. Also features Brian Wilson.					
United Arts. 5571	(S)	Spring	1972	10.00	25.00
SPRINGFIELD, DUSTY					
Also refer to the Springfields.					
Phillips PHM-200133	(M)	Stay Awhile	1964	6.00	15.00
Phillips PHS-600133	(S)	Stay Awhile	1964	8.00	20.00
Phillips PHM-200156	(M)	Dusty	1964	5.00	12.00
Phillips PHS-600156	(S)	Dusty	1964	6.00	15.00
Phillips PHM-200174	(M)	Oooooo Weeee!!!	1965	5.00	12.00
Phillips PHS-600174	(S)	Oooooo Weeee!!!	1965	6.00	15.00
Phillips PHM-200210	(M)	You Don't Have To Say You Love Me	1966	5.00	12.00
Phillips PHS-600210	(S)	You Don't Have To Say You Love Me	1966	6.00	15.00
Phillips PHM-200220	(M)	Golden Hits	1966	5.00	12.00
Phillips PHS-600220	(P)	Golden Hits (With "Goin' Back")	1966	6.00	15.00
Phillips PHS-600220	(P)	Golden Hits (Without "Goin' Back")	1967	5.00	12.00
Phillips PHM-200256	(M)	The Look Of Love	1967	5.00	12.00
Phillips PHS-600256	(S)	The Look Of Love	1967	6.00	15.00
Colgems 5005	(M)	Casino Royale (Sdtk)	1967	12.00	30.00
Colgems 5005	(S)	Casino Royale (Sdtk)	1967	45.00	90.00
United Arts. UAL-4158	(M)	The Corrupt Ones (Sdtk)	1967	12.00	30.00
United Arts. UAS-5158	(S)	The Corrupt Ones (Sdtk)	1967	14.00	35.00
20th Century TFS-S-4198	(S)	The Sweet Ride (Sdtk)	1968	6.00	15.00
Phillips PHM-200303	(M)	Everything's Coming Up Dusty	1967	5.00	12.00
Phillips PHS-600303	(S)	Everything's Coming Up Dusty	1967	6.00	15.00
Atlantic SD-8214	(S)	Dusty In Memphis	1969	4.00	10.00
Atlantic SD-8249	(S)	A Brand New Me	1970	4.00	10.00
Dunhill DSX-50128	(S)	Cameo	1973	4.00	10.00
United Arts. LA791	(S)	It Begins Again	1978	4.00	10.00
United Arts. LA936	(S)	Living Without Your Love	1979	4.00	10.00
SPRINGFIELDS, THE (TOM & DUSTY SPRINGFIELD)					
Phillips PHM-200052	(M)	Silver Threads And Golden Needles	1962	6.00	15.00
Phillips PHS-600052	(S)	Silver Threads And Golden Needles	1962	8.00	20.00
Phillips PHM-200076	(M)	Folksongs From The Hills	1963	6.00	15.00
Phillips PHS-600076	(S)	Folksongs From The Hills	1963	8.00	20.00
SPRINGSTEEN, BRUCE (& THE E STREET BAND)					
Columbia KC-31903	(S)	Greetings From Asbury Park	1973	6.00	15.00
Columbia KC-32432	(S)	Wild, The Innocent & The E Street Shuffle	1973	6.00	15.00
		(The title on the cover is in yellow.)			
Columbia PC-33795	(S)	Born To Run	1975	8.00	20.00
		(Producer Jon Landau's name is mis-spelled as "John" on the back cover.)			
Columbia PC-33795	(S)	Born To Run	1975	6.00	15.00
		(A strip correctly spelling Landau's name is added to the back cover.)			
Columbia PC-33795	(S)	Born To Run	1975	3.50	8.00
		(Landau's name is spelled correctly.)			
Columbia HC-33795	(S)	Born To Run (1/2 speed)	1980	14.00	35.00
Columbia HC-43795	(S)	Born To Run (1/2 speed)	1980	10.00	25.00
Columbia HC-45318	(S)	Darkness On The Edge Of Town (1/2 speed)	1981	14.00	35.00

Label		Title	Year	VG+	NM
STAFFORD, JO					
Also refer to Frank Sinatra and Gordon MacCrae.					
Capitol H-197 (10")	(M)	Autumn In New York		14.00	35.00
Columbia CL-2567 (10")	(M)	Guys And Dolls (Studio Cast)		14.00	35.00
Columbia CL-578	(M)	Musical Portrait Of New Orleans		12.00	30.00
		(With Frankie Laine.)			
Columbia CL-691	(M)	Happy Holiday		12.00	30.00
Columbia CL-910	(M)	Ski Trails		12.00	30.00
Columbia CL-968	(M)	Once Over Lightly		12.00	30.00
Columbia CL-1043	(M)	Songs Of Scotland	1957	14.00	35.00
Columbia CL-1124	(M)	Swingin' Down Broadway	1958	14.00	35.00
Columbia CL-1228	(M)	Jo Stafford's Greatest Hits	1959	14.00	35.00
Columbia CL-1280	(M)	I'll Be Seeing You	1959	8.00	20.00
Columbia CS-8080	(S)	I'll Be Seeing You	1959	12.00	30.00
Columbia CL-1339	(M)	Ballad Of The Blues	1959	8.00	20.00
Columbia CS-8139	(S)	Ballad Of The Blues	1959	12.00	30.00
Columbia CL-1561	(M)	Jo + Jazz	1960	6.00	15.00
Columbia CS-8361	(S)	Jo + Jazz	1960	10.00	25.00
		(Columbia albums above have six			
		black "eye" logos on each label.)			
Capitol T-1653	(M)	American Folk Songs	1962	5.00	12.00
Capitol ST-1653	(S)	American Folk Songs	1962	6.00	15.00
Capitol T-1696	(M)	Whispering Hope (With Gordon McRae)	1962	5.00	12.00
Capitol ST-1696	(S)	Whispering Hope (With Gordon McRae)	1962	6.00	15.00
Capitol T-1916	(M)	Peace In The Valley (With Gordon McRae)	1963	5.00	12.00
Capitol ST-1916	(S)	Peace In The Valley (With Gordon McRae)	1963	6.00	15.00
Capitol T-1921	(M)	The Hits Of Jo Stafford	1963	5.00	12.00
Capitol ST-1921	(S)	The Hits Of Jo Stafford	1963	6.00	15.00
Capitol T-2069	(M)	Sweet Hour Of Prayer	1964	5.00	12.00
Capitol ST-2069	(S)	Sweet Hour Of Prayer	1964	6.00	15.00
Capitol T-2166	(M)	Joyful Season	1964	5.00	12.00
Capitol ST-2166	(S)	Joyful Season	1964	6.00	15.00
Reprise R-6090	(M)	Getting Sentimental Over Tommy Dorsey		5.00	12.00
Reprise R9-6090	(S)	Getting Sentimental Over Tommy Dorsey		6.00	15.00
Dot DLP-3673	(M)	Do I Hear A Waltz?	1966	5.00	12.00
Dot DLP-25673	(S)	Do I Hear A Waltz?	1966	6.00	15.00
Dot DLP-3745	(M)	This Is Jo Stafford	1966	5.00	12.00
Dot DLP-25745	(S)	This Is Jo Stafford	1966	6.00	15.00
STAFFORD, TERRY					
Crusader CLP-1001	(M)	Suspicion!	1964	14.00	35.00
Crusader SC-1001	(P)	Suspicion!	1964	14.00	35.00
Tower T-5053	(M)	Dr. Goldfoot And The Girl Bombs (Sdtk)	1966	5.00	12.00
Tower DT-5053	(E)	Dr. Goldfoot And The Girl Bombs (Sdtk)	1966	4.00	10.00
Tower T-5082	(M)	Born Losers (Sdtk)	1967	6.00	15.00
Tower DT-5082	(E)	Born Losers (Sdtk)	1967	5.00	12.00
STAINED GLASS					
Capitol ST-154	(S)	Crazy Horse Roads	1969	8.00	20.00
Capitol ST-242	(S)	Aurora	1969	8.00	20.00
STANDELLS, THE					
Liberty LRP-3384	(M)	The Standells In Person At P.J.'s	1964	16.00	40.00
Liberty LST-7384	(S)	The Standells In Person At P.J.'s	1964	20.00	50.00
MGM E-4273	(M)	Get Yourself A College Girl (Sdtk)	1964	8.00	20.00
MGM SE-4273	(S)	Get Yourself A College Girl (Sdtk)	1964	10.00	25.00
Sunset SUM-1186	(M)	Live And Out Of Sight	1966	10.00	25.00
Sunset SUS-5186	(S)	Live And Out Of Sight	1966	12.00	30.00
Tower T-5027	(M)	Dirty Water	1966	14.00	35.00
Tower ST-5027	(S)	Dirty Water	1966	16.00	40.00
Tower T-5044	(M)	Why Pick On Me	1966	14.00	35.00
Tower ST-5044	(S)	Why Pick On Me	1966	16.00	40.00
Tower T-5049	(M)	Hot Ones	1966	14.00	35.00
Tower ST-5049	(S)	Hot Ones	1966	16.00	40.00
Tower T-5065	(M)	Riot On Sunset Strip (Sdtk)	1967	14.00	35.00
Tower DT-5065	(E)	Riot On Sunset Strip (Sdtk)	1967	12.00	30.00
Tower T-5098	(M)	Try It	1967	14.00	35.00
Tower ST-5098	(S)	Try It	1967	16.00	40.00
STANDLEY, JOHNNY					
Capitol T-732	(M)	Comedy Caravan		10.00	25.00

Label		Title	Year	VG+	NM
STANLEY, PAUL					
Casablanca NBLP-7123	(S)	Paul Stanley (With poster)	1978	6.00	15.00
Casablanca NBPIX-7123	(S)	Paul Stanley (Picture disc)	1979	10.00	25.00
STARFIRES, THE					
Ohio Recording Service 34	(M)	The Starfires Play	1964	20.00	50.00
La Brea LS-8018	(M)	Teenbeat A-Go-Go	1965	20.00	50.00
STARK NAKED					
RCA LSP-4592	(S)	Stark Naked	1971	10.00	25.00
STARR, KAY					
Capitol H-211 (10")	(M)	Songs By Starr	1952	12.00	30.00
Capitol T-211	(M)	Songs By Starr	1955	10.00	25.00
Capitol T-363	(M)	Kay Starr Style		10.00	25.00
Capitol T-415	(M)	The Hits Of Kay Starr		10.00	25.00
Capitol T-580	(M)	In A Blue Mood		10.00	25.00
		(Capitol albums above have turquoise labels.)			
Liberty LRP-9001	(M)	Swingin' With Kay Starr	1956	10.00	25.00
Modern 1203	(M)	Singin' Kay Starr, Swingin' Erroll Garner	1956	10.00	25.00
Rondo-Lette 3	(M)	Them There Eyes	1958	10.00	25.00
RCA LPM-1149	(M)	The One And Only Kay Starr	1955	10.00	25.00
RCA LPM-1549	(M)	Blue Starr	1957	10.00	25.00
RCA LPM-1720	(M)	Rockin' With Kay	1958	12.00	30.00
RCA LPM-2055	(M)	I Hear The Word	1959	6.00	15.00
RCA LSP-2055	(S)	I Hear The Word	1959	8.00	20.00
Capitol T-1254	(M)	Movin'	1959	6.00	15.00
Capitol ST-1254	(S)	Movin'	1959	8.00	20.00
Capitol T-1303	(M)	Losers, Weepers	1960	6.00	15.00
Capitol ST-1303	(S)	Losers, Weepers	1960	8.00	20.00
Capitol T-1358	(M)	One More Time	1960	5.00	12.00
Capitol ST-1358	(S)	One More Time	1960	6.00	15.00
Capitol T-1374	(M)	Movin' On Broadway	1960	5.00	12.00
Capitol ST-1374	(S)	Movin' On Broadway	1960	6.00	15.00
Capitol T-1438	(M)	Jazz Singer	1960	5.00	12.00
Capitol ST-1438	(S)	Jazz Singer	1960	6.00	15.00
Capitol T-1468	(M)	All Starr Hits	1961	5.00	12.00
Capitol ST-1468	(S)	All Starr Hits	1961	6.00	15.00
Capitol T-1681	(M)	I Cry By Night	1962	5.00	12.00
Capitol ST-1681	(S)	I Cry By Night	1962	6.00	15.00
		(Capitol albums above have black labels			
		with the Capitol logo on the left side.)			
Capitol T-1795	(M)	Just Plain Country	1962	5.00	12.00
Capitol ST-1795	(S)	Just Plain Country	1962	6.00	15.00
Capitol T-2106	(M)	Fabulous Favorites	1964	4.00	10.00
Capitol ST-2106	(S)	Fabulous Favorites	1964	5.00	12.00
Capitol T-2550	(M)	Tears And Heartaches	1966	4.00	10.00
Capitol ST-2550	(S)	Tears And Heartaches	1966	5.00	12.00
		(Capitol albums above have black labels			
		with the Capitol logo on top.)			
STARR, RINGO					
Apple SW-3365	(S)	Sentimental Journey	1970	6.00	15.00
Ode SP-99001	(S)	Tommy (Cast)	1970	6.00	15.00
Apple SWAL-3413	(S)	Ringo (With booklet)	1973	6.00	15.00
		(Cover and label list "Hold On.")			
Apple SWAL-3413	(S)	Ringo (With booklet)	1973	4.00	10.00
		(Cover and label list "Have You Seen My Baby.")			
Apple SWAL-3413	(S)	Ringo (With booklet)	1973	75.00	150.00
		(With a long version of "Six O'Clock.")			
Apple SMAS-3368	(S)	Beaucoups Of Blues	1970	6.00	15.00
Apple SW-3417	(S)	Goodnight Vienna	1974	4.00	10.00
Apple SW-3422	(S)	Blast From Your Past	1975	4.00	10.00
Atlantic SD-18193	(S)	Ringo's Photogravure	1976	2.50	6.00
Atlantic SD-19108	(S)	Ringo The Fourth	1977	2.50	6.00
Portrait JR-35378	(S)	Bad Boy	1978	2.50	6.00
Boardwalk NB1-33246	(S)	Stop And Smell The Roses	1981	2.50	6.00
STATLER BROTHERS, THE					
Columbia CL-2449	(M)	Flowers On The Wall	1966	5.00	12.00
Columbia CS-9249	(S)	Flowers On The Wall	1966	6.00	15.00

Label		Title	Year	VG+	NM
Columbia CL-2719	(M)	The Big Hits	1967	4.00	10.00
Columbia CS-9519	(S)	The Big Hits	1967	5.00	12.00
Columbia CS-9878	(S)	Oh Happy Day	1969	4.00	10.00

STATON, DAKOTA

Capitol T-876	(M)	The Late, Late Show	1957	12.00	30.00
Capitol T-1003	(M)	In The Night	1958	12.00	30.00
		(Capitol albums above have turquoise labels.)			
Capitol T-1054	(M)	Dynamic!	1958	8.00	20.00
Capitol T-1170	(M)	Crazy He Calls Me	1958	8.00	20.00
Capitol T-1241	(M)	Time To Swing	1959	6.00	15.00
Capitol ST-1241	(S)	Time To Swing	1959	8.00	20.00
Capitol T-1325	(M)	More Than The Most	1959	6.00	15.00
Capitol ST-1325	(S)	More Than The Most	1959	8.00	20.00
Capitol T-1387	(M)	Ballads And The Blues	1959	6.00	15.00
Capitol ST-1387	(S)	Ballads And The Blues	1959	8.00	20.00
Capitol T-1427	(M)	Softly	1960	6.00	15.00
Capitol ST-1427	(S)	Softly	1960	8.00	20.00
Capitol T-1490	(M)	Dakota	1960	6.00	15.00
Capitol ST-1490	(S)	Dakota	1960	8.00	20.00
Capitol T-1597	(M)	Round Midnight	1960	6.00	15.00
Capitol ST-1597	(S)	Round Midnight	1960	8.00	20.00
Capitol T-1649	(M)	Dakota At Storyville	1961	8.00	20.00
Capitol ST-1649	(S)	Dakota At Storyville	1961	8.00	20.00
		(Capitol albums above have black labels with the Capitol logo on the left side.)			
United Arts. UAL-3292	(M)	From Dakota With Love	1963	5.00	12.00
United Arts. UAS-6292	(S)	From Dakota With Love	1963	6.00	15.00
United Arts. UAL-3312	(M)	Live And Swinging	1963	5.00	12.00
United Arts. UAS-6312	(S)	Live And Swinging	1963	6.00	15.00
United Arts. UAL-3355	(M)	Dakota Staton With Strings	1964	5.00	12.00
United Arts. UAS-6355	(S)	Dakota Staton With Strings	1964	6.00	15.00

STATUS QUO, THE

Cadet Concept LPS-315	(E)	Messages From The Status Quo	1968	10.00	25.00

STEAMHAMMER

Epic BN-26490	(S)	Reflection	1969	8.00	20.00
Epic BN-26552	(S)	Steamhammer	1970	8.00	20.00

STEELEYE SPAN

Big Tree BTS-2004	(S)	Please To See The King	1971	8.00	20.00
Mobile Fidelity 1-027	(S)	All Around My Hat	1978	10.00	25.00

STEELY DAN

Command QD-40009	(Q)	Can't Buy A Thrill	1974	5.00	12.00
Command QD-40010	(Q)	Countdown To Ecstasy	1974	5.00	12.00
Command QD-40015	(Q)	Pretzel Logic	1974	5.00	12.00
Mobile Fidelity 1-007	(S)	Katy Lied	1978	20.00	50.00
Mobile Fidelity 1-033	(S)	Aja	1979	10.00	25.00

STEPHENS, LEIGH

Phillips PHS-600294	(S)	Red Weather	1969	12.00	30.00

STEPPENWOLF

Dunhill D-50029	(M)	Steppenwolf	1968	20.00	50.00
Dunhill DS-50029	(S)	Steppenwolf	1968	8.00	20.00
ABC OC-9	(S)	Candy (Sdtk)	1968	6.00	15.00
Dunhill D-50037	(M)	The Second	1968	20.00	50.00
Dunhill DS-50037	(S)	The Second	1968	6.00	15.00
Dunhill DSX-50060	(S)	Early Steppenwolf	1969	6.00	15.00

STEVENS, APRIL

Also refer to Nino Tempo & April Stevens.

Audio Lab AL-1534	(M)	Torrid Tunes	1959	20.00	50.00
Imperial LP-9055	(M)	Teach Me Tiger	1961	8.00	20.00
Imperial LP-12055	(S)	Teach Me Tiger	1961	10.00	25.00

STEVENS, CAT

Deram DE-18005	(M)	Matthew And Son	1967	6.00	15.00
Deram DES-18005	(E)	Matthew And Son	1967	5.00	12.00

Label		Title	Year	VG+	NM
Deram DES-18010	(S)	New Masters	1968	6.00	15.00
A&M QU-54280	(Q)	Tea For The Tillerman	1972	5.00	12.00
A&M QU-54313	(Q)	Teaser And The Firecat	1972	5.00	12.00
A&M QU-54365	(Q)	Catch Bull At Four	1972	5.00	12.00
A&M QU-54391	(Q)	Foreigner	1974	5.00	12.00
A&M QU-53623	(Q)	Buddha And The Chocolate Box	1974	5.00	12.00
A&M QU-54519	(Q)	Greatest Hits	1975	5.00	12.00
Mobile Fidelity 1-035	(S)	Tea For The Tillerman	1979	8.00	20.00
Mobile Fidelity 1-1035	(S)	Tea For The Tillerman (UHQR)	1984	16.00	40.00

STEVENS, CONNIE

Label		Title	Year	VG+	NM
Warners W-1208	(M)	Conchetta	1958	10.00	25.00
Warners W-1335	(M)	Hawaiian Eye (TV Sdtk)	1959	10.00	25.00
Warners WS-1335	(S)	Hawaiian Eye (TV Sdtk)	1959	12.00	30.00
Warners W-1382	(M)	Connie Stevens From "Hawaiian Eye"	1960	8.00	20.00
Warners WS-1382	(S)	Connie Stevens From "Hawaiian Eye"	1960	10.00	25.00
Warners W-1432	(M)	Connie	1961	8.00	20.00
Warners WS-1432	(S)	Connie	1961	10.00	25.00
Warners W-1460	(M)	The Hank Williams Songbook	1962	8.00	20.00
Warners WS-1460	(S)	The Hank Williams Songbook	1962	10.00	25.00
Warners W-1519	(M)	Palm Springs Weekend (Sdtk)	1963	8.00	20.00
Warners WS-1519	(S)	Palm Springs Weekend (Sdtk)	1963	10.00	25.00
Mercury SRM-1-1603	(S)	The Littlest Angel (TV Sdtk)	1969	6.00	15.00

STEVENS, DODIE

Label		Title	Year	VG+	NM
Dot DLP-3212	(M)	Dodie Stevens	1960	8.00	20.00
Dot DLP-25212	(S)	Dodie Stevens	1960	10.00	25.00
Dot DLP-3323	(M)	Over The Rainbow	1960	8.00	20.00
Dot DLP-25323	(S)	Over The Rainbow	1960	10.00	25.00
Dot DLP-3371	(M)	Pink Shoelaces	1961	8.00	20.00
Dot DLP-25371	(S)	Pink Shoelaces	1961	10.00	25.00

STEVENS, RAY

Label		Title	Year	VG+	NM
Mercury MG-20732	(M)	1,837 Seconds Of Humor	1962	8.00	20.00
Mercury SR-60732	(S)	1,837 Seconds Of Humor	1962	10.00	25.00
Mercury MG-20732	(M)	Ahab The Arab	1962	6.00	15.00
Mercury SR-60732	(S)	Ahab The Arab	1962	8.00	20.00
Mercury MG-20028	(M)	This Is Ray Stevens	1963	5.00	12.00
Mercury SR-60028	(S)	This Is Ray Stevens	1963	6.00	15.00

STEWART, AL

Label		Title	Year	VG+	NM
Mobile Fidelity 1-009	(S)	Year Of The Cat	1979	10.00	25.00
Mobile Fidelity 1-082	(S)	Time Passages	1981	6.00	15.00

STEWART, BILLY

Label		Title	Year	VG+	NM
Chess LP-1496	(M)	I Do Love You	1965	10.00	25.00
Chess LPS-1496	(S)	I Do Love You	1965	12.00	30.00
Chess LP-1499	(M)	Unbelievable	1965	8.00	20.00
Chess LPS-1499	(S)	Unbelievable	1965	10.00	25.00
Chess LP-1513	(M)	Teaches Old Standards New Tricks	1967	8.00	20.00
Chess LPS-1513	(S)	Teaches Old Standards New Tricks	1967	10.00	25.00
Chess LPS-1547	(S)	Billy Stewart Remembered	1968	8.00	20.00

STEWART, JOHN

Label		Title	Year	VG+	NM
Capitol T-2975	(M)	Signals Through The Glass	1968	5.00	12.00
Capitol ST-2975	(S)	Signals Through The Glass	1968	6.00	15.00
Capitol ST-203	(S)	California Bloodlines	1969	6.00	15.00

STEWART, RED

Label		Title	Year	VG+	NM
Audio Lab AL-1528	(M)	Favorite Old Songs	1959	20.00	50.00

STEWART, ROD

Label		Title	Year	VG+	NM
Mobile Fidelity 1-054	(S)	Blondes Have More Fun	1981	8.00	20.00

STIDHAM, ARBEE

Label		Title	Year	VG+	NM
Bluesville BV-1021	(M)	Tired Of Wandering	1961	10.00	25.00

STITES, GARY

Label		Title	Year	VG+	NM
Carlton LP-120	(M)	Lonely For You	1960	14.00	35.00
Carlton STLP-120	(S)	Lonely For You	1960	18.00	45.00

Label		Title	Year	VG+	NM
STONE, CLIFFIE (CLIFFIE STONE'S HOMBRES)					
Capitol T-1080	(M)	The Party's On Me	1958	12.00	30.00
Capitol T-1230	(M)	Cool Cowboy	1959	8.00	20.00
Capitol ST-1230	(S)	Cool Cowboy	1959	12.00	30.00
Capitol T-1286	(M)	Square Dance Promenade	1960	6.00	15.00
Capitol ST-1286	(S)	Square Dance Promenade	1960	8.00	20.00
Capitol KAO-1555	(M)	Original Cowboy Sing-A-Long	1961	6.00	15.00
Capitol SKAO-1555	(S)	Original Cowboy Sing-A-Long	1961	8.00	20.00
STONE, ROLAND					
Ace LP-1018	(M)	Just A Moment	1961	16.00	40.00
STONEGROUND					
Warners WS-1895	(S)	Stoneground	1971	4.00	10.00
Warners 2ZS-1956	(S)	Family Album	1971	6.00	15.00
Warners BS-2645	(S)	Stoneground 3	1972	4.00	10.00
Flat Out 101	(S)	Flat Out (Direct-to-disc)	1976	10.00	25.00
STONEMAN, POP, & HIS DIXIE MOUNTAINEERS					
Capitol T-1230	(M)	Cool Cowboy	1960	6.00	15.00
Capitol ST-1230	(S)	Cool Cowboy	1960	8.00	20.00
STOOGES, THE					
Elektra EKS-74051	(S)	The Stooges (Red label)	1969	10.00	25.00
Elektra EKS-74701	(S)	Fun House (Red label)	1970	10.00	25.00
Columbia KC-32111	(S)	Raw Power	1973	8.00	20.00
STORM, BILLY (& THE VALIANTS)					
Buena Vista BV-3315	(M)	Billy Storm	1963	30.00	60.00
Famous F-504	(M)	This Is The Night	1969	12.00	30.00
STORM, GALE					
Dot DLP-3011	(M)	Gale Storm	1956	10.00	25.00
Dot DLP-3017	(M)	Sentimental Me	1956	10.00	25.00
Dot DLP-3098	(M)	Gale Storm Hits	1958	8.00	20.00
Dot DLP-3197	(M)	Softly And Tenderly	1959	6.00	15.00
Dot DLP-25197	(S)	Softly And Tenderly	1959	8.00	20.00
Dot DLP-3209	(M)	Gale Storm Sings	1959	6.00	15.00
Dot DLP-25209	(S)	Gale Storm Sings	1959	8.00	20.00
STOWAWAYS, THE					
Justice	(S)	The Stowaways		180.00	300.00
STRANGE					
Outer Galaxie 1000	(S)	Translucent World	1973	30.00	60.00
Outer Galaxie 1001	(S)	Raw Power	1976	20.00	50.00
STRANGELOVES, THE					
Bang BLP-211	(M)	I Want Candy	1965	14.00	35.00
Bang BLPS-211	(S)	I Want Candy	1964	20.00	50.00
STRAWBERRY ALARM CLOCK, THE					
Uni 73014	(M)	Incense And Peppermints	1967	8.00	20.00
Uni 73014	(S)	Incense And Peppermints	1967	10.00	25.00
Uni 73025	(M)	Wake Up It's Tomorrow	1967	6.00	15.00
Uni 73025	(S)	Wake Up It's Tomorrow	1967	8.00	20.00
Sidewalk ST-5913	(S)	Psych-Out (Sdtk)	1968	8.00	20.00
Uni 73035	(S)	The World In A Sea Shell	1968	6.00	15.00
Uni 73054	(S)	Good Morning Starshine	1969	6.00	15.00
Decca DL7-34568	(S)	The Who/The Strawberry Alarm Clock	1969	20.00	50.00
Uni 73074	(S)	The Best Of The Strawberry Alarm Clock	1970	8.00	20.00
20th Century TFS-4211	(S)	Beyond The Valley Of The Dolls (Sdtk)	1970	16.00	40.00
Vocalion 73915	(S)	Changes	1971	6.00	15.00
STRAY					
Transatlantic TRA-216	(S)	Stray		12.00	30.00
Mercury SRM-1-611	(S)	Suicide	1971	6.00	15.00
Mercury SRM-1-624	(S)	Saturday Morning Pictures	1971	6.00	15.00

Gale Storm Hits. A successful actress (she starred in television's "My Little Margie"), Ms Storm's recorded six Top Ten hits in a three year period. This album contains them all.

The Sunglows, *Peanuts.* A novelty hit in 1965, "Peanuts" was subtitled the "La Cacahuata Polka." This album followed.

Label		Title	Year	VG+	NM
STREISAND, BARBRA					
Columbia OS-2210	(M)	Pins And Needles (Sdtk)	1962	10.00	25.00
Columbia KOL-5780	(M)	I Can Get It For You Wholesale (Sdtk)	1962	6.00	15.00
Columbia KOS-2180	(S)	I Can Get It For You Wholesale (Sdtk)	1962	8.00	20.00
Columbia CL-2007	(M)	The Barbra Streisand Album	1963	4.00	10.00
Columbia CS-8807	(S)	The Barbra Streisand Album	1963	5.00	12.00
Columbia CL-2054	(M)	Second Barbra Streisand Album	1963	4.00	10.00
Columbia CS-8854	(S)	Second Barbra Streisand Album	1963	5.00	12.00
Columbia CS-8854	(S)	Second Barbra Streisand Album (Blue vinyl)	1963	50.00	100.00
Columbia CL-2154	(M)	The Third Barbra Streisand Album	1964	4.00	10.00
Columbia CS-8954	(S)	The Third Barbra Streisand Album	1964	5.00	12.00
Capitol VAS-2059	(M)	Funny Girl (Original Cast)	1964	8.00	20.00
Capitol SVAS-2059	(S)	Funny Girl (Original Cast)	1964	10.00	25.00
Columbia CL-2215	(M)	People	1964	4.00	10.00
Columbia CS-9015	(S)	People	1964	5.00	12.00
Columbia CL-2336	(M)	My Name Is Barbra	1965	4.00	10.00
Columbia CS-9136	(S)	My Name Is Barbra	1965	5.00	12.00
Columbia CL-2409	(M)	My Name Is Barbra, Two	1965	4.00	10.00
Columbia CS-9209	(S)	My Name Is Barbra, Two	1965	5.00	12.00
Columbia CL-2478	(M)	Color Me Barbra	1966	4.00	10.00
Columbia CL-2478	(M)	Color Me Barbra (Red vinyl)	1966	35.00	70.00
Columbia CS-9278	(S)	Color Me Barbra	1966	5.00	12.00
Columbia CL-2547	(M)	Je M' Appelle Barbra	1966	4.00	10.00
Columbia CS-9347	(S)	Je M' Appelle Barbra	1966	5.00	12.00
Columbia CL-2682	(M)	Simply Streisand	1967	4.00	10.00
Columbia CS-9482	(S)	Simply Streisand	1967	5.00	12.00
Columbia CL-2757	(M)	Barbra's Christmas Album	1967	4.00	10.00
Columbia CS-9557	(S)	Barbra's Christmas Album	1967	5.00	12.00
Columbia BOS-3220	(S)	Funny Girl (Sdtk)	1968	6.00	15.00
Columbia CS-9710	(S)	A Happening In Central Park	1968	4.00	10.00
Columbia CS-9816	(S)	What About Today?	1969	4.00	10.00
Columbia CS-9968	(S)	Barbra Streisand's Greatest Hits	1970	4.00	10.00
		(Columbia albums above have "360 Sound" labels.)			
Columbia PCQ-30378	(Q)	Stoney End	1971	6.00	15.00
Columbia PCQ-30792	(Q)	Barbra Joan Streisand	1971	6.00	15.00
Columbia SQ-30992	(Q)	Funny Girl (Sdtk)	1972	6.00	15.00
Columbia PCQ-31760	(Q)	Live In Concert At The Forum	1972	6.00	15.00
Columbia PCQ-32801	(Q)	The Way We Were	1974	6.00	15.00
Columbia PCQ-33005	(Q)	Butterfly	1974	6.00	15.00
Columbia PCQ-33815	(Q)	Lazy Afternoon	1975	6.00	15.00
Arista AQ-9004	(Q)	Funny Lady (Sdtk)	1975	8.00	20.00
Columbia HC-45679	(S)	Greatest Hits, Volume 2 (1/2 speed)	1982	8.00	20.00
Columbia HC-46750	(S)	Guilty (1/2 speed)	1982	8.00	20.00
Columbia HC-47678	(S)	Memories (1/2 speed)	1982	8.00	20.00
STRONG, NOLAN, & THE DIABLOS					
Fortune LP-8010	(M)	Fortune Of Hits	1961	30.00	60.00
Fortune LP-8012	(M)	Fortune Of Hits, Volume 2	1962	30.00	60.00
Fortune LP-8015	(M)	Mind Over Matter	1963	30.00	60.00
STYX					
Mobile Fidelity 1-025	(S)	The Grand Illusion	1978	10.00	25.00
SUNGLOWS, THE					
Sunglow SLP-103	(M)	Peanuts		16.00	40.00
SUNNY & THE SUNLINERS					
Tear Drop 2000	(M)	Talk To Me/Rags To Riches	1963	12.00	30.00
Tear Drop 2019	(M)	All Night Worker		12.00	30.00
Sunglow 103	(M)	The Original Peanuts	1965	8.00	20.00
SUNNYLAND SLIM					
Bluesville BV-1016	(M)	Slim's Shout	1961	16.00	40.00
Prestige 7723	(S)	Slim's Shout	1969	6.00	15.00
World Pacific WPS-21890	(S)	Slim's Got His Thing Goin' On	1969	8.00	20.00
SUNRAYS, THE					
Tower T-5017	(M)	Andrea	1966	10.00	25.00
Tower ST-5017	(S)	Andrea	1966	14.00	35.00
Tower DT-5124	(E)	Hellcats (Sdtk)	1968	8.00	20.00

Label		Title	Year	VG+	NM
SUNSET SURF, THE					
Capitol T-1915	(M)	The Sunset Surf	1963	6.00	15.00
Capitol ST-1915	(S)	The Sunset Surf	1963	8.00	20.00
SUNSETS, THE					
Palace 752	(M)	Surfing With The Sunsets	1963	12.00	30.00
Palace 752	(S)	Surfing With The Sunsets	1963	16.00	40.00
SUPERSTOCKS, THE					
Capitol T-2060	(M)	Thunder Road	1964	35.00	70.00
Capitol ST-2060	(S)	Thunder Road	1964	40.00	80.00
Capitol T-2113	(M)	Surf Route 101	1964	40.00	80.00
Capitol ST-2113	(S)	Surf Route 101	1964	50.00	100.00
		(Includes a bonus single by Mr. Gasser.)			
Capitol T-2190	(M)	School Is A Drag	1964	35.00	70.00
Capitol ST-2190	(S)	School Is A Drag	1964	40.00	80.00
SUPERSISTER					
Dwarf PDLP-2001	(S)	Supersister		8.00	20.00
SUPERTRAMP					
Mobile Fidelity 1-005	(S)	Crime Of The Century	1978	10.00	25.00
Mobile Fidelity 1-005	(S)	Crime Of The Century (UHQR)		16.00	40.00
Mobile Fidelity 1-045	(S)	Breakfast In America	1980	5.00	12.00
SUPREMES, THE					
Motown M-606	(M)	Meet The Supremes	1964	150.00	250.00
		(The cover features the group seated on stools.)			
Motown M-606	(M)	Meet The Supremes	1964	8.00	20.00
Motown S-606	(S)	Meet The Supremes	1964	10.00	25.00
		(The cover features a close-up of the group.)			
Motown M-621	(M)	Where Did Our Love Go	1964	6.00	15.00
Motown S-621	(S)	Where Did Our Love Go	1964	8.00	20.00
Motown M-623	(M)	A Bit Of Liverpool	1964	12.00	30.00
Motown S-623	(S)	A Bit Of Liverpool	1964	14.00	35.00
Motown M-625	(M)	Country, Western And Pop	1965	8.00	20.00
Motown S-625	(S)	Country, Western And Pop	1965	10.00	25.00
Motown M-627	(M)	More Hits By The Supremes	1965	6.00	15.00
Motown S-627	(S)	More Hits By The Supremes	1965	8.00	20.00
Motown M-629	(M)	We Remember Sam Cooke	1965	8.00	20.00
Motown S-629	(S)	We Remember Sam Cooke	1965	10.00	25.00
Motown M-636	(M)	The Supremes At The Copa	1965	6.00	15.00
Motown S-636	(S)	The Supremes At The Copa	1965	8.00	20.00
Motown M-638	(M)	Merry Christmas	1965	8.00	20.00
Motown S-638	(S)	Merry Christmas	1965	10.00	25.00
Motown M-643	(M)	I Hear A Symphony	1966	6.00	15.00
Motown S-643	(S)	I Hear A Symphony	1966	8.00	20.00
Motown M-649	(M)	Supremes A' Go-Go	1966	6.00	15.00
Motown S-649	(S)	Supremes A' Go-Go	1966	8.00	20.00
Motown M-650	(M)	Holland-Dozier-Holland	1967	8.00	20.00
Motown S-650	(S)	Holland-Dozier-Holland	1967	10.00	25.00
Motown M-659	(M)	The Supremes Sing Rodgers And Hart	1967	8.00	20.00
Motown S-659	(S)	The Supremes Sing Rodgers And Hart	1967	10.00	25.00
Motown M-663	(M)	The Supremes' Greatest Hits	1967	12.00	30.00
Motown S-663	(S)	The Supremes' Greatest Hits	1967	12.00	30.00
		(With a large fold-open poster.)			
Motown M-665	(M)	Reflections	1968	6.00	15.00
Motown S-665	(S)	Reflections	1968	6.00	15.00
SURF SIDE FIVE, THE					
Intermountain 153	(M)	Recorded Live		75.00	150.00
SURFARIS, THE					
Dot DLP-3535	(M)	Wipe Out	1963	16.00	40.00
Dot DLP-25535	(S)	Wipe Out	1963	20.00	50.00
Dot DLP-3535	(M)	Wipe Out & Other Popular Selections	1963	14.00	35.00
Dot DLP-25535	(S)	Wipe Out & Other Popular Selections	1963	16.00	40.00
		(Back cover does not have a photo of the group.)			
Dot DLP-3535	(M)	Wipe Out & Other Popular Selections	1963	10.00	25.00
Dot DLP-25535	(S)	Wipe Out & Other Popular Selections	1963	12.00	30.00
		(The back cover has a photo of the group.)			

Label		Title	Year	VG+	NM
Decca DL-4470	(M)	The Surfaris Play Wipe Out	1963	14.00	35.00
Decca DL7-4470	(S)	The Surfaris Play Wipe Out	1963	16.00	40.00
Decca DL-4487	(M)	Hit City '64	1964	16.00	40.00
Decca DL7-4487	(S)	Hit City '64	1964	20.00	50.00
Decca DL-4560	(M)	Fun City, U.S.A.	1964	16.00	40.00
Decca DL7-4560	(S)	Fun City, U.S.A.	1964	20.00	50.00
Decca DL-9119	(M)	The Lively Set (Sdtk)	1964	8.00	20.00
Decca DL7-9119	(S)	The Lively Set (Sdtk)	1964	10.00	25.00
Decca DL-4614	(M)	Hit City '65	1965	16.00	40.00
Decca DL7-4614	(S)	Hit City '65	1965	20.00	50.00
Decca DL-4683	(M)	It Ain't Me, Babe	1965	16.00	40.00
Decca DL7-4683	(S)	It Ain't Me, Babe	1965	20.00	50.00

(Decca albums above have black labels with "Mfrd. by Decca" beneath the rainbow.)

SURFRIDERS, THE

Label		Title	Year	VG+	NM
Vault V-105	(M)	Surfbeat	1963	10.00	25.00
Vault VS-105	(S)	Surfbeat	1963	12.00	30.00

SURFSIDERS, THE

Label		Title	Year	VG+	NM
Design DLP-208	(M)	The Beach Boy's Songbook	1965	6.00	15.00
Design DLPS-208	(S)	The Beach Boy's Songbook	1965	8.00	20.00

SURPRISE PACKAGE

Label		Title	Year	VG+	NM
LHI S-12005	(S)	Free Up		10.00	25.00

SWAMP DOGG

Label		Title	Year	VG+	NM
Canyon LP-7706	(S)	Total Destruction To Your Mind		10.00	25.00
Elektra EKS-74089	(S)	Rat On	1971	6.00	15.00

SWEET INSPIRATIONS, THE

Label		Title	Year	VG+	NM
Atlantic SD-8155	(S)	The Sweet Inspirations	1968	6.00	15.00
Atlantic SD-8201	(S)	What The World Needs Now Is Love	1969	6.00	15.00
Atlantic SD-8225	(S)	Sweets For My Sweet	1969	6.00	15.00
Atlantic SD-8253	(S)	Sweet, Sweet Soul	1970	6.00	15.00

SWINGIN' MEDALLIONS, THE

Label		Title	Year	VG+	NM
Smash MGS-27083	(M)	Double Shot	1966	8.00	20.00
Smash SRS-67083	(S)	Double Shot	1966	10.00	25.00

SWINGING BLUE JEANS, THE

Label		Title	Year	VG+	NM
Imperial LP-9261	(M)	Hippy Hippy Shake	1964	50.00	100.00
Imperial LP-12261	(E)	Hippy Hippy Shake	1964	40.00	80.00

SYKES, ROOSEVELT

Label		Title	Year	VG+	NM
Bluesville BV-1006	(M)	The Return Of Roosevelt Sykes	1960	20.00	50.00
Bluesville BV-1014	(M)	The Honeydripper	1961	20.00	50.00

SYNDICATE OF SOUND, THE

Label		Title	Year	VG+	NM
Bell LP-6001	(M)	Little Girl	1966	14.00	35.00
Bell SLP-6001	(S)	Little Girl	1966	16.00	40.00

SYMS, SYLVIA

Label		Title	Year	VG+	NM
Version 103 (10")	(M)	After Dark		16.00	40.00
Atlantic 137 (10")	(M)	Songs By Sylvia Sims	1953	20.00	50.00
Atlantic 1243	(M)	Songs By Sylvia Sims (Black label)	1956	20.00	50.00
Version 103 (10")	(M)	After Dark	1954	12.00	30.00
Decca DL-8188	(M)	Sylvia Sims Sings	1955	10.00	25.00
Decca DL-8639	(M)	Songs Of Love	1958	10.00	25.00
Columbia CL-1443	(M)	Torch Song	1960	5.00	12.00
Columbia CS-8243	(S)	Torch Song	1960	6.00	15.00
Kapp KL-1236	(M)	That Man/Love Songs To Frank Sinatra	1961	5.00	12.00
Kapp KS-3236	(S)	That Man/Love Songs To Frank Sinatra	1961	6.00	15.00
20th Century 4123	(M)	The Fabulous Sylvia Sims	1964	5.00	12.00
20th Century S-4123	(S)	The Fabulous Sylvia Sims	1964	6.00	15.00
Prestige 7439	(M)	Sylvia Is!	1965	5.00	12.00
Prestige S-7439	(S)	Sylvia Is!	1965	6.00	15.00
Prestige 7489	(M)	For Once In My Life	1965	5.00	12.00
Prestige S-7489	(S)	For Once In My Life	1965	6.00	15.00

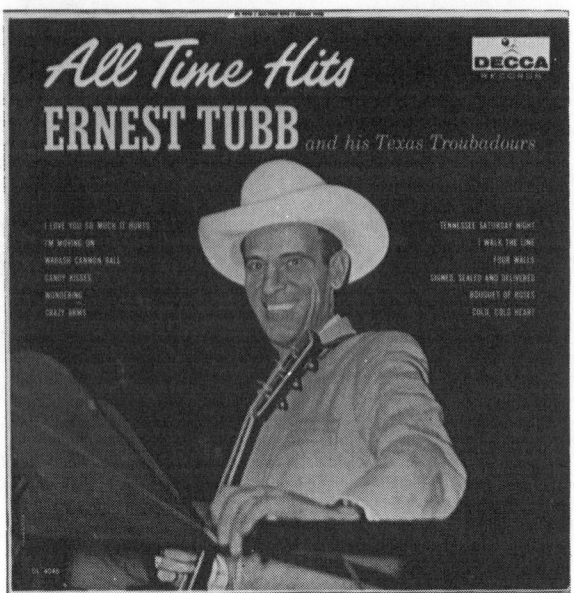

The All-Time Hits Of Ernest Tubb. A country music legend, Tubb's early works stand as classic of the genre. The influence he has had in the country field is immeasurable. Like all too many country artists, his records have long been overlooked by collectors, although that appears to be changing in the past few years.

Ike & Tina Turner, *River Deep-Mountain High.* Recorded in 1966 and prepared for release on Phil Spector's Philles label, most of the copies of that pressing were personally destroyed by Spector, making it one of the rarest and most valuable albums of all records. This, the first version released to the public, was issued by A&M in 1969, too late to capitalize on the publicity surrounding the phenomenal failure of the phenomenal title track.

Label		Title	Year	VG+	NM
T-BONES, THE					
Liberty LRP-3346	(M)	Boss Drag	1964	5.00	12.00
Liberty LST-7346	(S)	Boss Drag	1964	6.00	15.00
Liberty LRP-3363	(M)	Boss Drag At The Beach	1964	5.00	12.00
Liberty LST-7363	(S)	Boss Drag At The Beach	1964	6.00	15.00
Liberty LRP-3404	(M)	Doin' The Jerk	1965	4.00	10.00
Liberty LST-7404	(S)	Doin' The Jerk	1965	5.00	12.00
Liberty LRP-3439	(M)	No Matter What Shape	1966	5.00	12.00
Liberty LST-7439	(S)	No Matter What Shape	1966	6.00	15.00
Liberty LRP-3446	(M)	Sippin' And Chippin'	1966	4.00	10.00
Liberty LST-7446	(S)	Sippin' And Chippin'	1966	5.00	12.00
Liberty LRP-3471	(M)	Everyone's Gone To The Moon	1966	4.00	10.00
Liberty LST-7471	(S)	Everyone's Gone To The Moon	1966	5.00	12.00
T.C. ATLANTIC					
Dove LP-4459	(M)	T.C. Atlantic		50.00	100.00
T.I.M.E.					
Liberty LST-7558	(S)	T.I.M.E.	1968	5.00	12.00
Liberty LST-7605	(S)	Smooth Ball	1969	5.00	12.00
T-REX (TYRANNOSAURUS REX)					
A&M	(S)	My People Were Fair	1968	8.00	20.00
A&M	(S)	Prophets, Seers And Sages	1968	8.00	20.00
Blue Thumb BTS-7	(S)	Unicorn	1969	8.00	20.00
Blue Thumb BTS-18	(S)	A Beard Of Stars	1970	8.00	20.00
Reprise RS-6440	(S)	T-Rex	1971	6.00	15.00
Reprise RS-6466	(S)	Electric Warrior	1971	6.00	15.00
Reprise MS-2095	(S)	The Slider	1972	6.00	15.00
Reprise MS-2132	(S)	Tanx	1973	6.00	15.00
Casablanca NBLP-9006	(S)	Light Of Love	1974	5.00	12.00
T2					
London PS-583	(S)	It'll All Work Out In Boomland	1971	8.00	20.00
T.V. & THE TRIBESMEN					
Hanna Barbera H-9507	(M)	Barefootin'	1966	5.00	12.00
Hanna Barbera HST-9507	(S)	Barefootin'	1966	6.00	15.00
TAMPA RED					
Bluesville BV-1030	(M)	Don't Tampa With The Blues	1961	12.00	30.00
Bluesville BV-1043	(M)	Don't Jive With Me	1962	12.00	30.00
TAMS, THE					
ABC-Paramount 481	(M)	Presenting The Tams	1964	8.00	20.00
ABC-Paramount S-481	(E)	Presenting The Tams	1964	6.00	15.00
ABC-Paramount 499	(M)	Hey Girl Don't Bother Me	1964	6.00	15.00
ABC-Paramount S-499	(S)	Hey Girl Don't Bother Me	1964	8.00	20.00
ABC 596	(M)	Time For The Tams	1967	5.00	12.00
ABC S-596	(S)	Time For The Tams	1967	6.00	15.00
ABC S-673	(S)	A Portrait Of The Tams	1969	5.00	12.00
TANEGA, NORMA					
New Voice 2001	(M)	Walkin' My Cat Named Dog	1966	8.00	20.00
New Voice 2002	(S)	Walkin' My Cat Named Dog	1966	14.00	35.00
TANGERINE ZOO					
Mainstream S-6107	(S)	Tangerine Zoo	1968	8.00	20.00
Mainstream S-6116	(S)	Outside Looking In	1968	8.00	20.00
TANYET					
Vault LP-117	(S)	The Ceylib People	1968	6.00	15.00

Label		Title	Year	VG+	NM
TARRIERS, THE					
United Arts. UAL-4033	(M)	Hard Travelin'	1959	6.00	15.00
United Arts. UAS-5033	(S)	Hard Travelin'	1959	8.00	20.00
Atlantic 8042	(M)	Tell The World About This	1960	6.00	15.00
Atlantic SD-8042	(S)	Tell The World About This	1960	8.00	20.00
Decca DL-4342	(M)	The Tarriers	1962	5.00	12.00
Decca DL7-4342	(S)	The Tarriers	1962	6.00	15.00
Kapp KL-1349	(M)	The Original Tarriers	1963	5.00	12.00
Kapp KS-3349	(S)	The Original Tarriers	1963	6.00	15.00
TASTE					
Atco SD-33-296	(S)	Taste	1969	8.00	20.00
Atco SD-33-322	(S)	On The Boards	1970	8.00	20.00
TAVENER, JOHN					
Apple SMAS-3369	(S)	The Whale	1972	6.00	15.00
TAYLOR, BOBBY, & THE VANCOUVERS					
Gordy GS-930	(S)	Bobby Taylor And The Vancouvers	1968	6.00	15.00
Gordy GS-942	(S)	Taylor Made Soul	1968	5.00	12.00
TAYLOR, CATHIE					
Capitol T-1359	(M)	A Little Bit Of Sweetness	1960	5.00	12.00
Capitol ST-1359	(S)	A Little Bit Of Sweetness	1960	6.00	15.00
Capitol T-1448	(M)	The Tree Near My House	1961	5.00	12.00
Capitol ST-1448	(S)	The Tree Near My House	1961	6.00	15.00
Reprise R-6121	(M)	The Land And The People	1964	4.00	10.00
Reprise RS-6121	(S)	The Land And The People	1964	5.00	12.00
TAYLOR, EARL (& THE STONEY MOUNTAIN BOYS)					
United Arts. UAL-3049	(M)	Folk Songs From The Bluegrass	1960	6.00	15.00
United Arts. UAS-6049	(S)	Folk Songs From The Bluegrass	1960	8.00	20.00
Capitol T-2090	(M)	Bluegrass Taylor Made	1963	10.00	25.00
Capitol ST-2090	(S)	Bluegrass Taylor Made	1963	12.00	30.00
TAYLOR, JAMES					
Apple SKAO-3352	(S)	James Taylor	1969	6.00	15.00
Warners BS4-2866	(Q)	Gorilla	1975	5.00	12.00
TAYLOR, JOHNNIE					
Stax ST-715	(M)	Wanted: One Soul Singer	1967	8.00	20.00
Stax STS-715	(S)	Wanted: One Soul Singer	1967	8.00	20.00
Stax STS-2005	(S)	Who's Making Love?	1968	6.00	15.00
Stax STS-2008	(S)	Raw Blues	1969	6.00	15.00
Stax STS-2012	(S)	Rare Stamps	1969	6.00	15.00
Stax STS-2023	(S)	The Philosophy Continues	1969	6.00	15.00
Columbia PCQ-33951	(Q)	Eargasm	1976	5.00	12.00
Columbia PCQ-34401	(Q)	Rated Extraordinaire	1977	5.00	12.00
TAYLOR, KINGSIZE, & THE DOMINOS					
Midnight HLP-2101	(M)	Real Gonk Man		12.00	30.00
Midnight HST-2101	(S)	Real Gonk Man		14.00	35.00
TAYLOR, KOKO					
Chess LPS-1532	(S)	Koko Taylor	1968	6.00	15.00
TAYLOR, LITTLE JOHNNY					
Galaxy 203	(M)	Little Johnny Taylor	1963	10.00	25.00
Galaxy 8203	(S)	Little Johnny Taylor	1963	12.00	30.00
TAYLOR, MEL, & THE MAGICS					
Warners W-1624	(M)	Mel Taylor In Action	1966	6.00	15.00
Warners WS-1624	(S)	Mel Taylor In Action	1966	8.00	20.00
TAYLOR, TED					
OKeh 12104	(M)	Be Ever Wonderful	1963	6.00	15.00
OKeh 14104	(S)	Be Ever Wonderful	1963	8.00	20.00
OKeh 14109	(M)	Blues And Soul	1965	6.00	15.00
OKeh 14109	(S)	Blues And Soul	1965	8.00	20.00
OKeh 12113	(M)	Greatest Hits	1966	5.00	12.00
OKeh 14113	(S)	Greatest Hits	1966	6.00	15.00

The Teddy Bears. Featuring the soon-to-be "boy genius" Phil Spector, this album ranks as one of the most collectible of the '50s, mainly for its being one of the first true stereo rock releases. (And for Uncle Phil's involvement, of course.)

The Temptations Wish It Would Rain. This followed on the heels of the hit title tune and presented another strong showcase for the Temps unrivalled ensemble vocals, highlighted by David Ruffin's magnificent leads.

Label		Title	Year	VG+	NM
TEA COMPANY, THE					
Smash SRS-67105	(S)	Come And Have Some Tea	1968	8.00	20.00
TEDDY & THE PANDAS					
Tower ST-5125	(S)	Basic Magnetism	1968	10.00	25.00
TEDDY BEARS, THE					
Imperial LP-9067	(M)	The Teddy Bears Sing!	1959	180.00	300.00
Imperial SLP-12067	(S)	The Teddy Bears Sing!	1959	300.00	500.00
TEEMATES, THE					
Audio Fidelity DF-7042	(M)	Jet Set Dance Discotheque	1964	5.00	12.00
Audio Fidelity DFS-7042	(S)	Jet Set Dance Discotheque	1964	6.00	15.00
TEEN QUEENS, THE					
Crown CLP-5022	(M)	Eddie, My Love	1956	50.00	100.00
Crown CLP-5373	(M)	The Teen Queens	1963	16.00	40.00
TEENAGERS: *Refer to* **LYMON, FRANKIE, & THE TEENAGERS**					
TELEVISION					
Elektra 6E-133	(S)	Adventure	1978	6.00	15.00
Elektra 7E-1098	(S)	Marquee Moon	1976	6.00	15.00
TEMPO, NICK					
Liberty LRP-3023	(M)	Rock 'N Roll Beach Party	1958	16.00	40.00
TEMPO, NINO, & APRIL STEVENS					
Atco 33-156	(M)	Deep Purple	1963	8.00	20.00
Atco SD-33-156	(S)	Deep Purple	1963	10.00	25.00
Atco 33-162	(M)	Sing The Great Songs	1964	5.00	12.00
Atco SD-33-162	(S)	Sing The Great Songs	1964	6.00	15.00
Atco 33-180	(M)	Hey Baby	1966	5.00	12.00
Atco SD-33-180	(S)	Hey Baby	1966	6.00	15.00
White Whale 7113	(S)	All Strung Out	1969	5.00	12.00
TEMPOS, THE					
Justice 104	(M)	Speaking Of The Tempos	1966	210.00	350.00
TEMPTATIONS, THE					
Gordy G-911	(M)	Meet The Temptations	1964	8.00	20.00
Gordy GS-911	(S)	Meet The Temptations	1964	10.00	25.00
Gordy G-912	(M)	The Temptations Sing Smokey	1965	8.00	20.00
Gordy GS-912	(S)	The Temptations Sing Smokey	1965	10.00	25.00
Gordy G-914	(M)	Temptin' Temptations	1965	6.00	15.00
Gordy GS-914	(S)	Temptin' Temptations	1965	8.00	20.00
Gordy G-918	(M)	Gettin' Ready	1966	6.00	15.00
Gordy GS-918	(S)	Gettin' Ready	1966	8.00	20.00
Gordy G-919	(M)	The Temptations' Greatest Hits	1966	6.00	15.00
Gordy GS-919	(S)	The Temptations' Greatest Hits	1966	8.00	20.00
Gordy G-921	(M)	The Temptations Live	1967	6.00	15.00
Gordy GS-921	(S)	The Temptations Live	1967	8.00	20.00
Gordy G-922	(M)	With A Lot O' Soul	1967	6.00	15.00
Gordy GS-922	(S)	With A Lot O' Soul	1967	8.00	20.00
Gordy G-924	(M)	In A Mellow Mood	1967	6.00	15.00
Gordy GS-924	(S)	In A Mellow Mood	1967	8.00	20.00
Gordy GS-927	(S)	The Temptations Wish It Would Rain	1968	6.00	15.00
Gordy GS-933	(S)	The Temptations Show	1969	6.00	15.00
Gordy GS-938	(S)	Live At The Copa	1969	6.00	15.00
Gordy GS-939	(S)	Cloud Nine	1969	5.00	12.00
Gordy GS-947	(S)	Psychedelic Shack	1970	5.00	12.00
Gordy GS-949	(S)	Puzzle People	1969	5.00	12.00
Gordy GS-951	(S)	The Temptations' Christmas Album	1970	6.00	15.00
Gordy GS-953	(S)	Live At London's Talk Of The Town	1970	5.00	12.00
TEN YEARS AFTER					
Deram DES-18009	(S)	Ten Years After	1968	6.00	15.00
Deram DES-18016	(S)	Undead	1968	6.00	15.00
Deram DES-18021	(S)	Stonedhenge	1969	5.00	12.00
Deram DES-18029	(S)	Ssssh	1969	5.00	12.00
Deram DES-18038	(S)	Cricklewood Green	1970	5.00	12.00

Label		Title	Year	VG+	NM
Deram DES-18050	(S)	Watt	1970	5.00	12.00
Cotillion CT3-500	(S)	Woodstock (Sdtk)	1970	8.00	20.00
Cotillion CT2-400	(S)	Woodstock Two	1971	6.00	15.00
Columbia CQ-30801	(Q)	A Space In Time	1972	6.00	15.00

TERRELL, TAMMI
Also refer to Marvin Gaye and Chuck Jackson.

Motown 652	(M)	Irresistible Tammi	1967	6.00	15.00
Motown MS-652	(S)	Irresistible Tammi	1967	8.00	20.00

TEX, JOE

Checker 2993	(M)	Hold On	1964	12.00	30.00
King 935	(M)	The Best Of Joe Tex	1965	8.00	20.00
King KS-935	(S)	The Best Of Joe Tex	1965	10.00	25.00
Parrot 61002	(M)	The Best Of Joe Tex	1965	6.00	15.00
Parrot PAS-71002	(S)	The Best Of Joe Tex	1965	8.00	20.00
Atlantic 8106	(S)	Hold What You've Got	1965	6.00	15.00
Atlantic SD-8106	(S)	Hold What You've Got	1965	8.00	20.00
Atlantic 8115	(M)	The New Boss	1965	6.00	15.00
Atlantic SD-8115	(S)	The New Boss	1965	8.00	20.00
Atlantic 8124	(M)	The Love You Save	1966	6.00	15.00
Atlantic SD-8124	(S)	The Love You Save	1966	8.00	20.00
Atlantic 8133	(M)	I've Got To Do A Little Better	1966	5.00	12.00
Atlantic SD-8133	(S)	I've Got To Do A Little Better	1966	6.00	15.00
Atlantic 8144	(S)	The Best Of Joe Tex	1967	5.00	12.00
Atlantic SD-8144	(S)	The Best Of Joe Tex	1967	6.00	15.00
Atlantic SD-8156	(S)	Live And Lively	1968	5.00	12.00
Atlantic SD-8187	(S)	Soul Country	1968	5.00	12.00
Atlantic SD-8211	(S)	Happy Soul	1969	5.00	12.00
Atlantic SD-8231	(S)	Buying A Book	1969	5.00	12.00
Atlantic SD-8254	(S)	With Strings And Things	1970	4.00	10.00
Atlantic SD-8292	(S)	From The Roots Came The Rapper	1972	4.00	10.00

THEE IMAGE

Manticore MA6-50451	(S)	Thee Image	1975	5.00	12.00
Manticore MA6-50651	(S)	Inside The Triangle	1975	5.00	12.00

THEE MIDNIGHTERS

Chattahoochee CS-1001	(S)	Thee Midniters	1965	14.00	35.00
Whittier W-5000	(M)	Bring You Love Special Delivery	1966	10.00	25.00
Whittier W-5001	(M)	Unlimited	1966	10.00	25.00
Whittier WS-5002	(S)	The Giants	1967	10.00	25.00

THEE PROPHETS

Kapp KS-3596	(S)	Playgirl	1969	8.00	20.00

THEM

Parrot PS-61005	(M)	Them	1965	16.00	40.00
Parrot PAS-71005	(E)	Them	1965	14.00	35.00
Parrot PA-61008	(M)	Them Again	1966	12.00	30.00
Parrot PAS-71008	(S)	Them Again	1966	14.00	35.00
Tower ST-5104	(S)	Now And Them	1968	16.00	40.00
Tower ST-5116	(S)	Time Out! Time In For Them	1968	16.00	40.00
Happy Tiger 1004	(S)	Them	1969	16.00	40.00
Happy Tiger 1012	(S)	In Reality	1971	16.00	40.00

THIRD POWER, THE

Vanguard VSD-6554	(S)	The Third Power Believe	1970	6.00	15.00

THIRD RAIL, THE

Epic LN-24327	(M)	Id Music	1967	12.00	30.00
Epic BN-26327	(S)	Id Music	1967	14.00	35.00

THIRTEENTH FLOOR ELEVATORS, THE

International Arts. 1	(M)	Psychedelic Sounds	1967	16.00	40.00
International Arts. 1	(S)	Psychedelic Sounds	1967	12.00	30.00
International Arts. 5	(M)	Easter Everywhere	1967	16.00	40.00
International Arts. 5	(S)	Easter Everywhere	1967	12.00	30.00
International Arts. 8	(S)	Live	1968	12.00	30.00
International Arts. 9	(S)	Bull Of The Woods	1968	12.00	30.00

(Reissues have "Masterfonics" in the trail-off vinyL)

Label		Title	Year	VG+	NM
31ST OF FEBRUARY, THE					
Vanguard VSD-6503	(S)	The 31st Of February	1969	8.00	20.00
THOMAS, B.J.					
Pacemaker PLP-3001	(M)	B.J. Thomas And The Triumphs		16.00	40.00
Hickory LP-133	(M)	The Very Best Of B.J. Thomas	1966	8.00	20.00
Hickory LPS-133	(S)	The Very Best Of B.J. Thomas	1966	8.00	20.00
Scepter SP-535	(M)	I'm So Lonesome I Could Cry	1966	6.00	15.00
Scepter SPS-535	(S)	I'm So Lonesome I Could Cry	1966	8.00	20.00
Scepter SP-556	(M)	Tomorrow Never Comes	1966	5.00	12.00
Scepter SPS-556	(S)	Tomorrow Never Comes	1966	6.00	15.00
Scepter SP-561	(M)	B.J. Thomas Sings For Lovers And Losers	1967	5.00	12.00
Scepter SPS-561	(S)	B.J. Thomas Sings For Lovers And Losers	1967	6.00	15.00
THOMAS, CARLA					
Atlantic 8057	(M)	Gee Whiz	1961	30.00	60.00
Stax 709	(M)	Carla	1966	10.00	25.00
Stax STS-709	(S)	Carla	1966	12.00	30.00
Stax ST-706	(M)	Comfort Me	1966	10.00	25.00
Stax STS-706	(S)	Comfort Me	1966	12.00	30.00
Stax 716	(M)	The King And Queen (With Otis Redding)	1967	10.00	25.00
Stax S-716	(S)	The King And Queen (With Otis Redding)	1967	12.00	30.00
Stax 718	(M)	The Queen Alone	1967	10.00	25.00
Stax STS-718	(S)	The Queen Alone	1967	12.00	30.00
Atlantic SD-8232	(S)	The Best Carla Thomas	1969	8.00	20.00
Stax STS-2019	(S)	Memphis Queen	1969	6.00	15.00
Stax STS-2044	(S)	Love Means Carla Thomas	1971	6.00	15.00
THOMAS, IRMA					
Imperial LP-9266	(M)	Wish Someone Would Care	1964	8.00	20.00
Imperial LP-12266	(S)	Wish Someone Would Care	1964	10.00	25.00
Imperial 9302	(M)	Take A Look	1966	8.00	20.00
Imperial LP-12302	(S)	Take A Look	1966	10.00	25.00
Fungus FB-25150	(S)	In Between Tears	1973	6.00	15.00
THOMAS, JEANNIE					
Strand 1030	(M)	Jeannie Thomas Sings For The Boys	1961	6.00	15.00
THOMAS, JOE, & BILL ELLIOTT					
Sue 1025	(S)	Speak Your Piece	1964	6.00	15.00
THOMAS, JON					
ABC-Paramount 351	(M)	Heartbreak	1960	6.00	15.00
ABC-Paramount S-351	(S)	Heartbreak	1960	8.00	20.00
THOMAS, KID, & THE ALGIERS STOMPERS					
Riverside 9-386	(M)	New Orleans-Living Legends-Series	1961	8.00	20.00
THOMAS, RUFUS					
Stax 704	(M)	Walking The Dog	1963	20.00	50.00
THOMPSON, HANK (& THE BRAZOS VALLEY BOYS)					
Capitol H-418 (10")	(M)	Songs Of The Brazos Valley	1953	20.00	50.00
Capitol H-618 (10")	(M)	North Of The Rio Grande	1955	20.00	50.00
Capitol H-729 (10")	(M)	New Recordings Of Hank's All-Time Hits	1956	20.00	50.00
Capitol H-911 (10")	(M)	Hank Thompson Favorites	1956	20.00	50.00
Capitol T-418	(M)	Songs Of The Brazos Valley	1956	16.00	40.00
Capitol T-618	(M)	North Of The Rio Grande	1956	16.00	40.00
Capitol T-729	(M)	New Recordings Of Hank's All-Time Hits	1956	16.00	40.00
Capitol T-826	(M)	Hank	1957	14.00	35.00
Capitol T-911	(M)	Hank Thompson Favorites	1957	14.00	35.00
Capitol T-975	(M)	Hank Thompson's Dance Ranch	1958	14.00	35.00
		(Capitol albums above have turquoise or grey labels.)			
Capitol T-1111	(M)	Favorite Waltzes	1959	10.00	25.00
Capitol T-1246	(M)	Songs For Rounders	1959	8.00	20.00
Capitol ST-1246	(S)	Songs For Rounders	1959	10.00	25.00
Capitol T-1360	(M)	Most Of All	1960	8.00	20.00
Capitol ST-1360	(S)	Most Of All	1960	10.00	25.00
Capitol T-1469	(M)	This Broken Heart Of Mine	1960	8.00	20.00
Capitol ST-1469	(S)	This Broken Heart Of Mine	1960	10.00	25.00

Label		Title	Year	VG+	NM
Capitol T-1544	(M)	An Old Love Affair	1961	5.00	12.00
Capitol ST-1544	(S)	An Old Love Affair	1961	6.00	15.00
Capitol T-1632	(M)	At The Golden Nugget	1961	5.00	12.00
Capitol ST-1632	(S)	At The Golden Nugget	1961	6.00	15.00
Capitol T-1741	(M)	The #1 Country And Western Band	1962	6.00	15.00
Capitol DT-1741	(E)	The #1 Country And Western Band	1962	5.00	12.00
		(Capitol albums above have black labels			
		with the Capitol logo on the left side.)			
Capitol T-1775	(M)	Cheyenne Frontier Days	1962	5.00	12.00
Capitol ST-1775	(S)	Cheyenne Frontier Days	1962	6.00	15.00
Capitol T-1878	(M)	The Best Of Hank Thompson	1963	5.00	12.00
Capitol ST-1878	(P)	The Best Of Hank Thompson	1963	6.00	15.00
Capitol T-1955	(M)	At The State Fair Of Texas	1963	6.00	15.00
Capitol DT-1955	(E)	At The State Fair Of Texas	1963	5.00	12.00
Capitol T-2089	(M)	Golden Country Hits	1964	5.00	12.00
Capitol ST-2089	(S)	Golden Country Hits	1964	6.00	15.00
Capitol T-2154	(M)	It's Christmas Time	1964	5.00	12.00
Capitol ST-2154	(S)	It's Christmas Time	1964	6.00	15.00
Capitol T-2274	(M)	Breakin' In Another Heart	1965	5.00	12.00
Capitol ST-2274	(S)	Breakin' In Another Heart	1965	6.00	15.00
Capitol T-2342	(M)	The Luckiest Heartache In Town	1965	5.00	12.00
Capitol ST-2342	(S)	The Luckiest Heartache In Town	1965	6.00	15.00
Capitol T-2460	(M)	A Six Pack To Go	1966	6.00	15.00
Capitol DT-2460	(E)	A Six Pack To Go	1966	5.00	12.00
Capitol T-2575	(M)	Breakin' The Rules	1966	5.00	12.00
Capitol ST-2575	(S)	Breakin' The Rules	1966	6.00	15.00
Capitol T-2661	(M)	The Best Of Hank Thompson, Volume 2	1967	5.00	12.00
Capitol ST-2661	(S)	The Best Of Hank Thompson, Volume 2	1967	6.00	15.00
Capitol T-2826	(M)	Just An Old Flame	1967	5.00	12.00
Capitol ST-2826	(S)	Just An Old Flame	1967	6.00	15.00
		(Capitol albums above have black labels			
		with the Capitol logo on top.)			

THOMPSON, HAYDEN

Label		Title	Year	VG+	NM
Kapp KL-1507	(M)	Here's Hayden Thompson	1966	10.00	25.00
Kapp KS-3507	(S)	Here's Hayden Thompson	1966	12.00	30.00

THOMPSON, KAY

Label		Title	Year	VG+	NM
MGM E-3146	(M)	Kay Thompson		10.00	25.00

THOMPSON, SONNY

Label		Title	Year	VG+	NM
King 568	(M)	Moody Blues	1956	50.00	100.00
King 655	(M)	Mellow Blues For The Late Hours	1959	35.00	70.00

THOMPSON'S BRAZOS VALLEY BOYS, HANK

Label		Title	Year	VG+	NM
Warners W-1664	(M)	Where Is The Circus	1966	5.00	12.00
Warners WS-1664	(S)	Where Is The Circus	1966	6.00	15.00
Warners W-1679	(M)	The Countrypolitan Sound	1967	5.00	12.00
Warners WS-1679	(S)	The Countrypolitan Sound	1967	6.00	15.00
Warners W-1686	(M)	The Gold Standard Collection	1967	5.00	12.00
Warners WS-1686	(S)	The Gold Standard Collection	1967	6.00	15.00
Dot DLP-25978	(S)	The Instrumental Sound	1970	5.00	12.00

THORINSHIELD

Label		Title	Year	VG+	NM
Phillips PHS-600251	(S)	Thorinshield	1968	5.00	12.00

THORNTON, BIG MAMA

Label		Title	Year	VG+	NM
Mercury SRM-1-61225	(S)	Stronger Than Dirt	1969	8.00	20.00
Mercury SRM-1-61249	(S)	The Way It Is	1970	8.00	20.00
Roulette SR-42050	(S)	Maybe	1970	6.00	15.00
Back Beat BLP-68	(S)	She's Back	1970	6.00	15.00

THORNTON, TERI

Label		Title	Year	VG+	NM
Riverside 352	(M)	Devil May Care	1960	6.00	15.00
Riverside 9352	(S)	Devil May Care	1960	8.00	20.00
Dauntless 4306	(M)	Somewhere In The Night	1963	6.00	15.00
Dauntless 6306	(S)	Somewhere In The Night	1963	8.00	20.00
Columbia CL-2094	(M)	Open Highway	1963	6.00	15.00
Columbia CS-8894	(S)	Open Highway	1963	8.00	20.00

Three Dog Night, *It Ain't Easy*. At the height of their incredible popularity, Three Dog Night released this cover attired only in their birthday suits. It was deemed "unsuitable" and recalled to be replaced with the more familiar cover. This was not the first time one of their covers would cause a controversy...

The Trade Winds, *Excursions*. The Trade Winds scored with two moderate hits in the mid '70s, the now classic "New York's A Lonely Town" (which portrays the underside of Brian Wilson's California dream odes) and the mildly psychedelic "Mind Excursion." This, their sole LP release, is slowly gaining recognition amongst collectors of '60s pop.

Label		Title	Year	VG+	NM
THREE CHUCKLES, THE					
Vik LX-1067	(M)	The Three Chuckles	1956	40.00	80.00
THREE D'S, THE					
Capitol T-2171	(M)	New Dimensions In Folk Songs	1964	4.00	10.00
Capitol ST-2171	(S)	New Dimensions In Folk Songs	1964	5.00	12.00
THREE DOG NIGHT					
Dunhill DS-50048	(S)	Three Dog Night	1968	5.00	12.00
Dunhill DS-50078	(S)	It Ain't Easy	1970	16.00	40.00
		(The cover has a nude portrait of the group.)			
Dunhill DSD-50168	(S)	Hard Labor	1974	6.00	15.00
		(The cover depicts a hospital delivery with			
		a woman giving birth to a record album.)			
Dunhill DSD-50168	(S)	Hard Labor	1974	3.50	8.00
		(The delivery has a band-aid pasted over it.)			
Dunhill DSD-50168	(S)	Hard Labor	1974	2.50	6.00
		(The delivery has a band-aid printed over it.)			
Command QD-40014	(Q)	Hard Labor	1974	5.00	12.00
Command QD-40018	(Q)	Coming Down Your Way	1975	5.00	12.00
THREE FACES WEST					
Outpost 1000	(S)	Three Faces West		8.00	20.00
THREE FLAMES, THE					
Mercury MG-20239	(M)	At The Bon Soir	1957	12.00	30.00
THREE GIRLS					
Phantom BPL1-0955	(S)	The Deadly Nightshade	1975	4.00	10.00
THREE MAN ARMY					
Kama Sutra SKBS-2044	(S)	A Third Of A Lifetime	1971	8.00	20.00
		(Pink label, fold open cover.)			
Reprise MS-2150	(S)	Three Man Army	1973	6.00	15.00
Reprise MS-2182	(S)	Three Man Army Two	1974	6.00	15.00
THREE STOOGES, THE					
Vocalion VL7-3823	(E)	The Three Stooges Sing For Kids	1968	12.00	30.00
THREE SUNS, THE					
RCA LPM-1041	(M)	Soft And Sweet	1955	14.00	35.00
RCA LPM-1249	(M)	High Fi And Wide	1956	14.00	35.00
RCA LPM-1333	(M)	Midnight For Two	1957	14.00	35.00
THRILLINGTON, PERCY "THRILLS" (PAUL McCARTNEY)					
Capitol ST-11642	(S)	Thrillington	1977	20.00	50.00
THUNDER, JOHNNY					
Diamond D-5001	(M)	Loop De Loop	1963	20.00	50.00
Diamond SD-5001	(S)	Loop De Loop	1963	30.00	60.00
THUNDERBIRDS, THE					
Red Feather TH-1	(M)	Meet The Fabulous Thunderbirds		100.00	200.00
THUNDERCLAP NEWMAN					
Track SD-8264	(S)	Hollywood Dream	1970	8.00	20.00
TIDE, THE					
Mouth 7237	(S)	Almost Live		20.00	50.00
TIDES, THE					
Mercury MG-20714	(M)	Limbo Rock	1962	5.00	12.00
Mercury SR-60714	(S)	Limbo Rock	1962	6.00	15.00
Wing MGW-12248	(M)	The Best Of Bossa Nova	1963	5.00	12.00
Wing SRW-16248	(S)	The Best Of Bossa Nova	1963	6.00	15.00
Wing MGW-12265	(M)	Surf City And Other Surfin' Favorites	1963	8.00	20.00
Wing SRW-16265	(S)	Surf City And Other Surfin' Favorites	1963	10.00	25.00
TIEKIN, FREDDIE, & THE ROCKERS					
I.T. 2301	(M)	By Popular Demand	1957	20.00	50.00
I.T. 2304	(M)	Freddie Tieken And The Rockers	1958	20.00	50.00

Label		Title	Year	VG+	NM
TIFFANY SHADE					
Mainstream 56105	(S)	Tiffany Shade	1968	6.00	15.00
TIJUANA BEATLES, THE					
Alshire 5165	(S)	The Tijuana Beatles	1969	6.00	15.00
TIKIS, THE					
Phillips PHM-200043	(M)	The Tikis	1962	8.00	20.00
Phillips PHS-600043	(S)	The Tikis	1962	10.00	25.00
TIL, SONNY, & THE ORIOLES					
RCA LSP-4451	(S)	Sonny Til Returns	1970	6.00	15.00
RCA LSP-4538	(S)	Old Gold/New Gold	1970	6.00	15.00
TILLOTSON, JOHNNY					
Cadence 3052	(M)	Johnny Tillotson's Best	1961	10.00	25.00
Cadence CLP-25052	(P)	Johnny Tillotson's Best	1961	12.00	30.00
Cadence 3058	(M)	It Keeps Right On A-Hurtin'	1962	10.00	25.00
Cadence CLP-25058	(S)	It Keeps Right On A-Hurtin'	1962	12.00	30.00
Cadence CLP-3067	(M)	You Can Never Stop Me Loving You	1963	8.00	20.00
Cadence CLP-25067	(S)	You Can Never Stop Me Loving You	1963	10.00	25.00
MGM E-4188	(M)	Talk Back Trembling Lips	1964	5.00	12.00
MGM SE-4188	(S)	Talk Back Trembling Lips	1964	6.00	15.00
MGM E-4224	(M)	The Tillotson Touch	1964	5.00	12.00
MGM SE-4224	(S)	The Tillotson Touch	1964	6.00	15.00
MGM E-4270	(M)	She Understands Me	1964	5.00	12.00
MGM SE-4270	(S)	She Understands Me	1964	6.00	15.00
MGM E-4302	(M)	That's My Style	1965	5.00	12.00
MGM SE-4302	(S)	That's My Style	1965	6.00	15.00
MGM E-4328	(M)	Our World	1965	5.00	12.00
MGM SE-4328	(S)	Our World	1965	6.00	15.00
MGM E-4395	(M)	No Love At All	1966	5.00	12.00
MGM SE-4395	(S)	No Love At All	1966	6.00	15.00
MGM E-4402	(M)	The Christmas Touch	1966	5.00	12.00
MGM SE-4402	(S)	The Christmas Touch	1966	6.00	15.00
MGM E-4452	(M)	Here I Am	1967	5.00	12.00
MGM SE-4452	(S)	Here I Am	1967	6.00	15.00
TITANS, THE					
MGM E-3992	(M)	Today's Teen Beat	1961	10.00	25.00
MGM SE-3992	(S)	Today's Teen Beat	1961	12.00	30.00
TOAD HALL					
Liberty LST-7580	(S)	Toad Hall	1968	6.00	15.00
TOADS, THE					
Wiggins 64021	(M)	The Toads	1964	100.00	200.00
TOKENS, THE					
RCA LPM-2514	(M)	The Lion Sleeps Tonight	1961	16.00	40.00
RCA LSP-2514	(S)	The Lion Sleeps Tonight	1961	20.00	50.00
RCA LPM-2631	(M)	We, The Tokens, Sing Folk	1962	10.00	25.00
RCA LSP-2631	(S)	We, The Tokens, Sing Folk	1962	12.00	30.00
RCA LPM-2886	(M)	Wheels	1964	10.00	25.00
RCA LST-2886	(S)	Wheels	1964	12.00	30.00
RCA LPM-3685	(M)	The Tokens Again	1966	10.00	25.00
RCA LSP-3685	(S)	The Tokens Again	1966	12.00	30.00
B.T. Puppy 1000	(M)	I Hear Trumpets Blow	1966	8.00	20.00
B.T. Puppy S-1000	(P)	I Hear Trumpets Blow	1966	10.00	25.00
B.T. Puppy 1002	(M)	Back To Back (With the Happenings)	1967	5.00	12.00
B.T. Puppy S-1002	(S)	Back To Back (With the Happenings)	1967	6.00	15.00
B.T. Puppy S-1006	(S)	Tokens Of Gold	1969	10.00	25.00
B.T. Puppy S-1012	(S)	Greatest Moments	1970	10.00	25.00
B.T. Puppy S-1014	(S)	December 5th	1971	10.00	25.00
Buddah BDS-5059	(S)	Both Sides Now	1971	6.00	15.00
TOM & JERRY (CHARLIE TOMLINSON & JERRY KENNEDY)					
Mercury MG-20626	(M)	Guitar's Greatest Hits	1961	5.00	12.00
Mercury SR-60626	(S)	Guitar's Greatest Hits	1961	6.00	15.00
Mercury MG-20671	(M)	Guitars Play The Sound Of Ray Charles	1962	5.00	12.00
Mercury SR-60671	(S)	Guitars Play The Sound Of Ray Charles	1962	6.00	15.00

Label		Title	Year	VG+	NM
Mercury MG-20756	(M)	Guitar's Greatest Hits, Volume 2	1962	5.00	12.00
Mercury SR-60756	(S)	Guitar's Greatest Hits, Volume 2	1962	6.00	15.00
Mercury MG-20842	(M)	Surfin' Hootenanny	1963	6.00	15.00
Mercury SR-60842	(S)	Surfin' Hootenanny	1963	8.00	20.00

TOMORROW

Sire SES-97912	(S)	Tomorrow	1968	10.00	25.00

TONEY, OSCAR, JR.

Bell 6006	(M)	For Your Precious Love	1967	6.00	15.00
Bell S-6006	(S)	For Your Precious Love	1967	8.00	20.00

TONTO'S EXPANDING HEAD BAND

Embryo SD-732	(S)	Zero Time	1971	8.00	20.00

TOPSIDERS

Josie J-4000	(M)	Rock Goes Folk	1963	5.00	12.00
Josie JS-4000	(S)	Rock Goes Folk	1963	6.00	15.00

TORME, MEL

MGM 552 (10")	(M)	Songs	1952	16.00	40.00
Coral CRL-57012	(M)	Mel Torme At The Crescendo	1954	14.00	35.00
Coral CRL-57044	(M)	Musical Soundings	1954	14.00	35.00
Bethlehem BCP-34	(M)	It's A Blue World	1955	14.00	35.00
Bethlehem BCP-52	(M)	Mel Torme	1956	14.00	35.00
Bethlehem BCP-6013	(M)	Mel Torme Sings Fred Astaire	1958	14.00	35.00
Bethlehem BCP-6016	(M)	California Suite	1958	14.00	35.00
Bethlehem BCP-6020	(M)	Mel Torme At The Crescendo	1958	14.00	35.00
Bethlehem BCP-6031	(M)	Song For Any Taste	1959	14.00	35.00
Verve V-2105	(M)	Torme	1958	10.00	25.00
Verve V-2117	(M)	Ole Torme	1959	10.00	25.00
Verve V-2120	(M)	Back In Town	1959	10.00	25.00
Verve V-2132	(M)	Mel Torme Swings Schubert Alley	1960	10.00	25.00
Strand 1076	(M)	Mel Torme Sings	1960	8.00	20.00
Strand S-1076	(S)	Mel Torme Sings	1960	10.00	25.00
Verve V-2144	(M)	Swingin' On The Moon	1960	8.00	20.00
Verve V6-2144	(S)	Swingin' On The Moon	1960	10.00	25.00
Verve V-2146	(M)	Broadway Right Now	1961	8.00	20.00
Verve V6-2146	(S)	Broadway Right Now	1961	10.00	25.00
Verve V-8440	(M)	My Kind Of Music	1961	8.00	20.00
Verve V6-8440	(S)	My Kind Of Music	1961	10.00	25.00
Verve V-8491	(M)	I Dig The Duke, I Dig The Count	1961	8.00	20.00
Verve V6-8491	(S)	I Dig The Duke, I Dig The Count	1961	10.00	25.00
Atlantic 8066	(M)	Mel Torme At The Red Hill	1962	8.00	20.00
Atlantic SD-8066	(S)	Mel Torme At The Red Hill	1962	10.00	25.00
Atlantic 8069	(M)	Comin' Home, Baby	1962	10.00	25.00
Atlantic SD-8069	(S)	Comin' Home, Baby	1962	12.00	30.00
Atlantic 8091	(M)	Sunday In New York	1963	10.00	25.00
Atlantic SD-8091	(S)	Sunday In New York	1963	12.00	30.00
Columbia CL-2318	(M)	That's All	1964	6.00	15.00
Columbia CS-9118	(S)	That's All	1964	8.00	20.00
Metro 523	(M)	I Wished On The Moon	1965	5.00	12.00
Metro S-523	(S)	I Wished On The Moon	1965	6.00	15.00

TORNADOES, THE (THE HOLLYWOOD TORNADOES)

Josie 4005	(M)	Bustin' Surfboards	1963	50.00	100.00

TORNADOS, THE

London LL-3279	(M)	Telstar	1962	14.00	35.00
London LL-3293	(M)	The Sounds Of The Tornados	1963	12.00	30.00

TORQUES, THE

Wiggins 64010	(M)	Zoom!	1964	75.00	150.00
Lemco 604	(M)	Live		50.00	100.00

TOUCH, THE

Coliseum DS-51004	(S)	The Touch	1968	8.00	20.00

TOUCHSTONE

United Arts. UAS-5563	(S)	Tarot	1972	10.00	25.00

Label		Title	Year	VG+	NM
TOUSSAINT, ALLEN					
RCA LPM-1767	(M)	The Wild Sound Of New Orleans	1958	35.00	70.00
Scepter 24003	(S)	Toussaint	1971	6.00	15.00
Reprise MS-2062	(S)	Life, Love And Faith	1972	5.00	12.00
TOURISTS, THE					
Epic NJE-36386	(S)	Reality Effect	1979	4.00	10.00
Epic NJE-36757	(S)	Luminous Basement	1980	4.00	10.00
TOWER OF POWER					
San Francisco 204	(S)	East Bay Grease	1971	8.00	20.00
TOWNSEND, HENRY					
Bluesville BV-1041	(M)	Tired Of Bein' Mistreated	1962	10.00	25.00
TOWNSHEND, PETE					
Track 79189	(S)	Who Came First	1972	8.00	20.00
TOYS, THE					
DynoVoice 9002	(M)	A Lovers Concerto/Attack	1966	10.00	25.00
DynoVoice 9002	(S)	A Lovers Concerto/Attack	1966	12.00	30.00
TRADEWINDS, THE					
Kama Sutra KLP-8057	(M)	Excursions	1967	8.00	20.00
Kama Sutra KLPS-8057	(S)	Excursions	1967	10.00	25.00
TRAFFIC					
United Arts. UAS-6651	(S)	Heaven Is In Your Mind	1968	12.00	30.00
United Arts. UAS-6651	(S)	Mr. Fantasy		6.00	15.00
		(U.A. albums above have black labels.)			
United Arts. UAS-6676	(S)	Traffic	1968	5.00	12.00
United Arts. UAS-6702	(S)	Last Exit	1969	5.00	12.00
United Arts. UAS-5500	(S)	The Best Of Traffic	1969	5.00	12.00
		(U.A. albums above have purple & orange labels.)			
TRAMMELL, BOBBY LEE					
Atlantic LPM-1503	(M)	Arkansas Twist	1962	35.00	70.00
TRASHMEN, THE					
Garrett GA-200	(M)	Surfin' Bird	1964	30.00	60.00
Garrett GAS-200	(S)	Surfin' Bird	1964	35.00	70.00
TRAVELLERS, THE					
Kapp KL-1051	(M)	Journey With The Travellers	1960	5.00	12.00
Kapp KS-3051	(S)	Journey With The Travellers	1960	6.00	15.00
Epic LN-124013	(M)	Introducing The Travellers	1962	4.00	10.00
Epic BN-26013	(S)	Introducing The Travellers	1962	5.00	12.00
TRAVIS, MERLE					
Capitol T-650	(M)	The Merle Travis Guitar	1956	20.00	50.00
Capitol T-891	(M)	Back Home	1957	14.00	35.00
Capitol T-1391	(M)	Walkin' The Strings	1960	12.00	30.00
Capitol T-1664	(M)	Travis	1962	6.00	15.00
Capitol ST-1664	(S)	Travis	1962	8.00	20.00
Capitol T-1956	(M)	Songs Of The Coal Mines	1963	6.00	15.00
Capitol ST-1956	(S)	Songs Of The Coal Mines	1963	8.00	20.00
Capitol T-2662	(M)	The Best Of Merle Travis	1967	6.00	15.00
Capitol ST-2662	(P)	The Best Of Merle Travis	1967	5.00	12.00
Capitol ST-2938	(S)	Strictly Guitar	1969	4.00	10.00
Capitol ST-249	(S)	Great Songs Of The Delmore Brothers	1969	4.00	10.00
TREMELOES, THE					
Also refer to Brian Poole & the Tremeloes.					
Epic LN-24310	(M)	Here Comes My Baby	1967	10.00	25.00
Epic BN-26310	(E)	Here Comes My Baby	1967	8.00	20.00
Epic LN-24326	(M)	Even The Bad Times Are Good	1967	10.00	25.00
Epic BN-26326	(P)	Even The Bad Times Are Good	1967	8.00	20.00
Epic LN-24363	(M)	Suddenly You Love Me	1968	8.00	20.00
Epic BN-26363	(E)	Suddenly You Love Me	1968	6.00	15.00
Epic BN-26388	(S)	World Explosion '58/'68	1968	8.00	20.00

Label		Title	Year	VG+	NM
TRENIERS, THE					
Epic LG-3125	(M)	The Treniers On TV		20.00	50.00
Dot DLP-3257	(M)	Souvenir Album	1960	16.00	40.00
TROGGS, THE					
Atco 33-193	(M)	Wild Thing	1966	12.00	30.00
Atco SD-33-193	(E)	Wild Thing	1966	10.00	25.00
Fontana SR-27556	(M)	The Troggs	1966	10.00	25.00
Fontana SRF-67556	(E)	The Troggs	1966	8.00	20.00
Fontana SRF-67576	(E)	Love Ia All Around	1968	10.00	25.00
Sire SASH-3714-2	(M)	Vintage Years	1976	6.00	15.00
TROY, DORIS					
Atlantic 8088	(M)	Just One Look	1964	10.00	25.00
Atlantic SD-8088	(S)	Just One Look	1964	14.00	35.00
Apple ST-3371	(S)	Doris Troy	1970	8.00	20.00
TRUMPETEERS, THE					
Score 4021	(M)	Milky White Way		50.00	100.00
TUBB, ERNEST (& THE TEXAS TROUBADORS)					
Also refer to Loretta Lynn.					
Decca DL-5301 (10")	(M)	Favorites	1951	20.00	50.00
Decca DL-5334 (10")	(M)	Old Rugged Cross	1951	20.00	50.00
Decca DL-5336 (10")	(M)	Jimmie Rodgers Songs	1951	20.00	50.00
Decca DL-5497 (10")	(M)	Sing A Song Of Christmas	1954	20.00	50.00
Decca DL-8291	(M)	Favorites	1956	16.00	40.00
Decca DL-8553	(M)	The Daddy Of 'Em All	1956	16.00	40.00
Decca DL-8834	(M)	The Importance Of Being Ernest	1959	10.00	25.00
Decca DL7-8834	(S)	The Importance Of Being Ernest	1959	14.00	35.00
Decca DXA-159	(M)	The Ernest Tubb Story (With booklet)	1958	14.00	35.00
Decca DXSA7-159	(E)	The Ernest Tubb Story (With booklet)	1958	10.00	25.00
		(Decca albums above have black & silver labels.)			
Decca DL-4042	(M)	Record Shop	1960	8.00	20.00
Decca DL7-4042	(S)	Record Shop	1960	10.00	25.00
Decca DL-4045	(M)	Midnight Jamboree	1960	8.00	20.00
Decca DL7-4045	(S)	Midnight Jamboree	1960	10.00	25.00
Decca DL-4046	(M)	All Time Hits	1961	8.00	20.00
Decca DL7-4046	(S)	All Time Hits	1961	10.00	25.00
Decca D7-4118	(M)	Ernest Tubb's Golden Favorites	1961	8.00	20.00
Decca DL7-4118	(S)	Ernest Tubb's Golden Favorites	1961	10.00	25.00
Decca DL-4321	(M)	On Tour	1962	8.00	20.00
Decca DL7-4321	(S)	On Tour	1962	10.00	25.00
Decca DL-4385	(M)	Just Call Me Lonesome	1964	8.00	20.00
Decca DL7-4385	(S)	Just Call Me Lonesome	1964	10.00	25.00
Decca DL-4397	(M)	The Family Bible	1963	6.00	15.00
Decca DL7-4397	(S)	The Family Bible	1963	8.00	20.00
Decca DL-4514	(M)	Thanks A Lot	1964	6.00	15.00
Decca DL7-4514	(S)	Thanks A Lot	1964	8.00	20.00
Decca DL-4518	(M)	Blue Christmas	1964	6.00	15.00
Decca DL7-4518	(S)	Blue Christmas	1964	8.00	20.00
Decca DL-4640	(M)	My Pick Of The Hits	1965	6.00	15.00
Decca DL7-4640	(S)	My Pick Of The Hits	1965	8.00	20.00
Decca DL-4644	(M)	Country Dance Time	1965	6.00	15.00
Decca DL7-4644	(S)	Country Dance Time	1965	8.00	20.00
Decca DL-4681	(M)	Hittin' The Road	1965	6.00	15.00
Decca DL7-4681	(S)	Hittin' The Road	1965	8.00	20.00
Decca DL-4746	(M)	By Request	1966	6.00	15.00
Decca DL7-4746	(S)	By Request	1966	8.00	20.00
Decca DL-4772	(M)	Country Hits, Old And New	1966	6.00	15.00
Decca DL7-4772	(S)	Country Hits, Old And New	1966	8.00	20.00
		(Decca albums above have black labels with "Mfrd by Decca" beneath the rainbow.)			
TUBB'S TEXAS TROUBADORS, ERNEST					
Decca DL-4459	(M)	The Texas Troubadors	1964	6.00	15.00
Decca DL7-4459	(S)	The Texas Troubadors	1964	8.00	20.00
Decca DL-4745	(M)	Ernest Tubb's Fabulous Texas Troubadors	1966	6.00	15.00
Decca DL7-4745	(S)	Ernest Tubb's Fabulous Texas Troubadors	1966	8.00	20.00
Decca DL7-5017	(S)	The Terrific Texas Troubadors	1968	6.00	15.00

Label		Title	Year	VG+	NM
TUCKER, TOMMY					
Checker 2990	(M)	Hi Heel Sneakers	1964	20.00	50.00
TUNETOPPERS, THE					
Amy A-1	(M)	At The Madison Dance Party	1960	14.00	35.00
Amy A-1	(P)	At The Madison Dance Party	1960	20.00	50.00
TURNER, IKE AND TINA					
Sue LP-2001	(M)	The Sound Of Ike And Tina Turner	1961	30.00	60.00
Sue LP-2003	(M)	Dance With Ike And Tina Turner	1962	30.00	60.00
Sue LP-2004	(M)	Dynamite	1963	30.00	60.00
Sue LP-2005	(M)	Don't Play Me Cheap	1963	30.00	60.00
Sue LP-2007	(M)	It's Gonna Work Out Fine	1963	30.00	60.00
Sue LP-1038	(M)	Ike And Tina Turner's Greatest Hits	1965	20.00	50.00
Kent K-519	(M)	The Soul Of Ike And Tina	1961	5.00	12.00
Kent KST-519	(S)	The Soul Of Ike And Tina	1961	5.00	12.00
Kent K-538	(M)	Festival Of Live Performances	1962	6.00	15.00
Kent KST-538	(S)	Festival Of Live Performances	1962	5.00	12.00
Kent K-550	(M)	Please Please Please	1962	6.00	15.00
Kent KST-550	(S)	Please Please Please	1962	6.00	15.00
Kent K-5014	(M)	The Ike And Tina Turner Revue Live	1964	5.00	12.00
Kent KST-5014	(S)	The Ike And Tina Turner Revue Live	1964	6.00	15.00
Minit 24018	(M)	Ike And Tina Turner In Person		6.00	15.00
Warners W-1579	(M)	The Ike And Tina Turner Show Live	1965	6.00	15.00
Warners WS-1579	(S)	The Ike And Tina Turner Show Live	1965	6.00	15.00
Loma 5904	(M)	Live/The Ike And Tina Show	1966	5.00	12.00
Philles PHLP-4011	(M)	River Deep-Mountain High	1966	1,400.00	2,000.00
		(A small quantity was pressed with most destroyed by Phil Spector. No covers are known to have been manufactured.)			
Pompeii SD-6000	(S)	So Fine	1968	5.00	12.00
Pompeii SD-6004	(S)	Cussin,' Cryin' And Carryin' On	1969	5.00	12.00
Pompeii SD-6006	(S)	Get It Together	1969	5.00	12.00
A&M SP-4178	(S)	River Deep-Mountain High (Brown label)	1969	6.00	15.00
Warners WS-1810	(S)	Ike And Tina Turner's Greatest Hits	1969	4.00	10.00
Capitol ST-571	(S)	Her Man, His Woman	1969	4.00	10.00
Blue Thumb BTS-5	(S)	Outta Season	1969	5.00	12.00
Blue Thumb BTS-11	(S)	The Hunter	1969	5.00	12.00
Liberty LST-7637	(S)	Come Together	1970	4.00	10.00
Liberty LST-7650	(S)	Workin' Together	1970	4.00	10.00
United Arts. UAS-9953	(S)	What You Hear Is What You Get	1971	6.00	15.00
United Arts. UAS-5530	(S)	Nuff Said	1971	5.00	12.00
United Arts. UAS-5598	(S)	Feel Good	1972	4.00	10.00
United Arts. UAS-5660	(S)	Let Me Touch Your Mind	1973	4.00	10.00
United Arts. UAS-5667	(S)	Ike And Tina Turner's Greatest Hits	1972	4.00	10.00
United Arts. LA064	(S)	The World Of Ike And Tina Live	1973	4.00	10.00
United Arts. LA180	(S)	Nutbush City Limits	1973	6.00	15.00
TURNER, "BIG" JOE					
EmArcy 36014	(M)	Joe Turner And Pete Johnson	1955	20.00	50.00
Atlantic 1234	(M)	Boss Of The Blues	1956	35.00	70.00
Atlantic 1243	(M)	Kansas City Jazz	1956	35.00	70.00
Atlantic 8005	(M)	Joe Turner	1957	35.00	70.00
Atlantic 8023	(M)	Rockin' The Blues	1959	35.00	70.00
Atlantic 8033	(M)	Big Joe Is Here	1959	35.00	70.00
		(Atlantic albums above have black labels.)			
Atlantic 1332	(M)	Big Joe Rides Again	1960	20.00	50.00
Savoy MG-14012	(M)	Joe Turner And The Blues	1962	20.00	50.00
Savoy MG-14106	(M)	Careless Love	1963	20.00	50.00
Atlantic 8081	(M)	The Best Of Joe Turner	1963	20.00	50.00
BluesWay BL-6006	(M)	Singing The Blues	1967	5.00	12.00
BluesWay BLS-6006	(S)	Singing The Blues	1967	6.00	15.00
BluesWay BLS-6060	(S)	Roll 'Em	1973	4.00	10.00
Atco SD-33-376	(S)	His Greatest Recordings	1971	4.00	10.00
TURNER, MICKEY					
Edmar E-1040	(M)	The Mickey Turner Show	1966	10.00	25.00
TURNER, SAMMY					
Big Top 1301	(M)	Lavender Blue Mods		10.00	25.00
Big Top 1301	(S)	Lavender Blue Mods		12.00	30.00

Label		Title	Year	VG+	NM
TURNER, SPYDER					
MGM E-4450	(M)	Stand By Me	1967	6.00	15.00
MGM SE-4450	(S)	Stand By Me	1967	8.00	20.00
TURNER, TITUS					
Jamie JLP-70-3018	(M)	Sound Off	1961	8.00	20.00
Jamie JLP-3018	(S)	Sound Off	1961	10.00	25.00
TURTLES, THE					
White Whale 111	(M)	It Ain't Me Babe	1965	10.00	25.00
White Whale S-7111	(S)	It Ain't Me Babe	1965	12.00	30.00
White Whale 112	(M)	You Baby	1966	10.00	25.00
White Whale S-7112	(S)	You Baby	1966	12.00	30.00
Decca DL-4751	(M)	Out Of Sight (Sdtk)	1966	6.00	15.00
Decca DL7-4751	(S)	Out Of Sight (Sdtk)	1966	8.00	20.00
White Whale 114	(M)	Happy Together	1967	6.00	15.00
White Whale S-7114	(S)	Happy Together	1967	8.00	20.00
White Whale 115	(M)	The Turtles' Golden Hits	1967	5.00	12.00
White Whale S-7115	(S)	The Turtles' Golden Hits	1967	6.00	15.00
White Whale S-7118	(S)	The Battle Of The Bands	1968	5.00	12.00
White Whale S-7124	(S)	Turtle Soup	1969	5.00	12.00
White Whale S-7127	(S)	More Golden Hits	1970	4.00	10.00
White Whale S-7133	(S)	Wooden Head	1971	5.00	12.00
Sire SASH-3703	(S)	Happy Together Again	1974	8.00	20.00
TWIGGY					
Mercury SRM-1-138	(S)	Please Get My Name Right		6.00	15.00
Mercury SRM-1-1093	(S)	Twiggy		6.00	15.00
MGM 1SE-32	(S)	The Boy Friend (Sdtk)	1971	6.00	15.00
TWINK					
Sire SES-97022	(S)	Think Pink	1970	20.00	50.00
TWINS, THE					
RCA LPM-1708	(M)	Teenagers Love The Twins	1958	20.00	50.00
TWISTERS, THE					
Treasure TLP-890	(M)	Doin' The Twist	1962	12.00	30.00
TWISTIN' KINGS, THE					
Motown MLP-601	(M)	Twistin' The World Around	1960	16.00	40.00
TWITTY, CONWAY					
MGM E-3744	(M)	Conway Twitty Sings	1959	35.00	70.00
MGM SE-3744	(S)	Conway Twitty Sings	1959	50.00	100.00
		(MGM albums above have yellow & black labels.)			
MGM E-3786	(M)	Saturday Night With Conway Twitty	1959	35.00	70.00
MGM SE-3786	(S)	Saturday Night With Conway Twitty	1959	50.00	100.00
MGM E-3818	(M)	Lonely Blue Boy	1960	35.00	70.00
MGM SE-3818	(S)	Lonely Blue Boy	1960	50.00	100.00
MGM E-3849	(M)	Conway Twitty's Greatest Hits	1960	20.00	50.00
MGM SE-3849	(P)	Conway Twitty's Greatest Hits	1960	30.00	60.00
		(Issued with a poster, priced separately below.)			
		Conway Twitty's Greatest Hits Poster	1960	20.00	50.00
MGM E-3907	(M)	The Rock And Roll Story	1961	20.00	50.00
MGM SE-3907	(S)	The Rock And Roll Story	1961	30.00	60.00
MGM E-3943	(M)	The Conway Twitty Touch	1961	20.00	50.00
MGM SE-3943	(S)	The Conway Twitty Touch	1961	30.00	60.00
MGM E-4019	(M)	Portrait Of A Fool And Others	1962	16.00	40.00
MGM SE-4019	(S)	Portrait Of A Fool And Others	1962	20.00	50.00
MGM E-4089	(M)	R&B '63	1963	16.00	40.00
MGM SE-4089	(S)	R&B '63	1963	20.00	50.00
MGM E-4217	(M)	Hit The Road	1964	10.00	25.00
MGM SE-4217	(S)	Hit The Road	1964	12.00	30.00
		(MGM albums above have black labels.)			
Decca DL-4724	(M)	Conway Twitty Sings	1966	5.00	12.00
Decca DL7-4724	(S)	Conway Twitty Sings	1966	6.00	15.00
Decca DL-4828	(M)	Look Into My Teardrops	1966	5.00	12.00
Decca DL7-4828	(S)	Look Into My Teardrops	1966	6.00	15.00
		(Decca albums above have black labels with "Mfrd by Decca" beneath the rainbow.)			

Label		Title	Year	VG+	NM
TYLER, RED, & THE GYROS					
Ace LP-1006	(M)	Rockin' And Rollin'	1960	16.00	40.00
TYLER, T. TEXAS					
Sound 607	(M)	Deck Of Cards	1958	20.00	50.00
King LPS-664	(M)	T. Texas Tyler	1959	16.00	40.00
King LP-686	(M)	The Great Texan	1960	16.00	40.00
King LP-721	(M)	T. Texas Tyler	1961	16.00	40.00
King LP-734	(M)	Songs Along The Way	1961	16.00	40.00
Capitol T-1662	(M)	Salvation	1962	6.00	15.00
Capitol ST-1662	(S)	Salvation	1962	8.00	20.00
Capitol T-2344	(M)	The Hits Of T. Texas Tyler	1965	5.00	12.00
Capitol ST-2344	(S)	The Hits Of T. Texas Tyler	1965	6.00	15.00
Starday SLP-379	(M)	The Man With A Million Friends	1966	6.00	15.00
TYMES, THE					
Parkway P-7032	(M)	So Much In Love	1963	12.00	30.00
Parkway P-7038	(M)	The Sound Of Wonderful Tymes	1963	10.00	25.00
Parkway P-7039	(M)	Somewhere	1964	10.00	25.00
Columbia CS-9778	(S)	People	1969	6.00	15.00

U.F.O.					
Rare Earth RS-524	(S)	U.F.O.	1971	10.00	25.00
ULTIMATE SPINACH, THE					
MGM SE-4518	(S)	The Ultimate Spinach	1968	6.00	15.00
MGM SE-4570	(S)	Behold And See	1968	6.00	15.00
MGM SE-4600	(S)	The Ultimate Spinach	1969	6.00	15.00
UNBEATABLES, THE					
Fawn LP-5050	(M)	Live At Palisades Park	1964	35.00	70.00
UNDERGROUND SUNSHINE					
Intrepid IT-4003	(S)	Let There Be Light	1969	12.00	30.00
UNDERGROUNDS, THE					
Mercury MG-16337	(M)	Psychedelic Visions	1967	8.00	20.00
Mercury SR-16337	(S)	Psychedelic Visions	1967	10.00	25.00
UNFOLDING, THE					
Audio Fidelity 6184	(S)	How To Blow Your Mind		16.00	40.00
UNIQUES, THE					
Paula LP-2190	(M)	Uniquely Yours	1966	6.00	15.00
Paula LPS-2190	(S)	Uniquely Yours	1966	8.00	20.00
Paula LP-2194	(M)	Happening Now	1967	6.00	15.00
Paula LPS-2194	(S)	Happening Now	1967	8.00	20.00
Paula LPS-2199	(S)	Playtime	1968	8.00	20.00
Paula LPS-2204	(S)	The Uniques	1969	6.00	15.00
Paula LPS-2208	(S)	Golden Hits	1970	6.00	15.00
UNITED STATES DOUBLE QUARTET, THE					
B.T. Puppy 1005	(S)	Life Is Groovy	1969	12.00	30.00
UNITED STATES OF AMERICA, THE					
Columbia CS-9616	(S)	The United States Of America (With bag)	1968	12.00	30.00

Unit 4 + 2 #1. The percussive feel of the Units big hit, "Concrete And Clay," stood out in the guitar dominated summer of '65. This album followed shortly after and disappeared without a trace. The group briefly placed one more single, "You've Never Been In Love Like This Before," in the charts before following the album into obscurity.

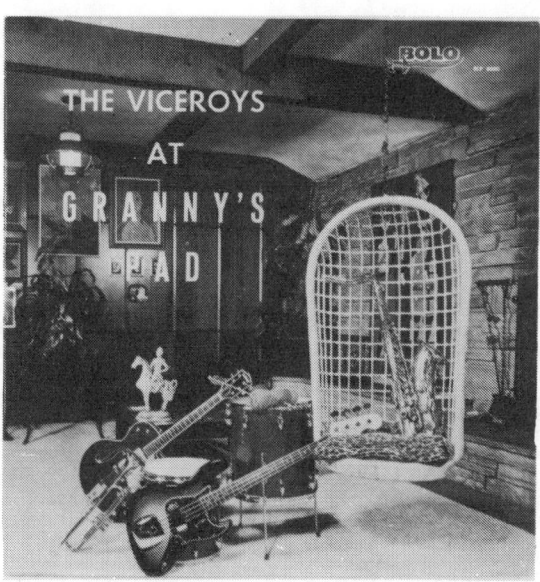

The Viceroys At Granny's Pad. While many collectors associate the Northwest sound only as that of the Wailers, the Sonics and Paul Revere's Raiders, these little recognized progenitors of the Northwest sound are highly sought-after.

Label		Title	Year	VG+	NM
UNIT FOUR PLUS TWO					
London LL-3427	(M)	Unit 4 Plus 2 #1	1965	16.00	40.00
London PS-427	(P)	Unit 4 Plus 2 #1	1965	20.00	50.00
UNUSUAL WE					
Pulsar 10608	(S)	Unusual We	1969	10.00	25.00

Label		Title	Year	VG+	NM
VALE, RICKY, & HIS SURFERS					
Strand SL-1104	(M)	Everybody's Surfin'	1963	8.00	20.00
Strand SLS-1104	(S)	Everybody's Surfin'	1963	10.00	25.00
VALENS, RITCHIE					
Del Fi 1201	(M)	Ritchie Valens	1959	35.00	70.00
Del Fi 1206	(M)	Ritchie	1959	35.00	70.00
Del Fi 1214	(M)	In Concert At Pacoima Jr. High	1960	45.00	90.00
Del Fi 1225	(M)	His Greatest Hits	1963	35.00	70.00
		(Del Fi albums above have black, blue & gold labels.)			
Del Fi 1247	(M)	His Greatest Hits, Volume 2	1965	30.00	60.00
MGM GAS-117	(E)	Ritchie Valens	1970	8.00	20.00
VALENTE, DINO					
Epic BN-26335	(S)	Dino Valente	1967	6.00	15.00
VALENTINE, HILTON					
Capitol ST-330	(S)	All In Your Head	1969	8.00	20.00
VALENTINO, MARK					
Swan LP-508	(M)	Mark Valentino	1963	14.00	35.00
VALIDS, THE					
Amber 802	(M)	Accapella		6.00	15.00
VALLEY, JIM					
Panorama 104	(S)	Harpo (With Don & The Goodtimes)		16.00	40.00
Light LS-5564	(S)	Family		6.00	15.00
VALLI, FRANKI					
Phillips PHM-200247	(M)	Solo	1967	8.00	20.00
Phillips PHS-600247	(S)	Solo	1967	10.00	25.00
Phillips PHS-600274	(S)	Timeless	1968	6.00	15.00
VAMPIRES, THE					
United Arts. UAL-3378	(M)	At The Monster Ball	1964	6.00	15.00
United Arts. UAS-6378	(S)	At The Monster Ball	1964	8.00	20.00
VAN DER GRAAF GENERATOR					
Mercury SR-61238	(S)	The Aerosol Grey Machine	1969	6.00	15.00
Probe 4515	(S)	The Least We Can Do Is Wave	1970	6.00	15.00
VAN DYKES, THE					
Bell 6004	(M)	Tellin' It Like It Is	1967	6.00	15.00
Bell 6004	(S)	Tellin' It Like It Is	1967	8.00	20.00
VAN RONK, DAVE					
Folkways F-3818	(M)	Ballads And Blues And Spirituals	1959	8.00	20.00
Prestige INT-13056	(M)	Dave Van Ronk, Folksinger	1962	6.00	15.00
Prestige F-14025	(M)	The Genius Of Dave Van Ronk	1964	6.00	15.00

Label		Title	Year	VG+	NM
Mercury MG-20908	(M)	Just Dave Van Ronk	1964	5.00	12.00
Mercury SR-60908	(S)	Just Dave Van Ronk	1964	6.00	15.00
Folkways FV-9006	(M)	Dave Van Ronk Sings The Blues	1965	5.00	12.00
Folkways FVS-9006	(S)	Dave Van Ronk Sings The Blues	1965	6.00	15.00
Folkways FV-9017	(M)	Gambler's Blues	1965	5.00	12.00
Folkways FVS-9017	(S)	Gambler's Blues	1965	6.00	15.00
Folkways FV-3009	(M)	No Dirty Names	1966	5.00	12.00
Folkways FVS-3009	(S)	No Dirty Names	1966	6.00	15.00
Prestige PR-7527	(M)	Dave Van Ronk, Folksinger	1967	5.00	12.00
Prestige PRS-7527	(S)	Dave Van Ronk, Folksinger	1967	6.00	15.00
Forecast FVS-3041	(S)	Dave Van Ronk And The Hudson Dusters	1968	6.00	15.00
Prestige PRS-7716	(S)	Inside Dave Van Ronk	1969	5.00	12.00
Polydor 24-4052	(S)	Van Ronk	1971	4.00	10.00
Fantasy 24170	(S)	Van Ronk	1972	5.00	12.00

VAN ZANDT, TOWNES

Label		Title	Year	VG+	NM
Poppy 40007	(S)	Townes Van Zandt	1969	6.00	15.00
Poppy LAOO-F4	(S)	The Late Great Townes Van Zandt	1973	6.00	15.00
Tomato 2-7001	(S)	Live At The Old Quarter, Houston, Texas	1977	5.00	12.00
Tomato 7011	(S)	The Late Great Townes Van Zandt	1978	4.00	10.00
Tomato 7012	(S)	High, Low And In Between	1978	4.00	10.00
Tomato 7013	(S)	Delta Momma Blues	1978	4.00	10.00
Tomato 7014	(S)	Townes Van Zandt	1978	4.00	10.00
Tomato 7015	(S)	Our Mother, The Mountain	1978	4.00	10.00
Tomato 7017	(S)	Flyin' Shoes	1978	4.00	10.00

VANNELLI, GINO

Label		Title	Year	VG+	NM
Mobile Fidelity 1-041	(S)	Powerful People		6.00	15.00

VANILLA FUDGE

Label		Title	Year	VG+	NM
Atco 33-224	(M)	Vanilla Fudge	1967	8.00	20.00
Atco SD-33-224	(S)	Vanilla Fudge	1967	8.00	20.00
Atco SD-33-237	(S)	The Beat Goes On	1968	6.00	15.00
Atco SD-33-244	(S)	Renaissance	1968	6.00	15.00
Atco SD-33-278	(S)	Near The Beginning	1969	5.00	12.00
Atco SD-33-303	(S)	Rock N' Roll	1969	5.00	12.00

VAUGHAN, SARAH

Label		Title	Year	VG+	NM
Columbia CL-6133 (10")	(M)	Sarah Vaughan	1950	16.00	40.00
Mercury MG-25188 (10")	(M)	Divine Sarah	1951	16.00	40.00
MGM E-165 (10")	(M)	Tenderly	1952	16.00	40.00
Remington 1024 (10")	(M)	Hot Jazz	1953	16.00	40.00
MGM E-544 (10")	(M)	Sarah Vaughan Sings	1954	16.00	40.00
EmArcy 26005 (10")	(M)	Images	1954	16.00	40.00
EmArcy MG-36004	(M)	Sarah Vaughan	1954	12.00	30.00
MGM E-3274	(M)	My Kinda Love	1955	12.00	30.00
EmArcy MG-36058	(M)	Sarah Vaughan In The Land Of Hi Fi	1955	12.00	30.00
Columbia CL-660	(M)	After Hours With Sarah Vaughan	1955	12.00	30.00
Mercury MG-20038	(M)	Vaughan And Violins	1955	8.00	20.00
Mercury MG-20041	(M)	Great Songs From Hit Shows	1955	8.00	20.00
Mercury MG-20045	(M)	Sarah Vaughan Sings George Gershwin	1955	10.00	25.00
Mercury MG-20078	(M)	Great Songs From Hit Shows, Volume 2	1956	8.00	20.00
Mercury MG-20094	(M)	Sarah Vaughan At The Blue Note	1956	8.00	20.00
Mercury MG-20110	(M)	The Magic Of Sarah Vaughan	1956	8.00	20.00
Mercury MG-20116	(M)	No Count Sarah	1956	8.00	20.00
Columbia CL-745	(M)	Sarah Vaughan In Hi Fi	1956	12.00	30.00
Columbia CL-914	(M)	Linger Awhile	1957	10.00	25.00
EmArcy MG-36109	(M)	Swingin' Easy	1957	10.00	25.00
Mercury MG-20219	(M)	Wonderful Sarah	1957	8.00	20.00
Mercury MG-20223	(M)	In A Romantic Mood	1957	8.00	20.00
Mercury MG-20255	(M)	Close To You	1957	8.00	20.00
Mercury MG-20316	(M)	Sarah Vaughan And Billy Eckstine Sing The Best Of Irving Berlin	1957	8.00	20.00
Mercury MG-20326	(M)	Sarah Vaughan At Mr. Kelly's	1958	8.00	20.00
Mercury MG-20383	(M)	After Hours At The London House	1958	8.00	20.00
Mercury MG-20441	(M)	No Count Sarah	1959	5.00	12.00
Mercury SR-60441	(S)	No Count Sarah	1959	6.00	15.00
Rondo-Lette 35	(M)	Songs Of Broadway	1959	10.00	25.00
Concord 3018	(M)	Sarah Vaughan Concert		6.00	15.00
Lion 70052	(M)	Sarah Vaughan	1959	8.00	20.00
Lion 70088	(M)	Billy And Sarah (With Billy Eckstine)	1959	8.00	20.00

Label		Title	Year	VG+	NM
Roulette R-52046	(M)	Dreamy	1960	5.00	12.00
Roulette SR-52048	(S)	Dreamy	1960	6.00	15.00
Roulette R-52060	(M)	Divine One	1960	5.00	12.00
Roulette SR-52060	(S)	Divine One	1960	6.00	15.00
Roulette R-52061	(M)	Count Basie/Sarah Vaughan	1960	5.00	12.00
Roulette SR-52061	(S)	Count Basie/Sarah Vaughan	1960	6.00	15.00
Roulette R-52070	(M)	After Hours	1961	5.00	12.00
Roulette SR-52070	(S)	After Hours	1961	6.00	15.00
Mercury MG-20617	(M)	My Heart Sings	1961	5.00	12.00
Mercury SR-60617	(S)	My Heart Sings	1961	6.00	15.00
Mercury MG-20645	(M)	Sarah Vaughan's Golden Hits	1962	5.00	12.00
Mercury SR-60645	(S)	Sarah Vaughan's Golden Hits	1962	6.00	15.00
Roulette R-52082	(M)	You're Mine, You	1962	5.00	12.00
Roulette SR-52082	(S)	You're Mine, You	1962	6.00	15.00
Roulette SR-52082	(S)	You're Mine, You (Red vinyl)	1962	12.00	30.00
Roulette R-52091	(M)	Snowbound	1962	5.00	12.00
Roulette SR-52091	(S)	Snowbound	1962	6.00	15.00
Roulette R-52092	(M)	The Explosive Side Of Sarah	1962	5.00	12.00
Roulette SR-52092	(S)	The Explosive Side Of Sarah	1962	6.00	15.00
Roulette R-52100	(M)	Star Eyes	1963	5.00	12.00
Roulette SR-52100	(S)	Star Eyes	1963	6.00	15.00
Roulette R-52104	(M)	Lonely Hours	1963	5.00	12.00
Roulette SR-52104	(S)	Lonely Hours	1963	6.00	15.00
Mercury MG-20831	(M)	Sassy Swings The Tivoli	1963	5.00	12.00
Mercury MG-60831	(S)	Sassy Swings The Tivoli	1963	6.00	15.00
Mercury MG-20882	(M)	Vaughan With Voices	1964	5.00	12.00
Mercury SR-60882	(S)	Vaughan With Voices	1964	6.00	15.00
Mercury MG-20941	(M)	Viva Vaughan	1964	5.00	12.00
Mercury SR-60941	(S)	Viva Vaughan	1964	6.00	15.00
Roulette R-52108	(M)	We Three	1964	5.00	12.00
Roulette SR-52108	(S)	We Three	1964	6.00	15.00
		(With Dinah Washington & Joe Williams.)			
Roulette R-52109	(M)	The World Of Sarah Vaughan	1964	5.00	12.00
Roulette SR-52109	(S)	The World Of Sarah Vaughan	1964	6.00	15.00
Roulette R-52112	(M)	Sweet 'N Sassy	1964	5.00	12.00
Roulette SR-52112	(S)	Sweet 'N Sassy	1964	6.00	15.00
Roulette R-52116	(M)	Sarah Sings Soulfully	1965	5.00	12.00
Roulette SR-52116	(S)	Sarah Sings Soulfully	1965	6.00	15.00
Roulette R-52118	(M)	Sarah Plus Two	1965	5.00	12.00
Roulette SR-52118	(S)	Sarah Plus Two	1965	6.00	15.00
Mercury MG-21009	(M)	Mancini Songbook	1965	5.00	12.00
Mercury SR-61009	(S)	Mancini Songbook	1965	6.00	15.00
Mercury MG-21069	(M)	The Pop Artistry Of Sarah Vaughan	1966	5.00	12.00
Mercury SR-61069	(S)	The Pop Artistry Of Sarah Vaughan	1966	6.00	15.00
Mercury MG-21079	(M)	New Scene	1966	5.00	12.00
Mercury SR-61079	(S)	New Scene	1966	6.00	15.00
Mercury MG-21116	(M)	Sassy Swings Again	1967	5.00	12.00
Mercury SR-61116	(S)	Sassy Swings Again	1967	6.00	15.00

VAUGHT, BOB, & THE RENEGADES

Label		Title	Year	VG+	NM
GNP/Crescendo 83	(M)	Surf Crazy	1963	8.00	20.00
GNP/Crescendo S-83	(S)	Surf Crazy	1963	10.00	25.00

VEE, BOBBY

Label		Title	Year	VG+	NM
Liberty LRP-3165	(M)	Bobby Vee Sings Your Favorites	1960	10.00	25.00
Liberty LST-7165	(S)	Bobby Vee Sings Your Favorites	1960	12.00	30.00
Liberty LRP-3181	(M)	Bobby Vee	1961	8.00	20.00
Liberty LST-7181	(S)	Bobby Vee	1961	12.00	30.00
Liberty LRP-3186	(M)	Bobby Vee With Strings And Things	1961	8.00	20.00
Liberty LST-7186	(S)	Bobby Vee With Strings And Things	1961	10.00	25.00
Liberty LRP-3205	(M)	Bobby Vee Sings Hits Of The Rockin' 50's	1961	10.00	25.00
Liberty LST-7205	(S)	Bobby Vee Sings Hits Of The Rockin' 50's	1961	12.00	30.00
Liberty LRP-3211	(M)	Take Good Care Of My Baby	1961	8.00	20.00
Liberty LST-7211	(S)	Take Good Care Of My Baby	1961	10.00	25.00
Liberty LRP-3228	(M)	Bobby Vee Meets The Crickets	1962	10.00	25.00
Liberty LST-7228	(S)	Bobby Vee Meets The Crickets	1962	12.00	30.00
Liberty LRP-3232	(M)	A Bobby Vee Recording Session	1962	6.00	15.00
Liberty LST-7232	(S)	A Bobby Vee Recording Session	1962	8.00	20.00
Liberty LRP-3245	(M)	Bobby Vee's Golden Greats	1962	5.00	12.00
Liberty LST-7245	(S)	Bobby Vee's Golden Greats	1962	6.00	15.00

Label		Title	Year	VG+	NM
Liberty LRP-3267	(M)	Merry Christmas From Bobby Vee	1962	5.00	12.00
Liberty LST-7267	(S)	Merry Christmas From Bobby Vee	1962	6.00	15.00
Liberty LRP-3285	(M)	The Night Has A Thousand Eyes	1963	6.00	15.00
Liberty LST-7285	(S)	The Night Has A Thousand Eyes	1963	8.00	20.00
Liberty LRP-3289	(M)	Bobby Vee Meets The Ventures	1963	6.00	15.00
Liberty LST-7289	(S)	Bobby Vee Meets The Ventures	1963	8.00	20.00
Liberty LRP-3336	(M)	I Remember Buddy Holly	1963	10.00	25.00
Liberty LST-7336	(S)	I Remember Buddy Holly	1963	12.00	30.00
Liberty LRP-3352	(M)	The New Sound From England!	1964	6.00	15.00
Liberty LST-7352	(S)	The New Sound From England!	1964	8.00	20.00
Liberty LRP-3385	(M)	30 Big Hits From The 60's	1964	8.00	20.00
Liberty LST-7385	(S)	30 Big Hits From The 60's	1964	10.00	25.00
Liberty LRP-3393	(M)	Bobby Vee Live On Tour	1965	6.00	15.00
Liberty LST-7393	(S)	Bobby Vee Live On Tour	1965	8.00	20.00
Liberty LRP-3430	(M)	C'Mon Let's Live A Little (Sdtk)	1966	6.00	15.00
Liberty LST-7430	(S)	C'Mon Let's Live A Little (Sdtk)	1966	8.00	20.00
		(Liberty albums above have black labels			
		with a gold logo on the left side.)			
Liberty LRP-3464	(M)	Bobby Vee's Golden Greats, Volume 2	1966	5.00	12.00
Liberty LST-7464	(S)	Bobby Vee's Golden Greats, Volume 2	1966	6.00	15.00
Liberty LRP-3480	(M)	Look At Me Girl	1966	4.00	10.00
Liberty LST-7480	(S)	Look At Me Girl	1966	5.00	12.00
Liberty LRP-3534	(M)	Come Back When You Grow Up	1967	4.00	10.00
Liberty LST-7534	(S)	Come Back When You Grow Up	1967	5.00	12.00
Liberty LST-7554	(S)	Just Today	1968	4.00	10.00
Liberty LST-7592	(S)	Do What You Gotta Do	1968	4.00	10.00
Liberty LST-7612	(S)	Gates, Grills And Railings	1969	4.00	10.00
United Arts. LA025	(S)	Legendary Masters	1973	6.00	15.00

VEGAS, PAT & LOLLY

Label		Title	Year	VG+	NM
Mercury MG-21059	(M)	At The Haunted House	1966	12.00	30.00
Mercury SR-61059	(S)	At The Haunted House	1966	14.00	35.00

VELEZ, MARTHA

Label		Title	Year	VG+	NM
Sire 97008	(S)	Friends And Angels	1969	10.00	25.00
Sire 7409	(S)	Matinee Weepers	1974	5.00	12.00

VELVET UNDERGROUND, THE

Label		Title	Year	VG+	NM
Verve V-5008	(M)	The Velvet Underground And Nico	1967	75.00	150.00
Verve V6-5008	(S)	The Velvet Underground And Nico	1967	50.00	100.00
		(Blue label. With a yellow, peel-off banana			
		sticker on the cover. The photo of the group			
		on the back cover is framed by a male torso.)			
Verve V-5008	(M)	The Velvet Underground And Nico	1967	50.00	100.00
Verve V6-5008	(S)	The Velvet Underground And Nico	1967	35.00	70.00
		(Blue label. With a yellow, peel-off banana			
		sticker on the cover. The photo of the group			
		on the back cover is covered with a sticker.)			
Verve V-5008	(M)	The Velvet Underground And Nico	1967	40.00	80.00
Verve V6-5008	(S)	The Velvet Underground And Nico	1967	20.00	50.00
		(Blue label. With a yellow, peel-off banana			
		sticker on the cover. The male torso on			
		the back cover is airbrushed out.)			
Verve V-5046	(M)	White Light/White Heat	1967	20.00	50.00
Verve V6-5046	(S)	White Light/White Heat	1967	16.00	40.00
		(Blue label. A black-on-black skull is in			
		lower left left corner of the cover.)			
MGM SE-4617	(S)	The Velvet Underground	1969	16.00	40.00
MGM GAS-131	(S)	The Velvet Underground	1970	10.00	25.00
Cotillion SD-9034	(S)	Loaded (Light Blue label)	1970	8.00	20.00
Mercury SRM-2-7504	(M)	Live 1969 (Fold-open cover)	1972	6.00	15.00

VENTURAS, THE

Label		Title	Year	VG+	NM
Drum Boy DB-1003	(M)	Here They Are	1964	20.00	50.00
Drum Boy DBS-1003	(S)	Here They Are	1964	30.00	60.00

VENTURES, THE

Label		Title	Year	VG+	NM
Dolton BLP-2003	(M)	Walk-Don't Run (Light blue label)	1960	8.00	20.00
Dolton BST-8003	(S)	Walk-Don't Run	1960	10.00	25.00
Dolton BLP-2004	(M)	The Ventures	1961	8.00	20.00
Dolton BST-8004	(S)	The Ventures	1961	10.00	25.00

Gene Vincent Rocks And The Blue Caps Roll. When Gene sent Capitol a demo of "Be-Bop-A-Lula," the record company had found their answer to Elvis. Drenched in an echo that was one step shy of absurd, Vincent gave the world one of the quintessential rock and roll records. While his albums showed a more diverse talent, with his gritty vocals wrapped around standards that would have made a lesser rocker twinge, he ranks with Elvis, Buddy and Jerry Lee as one of the pre-eminent white rockers of the '50s. All of his records are collectible, none more so than his first few Capitol albums.

The Velvet Underground, *Loaded.* While the VU's first three albums receive the lion's share of credit for their seeming never-ending influence on contemporary musicians, it was this, their final album as a group that remained in print while the others were deleted. A solid collection of rock and roll, this could easily stand as Lou Reed's first solo album *and* his finest hour in the studio. Good cover, too.

Label		Title	Year	VG+	NM
Dolton BLP-2006	(M)	Another Smash!!!	1961	8.00	20.00
Dolton BST-8006	(S)	Another Smash!!!	1961	10.00	25.00
Dolton BLP-2008	(M)	The Colorful Ventures	1961	8.00	20.00
Dolton BST-8008	(S)	The Colorful Ventures	1961	10.00	25.00
Dolton BLP-2010	(M)	Twist With The Ventures	1962	8.00	20.00
Dolton BST-8010	(S)	Twist With The Ventures	1962	10.00	25.00
Dolton BLP-2014	(M)	The Ventures' Twist Party, Volume 2	1962	8.00	20.00
Dolton BST-8014	(S)	The Ventures' Twist Party, Volume 2	1962	10.00	25.00
		(Dolton albums above have blue & silver labels.)			
Dolton BLP-2016	(M)	Mashed Potatoes And Gravy	1962	6.00	15.00
Dolton BST-8016	(S)	Mashed Potatoes And Gravy	1962	8.00	20.00
Dolton BLP-2017	(M)	Going To The Ventures' Dance Party!	1962	6.00	15.00
Dolton BST-8017	(S)	Going To The Ventures' Dance Party!	1962	8.00	20.00
Dolton BLP-2010	(M)	Dance!	1963	5.00	12.00
Dolton BST-8010	(S)	Dance!	1963	6.00	15.00
Dolton BLP-2014	(M)	Dance With The Ventures	1963	5.00	12.00
Dolton BST-8014	(S)	Dance With The Ventures	1963	6.00	15.00
Dolton BLP-2016	(M)	The Ventures' Beach Party	1963	5.00	12.00
Dolton BST-8016	(S)	The Ventures' Beach Party	1963	6.00	15.00
Dolton BLP-2019	(M)	Telstar, The Lonely Bull	1963	6.00	15.00
Dolton BST-8019	(S)	Telstar, The Lonely Bull	1963	8.00	20.00
Dolton BLP-2022	(M)	Surfing	1963	6.00	15.00
Dolton BST-8022	(S)	Surfing	1963	8.00	20.00
Liberty LRP-3289	(M)	Bobby Vee Meets The Ventures	1963	10.00	25.00
Liberty LST-7289	(S)	Bobby Vee Meets The Ventures	1963	12.00	30.00
Dolton BLP-2023	(M)	The Ventures Play The Country Classics	1963	5.00	12.00
Dolton BST-8023	(S)	The Ventures Play The Country Classics	1963	6.00	15.00
Dolton BLP-2024	(M)	Let's Go!	1963	5.00	12.00
Dolton BST-8024	(S)	Let's Go!	1963	6.00	15.00
Dolton BLP-2027	(M)	The Ventures In Space	1963	5.00	12.00
Dolton BST-8027	(S)	The Ventures In Space	1963	6.00	15.00
Dolton BLP-2029	(M)	The Fabulous Ventures	1964	5.00	12.00
Dolton BST-8029	(S)	The Fabulous Ventures	1964	6.00	15.00
Dolton BLP-2031	(M)	Walk, Don't Run, Volume 2	1964	5.00	12.00
Dolton BST-8031	(S)	Walk, Don't Run, Volume 2	1964	6.00	15.00
Dolton BLP-2033	(M)	The Ventures Knock Me Out!	1965	5.00	12.00
Dolton BST-8033	(S)	The Ventures Knock Me Out!	1965	6.00	15.00
Dolton BLP-2035	(M)	The Ventures On Stage Around The World	1965	5.00	12.00
Dolton BST-8035	(S)	The Ventures On Stage Around The World	1965	6.00	15.00
Dolton BLP-16501	(M)	Play Guitar With The Ventures	1965	8.00	20.00
Dolton BLP-2037	(M)	The Ventures A Go-Go	1965	5.00	12.00
Dolton BST-8037	(S)	The Ventures A Go-Go	1965	6.00	15.00
Dolton BLP-2038	(M)	The Ventures' Christmas Album	1965	6.00	15.00
Dolton BST-8038	(S)	The Ventures' Christmas Album	1965	8.00	20.00
		(Dolton albums above have blue labels			
		with a color logo on the left side.)			
Dolton BLP-16502	(M)	Play Guitar With The Ventures, Volume 2	1966	8.00	20.00
Dolton BLP-16503	(M)	Play Guitar With The Ventures, Volume 3	1966	8.00	20.00
Dolton BLP-16504	(M)	Play Guitar With The Ventures, Volume 4	1966	8.00	20.00
Dolton BLP-2040	(M)	Where The Action Is!	1966	5.00	12.00
Dolton BST-8040	(S)	Where The Action Is!	1966	6.00	15.00
Dolton BLP-2042	(M)	The Ventures	1966	5.00	12.00
Dolton BST-8042	(S)	The Ventures	1966	6.00	15.00
Dolton BLP-2042	(M)	Batman Theme	1966	8.00	20.00
Dolton BST-8042	(S)	Batman Theme	1966	10.00	25.00
Dolton BLP-2045	(M)	Go With The Ventures!	1966	5.00	12.00
Dolton BST-8045	(S)	Go With The Ventures!	1966	6.00	15.00
Dolton BLP-2047	(M)	Wild Things!	1966	5.00	12.00
Dolton BST-8047	(S)	Wild Things!	1966	6.00	15.00
Dolton BLP-2050	(M)	Guitar Freakout	1967	5.00	12.00
Dolton BST-8050	(S)	Guitar Freakout	1967	6.00	15.00
Liberty LRP-4052	(M)	Super Psychedelics	1967	5.00	12.00
Liberty LST-8052	(S)	Super Psychedelics	1967	6.00	15.00
Liberty LRP-4053	(M)	Golden Greats By The Ventures	1967	5.00	12.00
Liberty LST-8053	(S)	Golden Greats By The Ventures	1967	6.00	15.00
Liberty LRP-4054	(M)	$1,000,000.00 Weekend	1967	5.00	12.00
Liberty LST-8054	(S)	$1,000,000.00 Weekend	1967	6.00	15.00
Liberty LST-8055	(S)	Flights Of Fantasy	1968	6.00	15.00
Liberty LST-8057	(S)	The Horse	1968	6.00	15.00
Liberty LST-8059	(S)	Underground Fire	1969	6.00	15.00
Liberty LST-8060	(S)	More Golden Greats	1970	6.00	15.00

Label		Title	Year	VG+	NM
Liberty LST-8061	(S)	Hawaii Five-O	1969	6.00	15.00
Liberty LST-8062	(S)	Swamp Rock	1969	6.00	15.00
Liberty LST-35000	(S)	The Ventures' 10th Anniversary Album	1970	8.00	20.00
Liberty SCR-5	(S)	The Versatile Ventures (Record Club)		6.00	15.00

VERA, BILLY
Also refer to Judy Clay & Billy Vera.

Atlantic SD-8197	(S)	With Pen In Hand	1968	6.00	15.00

VERITY BAND, JOHN

Dunhill DSX-500170	(S)	The John Verity Band	1974	8.00	20.00

VERNE, LARRY

Era 104	(M)	Mister Larry Verne		14.00	35.00

VERNON, MILLI

Storyville 910	(M)	Introducing Milli Verdon	1956	12.00	30.00

VERSATONES, THE

RCA Victor LPM-1538	(M)	The Versatones	1957	16.00	40.00

VETTES, THE

MGM E-4193	(M)	Rev-Up	1963	8.00	20.00
MGM SE-4193	(S)	Rev-Up	1963	10.00	25.00

VIBRATIONS, THE

Checker 2978	(M)	Watusi	1961	16.00	40.00
OKeh OKM-4111	(M)	Shout	1965	12.00	30.00
OKeh OKS-14111	(S)	Shout	1965	14.00	35.00
OKeh OKM-4112	(M)	Misty	1966	10.00	25.00
OKeh OKS-14112	(S)	Misty	1966	12.00	30.00
OKeh OKS-14129	(S)	Greatest Hits	1969	16.00	40.00
Mandate 3006	(S)	Taking A New Step	1972	6.00	15.00

VICEROYS, THE

Bolo BLP-8000	(M)	The Viceroys At Granny's Pad	1963	16.00	40.00

VICTIMS OF CHANCE, THE

Crestview CRS-3052	(S)	The Victims Of Chance		6.00	15.00

VIGRASS & OSBORNE

Uni 73129	(S)	Queues	1971	8.00	20.00
Epic KE-33077	(S)	Steppin' Out	1975	4.00	10.00

VINCENT, GENE

Capitol T-764	(M)	Bluejean Bop!	1957	180.00	300.00
Capitol T-811	(M)	Gene Vincent & The Blue Caps	1957	180.00	300.00
Capitol T-970	(M)	Gene Vincent Rocks! & The Blue Caps Roll	1958	180.00	300.00
Capitol T-1059	(M)	A Gene Vincent Record Date	1958	180.00	300.00
Capitol T-1207	(M)	Sounds Like Gene Vincent	1959	150.00	250.00
Capitol T-1342	(M)	Crazy Times	1960	150.00	250.00
Capitol DKAO-380	(E)	Gene Vincent's Greatest	1969	8.00	20.00
Dandelion 9-102	(S)	I'm Back And I'm Proud	1970	14.00	35.00
Kama Sutra 2019	(S)	If Only You Could See Me Today	1970	14.00	35.00
Kama Sutra 2027	(S)	The Day The World Turned Blue	1971	14.00	35.00

VINSON, EDDIE "CLEANHEAD"

King 634	(M)	Battle Of The Blues, Volume 3	1959	270.00	450.00
		(Also features Jimmy Witherspoon.)			
King 668	(M)	Battle Of The Blues, Volume 4	1960	400.00	600.00
		(Also features Roy Brown and Wynonie Harris.)			
Riverside 3502	(M)	Backdoor Blues		12.00	30.00
Bethlehem BCP-5005	(M)	Eddie Cleanhead Vinson Sings		14.00	35.00
Aamco 312	(M)	Eddie Cleanhead Vinson Sings		8.00	20.00
BluesWay BL-6007	(M)	Cherry Red	1967	6.00	15.00
BluesWay BLS-6007	(S)	Cherry Red	1967	8.00	20.00
King 1087	(M)	Cherry Red	1969	5.00	12.00

VINTON, BOBBY

Epic BN-3727	(M)	Dancing At The Hop		8.00	20.00
Epic LN-579	(S)	Dancing At The Hop		10.00	25.00

Label		Title	Year	VG+	NM
Epic BN-3780	(M)	Young Man With A Big Band		6.00	15.00
Epic LN-597	(S)	Young Man With A Big Band		10.00	25.00
Epic LN-24020	(M)	Roses Are Red	1962	5.00	12.00
Epic BN-26020	(S)	Roses Are Red	1962	6.00	15.00
Epic LN-24035	(M)	Bobby Vinton Sings The Big Ones	1963	5.00	12.00
Epic BN-26035	(S)	Bobby Vinton Sings The Big Ones	1963	6.00	15.00
Epic LN-24049	(M)	The Greatest Hits Of The Greatest Groups	1963	6.00	15.00
Epic BN-26049	(S)	The Greatest Hits Of The Greatest Groups	1963	8.00	20.00
Epic LN-24068	(M)	Blue Velvet	1963	5.00	12.00
Epic BN-26068	(S)	Blue Velvet	1963	6.00	15.00
Epic LN-24081	(M)	There! I've Said It Again	1964	4.00	10.00
Epic BN-26081	(S)	There! I've Said It Again	1964	5.00	12.00
Epic LN-24098	(M)	Bobby Vinton's Greatest Hits	1964	4.00	10.00
Epic BN-26098	(S)	Bobby Vinton's Greatest Hits	1964	5.00	12.00
Epic LN-24113	(M)	Tell Me Why	1964	4.00	10.00
Epic BN-26113	(S)	Tell Me Why	1964	5.00	12.00
Epic LN-24122	(M)	A Very Merry Christmas	1964	4.00	10.00
Epic BN-26122	(S)	A Very Merry Christmas	1964	5.00	12.00
Epic LN-24136	(M)	Mr. Lonely	1965	4.00	10.00
Epic BN-26136	(S)	Mr. Lonely	1965	5.00	12.00
Epic LN-24154	(M)	Bobby Vinton Sings For Lonely Nights	1965	5.00	12.00
Epic BN-26154	(S)	Bobby Vinton Sings For Lonely Nights	1965	6.00	15.00
Epic LN-24170	(M)	Drive-In Movie Time	1965	5.00	12.00
Epic BN-26170	(S)	Drive-In Movie Time	1965	6.00	15.00
Epic LN-24182	(M)	Satin Pillows	1966	4.00	10.00
Epic BN-26182	(S)	Satin Pillows	1966	5.00	12.00
Epic LN-24187	(M)	More Of Bobby Vinton's Greatest Hits	1966	4.00	10.00
Epic BN-26187	(S)	More Of Bobby Vinton's Greatest Hits	1966	5.00	12.00
Epic LN-24188	(M)	Country Boy	1966	5.00	12.00
Epic BN-26188	(S)	Country Boy	1966	6.00	15.00
Epic LN-24203	(M)	Live At The Copa	1966	5.00	12.00
Epic BN-26203	(S)	Live At The Copa	1966	6.00	15.00
Epic LN-24245	(M)	Bobby Vinton Sings The Newest Hits	1967	4.00	10.00
Epic BN-26245	(S)	Bobby Vinton Sings The Newest Hits	1967	5.00	12.00
Epic LN-24341	(M)	Please Love Me Forever	1967	4.00	10.00
Epic BN-26341	(S)	Please Love Me Forever	1967	5.00	12.00
Epic BN-26382	(S)	Take Good Care Of Her	1968	4.00	10.00
Epic BN-26437	(S)	I Love How You Love Me	1969	4.00	10.00
		(Epic albums above have yellow labels.)			

VIOLA CRAYOLA, THE

Fautra 1	(S)	Music: Breaking Of Statues	1974	5.00	12.00

VIOLINAIRES, THE

Checker 2CK-10065	(M)	Please Answer This Prayer		10.00	25.00

VIRGIN INSANITY

Funky 71411	(S)	Illusions Of The Maintenance Man		8.00	20.00

VIRTUES, THE

Wynne WLP-111	(M)	Guitar Boogie Shuffle	1960	8.00	20.00
Strand SL-1061	(M)	Guitar Boogie Shuffle	1960	8.00	20.00
Strand SL-1061	(S)	Guitar Boogie Shuffle	1960	10.00	25.00

VISCOUNTS, THE

Madison 1001	(M)	The Viscounts	1960	40.00	80.00
Amy 8008	(M)	Harlem Nocturne	1965	12.00	30.00
Amy S-8008	(P)	Harlem Nocturne	1965	16.00	40.00

VOGUES, THE

Co&Ce 1229	(M)	Meet The Vogues	1965	10.00	25.00
Co&Ce 1229	(S)	Meet The Vogues	1965	12.00	30.00
Co&Ce 1230	(M)	Five O'clock World	1966	10.00	25.00
Co&Ce 1230	(S)	Five O'clock World	1966	12.00	30.00
Reprise RS-6314	(S)	Turn Around, Look At Me	1968	5.00	12.00
		(Brown & orange steamboat label.)			

VON SCHMIDT, ERIC

Prestige 7717	(S)	The Folk Blues Of Eric Von Schmidt	1969	6.00	15.00
Smash SRS-67124	(S)	Who Knocked The Brains Out Of The Sky	1969	6.00	15.00

Label		Title	Year	VG+	NM
WADE, ADAM					
Coed LPC-902	(M)	And The Came Adam	1960	12.00	30.00
Coed LPC-903	(M)	Adam And Evening	1961	10.00	25.00
Coed LPCS-903	(S)	Adam And Evening	1961	12.00	30.00
Epic LN-24019	(M)	Adam Wade's Greatest Hits	1962	6.00	15.00
Epic BN-26019	(S)	Adam Wade's Greatest Hits	1962	8.00	20.00
Epic LN-24026	(M)	One Is A Lonely Number	1962	6.00	15.00
Epic BN-26026	(S)	One Is A Lonely Number	1962	8.00	20.00
Epic LN-24044	(M)	What Kind Of Fool Am I?	1963	6.00	15.00
Epic BN-26044	(S)	What Kind Of Fool Am I?	1963	8.00	20.00
Epic LN-24056	(M)	A Very Good Year For Girls	1963	6.00	15.00
Epic BN-26056	(S)	A Very Good Year For Girls	1963	8.00	20.00
WAGONER, PORTER (& THE WAGONMASTERS)					
RCA LPM-1358	(M)	A Satisfied Mind	1956	16.00	40.00
RCA LPM-2447	(M)	A Slice Of Life-Songs Happy 'N' Sad	1962	8.00	20.00
RCA LSP-2447	(S)	A Slice Of Life-Songs Happy 'N' Sad	1962	10.00	25.00
RCA LPM-2529	(M)	Duets (With Skeeter Davis)	1962	8.00	20.00
RCA LSP-2529	(S)	Duets (With Skeeter Davis)	1962	10.00	25.00
RCA LPM-2650	(M)	The Porter Wagoner Show	1963	6.00	15.00
RCA LSP-2650	(S)	The Porter Wagoner Show	1963	8.00	20.00
RCA LPM-2706	(M)	Y'All Come	1963	6.00	15.00
RCA LSP-2706	(S)	Y'All Come	1963	8.00	20.00
		(Mono RCA albums above have "Long Play" on the bottom of the label. Stereo albums have "Living Stereo" on the bottom.)			
RCA LPM-2723	(M)	Three Country Gentlemen	1963	5.00	12.00
RCA LSP-2723	(S)	Three Country Gentlemen	1963	6.00	15.00
RCA LPM-2840	(M)	In Person (With Norma Jean)	1964	5.00	12.00
RCA LSP-2840	(S)	In Person (With Norma Jean)	1964	6.00	15.00
RCA LPM-2960	(M)	The Bluegrass Story	1964	5.00	12.00
RCA LSP-2960	(S)	The Bluegrass Story	1964	3.00	15.00
RCA LPM-3389	(M)	The Thin Man From West Plains	1965	5.00	12.00
RCA LSP-3389	(S)	The Thin Man From West Plains	1965	6.00	15.00
RCA LPM-3488	(M)	Grand Old Gospel	1966	5.00	12.00
RCA LSP-3488	(S)	Grand Old Gospel	1966	6.00	15.00
RCA LPM-3509	(M)	Live On The Road (With Norma Jean)	1966	5.00	12.00
RCA LSP-3509	(S)	Live On The Road (With Norma Jean)	1966	6.00	15.00
RCA LPM-3560	(M)	The Best Of Porter Wagoner	1966	4.00	10.00
RCA LSP-3560	(S)	The Best Of Porter Wagoner	1966	5.00	12.00
RCA LPM-3593	(M)	Confessions Of A Broken Man	1966	4.00	10.00
RCA LSP-3593	(S)	Confessions Of A Broken Man	1966	5.00	12.00
RCA LPM-3683	(M)	Soul Of A Convict	1967	4.00	10.00
RCA LSP-3683	(S)	Soul Of A Convict	1967	5.00	12.00
RCA LPM-3797	(M)	The Cold Hard Facts Of Life	1967	4.00	10.00
RCA LSP-3797	(S)	The Cold Hard Facts Of Life	1967	5.00	12.00
RCA LPM-3855	(M)	More Grand Old Gospel	1967	4.00	10.00
RCA LSP-3855	(S)	More Grand Old Gospel	1967	5.00	12.00
RCA LSP-3968	(S)	The Bottom Of The Bottle	1968	4.00	10.00
RCA LSP-3926	(S)	Just Between You And Me	1968	4.00	10.00
		(With Dolly Parton.)			
RCA LSP-4034	(S)	Gospel Country	1968	5.00	12.00
		(RCA albums above have black labels.)			
WAILERS, THE					
Golden Crest CR-3075	(M)	Fabulous Wailers	1959	20.00	50.00
Etiquette ALB-01	(M)	At The Castle	1962	12.00	30.00
Etiquette ALB-02	(M)	Merry Christmas (With the Sonics)		100.00	200.00
Etiquette ALB-022	(M)	Wailers And Company	1963	12.00	30.00
Imperial LP-9262	(M)	Tall Cool One	1964	8.00	20.00
Imperial LP-12262	(S)	Tall Cool One	1964	10.00	25.00
Etiquette ALB-023	(M)	Wailers, Wailers, Everywhere	1965	10.00	25.00

Label		Title	Year	VG+	NM
Etiquette ALB-026	(M)	Out Of Our Tree	1966	10.00	25.00
United Arts. UAL-3557	(M)	Out Burst	1966	8.00	20.00
United Arts. UAS-6557	(P)	Out Burst	1966	10.00	25.00
Bell 6016	(M)	Walk Thru The People	1968	8.00	20.00
WAKELY, JIMMY					
Capitol H-9004 (10")	(M)	Christmas On The Range		16.00	40.00
Capitol H-4008 (10")	(M)	Songs Of The West		16.00	40.00
Decca DL-8409	(M)	Santa Fe Trail	1956	14.00	35.00
Decca DL-8680	(M)	Enter And Rest And Pray	1957	14.00	35.00
Shasta SHLP-501	(M)	Country Million Sellers	1959	10.00	25.00
Shasta SHLP-502	(M)	Merry Christmas	1959	10.00	25.00
Shasta SHLP-505	(M)	Jimmy Wakely Sings	1960	10.00	25.00
Dot DLP-3711	(M)	Slippin' Around	1966	5.00	12.00
Dot DLP-25711	(S)	Slippin' Around	1966	6.00	15.00
Dot DLP-3754	(M)	Christmas With Jimmy Wakely	1966	5.00	12.00
Dot DLP-25754	(S)	Christmas With Jimmy Wakely	1966	6.00	15.00
WAKEMAN, RICK					
A&M QU-54361	(Q)	The Six Wives Of Henry VIII	1973	6.00	15.00
A&M QU-53621	(Q)	Journey To The Center Of The Earth	1975	6.00	15.00
A&M QU-54515	(Q)	Myths And Legends Of King Arthur	1975	6.00	15.00
WALES, HOWARD					
Douglas KZ-30589	(S)	Hooteroll (With Jerry Garcia)	1971	8.00	20.00
WALKER, CHARLIE					
Columbia CL-1691	(M)	Charlie Walker's Greatest Hits	1961	6.00	15.00
Columbia CS-8491	(S)	Charlie Walker's Greatest Hits	1961	8.00	20.00
WALKER, JERRY JEFF					
Atco SD-33-259	(S)	Mr. Bojangles	1968	8.00	20.00
Vanguard VSD-6521	(S)	Driftin' Way Of Life	1969	8.00	20.00
Atco SD-33-297	(S)	Jerry Jeff Walker	1969	12.00	30.00
Atco SD-33-336	(S)	Bein' Free	1970	8.00	20.00
Elektra 6E-163	(S)	Jerry Jeff		5.00	12.00
Elektra 6E-239	(S)	Too Old To Change		5.00	12.00
Decca 75384	(S)	Jerry Jeff Walker	1972	6.00	15.00
WALKER, JUNIOR (& THE ALL STARS)					
Soul 701	(M)	Shotgun	1965	8.00	20.00
Soul S-701	(S)	Shotgun	1965	10.00	25.00
Soul 702	(M)	Soul Session	1966	6.00	15.00
Soul S-702	(S)	Soul Session	1966	8.00	20.00
Soul 703	(M)	Road Runner	1966	6.00	15.00
Soul S-703	(S)	Road Runner	1966	8.00	20.00
Soul 705	(M)	Live	1967	5.00	12.00
Soul S-705	(S)	Live	1967	6.00	15.00
WALKER, LUCILLE					
Checker 1428	(M)	The Best Of Lucille Walker	1957	16.00	40.00
WALKER, T-BONE (AARON WALKER)					
Capitol H-370 (10")	(M)	Classics In Jazz	1953	75.00	150.00
Capitol T-370	(M)	Classics In Jazz	1953	50.00	100.00
Atlantic SD-8020	(M)	T-Bone Blues (Black label)	1959	35.00	70.00
Atlantic SD-8020	(M)	T-Bone Blues (Red label)		14.00	35.00
Imperial 9098	(M)	Sings The Blues	1959	20.00	50.00
Imperial 9116	(M)	Singing The Blues	1960	20.00	50.00
Imperial 9146	(M)	I Get So Weary	1961	20.00	50.00
Capitol T-1958	(M)	The Great Blues Vocals And Guitar	1963	14.00	35.00
Capitol ST-1958	(S)	The Great Blues Vocals And Guitar	1963	16.00	40.00
Delmark DS-633	(S)	I Want A Little Girl	1967	6.00	15.00
Wet Soul 1002	(M)	Stormy Monday Blues	1967	6.00	15.00
Wet Soul 1002	(S)	Stormy Monday Blues	1967	8.00	20.00
Brunswick BL-754126	(S)	The Truth	1968	6.00	15.00
Bluestime 29010	(S)	Blue Rocks	1968	6.00	15.00
BluesWay BLS-6014	(S)	Funky Town	1968	6.00	15.00
Atlantic SD-8256	(S)	T-Bone Blues	1970	6.00	15.00

Label		Title	Year	VG+	NM
WALKER BROTHERS, THE					
Smash MGS-27076	(M)	Introducing The Walker Brothers	1966	6.00	15.00
Smash SRS-67076	(P)	Introducing The Walker Brothers	1966	8.00	20.00
Smash MGS-27082	(M)	The Sun Ain't Gonna Shine Anymore	1967	6.00	15.00
Smash SRS-67082	(P)	The Sun Ain't Gonna Shine Anymore	1967	8.00	20.00
WALLER, JIM, & THE DELTAS					
Arvee A-432	(M)	Surfin' Wild	1963	12.00	30.00
Arvee AS-432	(S)	Surfin' Wild	1963	14.00	35.00
WARD, BILLY, & THE DOMINOES					
Federal 295-94 (10")	(M)	Billy Ward & His Dominoes	1954	800.00	1,200.00
Federal 395-548	(M)	Billy Ward & His Dominoes	1956	300.00	500.00
Federal LP-559	(M)	Clye McPhatter With Billy Ward	1957	300.00	500.00
King LP-548	(M)	Billy Ward & His Dominoes		150.00	250.00
King LP-559	(M)	Clye McPhatter With Billy Ward		150.00	250.00
King LP-733	(M)	Billy Ward & His Dominoes Featuring Clyde McPhatter And Jackie Wilson		100.00	200.00
Decca DL-8621	(M)	Billy Ward & His Dominoes	1958	75.00	150.00
Liberty LRP-3056	(M)	Sea Of Glass	1959	30.00	60.00
Liberty LRP-3083	(M)	Your's Forever	1959	30.00	60.00
Liberty LRP-3113	(M)	Pagan Love Song	1959	20.00	50.00
Liberty LST-7113	(S)	Pagan Love Song	1959	30.00	60.00
King LP-952	(M)	Twenty Four Songs	1966	20.00	50.00
WARD, ROBIN					
Dot DLP-35555	(M)	Wonderful Summer	1963	16.00	40.00
Dot DLP-25555	(S)	Wonderful Summer	1963	20.00	50.00
WARWICK, DEE DEE					
Mercury MG-21100	(M)	I Want To Be With You	1967	6.00	15.00
Mercury SR-61100	(S)	I Want To Be With You	1967	8.00	20.00
Mercury SR-61221	(S)	Dee Dee Warwick	1969	6.00	15.00
Atco SD-33-337	(S)	Turnin' Around	1970	5.00	12.00
WARWICK, DIONNE					
Scepter S-508	(M)	Presenting Dionne Warwick	1963	5.00	12.00
Scepter SS-508	(S)	Presenting Dionne Warwick	1963	6.00	15.00
Scepter S-517	(M)	Anyone Who Had A Heart	1964	4.00	10.00
Scepter SS-517	(S)	Anyone Who Had A Heart	1964	5.00	12.00
Scepter S-523	(M)	Make Way For Dionne Warwick	1964	4.00	10.00
Scepter SS-523	(S)	Make Way For Dionne Warwick	1964	5.00	12.00
Scepter S-528	(M)	The Sensitive Sound Of Dionne Warwick	1965	4.00	10.00
Scepter SS-528	(S)	The Sensitive Sound Of Dionne Warwick	1965	5.00	12.00
United Arts. UAL-4128	(M)	What's New, Pussycat? (Sdtk)	1965	4.00	10.00
United Arts. UAS-5128	(S)	What's New, Pussycat? (Sdtk)	1965	4.00	10.00
Scepter S-531	(M)	Here I Am	1966	4.00	10.00
Scepter SS-531	(S)	Here I Am	1966	5.00	12.00
Scepter S-534	(M)	Dionne Warwick In Paris	1966	4.00	10.00
Scepter SS-534	(S)	Dionne Warwick In Paris	1966	5.00	12.00
Scepter S-555	(M)	Here Where There Is Love	1966	4.00	10.00
Scepter SS-555	(S)	Here Where There Is Love	1966	5.00	12.00
Scepter S-559	(M)	On Stage And In The Movies	1967	4.00	10.00
Scepter SS-559	(S)	On Stage And In The Movies	1967	5.00	12.00
Scepter S-563	(M)	The Windows Of The World	1967	4.00	10.00
Scepter SS-563	(S)	The Windows Of The World	1967	5.00	12.00
Scepter S-565	(M)	Dionne Warwick's Golden Hits, Part One	1967	4.00	10.00
Scepter SS-565	(S)	Dionne Warwick's Golden Hits, Part One	1967	5.00	12.00
		(The Scepter albums above have orange labels.)			
Mobile Fidelity 2-098	(S)	Hot! Live And Otherwise		6.00	15.00
WASHINGTON, BABY (JEANETTE WASHINGTON)					
Sue LP-1014	(M)	That's How Heartaches Are Made	1963	16.00	40.00
Veep 16528	(S)	With You In Mind	1968	8.00	20.00
WASHINGTON, DINAH					
Also refer to Brook Benton.					
Mercury MG-25060 (10")	(M)	Dinah Washington Songs	1950	14.00	35.00
Mercury MG-25138 (10")	(M)	Dynamic Dinah	1951	14.00	35.00
Mercury MG-25140 (10")	(M)	Blazing Ballads	1951	14.00	35.00
Mercury MG-20120	(M)	Music For Late Hours		10.00	25.00

Label		Title	Year	VG+	NM
Mercury MG-20202	(M)	Dinah Washington Sings Fats Waller		10.00	25.00
EmArcy 26032 (10")	(M)	After Hours With Miss D	1954	12.00	30.00
EmArcy MG-36000	(M)	Dinah Jams	1954	10.00	25.00
EmArcy MG-36011	(M)	For Those In Love	1955	10.00	25.00
EmArcy MG-36028	(M)	After Hours With Miss D	1955	10.00	25.00
EmArcy MG-36065	(M)	Dinah	1956	10.00	25.00
EmArcy MG-36073	(M)	In The Land Of Hi Fi	1956	10.00	25.00
EmArcy MG-36104	(M)	The Swingin' Miss D		10.00	25.00
EmArcy MG-36119	(M)	Dinah Washington Sings Fats Waller	1957	10.00	25.00
EmArcy MG-36130	(M)	Dinah Washington Sings Bessie Smith	1958	10.00	25.00
Mercury MG-20479	(M)	What A Difference A Day Makes	1960	5.00	12.00
Mercury SR-60479	(S)	What A Difference A Day Makes	1960	6.00	15.00
Mercury MG-20532	(M)	Unforgettable	1961	5.00	12.00
Mercury SR-60532	(S)	Unforgettable	1961	6.00	15.00
Mercury MG-20604	(M)	I Concentrate On You	1961	5.00	12.00
Mercury SR-60604	(S)	I Concentrate On You	1961	6.00	15.00
Mercury MG-20614	(M)	For Lonely Lovers	1961	5.00	12.00
Mercury SR-60614	(S)	For Lonely Lovers	1961	6.00	15.00
Mercury MG-20638	(M)	September In The Rain	1961	5.00	12.00
Mercury SR-60638	(S)	September In The Rain	1961	6.00	15.00
Mercury MG-20661	(M)	Tears And Laughter	1962	5.00	12.00
Mercury SR-60661	(S)	Tears And Laughter	1962	6.00	15.00
Mercury MG-20729	(M)	I Wanna Be Loved	1962	5.00	12.00
Mercury SR-60729	(S)	I Wanna Be Loved	1962	6.00	15.00
Mercury MG-20788	(M)	This Is My Story, Volume 1	1963	5.00	12.00
Mercury SR-60788	(S)	This Is My Story, Volume 1	1963	6.00	15.00
Mercury MG-20789	(M)	This Is My Story, Volume 2	1963	5.00	12.00
Mercury SR-60789	(S)	This Is My Story, Volume 2	1963	6.00	15.00
Mercury MG-20829	(M)	The Good Old Days	1963	6.00	15.00
Mercury SR-60829	(E)	The Good Old Days	1963	5.00	12.00
Roulette R-52108	(M)	We Three	1964	5.00	12.00
Roulette SR-52108	(S)	We Three	1964	6.00	15.00
		(With Sarah Vaughan & Joe Williams.)			
Roulette R-52170	(M)	Dinah '62	1962	5.00	12.00
Roulette SR-52170	(S)	Dinah '62	1962	6.00	15.00
Roulette R-52180	(M)	In Love	1962	5.00	12.00
Roulette SR-52180	(S)	In Love	1962	6.00	15.00
Roulette R-52183	(M)	Drinking Again	1962	5.00	12.00
Roulette SR-52183	(S)	Drinking Again	1962	6.00	15.00
Roulette R-52189	(M)	Back To The Blues	1962	5.00	12.00
Roulette SR-52189	(S)	Back To The Blues	1962	6.00	15.00
Roulette R-52220	(M)	Dinah '63	1963	5.00	12.00
Roulette SR-52220	(S)	Dinah '63	1963	6.00	15.00
Roulette R-52244	(M)	In Tribute	1963	5.00	12.00
Roulette SR-52244	(S)	In Tribute	1963	6.00	15.00
Roulette R-52253	(M)	Stranger On Earth	1964	5.00	12.00
Roulette SR-52253	(S)	Stranger On Earth	1964	6.00	15.00
Roulette R-52269	(M)	Dinah Washington	1964	5.00	12.00
Roulette SR-52269	(S)	Dinah Washington	1964	6.00	15.00
Roulette R-52289	(M)	The Best Of Dinah Washington	1965	4.00	10.00
Roulette SR-52289	(S)	The Best Of Dinah Washington	1965	5.00	12.00
Mercury R-60928	(M)	The Queen And Quincy	1965	4.00	10.00
Mercury SR-60928	(S)	The Queen And Quincy	1965	5.00	12.00
Mercury MG-21119	(M)	Dinah Discovered	1967	4.00	10.00
Mercury SR-61119	(S)	Dinah Discovered	1967	5.00	12.00
Mercury PKW-2-121	(S)	The Original Queen Of Soul	1969	5.00	12.00
Mercury SRM-2-603	(S)	This Is My Story		6.00	15.00

WASHINGTON, JUSTINE

Sue 1042	(M)	Only Those In Love	1965	8.00	20.00
Sue S-1042	(S)	Only Those In Love	1965	10.00	25.00

WATERFORD, "CROWN PRINCE"

Aladdin 703 (10")	(M)	Party After Hours (Red vinyl)	1956	210.00	350.00
Aladdin 703 (10")	(M)	Party After Hours	1956	100.00	200.00
		(Fatures Wynonie Harris and Amos Milburn.)			

WATSON, DOC (& MERLE WATSON)

Folkways FA-2366	(M)	Doc Watson And Family	1963	6.00	15.00
Vanguard VSD-9152	(M)	Doc Watson	1964	5.00	12.00
Vanguard VSD7-9152	(S)	Doc Watson	1964	6.00	15.00

Label		Title	Year	VG+	NM
Vanguard VSD-9170	(M)	Doc Watson And Son	1965	5.00	12.00
Vanguard VSD7-9170	(S)	Doc Watson And Son	1965	6.00	15.00
Vanguard VSD-9213	(M)	Southbound	1966	5.00	12.00
Vanguard VSD7-9213	(S)	Southbound	1966	6.00	15.00
Vanguard VSD-9239	(M)	Home Again	1967	5.00	12.00
Vanguard VSD7-9239	(S)	Home Again	1967	6.00	15.00
Vanguard VSD7-9276	(S)	Good Deal	1968	6.00	15.00
Poppy PYS-5703	(S)	The Elementary Doc Watson	1972	4.00	10.00
Poppy LA022	(S)	Then And Now	1973	4.00	10.00
Poppy LA210	(S)	Two Days In November	1974	4.00	10.00

WATSON, JOHNNY "GUITAR"

Label		Title	Year	VG+	NM
King LP-857	(M)	Johnny Guitar Watson	1963	50.00	100.00
Chess 1490	(M)	Blues Soul	1965	20.00	50.00
OKeh OKM-4118	(M)	Bad	1967	8.00	20.00
OKeh OKS-14118	(S)	Bad	1967	10.00	25.00
OKeh OKM-4122	(M)	Two For The Price Of One	1967	8.00	20.00
OKeh OKS-14122	(S)	Two For The Price Of One (With Larry Williams.)	1967	10.00	25.00
OKeh OKM-4124	(M)	In The Fats Bag	1967	8.00	20.00
OKeh OKS-14124	(S)	In The Fats Bag	1967	10.00	25.00
Cadet 4056	(S)	I Cried For You	1967	8.00	20.00

WAVE CRESTS, THE

Label		Title	Year	VG+	NM
Viking VKS-6606	(M)	Surftime U.S.A.	1963	12.00	30.00

WAYFARERS, THE

Label		Title	Year	VG+	NM
RCA LPM-2666	(M)	Come Along With The Wayfarers	1963	5.00	12.00
RCA LSP-2666	(S)	Come Along With The Wayfarers	1963	6.00	15.00
RCA LPM-2735	(M)	The Wayfarers At The Hungry i	1963	5.00	12.00
RCA LSP-2735	(S)	The Wayfarers At The Hungry i	1963	6.00	15.00
RCA LPM-2946	(M)	The Wayfarers At The World's Fair	1964	5.00	12.00
RCA LSP-2946	(S)	The Wayfarers At The World's Fair	1964	6.00	15.00

WAYFARERS TRIO, THE

Label		Title	Year	VG+	NM
Mercury MG-20634	(M)	Songs Of The Blue And Grey	1961	5.00	12.00
Mercury SR-60634	(S)	Songs Of The Blue And Grey	1961	6.00	15.00

WAYNE, FRANCES

Label		Title	Year	VG+	NM
Atlantic 1263	(M)	The Warm Sound Of Frances Wayne		14.00	35.00
Epic LN-3222	(M)	Songs For My Man		10.00	25.00
Brunswick BL-54022	(M)	Frances Wayne		10.00	25.00

WAYNE, WEE WILLIE

Label		Title	Year	VG+	NM
Imperial LP-9144	(M)	Travelin' Mood	1961	35.00	70.00

WE FIVE, THE

Label		Title	Year	VG+	NM
A&M LP-111	(M)	You Were On My Mind	1965	5.00	12.00
A&M SP-4111	(S)	You Were On My Mind	1965	6.00	15.00
A&M LP-138	(M)	Make Someone Happy	1967	4.00	10.00
A&M SP-4138	(S)	Make Someone Happy	1967	5.00	12.00
A&M SP-4168	(S)	The Return Of We Five	1969	4.00	10.00

WEASELS, THE

Label		Title	Year	VG+	NM
Wing MGW-12282	(M)	The Liverpool Beat	1964	8.00	20.00
Wing SRW-16282	(S)	The Liverpool Beat	1964	10.00	25.00

WEAVERS, THE

Label		Title	Year	VG+	NM
Decca DL-8893	(M)	Best Of The Weavers		10.00	25.00
Decca DL-8909	(M)	Folk Songs Around The World		10.00	25.00
Decca DXB-173	(M)	Best Of The Weavers		10.00	25.00
Decca DXSB7-173	(P)	Best Of The Weavers		8.00	20.00
Vanguard VRS-2022	(M)	Travelling On With The Weavers		5.00	12.00
Vanguard VSD-2022	(S)	Travelling On With The Weavers		6.00	15.00
Vanguard VRS-2030	(M)	The Weavers At Home		5.00	12.00
Vanguard VSD-2030	(S)	The Weavers At Home		6.00	15.00
Vanguard VRS-2101	(M)	Almanac		5.00	12.00
Vanguard VSD-2101	(S)	Almanac		6.00	15.00
Vanguard VRS-2150	(M)	Reunion At Carnegie Hall	1963	5.00	12.00
Vanguard VSD-2150	(S)	Reunion At Carnegie Hall	1963	6.00	15.00
Vanguard VRS-9010	(M)	The Weavers At Carnegie Hall		6.00	15.00

Label		Title	Year	VG+	NM
Vanguard VRS-9013	(M)	The Weavers On Tour		6.00	15.00
Vanguard VRS-9075	(M)	The Weavers At Carnegie Hall, Volume 2		6.00	15.00
Vanguard VRS-9161	(M)	Reunion At Carnegie Hall	1965	5.00	12.00
Vanguard VSD7-9161	(S)	Reunion At Carnegie Hall	1965	6.00	15.00
Vanguard VRS-3001	(M)	Songbook	1967	5.00	12.00
Vanguard VSD7-3001	(S)	Songbook	1967	5.00	12.00
Vanguard VSD7-6533	(S)	The Weavers At Carnegie Hall	1970	4.00	10.00
Vanguard VSD-6537	(S)	The Weavers On Tour	1970	4.00	10.00

WEB, THE

Deram DES-18018	(S)	Fully Interlocking	1968	8.00	20.00

WEBB, JACK

Warners W-1207	(M)	You're My Girl		8.00	20.00
Warners WS-1207	(S)	You're My Girl		10.00	25.00

WEDGES, THE

Time T-2090	(M)	Hang Ten	1963	10.00	25.00
Time ST-2090	(S)	Hang Ten	1963	12.00	30.00

WEIR, BOB

Warners BS-2627	(S)	Ace	1973	14.00	35.00

WELCH, LENNY

Cadence CLP-5068	(M)	Since I Fell For You	1963	8.00	20.00
Cadence CLP-25068	(S)	Since I Fell For You	1963	10.00	25.00
Columbia CL-2430	(M)	Since I Fell For You	1965	6.00	15.00
Columbia CS-9230	(S)	Since I Fell For You	1965	8.00	20.00
Kapp KL-1457	(M)	Two Different Worlds	1965	5.00	12.00
Kapp KS-3457	(S)	Two Different Worlds	1965	6.00	15.00
Kapp KL-1481	(M)	Rags To Riches	1966	5.00	12.00
Kapp KS-3481	(S)	Rags To Riches	1966	6.00	15.00
Kapp KL-1517	(M)	Lenny	1967	5.00	12.00
Kapp KS-3517	(S)	Lenny	1967	6.00	15.00

WELLS, JUNIOR (AMOS WELLS, JR.)

Delmark 612	(M)	Hoodoo Man Blues	1966	10.00	25.00
Vanguard VRS-9231	(M)	It's My Life Baby	1966	6.00	15.00
Vanguard VSD-79231	(S)	It's My Life Baby	1966	8.00	20.00
Delmark 628	(S)	Southside Blues Jam	1967	6.00	15.00
Vanguard 79262	(S)	Comin' At You	1968	6.00	15.00
Blue Rock 64002	(S)	You're Tuff Enough	1968	6.00	15.00
Delmark 640	(S)	Blues Hit Big Town	1969	6.00	15.00

WELLS, KITTY

Decca DL-8293	(M)	Country Hit Parade	1956	14.00	35.00
Decca DL-8552	(M)	Winner Of Your Heart	1956	14.00	35.00
Decca DL-8858	(M)	Dust On The Bible	1959	10.00	25.00
Decca DL-8888	(M)	After Dark	1959	10.00	25.00
Decca DL-8979	(M)	Kitty's Choice	1960	8.00	20.00
Decca DL7-8979	(S)	Kitty's Choice	1960	10.00	25.00
		(Decca albums above have black & silver labels.)			
Decca DL-4075	(M)	Seasons Of My Heart	1960	6.00	15.00
Decca DL7-4075	(S)	Seasons Of My Heart	1960	8.00	20.00
Decca DL-4108	(M)	Kitty Wells' Golden Favorites	1961	6.00	15.00
Decca DL7-4108	(S)	Kitty Wells' Golden Favorites	1961	8.00	20.00
Decca DL-4109	(M)	Golden Favorites	1961	6.00	15.00
Decca DL7-4109	(E)	Golden Favorites	1961	5.00	12.00
Decca DL-4141	(M)	Heartbreak U.S.A.	1961	5.00	12.00
Decca DL7-4141	(S)	Heartbreak U.S.A.	1961	6.00	15.00
Decca DL-4197	(M)	Queen Of Country Music	1962	5.00	12.00
Decca DL7-4197	(S)	Queen Of Country Music	1962	6.00	15.00
Decca DL-4270	(M)	Singing On Sunday	1962	5.00	12.00
Decca DL7-4270	(S)	Singing On Sunday	1962	6.00	15.00
Decca DL-4349	(M)	Christmas With Kitty Wells	1962	5.00	12.00
Decca DL7-4349	(S)	Christmas With Kitty Wells	1962	6.00	15.00
Decca DXB-174	(M)	The Kitty Wells Story (With booklet)	1963	8.00	20.00
Decca DXSB7-174	(S)	The Kitty Wells Story (With booklet)	1963	10.00	25.00
Decca DL-4493	(M)	Especially For You	1964	5.00	12.00
Decca DL7-4493	(S)	Especially For You	1964	6.00	15.00

Label		Title	Year	VG+	NM
Decca DL-4554	(M)	Country Music Time	1964	5.00	12.00
Decca DL7-4554	(S)	Country Music Time	1964	6.00	15.00
Decca DL-4612	(M)	Burning Memories	1965	5.00	12.00
Decca DL7-4612	(S)	Burning Memories	1965	6.00	15.00
Decca DL-4658	(M)	Lonesome, Sad And Blue	1965	5.00	12.00
Decca DL7-4658	(S)	Lonesome, Sad And Blue	1965	6.00	15.00
Decca DL-4679	(M)	Family Gospel Sing	1965	5.00	12.00
Decca DL7-4679	(S)	Family Gospel Sing	1965	6.00	15.00
Decca DL-4741	(M)	Songs Made Famous By Jim Reeves	1966	5.00	12.00
Decca DL7-4741	(S)	Songs Made Famous By Jim Reeves	1966	6.00	15.00
Decca DL-4776	(M)	Country All The Way	1966	5.00	12.00
Decca DL7-4776	(S)	Country All The Way	1966	6.00	15.00
Decca DL-4831	(M)	The Kitty Wells Show	1966	5.00	12.00
Decca DL7-4831	(S)	The Kitty Wells Show	1966	6.00	15.00

(Decca albums above have black labels with
"Mfrd by Decca" beneath the rainbow.)

WELLS, MARY

Label		Title	Year	VG+	NM
Motown 600	(M)	Bye Bye Baby	1961	30.00	60.00
Motown 605	(M)	The One Who Really Loves You	1962	20.00	50.00
Motown 607	(M)	Two Lovers	1963	16.00	40.00
Motown 611	(M)	Live On Stage	1963	10.00	25.00
Motown 611	(S)	Live On Stage	1963	12.00	30.00
Motown 616	(M)	Greatest Hits	1964	10.00	25.00
Motown 617	(M)	My Guy	1964	14.00	35.00
Motown 630	(M)	Nothing But A Man (Sdtk)	1965	8.00	20.00
Motown MS-630	(S)	Nothing But A Man (Sdtk)	1965	10.00	25.00
20th Century TFM-3171	(M)	Mary Wells	1965	8.00	20.00
20th Century TFS-4171	(S)	Mary Wells	1965	10.00	25.00
20th Century TFM-3178	(M)	Love Songs To The Beatles	1965	14.00	35.00
20th Century TFS-4178	(S)	Love Songs To The Beatles	1965	16.00	40.00
Movietone 71010	(M)	Ooh	1966	8.00	20.00
Movietone 72010	(S)	Ooh	1966	10.00	25.00
Atco 33-199	(M)	Two Sides Of Mary Wells	1966	8.00	20.00
Atco SD-33-199	(S)	Two Sides Of Mary Wells	1966	10.00	25.00
Motown 653	(M)	Vintage Stock	1966	10.00	25.00
Motown 653	(S)	Vintage Stock	1966	12.00	30.00
Jubilee JGS-8018	(S)	Servin' Up Some Soul	1968	6.00	15.00

WEST, ADAM, & BURT WARD

Label		Title	Year	VG+	NM
20th Century TF-4180	(M)	Batman (Sdtk)	1966	20.00	50.00
20th Century TFS-4180	(S)	Batman (Sdtk)	1966	30.00	60.00

WEST, SPEEDY

Label		Title	Year	VG+	NM
Capitol H-520 (10")	(M)	Two Guitars Country Style	1954	75.00	150.00
Capitol T-520	(M)	Two Guitars Country Style	1956	40.00	80.00
Capitol T-956	(M)	West Of Hawaii	1958	20.00	50.00
Capitol T-1341	(M)	Steel Guitar	1960	16.00	40.00
Capitol ST-1341	(S)	Steel Guitar	1960	20.00	50.00
Capitol T-1835	(M)	Guitar Spectacular	1962	14.00	35.00
Capitol ST-1835	(S)	Guitar Spectacular	1962	16.00	40.00

WEST COAST POP ART EXPERIMENTAL BAND, THE

Label		Title	Year	VG+	NM
Fifo M101	(M)	West Coast Pop Art Experimental Band	1966	300.00	500.00
Amos AAS-7004	(S)	Where's My Daddy	1969	16.00	40.00
Reprise R-6247	(M)	Part One	1967	8.00	20.00
Reprise RS-6247	(S)	Part One	1967	10.00	25.00
Reprise R-6270	(M)	Volume 2	1967	8.00	20.00
Reprise RS-6270	(S)	Volume 2	1967	10.00	25.00
Reprise RS-6298	(S)	A Child's Guide To Good And Evil	1968	12.00	30.00

WESTON, KIM
Also refer to Marvin Gaye.

Label		Title	Year	VG+	NM
MGM E-4477	(M)	For The First Time	1967	6.00	15.00
MGM SE-4477	(S)	For The First Time	1967	8.00	20.00
Volt VOS-6014	(S)	Kim Kim Kim	1971	5.00	12.00

WHALEFEATHERS

Label		Title	Year	VG+	NM
Nasco 9003	(S)	Whalefeathers Declare	1969	20.00	50.00
Nasco 9005	(S)	Whalefeathers	1970	20.00	50.00

Label		Title	Year	VG+	NM
WHATNAUTS, THE					
Stang 1005	(S)	Introducing The Whatnauts	1970	6.00	15.00
Stang 1012	(S)	Reaching For The Stars	1971	6.00	15.00
WHITCOMB, IAN					
Tower T-5004	(M)	You Turn Me On	1965	8.00	20.00
Tower DT-5004	(E)	You Turn Me On	1965	6.00	15.00
Tower T-5042	(M)	Mod, Mod, Music Hall	1966	5.00	12.00
Tower ST-5042	(S)	Mod, Mod, Music Hall	1966	6.00	15.00
Tower T-5071	(M)	Yellow Underground	1967	5.00	12.00
Tower ST-5071	(S)	Yellow Underground	1967	6.00	15.00
Tower ST-5100	(S)	Sock Me Some Rock	1968	6.00	15.00
WHITE, JOSH					
Also refer to Leadbelly.					
Decca DL-5082 (10")	(M)	Ballads		16.00	40.00
Decca DL-5247 (10")	(M)	Ballads, Volume 2		16.00	40.00
London 338 (10")	(M)	Josh White		12.00	30.00
London 341 (10")	(M)	Josh White Program		12.00	30.00
Mercury MG-25015 (10")	(M)	Josh White Sings		14.00	35.00
Mercury MG-20203	(M)	Josh White's Blues		10.00	25.00
Decca DL-8665	(M)	Josh White		12.00	30.00
Elektra EKL-102	(M)	Josh At Midnight		8.00	20.00
Elektra EKL-114	(M)	Josh		8.00	20.00
Elektra EKL-123	(M)	25th Anniversary Album		8.00	20.00
Elektra EKL-158	(M)	Chain Gang Songs		8.00	20.00
Period 1209	(M)	Josh White And Big Bill Broonzy		10.00	25.00
Stinson 14 (10")	(M)	Blues		6.00	15.00
Stinson 15 (10")	(M)	Folk Songs		6.00	15.00
Mercury MG-20821	(M)	The Beginning	1963	6.00	15.00
Mercury SR-60821	(S)	The Beginning	1963	8.00	20.00
WHITE, TONY JOE					
Monument SLP-18114	(S)	Black And White	1969	6.00	15.00
Monument SLP-18133	(S)	Tony Joe White Continued	1969	5.00	12.00
Monument SLP-18142	(S)	Tony Joe	1970	5.00	12.00
WHITE CLOUD					
Good Medicine 3500	(S)	White Cloud	1972	5.00	12.00
WHITE DUCK					
Uni 73140	(S)	In Season	1972	6.00	15.00
Uni 73122	(S)	White Duck	1971	6.00	15.00
WHITE ELEPHANT					
Just Sunshine 3000	(S)	White Elephant	1973	6.00	15.00
WHITE LIGHT					
Century 39955	(S)	White Light		50.00	100.00
WHITE LIGHTNIN'					
ABC 690	(S)	File Under Rock	1969	6.00	15.00
WHITE WITCH					
Capricorn CPN-0107	(S)	White Witch	1973	6.00	15.00
Capricorn CPN-0129	(S)	A Spiritual Greeting	1974	5.00	12.00
WHITEHEAD, CHARLIE, & THE SWAMP DOGG BAND					
Fungus FB-25145	(S)	Charlie Whitehead		6.00	15.00
WHITING, MARGARET					
Also refer to Mel Torme.					
Capitol H-209 (10")	(M)	Margaret Whiting Sings Rodgers And Hart		14.00	35.00
Capitol T-410	(M)	Love Songs		12.00	30.00
Capitol T-685	(M)	Margaret Whiting Sings For The Starry-Eyed		12.00	30.00
Verve V-4038	(M)	The Jerome Kern Song Book		12.00	30.00
Verve V6-4038	(S)	The Jerome Kern Song Book		14.00	35.00
Dot DLP-3072	(M)	Goin' Places	1957	8.00	20.00
Dot DLP-3113	(M)	Margaret	1958	6.00	15.00
Dot DLP-25113	(S)	Margaret	1958	8.00	20.00

Label		Title	Year	VG+	NM
Dot DLP-3176	(M)	Margaret Whiting Great Hits	1959	6.00	15.00
Dot DLP-25176	(S)	Margaret Whiting Great Hits	1959	8.00	20.00
Dot DLP-3235	(M)	Ten Top Hits	1960	6.00	15.00
Dot DLP-25235	(S)	Ten Top Hits	1960	8.00	20.00
Dot DLP-3337	(M)	Just A Dream	1960	6.00	15.00
Dot DLP-25337	(S)	Just A Dream	1960	8.00	20.00
MGM E-4006	(M)	Past Midnight		5.00	12.00
MGM SE-4006	(S)	Past Midnight		6.00	15.00

WHITMAN, SLIM

Label		Title	Year	VG+	NM
RCA LPM-3217 (10")	(M)	Slim Whitman Sings And Yodels	1954	30.00	60.00
Imperial LP-3004 (10")	(M)	America's Favorite Folk Artist	1954	30.00	60.00
Imperial LP-9003	(M)	Favorites	1956	20.00	50.00
Imperial LP-9026	(M)	Slim Whitman Sings	1957	20.00	50.00
		(Imperial albums above have maroon labels.)			
Imperial LP-9056	(M)	Slim Whitman	1958	14.00	35.00
Imperial LP-9064	(M)	Sings	1959	14.00	35.00
Imperial LP-9077	(M)	Annie Laurie	1959	14.00	35.00
Imperial LP-9088	(M)	I'll Walk With God	1960	12.00	30.00
Imperial LP-9102	(M)	Million Record Hits	1960	12.00	30.00
Imperial LP-9135	(M)	First Visit To Britain	1960	10.00	25.00
Imperial LP-9137	(M)	Just Call Me Lonesome	1961	10.00	25.00
Imperial LP-9156	(M)	Once In A Lifetime	1961	10.00	25.00
Imperial LP-9194	(M)	Slim Whitman Sings	1962	10.00	25.00
Imperial LP-9209	(M)	Heart Songs And Love Songs	1962	10.00	25.00
Imperial LP-9226	(M)	I'm A Lonely Wanderer	1963	10.00	25.00
Imperial LP-9235	(M)	Yodeling	1963	10.00	25.00
Imperial LP-9245	(M)	Irish Songs, The Whitman Way	1963	10.00	25.00
Imperial LP-9252	(M)	All Time Favorites	1964	10.00	25.00
		(Imperial albums above have black labels with stars on top.)			
Imperial LP-9268	(M)	Country Songs/City Hits	1964	6.00	15.00
Imperial LP-12268	(S)	Country Songs/City Hits	1964	8.00	20.00
Imperial LP-9277	(M)	Love Song Of The Waterfall	1964	6.00	15.00
Imperial LP-12277	(S)	Love Song Of The Waterfall	1964	8.00	20.00
Imperial LP-9288	(M)	Reminiscing	1965	6.00	15.00
Imperial LP-12288	(S)	Reminiscing	1965	8.00	20.00
Imperial LP-9303	(M)	More Than Yesterday	1965	6.00	15.00
Imperial LP-12303	(S)	More Than Yesterday	1965	8.00	20.00
Camden CAL-954	(M)	Birmingham Jail	1966	8.00	20.00
Imperial LP-12032	(E)	I'll Walk With God	1966	5.00	12.00
Imperial LP-12077	(E)	Sweeter Than Flowers	1966	5.00	12.00
Imperial LP-12100	(E)	Country Hits, Volume 1	1966	5.00	12.00
Imperial LP-12102	(E)	Song Of The Old Waterwheel	1966	5.00	12.00
Imperial LP-12104	(E)	Country Hits, Volume 2	1966	5.00	12.00
Imperial LP-12105	(E)	My Best To You	1966	5.00	12.00
Imperial LP-12106	(E)	Country Favorites	1966	5.00	12.00
Imperial LP-12135	(E)	I'll Never Stop Loving You	1966	5.00	12.00
Imperial LP-12137	(E)	Portrait	1966	5.00	12.00
Imperial LP-12156	(E)	Cool Water	1966	5.00	12.00
Imperial LP-12171	(E)	Forever	1966	5.00	12.00
Imperial LP-12194	(E)	Anytime	1966	5.00	12.00
Imperial LP-12209	(E)	Heart Songs And Happy Songs	1966	5.00	12.00
Imperial LP-12226	(E)	I'm A Lonely Wanderer	1966	5.00	12.00
Imperial LP-12245	(E)	Irish Songs, The Whitman Way	1966	5.00	12.00
Imperial LP-12252	(E)	Favorites	1966	5.00	12.00
Imperial LP-9308	(M)	God's Hand In Mine	1966	5.00	12.00
Imperial LP-12308	(S)	God's Hand In Mine	1966	6.00	15.00
Imperial LP-9313	(M)	A Travelin' Man	1966	5.00	12.00
Imperial LP-12313	(S)	A Travelin' Man	1966	6.00	15.00
Imperial LP-9333	(M)	A Time For Love	1966	5.00	12.00
Imperial LP-12333	(S)	A Time For Love	1966	6.00	15.00
Imperial LP-9342	(M)	15th Anniversary	1967	5.00	12.00
Imperial LP-12342	(S)	15th Anniversary	1967	6.00	15.00
Imperial LP-9356	(M)	Country Memories	1967	5.00	12.00
Imperial LP-12356	(S)	Country Memories	1967	6.00	15.00
Imperial LP-12375	(S)	In Love, The Whitman Way	1968	5.00	12.00
Imperial LP-12411	(S)	Happy Street	1969	5.00	12.00
Imperial LP-12436	(S)	Slim	1969	5.00	12.00
Imperial LP-12448	(S)	The Slim Whitman Christmas Album	1969	5.00	12.00

Label		Title	Year	VG+	NM
WHO, THE					
Decca DL-4664	(M)	The Who Sing My Generation	1966	20.00	50.00
Decca DL7-4664	(E)	The Who Sing My Generation	1966	16.00	40.00
Decca DL-4892	(M)	Happy Jack	1967	16.00	40.00
Decca DL7-4892	(S)	Happy Jack	1967	12.00	30.00
Decca DL-4950	(M)	The Who Sell Out	1967	20.00	50.00
Decca DL7-4950	(S)	The Who Sell Out	1967	10.00	25.00
Decca DL7-5064	(P)	Magic Bus	1968	16.00	40.00
Decca DL7-34568	(P)	The Who/The Strawberry Alarm Clock	1969	20.00	50.00
Decca DXSW-7205	(S)	Tommy (With booklet)	1969	12.00	30.00
Decca DL7-9175	(S)	Live At Leeds	1970	12.00	30.00
		(Fold-open jacket includes twelve			
		different inserts, bios and photos.)			
Ode SP-99001	(S)	Tommy (Original Cast)	1970	8.00	20.00
Cotillion CT3-500	(S)	Woodstock (Sdtk)	1970	8.00	20.00
Decca DL7-9182	(S)	Who's Next	1971	6.00	15.00
Decca DL7-9184	(P)	Meaty, Beaty, Big And Bouncy	1971	6.00	15.00
Track 2126	(P)	Odds And Sods	1974	6.00	15.00
Track 2-4067	(S)	A Quick One/The Who Sell Out	1974	5.00	12.00
Track 2-4068	(P)	Magic Bus/The Who Sing My Generation	1974	5.00	12.00
Direct Disc 16610	(S)	Who Are You	1979	14.00	35.00
Mobile Fidelity 1-115	(S)	Face Dances	1984	6.00	15.00
WICHITA TRAIN WHISTLE, THE					
Dot DLP-25861	(S)	The Wichita Train Whistle Sings	1968	16.00	40.00
WILBURN BROTHERS, THE					
Decca DL-8576	(M)	The Wilburn Brothers	1957	10.00	25.00
Decca DL-8774	(M)	Side By Side	1958	8.00	20.00
Decca DL7-8774	(S)	Side By Side	1958	12.00	30.00
Decca DL-8959	(M)	Livin' In God's Country	1959	8.00	20.00
Decca DL7-8959	(S)	Livin' In God's Country	1959	12.00	30.00
		(Decca albums above have black & silver labels.)			
Decca DL-4058	(M)	The Big Heartbreak	1960	6.00	15.00
Decca DL7-4058	(S)	The Big Heartbreak	1960	8.00	20.00
Decca DL-4122	(M)	City Limits	1961	6.00	15.00
Decca DL7-4122	(S)	City Limits	1961	8.00	20.00
Decca DL-4142	(M)	The Wilburn Brothers Sing	1961	6.00	15.00
Decca DL7-4142	(S)	The Wilburn Brothers Sing	1961	8.00	20.00
King 746	(M)	The Wonderful Wilburn Brothers	1961	16.00	40.00
Decca DL-4225	(M)	Folk Songs	1962	5.00	12.00
Decca DL7-4225	(S)	Folk Songs	1962	6.00	15.00
Decca DL-4391	(M)	Trouble's Back In Town	1963	5.00	12.00
Decca DL7-4391	(S)	Trouble's Back In Town	1963	6.00	15.00
Decca DL-4464	(M)	Take Up Thy Cross	1964	5.00	12.00
Decca DL7-4464	(S)	Take Up Thy Cross	1964	6.00	15.00
Decca DL-4544	(M)	Never Alone	1964	5.00	12.00
Decca DL7-4544	(S)	Never Alone	1964	6.00	15.00
Decca DL-4615	(M)	Country Gold	1965	5.00	12.00
Decca DL7-4615	(S)	Country Gold	1965	6.00	15.00
Decca DL-4645	(M)	I'm Gonna Tie One On Tonight	1965	5.00	12.00
Decca DL7-4645	(S)	I'm Gonna Tie One On Tonight	1965	6.00	15.00
Decca DL-4721	(M)	The Wilburn Brothers Show	1966	6.00	15.00
Decca DL7-4721	(S)	The Wilburn Brothers Show	1966	8.00	20.00
Decca DL-4764	(M)	Let's Go Country	1966	5.00	12.00
Decca DL7-4764	(S)	Let's Go Country	1966	6.00	15.00
Decca DL-4824	(M)	Two For The Show	1967	5.00	12.00
Decca DL7-4824	(S)	Two For The Show	1967	6.00	15.00
		(Decca albums above have black labels with			
		"Mfrd by Decca" beneath the rainbow.)			
WILDCATS, THE					
United Arts. UAL-3031	(M)	Bandstand Record Hop	1958	12.00	30.00
WILDE, MARTY					
Epic LN-3686	(M)	Bad Boy	1960	20.00	50.00
Epic LN-3711	(M)	Wilde About Marty	1960	14.00	35.00
Epic BN-3575	(S)	Wilde About Marty	1960	16.00	40.00
WILDWEEDS, THE					
Vanguard VSD-6552	(S)	Wildweeds	1970	6.00	15.00

Label		Title	Year	VG+	NM
WILEY, LEE					
Columbia CL-6125 (10")	(M)	Lee Wiley Sings Vincet Youmans		14.00	35.00
Columbia CL-6126 (10")	(M)	Lee Wiley Sings Irving Berlin		14.00	35.00
Columbia CL-656	(M)	Night In Manhattan		10.00	25.00
Storyville 312 (10")	(M)	Lee Wiley Sings Rodgers And Hart		14.00	35.00
Storyville 911	(M)	Duologue		10.00	25.00
RCA LPM-1408	(M)	West Of The Moon	1957	10.00	25.00
RCA LPM-1566	(M)	A Touch Of The Blues	1957	10.00	25.00
Ric MS-2002	(S)	One And Only Lee Wiley	1965	10.00	25.00
WILKINSON TRI-CYCLE					
Date TES-4016	(S)	Wilkinson Tri-cycle	1969	6.00	15.00
WILLETT, SLIM					
Audio Lab 1542	(M)	Slim Willett		20.00	50.00
WILLETTE, BABY FACE					
Argo 739	(S)	Mo-Roc	1964	6.00	15.00
WILLIAMS, BIG JOE					
Folkways F-3820	(M)	Mississippi's Big Joe Williams	1962	8.00	20.00
Folkways FS-3820	(S)	Mississippi's Big Joe Williams	1962	10.00	25.00
Delmark D-604	(M)	Blues On Highway 49	1962	10.00	25.00
Bluesville BV-1056	(M)	Blues For Nine Strings	1963	8.00	20.00
Bluesville BV-1067	(M)	Big Joe Williams At Folk City	1963	8.00	20.00
Bluesville BV-1083	(M)	Studio Blues	1964	8.00	20.00
Delmark D-609	(M)	Starvin' Chain Blues	1966	6.00	15.00
Delmark SD-609	(S)	Starvin' Chain Blues	1966	8.00	20.00
Milestone 3001	(M)	Classic Delta Blues	1966	6.00	15.00
Folkways 31004	(M)	Hell Bound And Heaven Sent	1967	6.00	15.00
World Pacific 21897	(S)	Big Joe Williams	1969	6.00	15.00
WILLIAMS, BILLY					
Coral CRL57184	(M)	Billy Williams	1957	16.00	40.00
MGM E-3400	(M)	The Billy Williams Quartet	1957	16.00	40.00
Mercury MG-20317	(M)	Billy Williams Singing Oh Yeah	1958	16.00	40.00
Wing MGW-12131	(M)	Vote For Billy Williams	1959	16.00	40.00
Coral CRL-57251	(M)	Half Sweet, Half Beat	1959	16.00	40.00
Coral CRL-57343	(M)	The Billy Williams Revue	1960	16.00	40.00
WILLIAMS, BILLY DEE					
Prestige LA-30001	(M)	Let's Misbehave	1961	6.00	15.00
WILLIAMS, HANK (LUKE THE DRIFTER)					
MGM E-107 (10")	(M)	Hank Williams Sings	1952	40.00	80.00
MGM E-168 (10")	(M)	Moanin' The Blues	1952	35.00	70.00
MGM E-202 (10")	(M)	Hank Williams Memorial Album	1953	35.00	70.00
MGM E-203 (10")	(M)	Hank Williams As Luke The Drifter	1953	40.00	80.00
MGM E-242 (10")	(M)	Honky Tonkin'	1954	35.00	70.00
MGM E-243 (10")	(M)	I Saw The Light	1954	35.00	70.00
MGM E-291 (10")	(M)	Ramblin' Man	1954	35.00	70.00
MGM E-3219	(M)	Ramblin' Man	1955	30.00	60.00
MGM E-3267	(M)	Hank Williams As Luke The Drifter	1955	35.00	70.00
MGM E-3272	(M)	Hank Williams Memorial Album	1955	30.00	60.00
MGM E-3330	(M)	Moanin' The Blues	1956	30.00	60.00
MGM E-3331	(M)	I Saw The Light (Green picture cover)	1956	30.00	60.00
MGM E-3412	(M)	Honky Tonkin'	1957	30.00	60.00
MGM 3E-2	(M)	36 Of Hank Williams' Greatest Hits	1957	50.00	100.00
MGM 3E-4	(M)	36 More Of Hank Williams' Greatest Hits	1958	50.00	100.00
MGM E-3560	(M)	Sing Me A Blue Song	1958	20.00	50.00
MGM E-3605	(M)	The Immortal Hank Williams	1958	20.00	50.00
MGM E-3733	(M)	The Unforgettable Hank Williams	1959	20.00	50.00
		(MGM albums above have yellow labels.)			
MGM E-3803	(M)	The Lonesome Sound Of Hank Williams	1960	12.00	30.00
MGM E-3850	(M)	Wait For The Light To Shine	1960	12.00	30.00
MGM E-3918	(M)	Hank Williams' Greatest Hits	1961	12.00	30.00
MGM E-3923	(M)	Hank Williams Lives Again	1961	12.00	30.00
MGM E-3924	(M)	Let Me Sing A Blue Song	1961	12.00	30.00
MGM E-3925	(M)	Wanderin' Around	1961	12.00	30.00
MGM E-3926	(M)	I'm Blue Inside	1961	12.00	30.00
MGM E-3927	(M)	Luke The Drifter	1961	14.00	35.00

Label		Title	Year	VG+	NM
MGM E-3928	(M)	First, Last And Always	1961	14.00	35.00
MGM E-3955	(M)	The Spirit Of Hank Williams	1961	14.00	35.00
MGM E-3999	(M)	On Stage! Hank Williams Recorded Live	1961	16.00	40.00
MGM E-3999	(M)	Hank Williams On Stage Recorded Live	1962	12.00	30.00
MGM SE-3999	(E)	Hank Williams On Stage Recorded Live	1962	10.00	25.00
MGM E-4040	(M)	14 More Greatest Hits	1961	10.00	25.00
MGM E-4138	(M)	Beyond The Sunset	1961	12.00	30.00
MGM E-4140	(M)	14 More Greatest Hits, Volume 3	1962	10.00	25.00
MGM E-4168	(M)	The Very Best Of Hank Williams	1963	8.00	20.00
MGM SE-4168	(E)	The Very Best Of Hank Williams	1963	5.00	12.00
MGM E-4227	(M)	The Very Best Of Hank Williams, Volume 2	1964	8.00	20.00
MGM SE-4227	(E)	The Very Best Of Hank Williams, Volume 2	1964	5.00	12.00
MGM E-4254	(M)	Lost Highway And Other Folk Ballads	1964	8.00	20.00
MGM E-4267	(M)	The Hank Williams Story	1966	20.00	50.00
MGM E-4300	(M)	Kaw-Liga And Other Humorous Songs	1965	8.00	20.00
MGM SE-4300	(E)	Kaw-Liga And Other Humorous Songs	1965	5.00	12.00
Metro M-509	(M)	Hank Williams	1965	8.00	20.00
Metro MS-509	(E)	Hank Williams	1965	5.00	12.00
Metro M-547	(M)	Mr. And Mrs. Hank Williams	1965	8.00	20.00
Metro MS-547	(E)	Mr. And Mrs. Hank Williams	1965	5.00	12.00
Metro M-602	(M)	The Immortal Hank Williams	1966	8.00	20.00
Metro MS-602	(E)	The Immortal Hank Williams	1966	5.00	12.00
MGM E-4377	(M)	Hank Williams With Strings	1966	8.00	20.00
MGM SE-4377	(E)	Hank Williams With Strings	1966	5.00	12.00
MGM E-4380	(M)	Movin' On	1966	8.00	20.00
MGM SE-4380	(E)	Movin' On	1966	5.00	12.00
MGM E-4429	(M)	More Hank Williams And Strings	1966	8.00	20.00
MGM SE-4429	(E)	More Hank Williams And Strings	1966	5.00	12.00
MGM E-4481	(M)	I Won't Be Home No More	1967	8.00	20.00
MGM SE-4481	(E)	I Won't Be Home No More	1967	5.00	12.00
		(MGM albums above have black labels.)			
MGM E-4529	(M)	Hank Williams With Strings, Volume 3	1968	8.00	20.00
MGM SE-4529	(E)	Hank Williams With Strings, Volume 3	1968	5.00	12.00
MGM SE-4755	(E)	24 Of Hank Williams' Greatest Hits	1968	8.00	20.00
MGM E-4576	(M)	In The Beginning	1968	8.00	20.00
MGM SE-4576	(E)	In The Beginning	1968	5.00	12.00

WILLIAMS, HANK, & HANK WILLIAMS, JR.

Label		Title	Year	VG+	NM
MGM E-4276	(M)	Hank Williams, Sr., & Hank Williams. Jr.	1965	5.00	12.00
MGM SE-4276	(P)	Hank Williams, Sr., & Hank Williams. Jr.	1965	6.00	15.00
MGM E-4378	(M)	Again	1966	5.00	12.00
MGM SE-4378	(P)	Again	1966	6.00	15.00

WILLIAMS, HANK, JR. (& THE CHEATIN' HEARTS)

Label		Title	Year	VG+	NM
MGM E-4213	(M)	Songs Of Hank Williams	1963	6.00	15.00
MGM SE-4213	(S)	Songs Of Hank Williams	1963	8.00	20.00
MGM E-4251	(M)	Great Country Favorites	1964	6.00	15.00
MGM SE-4251	(S)	Great Country Favorites	1964	8.00	20.00
		(With Connie Francis.)			
MGM E-4260	(M)	Your Cheatin' Heart (Sdtk)	1964	6.00	15.00
MGM SE-4260	(S)	Your Cheatin' Heart (Sdtk)	1964	8.00	20.00
MGM E-4316	(M)	Ballads Of The Hills And Plains	1965	5.00	12.00
MGM SE-4316	(S)	Ballads Of The Hills And Plains	1965	6.00	15.00
MGM E-4344	(M)	Blue's My Name	1966	5.00	12.00
MGM SE-4344	(S)	Blue's My Name	1966	6.00	15.00
MGM E-4391	(M)	Country Shadows	1966	5.00	12.00
MGM SE-4391	(S)	Country Shadows	1966	6.00	15.00
MGM E-4428	(M)	In My Own Way	1967	5.00	12.00
MGM SE-4428	(S)	In My Own Way	1967	6.00	15.00
MGM E-4513	(M)	The Best Of Hank Williams, Jr.	1967	5.00	12.00
MGM SE-4513	(S)	The Best Of Hank Williams, Jr.	1967	6.00	15.00
		(MGM albums above have black labels.)			

WILLIAMS, JOE

Label		Title	Year	VG+	NM
Regent 6002	(M)	Joe Williams Sings Everyday	1956	14.00	35.00
Roulette R-52005	(M)	Man Ain't Supposed To Cry	1958	10.00	25.00
Roulette RS-52005	(S)	Man Ain't Supposed To Cry	1958	12.00	30.00
Roulette R-52021	(M)	Memories Ad Lib	1959	10.00	25.00
Roulette RS-52021	(S)	Memories Ad Lib	1959	12.00	30.00
Roulette R-52030	(M)	Joe Williams Sings About You!	1959	10.00	25.00
Roulette RS-52030	(S)	Joe Williams Sings About You!	1959	12.00	30.00

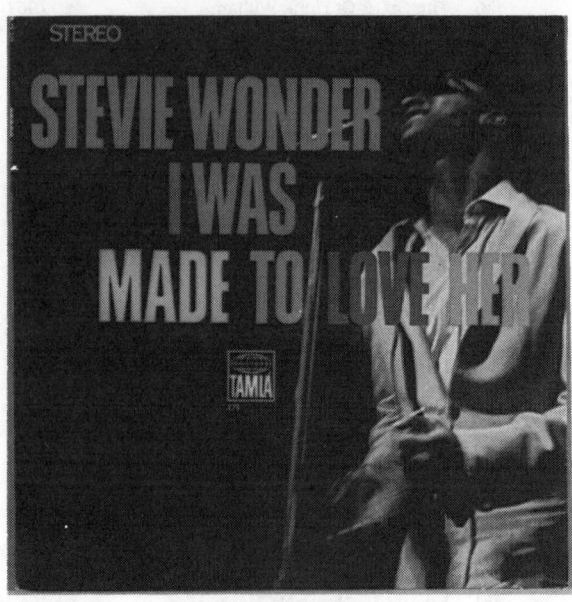

Stevie Wonder, *I Was Made To Love Her*. Built around the triumphant title tune, this was a typical Motown product of the time, with Stevie interpreting the hits of his stable mates and those of his predecessors with a few originals thrown in.

Dinah Washington, *Back To The Blues*. Best known for her 1959 hit, "What A Diff'rence A Day Makes," Ms. Washington was a successful jazz singer for years before making the popular charts. A blues stylist whose long-ranging influence vastly outweighs her current popularity.

Label		Title	Year	VG+	NM
Roulette R-52033	(M)	Everyday I Have The Blues	1959	10.00	25.00
Roulette RS-52033	(S)	Everyday I Have The Blues	1959	12.00	30.00
Roulette R-52039	(M)	That Kind Of Woman	1959	10.00	25.00
Roulette RS-52039	(S)	That Kind Of Woman	1959	12.00	30.00
Roulette R-52054	(M)	Just The Blues	1960	10.00	25.00
Roulette RS-52054	(S)	Just The Blues	1960	12.00	30.00
Roulette R-52066	(M)	Sentimental And Melancholy	1960	8.00	20.00
Roulette RS-52066	(S)	Sentimental And Melancholy	1960	10.00	25.00
Roulette R-52069	(M)	Together	1961	8.00	20.00
Roulette RS-52069	(S)	Together	1961	10.00	25.00
Roulette R-52071	(M)	Have A Good Time	1961	6.00	15.00
Roulette RS-52071	(S)	Have A Good Time	1961	8.00	20.00
Roulette R-52085	(M)	Swingin' Night At Birdland	1962	6.00	15.00
Roulette RS-52085	(S)	Swingin' Night At Birdland	1962	8.00	20.00
Roulette R-52102	(M)	One Is A Lonesome Number	1962	6.00	15.00
Roulette RS-52102	(S)	One Is A Lonesome Number	1962	8.00	20.00
Verve V-8488	(M)	Count Basie Swings/Joe Williams Sings	1962	5.00	12.00
Verve V6-8488	(S)	Count Basie Swings/Joe Williams Sings	1962	6.00	15.00
RCA LPM-2713	(M)	Jump For Joy	1963	5.00	12.00
RCA LSP-2713	(S)	Jump For Joy	1963	6.00	15.00
RCA LPM-2762	(M)	Joe Williams At Newport '63	1963	5.00	12.00
RCA LSP-2762	(S)	Joe Williams At Newport '63	1963	6.00	15.00
RCA LPM-2879	(M)	Me And The Blues	1963	5.00	12.00
RCA LSP-2879	(S)	Me And The Blues	1963	6.00	15.00
Roulette R-52105	(M)	New Kind Of Love	1964	5.00	12.00
Roulette RS-52105	(S)	New Kind Of Love	1964	6.00	15.00
Roulette R-52108	(M)	We Three	1964	5.00	12.00
Roulette RS-52108	(S)	We Three	1964	6.00	15.00
		(With Sarah Vaughan & Dinah Washington.)			
RCA LPM-3433	(M)	Song Is You	1965	5.00	12.00
RCA LSP-3433	(S)	Song Is You	1965	6.00	15.00
RCA LPM-3461	(M)	The Exciting Joe Williams	1965	5.00	12.00
RCA LSP-3461	(S)	The Exciting Joe Williams	1965	6.00	15.00

WILLIAMS, LARRY

Label		Title	Year	VG+	NM
Specialty SP-2109	(M)	Here's Larry Williams	1959	50.00	100.00
		(Black & gold label.)			
OKeh OKM-4122	(M)	Two For The Price Of One	1967	8.00	20.00
OKeh OKS-14122	(S)	Two For The Price Of One	1967	10.00	25.00
		(With Johnny "Guitar" Watson.)			
OKeh OKM-2123	(M)	Greatest Hits	1967	8.00	20.00
OKeh OKS-12123	(S)	Greatest Hits	1967	10.00	25.00

WILLIAMS, MAURICE, & THE ZODIACS

Label		Title	Year	VG+	NM
Herald HLP-1014	(M)	Stay	1961	50.00	100.00
Sphere Sound SSR-7007	(E)	Stay		12.00	30.00
Snyder 5586	(M)	At The Beach		16.00	40.00

WILLIAMS, MEL, & JOHNNY OTIS

Label		Title	Year	VG+	NM
Dig 103	(M)	All Through The Night	1955	50.00	100.00

WILLIAMS, OTIS, & THE CHARMS

Label		Title	Year	VG+	NM
Deluxe 750	(M)	Their All Time Hits	1957	150.00	250.00
King 560	(M)	Their All Time Hits	1957	50.00	100.00
King 614	(M)	This Is Otis Williams And The Charms	1959	50.00	100.00

WILLIAMS, TEX

Label		Title	Year	VG+	NM
Decca DL-5565	(M)	Dance-O-Rama	1955	30.00	60.00
Camden CAL-363	(M)	Tex Williams' Best	1958	10.00	25.00
Capitol T-1463	(M)	Smoke! Smoke! Smoke!	1960	8.00	20.00
Capitol ST-1463	(S)	Smoke! Smoke! Smoke!	1960	12.00	30.00
Decca DL-4295	(M)	Country Music Time	1962	8.00	20.00
Liberty LRP-3304	(M)	Tex Williams In Las Vegas	1963	5.00	12.00
Liberty LST-7304	(S)	Tex Williams In Las Vegas	1963	6.00	15.00
Imperial LP-9309	(M)	The Voice Of Authority	1966	4.00	10.00
Imperial LP-12309	(S)	The Voice Of Authority	1966	5.00	12.00

WILLIAMS, TONY

Label		Title	Year	VG+	NM
Mercury MG-20454	(M)	A Girl Is A Girl Is A Girl	1959	8.00	20.00
Mercury SR-60138	(S)	A Girl Is A Girl Is A Girl	1959	10.00	25.00

Label		Title	Year	VG+	NM
Reprise R-6006	(M)	His Greatest Hits	1961	6.00	15.00
Reprise R9-6006	(S)	His Greatest Hits	1961	8.00	20.00
Phillips PHM-200051	(M)	Magic Touch Of Tony	1962	6.00	15.00
Phillips PHS-600051	(S)	Magic Touch Of Tony	1962	8.00	20.00

WILLIAMSON, SONNY BOY (ALEC "RICE" WILLIAMSON)

Label		Title	Year	VG+	NM
Checker 1437	(M)	Sonny Boy Williamson		50.00	100.00
Chess 1437	(S)	Down And Out Blues	1964	20.00	50.00
Chess 1503	(M)	The Real Folk Blues	1966	14.00	35.00
Chess 1509	(M)	More Real Folk Blues	1966	14.00	35.00
Mercury MG-21071	(M)	Sonny Boy Williamson And The Yardbirds	1966	12.00	30.00
Mercury SR-61071	(S)	Sonny Boy Williamson And The Yardbirds	1966	16.00	40.00
Chess 1536	(S)	Bummer Road	1969	8.00	20.00

WILLING, FOY, & THE RIDERS OF THE PURPLE SAGE

Label		Title	Year	VG+	NM
Roulette R-25035	(M)	Cowboy	1958	10.00	25.00
Jubilee 5028	(M)	The New Sound Of American Folk	1962	6.00	15.00

WILLIS, CHUCK

Label		Title	Year	VG+	NM
Atlantic 8018	(M)	The King Of The Stroll (Black label.)	1958	75.00	150.00
Epic LN-3425	(M)	Chuck Willis Wails The Blues	1958	75.00	150.00
Epic LN-3728	(M)	A Tribute To Chuck Willis	1960	50.00	100.00
Atlantic 8079	(M)	I Remember Chuck Willis	1963	16.00	40.00
Atlantic SD-8079	(P)	I Remember Chuck Willis	1963	20.00	50.00
Epic LN-3425	(M)	Wails The Blues	1958	50.00	100.00
Atlantic 8018	(M)	The King Of The Stroll (Black label)	1958	50.00	100.00
Atlantic 8018	(M)	The King Of The Stroll (Red label)	1959	30.00	60.00
Epic LN-3728	(M)	A Tribute To Chuck Willis	1960	50.00	100.00
Atlantic 8079	(M)	I Remember Chuck Willis	1963	20.00	50.00
Atlantic SD-8079	(P)	I Remember Chuck Willis	1963	30.00	60.00
Atco SD-33-373	(P)	His Greatest Recordings	1971	6.00	15.00

WILLS, BOB (& HIS TEXAS PLAYBOYS)

Label		Title	Year	VG+	NM
MGM E-91 (10")	(M)	Ranch House Favorites	1951	50.00	100.00
Columbia HL-9003 (10")	(M)	Bob Wills Round-Up		50.00	100.00
Decca DL-5562 (10")	(M)	Dance-O-Rama	1955	50.00	100.00
Antones LP-6000 (10")	(M)	Old Time Favorites		50.00	100.00
Antones LP-6010 (10")	(M)	Old Time Favorites		50.00	100.00
MGM E-3352	(M)	Ranch House Favorites	1956	50.00	100.00
Harmony HL-7036	(M)	Bob Wills Special	1957	14.00	35.00
Decca DL-8727	(M)	Bob Wills And His Texas Playboys	1957	30.00	60.00
Liberty LRP-3182	(M)	Living Legend	1961	8.00	20.00
Liberty LST-7182	(S)	Living Legend	1961	10.00	25.00
Liberty LRP-3173	(M)	Together Again (With Tommy Duncan)	1960	8.00	20.00
Liberty LST-7173	(S)	Together Again (With Tommy Duncan)	1960	10.00	25.00
Liberty LRX-1912	(M)	Bob Wills And Tommy Duncan	1961	8.00	20.00
Liberty LSX-1912	(S)	Bob Wills And Tommy Duncan	1961	10.00	25.00
Liberty LRP-3194	(M)	Mr. Words And Music	1961	8.00	20.00
Liberty LST-7194	(S)	Mr. Words And Music	1961	10.00	25.00
Liberty LRP-3303	(M)	Bob Wills Sings And Plays	1963	8.00	20.00
Liberty LST-7303	(S)	Bob Wills Sings And Plays	1963	10.00	25.00
Harmony HL-7304	(M)	The Best Of Bob Wills	1963	8.00	20.00
Harmony HL-7345	(M)	The Great Bob Wills	1965	8.00	20.00
Longhorn LP-001	(M)	Keepsake Album #1	1965	20.00	50.00
Vocalion VL-3735	(M)	Western Swing Band	1965	8.00	20.00
Vocalion VL7-3735	(E)	Western Swing Band	1965	5.00	12.00
Starday SLP-375	(M)	San Antonio Rose	1965	8.00	20.00
Metro M-594	(M)	Bob Wills	1967	6.00	15.00
Metro MS-594	(S)	Bob Wills	1967	4.00	10.00
Kapp KL-1506	(M)	From The Heart Of Texas	1967	6.00	15.00
Kapp KS-3506	(S)	From The Heart Of Texas	1967	6.00	15.00
Kapp KL-1523	(M)	King Of Western Swing	1967	6.00	15.00
Kapp KS-3523	(S)	King Of Western Swing	1967	6.00	15.00
Kapp KS-3542	(S)	Here's That Man Again	1968	6.00	15.00
Kapp KS-3587	(S)	The Living Legend	1969	6.00	15.00
Kapp KS-3601	(S)	The Greatest String Band Hits	1969	6.00	15.00
Kapp KS-3569	(S)	Time Changes Everything	1969	6.00	15.00
Kapp KS-3639	(S)	Bob Wills In Person	1970	6.00	15.00
Kapp KS-3641	(S)	The Best Of Bob Wills	1971	5.00	12.00
United Arts. UAS-9962	(P)	Legendary Masters	1971	6.00	15.00

Label		Title	Year	VG+	NM
WILMER & THE DUKES					
Aphrodisiac 6001	(S)	Wilmer And The Dukes	1969	10.00	25.00
WILSON, DENNIS					
Caribou PZ-35354	(S)	Pacific Ocean Blue	1977	6.00	15.00
WILSON, J. FRANK, & THE CAVALIERS					
Josie JS-4006	(S)	Last Kiss	1964	16.00	40.00
WILSON, JACKIE					
Also refer to Billy Ward & The Dominoes.					
Brunswick BL-54042	(M)	He's So Fine	1959	35.00	70.00
Brunswick BL-54045	(M)	Lonely Teardrops	1959	35.00	70.00
Brunswick BL-54050	(M)	So Much	1960	12.00	30.00
Brunswick BL7-54050	(S)	So Much	1960	16.00	40.00
Brunswick BL-54055	(M)	Jackie Sings The Blues	1960	12.00	30.00
Brunswick BL7-54055	(S)	Jackie Sings The Blues	1960	16.00	40.00
Brunswick BL-54058	(M)	My Golden Favorites	1960	12.00	30.00
Brunswick BL7-54058	(S)	My Golden Favorites	1960	16.00	40.00
Brunswick BL-54059	(M)	A Woman, A Lover, A Friend	1961	12.00	30.00
Brunswick BL7-54059	(S)	A Woman, A Lover, A Friend	1961	14.00	35.00
Brunswick BL-54100	(M)	You Ain't Heard Nothin' Yet	1961	10.00	25.00
Brunswick BL7-54100	(S)	You Ain't Heard Nothin' Yet	1961	12.00	30.00
Brunswick BL-54101	(M)	By Special Request	1961	10.00	25.00
Brunswick BL7-54101	(S)	By Special Request	1961	12.00	30.00
Brunswick BL-54105	(M)	Body And Soul	1962	10.00	25.00
Brunswick BL7-54105	(S)	Body And Soul	1962	12.00	30.00
Brunswick BL-54106	(M)	The World's Greatest Melodies	1962	10.00	25.00
Brunswick BL7-54106	(S)	The World's Greatest Melodies	1962	12.00	30.00
Brunswick BL-54108	(M)	Jackie Wilson At The Copa	1962	8.00	20.00
Brunswick BL7-54108	(S)	Jackie Wilson At The Copa	1962	10.00	25.00
		(Brunswick albums above have black & silver labels.)			
Brunswick BL-54110	(M)	Baby Workout	1963	8.00	20.00
Brunswick BL7-54110	(S)	Baby Workout	1963	10.00	25.00
Brunswick BL-54112	(M)	Merry Christmas From Jackie Wilson	1963	8.00	20.00
Brunswick BL7-54112	(S)	Merry Christmas From Jackie Wilson	1963	10.00	25.00
Brunswick BL-54113	(M)	Shake A Hand	1963	6.00	15.00
Brunswick BL7-54113	(S)	Shake A Hand	1963	8.00	20.00
Brunswick BL-54115	(M)	My Golden Favorites, Volume 2	1964	6.00	15.00
Brunswick BL7-54115	(S)	My Golden Favorites, Volume 2	1964	8.00	20.00
Brunswick BL-54117	(M)	Somethin' Else	1964	6.00	15.00
Brunswick BL7-54117	(S)	Somethin' Else	1964	8.00	20.00
Brunswick BL-54118	(M)	Soul Time	1965	6.00	15.00
Brunswick BL7-54118	(S)	Soul Time	1965	8.00	20.00
Brunswick BL-54119	(M)	Spotlight On Jackie Wilson	1965	6.00	15.00
Brunswick BL7-54119	(S)	Spotlight On Jackie Wilson	1965	8.00	20.00
Brunswick BL-54120	(M)	Soul Galore	1966	6.00	15.00
Brunswick BL7-54120	(S)	Soul Galore	1966	8.00	20.00
Brunswick BL-54112	(M)	Whispers	1967	6.00	15.00
Brunswick BL7-54112	(S)	Whispers	1967	6.00	15.00
Brunswick BL-54130	(M)	Higher And Higher	1967	6.00	15.00
Brunswick BL7-54130	(S)	Higher And Higher	1967	6.00	15.00
Brunswick BL7-54138	(S)	I Get The Sweetest Feeling	1968	6.00	15.00
Brunswick BL7-54134	(S)	Manufacturers Of Soul	1968	6.00	15.00
		(Brunswick albums above have black labels with a "Division of Decca Records" on the left side.)			
WILSON, JULIE					
Vik 1095	(M)	My Old Flame		8.00	20.00
Vik 1118	(M)	Julie Wilson At The St. Regis		8.00	20.00
Dolphin 6	(M)	Love		8.00	20.00
Cameo C-1021	(M)	Meet Julie Wilson		6.00	15.00
WINCHESTER, JESSE					
Ampex A-10104	(S)	Jesse Winchester	1970	8.00	20.00
WIND					
Life LLPS-2000	(S)	Make Believe	1969	6.00	15.00
WIND IN THE WILLOWS, THE					
Capitol SKAO-2956	(S)	The Wind In The Willows	1968	8.00	20.00

Label		Title	Year	VG+	NM
WINGS					
Dunhill DS-50046	(S)	Wings	1968	6.00	15.00
WINTER, EDGAR (& WHITE TRASH)					
Epic EQ-31584	(Q)	They Only Come Out At Night	1973	5.00	12.00
Epic PEQ-32461	(Q)	Shock Treatment	1974	5.00	12.00
Blue Sky PZQ-33483	(Q)	Jasmine Nightdreams	1975	5.00	12.00
Blue Sky PZQ-33798	(Q)	Edger Winter Group With Rick Derringer	1975	5.00	12.00
WINTER, JOHNNY					
Imperial 12431	(S)	The Progressive Blues Experiment	1969	8.00	20.00
GRT 10010	(S)	The Johnny Winter Story	1969	6.00	15.00
Buddah BDS-7513	(S)	First Winter	1969	6.00	15.00
Janus 3008	(S)	About Blues	1969	6.00	15.00
Janus 3056	(S)	Before The Storm	1970	6.00	15.00
Columbia CS-9826	(S)	Johnny Winter ("360 Sound" label)	1969	6.00	15.00
Columbia CS-9947	(S)	Second Winter ("360 Sound" label)	1969	8.00	20.00
Columbia CQ-32188	(Q)	Still Alive And Well	1973	6.00	15.00
Columbia CQ-32715	(Q)	Saints And Sinners	1974	6.00	15.00
Blue Sky PZQ-33292	(Q)	John Dawson Winter III	1974	6.00	15.00
WINWOOD, STEVE					
United Arts. UAS-9950	(S)	Winwood (With booklet)	1971	8.00	20.00
WISEMAN, MAC					
Also refer to Lester Flatt.					
Dot DLP-3084	(M)	Tis Sweet To Be Remembered	1958	8.00	20.00
Dot DLP-3135	(M)	Beside The Still Waters	1959	8.00	20.00
Dot DLP-25135	(S)	Beside The Still Waters	1959	10.00	25.00
Dot DLP-3213	(M)	Great Folk Ballads	1959	8.00	20.00
Dot DLP-25213	(S)	Great Folk Ballads	1959	10.00	25.00
Dot DLP-3313	(M)	12 Great Hits	1960	6.00	15.00
Dot DLP-25313	(S)	12 Great Hits	1960	8.00	20.00
Dot DLP-3336	(M)	Keep On The Sunnyside	1960	8.00	20.00
Dot DLP-3373	(M)	Best Loved Gospel Hymns	1961	5.00	12.00
Dot DLP-25373	(S)	Best Loved Gospel Hymns	1961	6.00	15.00
Dot DLP-3408	(M)	Fireball Mail	1961	8.00	20.00
Capitol T-1800	(M)	Bluegrass Favorites	1962	6.00	15.00
Capitol ST-1800	(S)	Bluegrass Favorites	1962	8.00	20.00
Hamilton HLP-12130	(M)	Sincerely	1964	5.00	12.00
Hamilton HLP-12130	(S)	Sincerely	1964	6.00	15.00
Hamilton HLP-12167	(M)	Songs Of The Dear Old Days	1966	5.00	12.00
Hamilton HLP-12167	(S)	Songs Of The Dear Old Days	1966	6.00	15.00
Dot DLP-3697	(M)	This Is Mac Wiseman	1966	5.00	12.00
Dot DLP-25697	(S)	This Is Mac Wiseman	1966	6.00	15.00
Dot DLP-3730	(M)	A Master At Work	1966	5.00	12.00
Dot DLP-25730	(S)	A Master At Work	1966	6.00	15.00
Dot DLP-3731	(M)	Bluegrass	1966	5.00	12.00
Dot DLP-25731	(S)	Bluegrass	1966	6.00	15.00
WITHERSPOON, JIMMY					
Atlantic 1266	(M)	New Orleans Blues	1956	20.00	50.00
RCA LPM-1639	(M)	Goin' To Kansas City Blues	1958	12.00	30.00
King 634	(M)	Battle Of The Blues, Volume 3	1959	270.00	450.00
		(*Also features Eddie Vinson.*)			
Hi Fi 421	(M)	At The Monterey Jazz Festival	1959	10.00	25.00
Hi Fi 422	(M)	Feelin' The Spirit	1959	10.00	25.00
Hi Fi 426	(M)	Jimmy Witherspoon At The Renaissance	1959	10.00	25.00
World Pacific 1267	(M)	Singin' The Blues	1959	12.00	30.00
World Pacific 1402	(M)	There's Good Rockin' Tonight	1961	10.00	25.00
Reprise R-2008	(M)	Spoon	1961	6.00	15.00
Reprise R9-2008	(S)	Spoon	1961	8.00	20.00
Reprise R-6012	(M)	Hey, Mrs. Jones	1962	6.00	15.00
Reprise R9-6012	(S)	Hey, Mrs. Jones	1962	6.00	15.00
Reprise R-6059	(M)	Roots	1962	6.00	15.00
Reprise R9-6059	(S)	Roots	1962	8.00	20.00
Prestige PR-7290	(M)	Baby, Baby, Baby	1963	5.00	12.00
Prestige PRS-7290	(S)	Baby, Baby, Baby	1963	6.00	15.00
Prestige PR-7300	(M)	Evenin' Blues	1964	5.00	12.00
Prestige PRS-7300	(S)	Evenin' Blues	1964	6.00	15.00

Label		Title	Year	VG+	NM
Prestige PR-7314	(M)	Goin' To Chicago Blues	1964	5.00	12.00
Prestige PRS-7314	(S)	Goin' To Chicago Blues	1964	6.00	15.00
Prestige PR-7327	(M)	Blue Spoon	1964	5.00	12.00
Prestige PRS-7327	(S)	Blue Spoon	1964	6.00	15.00
Prestige PR-7356	(M)	Some Of My Best Friends Are The Blues	1964	5.00	12.00
Prestige PRS-7356	(S)	Some Of My Best Friends Are The Blues	1964	6.00	15.00
Constellation M-1422	(M)	Take This Hammer	1964	8.00	20.00
Surrey S-1106	(M)	Blues For Spoon And Groove	1965	5.00	12.00
Surrey SS-1106	(S)	Blues For Spoon And Groove	1965	6.00	15.00
Prestige PR-7418	(M)	Spoon In London	1965	5.00	12.00
Prestige PRS-7418	(S)	Spoon In London	1965	6.00	15.00
Verve V-5007	(M)	Blue Point Of View	1966	6.00	15.00
Verve V6-5007	(S)	Blue Point Of View	1966	8.00	20.00
Prestige PR-7475	(M)	Blues For Easy Livers	1967	5.00	12.00
Prestige PRS-7475	(S)	Blues For Easy Livers	1967	6.00	15.00
Prestige PRS-7713	(S)	The Best Of Jimmy Witherspoon	1969	5.00	12.00
Verve V6-5050	(S)	A Spoonful Of Soul	1968	6.00	15.00
ABC S-717	(S)	Handbags And Gladrags	1970	4.00	10.00
BluesWay BLS-6026	(S)	Blues Singer	1970	4.00	10.00
MGM SE-4791	(S)	Guilty (With Eric Burdon)	1971	4.00	10.00

WIZARD

Peon 1069	(S)	Original Wizard	1971	50.00	100.00

WIZARDS FROM KANSAS, THE

Mercury SR-61309	(S)	The Wizards From Kansas	1970	14.00	35.00

WOMENFOLK, THE

RCA LPM-2821	(M)	We Give A Hoot	1963	6.00	15.00
RCA LSP-2821	(S)	We Give A Hoot	1963	8.00	20.00
RCA LPM-2832	(M)	The Womenfolk	1964	5.00	12.00
RCA LSP-2832	(S)	The Womenfolk	1964	6.00	15.00
RCA LPM-2919	(M)	Never Underestimate The Power	1964	5.00	12.00
RCA LSP-2919	(S)	Never Underestimate The Power	1964	6.00	15.00
RCA LPM-2991	(M)	The Womenfolk At The Hungry i	1965	5.00	12.00
RCA LSP-2991	(S)	The Womenfolk At The Hungry i	1965	6.00	15.00
RCA LPM-3527	(M)	Man, Oh Man	1966	5.00	12.00
RCA LSP-3527	(S)	Man, Oh Man	1966	6.00	15.00

WONDER, STEVIE

Tamla TS-232	(M)	A Tribute To Uncle Ray	1963	30.00	60.00
Tamla TS-233	(M)	The Jazz Soul Of Stevie Wonder	1963	40.00	80.00
Tamla TS-240	(M)	12 Year Old Genius	1963	20.00	50.00
Tamla TS-248	(M)	Workout Stevie, Workout	1963	20.00	50.00
Tamla T-250	(M)	With A Song In My Heart	1964	16.00	40.00
Tamla T-255	(M)	At The Beach	1964	10.00	25.00
Tamla TS-255	(S)	At The Beach	1964	14.00	35.00
Motown MT-630	(M)	Nothing But A Man (Sdtk)	1965	8.00	20.00
Motown S-630	(S)	Nothing But A Man (Sdtk)	1965	10.00	25.00
Tamla T-268	(M)	Up-Tight	1966	10.00	25.00
Tamla TS-268	(S)	Up-Tight	1966	12.00	30.00
Tamla 272	(M)	Down To Earth	1967	8.00	20.00
Tamla TS-272	(S)	Down To Earth	1967	10.00	25.00
Tamla 279	(M)	I Was Made To Love Her	1967	6.00	15.00
Tamla TS-279	(S)	I Was Made To Love Her	1967	8.00	20.00
Tamla T-281	(M)	Someday At Christmas	1967	12.00	30.00
Tamla TS-281	(S)	Someday At Christmas	1967	14.00	35.00
Gordy GS-932	(S)	Eivets Rednow	1968	8.00	20.00
Tamla TS-282	(S)	Stevie Wonder's Greatest Hits	1968	6.00	15.00
Tamla TS-291	(S)	For Once In My Life	1968	6.00	15.00
Tamla TS-296	(S)	My Cherie Amour	1969	6.00	15.00
Tamla TS-298	(S)	Stevie Wonder Live	1970	6.00	15.00
Tamla TS-304	(S)	Signed, Sealed And Delivered	1970	5.00	12.00
Tamla TS-308	(S)	Where I'm Coming From	1971	5.00	12.00

WOOD, BRENTON

Double Shot 1002	(M)	Oogum Boogum	1967	8.00	20.00
Double Shot 5002	(S)	Oogum Boogum	1967	6.00	15.00
Double Shot 1003	(M)	Baby You Got It	1967	8.00	20.00
Double Shot 5003	(S)	Baby You Got It	1967	6.00	15.00

Label		Title	Year	VG+	NM
WOODY'S TRUCK STOP					
Smash SRS-67111	(S)	Woody's Truck Stop	1969	8.00	20.00
WOOL					
ABC S-676	(S)	Wool	1969	8.00	20.00
WOOLEY, SHEB (BEN COLDER)					
MGM E-3299	(M)	Sheb Wooley	1956	16.00	40.00
MGM E-4026	(M)	That's My Ma And That's My Pa	1962	5.00	12.00
MGM SE-4026	(S)	That's My Ma And That's My Pa	1962	6.00	15.00
MGM E-4136	(M)	Tales Of How The West Was Won	1963	5.00	12.00
MGM SE-4136	(S)	Tales Of How The West Was Won	1963	6.00	15.00
MGM E-4275	(M)	The Very Best Of Sheb Wooley	1965	5.00	12.00
MGM SE-4275	(S)	The Very Best Of Sheb Wooley	1965	6.00	15.00
MGM E-4325	(M)	It's A Big Land	1965	5.00	12.00
MGM SE-4325	(S)	It's A Big Land	1965	6.00	15.00
WOOLIES, THE					
Split 9645-2001	(S)	Basic Rock		8.00	20.00
WORLD OF OZ, THE					
Deram DES-18022	(S)	The World Of Oz	1969	6.00	15.00
WORTH, MARION					
Columbia CL-2011	(M)	Marion Worth's Greatest Hit	1963	5.00	12.00
Columbia CS-8811	(S)	Marion Worth's Greatest Hit	1963	6.00	15.00
Columbia CL-2287	(M)	Marion Worth Sings Marty Robbins	1964	5.00	12.00
Columbia CS-9087	(S)	Marion Worth Sings Marty Robbins	1964	6.00	15.00
Decca DL-4936	(M)	A Woman Needs Love	1967	5.00	12.00
Decca DL7-4936	(S)	A Woman Needs Love	1967	6.00	15.00
WRAY, LINK (& HIS WRAYMEN)					
Epic LN-3661	(M)	Link Wray And The Wraymen	1960	30.00	60.00
Vermillion 1924	(M)	Great Guitar Hits		20.00	50.00
Vermillion 1925	(M)	Link Wray Sings And Plays Guitar		20.00	50.00
Swan SLP-510	(M)	Jack The Ripper	1963	20.00	50.00
Record Factory 1929	(S)	Yesterday And Today		8.00	20.00
WRAY, VERNON					
Vermillion 1972	(S)	Wasted (With Link Wray)		12.00	30.00
WRIGHT, BETTY					
Atco SD-33-260	(S)	My First Time Around	1968	6.00	15.00
WRIGHT, NAT					
Warwick 2040	(M)	The Biggest Voice In Jazz	1960	12.00	30.00
WRIGHT, O.V.					
Back Beat 61	(M)	If It's Only For Tonight	1965	6.00	15.00
Back Beat 61	(S)	If It's Only For Tonight	1965	8.00	20.00
Back Beat 67	(S)	Nucleus Of Soul	1969	6.00	15.00
Back Beat 70	(S)	A Nickle And A Nail And Ace Of Spades	1972	5.00	12.00
WYMAN, BILL					
Roll. Stones COC-79100	(S)	Monkey Grip	1974	5.00	12.00
Roll. Stones QD-79100	(Q)	Monkey Grip	1974	6.00	15.00
Roll. Stones COC-79103	(S)	Stone Alone	1976	5.00	12.00
Roll. Stones QD-79103	(Q)	Stone Alone	1976	6.00	15.00
WYNETTE, TAMMY					
Epic LN-24305	(M)	Your Good Girl's Gonna Go Bad	1967	5.00	12.00
Epic BN-26305	(S)	Your Good Girl's Gonna Go Bad	1967	6.00	15.00
Epic BN-26353	(S)	Take Me To Your World	1968	5.00	12.00
Epic BN-26392	(S)	D-I-V-O-R-C-E	1968	5.00	12.00
Epic BN-26423	(S)	Inspiration	1969	4.00	10.00
Epic BN-26451	(S)	Stand By Your Man	1969	4.00	10.00
Epic BN-26474	(S)	Run, Angel, Run (Sdtk)	1969	6.00	15.00
Epic BN-26486	(S)	Tammy's Greatest Hits	1969	4.00	10.00
Epic BN-26519	(S)	The Ways To Love A Man	1970	4.00	10.00
Epic BN-26549	(S)	Tammy's Touch	1970	4.00	10.00

(Epic albums above have yellow labels.)

Label		Title	Year	VG+	NM
X					
Slash 104	(S)	Los Angeles	*1980*	**5.00**	**12.00**
Slash 107	(S)	Wild Gift	*1981*	**5.00**	**12.00**

YANCEY, JIMMY & MAMA

Atlantic 103 (10")	(M)	Yancey Special		**30.00**	**60.00**
Atlantic 130 (10")	(M)	Jimmy And Mama Yancey		**30.00**	**60.00**
Atlantic 134 (10")	(M)	Jimmy And Mama Yancey		**30.00**	**60.00**
Atlantic 1231	(M)	Pure Blues		**20.00**	**50.00**
Atlantic SD-7229	(S)	Blues Originals	*1972*	**5.00**	**12.00**

YANKEE DOLLAR, THE

Dot DLP-25874	(S)	The Yankee Dollar	*1968*	**12.00**	**30.00**

YANOVSKY, ZALMAN

Buddah BDS-5019	(S)	Alive And Well In Argentina	*1968*	**8.00**	**20.00**
Kama Sutra KSBS-2030	(S)	Alive And Well In Argentina	*1971*	**5.00**	**10.00**

YARBROUGH, GLENN

RCA LPM-2905	(M)	One More Sound	*1964*	**3.50**	**8.00**
RCA LSP-2905	(S)	One More Sound	*1964*	**4.00**	**10.00**
RCA LPM-3301	(M)	Come Share My Life	*1965*	**3.50**	**8.00**
RCA LSP-3301	(S)	Come Share My Life	*1965*	**4.00**	**10.00**
RCA LPM-3422	(M)	Baby, The Rain Must Fall	*1965*	**3.50**	**8.00**
RCA LSP-3422	(S)	Baby, The Rain Must Fall	*1965*	**4.00**	**10.00**
RCA LPM-3472	(M)	It's Gonna Be Fine	*1965*	**2.50**	**6.00**
RCA LSP-3472	(S)	It's Gonna Be Fine	*1965*	**3.50**	**8.00**
RCA LPM-3539	(M)	The Lonely Things	*1966*	**2.50**	**6.00**
RCA LSP-3539	(S)	The Lonely Things	*1966*	**3.50**	**8.00**
RCA LPM-3661	(M)	Live At The Hungry i	*1966*	**2.50**	**6.00**
RCA LSP-3661	(S)	Live At The Hungry i	*1966*	**3.50**	**8.00**
RCA LPM-3801	(M)	For Emily, Whenever I May Find Her	*1967*	**2.50**	**6.00**
RCA LSP-3801	(S)	For Emily, Whenever I May Find Her	*1967*	**3.50**	**8.00**
RCA LPM-3860	(M)	Honey And Wine	*1967*	**2.50**	**6.00**
RCA LSP-3860	(S)	Honey And Wine	*1967*	**3.50**	**8.00**

YARDBIRDS, THE

Epic LN-24167	(M)	For Your Love	*1965*	**20.00**	**50.00**
Epic BN-26167	(P)	For Your Love	*1965*	**20.00**	**50.00**
Epic LN-24177	(M)	Having A Rave Up	*1965*	**16.00**	**40.00**
Epic BN-26177	(E)	Having A Rave Up	*1965*	**12.00**	**30.00**
Mercury MG-21071	(M)	Sonny Boy Williamson And The Yardbirds	*1966*	**12.00**	**30.00**
Mercury SR-61071	(M)	Sonny Boy Williamson And The Yardbirds	*1966*	**16.00**	**40.00**
Epic LN-24210	(M)	Over Under Sideways Down	*1966*	**16.00**	**40.00**
Epic BN-26210	(E)	Over Under Sideways Down	*1966*	**12.00**	**30.00**
Epic LN-24246	(M)	The Yardbirds' Greatest Hits	*1966*	**12.00**	**30.00**
Epic BN-26246	(E)	The Yardbirds' Greatest Hits	*1966*	**10.00**	**25.00**
MGM E-4447	(M)	Blow-Up (Sdtk)	*1967*	**10.00**	**25.00**
MGM SE-4447	(S)	Blow-Up (Sdtk)	*1967*	**12.00**	**30.00**

Label		Title	Year	VG+	NM
Epic LN-24313	(M)	Little Games	1967	16.00	40.00
Epic BN-26313	(S)	Little Games	1967	20.00	50.00
Epic EG-30135	(P)	The Yardbirds	1970	16.00	40.00
Epic KE-30615	(S)	Live Yardbirds Featuring Jimmy Page	1971	20.00	50.00
Columbia P-13311	(S)	Live Yardbirds Featuring Jimmy Page	1972	16.00	40.00
Epic PE-34490	(P)	Yardbirds Favorites	1977	2.50	6.00
Epic PE-34491	(P)	Great Hits	1977	2.50	6.00
Epic HE-38455	(P)	The Yardbirds (1/2 speed)	1983	12.00	30.00

YELLO

Label		Title	Year	VG+	NM
Ralph YL-8059	(S)	Solid Pleasure		4.00	10.00
Ralph YL-8159	(S)	Claro Que Si		4.00	10.00

YELLOW BALLOON, THE

Label		Title	Year	VG+	NM
Canterbury CLPM-1502	(M)	The Yellow Balloon	1967	10.00	25.00
Canterbury CLPS-1502	(S)	The Yellow Balloon	1967	12.00	30.00

YELLOW PAYGES, THE

Label		Title	Year	VG+	NM
Uni 73045	(S)	The Yellow Pages, Volume 1	1969	8.00	20.00

YES

Label		Title	Year	VG+	NM
Atlantic SD-8243	(S)	Yes	1969	5.00	12.00
Atlantic SD-8273	(S)	Time And A Word	1960	5.00	12.00
Mobile Fidelity 1-077	(S)	Close To The Edge	1970	8.00	20.00

YESTERDAY'S CHILDREN

Label		Title	Year	VG+	NM
Map 3012	(S)	Yesterdays Children		6.00	15.00

YOKOHAMA KNIGHTS, THE

Label		Title	Year	VG+	NM
GRT 10002	(S)	Yokohama Knights	1969	6.00	15.00

YORK BROTHERS, THE

Label		Title	Year	VG+	NM
King 586	(M)	The York Brothers	1958	16.00	40.00
King 591	(M)	The York Brothers, Volume 2	1958	16.00	40.00
King 820	(M)	16 Great Country And Western Hits	1963	12.00	30.00

YOU KNOW WHO GROUP, THE

Label		Title	Year	VG+	NM
International Allied 420	(M)	The You Know Who Group	1965	30.00	60.00

YOUNG, FARON

Label		Title	Year	VG+	NM
Capitol T-778	(M)	Sweethearts Or Strangers	1957	12.00	30.00
Capitol T-1004	(M)	The Object Of My Affection	1958	10.00	25.00
Capitol T-1096	(M)	This Is Faron Young	1959	10.00	25.00
		(Capitol albums above have turquoise labels.)			
Capitol T-1185	(M)	My Garden Of Prayer	1959	6.00	15.00
Capitol T-1245	(M)	Talk About Hits	1959	6.00	15.00
Capitol ST-1245	(S)	Talk About Hits	1959	8.00	20.00
Capitol T-1450	(M)	The Best Of Faron Young	1960	5.00	12.00
Capitol T-1528	(M)	Hello Walls	1961	6.00	15.00
Capitol T-1634	(M)	The Young Approach	1961	5.00	15.00
Capitol ST-1634	(S)	The Young Approach	1961	6.00	15.00
		(Capitol albums above have black labels with the Capitol logo on the left side.)			
Capitol T-1876	(M)	The All-Time Great Hits Of Faron Young	1963	5.00	12.00
Mercury MG-20785	(M)	This Is Faron	1963	4.00	10.00
Mercury SR-60785	(S)	This Is Faron	1963	5.00	12.00
Mercury MG-20840	(M)	Faron Young Aims At The West	1963	4.00	10.00
Mercury SR-60840	(S)	Faron Young Aims At The West	1963	5.00	12.00
Mercury MG-20896	(M)	Story Songs For Country Fans	1964	4.00	10.00
Mercury SR-60896	(S)	Story Songs For Country Fans	1964	5.00	12.00
Mercury MG-20931	(M)	Country Dance Favorites	1964	4.00	10.00
Mercury SR-60931	(S)	Country Dance Favorites	1964	5.00	12.00
Mercury MG-20971	(M)	Story Songs Of Mountains And Valleys	1964	4.00	10.00
Mercury SR-60971	(S)	Story Songs Of Mountains And Valleys	1964	5.00	12.00
Capitol T-2037	(M)	Memory Lane	1964	5.00	12.00
Capitol ST-2037	(E)	Memory Lane	1964	4.00	10.00
Capitol T-2307	(M)	Falling In Love	1965	5.00	12.00
Capitol ST-2307	(E)	Falling In Love	1965	4.00	10.00
Mercury MG-21007	(M)	Pen And Paper	1965	4.00	10.00
Mercury SR-61007	(S)	Pen And Paper	1965	5.00	12.00

Label		Title	Year	VG+	NM
Mercury MG-21047	(M)	Faron Young's Greatest Hits	1965	4.00	10.00
Mercury SR-61047	(S)	Faron Young's Greatest Hits	1965	5.00	12.00
Mercury MG-21058	(M)	The Best Of Jim Reeves	1966	4.00	10.00
Mercury SR-61058	(S)	The Best Of Jim Reeves	1966	5.00	12.00
Capitol T-2536	(M)	If You Ain't Lovin,' You Ain't Livin'	1966	5.00	12.00
Capitol ST-2536	(E)	If You Ain't Lovin,' You Ain't Livin'	1966	4.00	10.00
Tower T-5022	(M)	It's A Great Life	1966	5.00	12.00
Tower DT-5022	(E)	It's A Great Life	1966	4.00	10.00
Mercury MG-21110	(M)	Unmitigated Gall	1967	4.00	10.00
Mercury SR-61110	(S)	Unmitigated Gall	1967	5.00	12.00

YOUNG, JESSE COLIN

Label		Title	Year	VG+	NM
Capitol T-2070	(M)	Soul Of A City Boy	1964	8.00	20.00
Capitol ST-2070	(S)	Soul Of A City Boy	1964	10.00	25.00
Mercury MG-21005	(M)	Young Blood	1965	8.00	20.00
Mercury SR-61005	(S)	Young Blood	1965	10.00	25.00

YOUNG, KATHY, & THE INNOCENTS

Label		Title	Year	VG+	NM
Indigo 503	(M)	Innocenty Yours	1961	50.00	100.00
Indigo 504	(M)	The Sound Of Cathy Young	1961	50.00	100.00

YOUNG, NEIL

Label		Title	Year	VG+	NM
Reprise RS-6317	(S)	Neil Young	1968	20.00	50.00
		(The album's title, "Neil Young," does not appear at the top of the front cover.)			

YOUNG RASCALS, THE (THE RASCALS)

Label		Title	Year	VG+	NM
Atlantic 8123	(M)	The Young Rascals	1966	10.00	25.00
Atlantic SD-8123	(S)	The Young Rascals	1966	12.00	30.00
Atlantic 8134	(M)	Collections	1967	6.00	15.00
Atlantic SD-8134	(S)	Collections	1967	8.00	20.00
Atlantic 8148	(M)	Groovin'	1967	6.00	15.00
Atlantic SD-8148	(S)	Groovin'	1967	8.00	20.00
Atlantic SD-8169	(S)	Once Upon A Dream	1968	6.00	15.00
Atlantic SD-8190	(S)	Time Peace/The Rascals' Greatest Hits	1968	3.50	8.00
Atlantic SD-2-091	(S)	Freedom Suite	1969	4.00	10.00
Atlantic SD-8246	(S)	See	1970	3.50	8.00
Atlantic SD-8276	(S)	Search And Nearness	1971	3.50	8.00
Columbia 30462	(S)	Peaceful World	1971	3.50	8.00
Columbia 31103	(S)	The Island Of Real	1972	3.50	8.00

YOUNGBLOODS, THE

Label		Title	Year	VG+	NM
RCA LPM-3724	(M)	The Youngbloods	1967	6.00	15.00
RCA LSP-3724	(S)	The Youngbloods (Black label)	1967	4.00	10.00
RCA LPM-3865	(M)	Earth Music	1967	6.00	15.00
RCA LSP-3865	(S)	Earth Music (Black label)	1967	4.00	10.00
RCA LSP-4150	(S)	Elephant Mountain (Orange label)	1969	4.00	10.00
Mercury SR-61273	(S)	Two Trips	1970	6.00	15.00
MGM SE-4468	(S)	Zabriskie Point (Sdtk)	1970	6.00	15.00

YOUR GANG

Label		Title	Year	VG+	NM
Mercury MG-21094	(M)	If You Want To Buy 'Em	1966	5.00	12.00
Mercury SR-61094	(S)	If You Want To Buy 'Em	1966	6.00	15.00

YUM YUM KIDS, THE

Label		Title	Year	VG+	NM
MGM E-4396	(M)	Yummy In Your Tummy	1966	6.00	15.00
MGM SE-4396	(S)	Yummy In Your Tummy	1966	8.00	20.00

YURO, TIMI

Label		Title	Year	VG+	NM
Liberty LRP-3208	(M)	Hurt	1961	10.00	25.00
Liberty LST-7208	(S)	Hurt	1961	12.00	30.00
Liberty LRP-3212	(M)	Soul	1962	5.00	12.00
Liberty LST-7212	(S)	Soul	1962	6.00	15.00
Liberty LRP-3234	(M)	Let Me Call You Sweetheart	1962	5.00	12.00
Liberty LST-7234	(S)	Let Me Call You Sweetheart	1962	6.00	15.00
Liberty LRP-3263	(M)	What's A Matter, Baby?	1962	5.00	12.00
Liberty LST-7263	(S)	What's A Matter, Baby?	1962	6.00	15.00
Liberty LRP-3286	(M)	The Best Of Timi Yuro	1963	5.00	12.00
Liberty LST-7286	(S)	The Best Of Timi Yuro	1963	6.00	15.00
Liberty LRP-3319	(M)	Make The World Go Away	1963	5.00	12.00
Liberty LST-7319	(S)	Make The World Go Away	1963	6.00	15.00

Label		Title	Year	VG+	NM
Mercury MG-20963	(M)	The Amazing Timi Yuro	1964	4.00	10.00
Mercury SR-60963	(S)	The Amazing Timi Yuro	1964	5.00	12.00
Sunset SUM-1107	(M)	Timi Yuro	1966	4.00	10.00
Sunset SUS-5107	(S)	Timi Yuro	1966	5.00	12.00
Colgems COS-5007	(S)	Interlude (Sdtk)	1968	10.00	25.00
Liberty LST-7594	(S)	Something Bad On My Mind	1968	5.00	12.00

Z

ZZ TOP

London PS-584	(S)	First Album	1971	4.00	10.00
London PS-612	(S)	Rio Grande Mud	1972	4.00	10.00
London XPS-631	(S)	Tres Hombres	1973	4.00	10.00
London PS-656	(S)	Fandango	1975	4.00	10.00
London PS-680	(S)	Tejas	1977	4.00	10.00

ZABACH, FLORIAN

Decca DL-5367 (10")	(M)	The Hot Canary		8.00	20.00

ZACHERLY, JOHN

Elektra EKL-7190	(M)	Spook Along With Zacherley	1960	14.00	35.00
Elektra EKS-7190	(S)	Spook Along With Zacherley	1960	16.00	40.00
Parkway P-7018	(M)	Monster Mash	1962	16.00	40.00
Parkway P-7023	(M)	Scary Tales	1963	16.00	40.00
Crestview CR-803	(M)	Zacherley's Monster Gallery	1963	14.00	35.00
Crestview CRS7-803	(S)	Zacherley's Monster Gallery	1963	16.00	40.00

ZAPPA, FRANK (& THE MOTHERS OF INVENTION)

Verve V-5005	(M)	Freak Out!	1966	20.00	50.00
Verve V6-5005	(S)	Freak Out!	1966	16.00	40.00
		(Some copies were issued with a map, priced separately below.)			
		Freak Out! Map	1966	20.00	50.00
		(A map of "freak out hot spots" in L.A.)			
Verve V-5013	(M)	Absolutely Free	1967	30.00	60.00
Verve V6-5013	(S)	Absolutely Free	1967	20.00	50.00
Verve V-5045	(M)	We're Only In It For The Money	1968	30.00	60.00
Verve V6-5045	(S)	We're Only In It For The Money	1968	20.00	50.00
		(With a "Sgt Pepper" parody insert.)			
Verve V-5045	(M)	We're Only In It For The Money	1968	40.00	80.00
Verve V6-5045	(S)	We're Only In It For The Money	1968	35.00	70.00
		(Edited version with the line "I will love the police as they kick the shit out of me" deleted from "Who Needs The Peace Corps?")			
Verve V6-5055	(S)	Cruising With Ruben And The Jets	1968	16.00	40.00
		(Some copies were issued with a set of bonuses, priced separately below.)			
		Cruising With Ruben And The Jets Inserts	1968	30.00	60.00
		(Three bonuses were issued: an insert with "The Story Of Ruben & The Jets," an insert with "How To Comb & Set A Jellyroll," and a guide on how to do the "bop.")			
Verve V6-8741	(S)	Lumpy Gravy	1968	20.00	50.00
Verve V6-5068	(S)	Mothermania/The Best Of The Mothers	1969	20.00	50.00
Verve V6-5074	(S)	The XXXX Of The Mothers Of Invention	1969	16.00	40.00
MGM GAS-112	(S)	The Mothers Of Invention	1970	16.00	40.00
MGM SE-4754	(S)	The Worst Of The Mothers	1971	16.00	40.00
Bizarre MS-2024	- (S)	Uncle Meat (With booklet)	1969	16.00	40.00
Bizarre RS-6356	(S)	Hot Rats	1969	6.00	15.00
Bizarre RS-6370	(S)	Burnt Weenie Sandwich (With booklet)	1969	10.00	25.00

Label		Title	Year	VG+	NM
Warner PRO-368	(S)	Zapped (Collage cover)	1969	16.00	40.00
Warner PRO-368	(S)	Zapped (Photo cover)	1969	10.00	25.00
Bizarre MS-2028	(S)	Weasels Ripped My Flesh	1970	6.00	15.00
Bizarre MS-2030	(S)	Chunga's Revenge	1970	6.00	15.00
United Arts. UAS-9956	(S)	Frank Zappa's 200 Motels (With insert)	1971	12.00	30.00
Bizarre MS-2042	(S)	Fillmore East, June 1971	1971	6.00	15.00
Bizarre MS-2075	(S)	Just Another Band From L.A.	1972	6.00	15.00
Bizarre MS-2093	(S)	The Grand Wazoo	1972	6.00	15.00
Bizarre MS-2094	(S)	Waka/Jawaka	1972	6.00	15.00
		(Bizarre albums above have blue labels.)			
DiscReet MS-2149	(S)	Over-Nite Sensation	1973	8.00	20.00
DiscReet MS4-2149	(Q)	Over-Nite Sensation	1973	16.00	40.00
DiscReet DS-2175	(S)	Apostrophe	1974	6.00	15.00
DiscReet DS4-2175	(Q)	Apostrophe	1974	14.00	35.00
DiscReet DSS-2202	(S)	Roxy & Elsewhere	1974	8.00	20.00
DiscReet DS-2216	(S)	One Size Fits All	1975	6.00	15.00
DiscReet DS-2234	(S)	Bongo Fury (With Captain Beefheart)	1975	6.00	15.00
Warners BS-2970	(S)	Zoot Allures	1976	6.00	15.00
DiscReet DSK-2288	(S)	Over-Nite Sensation	1977	8.00	20.00
DiscReet 2D-2290	(S)	Zappa In New York	1978	8.00	20.00
DiscReet DSK-2291	(S)	Studio Tan	1978	6.00	15.00
DiscReet DSK-2292	(S)	Sleep Dirt	1979	6.00	15.00
Zappa SRZ-2-1501	(S)	Sheik Yerbouti	1979	6.00	15.00
DiscReet DSK-2294	(S)	Orchestral Favorites	1979	6.00	15.00
Zappa SRZ-1-1603	(S)	Joe's Garage, Act I	1979	5.00	12.00
Zappa SRZ-2-1502	(S)	Joe's Garage, Acts II and III	1979	6.00	15.00
ZEPHYR					
Probe CPLP-4510	(S)	Zephyr	1969	16.00	40.00
Warners BS-1897	(S)	Going Back To Colorado	1971	12.00	30.00
Warners BS-2603	(S)	Sunset Ride	1972	12.00	30.00
ZIG ZAG PEOPLE					
Decca DL-75110	(S)	Take Bubble Gum Music Underground	1969	8.00	20.00
ZIP CODES					
Liberty LRP-3367	(M)	Mustang	1964	10.00	25.00
Liberty LST-7367	(S)	Mustang	1964	12.00	30.00
ZOMBIES					
Parrot PAR-1001	(M)	The Zombies	1965	16.00	40.00
Parrot PAS-71001	(E)	The Zombies	1965	12.00	30.00
RCA LOC-1115	(M)	Bunny Lake Is Missing (Sdtk)	1965	14.00	35.00
RCA LSO-1115	(S)	Bunny Lake Is Missing (Sdtk)	1965	16.00	40.00
Date TES-4013	(S)	Odessey And Oracle	1968	8.00	20.00
London PS-557	(P)	Early Days	1969	5.00	12.00
ZOO					
Sunburst 7500	(S)	The Zoo Presents The Chocolate Mouse	1968	10.00	25.00
Mercury SR-61300	(S)	The Zoo	1970	6.00	15.00

Neal Umphred: A Brief Bio

Photo by Don Morrisey

Born to a modest family of registered Democrats in Wilkes-Barre, Pennsylvania, in 1951, I can honestly count Marcel Duchamp and burning culm banks as pivotal influences on my psyche. While my baby book, since lost in the Great Flood of '72, claimed my favorite song in those preliterate years to have been "Sh-Boom," I *remember* "Hound Dog"...

By the age of ten I had passed through dinosaurs, the Civil War, military aircraft of the First World War and baseball cards. I spent many a Saturday traipsing over to the Back-Date Book Store, where I could buy six comic books for a quarter, and then spend the rest of the day at my Gramma's apartment, stacking old 45s on my aunt's record player.

In 1965 everything turned inside out upon hearing the Byrds' "Mr. Tambourine Man," which, with the aforementioned "Hound Dog," makes for an odd pairing as my two faverave singles of all time. Around 1970 it dawned on me that *Pet Sounds* was the single greatest rock album ever made, a belief I still hold and is only occasionally challenged when I am listening to *Beggar's Banquet* or *Blonde On Blonde*.

At the ripe old age of 37, with some assistance from my wife, Elaine, I became a father for the first time and am in awe of my daughter, Ananda. Ananda is Sanskrit and means "bliss," a concept and experience noticeably lacking in Western culture.

My favorite writers are John Barth and Philip Dick; my favorite cartoonists are George Herriman, Dave Sheridan and Wally Wood; Woody Allen and Cerebus and the Aardvark always make me laugh; and I will die a devoted Philadelphia Phillies fan, possibly due to some bad kharma in a previous life.

I am one of three siblings: my brother, Charles, is a (literally) born-again multi-level marketeer while my sister, Mary Alice, is a gorgeous, head-strong agoraphobiac. Finally, I would like to take this opportunity to say "Hi, Mom... Hi, Dad."

Neal Umphred is the author of O'Sullivan Woodside's two most acclaimed books, the sixth edition of the *Rock Record Album Price Guide* and the third edition of *The Elvis Presley Record Price Guide*. Neal is also a regular contributor to *Goldmine* magazine.

FRANKENSTEIN!
(Odeon OSX 228) — $2000

The Beatles Featuring T. Sheridan
(Brunswick ST 2911111), White
Label Silver Series — $750

Beatles & T. Sheridan
(Polydor ST237639) — $1000

THE ULTIMATE!
(Odeon OSX 231) — $3000

Beat Bros. (Polydor 237629)
Commercial Issue — $1000
Promo — $2000

T. Sheridan & Beat Bros.
(Polydor 237112) — $1000

U.S. Beatles & T. Sheridan
**Military Promo LP w/CUSTOM
SLEEVE!** — $2000

T. Sheridan '62 Polydor Promo LP
Informationsplatte — $2000

P. DIXON (617) 767-0558